ELMHURST COLLEGE
THEATRE

Oral Interpretation

Oral Interpretation
SEVENTH EDITION

Charlotte I. Lee
Professor Emeritus, Northwestern University

Timothy Gura
Brooklyn College, City University of New York

HOUGHTON MIFFLIN COMPANY Boston

Dallas   Geneva, Ill.   Lawrenceville, N.J.   Palo Alto

Cover: "The New Year" by Pablo Picasso, Musée Saint-Denis / Cliché des Musées Nationaux, Paris / © SPADEM, Paris / VAGA, New York.

Chapter openers and selection illustrations by Michael Crawford.

Acknowledgments begin on page 519.

Printed in the U.S.A.

Library of Congress Catalog Card Number: 86-81107
ISBN: 0-395-42440-2

ABCDEFGHIJ-H-9876

Contents

To the Student   xiii

To the Instructor   xvii

I.   Basic Principles   1

1   A Beginning and an End   3

Sources of Material   7
Choosing the Selection: Three Touchstones   8
Bibliography   15

2   Analyzing the Selection   19

Climax   21
Persona   23
Locus   24
Intrinsic Factors   26
    Unity and Harmony   27
    Variety and Contrast   28
    Balance and Proportion   28
    Rhythm   30
A Sample Analysis of a Story   32
A Sample Analysis of a Poem   38
Synthesis   44
Analyzing the Performance   45
Selections for Analysis and Oral Interpretation   47
    WALT WHITMAN *When I Heard the Learn'd Astronomer*   47
    JOHN KEATS *Sonnet*   48
    GERARD MANLEY HOPKINS *The Starlight Night*   48
    TRUMAN CAPOTE From *A Christmas Memory*   49

ANNE SEXTON *Ringing the Bells* 51

ROBERT FROST *Wild Grapes* 52

EMILY DICKINSON *Because I Could Not Stop for Death* 54

WILLIAM SHAKESPEARE *Sonnet 18* 55

WILLIAM SHAKESPEARE *Sonnet 130* 56

DEBORAH SHERMAN *Dulce* 56

PETER CAMERON *Homework* 59

CLAIRE MORRILL *Miss Lizzie* 66

Bibliography 72

3 Voice Development for Oral Interpretation 75

Breath Control 75

Volume and Projection 80

Focus of Projection 81

Pitch and Quality 83

Rate and Pause 85

Intelligibility of Speech 87

Selections for Analysis and Oral Interpretation 89

GARRISON KEILLOR From *Lake Wobegon Days* 89

LEWIS CARROLL *Jabberwocky* 92

ELIZABETH BOWEN From *The Little Girls* 93

JOHN DONNE *A Hymn to God the Father* 97

JOHN UPDIKE *A & P* 98

MATTHEW ARNOLD *Dover Beach* 104

JOAN DIDION From *The White Album* 105

NAOMI LONG MADGETT *Her Story* 107

CHIEF SEATTLE *My People* 108

NAVAJO CEREMONIAL CHANT, TRANSLATED BY JOHN BIERHORST From *The Night Chant* 111

WILLIAM LEAST HEAT MOON From *Blue Highways* 111

Bibliography 114

4 The Use of the Body in Oral Interpretation 117

Posture 119

Gesture 120

Kinesics and Muscle Tone 121

Sense Imagery 123

Empathy 126

Hints for Preparation 129

Analyzing the Performance 129

Selections for Analysis and Oral Interpretation   131
    WILLIAM BUTLER YEATS *The Second Coming*   132
    ALFRED, LORD TENNYSON *Ulysses*   133
    ISAAC BASHEVIS SINGER From *A Crown of Feathers*   135
    RODNEY JONES *The Mosquito*   141
    EUDORA WELTY From *One Writer's Beginnings*   142
    RONALD WALLACE *The Art of Love*   145
    TED JOANS *The .38*   146
    SHARON OLDS *The Race*   148
    LANGSTON HUGHES *The Negro Speaks of Rivers*   150
    THEODORE ROETHKE *Old Lady's Winter Words*   151
    WILLIAM SHAKESPEARE From *As You Like It*   153
    MAYA ANGELOU *Phenominal Woman*   154
    MAYA ANGELOU From *I Know Why the Caged Bird Sings*   155
    THOMAS HARDY *In Church*   158
Bibliography   158

II.   The Interpretation of Prose   161

5   Some Aspects of Prose   163

Style   164
   Paragraphs   164
   Sentences   165
   Speech Phrases   168
   Balancing Sentences   170
   Choice of Words   171
   Tone Color   172
   Prose Rhythm   173
   Description   174
Types of Prose   176
   Factual Prose   176
   The Personal Essay   177
   Journals, Diaries, Letters, Testimony, and Paraliterature   178
Selections for Analysis and Oral Interpretation   181
    EUDORA WELTY From *June Recital*   181
    JUDITH MARTIN From *Miss Manners'® Guide to Excruciatingly
      Correct Behavior*   183
    JOHN C. DANN, ED. From *The Revolution Remembered*   185
    WILLIAM FAULKNER From *Dry September*   187
    ST. PAUL From *The New Testament*   189
    HENRY JAMES *Letter to Grace Norton*   190

LILLIAN HELLMAN AND PETER FEIBLEMAN From *Eating Together*   191
LILLIAN SCHLISSEL, ED. From *Women's Diaries of the
    Westward Journey*   194
STUDS TERKEL From *Working*   197
Bibliography   201

6 **Narration**   203

Point of View   204
    First-Person Narrators   205
    Third-Person Narrators   208
Action and Plot   211
Character   212
Dialogue   213
Setting   217
Cutting and Excerpting   218
Analyzing the Performance   220
Selections for Analysis and Oral Interpretation   223
    BERNARD MALAMUD *The Prison*   223
    DORIS BETTS From *The Ugliest Pilgrim*   229
    MADISON SMARTT BELL *The Naked Lady*   238
    OVID From *The Metamorphoses*   242
    TONI MORRISON From *Sula*   246
    THE TORAH *Genesis I: 1–16*   248
    ARCHIBALD MARSHALL *The Detective*   249
    PHILIP ROTH From *The Conversion of the Jews*   252
Bibliography   257

III.   **The Interpretation of Drama**   261

7 **The Solo Performance of Drama**   263

The Purpose of Solo Performance   265
Acting and Interpretation   266
Structural Elements of a Play   268
Working a Scene   274
Rhythm   281
Style   282
Scenography   283
Putting It Together   285
Selections for Analysis and Oral Interpretation   287
    LANFORD WILSON From *Fifth of July*   287
    EUGENE IONESCO From *The Bald Soprano*   290

GEORGE BERNARD SHAW From *Caesar and Cleopatra*   291
JOHN DRYDEN From *All for Love*   294
WILLIAM SHAKESPEARE From *Antony and Cleopatra*   297
Bibliography   299

8 Technique in Drama   303

Technique in Interpretation   303
   Control   304
   Memorizing Lines   305
   Setting the Scene   306
Properties   308
Embodying Characters   309
Building Bodies and Voices of Characters   311
Physical Contact   314
Interplay of Characters   315
   Picking Up Cues   316
Physical Focus   317
   Angle of Placement   319
The Reading Stand   320
Cutting and Excerpting   321
Analyzing the Performance   322
Selections for Analysis and Oral Interpretation   325
   STEPHEN SONDHEIM From *Sunday in the Park with George*   325
   WILLIAM SHAKESPEARE From *Romeo and Juliet*   326
   HUGH LEONARD From *Da*   329
   HAROLD PINTER From *Betrayal*   335
   SOPHOCLES From *Oedipus the King*   341
Bibliography   345

IV. The Interpretation of Poetry   347

9 The Language of Poetry   349

Poetic Content   349
Narrative Poetry   352
Lyric Poetry   354
Dramatic Poetry   357
Figurative Language   359
   Allusions   360
   Figures of Speech   360
   Sensory Appeals   363

Stanzas   365
Poetic Syntax   366
Tone Color   368
Titles   371
Selections for Analysis and Oral Interpretation   372
   GERARD MANLEY HOPKINS *The Windhover*   372
   ANDREW MARVELL *To His Coy Mistress*   373
   NIKKI GIOVANNI *Nikki-Rosa*   375
   DYLAN THOMAS *In My Craft or Sullen Art*   376
   MARCIA LEE MASTERS *The Heart's Place*   377
   ADRIENNE RICH *A Woman Mourned by Daughters*   379
   WALLACE STEVENS *The Idea of Order at Key West*   380
   CORRINE HALES *Power*   381
   STANLEY KUNITZ *Open the Gates*   383
   JOHN CROWE RANSOM *Bells for John Whiteside's Daughter*   384
   ROBERT BROWNING *Soliloquy of the Spanish Cloister*   385
   JAMES DICKEY *The Hospital Window*   387
   IMAMU AMIRI BARAKA *Preface to a Twenty Volume Suicide Note*   389
Bibliography   389

10   **The Structure of Poetry**   391

The Stanza   393
The Line   394
   Foot Prosody   394
   Stress Prosody   397
   Syllabic Prosody   397
   The Interpreter's Use of Line Lengths   399
Cadences   401
Rhyme   405
Analyzing the Performance   408
Selections for Analysis and Oral Interpretation   409
   THEODORE ROETHKE *Child on Top of a Greenhouse*   409
   THEODORE ROETHKE *The Waking*   410
   JOHN CIARDI *As I Would Wish You Birds*   411
   T. S. ELIOT *Journey of the Magi*   412
   JAMES WRIGHT *A Blessing*   413
   JOHN DONNE *Go and Catch a Falling Star*   415
   E. E. CUMMINGS *Spring is like a perhaps hand*   416
   WALT WHITMAN From *Song of Myself*   416
   CHARLES BATTEL LOOMIS *Jack and Jill*   418
   WILLIAM SHAKESPEARE *Sonnet 29*   420
   JOHN MILTON *On His Blindness*   420

ROBERT BROWNING *My Last Duchess*   421

MAYA ANGELOU *I Almost Remember*   423

MICHAEL DRAYTON *Since There's No Help*   424

EDNA ST. VINCENT MILLAY *Sonnet XXX*   424

VICTOR HERNANDEZ CRUZ *Today Is a Day of Great Joy*   425

ALICE WALKER From *Horses Make a Landscape Look
    More Beautiful*   426

Bibliography   428

V.   Group Performance   433

11   The Group Performance of Literature   435

Readers Theatre   436

Chamber Theatre   441

Group Performance of Compiled Scripts   449

Other Kinds of Literature   452

Some Concluding Cautions   454

Analyzing the Performance   454

Selections for Analysis and Oral Interpretation   456

RETOLD BY VIRGINIA HAMILTON *The People Could Fly*   456

ANNE SEXTON *Cinderella*   460

X. J. KENNEDY *B Negative*   463

AL SANTOLI From *Everything We Had*   465

BERTOLT BRECHT From *The Caucasian Chalk Circle*   467

ROGER McGOUGH *40 – Love*   470

MARY ELLEN SOLT *Forsythia*   471

REINHARD DÖHL *Apfel*   472

NTOZAKE SHANGE From *For Colored Girls Who Have Considered
    Suicide/When the Rainbow Is Enuf*   473

CHRISTINA GEORGINA ROSSETTI *Goblin Market*   477

Bibliography   490

Appendix A
Some Notes on Directing the Group Performance   493

Appendix B
Building and Presenting a Program   498

Selecting Material   499

Unifying the Program: A Traditional Method   500

Using Multiple Readers, Different Types of Literature,
    and Multimedia   502
Adapting to the Audience   506
Timing   507

Appendix C
A Brief History of Theories of Interpretation   509

Subject Index   525

Selections Index   531

To the Student

At first this book — and the course of study it suggests — may strike you as difficult and indeed perhaps strange. For most of our lives we have been taught to read silently, not to move our lips, and to get through the material as rapidly as possible. Moreover, we have been asked to look at poems, plays, or stories much as we look at rocks in the geology laboratory or dissect frogs in biology. We are frequently encouraged to point out metaphors, tragic flaws, or third-person narrators, as if literature were aggregates of those items. Too often this approach leads to study *around* the work. When finished, we are left with masses of facts about the text but not much of the excitement or delight we felt when we enjoyed the reading itself.

Interpretation, on the other hand, asks you to speak up, move your lips, respond to the fullness of the story, and take time to experience what the characters are undergoing. All of the "facts" you have discovered about literature in other courses can be used here to refine and clarify your own performance, because interpretation goes several steps beyond the mere vocalization of silent reading. It requires a full appreciation of your material as a work of literary art, and it demands that you communicate that work of art through your voice and body. You will be asked to respond fully — intellectually and emotionally — and to control and channel your understanding and emotion to elicit the appropriate response from your audience. Interpretation is built on scholarship, technical know-how, sensitivity, and the desire to share. It demands total synthesis of all of these.

Like any other art, interpretation requires practice and study. Just as a musician translates written notes into sounds and thus conveys the achievement of the composer to the listener, so you, the interpreter, bring to life the printed words that preserve the ideas and experiences of humankind. Your instruments are your voice and your body; as is true for musicians, using these instruments requires skill developed by rehearsal. Success is rarely immediate; learning to read aloud requires care and effort.

Oral interpretation enhances any kind of vocational training. Many people, as we all know, spend their most prized hours outside of their jobs. Even the most ambitious of us is unlikely to spend more than a third of a week pursuing commercial success. On the weekends, on vacations, during free evenings, many people feel a desire for something more out of life and themselves than another beer and a rented movie on television. They want something that enhances their sense of being human. Studying literature accomplishes this; and the oral interpretation of literature is not only the fullest way to enjoy stories and poems and plays: it also allows us to share our experiences and our pleasures with people who care about literature as we do.

The opening chapters of the book suggest a method of detailed analysis that will help you to develop your own responses to the literature you have chosen and provide the foundation upon which you can build your performance. Part II applies these principles to prose and contains additional clues to what to look for. Part III is concerned with drama and offers suggestions about character and scene analysis as well as helpful tips about the techniques for creating those characters and scenes vividly in the minds of your audience. Part IV deals with poetry, although numerous poems appear earlier in the book. Group performance is discussed last because it includes poetry, prose, and drama and because the success of any group depends upon the preparation and technical skill of every individual involved in it.

If you are already a performer, you will find that the literary analysis we encourage gives you greater confidence and increases your flexibility in handling various moods or kinds of material. As it has been said, "Chance favors the prepared mind." If you are new to performing or if you have spent most of your time studying literature by other methods, you will find that performance before an intelligent audience is a valuable test of your thoroughness and accuracy. You will also discover why others find performing so enjoyable. Whatever your previous experience in performance, you will find this book full of what we hope are intriguing questions. In Chapters 2, 4, 6, 8, 10, and 11 you will find a series of questions that will help you to analyze your performance and will assist you in discussing the performances of your classmates. These questions are not rules or recipes; they are ways to help you think carefully and precisely about all the choices that made your performance uniquely yours. And each of the selections is followed by a question or two which asks you to consider a central performance problem in that text. Thus *Oral Interpretation* offers both practical suggestions for solving specific problems and a wide choice of literary selections at various levels of sophistication and degrees of difficulty.

One final word about the selections at the ends of the chapters: each is substantial and challenging and each contains clear clues to help you embody that special experience. Some may even "remind you of something you did not know you knew," as Robert Frost has put it. But if one selection seems difficult, don't give up on it right away: walk around a bit in its shoes before dismissing it. You may be surprised at how much you discover about yourself as you reach out to understand the literature. Like what you get out of any other book (or any other course), what you derive from *Oral Interpretation* will depend on how much of yourself you are willing to invest.

To the Instructor

Much has changed in the field of oral interpretation since the first edition of this book appeared in 1952. Frequently, as we re-examined that book and its five descendants, we remembered the axiom that change does not necessarily imply progress. Scrutiny of this seventh edition of *Oral Interpretation* will show a number of similarities to those predecessors as well as some substantial innovations.

The fundamental theory of the book remains the same: only when a student fully understands a literary selection can any reliable performance preparation begin. Thus we have continued our emphasis on the analysis of literary selections as a guide to their appreciation and, more immediately, as the indispensable first step of any rehearsal. The process of analysis described here emphasizes the writer's relationship with the reader and thus the position the interpreter takes in re-creating the experience, whether that experience is an author's personal discovery or the sensibilities of a created character. In addition to an awareness of the work's complexities, oral performance demands a flexible voice and body able to suggest all the subtleties discovered through close analysis. Throughout the process, the only reliable yardstick of the success of performance remains the text itself. Thus, interpreters and critics have as their ultimate recourse that with which they began: the literature being performed.

These principles, of course, have characterized the previous editions of this book. The most immediately apparent difference in this edition is the inclusion of six sections called "Analyzing the Performance," which appear in Chapters 2, 4, 6, 8, 10, and 11. Each of the sections contains practical hints for describing and evaluating student performances and concludes with several general questions we have found useful in guiding students to analyze both their own performances and those of classmates. These questions are not check lists, rating sheets, or score cards. Rather, they are suggestions that probe the concerns raised in the preceding pages. Furthermore, in addition to the headnotes, which provide sound performance advice, each selection for oral interpretation is now followed by specific questions that address problems most often encountered by performers of the work. We hope that these new features of the text will help focus students' attention on what we believe to be the most important post-performance question: How fully did *this* reader communicate *this* selection to *this* audience?

Also new to this edition is a reorganization and revision of the section on the performance of prose, with particular attention to narration and character. Problems in the creation of character are also discussed in the chapters on the solo performance of drama, as are the technical difficulties that surround the single performer's attempt to suggest simultaneity and spectacle in drama. A chapter on the group performance of literature concludes the book, buttressed by three appendices: a section entirely devoted to practical suggestions for beginning directors of group performances, a discussion of program building for individuals and groups, and a brief review of the history of interpretation. Chapter bibliographies have been significantly updated and modified by John M. Allison, Louisiana State University, Baton Rouge, Louisiana.

These changes mean that there may be more material here than can be covered comfortably in a single term, but the general format of this edition will be familiar to readers of earlier editions. We suggest beginning study with the introductory material of Part I. Here we examine the fundamental principles of analysis, selection, and evaluation of literature and apply these principles to a brief story and a poem. We then look at the ways interpreters can use their bodies and their voices. The early chapters establish the basic principles common to all kinds of literature and complement the modal, rhetorical, or dramatistic approaches. Then the course may either concentrate on one or two areas or briefly survey all genres in the parts that follow. Part II, devoted to the interpretation of prose, pays particular attention both to the embodiment and evocation of prose style and to the problems inherent in narration. Part III deals with drama, with specific attention given to the structure of a play, character analysis, and style in dialogue, in addition to practical advice about technique. Although many poems appear in earlier parts of the book, as well as some selections from verse drama and epic poetry, the interpretation of poetry *per se* is not discussed until Part IV, where the analysis is as detailed as befits the condensation and complexity of a successful poem, no matter how brief. Part V concerns group interpretation and makes a basic distinction between Readers Theatre and Chamber Theatre as a guide to preparation of scripts and the implementation of production and performance.

The literary selections included in this edition encompass a broad range of interests, topics, and levels of sophistication. Among the new selections in this edition are excerpts from Garrison Keillor's *Lake Wobegon Days,* William Least Heat Moon's *Blue Highways,* and Studs Terkel's *Working;* poems by Corinne Hales, Alice Walker, Sharon Olds, and Roger McGough; and drama by Harold Pinter, Stephen Sondheim, and Bertolt Brecht. Performing any of the selections is richly rewarding — in different ways with different students, of course. None of the selections is simple, because we are convinced of the superior educational benefit of the gallant struggle over the easy victory. We encourage you to use the selections in the text whenever possible, since it is important that students have a copy of the literature to consult *after* — not during — the reading as a guide to their criticism. We have found it valuable — and expeditious — to hold all critiques until the performers scheduled for a given day have finished. There are usually some common problems, and students find it agonizing to analyze others' readings when they are still concentrating on their own. Criticism of material about which we know nothing tends to focus on technical proficiencies that can obscure or even obliterate the very work we seek to enjoy.

The success of this edition will depend in large measure on those two intangibles that improved the earlier editions: the interest and enthusiasm of the individual student and the spark that only a dedicated teacher can give any body of knowledge. We have tried to create a book that can guide, encourage, and challenge its readers in the hope that if our suggestions seem inadequate, students and teacher together will discover a fuller, richer response. All disciplines require such discoveries in order to grow. In them we see most clearly the difference between change and progress.

By their questions and responses to previous editions, our colleagues throughout the country — and their students — have substantially improved this edition. Lee Beltzer and Leland Croghan were particularly helpful in discovering new ways to solve old performance problems. Many will find in these pages theories or practices we discovered together. In their admirable refusal to accept easy answers, students across the country helped us to refine our thinking on the practical application of several theories. We are grateful to the following colleagues who agreed to review the book and recommend improvements: William Alfred Boyce, Wayne State University; Earline G. Grizzle, Victoria College; William B. Kennedy, John Carroll University; Christie Logan, California State University,

Northridge; Gail T. Miller, Arizona State University; Newton Neely, University of Montevallo; Ronald J. Pelias, Southern Illinois University; and Janice Rice, University of Rhode Island. As before, some singular contributions deserve special mention: Frank Galati's genial imagination continues to brighten this edition in countless unacknowledged ways, and Karen Owsley's skill, speed, and intelligence were invaluable. Finally, we note with gratitude that, like Faulkner's Dilsey, Eleanor Huff and Mark Gallaher endured.

I. Basic Principles

1 A Beginning and an End

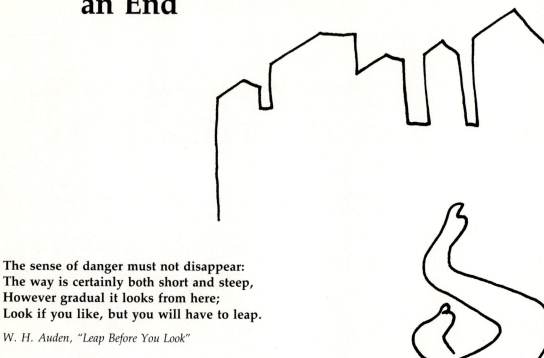

The sense of danger must not disappear:
The way is certainly both short and steep,
However gradual it looks from here;
Look if you like, but you will have to leap.

W. H. Auden, "Leap Before You Look"

*I*nterpretation is the art of communicating to an audience a work of literary art in its intellectual, emotional, and aesthetic entirety.

Interpretation is the art of communicating . . . By its very definition, art implies skill in performance. It requires discipline and training in the use of the appropriate tools, as well as intelligence, experience, and the ability to order both experience and response into meaningful form. The writer of a literary selection is a creative artist who orders ideas, words, sounds, and rhythms into a particular form, putting them into written symbols. The interpreter, in turn, takes these symbols printed on a page and brings personal experience and insight to bear on the clues the author has given. He or she then submits subjective experience and responses to the order imposed by the creative artist and assumes the responsibility of re-creating the literary entity. This process demands thorough analysis, painstaking rehearsal, and strict discipline in the use of voice and body.

The writer is the creative artist; you, the interpreter, are also a creative artist. You have the privilege of choosing a meaningful example of literary art and bringing it, with its aesthetic qualities intact, to an audience. The introduction, transitions, and program arrangement become part of a *new* artistic product, which, though it owes its first responsibility to the creative artist, in fact becomes a creative act of the interpreter. You are director, arranger, and performer, all in one. The oral interpreter's art is comparable to the art of a musician playing the work of an artist-composer.

The truest and finest art is disarming in its seeming simplicity. Observers are aware of the result, not of the means used to attain the result. Technical display is not art. Art implies the systematic application of knowledge and skill in effecting a desired result, and the desired result in interpretation is precisely the same as that in any other phase of speech: communication. In your case this communication involves *sharing* an *experience*, first with the writer or the speaker of a selection, and then with an audience.

It is the perfect tribute when the members of the audience are captured so thoroughly by the experience of the material that they cannot immediately break the spell to applaud. If an audience says, "What a beautiful voice!" or "What graceful gestures!", the interpreter has failed. When the audience's attention is held by the effect of the material presented, the interpreter has succeeded. But this unobtrusiveness on your part does not result from casual preparation or from a feeling that since the literature is the important thing, you need do no more than face the audience, open the book, and open your mouth. On the contrary, your effectiveness is the result of a preparation so thorough and a technique so perfectly coordinated that the audience cannot see the wheels go around.

. . . *communicating to an audience* . . .   An audience may consist of one person or several thousand. No matter what the size or nature of the audience, your responsibilities are the same. You should communicate as skillfully as possible what is on the printed page, making intelligent use of every detail to achieve the organic whole. The listeners' understanding, their mental and emotional responses to the content and to the form in which it is presented, depend to a large degree on your ability to discover these elements and to project them satisfactorily in their proper relationship.

How do you communicate these elements to the audience? You use your voice and body, which work together and are controlled by an alert and informed mind. Interpreters train their voices and bodies in order to respond to the particular requirements of a work of literature. They strive to eliminate mannerisms that may distract the audience; they are aware of the effect of posture, muscle tone, and general platform presence; and they try to discipline physical action so that it aids communication and in no way calls attention to itself. Interpreters work with their voices during practice periods so that they may be heard and understood. They are aware of the need for flexibility in range, force, stress, and volume, if they are to do justice to the writing and bring out whatever strength and beauty the author has achieved through the sounds and relationships of the words. Their concentration on communicating, on sharing, the material at hand must be strong and continuous. During early rehearsals, interpreters stop to work on difficult segments, as pianists repeatedly finger complicated passages. In later rehearsals, when the selection is thoroughly in mind, and has indeed become a part of them, they turn their attention out to an imagined audience, being careful not to become distracted from the essence of the material that they wish to share with that audience.

Modern interpreters often choose not to memorize selections completely. The time it would take to commit the words to memory might be better spent in studying the material and in perfecting the techniques of communication. Technically speaking, it does not matter in the least whether or not the material is completely memorized. If you choose to memorize, you must concentrate on embodying and sharing the literature rather than on the act of remembering. If you choose not to memorize completely, you must be free enough of the text to concentrate on communicating with the audience rather than on reading. By the time you have analyzed the material in detail, put it back together again, and practiced conscientiously, you will have your selection so firmly implanted in your mind that you will need to glance at the page only occasionally.

Whether the selection is memorized or not, most modern interpreters have the book — or a typescript of the selection — with them during performance. Its presence serves two important purposes. First, it establishes the interpreter as the intermediary between the author and the audience. The printed page is a tool, a medium. Neither the pages in a book nor the words on the page constitute a literary work of art. Printed words are merely a record, a way to preserve word symbols through which an author has set down certain thoughts, emotions, and attitudes. Through the interpreter's voice and body the symbols on the page come alive, and the ideas and experience they symbolize are created anew.

Second, the presence of the book or manuscript serves an aesthetic purpose. It alerts the audience to the fact that the emotions and concepts presented belong to the author, or the speaker, or the characters in the writing. Thus, the book allows the audience to keep some psychological and aesthetic distance from the personality of the interpreter so they can respond to the literature out of their own experience. As an interpreter, you should respond thoroughly to the emotions evident in the selection; however, when your own personal experience is substituted for the experience conveyed by the literature, an audience may become uncomfortable. The presence of the book or manuscript can help to avoid this problem.

. . . a work of literary art in its intellectual, emotional, and aesthetic entirety . . . Your concern is to communicate the total effect of the literary work of art. This does not mean that you should present only complete works, or that you cannot use excerpts. Neither does it mean that the listeners will always receive the full impact of the author's achievement. For instance, they may be able to respond to a complex contemporary poem in only a general way. How fully they respond depends in part on their backgrounds and their familiarity with the work. You should always strive to present the literature in its "intellectual, emotional, and aesthetic entirety." The elements of good writing work so interdependently that to ignore or eliminate any one element is to misread the work.

Listening is a wholly time-bound activity. You, the interpreter, are able to go back and reread certain passages in rehearsal to clarify their relationship with the whole. You know where the entire selection is going and how it gets there. However, your audience has only the fraction of a second to hear words, to translate them into ideas, and to add associations and responses, which are guided by your skillful suggestion in voice and body. Thus, if you understand only half of what you hope to share with the members of your audience, their chances of comprehension and response become minimal. All the various qualities that contribute to the total effect of a selection must be held in their proper relation to the whole.

For purposes of analysis, it is convenient to break a work down into its parts. However, you should always remember that such arbitrary division is only a device to facilitate your understanding. We may conveniently speak of content and structure, of logical meaning, and of emotive quality. But separating literature into these elements is useful *only* as a way of getting at full understanding. Content and structure do not exist as separate entities; they work together to form one organic whole. You should always examine them in relation to each other as you attempt to arrive at the writer's total achievement, which is undeniably more than the sum of its various parts. You should always put the material back together after each step in your analysis of it.

Analysis is one of the most difficult aspects of interpretation, but also one of the most rewarding. We will refer to it frequently in the chapters that follow. As soon as you have discovered one or more clues given by the author, reread the entire selection aloud, seeing how what you have just discovered works within the whole. You should always rehearse aloud even before you are ready to pay particular attention to vocal techniques. Then go back to your analysis and repeat the reading aloud of the entire selection each time you discover more and more helpful details.

Although it is very difficult to isolate and discuss separately certain aspects of a work of art, a full appreciation of the whole is enhanced by careful analysis of the particulars. To begin, you should distinguish the content from the structure of a piece of literature. In the broadest sense, *content* has to do with what is being said, *structure* with the way it is said. Content has two aspects. The first is the *intellectual* or *logical* aspect, which is simply what the material says. It involves an intellectual understanding of the meanings of the words and the relationships between words and groups of words. The other aspect of content is its *emotive* quality, the capacity of both meaning and sound to arouse pleasure or pain, to stimulate the reader and listeners to activity or repose through association. Words seldom have meaning independent of association or have emotion-arousing qualities without meaning. Consequently, for all purposes except analysis the logical and emotive qualities of a work of art can never be divorced. Since understanding takes place simultaneously on the intellectual and emotional levels, you must find out exactly what the author is saying, experience emotionally what is said, and communicate the total response — intellectual and emotional — to the audience.

Structure involves the way a writer has organized the expression of ideas, his or her choice of words, and the relationship of the parts to each other and to the whole. Structure is concerned with the manner of expression, ranging from simple lucidity to the most complex ornamentations of language. The structure of prose, for instance, includes the patterns of phrases and individual sentences, as well as the effect created by several sentences in combination. The structure of drama involves the rhythm of the characters' speeches, their choice of words, the structure of the sentences, and the interrelationship of the speeches, scenes, and acts of the entire play. The structure of poetry includes all the contributions to the sound patterns, the sounds of words in combination, stanzaic structure, scansion, rhyme, and length of line. These elements will be examined in more detail as these types of writing are discussed in later chapters.

. . . aesthetic entirety . . .   The phrase "aesthetic entirety" embraces all the qualities that must be considered to appreciate a piece of writing as a successful work of literary art. These elements should always be evaluated in relation to each other and to the whole.

Aesthetics deals with the theory of the fine arts and the individual's response to the arts. Although the field of aesthetics includes all areas of art, our primary concern in this book is literary art. As a study, aesthetics concerns itself with the ordering of the parts of a work of art, as well as with the response of the beholder. In our case, the interpreter and the listeners are the beholders. Some books for further reading about the topic of aesthetics are listed in the bibliography at the end of this chapter. At the moment, we need to be aware only that there are aesthetic standards for the way that parts work together to create a literary whole. It is this whole, with all its elements intact and correlated, that is to be shared with the audience.

Sources of Material

Interpreters can choose from an almost unlimited range of material. They may use prose, poetry, or drama in epic, lyric, or dramatic modes. Their major considerations are the literary value of the selection, its suitability for the audience, and their own personal interests. This freedom of choice is a distinct advantage for an experienced interpreter, but it may present the beginning student with a problem. From the wealth of available material, where does one begin to select something?

The first question, obviously, is where to look. The selections at the ends of chapters in this book should be helpful. They offer a wide variety of material, much of which can be used with several chapters. If, however, part of your assignment is to find your own material, literary anthologies are a good place to begin your search.

Anthologies are especially valuable to the beginning student of interpretation because they offer a wide selection in a single volume. You will find collections of all types of prose: essays, short stories, humorous and satirical pieces, biographies, letters, diaries, and even novels. You will find poetry classified by kind, such as lyric, narrative, humorous, or didactic; by period or nation, such as Elizabethan, Russian, or contemporary American; and by subject or spirit, such as poems about nature, love, religion, Christmas, protest, or patriotism. If you decide to try drama, you will find many volumes that include either entire plays, both one-act and full-length, or selected scenes. There are also anthologies that cut across these classifications, presenting, for example, chronological surveys of a particular type of literature or examples of regional writing. Of course there are volumes of selected works by individual authors. Dozens of useful anthologies are available in inexpensive editions in any bookstore or in hardback editions in any library.

After your first few assignments, you will have a better idea of the kind of material that appeals to you and where to look for it. You could begin by asking yourself, "What am I most interested in?" Is it the city or the country? Some exotic part of the world or your own home state? Perhaps you are much more interested in people than in places. What kind of people? In what circumstances?

Choosing the Selection: Three Touchstones

To choose material because of its interesting subject matter does not imply that you should make no effort to evaluate its literary worth. On the contrary, throughout this book there is constant concern with evaluation of material through analysis.

Most of us are attracted first to a piece of writing by what it says — its content. As we become more sophisticated, we appreciate more fully the complex relationship between meaning and structure. Although there are numerous ways to treat any subject, some ways are more effective than others. You are probably very fond of certain poems, plays, or stories because of early associations. You are not expected to give up those feelings, but you should not impose them on an audience that does not share your associations, unless your selections are also successful as works of literary art. Neither, of course, should you reject a piece of writing as "bad" because the author did not do what you wish he or she had done. If you do not enjoy a selection, you certainly do not need to choose to read it. Be careful, though, not to limit yourself to what you have always liked and known. Be willing to broaden your horizons. The important thing is not so much to know what you like as to establish criteria for evaluating a literary artist's success or failure. It is important to admit why you do or do not wish to study a certain selection. Even though you may not come to like it, you may learn to respect its qualities as good literature.

Let us assume that you have made a tentative choice of material, or have narrowed down the possibilities to two or three selections that are equally appealing as far as content is concerned. Before making a final decision, you wish to evaluate the choices as pieces of literature. You will do well to consider three factors as touchstones: universality, individuality, and suggestion.

Universality does not mean that the material will immediately appeal to all persons regardless of their intellectual or cultural backgrounds. It means, rather, that the idea expressed is potentially interesting to all people because it touches on a common experience. The emotional response it evokes is one that most readers (and listeners) have felt at one time or another: love or hate, hope or fear, joy or despair.

Literature draws its material from life, but literature is not exactly like life. A writer endeavors to select and control attitudes and motivations, to impose order on the flux and change of human existence, and to give us clues that direct us in relating our own experiences to the order he or she has chosen. Even deliberately distorted events can have relevance to our existence. When writing has universality, you will be able to call on your own background and experience to respond to it. When you communicate all the levels of meaning to an audience, they in turn will have a basis for identification with their own experiences.

However, you should be careful to test your own experience against that recorded by the author. You possibly have not had the identical experience, but you certainly have known, to at least some degree, the emotions of joy or sorrow, fear or yearning, hope or love that the experience recorded calls forth. Your own reaction to the specific situation might not be the same as the author's, but you should strive to identify with the literature even if you must adjust some of the details of a remembered event in order to make your response relevant to that which the author has put down.

The second touchstone of good writing is *individuality* — the writer's own fresh approach to a universal subject. This quality is revealed in choice of words, images, and method of organization. You cannot decide whether or not the author has handled the subject with individuality unless you have had some acquaintance with a wide variety of literature. After some time and experience, you will be able to recognize that individuality results in large part from the author's selectivity and control and is reflected in both content and structure. We shall take a closer look at the element of individuality when we compare two poems later in the chapter.

The subtlest and most rewarding writing is characterized by *suggestion*. The readers are left with something to do: they are not told everything on an immediate, purely logical level. This does not mean that the writing is obscure. It means, rather, that the author has chosen references and words that allow the readers to enrich the subject matter from their own backgrounds. However, there must be enough clear signals for the readers' imaginations to follow. Frequently, considerable analysis is necessary to find and use these signals properly. But once the possibilities for relevant association are realized, the writing continues to grow in meaning and in emotional impact for both the reader-interpreter and the audience. We shall touch on this aspect, too, in our later comparison.

It is obvious, of course, that these three touchstones — universality, individuality, and suggestion — are closely related and serve to enhance and balance each other in effective writing. The author's idea has been drawn from an experience that all people are able to share; the method of expressing the idea is different from that used by other authors; and the suggestion of associated ideas and responses points the way for the reader's imagination to follow and allows for continuing enrichment through the various levels of meaning. Sometimes these three qualities are not present in equal force in a selection, and it is not necessary for them to be. But if any one quality is totally absent or patently weak, you will do well to look elsewhere for material that interests and moves your audience.

To illustrate, let us look at two brief poems, one by Helen Hoyt and one by Emily Dickinson. Each poem contains an intensely personal experience and is written in the first person.

The Sense of Death
HELEN HOYT

Since I have felt the sense of death,
Since I have borne its dread, its fear —
Oh, how my life has grown more dear
Since I have felt the sense of death!
Sorrows are good, and cares are small,
Since I have known the loss of all.

Since I have felt the sense of death,
And death forever at my side —
Oh, how the world has opened wide
Since I have felt the sense of death!
My hours are jewels that I spend,
For I have seen the hours end.

Since I have felt the sense of death,
Since I have looked on that black night —
My inmost brain is fierce with light
Since I have felt the sense of death.
O dark, that made my eyes to see!
O death, that gave my life to me!

Before we look at the second poem, a word of explanation may
be in order. Emily Dickinson did not give her poems titles and in fact
never readied them for publication. Consequently, some of the poems
have several versions, each differing in punctuation and even in word
choice. Dickinson's use of capital letters and dashes is unique. She
frequently capitalizes all the nouns and sometimes uses dashes instead
of commas. The dashes seem compatible with interrupted or suspended thought units.

I Felt a Funeral

EMILY DICKINSON

I felt a Funeral, in my Brain,
And Mourners to and fro
Kept treading — treading — till it seemed
That Sense was breaking through —

And when they all were seated,
A Service, like a Drum —
Kept beating — beating — till I thought
My Mind was going numb —

And then I heard them lift a Box
And creak across my Soul
With those same Boots of Lead, again,
Then Space — began to toll,

As all the Heavens were a Bell,
And Being, but an Ear,
And I, and Silence, some strange Race
Wrecked, solitary, here —

And then a Plank in Reason, broke,
And I dropped down, and down —
And hit a World, at every Crash,
And Got through knowing — then —

The universality of the fact of death and the effect of death cannot
be denied. However, these two poems present this universal experience in markedly different ways. In her poem, Hoyt is talking about
the aftermath of having *sensed* death, probably physical death. Dickinson is talking about the *period* of the *sensing*. She probably is also
talking about despair, a kind of spiritual death so numbing and soul
shattering that it became a "funeral" in her brain. Hoyt uses
straightforward language and sentences that are linked together
loosely without a steady progression of thought. Dickinson also uses
straightforward language, but she introduces the extended metaphor
of a funeral service, which gives pace and progress to her writing.
Finally, Hoyt draws definite, even moralistic, conclusions. Dickinson
merely describes the experience and draws no conclusions.

Hoyt obviously wishes to place death in sharp contrast to a resulting acute appreciation of life. A quick count reveals that half of the
lines are concerned with death and half with life, and this is a very
comfortable balance. Yet the distinct impression remains that this
poem is more about death than life.

She asks us to take "Since" in the sense of "after," as well as in
the sense of cause and effect. She repeats her title as six of the eighteen lines of the poem, and approximates it by parallel construction
in three more. Such repetition could be most effective in creating a
driving, insistent impact. However, the phrase "felt the sense of
death" does not cut into our consciousness with much force. The
word "sense" implies recognition or perception. It is quite possible
to "feel" a "perception," of course, but let us look at the details she
has chosen to give us this perception of death. Death is characterized
by "dread," "fear," "forever at my side," "the hours end," "black
night," and "O dark." None of these references is fresh or individual.
Each has been used in the same connection for so many centuries
that it has become trite. Taken separately and skillfully developed,
each could carry a wealth of suggestion, but Hoyt gives us no time
or incentive to establish an individual identification with what the
"sense" of death was for her, or indeed might be for us.

Admittedly, Hoyt's insistent use of "Since" in nine of the eighteen lines clearly tells us that the experience of sensing death led her
to a new awareness of the value of life. Unfortunately, her references
to life are equally vague and familiar. Life is referred to in "grown
more dear," "Sorrows are good," "cares are small," "world has

opened wide," "hours are jewels that I spend," "inmost brain is fierce with light," "eyes to see," and "gave my life to me." "Sorrows" is so inclusive and allows for such a weight of personal association that we cannot fix on the paradox of sorrows being "good" before we are whisked on to "cares" that are "small." Presumably, this line is intended to set up a balance, but it is not entirely successful, partly because of the inclusiveness and permissiveness of "sorrows" and "cares," and partly because even small cares are not "good," as she asks us to believe sorrows have become. The use of the singular form of "sorrow" and "care" would at least have allowed us to accept these terms in a more abstract sense and hence to identify more easily with the emotional implication. There is, too, a disturbingly familiar ring in the phrase "hours are jewels" and in the verb "spend." It may be quibbling to say that one does not "spend" jewels unless one lives in a medieval economy; nevertheless, the association here is strained. The phrase "inmost brain is fierce with light" is probably the strongest line of the poem, particularly since the poet has set it carefully against "black night." But, again, it goes nowhere — except back to the already quite familiar refrain.

Further study of this poem reveals little individuality, in either the selection of details or the way they are expressed. The element of suggestion is also poorly established beyond the poem's basic premise: after one comes close to death, whether in the actual physical sense or in having been made aware of its omnipresence, life becomes more precious. The words and figures of speech chosen to develop this premise lack the force, freshness, sharpness of focus, and emotive quality that would make us feel that the poet has made us think about something important in an entirely new way.

Dickinson also begins her poem with "I felt," but the clear positioning of the event in time past and its implied completion put it firmly in perspective. Moreover, we are at once drawn into strong suggestion with the word "funeral." A funeral carries a complex weight of values and images; we are bombarded by associations of grief, dignity, ritual, the presence of the body, and a mixture of respect and grim, formal, finality. To "feel" a funeral goes beyond merely attending one. And to feel a funeral *in the brain* goes still further. We immediately are aware of a new and individual approach to the universal subject of death, of spiritual death that destroys the life of the senses, crushes hope, and even denies the power of the soul.

We are given time to develop associations suggested here, and our focus is sharpened by the mourners going to and fro and by the sound they make "treading — treading." We then are returned to sensation in the last line of the first stanza. Two suggested interpretations of this line, rather than being contradictory, provide a thin thread of suspense, strengthened by "till it seemed." On one level, "Sense" may be taken to mean the mind bending under the strain of the "treading." This interpretation is strongly suggested by the word "Brain" in the opening line. But Dickinson may also mean that awareness — "Sense" — had become so acute that the sensation was unbearable. These two interpretations are not mutually exclusive, and both can operate well here in a deliberate and disturbing ambiguity.

The balancing of the concrete elements of a funeral service with the sensation felt in the brain continues to the last line of the third stanza. It is held together and kept vivid by a strict chronological progression, as well as by constant references to sound, already prepared for by "treading — treading." Sound reaches an almost unbearable intensity as "Space — began to toll," and it becomes overwhelming in the opening lines of the next stanza. Our attention is snatched from this climax of sound by "and Silence," which by its very contrast is equally deafening.

At the same time, the mourners and the pallbearers disappear abruptly, leaving the senses "solitary." But the experience does not stop there. It continues in a swift downward pattern, suggesting a lowering into the grave and much more. The breaking "Plank in Reason" suggests a wealth of associations and adds still another dimension to the horror of the drop "down, and down —," which culminates in the highly graphic "hit" and "Crash" in the next-to-last line. The repeated use of "and" involves us in this swift and helpless dropping.

The last line, like several of the others, carries deliberate ambiguity and moves on more than one level. "Got through" may mean "finished" with a mortal type of knowledge. It also may imply having "broken through" into a superhuman, mystical type of knowledge that is possible only after death or a great spiritual crisis. The " — then — " also functions on more than one level. It completes the chronological progression; it terminates the immediate recorded experience; it teases us with a hint that there was more. A skilled interpreter can convey this multiplicity of meanings to the audience.

In our brief analysis of Hoyt's poem, we pointed out the weakness in her balancing of life and death. Dickinson is not talking about life and death as contrasting states, but she manages very skillfully to keep us aware of the world of the living. The reference to those who are attending the "funeral" that she felt in her brain is strong through the first three stanzas, but it is held constantly within the framework of her point of view. Even in the sensation responses there is a quality of living awareness. "Sense," "Mind," "Soul," "Being," "Ear," "Race," and "Reason" all relate to but do not parallel "knowing" in the final line. There is also an alive, human quality in "hit a World," and "every Crash," because they are so essentially physical.

Thus, from the opening line we are aware of a fresh, individual approach to the sensation that Dickinson is writing about. It catches and holds our interest, because it is an unusual but certainly acceptable way of talking about a subject whose universality cannot be denied. It is a succinct, compressed statement that cuts into our awareness and increases our understanding.

During the discussion of Dickinson's poem we mentioned the term "deliberate ambiguity." *Ambiguity* is sometimes confused with lack of clarity, but the term as it is used today in literary criticism means "having more than one possible meaning, all of which are relevant and congruent within the organic whole of the piece of writing." Ambiguity may result in some obscurity, but it must not defy careful study or split the literary selection into incompatible segments. The kind of ambiguity we have been discussing is one of the richest sources of suggestion for the very reason that it does not narrowly circumscribe the experience of the poem.

Hoyt uses outworn and too-familiar references to suggest the terror of death and the glory of life. Dickinson uses images that stir the senses and cause us to respond both emotionally and physically. At the same time, she engages our minds by juxtaposing unexpected and strongly suggestive words. Almost any line serves as an example, but two of the most striking are the opening line and the reference to "a Plank in Reason." At its best, then, suggestion takes us beyond the poem without taking us out of the poem. Suggestion and individuality go hand in hand.

There are numerous matters that we have not even touched on in our evaluation of these two poems, such as rhythm, sound patterns, and the structural complexities of verse. We shall refer to these matters in succeeding chapters when we work with analysis. It was not our intention here — although it was a temptation — to do more than illustrate how the three touchstones of universality, individuality, and suggestion can operate within a piece of literature.

Bibliography

As we mentioned in the chapter, there is a wide range of anthologies, many of them in inexpensive editions, in which you will find a wealth of material. Also, most current textbooks in interpretation contain a large variety of selections. The following books will help you in clarifying terms and in understanding the various approaches to criticism and analysis. Each provides an extensive bibliography.

Abrams, M. H. *The Mirror and the Lamp: Romantic Theory and the Critical Tradition.* New York: Oxford University Press, 1953.
A classic in the expressive theory of criticism, most often remembered for its model whereby all critical theories can be classified according to their primary focus.

Adams, Hazard, ed. *Critical Theory Since Plato.* New York: Harcourt Brace Jovanovich, 1971.
Anthology of major theoretical statements by literary critics from Plato to the present with brief, helpful introductions to each critic and sources for further study.

Barnet, Sylvan, Morton Berman, and William Burto. *A Dictionary of Literary Terms.* Boston: Little, Brown and Company, 1960.
A paperback of brief definitions with cross-references.

Beckson, Karl, and Arthur Ganz. *A Reader's Guide to Literary Terms.* New York: Farrar, Straus & Giroux, 1960.
Similar to *A Dictionary of Literary Terms,* but somewhat more complex.

Booth, Wayne C. *Critical Understanding: The Powers and Limits of Pluralism.* Chicago: University of Chicago Press, 1979.
An examination of M. H. Abrams, Kenneth Burke, and R. S. Crane as pluralist critics and an attempt to formulate an overarching pluralism. An important work in that it argues the significance of all forms of literary criticism and calls for understanding rather than warfare among critics.

Butcher, Samuel Henry. *Aristotle's Theory of Poetry and Fine Art, with a Critical Text and Translation of the Poetics.* 4th ed. New York: Dover Publications, 1951.
A useful and readable translation of Aristotle's classic study, with an essay on Aristotelian criticism by John Gassner.

Gardner, Helen. *The Business of Criticism.* New York: Oxford University Press, 1963.
A defense of the historical method of criticism and a plea for the realliance of criticism with scholarship.

Gilbert, Allan H., ed. *Literary Criticism.* Vol. 1, *Plato to Dryden;* Vol. 2, *Pope to Croce.* Detroit: Wayne State University Press, 1962.
Brief, helpful comments on excerpts from the great critics. Extended bibliographies for each period plus a general bibliography. Carefully indexed for cross-reference.

Grambs, David. *Words About Words.* New York: McGraw-Hill Book Company, 1984.
A dictionary of prose terminology containing entries not often found in traditional literary handbooks. Although many of the entries are technical, this dictionary is a helpful companion to *A Dictionary of Literary Terms.*

Hoffman, Daniel, ed. *Harvard Guide to Contemporary American Writing.* Cambridge, Mass.: Harvard University Press, 1979.

An outstanding critical survey of trends in American prose, poetry, and drama from the 1940s through the 1970s.

Kaplan, Charles, ed. *Criticism: The Major Statements.* 2nd ed. New York: St. Martin's Press, 1985.
Representative essays on criticism from Plato to Barthes.

McGuire, Richard. *Passionate Attention: An Introduction to Literary Study.* New York: W. W. Norton and Company, 1973.
A clear discussion of four approaches to literary criticism based on the first chapter of M. H. Abrams's *The Mirror and the Lamp.*

Scott, Wilbur. *Five Approaches to Literary Criticism.* New York: Collier Books, 1962.
Brief discussions of moral, psychological, sociological, formalistic, and archetypal approaches to criticism followed by essays that illustrate each of these forms.

Shipley, Joseph T., ed. *Dictionary of World Literature: Criticism-Form-Techniques.* 2nd ed. New York: Philosophical Library, 1945.
A complete, scholarly sourcebook of literary terms and genres.

Tomkins, Jane, ed. *Reader-Response Criticism: From Formalism to Post-Structuralism.* Baltimore: Johns Hopkins University Press, 1980.
A collection of essays that traces the re-emergence of the reader in critical theory since 1950.

Wimsatt, W. K., Jr., and Cleanth Brooks. *Literary Criticism: A Short History.* New York: Alfred A. Knopf, 1957.
A clearly presented, succinct account of the development of the field of literary criticism.

The following three collections are among the most popular paperback anthologies available today.

Barnet, Sylvan, Morton Berman, and William Burto. *An Introduction to Literature.* 7th ed. Boston: Little, Brown and Company, 1981.
This impressive edition includes an excellent collection of poems, stories, and plays with useful, brief discussions of genres and modes.

Cassill, R. V. *The Norton Anthology of Short Fiction.* New York: W. W. Norton and Company, 1978.
These short stories, collected from classic and contemporary sources, offer rich and diverse challenges to the performer.

Main, C. F., and Peter J. Seng. *Poems.* 4th ed. Belmont, Calif.: Wadsworth Publishing Company, 1978.
A brief discussion of poetic techniques with a collection of poems from all periods.

2

Analyzing the Selection

It may be the case that you expected what you are hearing now. But even in that case you expected something different.

Peter Handke, "Offending the Audience"

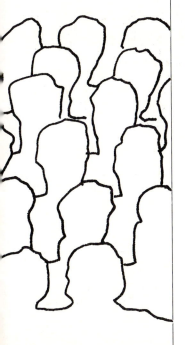

In Chapter 1 we used the three touchstones of universality, individuality, and suggestion to compare two short poems. This brief examination revealed some differences between the two selections. It also presented a starting point for interpreters who need to know how to choose a selection to which they can respond and that will interest an audience by providing a fresh look at a rich universal experience.

After making a selection, you should thoroughly investigate everything that's found within that particular piece of literature. You should know precisely what the author has given you to work with, accepting responsibility for discovering and making proper use of the author's organization and method of presentation. Only when you fully understand the author's achievement can you decide how to use your own technique to create the experience for the audience.

In order to evoke a desired response, an interpreter should be constantly concerned with the selection, arrangement, and expression of the author's ideas. First, of course, you should try to find out precisely what the literature is saying. You may easily understand the general meaning of a selection and yet find some specific lines or phrases that are not entirely clear. If so, look up the unfamiliar words and references. You cannot afford to gloss over them. The word or allusion is there because the author felt that it expresses exactly what he or she wished to say. For the author, it is not *almost* the right word; it is *precisely* the word that is needed. Consequently, you cannot hope to achieve the author's full purpose with only a vague idea of the definitions or connotations of the words. In fact, an idea may be distorted if you mistake the full meaning of a word or phrase.

The dictionary is, of course, the first source to consult. The dictionary gives primarily *denotative* meanings — what a word means *explicitly*. For example, it defines "funeral" as "the ceremonies held in connection with the burial or cremation of the dead." But of course we all know perfectly well what the denotative meaning of "funeral" is. However, as we look at the word in Emily Dickinson's poem in Chapter 1, a cluster of associations grows out of our experience with "funeral." Gradually, the word begins to mean more than its bare dictionary definition. The "more" is the *connotative* meaning: suggestions of associations and overtones that go beyond the explicit, or denotative, meaning. Connotative meaning is an associated meaning and often is partially based on subjective values. But successful writers give the reader enough clues to the way the word should be taken so that the connotative meaning is not entirely subjective. We should remember that connotation suggests *"in addition* to," not "instead of."

Connotation is most important when we consider the emotive quality of content, but it must not be overlooked or misunderstood when determining logical content. When a writer selects a particular word from several possible choices, it is because that word conveys something over and above what it "means." What that something else is, what special flavor it adds to the whole, is for you to ferret out and convey to the audience. We shall have more to say about connotation when we examine the various ways in which it operates in the major types of literature.

Closely allied with connotative meaning is the function of allusions. *Allusions* are references to persons, places, or events, real or mythological, that call up relevant associations. Allusions are useful, because in a word or phrase they can establish an entire complex of connotations. Tennyson's "Ulysses" (Chapter 4), for example, is based on allusion. The name Ulysses immediately brings to mind the great adventurer and leader in *The Odyssey* by Homer.

The consideration of connotative or associational meanings links interpretation to the whole field of semantics, which is the study of meanings and the relationship of "sets of signs." In literature, these signs are the words and the arrangement of them by which the author has chosen to express his or her ideas and share his or her experience. They are also the nonverbal signs that the interpreter sends out to the audience during performance. Consideration of connotative meanings also touches on the newer and somewhat broader field of semiotics. The terms *semantics* and *semiotics* are both derived from the same stem as the word *semaphore*, which is the translation of the positioning of objects, usually flags, into messages. (Used in its broadest sense, semiotics examines the general principles underlying all sign systems.)

For some interpreters, semiotics provides a method of accounting for the many complex constraints that affect performance. An interpreter speaks the words of the text, of course. But while doing so the interpreter also gestures, intones, glances, and allows the muscles of his or her entire body to respond to the emotions in the literature. And at the same time the world surrounding the performer sends its own conflicting signals to an audience: horns honking, doors slamming. Each variable articulates its own message, and this message may complement the text or conflict with it. Watching and listening, each person in the audience then receives all the signs and creates within himself or herself the text being communicated. The audience also incorporates what fulfills some of the performer's cues. At the same time, they discard potential conflicts and, in the process, return signs to the performer (laughter on an unexpected line, for example).

These signs in turn refine and enrich the performer's knowledge of the text.[1]

Our primary concern in this text is the words of the literature and their "messages," which become complex appeals to our own universal experiences. The individuality in an author's choice of "signals" gives us a basis for making our reponses relevant to the experiences the author is sharing. After making sure of the full meaning of the words, the interpreter must examine the organization of ideas. Most material divides rather easily into three parts: the introduction or lead-in portion, the body of the material, and the conclusion or tying-up unit. Usually, the body of the material contains the author's main point. However, it is important to make careful use of the selection and arrangement of details and ideas in each unit if the listeners are to perceive each section in its proper relation to the whole.

Within each unit there are key sentences or phrases on which the logical and emotional progression depends. They may contain a new idea or another aspect of an idea introduced previously. The interpreter should know the position and function of each key so that it can be clearly established in the minds of the audience in its proper relationship to all the other phrases and sentences and to the whole unit.

Climax

As you discover the key details within the introduction, body, and conclusion of the selection and evaluate each one in its relationship to the whole, you will find that they vary in importance. Occasionally they merely implant an idea or clue that becomes important later in the development of plot or action. Frequently, however, they indicate a high point of logical development or of emotional impact and may be considered *climaxes*. There are often several minor climaxes leading up to and/or following the major climax. A climax may be the culmination of the logical content, the high point of emotional impact, or a combination of both. Thus we may speak of *logical climax* and *emotional climax*, remembering that this separation is only for convenience in analysis and that ultimately we shall put them back together as they operate within the whole.

1. These sentences vastly oversimplify modern theories of semiotics. A good introduction is A. A. Berger's *Signs in Contemporary Culture* (New York: Longman, 1984). The authoritative discussion remains Umberto Eco's in *A Theory of Semiotics* (Bloomington: Indiana University Press, 1976).

In a play or story, the logical climax is often called the *crisis*. The crisis is the point at which the conflict becomes so intense that a resolution must occur and after which only one outcome is possible. In an essay, the logical climax occurs when the writer makes the main point with such clarity that the conclusion is inevitable. In a poem, it is the point at which the author completes the logical development upon which the emotional content is based.

The emotional climax is the moment of highest emotional impact and involvement for the reader. If this seems to be a completely subjective matter, we should remember that the writer gives us clues to follow. If our analysis is careful and we let the author lead the way, we generally will be moved most strongly at the point of emotional climax. It is important to be sure that we take into account the *whole* selection in our response. Because there are many degrees of emotion, the emotional climax may be as gentle as that in Hopkins's "The Starlight Night" at the end of this chapter or as dramatic as that in Sophocles' *Oedipus the King* (Chapter 8). If you use only part of a long selection, locating the climax or climaxes within that unit is especially important in making the audience feel that they have received a complete, unified, and fulfilling experience.

Sometimes the highest emotional intensity coincides with the logical climax. Often, however, this is not the case. The logical climax may precede and prepare for the emotional high point. This happens when the emotional climax depends on a character's or speaker's response to a completed cycle of events. On the other hand, if the outcome of events depends on an emotional reaction, the emotional climax precedes the logical climax, as it does in Dickinson's poem in Chapter 1. Here the impact of space, silence, and solitude precedes the completion of the fall.

You may find this dual aspect of climax difficult to convey, but understanding and experience will help you to cope with the problem. The logical climax, for instance, probably needs a particularly high degree of definition on the part of the interpreter. However, if you drive too hard at your listeners with this concept, the impact of the emotional climax may suffer. The audience will receive the full emotional impact only if you respond personally while reading. This does not mean that you should pull out all the stops and burst into tears or shake your fists in fury. You should, however, train yourself to respond in such a way that your nonverbal communication or body signals are in harmony with what the words are saying. It is important to be aware that literature moves on several levels and consequently may achieve its high point of logical development in one place and its emotional climax in another, although neither climax may be said to occur independently of the other. After each step in analysis, remember to put the material back together so that you may look again at the selection in its entirety as a guide to the use of performance techniques.

The discussion above is particularly pertinent if you choose to use an excerpt from a long selection. Many of the selections in this text are too long to be practical for a class assignment, but most of them offer units that may be used for excerpts. In general, poetry should not be cut because of its compactness and because cutting individual lines destroys a poem's structural unity.

When you choose an excerpt from a play or a piece of narrative prose, be sure to select a unit with at least a minor climax, so that your audience gets a sense of something happening. You need to be aware of the key sentences or phrases in earlier sections that your audience must know about in order to understand and respond to the climax. Often you can use the paragraph in which the key appears and then make a transition, probably in your own words, to the climactic unit you are reading. Sometimes it is clearer and smoother to include a reference to the key in your introduction. Although your introduction and transitions do not tell the audience what they are going to hear (except, of course, for the title), they do get your listeners ready, often with subtle cues, for what is to come.

Keep in mind that your introduction and transitions should be as brief as possible, and their style should be in harmony with the mood you want to create. You should address them directly to the audience, without using written notes. Your listeners want to believe that this is a special performance just for them, and the introduction and transitions should appear to be spontaneous. They are an important part of your performance.

Persona

Personae, the plural form of *persona,* has traditionally meant the characters in a piece of fictional writing such as a narrative or a play. Recently the singular, *persona,* has been used to indicate the speaker, the one who relates the experience in a piece of literature, whether it is fictional or true, poetry or prose, dramatic or nondramatic. The speaker may be someone who closely resembles the author in thoughts and attitudes, as in Capote's *A Christmas Memory* (at the end of this chapter), or the character may be quite different from the author, as in Browning's "Soliloquy of the Spanish Cloister" (Chapter 9) and in Betts's "The Ugliest Pilgrim" (Chapter 6).

In drama, obviously, there may be many speakers, and although all are under the control of the author, the speaking character's motivation and reactions will arise from the dramatic situation and from his or her relationships with other characters. In some cases, one or more of these characters may seem to speak directly for the playwright, indicating a particular attitude toward the world, human nature, or the events of the play. Such a character may even resemble the playwright in biographical details. An excellent example of this sort of character is found in Leonard's *Da* (Chapter 8): from time to time, Charlie addresses the audience directly, in character, bridging the passage of time and telling us certain things about the other characters that even they are not fully aware of.

In narratives, the narrator is clearly the controlling voice that tells us what we need to know about background and plot progression. The narrator may be a character in the story and involved directly in the events; in this case he or she speaks in his or her own person as that character, as in Sherman's "Dulce" or in Cameron's "Homework" (both at the end of this chapter). Or the speaker may be a benevolently objective reporter, as Morrill is in "Miss Lizzie" (also at the end of this chapter).

In lyric poetry the persona is often the poet speaking. Of course, authors change their minds and their moods. We have only to look at the two sonnets by Shakespeare at the end of this chapter to be aware that they exhibit quite different attitudes. There can be no doubt that both Dickinson and Hoyt (in Chapter 1) are sharing their own highly personal experiences, as are Whitman, Keats, and Hopkins in the three poems about stars that appear at the end of this chapter. It is not unusual, however, for a poet to create a thinly veiled mouthpiece to express ideas and reactions. This is certainly the case with Frost's "Wild Grapes" (at the end of this chapter), where the speaker is a woman "grown to wisdom": one critic has said of her, "She speaks in Robert Frost's tone of voice." In Roethke's "Child on Top of a Greenhouse" (Chapter 10), Roethke is recalling an experience out of his own childhood. The speaker is not the little boy who got himself into such an exciting predicament; rather, it is the poet, who remembers how it felt. The language and images are not a child's. In Roethke's "Old Lady's Winter Words" (Chapter 4), however, the persona is the old lady, as Roethke carefully indicates in the title.

Locus

Closely allied to the concept of persona is the theory of *locus*. Locus is the physical and psychological position of the persona in relation to the experience. Locus encompasses both time and space. It refers, initially, to place, deriving from the Latin root that underlies our words *location*, *locale*, and *locate*. Actors and directors who refer to shooting films "on location," or writers who speak of searching for a "new locale" for a story, are concerned with locus. In the term's broadest sense, then, the locus of a work of literature is the place where the action of the story occurs. In Tennyson's "Ulysses," the locus is the hearthside at which the hero muses about his past and future. In "Dulce," the locus is sharply focused on the grave during most of the story. The locus affects and is reflected in the mood and attitude of the speaker.

Locus includes more than simply the locale or setting for the action. It also involves the relationship between the speaker of a given line and all the surrounding world — not just the physical world of trees or hills or country, but also the audience to whom that speaker addresses that line and the relationship that speaker enjoys with that audience. In *Romeo and Juliet* (Chapter 8), when Juliet addresses her mother, it should be clear that she has a definite established relationship with her, a relationship that is very different from the ones she has established with the Nurse and with Romeo. She addresses her mother in a way appropriate to their particular relationship.

Less immediately obvious, on the other hand, is the situation of the speaker in Roethke's "Old Lady's Winter Words." What is her environment? Is she speaking these words to herself or to someone else? Where is this person who is being addressed? What would an audience at your performance of this poem see and hear as your relationship with the world of the poem?

These examples all involve questions of locus, because they all entail the speaker's relationship to his or her surroundings. If the persona is addressing another character, the performer envisions that character slightly above and beyond the audience. If the speaker is speaking or musing to herself, the performer may keep the scene and the surrounding environment out front, in the audience area, without, of course, singling out any specific audience member as the object of the words.[2] Obviously there are other choices you can make. Answer these questions: What is the relationship between the speaker and the audience? Is the audience overhearing

---

2. Some interpreters describe this last suggestion as a "closed" situation, as opposed to an "open" situation, in which a character directly addresses an audience. See, for example, Wallace Bacon, *The Art of Interpretation*, 3rd ed. (New York: Holt, Rinehart and Winston, 1979), p. 74. See also Alethea Smith Mattingly and Wilma Grimes, *Interpretation: Writer, Reader, Audience*, 2nd ed. (Belmont, Calif.: Wadsworth, 1970), pp. 18–19. Both books provide useful discussions of locus, with interesting and helpful aspects of locus discussed and illustrated.

what the character is saying? Is the character talking directly to them? If the character is speaking to an audience in the story, what will the audience at the performance see and hear? Each of these questions presumes a different environment, a different attitude, because each one demonstrates a different locus.

Finally, for some interpreters, locus refers to the story's attitude about the events it describes. Just as a camera describes the point of view of the action, viewing an incident from a sweeping panorama or focusing closely on a specific detail, such as the way the chef ever so carefully pipes the icing on the cake, so does a story or a poem or a play evoke an attitude toward the events it recounts. This attitude is not simply the same perspective as the point of view of the narrator, although the narrator's position is a part of it. We may feel some revulsion at an incident or character attribute within a selection, but perhaps no such revulsion is expressed by any of the characters or even by the narrator. In this, its fullest sense, locus includes the relationship between the entire tale and the world it inhabits and describes. Only when the locus of the line or speech or scene is clear in your mind can you make those performance choices that convey most fully the literature you have chosen.

Intrinsic Factors

So far we have been concerned largely with a general view of the material the interpreter chooses to use. Now we shall turn our attention to the details that work together to produce certain clearly discernible factors in a work of art. These factors, which we shall call the *intrinsic factors*, are found in varying degrees in all successful writing. Our interest here goes beyond illustration to an examination of how these factors function for the interpreter's more complete understanding and communication, and how the matters we have discussed thus far relate to the effectiveness of these intrinsic factors.

The intrinsic factors are *unity* and *harmony*, *variety* and *contrast*, *balance* and *proportion*, and *rhythm*. They are termed intrinsic because they are clearly discernible within the printed selection and because they appear the same to all qualified judges. To appreciate them, one does not depend on the uniqueness and range of one's personal experience, but rather on judgment of the selection itself. Since these elements are evident in content and structure and in the relationship between the two, you will need to know exactly how they operate within the selection. You will also learn to appreciate the author's skill in handling these intrinsic factors and thus acquire another standard by which to make critical judgments.

The intrinsic factors should not be thought of as separate entities. They should be considered in relation to all the other qualities of the selection if they are to make their true contribution to the total effect. They have bearing on and are affected by both the arrangement and organization of the material, and also its logical meaning and emotive quality. After you have thoroughly analyzed the material in terms of these factors, you should, as always, put it back together again. The audience must never be aware of any one of the factors in itself, only of the total effect. As a matter of fact, analysis will show that no one factor can be completely separated from the others. They overlap, correlate with, and affect each other. Many elements in the writing may contribute to more than one of these factors within a single selection. Yet each makes its own subtle contribution to the whole. We shall discuss the intrinsic factors briefly and then identify and examine them in both a story and a poem.

Unity and Harmony

Unity is the combining and ordering of all the parts that make up the whole. It consists of those elements of content and form that hold the writing together and keep the readers' and listeners' minds focused on the total effect.

Unity may be achieved in any number of ways. The persona is a strong unifying factor, as is locus. The setting and time may change within a piece of narrative, but the locus, the physical and psychological relationship of the persona to the events that control the persona's point of view, usually remains constant. Sometimes the persona or the characters go through a clear and unmistakable process of development, which in its progression unifies the material. As you look at a selection, you should observe all of the details that help to accomplish this unification. Connectives, such as "and," "then," "next," "a few hours later," and "after this," are important. It is impossible for us to list all of the possible contributions to unity that occur in a wide range of literature. You should approach each selection as a new problem and analyze it carefully to find everything that has been provided for holding the material together.

Harmony is the appropriate adjustment of parts to one another to form a satisfying whole. In literature it is the concord between the idea and the way that idea is expressed. Harmony is achieved in part through the author's choice of words, the sentence structure, and the relationship of phrases and clauses within the sentences. Obviously, then, it depends to a large extent on elements of style. In poetry, rhythmic elements serve to enhance harmony. Another important source of harmony is the selection of details that set up associations in the readers' minds. Thus, harmony is paired with unity. Although these two factors differ in definition, they are clearly interdependent and must function together if the writing is to achieve its intended effect.

Variety and Contrast

A picture painted in only one color or a musical composition with only one repeated melody is generally dull and uninteresting. In the same way, a piece of literature that lacks variety and contrast is not likely to hold a reader's attention for long.

Variety is provided when two things of the same general kind differ from each other in one or more details. For example, several characters of the same age, sex, and social background essentially may agree but express themselves differently. Or one character, at two or more points of his or her development, may retain unifying qualities but may demonstrate reactions in varying ways.

Contrast implies a sharper differentiation. It is concerned with the opposition or differences between associated things. Two characters may be set against each other by their opposing responses to a situation, or by different actions and motivations. Characters may be contrasted in appearance, age, wisdom, emotion, or any number of other attributes. One place or time may be contrasted with another. Quiet may be set against noise, dark against light, hope against despair, positive elements against negative.

Thus, variety and contrast are closely related. They function together to provide a change of emphasis or to heighten an effect. They are extremely effective in holding attention. You will find them invaluable in the clues they give for vocal and physical vividness. At no time, however, should either the writer or the interpreter allow variety and/or contrast to become so strong that they destroy the proper relationship of the parts to the whole. These two factors always must be held within the bounds of unity and harmony.

Balance and Proportion

Balance and *proportion* are more difficult to evaluate. The test to apply is how well they implement the other factors and contribute to the effect of the whole.

Since proportion provides balance, the two factors should be considered together. A seesaw balances when the fulcrum is exactly the same distance from each end of the board. When equal weights are placed at each end, that balance is retained. But when a heavier weight is placed on one end of the board, the balance is destroyed. Balance can be restored by an adjustment of proportions, either by moving the fulcrum toward the end on which the heavier weight rests or by moving the heavier object closer to the fulcrum.

When equal weights or quantities lie at equal distances from a central point, the balance is said to be symmetrical. For example, identical candlesticks placed equidistant from the center of a mantel-piece provide a symmetrical balance. Perfect balance is satisfying to the senses, but sometimes the asymmetrical or unequal balance achieved by an adjustment of distance, weights, and masses may be more interesting and effective. Instead of the candlesticks on the mantel, there may be a tall plant at one end and a low, bright-colored bowl at the other. These two objects do not agree in size and shape, but the bulk, height, or weight of the one is somehow balanced by the intensity of color in the other.

Balance also exists within a piece of literature. It is brought about by the intensity or the proportion of content on either side of the point at which the entire selection seems to pivot and change direc-tion. This point of balance occurs at the *crisis* in a story or a play. In a poem, as on a seesaw, it is called the *fulcrum*. The fulcrum or point of balance may or may not coincide with either the logical or the emotional climax.

The principle of point of balance is more important in the consid-eration of brief, compact selections than of longer units, and you will find it particularly helpful when you analyze poetry. As we men-tioned in Chapter 1, in the twelfth line of Dickinson's "I Felt a Fu-neral," attention shifts from the funeral and things of the earth to "Space." This, then, is the fulcrum of the poem.

Some selections seem to reach a balance point almost exactly in the middle: there is about the same amount of material leading up to and following the fulcrum. This is clearly the case with Chopin's "The Story of an Hour" (analyzed later in this chapter) or Alice Walker's untitled poem (Chapter 10). Such symmetrical balance gives the interpreter a fairly easy task. You need only to be sure to build to the proper point and not to allow the audience's interest to wane thereafter. If the author has arranged the material so that such han-dling is achieved without too much difficulty, he or she may be con-sidered successful in the use of symmetrical balance.

Frequently, however, the balance is off center, especially in con-temporary writing. In many cases, the greater proportion of the total material precedes the fulcrum. For example, Roethke's "Child on Top of a Greenhouse" (Chapter 10) turns on the last line.

Asymmetrical balance is effective in producing sudden shock, or a feeling of unrest, or a spark of humor. It is effective, however, only when the author has been careful to weight the smaller proportion of material with enough vividness and emotional intensity to enable it to hold its own against the greater number of words it must balance. When this has been taken care of in the writing, you need only to make use of the author's clues and add the proper amount of emotional intensity, emphasis, and stress to the smaller unit to achieve perfect balance in your performance.

Rhythm

In literature *rhythm* is usually thought of as an element of poetic structure, such as the relationship between stressed and unstressed syllables. But rhythm is an important aspect of content as well. Rhythm of content is found in both logical and emotional content as they operate together. We shall delay a discussion of structural rhythm until the later chapters on prose style and poetic structure.

Rhythm of content may be established in many ways in both prose and poetry, and it will begin to emerge as you study details of organization and style. For example, in Dickinson's "I Felt a Funeral," there is a steady alternation between references to the speaker in the poem and to "them." The briefer the selection, the more important this factor is likely to be.

The selection from Genesis I (Chapter 6) provides a very clear example of the rhythm of content in prose. Here the style so clearly underscores the progression of events that the effect is one of a steady build-up to the climax: the creation of humanity. Each step in the process leading up to this climax — the creation of the firmament, the waters, the trees and plants and animals — has its own introduction, its own point of completion, and its own conclusion. Each step is introduced by a low-key declaration of God's intention. Immediately the command is given, with the full assurance that it will be carried out. The act is performed, and God's approval is stated. Thus, each unit builds to its own minor climax, and each of the succeeding steps increases in its importance to us until we reach the creation of humanity.

Rhythm of content is also established by the location, frequency, and intensity of emotional build-ups and minor climaxes. This is certainly the technique in Genesis I. It is also a factor in "I Felt a Funeral," as we point out in our detailed analysis of this short poem later in this chapter.

Drama has a rhythm set up by its acts and scenes, as well as by the dialogue within the scenes. In addition to shifts in focus of attention from one character to another and the build-ups and drops in emotional content and tension, scenes often alternate between the active and the static. Some scenes suspend the main plot in order to develop a subplot or humor. Shakespeare uses this technique with particular skill in many of his plays.

Thus a rhythm of content can be set up by the recurrent shift of attention from one character to another or from one place or time to another, or by the alternation of description and narration or dialogue and exposition. The rhythm of emotional quality can be measured by the increased and decreased intensity of the reader's response, and it becomes evident as the minor climaxes are discovered. As we analyze more deeply, we shall discover many more ways of identifying and expressing this factor.

Rhythm of content is important to an interpreter, because it is closely related to holding an audience's attention. Most people are able to concentrate fully and exclusively on an idea for only a brief time. The skillful writer allows for this fatigue or wavering of attention and permits the reader to relax from time to time. By understanding and conveying this rhythm of concentration, you can do the same for your audience.

Furthermore, listeners cannot be held at a high emotional pitch for very long periods of time. In spite of themselves, and in spite of the interpreter's best efforts, they experience a sense of relaxation following the high points of emotional response. The wise writer and the informed interpreter will provide for this relaxation so that the emotional climaxes may be more effective, especially if they depend on accumulation of feeling. Be careful, however, not to break your own concentration. As we have seen, rhythm is also an excellent device for keeping variety and contrast in control within the essential frame of unity.

You will receive a great deal of help from the intrinsic factors within a piece of literature. The problem is how to go about finding them and using the understanding gained from this analysis in preparation and performance. Each selection differs from every other in the degree of importance that should be attached to the various factors. You should let the author lead the way, using what is actually *in* the writing rather than trying to fit the selection to a preconceived pattern. The first step should always be to look at the selection carefully and try to discover everything that the author has given you to work with. Then, and only then, should you be concerned specifically with unity and harmony, variety and contrast, balance and proportion, and rhythm. A careful consideration of these intrinsic factors will help you to put the piece of literature back together so that all the elements operate within the organic whole.

A Sample Analysis of a Story

All of these devices of analysis are really only tools to help you understand both what the author wrote and how it was written. Your close analysis using these tools will be different with each selection you perform, because each piece of literature is different and because you change each time you perform. Do not allow yourself to pass by the analysis stage, however. You wouldn't begin a long car journey to a place you've never been without carefully consulting a good map. Literary analysis, as we have said, is not an end in itself but a means to achieve an informed and rich rehearsal period and the fullest possible performance.

We provide sample analyses of a very short story and a poem. These discussions are obviously different in several respects, in part because poems and stories are frequently very different. The two works themselves — about superficially similar concerns such as life, death, and the realization of how both are ingeniously intertwined — present different performance problems and suggest different solutions. Do not be concerned that any other selection you make — another poem or another story — may not demonstrate exactly the same relationships between variety and contrast or the same use of balance and proportion as these do. Use these works as *examples*. You may discover aspects of the literature we have not mentioned, or you may emphasize something we have only touched upon. Remember: informed discussion requires information. Look carefully, gauge cautiously; an exciting journey is about to begin.

"The Story of an Hour" was written around the turn of the century by the American author Kate Chopin. Read it carefully once or twice before reading the analysis. (We have numbered the paragraphs for easy reference.)

The Story of an Hour
KATE CHOPIN

1 Knowing that Mrs. Mallard was afflicted with a heart trouble, great care was taken to break to her as gently as possible the news of her husband's death.

2   It was her sister Josephine who told her, in broken sentences, veiled hints that revealed in half concealing. Her husband's friend Richards was there, too, near her. It was he who had been in the newspaper office when intelligence of the railroad disaster was received, with Brently Mallard's name leading the list of "killed." He had only taken the time to assure himself of its truth

by a second telegram, and had hastened to forestall any less careful, less tender friend in bearing the sad message.

3   She did not hear the story as many women have heard the same, with a paralyzed inability to accept its significance. She wept at once, with sudden, wild abandonment, in her sister's arms. When the storm of grief had spent itself she went away to her room alone. She would have no one follow her.

4   There stood, facing the open window, a comfortable, roomy armchair. Into this she sank, pressed down by a physical exhaustion that haunted her body and seemed to reach into her soul.

5   She could see in the open square before her house the tops of trees that were all aquiver with the new spring life. The delicious breath of rain was in the air. In the street below a peddler was crying his wares. The notes of a distant song which some one was singing reached her faintly, and countless sparrows were twittering in the eaves.

6   There were patches of blue sky showing here and there through the clouds that had met and piled above the other in the west facing her window.

7   She sat with her head thrown back upon the cushion of the chair quite motionless, except when a sob came up into her throat and shook her, as a child who has cried itself to sleep continues to sob in its dreams.

8   She was young, with a fair, calm face, whose lines bespoke repression and even a certain strength. But now there was a dull stare in her eyes, whose gaze was fixed away off yonder on one of those patches of blue sky. It was not a glance of reflection, but rather indicated a suspension of intelligent thought.

9   There was something coming to her and she was waiting for it, fearfully. What was it? She did not know; it was too subtle and elusive to name. But she felt it, creeping out of the sky, reaching toward her through the sounds, the scents, the color that filled the air.

10   Now her bosom rose and fell tumultuously. She was beginning to recognize this thing that was approaching to possess her, and she was striving to beat it back with her will — as powerless as her two white slender hands would have been.

11   When she abandoned herself a little whispered word escaped her slightly parted lips. She said it over and over under her breath: "Free, free, free!" The vacant stare and the look of terror that had followed it went from her eyes. They stayed keen and bright. Her pulses beat fast, and the coursing blood warmed and relaxed every inch of her body.

12   She did not stop to ask if it were not a monstrous joy that held her. A clear and exalted perception enabled her to dismiss the suggestion as trivial.

13   She knew that she would weep again when she saw the kind, tender hands folded in death; the face that had never looked save with love upon her, fixed and gray and dead. But she saw beyond that bitter moment a long procession of years to come that would belong to her absolutely. And she opened and spread her arms out to them in welcome.

14   There would be no one to live for during those coming years; she would live for herself. There would be no powerful will bending her in that blind persistence with which men and women believe they have a right to impose a private will upon a fellow-creature. A kind intention or a cruel intention made the act seem no less a crime as she looked upon it in that brief moment of illumination.

15   And yet she had loved him — sometimes. Often she had not. What did it matter! What could love, the unsolved mystery, count for in face of this possession of self-assertion which she suddenly recognized as the strongest impulse of her being.

16   "Free! Body and soul free!" she kept whispering.

17   Josephine was kneeling before the closed door with her lips to the keyhole, imploring for admission. "Louise, open the door! I beg; open the door — you will make yourself ill. What are you doing, Louise? For heaven's sake open the door."

18   "Go away. I am not making myself ill." No; she was drinking in a very elixir of life through that open window.

19   Her fancy was running riot along those days ahead of her. Spring days, and summer days, and all sorts of days that would be her own. She breathed a quick prayer that life might be long. It was only yesterday she had thought with a shudder that life might be long.

20   She arose at length and opened the door to her sister's importunities. There was a feverish triumph in her eyes, and she carried herself unwittingly like a goddess of Victory. She clasped her sister's waist, and together they descended the stairs. Richards stood waiting for them at the bottom.

21   Some one was opening the front door with a latchkey. It was Brently Mallard who entered, a little travel-stained, composedly carrying his grip-sack and umbrella. He had been far from the scene of accident, and did not even know there had been one. He stood amazed at Josephine's piercing cry; at Richards' quick motion to screen him from the view of his wife.

22   But Richards was too late.

23   When the doctors came they said she had died of heart disease — of joy that kills.

The most important questions an interpreter confronts when studying a story are "Who is telling this story?" and "What is happening during the story?" All of the devices of structure we have mentioned, all of the intrinsic factors, all of the author's skill, give clues to help you discover the answer to these questions. "The Story of an Hour" provides a rich opportunity to examine the ways in which an author creates a storyteller and a story to tell.

Often, the best way to understand the nature of the narrator and the tale being told is to examine the story very closely. First, of course, we have to be sure we understand the dictionary meanings of all of the words. Are you sure that "elixir" (paragraph 18) refers to a cure-all? Are Josephine's "importunities" (paragraph 20) requests or demands or both? Have you ever seen a picture of a "goddess of Victory"? There are several famous sculptures on this theme. How does Mrs. Mallard carry herself in order to look like such a figure? Once these questions are answered, we can investigate the story in more depth.

In the space of this hour (although performing the story takes little more than five minutes), Mrs. Mallard undergoes an extraordinary change. On one hand, the characters in the story see only a woman distraught with grief who appears to die from joy at the appearance of the husband she thought dead. Balancing that view, we know that within this hour Mrs. Mallard begins to live another, richer, more fearful life of independence, a life of her own. When her old life returns (in the person of her husband), she knows that the rich new life she had embraced will never be possible, and she dies from a "joy that kills." The narrator lets us imagine what pained disappointment goes through her mind when she sees her husband again. But just as we did not share her thoughts when she learned of her husband's death, we do not share her thoughts when she sees he lives. Because we were with her only for the time she began to live, we know Mrs. Mallard better than any of her family or friends.

"Who is telling this story?" The storyteller is unnamed but clearly knows all the people in the tale. For all of them — storyteller and characters — Mrs. Mallard is the center of the tale, from the first paragraph to the last. The other characters — Josephine, Richards, and Brently — exist only as agents in her life. The narrator describes Mrs. Mallard's grief over her husband's presumed death, notes care-

fully her fears and concerns, and dwells at length on the impending
changes his death carries. In so brief a story, her victory is scrupulously described. Clearly, the narrator has a close, sensitive relationship with Mrs. Mallard.

We understand this relationship more fully when the narrator
tells us of Mrs. Mallard's change. After having expended "the storm
of grief," Mrs. Mallard "went away to her room alone. She would
have no one follow her" (paragraph 3). But *we* follow her closely,
guided by the narrator, who describes for us the furnishings of this
room barred to everyone else (paragraph 4), the view only Mrs. Mallard can see (paragraphs 5–6), Mrs. Mallard's very private behavior
(paragraph 7), and her physical features as she is experiencing the
change (paragraph 8). Because of the narrator's special access to Mrs.
Mallard, we are privileged to know her in complex ways others cannot. And our view gets richer. We move from the world outside Mrs.
Mallard to the world inside her. In contrast to what others hear
through the doors, we see a woman confronting independence.
Thus, by varying the ways in which the narrator reveals Mrs. Mallard
to us, the author contrasts her inner and outer worlds.

As Mrs. Mallard begins to consider life without her husband, the
narrator carefully describes the internal turmoil Mrs. Mallard experiences — how she feels, what she thinks, how her body throbs with
anxiety and fear (paragraphs 9 and 10). Only because the narrator
tells us are we permitted to hear her whispered cries (paragraph 11).
Solely because the narrator shows us do we see how she starts to live
without a husband (paragraphs 12–14). Her new status both dismays
and exhilarates her. It seems to have rushed in upon her after the
stately opening paragraphs, but there is something splendid about it
all the same. Dauntless, she continues to repeat the exhilarating word
"Free!" (paragraph 16).

To balance this internal view, at this point the narrator returns
us to the world outside the bedroom. Josephine's concern about Mrs.
Mallard and her fear that she will make herself ill contrast sharply
with what we know about how exciting these glimpses of freedom
have been. Given just these few moments of freedom, Mrs. Mallard
now sees an extraordinary life ahead of her, eagerly anticipates what
her own life might become, and remembers how little she had to look
forward to only yesterday (paragraph 19). With this realization of her
future she rises to confront at last the old world she inhabited.
Triumphing over her past, she now sees the future she had never
even been able to hope for (paragraph 20). And, just as at the beginning of the story, she again receives news about her husband.

The final scene moves quickly. Note that the narrator tells us that
"some one" opens the front door (paragraph 21). In suspense, we

join the world of the story for a moment, not knowing who will appear. All in the hall turn to see who is intruding on this scene of grief (or, in Mrs. Mallard's case, joy), only to discover Brently's return. Richards again tries to help but is too late (just as earlier he had been too hasty). The doctors diagnose Mrs. Mallard's death of a heart overjoyed. We know better.

The language the narrator chooses describes both Mrs. Mallard and the narrator. The opening paragraphs of the story contain formal, rather stilted grammar and vocabulary: the passive voice ("was afflicted," "was taken") and the legalistic "It was" introducing the summarized action of the story. Such forms tend to remove action from immediate experience, making it seem something that happened to someone else. The rhythm is stately and gradual. The Mrs. Mallard of the opening paragraphs is thus different from the rejuvenated woman who emerges ready to face a new life. In paragraphs 9 through 13, colorful language conveys the terror of her acceptance. "Powerful will bending" and "blind persistence" describe the relationship between men and women (paragraph 14). The forces of life seem to rush in on her. Love is characterized as "an unsolved mystery" that pales in front of the "possession of self-assertion," which becomes "the strongest impulse of her being," an "elixir" transforming her into a "goddess of Victory" over the past she has known (paragraphs 15–20). But as the story concludes, the language returns to its placid depiction of the opening, and the tempo resumes its slow, stately progress. The events again seem to happen to someone we do not know. Brently Mallard's appearance and the subsequent events are narrated from afar. He "stood amazed" at the cry of his sister-in-law and at his partner's attempt to "screen him from the view of his wife" (a tantalizingly rich phrase). All the narrator tells us about Mrs. Mallard's death is in one paragraph of six syllables. Only afterward does the word "died" appear, placed in the mouths of the doctors who, like everyone else in Mrs. Mallard's world, misunderstood her life.

Several other clues inform us about this narrator. He or she is sensitive to the natural world as the appropriate order of things, relies on the good sense and the justness of personal integrity, is sympathetic, and clearly understands what living in the world requires. Josephine and Richards are compassionate characters who care deeply about Mrs. Mallard. Her husband is kindly and enjoys his wife's affection. But this narrator knows that none of them understand who *she* is. Ironically, her family's loving concern simply reinforces her sense of living the trapped, airless life. With her discovery that she can — and must — live her own life, she also sees how she could no longer live any other way. And she doesn't.

Finally, of course, this narrator is supremely interested in life's ironies. Little ironies abound. The sad message of Brently Mallard's death actually brings a kind of joy to his wife. Richards's haste at the beginning to protect Mrs. Mallard and his tardiness at the end eventually contribute to her death. The doctors' diagnosis is true, but not at all in the way they mean or everyone else believes. Mrs. Mallard begins to live after years of marriage have been violently ended. In the springtime of the year she, too, comes to a new life, but she dies just as she is beginning to know what her new life is like.

Variety and contrast in tempo and character, balance and proportion in narrative and scene, unity and harmony of theme and incident, rendered with delicate but clear changes of rhythm that seem almost effortless: these have been the characteristics of successful storytelling for centuries. This story, then, is built in a classic form: an opening scene summarized initiates the rising action leading to the carefully described scene at the emotional fulcrum of the story. The moment of self-discovery leads inevitably to the emotional and thematic climax of the story in the last two paragraphs. By using suspense, surprise, understatement, and irony, the storyteller captures in a brief moment a story to resonate beyond an hour.

Mrs. Mallard's life and death — the story the narrator wants us to understand — causes us to wonder about what it means to be a human being living with other human beings, how love can both free and imprison, how human freedom is essential to happiness. To understand the story of Mrs. Mallard's last — and first — hour of life is to understand something about human integrity and human need. To tell such a story, then, becomes a profound act of sharing truth.

A Sample Analysis of a Poem

In Chapter 1 we observed that Dickinson's poem is somewhat more successful than Hoyt's when measured against the touchstones of universality, individuality, and suggestion. Let us look again at Dickinson's "I Felt a Funeral" to discover how the details of the intrinsic factors work together as well. Since the poem is so brief, it is repeated here, and the lines are numbered for easier reference.

1   I felt a Funeral, in my Brain,
2   And Mourners to and fro
3   Kept treading — treading — till it seemed
4   That Sense was breaking through —

5   And when they all were seated,
6   A Service, like a Drum —
7   Kept beating — beating — till I thought
8   My Mind was going numb —

9   And then I heard them lift a Box
10   And creak across my Soul
11   With those same Boots of Lead, again,
12   Then Space — began to toll,

13   As all the Heavens were a Bell,
14   And Being, but an Ear,
15   And I, and Silence, some strange Race
16   Wrecked, solitary, here —

17   And then a Plank in Reason, broke,
18   And I dropped down, and down —
19   And hit a World, at every Crash,
20   And Got through knowing — then —

There are probably no words in this poem that you need to look up in the dictionary. In our earlier discussion, we touched briefly on the connotation of some of the words. We shall come back to this matter later, for it is impossible to avoid it in a selection so filled with suggestion. For the moment we shall move on to organization.

The first line gives the complete opening situation. We know that she "felt" rather than saw a funeral, and that she felt it in her brain. Immediately the possibility opens up that this poem is not about an actual funeral but about a sensation and thus is, in a highly poetic way, an analogy. It may be about the sense of death, or despair, or both. In any case, it is about sensation within the rational part of one's body. That is a paradox in itself. To establish this essential paradox, Dickinson takes two stanzas, which we may consider as the introduction. The third and fourth stanzas take us from the tightly enclosed earthly place to "Space" and the almost intolerable tolling followed by silence. On the opening line of the final stanza, we begin the descent and the conclusion of the experience. Thus the organization is really very simple and unified. The logical climax is located in the last line, where the experience reaches its only possible outcome.

Although each stanza has its own emotional build-up, the major emotional climax coincides with the fulcrum, where heaviness is suddenly replaced by space and sound swells to sudden silence. In the final line of the middle stanza, the poem turns from earth and people, in a sense, to space and solitude. After the weight of the box, the "creak across my Soul," which strongly suggests a creak across a floor, and the "Boots of Lead," we are suddenly confronted with the sharply contrasting vast and empty expanse of space. This is, as we have said, the fulcrum. It is approximately in the center of the poem and causes no trouble as far as balance and proportion of stanzas is concerned.

The poem gives us a sense of continuing development, and yet without real speed except for lines 19 and 20, where the drop occurs. This is achieved in part by the structure. The effect of steady continuation first suggested in "to and fro" is strengthened by the connectives "and," "till," "and when," and "and then." It is interesting that the use of the word "and" increases sharply in the last stanza so that the drop picks up speed, and the experience is terminated with the final "then."

The verb forms also help to create this effect. Although the entire poem is in the past tense, there is a subtle variation within it. The repetition in "Kept treading — treading," "Kept beating — beating," and "down, and down," combined with the imperfect tense of "was breaking," and "was going," gives a feeling of action continuing over a period of time. It is interesting to notice, however, that at the fulcrum there is a shift into the infinitive with "began to toll," followed immediately by a subjunctive form throughout the entire fourth stanza ("As" in line 13 certainly implies "as if"). The subjunctive is used to speak of a hypothesis or a condition contrary to fact. The final stanza returns to the simple past with "broke," "dropped," "hit," and "Got through" — about as completed a past as one can have!

We have already mentioned the use of "I felt" in the opening line. Taking the first person singular *I*, we find that the poem moves from "I felt" to "I thought," "I heard," "And I, and Silence" to "I dropped," "[I] hit," and "[I] Got through." Although the first four *I*'s are evenly spaced one to a stanza, the last three occur in quick succession in the last three lines. Our attention is focused on the *I* at the opening of the poem, and then we are quickly introduced to the mourners. The rhythm of attention alternates, although not with perfect regularity, until line 12, when "Space" is introduced. We have no references to the mourners or to the funeral after that, and the next reference to *I* is "I, and Silence." A look at the funeral references reveals that they continue at least by implication through line 13 with "toll" and "Bell," but it is really "Space" that begins to toll and "the Heavens" that are a bell.

A specific set of references that a writer often returns to is called a *motif*. A motif in music, design, or literature is any detail repeated often enough to become significant. In music, it may be a phrase of melody or a set of chords. In design, it may be a leaf, a flower, or any particular element used in a pattern. In literature, the repeated reference need not be an *exact* repetition of images or ideas. It may present recurring references to a concept like the elements: storms, clouds, or sunshine. It may refer repeatedly to things related to each other, such as colors, nature, or animals.

The first line of Dickinson's poem refers to "my Brain," and this reference is strengthened and at the same time is made more specific three lines later by "Sense," which we discussed in Chapter 1 when we talked about suggestion. Thus we go from "my Brain" to "it seemed," "Sense," "I thought," and "My Mind." This mental motif does not reappear until the final stanza, which opens with a reference to "Reason" and closes with "knowing." We are very carefully returned to the poet with "I" in line 15; "Reason" and "knowing" are in identical positions with "Brain" and "Sense" in the opening stanza. Although psychologists might disagree, "heard" in line 9 appears to be more physical than emotional. The next reference is to "Soul," then to "Being," and then to "Race," a large, general, abstract category rather than a specific personal reference. Moreover, the race is "strange," "Wrecked," and, most important, "solitary." Even more subtle is the use of "Ear" with "Being." Thus, lines 9 through 16 form a unit that differs from the rest of the poem in motif. As we have remarked, there is also a shift in verb form, and this is the only place in the poem where a sentence continues past the stanza break without being broken by a dash.

A simple listing by line (see the table on the following page) makes this discussion more graphic. We should remember, however, that a list is not a poem. It is useful only as a step in analysis. In the interest of clarity we shall not follow Dickinson's use of capital letters.

Remembering that the intrinsic factors are closely related and that a detail may contribute to more than one of them, let us see how what we have found relates to unity and harmony, variety and contrast, balance and proportion, and rhythm.

The use of "I" and "my" is a strong unifying factor. It is clearly established in the first ten lines and returned to in line 15 and throughout the final stanza. The connectives and the simple progression of events also help to hold the poem together. The psychological motif opens and closes the poem and is constant throughout, except in the middle portion, where it is weaker but still operating in "heard" and "as [if]." The sound motif with the contrasting silence is heavy in the beginning, reaches a high level at the fulcrum, is somehow strengthened by the sudden silence, and returns with force in the final stanza. A feeling of weight and heaviness begins in the first stanza, reaches its peak in "lift a Box" and "Boots of Lead," and recurs in "Plank . . . broke" in lines 18 and 19.

Line	Persons	Mental and Physical Motifs	Connectives	Verb Forms	Funeral Motifs	Sound and Silence
1	I my	I felt my brain		I felt	funeral	
2	mourners		and		mourners	
3	they (implied)	it seemed	till	kept treading treading it seemed		treading treading
4	my (implied)	sense		was breaking		
5	they (mourners)		and when	were seated		
6					service drum	drum
7	I	I thought	till	kept beating beating I thought		beating beating
8	my	my mind		was going		
9	I them (mourners)	I heard	and then	I heard lift	box	heard them
10	them (implied) my	my soul	and	creak		creak across
11	their (implied)				lead	boots of lead
12		space	then	began to toll	toll	toll FULCRUM
13		heavens		as [if] . . . were	bell	bell
14		being ear	and	as [if] . . . were (implied)		ear
15	I and silence	race	and . . . and	as [if] . . . were (implied)		silence
16				as [if] . . . were (implied)		solitary
17		reason	and then	broke		plank broke
18	I		and . . . and	dropped		
19	I (implied)		and	hit		crash
20	I (implied)	knowing	and then	got through		

We cannot fully appreciate harmony until we have examined poetic structure, but certainly the heaviness just referred to and the continuing, unbroken downward progression are harmonious with the sensation that Dickinson describes. "Drum" suggests funeral drums; a tolling bell, also associated with funerals, prolongs the mood. "Wrecked," "broke," and "Crash" help to suggest the destruction following the tolling of "Space." Careful examination reveals a remarkable harmony between what is being said and the connotations and sounds of the words that say it.

Within the unity of this brief poem, we find enough variety and contrast to hold our interest. A look at the funeral motif and the sound motif indicates that Dickinson used very subtle variety indeed. Too much variety within so brief a poem would seriously threaten unity, especially since contrast is so sharp. The poet's isolation is contrasted with the multiplicity of people in "Mourners" and "they all," until the isolation reaches its culmination in "I, and Silence . . . solitary." Their actions are contrasted with her immobility and numbing sensations. Space and the heavens are set off against weight and the tangible things of earth. Silence is set against a crescendo of sound. It is, in fact, because of these contrasts that the fulcrum operates so successfully.

Balance and proportion offer no real problem here, since there are almost an equal number of lines and amount of emotional weight on either side of the fulcrum. The build-up to the fulcrum is steady. Immediately after the point of balance is reached, the action ceases momentarily; even though the emotional and logical climaxes fall in the second portion of the poem, they do not overbalance the heaviness and familiarity of the funeral motif in the first section. Moreover, the emotional climax is controlled by the abstractions: "the Heavens," "Being," and "strange Race." After the emotional climax, the speed picks up, and the repeated use of "and" tightens the progression to the conclusion.

Rhythm of content is strongest in the shifts from the poet to the mourners that we mentioned earlier and in the focus on their actions and then on her responses. Again, there is not enough room for a very elaborate pattern of rhythm of content in twenty short lines. As we continue to look at the poem, however, we are aware that both the variety and the contrast make a rhythmic contribution, as do some of the elements in unity.

There are innumerable small details that also contribute to the intrinsic factors. We cannot resist calling attention to the remarkable spacing of "treading," "creak across," and "Plank," all of which suggest floor boards. They are placed with mathematical precision in lines 3, 10, and 17. The use of the already familiar "I" with "heard" controls the unity, and "heard" prepares us for "toll," "Bell," "Ear," "Silence," "Plank . . . broke," and finally "Crash."

Now the question of what you should do with all this discovery arises. The answer is that you use it fully and with complete confidence in the author. Whether or not the writer was conscious of using all the elements, or indeed of the intrinsic and extrinsic factors, as such, is beside the point. It is your responsibility to find everything the writer has given you to work with.

Synthesis

The difficult task of synthesis comes next. In this process the interpreter begins to work as an artist. Slowly, step by step, all the parts are reassembled so that the selection is once more an ordered work of literary art and not a mere listing of details. Don't expect to do it all at once. Putting a literary selection back together after analysis is as complex as reassembling a delicate watch or a complicated stereo set or the engine of a car. Every piece must go where it belongs in order to function properly with every other piece. The process may seem like a juggling act the first few times you try it, but it will get easier and more interesting each time you do it. You may not be entirely satisfied with your first few performances, but that is because now you know much more and no longer need to rely on good luck or slick tricks that you hope will work.

It is impossible to set up a system that will work for every selection, because each piece of literature presents its own problems and opportunities. However, the following procedure may give you a general working outline.

Read the material aloud over and over and over, paying attention first to meaning, both what it means and how it means it.

Next, give some attention to the method of organization. Key words, phrases, and sentences come into play here, as do the denotations and connotations of words. Settle on the location of the climax, or the fulcrum, if you are reading a poem, and determine how the author brings the material to a close so that your audience will know where the selection is going and when it gets there.

Look at all the elements that contribute to unity and harmony. What holds the selection together and keeps it moving?

Spend some time examining the imagery in the selection for a full response with your mind and emotions. How does the imagery contribute to unity and harmony, and how and where does it provide variety and contrast? Don't forget about the importance of connotation here.

Who is speaking in the selection? Is this persona thinking aloud for us to overhear, or addressing another person specifically? How would he or she respond to the connotation and imagery you have worked on? What is the locus — the physical, psychological, and temporal position — of the persona in relation to the experience being shared? Is it memory of the past, is it the present, or is it the future?

What help does the author give you in keeping the two parts on either side of the fulcrum in balance? Is there a strong rhythm of content either in the emotional build-ups and drops or in the alternation of attention to activity and passivity, past and present, or any other aspect?

Keep reading the selection aloud as you fit these pieces together. Start several days ahead so you have time to allow it to mellow. Be sure your vocal technique is serving all the things you have discovered. Let the imagery and connotations be reflected in your voice quality, pace, and volume. Give every word its full value of sound.

As you work on a piece of literature aloud, you gain new insights and hear new melodies. Thus it is wise to begin oral preparation well in advance of performance. You need to let the writing work on you as you work on it. You should always start your rehearsal session by reading the entire selection aloud.

You will not always need to make a chart like the table we have used to discover the contribution of the intrinsic factors and the details that make them up. As you work on the material and know what you are looking for, these elements will become evident. Each time you put a selection back together, the task will become simpler and the relationships clearer.

As an interpreter, you should remember that your audience does not want to hear your analysis: it wants to share the experience of the literature. If the analysis has been thorough and the preparation sound, you may trust the author and yourself to give your full concentration to sharing the selection in its entirety. But unless you know exactly what the author has done, you cannot possibly perform the work to its full potential.

Analyzing the Performance

After you have finished your first performance, you must wait a few minutes before you have any realistic idea of how it went. In fact, it may not be until some hours later that you can get a clear evaluation of your success and your shortcomings. The line you "blew" or your break in concentration will stand blazing in your mind. Try not to lose your perspective. After you have settled back to normal and the adrenalin of performance has subsided, ask yourself some questions.

Did you keep your concentration steady from what the author had given you to your appropriate response and then out to communicate with the audience? If not, what caused the break? Where did it occur? Why there?

Did you control and preserve the unity so that there was an effective beginning, middle, and conclusion?

Did your introduction tell the audience what they needed for background, especially in the case of an excerpt? Did it set the proper mood for the selection? Was it too long?

Were variety and contrast allowed to work effectively while remaining well within the essential unity and harmony? Did you allow for the rhythm of content while keeping the thread of unity firm and clear?

Did the audience respond as you expected? Did any of your performance mannerisms distract the audience from what they were hearing?

Part of your responsibility — and pleasure — in an interpretation class is to be a good audience. Put your own worries aside for a time and really *listen* and react to the readings of others. Often you learn as much or more from someone else's performance as from your own. Your instructor's comment may seem vague or theoretical until you see or hear someone else doing the same thing; suddenly you see how what someone else did helped communicate the selection or detracted from it.

You will probably be asked to comment about others' readings. In your comments about these performances, try to describe to the interpreter exactly what you saw and heard. Avoid such comments as "I liked it" or "It was nice." Of course, the reader will be pleased that you liked it, but without any more specific comments on why you liked it, he or she will not know how to improve. Mention instead a specific moment in the performance. A comment like "The way you held your head made Mrs. Mallard seem very stern and cold at the end of the story" or "Your voice at the opening of 'I Felt a Funeral' was very high-pitched and sounded as if you were about to scream" will help the performer focus specifically on exactly what happened during the performance. Only in this way can the performer learn what he or she successfully communicated to you. Together you and the reader can examine the selection to see if it calls for the actions or mannerisms you describe. And you can compare your responses with those of other audience members to be sure that the performance was equally effective throughout the audience. Finally, we have found that performers are more likely to listen carefully if they think you enjoyed some aspect of the reading; why not begin your comment with something specific that succeeded in the performance and then move on to the elements that still need work?

Selections for Analysis and Oral Interpretation

Each of these selections must be analyzed thoroughly. Do not try to make each one follow the pattern of the Dickinson poem, however, because every piece of writing is unique. Look for all the details that we have discussed. Then decide which ones contribute to unity and harmony and see where variety and contrast exist within the unity and harmony. Find the fulcrum and climaxes, and consider balance and proportion. Look carefully for rhythm of content. Remember that details may contribute to more than one of the intrinsic factors.

Begin with the whole selection and let it work on you until you feel comfortable with it. Then move into an objective analysis. After each step, go back to the complete selection and see how the pieces fit together. Remember that your audience wants the total effect, not the separate pieces. Each selection is followed by one or two bulleted questions to assist you in rehearsal or to begin class discussion.

Although these three poems all have stars as their main motif, they vary considerably in the ways this theme is treated. Each poem shows strong marks of individuality. In each case the persona is clearly the poet and the locus is here on earth. The poems make an interesting comparison. In the first poem, by Walt Whitman, repetition creates both frustration and relief. The exquisite delay that culminates in the last syllable of the last line must never become sluggish.

When I Heard the Learn'd Astronomer
WALT WHITMAN

When I heard the learn'd astronomer,
When the proofs, the figures, were ranged in columns before me,
When I was shown the charts and diagrams, to add, divide, and
     measure them,
When I sitting heard the astronomer where he lectured with much
     applause in the lecture-room,
How soon unaccountable I became tired and sick,
Till rising and gliding out I wander'd off by myself,
In the mystical moist night-air, and from time to time,
Look'd up in perfect silence at the stars.

▌ How can you demonstrate the persona's growing dismay?
▌ At what word did your persona first see the stars?

Sonnet

JOHN KEATS

Bright star! would I were as steadfast as thou art —
   Not in lone splendor hung aloft the night
And watching, with eternal lids apart,
   Like nature's patient, sleepless Eremite,
The moving waters at their priest-like task
   Of pure ablution round earth's human shores,
Or gazing on the new soft fallen mask
   Of snow upon the mountains and the moors —
No — yet still steadfast, still unchangeable,
   Pillow'd upon my fair love's ripening breast,
To feel forever its soft fall and swell,
   Awake for ever in a sweet unrest,
Still, still to hear her tender-taken breath,
   And so live ever — or else swoon to death.

❚ How did your performance of the *still*'s in the ninth line differ
from the *still*'s in the thirteenth line? Why?

The Starlight Night

GERARD MANLEY HOPKINS

Look at the stars! look, look up at the skies!
   O look at all the fire-folk sitting in the air!
   The bright boroughs, the circle-citadels there!
Down in dim woods the diamond delves! the elves'-eyes!
The grey lawns cold where gold, where quickgold lies!
   Wind-beat whitebeam! airy abeles set on a flare!
   Flake doves sent floating forth at a farmyard scare!
Ah well! it is all a purchase, all is a prize.

Buy then! bid then! — What? — Prayer, patience, alms, vows.
Look, look: a May-mess, like on orchard boughs!
   Look! March-bloom, like on mealed-with-yellow sallows!
These are indeed the barn; withindoors house
The shocks. This piece-bright paling shuts the spouse
   Christ home, Christ and his mother and all his hallows.

❚ Did you see each manifestation of stars before moving on to
the next?
❚ Did your audience see the auction that begins in the ninth line?

The narrator in this excerpt is clearly the grown man remembering a special time in his childhood. Although the characters vary considerably in age, their attitudes are perfectly attuned. All the speeches are given to the woman. Her short sentences have the excitement and vitality of immediacy, which gives nice contrast to the quieter but warm and happy memory of the narrator, thus providing an essential rhythm.

FROM *A Christmas Memory*

TRUMAN CAPOTE

Imagine a morning in late November. A coming of winter morning more than twenty years ago. Consider the kitchen of a spreading old house in a country town. A great black stove is its main feature; but there is also a big round table and a fireplace with two rocking chairs placed in front of it. Just today the fireplace commenced its seasonal roar.

A woman with shorn white hair is standing at the kitchen window. She is wearing tennis shoes and a shapeless gray sweater over a summery calico dress. She is small and sprightly, like a bantam hen; but, due to a long youthful illness, her shoulders are pitifully hunched. Her face is remarkable — not unlike Lincoln's, craggy like that, and tinted by sun and wind; but it is delicate too, finely boned, and her eyes are sherry-colored and timid. "Oh my," she exclaims, her breath smoking the windowpane, "it's fruitcake weather!"

The person to whom she is speaking is myself. I am seven; she is sixty-something. We are cousins, very distant ones, and we have lived together — well, as long as I can remember. Other people inhabit the house, relatives; and though they have power over us, and frequently make us cry, we are not, on the whole, too much aware of them. We are each other's best friend. She calls me Buddy, in memory of a boy who was formerly her best friend. The other Buddy died in the 1880's, when she was still a child. She is still a child.

"I knew it before I got out of bed," she says, turning away from the window with a purposeful excitement in her eyes. "The courthouse bell sounded so cold and clear. And there were no birds singing; they've gone to warmer country, yes indeed. Oh, Buddy, stop stuffing biscuit and fetch our buggy. Help me find my hat. We've thirty cakes to bake."

It's always the same: a morning arrives in November, and my friend, as though officially inaugurating the Christmas time of year that exhilarates her imagination and fuels the blaze of her heart, announces: "It's fruitcake weather! Fetch our buggy. Help me find my hat."

The hat is found, a straw cartwheel corsaged with velvet roses out-of-doors has faded: it once belonged to a more fashionable relative. Together, we guide our buggy, a dilapidated baby carriage, out to the garden and into a grove of pecan trees. The buggy is mine, that is, it was bought for me when I was born. It is made of wicker, rather unraveled, and the wheels wobble like a drunkard's legs. But it is a faithful object; springtimes, we take it to the woods and fill it with flowers, herbs, wild fern for our porch pots; in the summer, we pile it with picnic paraphernalia and sugar-cane fishing poles and roll it down to the edge of a creek; it has its winter uses, too: as a truck for hauling firewood from the yard to the kitchen, as a warm bed for Queenie, our tough little orange and white rat terrier, who has survived distemper and two rattlesnake bites. Queenie is trotting beside it now.

Three hours later we are back in the kitchen hulling a heaping buggyload of windfall pecans. Our backs hurt from gathering them: how hard they were to find (the main crop having been shaken off the trees and sold by the orchard's owners, who are not us) among the concealing leaves, the frosted deceiving grass. Caarackle! A cheery crunch, scraps of miniature thunder sound as the shells collapse and the golden mound of sweet oily ivory meat mounts in the milk-glass bowl. Queenie begs to taste, and now and again my friend sneaks her a mite, though insisting we deprive ourselves. "We musn't, Buddy: If we start, we won't stop. And there's scarcely enough as there is. For thirty cakes." The kitchen is growing dark. Dusk turns the window into a mirror: our reflections mingle with the rising moon as we work by the fireside in the firelight. At last, when the moon is quite high, we toss the final hull into the fire and with joined sighs, watch it catch flame. The buggy is empty, the bowl is brimful.

▌ Did your audience see, hear, touch, smell, and taste all of the elements described? Did you allow time for each image to sink in?

Anne Sexton is often spoken of as a poet of the "confessional" school. This poem is an outgrowth of her actual experience in an institution, but her skill takes it beyond fact. The long sentence with its nursery rhyme construction of clauses must be used as a connected unit. The last sentence is an important contrast. The speaker's mental disturbance must not be overplayed. She is perfectly, but detachedly, in control of her logic. Locus is obviously of great importance here.

Ringing the Bells

ANNE SEXTON

        And this is the way they ring
the bells in Bedlam
and this is the bell-lady
who comes each Tuesday morning
to give us a music lesson
and because the attendants make you go
and because we mind by instinct,
like bees caught in the wrong hive,
we are the circle of crazy ladies
who sit in the lounge of the mental house
and smile at the smiling woman
who passes us each a bell,
who points at my hand
that holds my bell, E flat,
and this is the gray dress next to me
who grumbles as if it were special
to be old, to be old,
and this is the small hunched squirrel girl
on the other side of me
who picks at the hairs over her lip,
who picks at the hairs over her lip all day
and this is how the bells really sound,
as untroubled and clean
as a workable kitchen,
and this is always my bell responding
to my hand that responds to the lady
who points at me, E flat;
and although we are no better for it,
they tell you to go. And you do.

▌ How did you show your audience everyone else in "the circle
    of crazy ladies"?

"Wild Grapes" calls for considerable attention to locus. The narrative lines, of course, should be directed to the audience. The brother's first instructions are delivered as he stands beside the little girl; his "loud cries" are directed to her as she hangs suspended in the air.

Wild Grapes

ROBERT FROST

What tree may not the fig be gathered from?
The grape may not be gathered from the birch?
It's all you know the grape, or know the birch.
As a girl gathered from the birch myself
Equally with my weight in grapes, one autumn,
I ought to know what tree the grape is fruit of.
I was born, I suppose, like anyone,
And grew to be a little boyish girl
My brother could not always leave at home.
But that beginning was wiped out in fear
The day I swung suspended with the grapes,
And was come after like Eurydice
And brought down safely from the upper regions;
And the life I live now's an extra life
I can waste as I please on whom I please.
So if you see me celebrate two birthdays,
And give myself out as two different ages,
One of them five years younger than I look —
One day my brother led me to a glade
Where a white birch he knew of stood alone,
Wearing a thin head-dress of pointed leaves,
And heavy on her heavy hair behind,
Against her neck, an ornament of grapes.
Grapes, I knew grapes from having seen them last year.
One bunch of them, and there began to be
Bunches all round me growing in white birches,
The way they grew round Leif the Lucky's German;
Mostly as much beyond my lifted hands, though,
As the moon used to seem when I was younger,
And only freely to be had for climbing.

My brother did the climbing; and at first
Threw me down grapes to miss and scatter
And have to hunt for in sweet fern and hardhack;
Which gave him some time to himself to eat,
But not so much, perhaps, as a boy needed.

So then, to make me wholly self-supporting,
He climbed still higher and bent the tree to earth
And put it in my hands to pick my own grapes.
"Here, take a tree-top, I'll get down another.
Hold on with all your might when I let go."
I said I had the tree. It wasn't true.
The opposite was true. The tree had me.
The minute it was left with me alone
It caught me up as if I were the fish
And it the fishpole. So I was translated
To loud cries from my brother of "Let go!
Don't you know anything, you girl? Let go!"
But I, with something of the baby grip
Acquired ancestrally in just such trees
When wilder mothers than our wildest now
Hung babies out on branches by the hands
To dry or wash or tan, I don't know which,
(You'll have to ask an evolutionist) —
I held on uncomplainingly for life.
My brother tried to make me laugh to help me.
"What are you doing up there in those grapes?
Don't be afraid. A few of them won't hurt you.
I mean, they won't pick you if you don't them."
Much danger of my picking anything!
By that time I was pretty well reduced
To a philosophy of hang-and-let-hang.
"Now you know how it feels," my brother said,
"To be a bunch of fox-grapes, as they call them,
That when it thinks it has escaped the fox
By growing where it shouldn't — on a birch,
Where a fox wouldn't think to look for it —
And if he looked and found it, couldn't reach it —
Just then come you and I to gather it.
Only you have the advantage of the grapes
In one way: you have one more stem to cling by,
And promise more resistance to the picker."

One by one I lost off my hat and shoes,
And I still clung. I let my head fall back
And shut my eyes against the sun, my ears
Against my brother's nonsense; "Drop," he said,
"I'll catch you in my arms. It isn't far."
(Stated in lengths of him it might not be.)
"Drop or I'll shake the tree and shake you down."

Grim silence on my part as I sank lower,
My small wrists stretching till they showed the banjo strings.
"Why, if she isn't serious about it!
Hold tight awhile till I think what to do.
I'll bend the tree down and let you down by it."
I don't know much about the letting down;
But once I felt ground with my stocking feet
And the world came revolving back to me,
I know I looked long at my curled-up fingers,
Before I straightened them and brushed the bark off.
My brother said: "Don't you weigh anything?
Try to weigh something next time, so you won't
Be run off with by birch trees into space."

It wasn't my not weighing anything
So much as my not knowing anything —
My brother had been nearer right before.
I had not taken the first step in knowledge;
I had not learned to let go with the hands,
As still I have not learned to with the heart,
And have no wish to with the heart — nor need,
That I can see. The mind — is not the heart.
I may yet live, as I know others live,
To wish in vain to let go with the mind —
Of cares, at night, to sleep; but nothing tells me
That I need to learn to let go with the heart.

▌ Did you make the remembered scene vivid and present to
your audience? How?

The choice of words in this poem provides an interesting contrast to that of
the Dickinson poem we have already analyzed within the chapter.

Because I Could Not Stop for Death
EMILY DICKINSON

Because I could not stop for Death —
He kindly stopped for me —
The Carriage held but just Ourselves —
And Immortality.

We slowly drove — He knew no haste
And I had put away

My labor and my leisure too,
For His Civility —

We passed the School, where Children strove
At Recess — in the Ring —
We passed the Fields of Gazing Grain —
We passed the Setting Sun —

Or rather — He passed Us —
The Dews drew quivering and chill —
For only Gossamer, my Gown —
My Tippet — only Tulle —

We paused before a House that seemed
A Swelling of the Ground —
The Roof was scarcely visible —
The Cornice — in the Ground —

Since then — 'tis Centuries — and yet
Feels shorter than the Day
I first surmised the Horses' Heads
Were toward Eternity —

■ Did you perform the dashes in this poem? Do they all mean
the same thing?

These two sonnets by Shakespeare offer a strong contrast to each other. You
need to understand the grammatical structure of the sentences in order to
make the references clear when you read them aloud.

Sonnet 18

WILLIAM SHAKESPEARE

Shall I compare thee to a summer's day?
Thou art more lovely and more temperate:
Rough winds do shake the darling buds of May,
And summer's lease hath all too short a date:
Sometime too hot the eye of heaven shines,
And often is his gold complexion dimm'd;
And every fair from fair sometimes declines,
By chance, or nature's changing course untrimm'd;
But thy eternal summer shall not fade,
Nor lose possession of that fair thou ow'st,

Nor shall death brag thou wander'st in his shade,
When in eternal lines to time thou grow'st;
    So long as man can breathe, or eyes can see,
    So long lives this, and this gives life to thee.

▌ Who is being addressed here? Does the persona see the beloved clearly?

Sonnet 130
WILLIAM SHAKESPEARE

My mistress' eyes are nothing like the sun;
Coral is far more red than her lip's red:
If snow be white, why then her breasts are dun;
If hairs be wires, black wires grow on her head.
I have seen roses damask'd, red and white,
But no such roses see I in her cheeks;
And in some perfumes is there more delight
Than in the breath that from my mistress reeks.
I love to hear her speak, yet well I know
That music hath a far more pleasing sound:
I grant I never saw a goddess go;
My mistress, when she walks, treads on the ground:
    And yet, by heaven, I think my love as rare
    As any she belied with false compare.

▌ What did you do to mark the change between the twelfth and thirteenth lines?

The unity of this story is very tightly controlled by the first-person narrator as she moves from the road to the grave and finally to join Lambert after the burial. She is certainly not an objective witness, despite her noncommital replies to Lambert's questions. The variety among the characters is held within the unity by the continued sharply focused locus on the small area of the grave. We do not follow them as they leave the area but wait with the narrator and Lambert for their return. The narrator remains alone after the actual burial to solidify our focus.

Dulce
DEBORAH SHERMAN

I can still hear the pick hitting the caliche, Lambert breathing hard, sweat at the edge of his gray hair. I knew that the difficulty in breath-

wasn't just from the steady swinging of the heavy pick, nor was it because of his age. He said later that he couldn't cry and yet his eyes were red and I could see the tears.

When I saw Dulce lying there, the blood still wet, a small pool on the pavement, I couldn't touch her or move her. I ran to get Lambert, the one person who Dulce would never leave. "Damn it," he said. "Son of a bitches." Slowly, with Paula Sue at his side, bow-legged and tired, he walked down to the highway. I didn't have to watch him to know that he touched every part of Dulce to make sure that it was really true. He came so quietly up the driveway, carrying Dulce the way one carries a butchered lamb, holding the front paws in one hand and the back in the other, her head hanging by his legs. Gently, caressing her, he laid her on the grass by the ditch where he had buried Trixie a few years ago, then he went to put on his boots and get the pick and shovel. When he came back he looked at me. "Do you think that animals do things like this because they don't want to live?"

"No Lambert," I said, "it was just an accident, a stupid accident."

"Maybe they're unhappy and don't want to live."

"No Lambert."

"When Barbara and I first lived here, the house was right over there, and this tree was our tree." He kept digging. "When I put Trixie here I told Trixie this is your tree now. Now it's Duls' too." He got on his hands and knees, loosening a big rock. "Do you think this is wide enough? Enough room for her feet?"

"Ya, I think so Lambert."

But he widened it anyway.

"Do you think this is deep enough? I made it deeper than this for Trixie."

"Ya, I think so Lambert."

But he made it deeper anyway.

"Paula Sue," he said, "go get the hoe, the little one, in the shed."

His breathing was becoming labored, strained. Dulce was lying beside him. It was almost as if she were asleep, out in the pasture keeping him within view at all times even if she dozed off, waiting for him to finish whatever little chore he was occupied with. He looked down at her. "Do you think those who are supposed to die suffer later for being kept alive past their time?" The pick stopped. "When it's your time it's your time."

"I don't know, Lambert," I said, watching him climb slowly out of the hole.

When Paula Sue came back with the hoe he got in the hole again and carefully scraped the earth from the corners, making the surface flat and smooth. "Go ask Barbara for some rags, I know she has some," he said quietly, so slowly, so gently.

Paula Sue walked up with an old blanket. "It has pee on it though."

I looked at the blanket. "That's okay."

"No, that's not good for Duls. Barbara has other ones. Go ask her."

"It's okay, Lambert," I said. But Paula Sue had already dropped the blanket and was walking toward the house.

This time when Paula Sue came back, she brought the old patchwork quilt that used to be her bedspread. Lambert put down his hoe and looked at the quilt. A neighbor had made it. "It's too good."

"No," said Paula Sue, "it's got lots of tears in it."

I smiled, watching her pointing out each tear. "It's okay, Lambert."

He took the quilt and laid it in the hole, smoothing out each wrinkle. And then he went to Dulce, his hand petting her, automatically. He picked her up gently, as if afraid of disturbing her, and lowered her onto the blanket. "Let's clean up your nose, Duls," he said, as he took his glove and wiped the blood from her face. He wrapped her in the blanket.

"Are you ready Lambert?" I said. He just nodded, and I started shoveling the dirt over her as fast as I could. Ma had come out to see her lowered into the hole and as the colors disappeared she said that it was only right that Dulce have that quilt.

Lambert bent down and laid his hand on the earth, "Bye Duls, bye Duls." He picked up his worn tools and, dragging the old blanket that Canoncito had peed on, he walked back up to the house.

When I came around the corner, he was on the portal, sitting on the bench, his head bent down, his hands holding Dulce's white bowl. He just sat there, not moving. All the other dogs were at his feet, as if they knew that something had happened.

"Just a few minutes ago. We were in the shop and Duls was lying there on the chair, the old chair from Denver. We shared a cheese, what do you call it, a cheese ball. We ate together, Duls and me. Just a few minutes ago."

▌ How did your performance clearly convey the distress of this speaker?

▌ What is she doing to conceal her feelings?

Here is another, quite different, story about the death of a pet. (It can be useful to compare these two narrators and their reactions to the same event.) The present tense here increases the immediacy of the tale as it moves Michael (the storyteller) closer to us. Try to determine precisely what Keds's death means to him.

Homework

PETER CAMERON

My dog, Keds, was sitting outside of the A. & P. last Thursday when he got smashed by some kid pushing a shopping cart. At first we thought he just had a broken leg, but later we found out he was bleeding inside. Every time he opened his mouth, blood would seep out like dull red words in a bad silent dream.

Every night before my sister goes to her job she washes her hair in the kitchen sink with beer and mayonnaise and eggs. Sometimes I sit at the table and watch the mixture dribble down her white back. She boils a pot of water on the stove at the same time; when she is finished with her hair, she steams her face. She wants so badly to be beautiful.

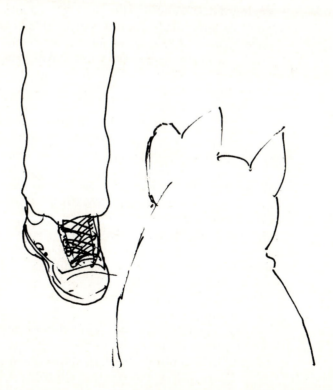

I am trying to solve complicated algebraic problems I have set for myself. Since I started cutting school last Friday, the one thing I miss is homework. Find the value for *n*. Will it be a whole number? It is never a whole number. It is always a fraction.

"Will you get me a towel?" my sister asks. She turns her face toward me and clutches her hair to the top of her head. The sprayer hose slithers into its hole next to the faucet.

I hand her a dish towel. "No," she says. "A bath towel. Don't be stupid."

In the bathroom, my mother is watering her plants. She has arranged them in the tub and turned the shower on. She sits on the toilet lid and watches. It smells like outdoors in the bathroom.

I hand my sister the towel and watch her wrap it round her head. She takes the cover off the pot of boiling water and drops lemon slices in. Then she lowers her face into the steam.

This is the problem I have set for myself:

$$\frac{245\,(n+17)}{34} = 396\,(n-45)$$

$$n =$$

Wednesday, I stand outside the high-school gym doors. Inside, students are lined up doing calisthenics. It's snowing, and prematurely dark, and I can watch without being seen.

"Well," my father says when I get home. He is standing in the garage testing the automatic door. Every time a plane flies overhead, the door opens or closes, so my father is trying to fix it. "Have you changed your mind about school?" he asks me.

I lock my bicycle to a pole. This infuriates my father, who doesn't believe in locking things up in his own house. He pretends not to notice. I wipe the thin stripe of snow off the fenders with my middle finger. It is hard to ride a bike in the snow. This afternoon on my way home from the high school I fell off, and I lay in the snowy road with my bike on top of me. It felt warm.

"We're going to get another dog," my father says.

"It's not that," I say. I wish everyone would stop talking about dogs. I can't tell how sad I really am about Keds versus how sad I am in general. If I don't keep these things separate, I feel as if I'm betraying Keds.

"Then what is it?" my father says.

"It's nothing," I say.

My father nods. He is very good about bringing things up and then letting them drop. A lot gets dropped. He presses the button on the automatic control. The door slides down its oiled tracks and falls shut. It's dark in the garage. My father presses the button again and the door opens, and we both look outside at the snow falling in the driveway, as if in those few seconds the world might have changed.

My mother has forgotten to call me for dinner, and when I confront her with this she tells me that she did, but that I was sleeping. She is loading the dishwasher. My sister is standing at the counter, listening, and separating eggs for her shampoo.

"What can I get you?" my mother asks. "Would you like a meatloaf sandwich?"

"No," I say. I open the refrigerator and survey its illuminated contents. "Could I have some scrambled eggs?"

"O.K.," says my mother. She comes and stands beside me and puts her hand on top of mine on the door handle. There are no eggs in the refrigerator. "Oh," my mother says; then, "Julie?"

"What?" my sister says.

"Did you take the last eggs?"

"I guess so," my sister says. "I don't know."

"Forget it," I say. "I won't have eggs."

"No," my mother says. "Julie doesn't need them in her shampoo. That's not what I bought them for."

"I do," my sister says. "It's a formula. It doesn't work without the eggs. I need the protein."

"I don't want eggs," I say. "I don't want anything." I go into my bedroom.

My mother comes in and stands looking out the window. The snow has turned to rain. "You're not the only one who is unhappy about this," she says.

"About what?" I say. I am sitting on my unmade bed. If I pick up my room, my mother will make my bed: that's the deal. I didn't pick up my room this morning.

"About Keds," she says. "I'm unhappy too. But it doesn't stop me from going to school."

"You don't go to school," I say.

"You know what I mean," my mother says. She turns around and looks at my room, and begins to pick things off the floor.

"Don't do that," I say. "Stop."

My mother drops the dirty clothes in an exaggerated gesture of defeat. She almost — almost — throws them on the floor. The way she holds her hands accentuates their emptiness. "If you're not going to go to school," she says, "the least you can do is clean your room."

In the algebra word problems, a boat sails down a river while a jeep drives along the bank. Which will reach the capital first? If a plane flies at a certain speed from Boulder to Oklahoma City and then at a different speed from Oklahoma City to Detroit, how many cups of coffee can the stewardess serve, assuming she is unable to serve during the first and last ten minutes of each flight? How many times can a man ride the elevator to the top of the Empire State Building while his wife climbs the stairs, given that the woman travels one stair slower each flight? And if the man jumps up while the elevator is going down, which is moving — the man, the woman, the elevator, or the snow falling outside?

The next Monday I get up and make preparations for going to school. I can tell at the breakfast table that my mother is afraid to acknowledge them for fear it won't be true. I haven't gotten up before ten o'clock in a week. My mother makes me French toast. I sit at the table and write the note excusing me for my absence. I am eighteen, an adult, and thus able to excuse myself from school. This is what my note says:

> DEAR MR. KELLY [my homeroom teacher]:
>   Please excuse my absence February 17–24. I was unhappy and did not feel able to attend school.
>
>   Sincerely,
>   MICHAEL PECHETTI

This is the exact format my mother used when she wrote my notes, only she always said, "Michael was home with a sore throat," or "Michael was home with a bad cold." The colds that prevented me from going to school were always bad colds.

My mother watches me write the note but doesn't ask to see it. I leave it on the kitchen table when I go to the bathroom, and when I come back to get it I know she has read it. She is washing the bowl she dipped the French toast into. Before, she would let Keds lick it clean. He liked eggs.

In Spanish class we are seeing a film on flamenco dancers. The screen wouldn't pull down, so it is being projected on the blackboard, which is green and cloudy with erased chalk. It looks a little as if the women are sick, and dancing in Heaven. Suddenly the little phone on the wall buzzes.

Mrs. Smitts, the teacher, gets up to answer it, and then walks over to me. She puts her hand on my shoulder and leans her face close to mine. It is dark in the room. "Miguel," Mrs. Smitts whispers, *"Tienes que ir a la oficina de* guidance."

"What?" I say.

She leans closer, and her hair blocks the dancers. Despite the clicking castanets and the roomful of students, there is something intimate about this moment. *"Tienes que ir a la oficina de* guidance," she repeats slowly. Then, "You must go to the guidance office. Now. *Vaya.*"

My guidance counsellor, Mrs. Dietrich, used to be a history teacher, but she couldn't take it anymore, so she was moved into guidance. On her immaculate desk is a calendar blotter with "LUNCH" written across the middle of every box, including Saturday and Sunday. The only other things on the desk are an empty photo cube and my letter to Mr. Kelly. I sit down, and she shows me the letter as if I haven't yet read it. I reread it.

"Did you write this?" she asks.

I nod affirmatively. I can tell Mrs. Dietrich is especially nervous about this interview. Our meetings are always charged with tension. At the last one, when I was selecting my second-semester courses, she started to laugh hysterically when I said I wanted to take Boys' Home Ec. Now every time I see her in the halls she stops me and asks me how I'm doing in Boys' Home Ec. It's the only course of mine she remembers.

I hand the note back to her and say, "I wrote it this morning," as if this clarified things.

"This morning?"

"At breakfast," I say.

"Do you think this is an acceptable excuse?" Mrs. Dietrich asks. "For missing more than a week of school?"

"I'm sure it isn't," I say.

"Then why did you write it?"

Because it is the truth, I start to say. It is. But somehow I know that saying this will make me more unhappy. It might make me cry. "I've been doing algebra at home," I say.

"That's fine," Mrs. Dietrich says, "but it's not the point. The point is, to graduate you have to attend school for a hundred and eighty days, or have legitimate excuses for the days you've missed. That's the point. Do you want to graduate?"

"Yes," I say.

"Of course you do," Mrs. Dietrich says.

She crumples my note and tries to throw it into the wastepaper basket but misses. We both look for a second at the note lying on the floor, and then I get up and throw it away. The only other thing in her wastepaper basket is a banana peel. I can picture her eating a banana in her tiny office. This, too, makes me sad.

"Sit down," Mrs. Dietrich says.

I sit down.

"I understand your dog died. Do you want to talk about that?"

"No," I say.

"Is that what you're so unhappy about?" she says. "Or is there something else?"

I almost mention the banana peel in her wastebasket, but I don't. "No," I say. "It's just my dog."

Mrs. Dietrich thinks for a moment. I can tell she is embarrassed to be talking about a dead dog. She would be more comfortable if it were a parent or a sibling.

"I don't want to talk about it," I repeat.

She opens her desk drawer and takes out a pad of hall passes. She begins to write one out for me. She has beautiful handwriting. I think of her learning to write beautifully as a child and then growing up to be a guidance counsellor, and this makes me unhappy.

"Mr. Neuman is willing to overlook this matter," she says. Mr. Neuman is the principal. "Of course, you will have to make up all the work you've missed. Can you do that?"

"Yes," I say.

Mrs. Dietrich tears the pass from the pad and hands it to me. Our hands touch. "You'll get over this," she says. "Believe me, you will."

My sister works until midnight at the Photo-Matica. It's a tiny booth in the middle of the A. & P. parking lot. People drive up and leave their film and come back the next day for the pictures. My sister wears a uniform that makes her look like a counterperson in a fast-food restaurant. Sometimes at night when I'm sick of being at home I walk downtown and sit in the booth with her.

There's a machine in the booth that looks like a printing press, only snapshots ride down a conveyor belt and fall into a bin and then disappear. The machine gives the illusion that your photographs are being developed on the spot. It's a fake. The same fifty photographs roll through over and over, and my sister says nobody notices, because everyone in town is taking the same pictures. She opens up the envelopes and looks at them.

Before I go into the booth, I buy cigarettes in the A. & P. It is open twenty-four hours a day, and I love it late at night. It is big and bright and empty. The checkout girl sits on her counter swinging her legs. The Muzak plays "If Ever I Would Leave You." Before I buy the cigarettes, I walk up and down the aisles. Everything looks good to eat, and the things that aren't edible look good in their own way. The detergent aisle is colorful and clean-smelling.

My sister is listening to the radio and polishing her nails when I get to the booth. It is almost time to close.

"I hear you went to school today," she says.

"Yeah."

"How was it?" she asks. She looks at her nails, which are so long it's frightening.

"It was O.K.," I say. "We made chili dogs in Home Ec."

"So are you over it all?"

I look at the pictures riding down the conveyor belt. I know the order practically by heart: graduation, graduation, birthday, mountains, baby, baby, new car, bride, bride and groom, house . . . "I guess so," I say.

"Good," says my sister. "It was getting to be a little much." She puts her tiny brush back in the bottle, capping it. She shows me her nails. They're an odd brown shade. "Cinnamon," she says. "It's an earth color." She looks out at the parking lot. A boy is collecting the abandoned shopping carts, forming a long silver train, which he noses back toward the store. I can tell he is singing by the way his mouth moves.

"That's where we found Keds," my sister says, pointing to the Salvation Army bin.

When I went out to buy cigarettes, Keds would follow me. I hung out down here at night before he died. I was unhappy then, too. That's what no one understands. I named him Keds because he was all white with big black feet and it looked as if he had high-top sneakers on. My mother wanted to name him Bootie. Bootie is a cat's name. It's a dumb name for a dog.

"It's a good thing you weren't here when we found him," my sister says. "You would have gone crazy."

I'm not really listening. It's all nonsense. I'm working on a new problem: Find the value for n such that n plus everything else in your life makes you feel all right. What would n equal? Solve for n.

▌ How did you help your audience understand why Michael tells us this story?

This selection easily lends itself to being excerpted. You may wish to follow the thread of Miss Lizzie's encounters with Mr. Pitcher, her business transactions, her first taste of freedom, or her experiences in California. In any case, you will need to supply some background for your audience in your introduction.

We have here an amusing blend of affection and humor. Notice how the narrator often reflects Miss Lizzie's attitude even when she is not using direct discourse, as in the Anderson Girls' feeling about Uncle's advice not to sell the land. Be careful not to make Miss Lizzie a caricature. She is unsophisticated, but she is not senile.

Miss Lizzie
CLAIRE MORRILL

That morning, when Lizzie crossed the road to see Mr. Pitcher, he had a big new gadget hanging down from the ceiling in front of his livingroom window. It seemed to be made of thin rods of different lengths, some wire, and a number of crystal balls.

"What is it?" she asked.

"Why, it's a mobile, Lizzie," Otto said.

"What does it do?"

"It doesn't do anything," he told her. "It just hangs there."

"Oh," she said.

The next time Miss Lizzie came, she surveyed the mobile again with a thoughtful eye.

"When do you light it up?" she asked.

Mr. Pitcher shook his head. "It doesn't light up. It doesn't do anything. It's an ornament."

On her third try a few days later Miss Lizzie took still a different tack.

"I expect it makes music," she said craftily.

"No," said Otto, "it doesn't make music; it doesn't light up. It doesn't do anything. It just hangs there."

Not long afterward, on the street in Taos, Otto ran into Mrs. John Dunn.

"I understand from Lizzie Anderson," she said slyly, "that you've got the only indoor lightning rod in Taos."

Otto was devoted to Miss Lizzie. Her sister Miss Jennie was another matter. But he saw quite a lot of both of them during those several years when he served as neighbor, chauffeur, advisor, and general troubleshooter for the Anderson Girls on their farm across the road from his house.

His volunteer unpaid services were often called upon at extremely short notice. For if the Andersons took no thought for the morrow, it was because the morrow seemed too far away. When they needed feed for their 120 chickens, they needed it *now*. When Miss Lizzie summoned Mr. Pitcher to drive her to town for chicken feed, he knew the hens were facing immediate famine and that he must hastily drop any of his own concerns and do something about it.

In willingly spending so much time with Miss Lizzie, Otto was admittedly motivated by more than his affection for her and a humanitarian concern for the state of affairs in the henhouse. As an old pro actor, he was enormously diverted by his role of straight man in the deadpan, inadvertently comic routines Miss Lizzie continually provided.

Though Miss Jennie was in her eighties and her sister coming along only five years behind, they carried their water, winter and summer, from a spring three or four hundred feet from their dilapidated Victorian frame house. But when he was not home, they accepted his neighborly offer to get it from Otto's house instead. After the first of these periods, Miss Lizzie approached him in a state of bright-eyed wonderment.

"Do you know, Mr. Pitcher," she asked, "that if you turn on that *other* tap, *hot* water comes out?"

Uncle Alex Anderson, when he had died forty years ago, had left the girls a hundred acres including some of the best land in Taos County, plus a few more acres and a small mine in Arroyo Seco, not far away. But Uncle had told them never to sell any of it. And he had known all about such matters.

Uncle had been a businessman and a man of property. He had owned the grist mill, with its sluice and waterwheel and its grain storage building, an establishment part of which has now become Otto's house. Besides this and the mine, with its showing of copper and a few other ores, he had had thirty beehives and sold the honey. He had raised prize Dahlias and marketed them wholesale.

Furthermore, Uncle was much more than a memory. They were still grateful to him and loved him. They had first lived in Embudo, twenty-five miles south of Taos, where their father had worked in a little mine and had to be away from home a lot of the time. And when their mother had had a mental break and had to be taken away, Uncle had brought the two little girls home with him to Taos and given them solicitous care. So when he told them never to sell the land, they knew he was right. No matter how scarce cash got over the years, they hung on grimly.

For years they prepared dinners in the old house in Los Cordovas, three or four miles from Taos, for the town's elite. There would be chicken, potatoes cooked in two to seven ways at the same meal, three kinds of salad or slaw, two or three kinds of pie, and cake with ice cream.

Of course, no matter what time the guests arrived, dinner was never ready, for there were still the dishes to do from previous meals, and one of the gentlemen had to be detailed to turn the ice cream freezer. Nor could you, in contemporary Taos fashion, fill in the wait with a sociable highball. The girls didn't hold with any such sinfulness, which had to be carried on, if at all, surreptitiously among the lilacs at the side of the house. So strongly did they feel on this subject that in later years, when Miss Lizzie saw a bottle of rum with which Otto was mellowing a Christmas cake, she sadly reported to Elsie Weimer, "Mr. Pitcher has taken to drink."

As age began to catch up with the Anderson Girls and more and fancier restaurants opened in Taos, they gave up serving dinners and settled for selling eggs, the cream from their four cows, and the angel-food cakes which they still liked to bake. Miss Lizzie brought these to town on weekly trips.

I don't think I ever laid eyes on Miss Jennie. She couldn't, she felt, leave the property unprotected. This was the reason why, after the road commission had ripped out Uncle's old wooden bridge, replaced it with a culvert, and piled the old timbers up at the side of the road, Miss Jennie broke out her shotgun and sat by the pile through all of one chilly autumn night. If she hadn't you never could tell who would have stolen her timber.

But while Miss Jennie seldom left the old homestead, I saw Miss Lizzie about every week, though, since we bought only eggs, we never saw her during those periods when the hens were moulting. It was, it appeared, impossible for them to lay when they were moulting or else to moult when they were laying. Whichever it was, these physiological phenomena never occurred simultaneously, the fact interrupting Miss Lizzie's visits to us.

Her spare New Englandish figure was garbed in winter in a long dogskin coat; in spring and fall in a long fitted black one of cloth. In summer she came in her countrywoman's dress of cotton. Her wide-brimmed hats, felt in winter and black straw in summer, were anchored in place with a scarf that tied under her chin and produced a sunbonnet effect.

Her speech, coming out in a high, thin voice, was brisk and chipper. But it was hard for me to keep my mind on what she was saying because of the interruptions that happened once or twice in each sentence when her upper dentures began to slip from their proper place. When this happened, she was, of course, forced to arrest their fall by a brisk upward movement of her lower jaw, and so had her choice of muttering through clenched teeth or waiting until things settled down and she could reopen her mouth to finish her sentence. This had to be accomplished with all possible speed before the same thing began to happen again.

The procedure, fascinating to see, caused Miss Lizzie no concern or embarrassment. And if, after she had brought out the eggs from one of the two pasteboard cartons she carried by their rope fastenings, her visits were always short, it was only because she had to hurry to the Safeway to meet Mr. Pitcher and get a ride home.

At the Safeway she would buy an Eskimo Pie, an addiction she had learned to finance by raising the price of eggs to a few cents above the figure she would report to Miss Jennie. Then on the way home, Mr. Pitcher would have to stop the car under a friendly shade tree, while she ate the delicacy with leisurely relish.

When Miss Jennie finally slipped on an icy spot and died as an indirect result of a broken hip, everyone worried about Miss Lizzie. What would she do now, all by herself in that old rattletrap of a house? Miss Jennie had always taken the lead; what would Miss Lizzie do without her?

But Otto was not apprehensive. He knew Miss Lizzie had only been scared to death of her sister.

He was out of town when Miss Jennie died, and got home a few days after the funeral. When Miss Lizzie asked him to drive her over to the cemetery, he complied with more than his usual alacrity. There was something he was curious about.

He knew there was room for five graves in the Anderson family plot. Father and Mother and Uncle Alex had long been there, side by side in a neat row. There was one more prized spot, right next to Uncle. But the fifth Anderson would have to settle for a crosswise place at the foot of the row.

As he and Miss Lizzie reached the plot and stood looking down, she nudged Otto's elbow and a slow grin spread over her face.

"See where Jennie is," she said. "Across the feet."

Now after more than eighty years, Miss Lizzie discovered freedom. For one thing, she sold some land. Though this radical move was rather forced upon her by the staggering size of the bills attending Miss Jennie's passing, she decided to use what money was left over to pay back the loans that had been made to them over the years by some of their longtime friends. She was touched when most of them refused the payments; they'd written those loans off years ago. Miss Lizzie was pleased, too, with the new checkbook she took around to use in paying the debts.

It was during this period that somebody paid her a check that bounced.

"Well, Mr. Pitcher," she said, "I see the bank's run out of money."

"Oh, I don't think so," Otto replied. "How do you know?"

"Well," said Miss Lizzie, "I took in this check and they didn't give me the money. They said they didn't have any more."

Soon she made another bold move — she went up in the attic. Miss Jennie had never allowed her to go up there; she might fall down the stairs and break a hip. But now in the attic she came upon Uncle's old wind-up phonograph and a bunch of cylinder records. There was one, though, that she didn't find that she wanted to hear again. She was especially fond of "Birmingham Jail." Mr. Pitcher, when she asked him about it, didn't have this record either, but he did have a tape recording. Miss Lizzie watched his contraption with interest.

"That's the funniest phonograph I ever saw," she declared. "It eats up the record as it goes along."

Now she decided to fix up an old radio that Mabel Luhan had once given them for Christmas. You could run it with batteries or you could plug it into the wall. Miss Lizzie tried to find batteries but the model was obsolete, so she had the kitchen wired for electricity and put in just one outlet where she could plug in the radio. Otto discovered her there one evening, blissfully listening in a dim room still lighted by an old kerosene lamp.

"What, no electric light?" he inquired.

"Oh, that's too expensive," Miss Lizzie said. Unless it cost too much, nobody who had electricity in his house would eat his dinner by candlelight, as she had often seen Mr. Pitcher doing. But after he had explained that he just thought it was nicer to have candles at dinner, she agreed to have an electric light, so Otto went to a rummage sale, found an old lamp, and hitched it up with a double plug to the radio outlet.

Thus reassured on the question of expense, she soon afterward bought an electric refrigerator. And the first thing she got to go into it was a hundred Eskimo Pies.

But her pleasure in what you could do by plugging things into the wall was dashed one day when she overloaded the line and blew out a fuse. Again she repaired to Otto's house, this time at seven o'clock in the morning.

"Mr. Pitcher," she asked, "have you used up all *your* electricity yet?"

"I don't think so," he said, flipping a switch.

"Well, I guess I've used all of mine," she said. "The radio hasn't said a word since six o'clock."

Now she settled down to enjoy life. She sold some more land and drilled a well. In fact, life was improving so much that she didn't accept when her cousin in California wrote and asked her to come and live with him and his wife. He'd visited her once and he liked her. He worried about her there all alone in the winters in that old, cold house with its woodburning stoves. But she was not yet ready to go.

Nor did she get ready until it finally happened — Miss Lizzie fell and struck her head against the cast-iron oven door of the kitchen stove. The door broke, and while her own injuries were, comparatively speaking, less serious, the neighbors took her off to the hospital, where she stayed for three weeks.

When the time came to go home, she found she couldn't face that cold house. In the hospital the heat sort of came out of the walls; hot water came out of the other tap there, too; and somebody cooked your meals and brought them right to you.

She went home only long enough to sell her house and the rest of her land. They brought enough money to live on the rest of her life. When her cousin came to take her to California, she walked out of the house with only two suitcases and scarcely a backward glance. Miss Lizzie knew she had had it.

And California was wonderful. Her cousins lived in Concord, just outside San Francisco. Their house was warm and pretty, and they were pleasantly attentive. Not too attentive, either. She could come and go as she liked. And Miss Lizzie, who had been known to get lost in Taos, found she could get around out there with no trouble at all. The thing was, there were so many policemen.

She did slide into things gradually. At first she just went to the supermarket, which was only a block or two away. Then she saw she could range farther afield on the bus that stopped right in front of the supermarket and stopped there again on its way back. And if you got off downtown and didn't know how to get home again, you could just ask one of those nice policemen. He wouldn't just tell you how to get home; he'd *take* you there in his car.

Things got more and more interesting. If you wanted to you could just stay on the bus and ride for two hours for twenty-five cents, up through Lafayette and Walnut Grove and back again, and get off at the supermarket. Her cousins got so they didn't even worry about her much. There seemed to be lots of policemen.

Emboldened by these successes, she remembered some other cousins in Glendale and went off to visit them, an all-day trip on the train. There were some relatives in Vancouver, too, and Miss Lizzie even went up there, two or three times, to help them pick strawberries.

These trips she made by herself, though of course when she took in the World's Fair in New York, she went with her cousins.

A while ago she jetted in from San Francisco to Albuquerque to visit an old friend, and came up to Taos for a day. Otto said he missed seeing her, but Pat McCarthy saw her.

"Just as full of juice as ever," was the way Pat put it.

And, of course, why not? She was only eighty-seven.

Here in Taos she is still the subject of amused and affectionate remembrance. At least, every time a few people gather at Otto's somebody is sure to ask, "Now just what was it Miss Lizzie said about the mobile?"

And I will say, Otto always tells it the same way.

▮ What physical and vocal characteristics did you use to convey Miss Lizzie's toughness and Otto's respect for her?

▮ How did you show her different solutions to the mystery of the mobile?

Bibliography

These works discuss in different ways and with different goals some of the chief philosophical foundations of literature, criticism, and the interrelationship of performance and criticism. Many of their arguments and conclusions complement positions taken in this chapter and elsewhere in this book.

Beardsley, Monroe, Robert Daniel, and Glenn Leggett. *Theme and Form.* Englewood Cliffs, N.J.: Prentice-Hall, 1956.
Brief essays on the structure of the various modes of literature combined with an anthology arranged according to themes.

Geiger, Don. *The Sound, Sense, and Performance of Literature.* Glenview, Ill.: Scott, Foresman and Company, 1963.
The performer of literature is the focal point of this book, which is built on the premise that oral interpretation is in itself an act of criticism.

Langer, Susanne K. *Philosophy in a New Key.* Cambridge, Mass.: Harvard University Press, 1942.
Discussion of art as cognitive discourse.

————. *Mind: An Essay on Human Feeling.* Vols. 1–3. Baltimore: Johns Hopkins University Press, 1967, 1972, 1982.
Further development of the *act* as a basic unit of life forms.

Pepper, Stephen. *The Work of Art.* Bloomington: Indiana University Press, 1955.
Propounds the author's theory of funding and fusion in response and contains a clarification of object and vehicle.

Richards, I. A. *Principles of Literary Criticism*. New York: Harcourt, Brace and Company, 1925.
One of the classic works on modern literary criticism.

Rosenblatt, Louise M. *The Reader, the Text, the Poem: The Transactional Theory of a Literary Work*. Carbondale, Ill.: Southern Illinois University Press, 1978.
An excellent and persuasive discussion of the reader's role as co-creator of a poem in the reading event. Explores implications for change in methods of evaluation that can easily be adapted to performance.

Vivas, Eliseo, and Murray Krieger. *The Problem of Aesthetics*. New York: Holt, Rinehart and Winston, 1935.
Essays on the nature and problems of aesthetics as a discipline and on criteria for judgment.

Wellek, Rene, and Austin Warren. *Theory of Literature*. 3rd ed. New York: Harcourt, Brace and World, 1966.
A discussion of the nature and function of literature, with helpful notes and a good bibliography.

Wheelwright, Philip. *Metaphor and Reality*. Bloomington: Indiana University Press, 1962.
A cogent discussion of the relationship between being, presence, and reality.

3

Voice Development for Oral Interpretation

. . . human voices vary even more. Each one possesses more notes than the richest instrument of music. And the combinations in which the voice groups these notes are as inexhaustible as the infinite variety of personalities.

Marcel Proust, Within a Budding Grove

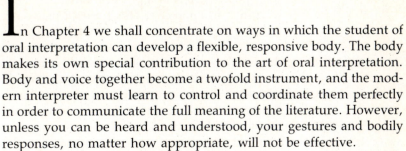

In Chapter 4 we shall concentrate on ways in which the student of oral interpretation can develop a flexible, responsive body. The body makes its own special contribution to the art of oral interpretation. Body and voice together become a twofold instrument, and the modern interpreter must learn to control and coordinate them perfectly in order to communicate the full meaning of the literature. However, unless you can be heard and understood, your gestures and bodily responses, no matter how appropriate, will not be effective.

Most people speak adequately for general conversation and informal communication. But the oral interpretation of literature requires additional vocal flexibility and special control. The fact that you use a normal speaking voice every day and have done so since childhood is no guarantee that your voice is an adequate instrument for artistic re-creation. You need to know first of all just how your voice functions and how you can control and develop it in order to provide wider range in pitch, greater flexibility in volume and stress, richer variations in quality, and finer degrees of subtlety in duration and rate. Once you understand these factors, you should work to develop your voice as deliberately as a singer does. As your voice control improves, you will be increasingly able to meet, with intelligence and sensitivity, the demands of the various kinds of literary material.

Students who have had voice training may find the following discussion useful only as a review. We have made an effort, however, to apply some of the principles of voice training to specific problems facing interpreters. You will find that a few minutes spent on the exercises will be most valuable during rehearsal periods when you are working on a particularly demanding selection.

Breath Control

The first concern of anyone interested in voice improvement should be breath control, because it is impossible to produce good vocal tone without adequate breath properly controlled. Proper use of the normal breathing mechanism is simple. Any difficulties are probably due to bad habits, which may be the result of physical or psychological tensions. An understanding of the muscles involved in the breathing process and of the functions they perform may help to locate and release some of these tensions.

In *inhalation* — intake of air — the major concern is with the amount; in *exhalation* — letting out of air — the major concern is with control. The whole process of breathing rests on two aspects of a basic physiological and physical principle: the balance of tension and relaxation in opposing sets of muscles serves to control the creation of a vacuum.

When we inhale and pull a quantity of air into the body, the diaphragm — the large dome-shaped muscle at the floor of the chest — lowers and pushes downward against the *relaxed* abdominal muscles; thus the lengthwise expansion of the chest is increased. As this action is taking place, the muscles between the outer surfaces of the ribs lift and extend the rib cage, and the side-to-side and front-to-back expansion of the chest is accomplished. This increase in size creates a vacuum inside the chest cavity. Atmospheric pressures force air into the vacuum, so that the pressure inside and outside of the body is equalized. The air is forced down through the windpipe (trachea) and through the bronchial tubes and finally comes to rest in the flexible air sacs in the lungs in which the bronchioli terminate. The air sacs in the lungs inflate as the air enters, and when the lungs are thus extended, the process of inhalation is complete. Obviously, breathing is an active muscular process.

When the mechanism is ready for the process of exhalation to take place (following the exchange of oxygen and carbon dioxide in the blood), the muscles in the diaphragm relax, and the diaphragm rises into the dome-shaped position again. The muscles on the outside of the rib cage relax as the ones between the ribs on the inside contract. This action pulls the extended rib cage inward. All of this pressure upward and inward acts on the elastic lung tissue containing the air that was forced in during inhalation. The elastic tissue begins to collapse, and the air is forced out of the lungs, up through the bronchial tubes and windpipe and finally out of the nose or mouth. Thus one cycle of respiration is completed.

In exhaling for speech, however, there is frequently another action besides the relaxing of the diaphragm in the lower chest area. This action is the firm contraction of the abdominal muscles that are relaxed for inhalation. As they contract for exhalation, they support the action accomplished by the relaxing of the diaphragm and in this way help to control the outflow of air. This process is known as *forced exhalation*. The term is somewhat misleading, perhaps, because the contraction of the abdominal muscles should be an easy and natural process, particularly for a trained speaker who wishes support for a tone projected by sustained exhalation. Forced exhalation is simply the continuation of the action that takes place in the process of exhalation during silent breathing.

Where should you begin exercises to achieve greater breath capacity and better control over exhalation? You may want these muscular processes to function effectively to give smooth interpretation to long flowing lines of poetry. You may want to force a swift exhalation for command or expression of emotion in dramatic dialogue.

The first thing to remember is that proper breathing is possible only when your posture is good. If each muscle is to perform its assigned function, your body should be in a state of controlled relaxation — that is, in a state of nicely balanced relaxation and essential tension. Wrongly induced tension inhibits the flexibility of muscles that control the intake and the outward flow of air. One of the most frequent errors in breathing practice is forcing the muscles of the rib cage and the abdomen into a rigid position. These muscles must be firm, but they cannot function if they are locked.

In exercises for improved breathing habits, it is particularly important, when standing, to have your weight easily and comfortably supported by your feet and legs; to have your spinal column erect but not forced into position; and to have your shoulders level and the muscles that support your shoulders free from tension. Strong lifting of the shoulders, a common error in inhalation, serves only to put tension in the wrong area and has a negative effect on the vocal tone.

A simple four-step exercise to demonstrate the proper balance between tension and relaxation in the special muscles of respiration should be profitable. This exercise also tends to show *where* concentration of energy should be — at the beltline rather than in the throat. Lie on your back the first few times you do the first step so that you get used to the easy, relaxing in-and-out movement of the muscles at the base of your ribs and below them.

1. Take a deep, comfortable breath and hold it. Contract your abdominal muscles *sharply* and force the air out of your chest on a single vocalization, such as "Ah — h — h," as if audibly sighing. Hold the contraction of these muscles an appreciable instant, and then *suddenly* release the tension. Notice that the air rushes into the chest and fills the lower portion of the lungs (or perhaps more) upon the release of the tension. Exhale by forcing air out of your chest with the gradual contraction of your abdominal muscles as your diaphragm relaxes and returns to its dome-shaped position.

2. Stand easily erect and repeat the process described in step 1. As the air rushes in on the release of tension in the abdominal muscles, make a conscious effort to lift your upper rib cage slightly. (Be careful *not* to lift your shoulders!) More space will be created in your upper chest, and your whole chest will be well extended and able to accommodate a large intake of air. The upper portion of your lungs, as well as the lower, should be filled now. Exhale,

pushing the air out with the relaxing of your diaphragm and the gradual contracting of your abdominal muscles and lowering of your rib cage. (Don't collapse and let your shoulders sag!)

3. Place your hands, palm in, on the lower portion of your rib cage so that your fingers are touching. Begin to inhale slowly. As you inhale, your ribs should push your hands apart. When the lower part of your breath cavity is full and you have allowed your chest to lift *slightly* until it, too, is full, you should have a full breath. Hold it for a second or two and let it out in a whoosh!

4. Repeat step 3, and when you have a full breath, tuck in your abdominal muscle slightly and hold your breath for a second until you feel in complete control. Now, as you start to exhale the full breath, begin to count aloud. As you begin to run out of breath for vocalizing, gradually contract your abdominal muscles (*not* the upper chest ones) as you continue counting. When you can no longer force air out of your chest by the strong but comfortable contraction of your abdominal muscles, stop the vocalized counting. Don't sacrifice a good quality of tone in the effort to "squeeze out" more sound. This will result only in undue tension in your upper chest and throat muscles — the very thing you want to avoid.

This exercise is basic to developing good breath control and should be used to begin any period of exercise. Many instructions say: "Breathe in," *then* "breathe out." This exercise suggests breathing out first, in order to empty your chest of air at the beginning of the exercise. In this way, a "stuffing" of the chest is avoided. Then comes the breathing in, followed by the controlled breathing out. This is the inevitable order, whether or not you are "exercising," for you cannot hold your breath forever.

You should not continue to work steadily at this or any other exercise after you begin to feel tired. Until you grow used to a changed method of control or a marked effort to increase capacity, you should go back to your usual manner of breathing for a rest. As you follow this type of exercise, it should become increasingly clear that the sooner you can make this method automatic, the easier the whole breathing process will be.

As you become able to take in larger amounts of air with ease and to continue exhalation to support the tone, you should be able to count more numbers on one breath. With each exercise period try to say a few more, always being careful that there is no strain in your throat, no forcing of the tone, and no sacrifice of quality. You should count at what seems an easy volume and at a pleasing level of pitch.

Practice breath control on the following passage. Keep an unbroken flow of sound to the end of each sentence, without doing violence to the meaning and the connotation of the words.

FROM *The Pied Piper of Hamelin*
ROBERT BROWNING

And out of the houses the rats came tumbling.
Great rats, small rats, lean rats, brawny rats,
Brown rats, black rats, gray rats, tawny rats,
Grave old plodders, gay young friskers,
   Fathers, mothers, uncles, cousins,
Cocking tails and pricking whiskers,
   Families by tens and dozens,
Brothers, sisters, husbands, wives —
Followed the Piper for their lives.

Obviously, it violates the author's intention to complete the long sentence in a single breath. To do so would threaten the clarity of the thought and the relationship of the phrases to one another as well as the contribution of line units and rhyme. When the material is read aloud, some of the phrasal units need to be separated by pauses of varying lengths. During these pauses you have an opportunity to replenish your supply of breath. Take care not to let the pauses break the continuity of thought. The position and duration of the pauses should always grow out of the relationship of the phrases to each other and to the complete thought being expressed. You should learn to breathe where you must pause, not pause in order to breathe. It is usually impossible to get a full breath except in the major pauses that complete the units of thought. Therefore, the final step in breath control is to learn to inhale quickly and unobtrusively, while still using the proper muscles.

Frequently a speaker inhales properly and uses the full capacity for breath but still cannot sustain a long flow of sound. Here the problem is not an insufficient supply of air but inadequate control of exhalation. This is one of the major causes of dropping final words or syllables so that they do not carry to the last row of the audience. A simple exercise will help to determine whether the control muscles collapse instead of exerting steady pressure as they relax.

Inhale a full, comfortable breath. Be sure that your shoulders are relaxed. Hold a lighted match directly in front of your lips as close as your profile will allow. Start to count aloud in full voice. You should be able to continue counting until the match burns down. If you blow out the flame, check the state of control of the muscles in and around your rib cage. Most of us exhale more than we need to on certain sounds, such as *"two"* or *"three"* or *"four."* Light another match, take another deep breath, and try the exercise again, speaking very softly with conscious control of the rate of relaxation of the muscles involved. You will feel as if you may explode, but you won't, and you will become aware of where the control must be exercised. As you gradually increase your volume to normal, you will find that the flame flickers but that you will not extinguish it by a sudden uncontrolled spurt of air.

Volume and Projection

Volume and projection are so important in communication that they must always be of utmost concern to the reader, actor, or speaker. Anyone who has been in an audience and strained to hear the speaker knows the tremendous importance of sufficient volume and good projection. After all, your purpose is to share your material with the audience. If you cannot be heard, you obviously have failed in your primary objective.

Actually, the words *volume* and *projection* are sometimes used interchangeably. Indeed, they are both part of your ability to be heard and understood. For greater clarity in this discussion, we shall consider *volume* to be the degree of loudness and *projection* to be the act of directing the voice to a specific target.

You should be able to make your voice fill the room in which the audience is gathered. You should learn to control the volume of your voice to fill a large space easily without distorting your voice and without blasting it down the back wall if space is limited. With practice, you will learn how much volume is required and how to achieve the greatest possible flexibility within that requirement.

Being understood also depends to a degree on the speaker's control of projection. The first requirement of adequate projection is to have enough volume and support so that the tone will carry as far as the material and situation demand. The second requirement is to have the proper mental attitude. Good communication is a product not only of breath control but also of your constant awareness of the listeners. This awareness is often spoken of in the theatre as *audience sense.* Although this sense is a difficult thing to explain, it has its base in the speaker's attitude of reaching out toward an audience with every line. Regardless of the energy of the ideas or emotions being expressed, readers or actors with a fine sense of audience participation should have a psychological set that helps their voices reach out to the audience. Interpreters, as well as actors, should keep in mind the old adage of show business and "play to the balcony." In other words, you should keep the back row of listeners in mind and be sure that your words reach them. This advice applies to an audience of a few people grouped around a fireplace as well as to several hundred listeners gathered in an auditorium or theatre.

This mental attitude toward communication has a direct and observable effect on the physiological control of projection. By thinking *to* your listeners as well as *of* them, wanting to be sure that they hear and share the full effect of the literature, you will tend to keep your body erect and your head lifted slightly so that your throat is free from tension.

Focus of Projection

It is sometimes helpful to think of your voice as a tangible thing — an object to be aimed and thrown at a target. This trick of *throwing the voice* may smack of ventriloquism, yet it is a practice everyone uses at times. A child calling to attract the attention of playmates down the street sends his voice to where they are. Football fans shouting advice to the players on the field direct their voices without conscious thought to the exact spot where their attention is focused. When carrying on a conversation in a room full of people, one person may project across the room to answer a remark or add to a discussion. When people wish to be confidential, they let their voices drop, and their circle of mental directness narrows to fill only the desired area.

The following exercises for focus of projection can be practiced most effectively in a large room. They have been conceived primarily to apply to an imagined concrete situation. By thinking specifically of what to do and by using any words that come to mind, the interpreter can concentrate on the suggested volume and focus.

1. You are seated at a desk in the center front of the room. You see a friend at the door; you call an easy greeting. She waves and goes on. You think of something that you ought to tell her. You call her name quickly, but she apparently doesn't hear, for she keeps on going. Without leaving your place, call again; have a good full breath as you start to call and direct the sound at her quickly disappearing back. Do the same thing again with more volume and longer sounds supported by forced exhalation. Be sure that you catch her this time.

2. You are giving directions to a group of people about how to work out a diagram. The room is large, and everyone must hear. Direct your remarks to various places, thinking of certain people who

might be there. After you have given instructions and the group starts to work, a person in the front of the group asks a question. You shift your focus of projection, reduce your volume, and answer the person who asked the question. Then you decide that others might need that special information, too. You raise your volume and expand your area of projection to attract everyone's attention, and then repeat to the group what you have said to the individual. As you do this, take care to direct your voice to the various parts of the room so that everyone will hear.

When you have made some progress in projection through these exercises, move on to practice with literary material.

An interesting problem in projection is found in Shakespeare's *Julius Caesar*. As Brutus goes up into the pulpit to make his famous speech to the crowd, he addresses a single remark to those near him. In the opening sentence, try to get the feeling of first speaking to those who stand around you, and then including the several hundred citizens who are milling around the Forum. It is necessary to quiet the crowd during the early part of the speech.

> **BRUTUS:** Be patient till the last. Romans, countrymen, and lovers! hear me for my cause, and be silent, that you may hear; believe me for mine honor, and have respect to mine honor, that you may believe; censure me in your wisdom, and awake your senses, that you may the better judge. If there be any in this assembly, any dear friend of Caesar's, to him I say, that Brutus' love to Caesar was no less than his. If then that friend demand why Brutus rose against Caesar, this is my answer: Not that I lov'd Caesar less, but that I lov'd Rome more.

In the following lines from the famous trial scene of Shakespeare's *The Merchant of Venice*, two characters are speaking. Our primary concern here is not with the difference in their voices or mental attitudes, but rather with the changes in focus and consequent projection in their speeches. (The parenthetical stage directions are inserted for this specific exercise. They do not appear in the text of the play.) The Duke speaks to Portia at close range on his greeting and first question and on the opening line of his second speech. After "take your place," it is assumed that she moves away from him; thus, his question "Are you acquainted with the difference/That holds this present question in the court?" must carry over a greater distance than his first remarks but should still be addressed directly to Portia. His order to Antonio and Shylock to "stand forth" may be thought of as carrying even farther, since they are probably among a group of people outside the judge's area. Practice the Duke's speeches until you can place them where you want them, and then follow the same procedure in Portia's speeches.

DUKE: Give me your hand. Came you from old Bellario?
PORTIA: (To Duke as she gives him her hand) I did, my lord.
DUKE: You are welcome; take your place.
   Are you acquainted with the difference
   That holds this present question in the court?
PORTIA: (From her place a few feet away from the Duke) I am informed thoroughly of the cause.
   (To the assemblage) Which is the merchant here, and which the Jew?
DUKE: Antonio and old Shylock, both stand forth.
PORTIA: (To Shylock after he has stepped forward from the crowd) Is your name Shylock?

In working to develop volume and projection, you are concentrating on one of the basic requirements of all speech: that it reach its audience. Volume depends largely on adequate breath supply and proper support in exhalation. Projection combines these physical aspects with the psychological aspect of mental directness. We shall discuss this concept of physical and mental focus more fully in later chapters. For the moment it is enough to recognize the relationship.

Pitch and Quality

Although pitch and quality are different attributes of sound, they are so closely related in origin and control in the human voice that they may be considered together. The way the vocal bands vibrate basically determines both the pitch and the quality of the vocal tone: the pitch is formed by the rate of vibration, the quality by the complexity of the vibration.

The *pitch* of a sound is its place on the musical scale. It is located very generally, in terms of the scale range, as high, medium, or low pitch. It is important for interpreters to become skillful in using pitch to suggest shades of meaning and to build to climaxes. Changes in pitch give variety and contrast to the material being read and help to hold the audience's attention. Since a change of pitch produces *inflection*, a speaker's *inflection range* is the entire pitch span between the highest and lowest tones that he or she is capable of making.

Any pattern in the variation of levels of pitch results in *melody*. When there are no discernible changes of pitch, the result is a *monotone*. Melody is an asset to the interpreter, but it can also become a problem. Most individuals have in their daily speech a characteristic pattern of inflections, which is part of their own personalities. This is highly commendable, and certainly it is to be expected that some of that pattern will be carried over into their work before an audience. It often happens, however, that a reader's pattern is so marked that it calls attention to itself and thus gets in the way of re-creation of the material. For example, one of the most common and annoying vocal patterns in reading poetry permits each line or each new thought to start on a high pitch and drift to a low tone at the close. The following lines are an example of poetic structure in which this problem must be controlled.

The Wild Honeysuckle
PHILIP FRENEAU

Fair flower, that dost so comely grow,
Hid in this silent, dull retreat,
Untouched thy honied blossoms blow,
Unseen thy little branches greet:
    No roving foot shall crush thee here,
    No busy hand provoke a tear.

And again, in less conventional poetry:

FROM I Hear America Singing
WALT WHITMAN

I hear America singing, the varied carols I hear,
Those of mechanics, each one singing his as it should be blithe and
    strong,
The carpenter singing his as he measures his plank or beam,
The mason singing his as he makes ready for work, or leaves off
    work . . .

Quality, more difficult to define distinctively, can be described best as the characteristic of a tone that distinguishes it from all other tones of the same pitch and intensity. This is sometimes called *timbre,* or to use the German word, *Klang,* meaning the "ring" of the tone. In describing quality, one frequently uses words that suggest color — a *golden* tone, a *silver-voiced* orator, a *blue* note.

    Quality of tone is perhaps most closely associated with mood and feeling. Connotation and emotional response have a strong effect on quality, and empathy (which we shall discuss more fully in the next chapter) plays its part in the degree of tension or relaxation it imposes on the vocal mechanism. Vocal quality is influenced by your empathic response to whatever elements of emotion, strength, and beauty are inherent in the material. An interpreter who is true to the art never adopts a certain quality and imposes it on the selection. A display of "rich" quality or of a variety of qualitative effects, like every other display of technique for its own sake, is in poor taste and violates the fundamental rule of unobtrusiveness.

Pitch and quality working together, then, are invaluable in helping you to bring out the universality and suggestion in a piece of literature. Pay particular attention to the control of these two aspects of vocal technique, because they contribute a great deal to the communication of emotional content.

Rate and Pause

The *rate* at which people speak is often habitual, a part of their personalities and their entire backgrounds. It probably serves them very well for ordinary conversation, but they may need to adjust their habitual rate to do justice to an author's style and purpose. Interpreters must learn to hear themselves in rehearsal and in conversation. There is no magic formula for slowing a too-rapid pace; to do this requires constant attention. It is helpful to select material that by its style and connotation encourages a slow pace of delivery. Very frequently the mere physical process of forming a sequence of sounds affects the rate at which a sentence can be read intelligibly and effectively. Interpreters should control their rate of speaking so that they can form every sound accurately. Also, by changing the rate, interpreters can express subtle variety in a selection. Emotion, connotation, suggestion, and the combination of vowels and consonants all provide clues for knowing when to speed up one's speaking pace, and when to slow it down.

Rate is determined not only by the speed with which sounds are uttered in sequence but also by the length and frequency of pauses that separate the sequences of sounds. It is essential to recognize the *phrasal pause* that clarifies the relationships of words in phrases in order to convey units of thoughts. The pause also may become one of your most effective tools for building suspense and climaxes and for reinforcing emotional content.

Beginning interpreters are often afraid to hold the pause long enough for its dramatic effect to register with their listeners. If a pause is motivated by real understanding, by identification with the feeling suggested, it may be sustained for a much longer time and with greater effect than you might realize. You need only be sure that during the pause something relevant to the material is going on in your own mind and consequently in the minds of your listeners.

Usually a pause provides a bridge between thoughts. It should always stay within the total concept of the selection and supply whatever transition or suspense is needed. You should work not only to
use pauses in the most effective places but also to vary and sustain
the lengths of the pauses as the material demands. Punctuation is
used on the printed page to signal the eyes. It guides the reader in
establishing the relationship of words and phrases and their division
into sentences. Interpreters can change pitch, quality, or emphasis or
use a combination of these to signal the ears of their listeners. You
do not always need to use a pause. Moreover, you should remember
that rules and fashions change in punctuation as they do in everything else. Your full understanding of and response to your material,
together with a sense of responsibility to your audience, are the final
determining factors in your use of pauses.

In the following scene from Edmond Rostand's *Cyrano de Bergerac,*
Cyrano is speaking of his monstrous nose and its effect on his entire
being. You can make exquisite use of pause here. As you work on
the interpretation, you will realize that the tempo of the scene
changes with "Oh, not that ever!" You will see how this change to a
faster, more smoothly flowing rate is effected. You also will realize
that the change goes hand in hand with Cyrano's struggle to turn
from his romantic, self-revelatory mood to his customary half-comic
acceptance of his nose.

> **CYRANO:**   My old friend — look at me,
> And tell me how much hope remains for me
> With this protuberance! Oh I have no more
> Illusions! Now and then — bah! I may grow
> Tender, walking alone in the blue cool
> Of evening, through some garden fresh with flowers
> After the benediction of the rain;
> My poor big devil of a nose inhales
> April . . . and so I follow with my eyes
> Where some boy, with a girl upon his arm,
> Passes a patch of silver . . . and I feel
> Somehow, I wish I had a woman too,
> Walking with little steps under the moon,
> And holding my arm so, and smiling. Then
> I dream — and I forget. . . .
>   And then I see
> The shadow of my profile on the wall!
> **LEBRET:** My friend! . . .
> **CYRANO:**   My friend, I have my bitter days,
> Knowing myself so ugly, so alone.
> Sometimes —

LEBRET: You weep?
CYRANO: *(Quickly)* Oh, not that ever! No,
        That would be too grotesque — the tears trickling down
        All the long way along this nose of mine?
        I will not so profane the dignity
        Of sorrow. Never any tears for me!

To develop additional skill in your use of rate of speaking, try to work on selections that demand basically different rate patterns. As you read the material aloud with feeling, you will realize that you should effectively observe the *quantity*, or length, of the individual vowel and consonant sounds, as well as the length of pauses between sounds. In a prevailing rapid rate, the sounds as well as the pauses are often short; in a slower rate, they are long.

Many of the lyrics of the Gilbert and Sullivan operettas are wonderful examples of the way in which sound suggests rate. Note particularly the fast-moving "Nightmare Song" from *Iolanthe:*

When you're lying awake with a dismal headache,
     And repose is taboo'd by anxiety —
I conceive you may use any language you choose
     To indulge in, without impropriety . . .

Intelligibility of Speech

We already have mentioned that in order to fulfill its basic function of communication, speech must be understandable and intelligible; hence, it must be heard. But to be fully intelligible, speech should be not only audible, but also distinct and accurate. Listeners cannot keep their attention on the material if they must constantly "translate" unclear speech sounds or mispronunciations. Therefore, all speech sounds should be correct, as well as distinct and pleasing. It is true that few things are more irritating to the listener than a speaker's self-conscious, overly careful mouthing of vowels and consonants. This conveys affectation and insincerity. Moreover, it violates the cardinal rule of interpretation, because it draws attention to the reader's technique and away from the material. On the other hand, a reader who cannot be understood certainly cannot communicate. Consequently, you should learn to pronounce and articulate words with such clarity and accuracy that any audience is able to understand you.

A distinction between pronunciation and articulation may be helpful. *Pronunciation* refers to the *correctness* of sounds and accents in spoken words. *Articulation,* on the other hand, refers to the *shaping* of the sounds by the speaker's lips, teeth, tongue, and hard and soft palates.

Pronunciation is considered to be acceptable when all the sounds of a word are uttered correctly in their proper order and with accent (stress) on the proper syllable. There is a big difference, for instance, between *refúse* and *réfuse.* Current good usage is the guide to correct pronunciation. A standard dictionary is the final authority. Unfamiliar polysyllabic words are not always the ones that trip up readers. Since you may distrust your pronunciation of such words, you probably will look them up in the dictionary. The real pitfalls are the common, everyday words that you may have fallen into the habit of pronouncing incorrectly. A mispronunciation can ruin a fine oral line. In addition, it may distract listeners so much that they momentarily lose the thought that you are trying to communicate.

Most of us have ingrained in our speech patterns certain regional or ethnic influences. These are usually slight deviations (from so-called standard speech) in some individual sounds and/or the melody pattern. For instance, one need only consider the difference in pronunciation of *r* as one travels from New England through the Midwest and into the South to be aware that Standard American Speech is "standard" for very few of us. Further, audiences have a tendency to associate accents or dialects with certain stereotypes. Therefore, some effort should be made to develop Standard American Speech, if only to use it "on special occasions," when material and audiences are better served by the elimination of any regionalisms or obtrusive vocal mannerisms.

Dialect, or accent, is basically a matter of the way separate sounds are formed and, far more important, the use of a melodic or rhythmic flow as the sounds go together. When an author wants dialect to provide a part of the character clues, he or she will indicate this through spelling or syntax. Because a writer is black or Chicano or British or from New England does not mean that the interpreter should strive for such regional speech. If the author wrote in dialect, you should read it as well as you can. If he or she did not, read the selection the way it was written with careful attention to all the elements of style. Make your own speech sufficiently flexible to conform to the total demand of the selection you have chosen. When an interpreter's own dialect seems incongruous for the speaker in the selection, the contradiction can distract the listeners.

When you know what correct pronunciation is and have checked your own everyday speech, you may profitably turn your attention both to improving the ways in which you form sounds and to strengthening your projection of them. Faulty projection of distinct sounds is closely related to the position of the sounds in the word or phrase. The end of a word or phrase often may be slighted or left off, even though the preceding sounds are distinct enough. In the exercises for control of sustained exhalation, we pointed out that you need adequate control in order to complete fully the ends of lines and sentences. This control and the accurate shaping of end sounds are closely allied. An interpreter's failure to finish words is one of the faults that interfere most with good communication, especially during a performance in a large auditorium or theatre.

After checking on individual sounds and words, you should occasionally test your progress by trying pieces of material that involve difficult combinations of sounds. Even experienced interpreters profit from an occasional session of careful listening for careless articulation. Of course, this attention to vocal technique belongs in rehearsal periods; in performance you should concentrate on the literature you are sharing, not on your articulation.

Selections for Analysis and Oral Interpretation

In analyzing these selections, pay particular attention to the vocal problems each one presents. Almost all of the selections require more than a normal supply of breath, because they either contain long, flowing sentences or demand an unusual amount of volume or force. Some pieces present interesting problems in projection. They all require that you work with a maximum flexibility of range in order to communicate the richness of sounds effectively. They also demand an awareness of your bodily responses.

The telling is almost more important than the tale itself in this segment from *Lake Wobegon Days*. Don't try to imitate Keillor's distinctive radio voice. Rather, focus on what interests this narrator most: the responsiveness of the people to the need they perceived. And be sure we see all of these characters as real people; no one is being mocked here.

FROM *Lake Wobegon Days*
GARRISON KEILLOR

People who visit Lake Wobegon come to see somebody, otherwise they missed the turn on the highway and are lost. *Ausländers*, the Germans call them. They don't come for Toast 'n Jelly Days, or the Germans' quadrennial Gesuffa Days, or Krazy Daze, or the Feast Day of St. Francis, or the three-day Mist County Fair with its exciting

Death Leap from the top of the grandstand to the arms of the haystack for only ten cents. What's special about here isn't special enough to draw a major crowd, though Flag Day — you could drive a long way on June 14 to find another like it.

Flag Day, as we know it, was the idea of Herman Hochstetter, Rollie's dad, who ran the dry goods store and ran Armistice Day, the Fourth of July, and Flag Day. For the Fourth, he organized a double-loop parade around the block which allowed people to take turns marching and watching. On Armistice Day, everyone stepped outside at 11 A.M. and stood in silence for two minutes as Our Lady's bell tolled eleven times.

Flag Day was his favorite. For a modest price, he would install a bracket on your house to hold a pole to hang your flag on, or he would drill a hole in the sidewalk in front of your store with his drill gun powered by a .22 shell. *Bam!* And in went the flag. On patriotic days, flags flew all over; there were flags on the tall poles, flags on the short, flags in the brackets on the pillars and the porches, and if you were flagless you could expect to hear from Herman. His hairy arm around your shoulder, his poochlike face close to yours, he would say how proud he was that so many people were proud of their country, leaving you to see the obvious, that you were a gap in the ranks.

In June 1944, the day after D-Day, a salesman from Fisher Hat called on Herman and offered a good deal on red and blue baseball caps. "Do you have white also?" Herman asked. The salesman thought that white caps could be had for the same wonderful price. Herman ordered two hundred red, two hundred white, and one hundred blue. By the end of the year, he still had four hundred and eighty-six caps. The inspiration of the Living Flag was born from that overstock.

On June 14, 1945, a month after V-E Day, a good crowd assembled in front of the Central Building in response to Herman's ad in the paper:

> Honor "AMERICA" June 14 AT 4 p.m. Be proud of "Our Land & People". Be part of the "LIVING FLAG". Don't let it be said that Lake Wobegon was "Too Busy". Be on time. 4 p.m. "Sharp".

His wife Louise handed out the caps, and Herman stood on a stepladder and told people where to stand. He lined up the reds and whites into stripes, then got the blues into their square. Mr. Hanson climbed up on the roof of the Central Building and took a photograph, they sang the national anthem, and then the Living Flag dispersed. The photograph appeared in the paper the next week. Herman kept the caps.

In the flush of victory, people were happy to do as told and stand in place, but in 1946 and 1947, dissension cropped up in the ranks: people complained about the heat and about Herman — what gave *him* the idea he could order *them* around? "People! Please! I need your attention! You blue people, keep your hats on! Please! Stripe No. 4, you're sagging! You reds, you're up here! We got too many white people, we need more red ones! Let's do this without talking, people! I can't get you straight if you keep moving around! Some of you are not paying attention! Everybody shut up! Please!"

One cause of resentment was the fact that none of them got to see the Flag they were in; the picture in the paper was black and white. Only Herman and Mr. Hanson got to see the real Flag, and some boys too short to be needed down below. People wanted a chance to go up to the roof and witness the spectacle for themselves.

"How can you go up there if you're supposed to be down here?" Herman said. "You go up there to look, you got nothing to look at. Isn't it enough to know that you're doing your part?"

On Flag Day, 1949, just as Herman said, "That's it! Hold it now!" one of the reds made a break for it — dashed up four flights of stairs to the roof and leaned over and had a long look. Even with the hole he left behind, it was a magnificent sight. The Living Flag filled the street below. A perfect Flag! The reds so brilliant! He couldn't take his eyes off it. "Get down here! We need a picture!" Herman yelled up to him. "How does it look?" people yelled up to him. "Unbelievable! I can't describe it!" he said.

So then everyone had to have a look. "No!" Herman said, but they took a vote and it was unanimous. One by one, members of the Living Flag went up to the roof and admired it. It *was* marvelous! It brought tears to the eyes, it made one reflect on this great country and on Lake Wobegon's place in it. One wanted to stand up there all afternoon and just drink it in. So, as the first hour passed, and only forty of the five hundred had been to the top, the others got more and more restless. "Hurry up! Quit dawdling! *You've* seen it! Get down here and give someone else a chance!" Herman sent people up in groups of four, and then ten, but after two hours, the Living Flag became the Sitting Flag and then began to erode, as the members who had had a look thought about heading home to supper, which infuriated the ones who hadn't. "Ten more minutes!" Herman cried, but ten minutes became twenty and thirty, and people snuck off and the Flag that remained for the last viewer was a Flag shot through by cannon fire.

In 1950, the Sons of Knute took over Flag Day. Herman gave them the boxes of caps. Since then, the Knutes have achieved several good Flags, though most years the attendance was poor. You need at least four hundred to make a good one. Some years the Knutes made a "no-look" rule, other years they held a lottery. One year they experimented with a large mirror held by two men over the edge of the roof, but when people leaned back and looked up, the Flag disappeared, of course.

▮ How did your performance demonstrate the narrator's affection for the inhabitants of his town? Did they disappoint him?

You can find a classic example of the value of sound combinations in this familiar nonsense poem.

Jabberwocky
LEWIS CARROLL

'Twas brillig, and the slithy toves
   Did gyre and gimble in the wabe:
All mimsy were the borogoves,
   And the mome raths outgrabe.

"Beware the Jabberwock, my son!
   The jaws that bite, the claws that catch!
Beware the Jubjub bird, and shun
   The frumious Bandersnatch!"

He took his vorpal sword in hand;
   Long time the manxome foe he sought —
So rested he by the Tumtum tree,
   And stood awhile in thought.

And, as in uffish thought he stood,
   The Jabberwock, with eyes of flame,
Came whiffling through the tulgey wood,
   And burbled as it came!

One, two! One, two! And through and through
   The vorpal blade went snicker-snack!
He left it dead, and with its head
   He went galumphing back.

"And hast thou slain the Jabberwock?
    Come to my arms, my beamish boy!
O frabjous day! Callooh, Callay!"
    He chortled in his joy.

'Twas brillig, and the slithy toves
    Did gyre and gimble in the wabe:
All mimsy were the borogoves,
    And the mome raths outgrabe.

▌ There is nothing silly for the personae in this tale. How did
your voice distinguish among the speakers?

There is great opportunity for vocal variety here. Let the young "interpreters"
in the story enjoy the elocutionary aspects of their selections. Note carefully
the narrator's descriptions of each of the girls' antics. Don't caricature these
young women — each is a character in herself.

FROM *The Little Girls*

ELIZABETH BOWEN

Thick cream glazed blinds were pulled most of the way down. Failing
to keep out the marine sunshine, they flopped lazily over the open
windows in the hot June breath rather than breeze haunting the garden. St. Agatha's had been a house, IV-A Classroom probably the
morning-room. The blinds were lace-bordered. There was a gar-
landed wallpaper — called to order by having on it a bald, pontifical
clock, only a size or two smaller than a station one, a baize board
clustered with lists and warnings, and sepia reproductions of inspir-
ing pictures, among them "Hope," framed in oak. Of oak were the
desks, to which were clamped high-backed seats. An aroma of Plas-
ticine came from the models along the chimneypiece, and from jars
of botanical specimens near a window whiffs of water slimy with
rotting greenery were fanned in — the girl in charge of the specimens
being absent with one of her summer colds. Chalk in the neighbour-
hood of the blackboard and ink thickening in china wells in the desks
were the only other educational smells.
    A dozen or so girls, most of them aged eleven, some ten, some
twelve, sat at the desks. All wore their summer tunics of butcher-
blue. By turning their heads, left, they could have seen strips of
garden, parching away, between restless lace and stolid white window sills. Politely, however, most of them faced their teacher; this
they could do for Miss Kinmate, if little else. This was the first lesson

after mid-morning break with its milk and biscuits — even the slight feast had thrown IV-A into a gorged condition. But this also was the Tuesday poetry hour, to which Miss Kinmate attached hopes. Each girl (the idea was) chose for herself the short poem or portion of longer one which, got by heart, she was to recite.

One more of them had just taken the stand.

"There *was* a time when meadow, grove and stream,
The earth and —"

"Stop!" cried Miss Kinmate. "Before we begin, not *too* much expression. Wordsworth was not as regretful as all that."

"I thought he was. Like some old, fat person saying, 'There *was* a time when I could jump over a ten-foot wall.'"

"That would be silly."

"Well, this is silly, in a way."

"Your old, fat man would not be speaking the truth. Have you any idea how high a ten-foot wall is?"

"Yes."

"I wonder whether you have. Because, even a Greek athlete could probably not jump over that." (From a back desk, a hand shot up.)

"*Yes*, Olive?"

"How high could a Greek athlete probably jump?"

"That would depend."

The child Clare, during this intermission, stood stonily contemplating her audience — hands behind her, back to the blackboard, feet planted apart, tongue exploring a cavity in a lower molar. At a moody sign from Miss Kinmate, she went on:

"— and every common sight,
To *me* did seem
Apparell'd in celestial *light*,
The glory and freshness of a dream.
It is *not* now as it has been of yore; —
Turn whereso'er I may,
By night *or* day,
The things which —"

"Stop! Oh dear, what are we to do?"

"I thought —"

"Well, don't — *try!* Otherwise, go and sit down. Ruining that beautiful poem!"

"Yes, Miss Kinmate."

"And don't make eyes at the others. Next time, choose a poem you understand."

"I do know another. Shall I try that?"

Miss Kinmate looked at the clock. The whole class (but for Sheila Beaker, who couldn't be bothered, and Muriel Borthwick, who having picked at a good big scab on her arm now dabbed blotting-paper at the resultant blood) did likewise, in an awed, considering way. "Very well," Miss Kinmate conceded. "Go on, Clare — though remember, there are others to come."

The child, having drawn a breath twice her size, launched with passion into her second choice:

> "Last night among his fellow roughs
> He jested, quaff'd and swore:
> A drunken private of the Buffs,
> Who never look'd before.
> Today, beneath the foeman's frown,
> He stands in Elgin's place,
> Ambassador from Britain's crown,
> And type of all her race.
>
> Poor, reckless, rude, low-born, untaught,
> Bewilder'd and alone,
> A heart, with English instinct fraught,
> He yet can call his own.
> *Ay! tear* his body limb from limb,
> Bring *cord*, or *axe*, or *flame*! —
> He only knows, that not through him
> Shall England come to shame.
>
> Fair Kentish hopfields round him seemed
> Like dreams to come and go;
> Bright leagues of cherry blossom —"

"Stop! Time's up, I'm afraid. A pity, because you were doing better." Miss Kinmate's eye roved round. "Diana, try and not sit with your mouth open — wake up! What is the name of the poem Clare's just recited?"

"'The Drunken Private of the Buffs.'"

"Not exactly. — Well, who and whose poem next? Muriel: you!"

"I think I'm bleeding too much."

"What, cut yourself?"

"Not exactly."

"Better go and find Matron."

Gory Muriel left. Miss Kinmate had to cast round all over again. "*Sheila*, then. Sheila, we'll hear you now."

Southstone's wonder, the child exhibition dancer, rose, tossed back her silver-gold plaits, and habituatedly stepped forward into the limelight. An ornate volume, open at the required page and gildedly looking like a school prize (which it was, though not awarded to her), was bestowed by her upon Miss Kinmate, with what was less a bow than a flowerlike inclination of the head. She then half-turned, with a minor swirl of the tunic, and, facing the footlights, glided three steps sideways into the place of doom left vacant by Clare. Here reality struck the prodigy amidships. Bewitched, since she rose from her desk, by her own performance, she had lost sight for that minute or two of her entrance's true and hideous purpose. She was to be called upon not to spring about but to give tongue. A badgered hatred of literature filled her features. She did deliver her poem, though in the manner of one voicing, with wonderful moderation, a long-nursed and justifiable complaint:

"Up the airy mountain,
Down the rushing glen,
We daren't *go* a-hunting
For fear of little *men;*
Wee folk, good folk,
Trooping all together;
Green jacket, red cap,
And white owl's feather!

Down on the rocky *shore*
Some make their home;
They *live* on crispy pancakes
Of yellow tide-foam;
Some, in the reeds
Of the black mountain-lake,

With frogs for *their* watch-dogs,
All night awake.

High on the hill-top
The old *King* sits.
He is now so old and grey
He's nigh lost . . . ?
. . . his bridge of white wits?
. . . his mist of white wits?
. . . *his* bridge?
. . . *his* wits . . . ?"

She ran down, ticked over uncertainly, gave right out, and turned on Miss Kinmate a look as much as to say: "Well, there you are. What else would you expect?"

"Never mind," Miss Kinmate hastened to say. "It went nicely so far. Though a little mournful — fairies are gay things, aren't they?"

Sheila had no idea.

"And one word wrong in your second line. It should be 'rushy,' not 'rushing.' How could a glen rush?"

"I thought it meant they were all rushing about," said Sheila Beaker, still more deeply aggrieved.

"Sheila chose a delightful poem, at any rate," Miss Kinmate informed the class — who knew to a girl whose the choice had been: Mrs. Beaker's.

▌ How did you demonstrate Miss Kinmate's growing dismay?

Pay particular attention to control of inflection and emphasis when reading this poem in order to make its important pun clear and meaningful when the words are heard rather than seen on the page.

A Hymn to God the Father
JOHN DONNE

Wilt thou forgive that sin where I begun,
    Which is my sin though it were done before?
Wilt thou forgive those sins through which I run,
    And do them still, though still I do deplore?
When thou hast done, thou hast not done,
        For I have more.

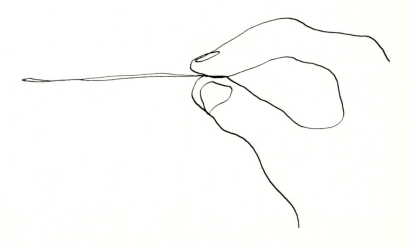

Wilt thou forgive that sin by which I've won
   Others to sin, and made my sin their door?
Wilt thou forgive that sin which I did shun
   A year or two, but wallow'd in a score?
When thou hast done, thou hast not done,
     For I have more.

I have a sin of fear, that when I've spun
   My last thread, I shall perish on the shore;
Swear by thyself at my death thy Sun
   Shall shine as it shines now, and heretofore;
And having done that, thou hast Donne.
     I have no more.

▌ How did you communicate the increasing gravity of the sins
the speaker confesses?

The narrator of this story by John Updike treats us as his friends, and the events he tells us about have affected him deeply, but he is not lugubrious. Don't let him become overbearing or dimwitted, either. Why does he quit his job?

A & P

JOHN UPDIKE

In walks these three girls in nothing but bathing suits. I'm in the third checkout slot, with my back to the door, so I don't see them until they're over by the bread. The one that caught my eye first was the one in the plaid green two-piece. She was a chunky kid, with a good tan and a sweet broad soft-looking can with those two crescents of white just under it, where the sun never seems to hit, at the top of the backs of her legs. I stood there with my hand on a box of HiHo crackers trying to remember if I rang it up or not. I ring it up again and the customer starts giving me hell. She's one of these cash-register-watchers, a witch about fifty with rouge on her cheekbones and no eyebrows, and I know it made her day to trip me up. She'd been watching cash registers for fifty years and probably never seen a mistake before.

    By the time I got her feathers smoothed and her goodies into a bag — she gives me a little snort in passing, if she'd been born at the right time they would have burned her over in Salem — by the time I get her on her way the girls had circled around the bread and were coming back, without a pushcart, back my way along the counters, in the aisle between the checkouts and the Special bins. They didn't even have shoes on. There was this chunky one, with the two-piece — it was bright green and the seams on the bra were still sharp and her belly was still pretty pale so I guessed she just got it (the suit) — there was this one, with one of those chubby berry-faces, the lips all bunched together under her nose, this one, and a tall one, with black hair that hadn't quite frizzed right, and one of these sunburns right across under the eyes, and a chin that was too long — you know, the kind of girl other girls think is very "striking" and "attractive" but never quite makes it, as they very well know, which is why they like her so much — and then the third one, that wasn't quite so tall. She was the queen. She kind of led them, the other two peeking around and making their shoulders round. She didn't look around, not this queen, she just walked straight on slowly, on these long white prima-donna legs. She came down a little hard on her heels, as if she didn't walk in her bare feet that much, putting down her heels and then letting the weight move along to her toes as if she was testing the floor with every step, putting a little deliberate extra action into it. You never know for sure how girls' minds work (do you really think it's a mind in there or just a little buzz like a bee in a glass jar?) but you got the idea she had talked the other two into coming in here with her, and now she was showing them how to do it, walk slow and hold yourself straight.

She had on a kind of dirty-pink — beige maybe, I don't know — bathing suit with a little nubble all over it and, what got me, the straps were down. They were off her shoulders looped loose around the cool tops of her arms, and I guess as a result the suit had slipped a little on her, so all around the top of the cloth there was this shining rim. If it hadn't been there you wouldn't have known there could have been anything whiter than those shoulders. With the straps pushed off, there was nothing between the top of the suit and the top of her head except just *her*, this clean bare plane of the top of her chest down from the shoulder bones like a dented sheet of metal tilted in the light. I mean, it was more than pretty.

She had sort of oaky hair that the sun and salt had bleached, done up in a bun that was unraveling, and a kind of prim face. Walking into the A & P with your straps down, I suppose it's the only kind of face you *can* have. She held her head so high her neck, coming up out of those white shoulders, looked kind of stretched, but I didn't mind. The longer her neck was, the more of her there was.

She must have felt in the corner of her eye me and over my shoulder Stokesie in the second slot watching, but she didn't tip. Not this queen. She kept her eyes moving across the racks, and stopped, and turned so slow it made my stomach rub the inside of my apron, and buzzed to the other two, who kind of huddled against her for relief, and then they all three of them went up the cat-and-dog-food-breakfast-cereal-macaroni-rice-raisins-seasonings-spreads-spaghetti-soft-drinks-crackers-and-cookies aisle. From the third slot I look straight up this aisle to the meat counter, and I watched them all the way. The fat one with the tan sort of fumbled with the cookies, but on second thought she put the package back. The sheep pushing their carts down the aisle — the girls were walking against the usual traffic (not that we have one-way signs or anything) — were pretty hilarious. You could see them, when Queenie's white shoulders dawned on them, kind of jerk, or hop, or hiccup, but their eyes snapped back to their own baskets and on they pushed. I bet you could set off dynamite in an A & P and the people would by and large keep reaching and checking oatmeal off their lists and muttering "Let me see, there was a third thing, began with A, asparagus, no, ah, yes, applesauce!" or whatever it is they do mutter. But there was no doubt, this jiggled them. A few houseslaves in pin curlers even looked around after pushing their carts past to make sure what they had seen was correct.

You know, it's one thing to have a girl in a bathing suit down on the beach, where what with the glare nobody can look at each other much anyway, and another thing in the cool of the A & P, under the fluorescent lights, against all those stacked packages, with her feet paddling along naked over our checkerboard green-and-cream rubber-tile floor.

"Oh Daddy," Stokesie said beside me. "I feel so faint."

"Darling," I said. "Hold me tight." Stokesie's married, with two babies chalked up on his fuselage already, but as far as I can tell that's the only difference. He's twenty-two, and I was nineteen this April.

"Is it done?" he asks, the responsible married man finding his voice. I forgot to say he thinks he's going to be manager some sunny day, maybe in 1990 when it's called the Great Alexandrov and Petrooshki Tea Company or something.

What he meant was, our town is five miles from a beach, with a big summer colony out on the Point, but we're right in the middle of town, and the women generally put on a shirt or shorts or something before they get out of the car into the street. And anyway these are usually women with six children and varicose veins mapping their legs and nobody, including them, could care less. As I say, we're right in the middle of town, and if you stand at our front doors you can see two banks and the Congregational church and the newspaper store and three real-estate offices and about twenty-seven old freeloaders tearing up Central Street because the sewer broke again. It's not as if we're on the Cape; we're north of Boston and there's people in this town haven't seen the ocean for twenty years.

The girls had reached the meat counter and were asking McMahon something. He pointed, they pointed, and they shuffled out of sight behind a pyramid of Diet Delight peaches. All that was left for us to see was old McMahon patting his mouth and looking after them sizing up their joints. Poor kids, I began to feel sorry for them, they couldn't help it.

Now here comes the sad part of the story, at least my family says it's sad, but I don't think it's so sad myself. The store's pretty empty, it being Thursday afternoon, so there was nothing much to do except lean on the register and wait for the girls to show up again. The whole store was like a pinball machine and I didn't know which tunnel they'd come out of. After a while they come around out of the far aisle, around the light bulbs, records at discount of the Caribbean Six or Tony Martin Sings or some such gunk you wonder they waste the wax on, sixpacks of candy bars, and plastic toys done up in cellophane that fall apart when a kid looks at them anyway. Around they come, Queenie still leading the way, and holding a little gray jar in her hand. Slots Three through Seven are unmanned and I could see her wondering between Stokes and me, but Stokesie with his usual luck draws an old party in baggy gray pants who stumbles up with four giant cans of pineapple juice (what do these bums *do* with all that pineapple juice? I've often asked myself) so the girls come to me. Queenie puts down the jar and I take it into my fingers icy cold. Kingfish Fancy Herring Snacks in Pure Sour Cream: 49¢. Now her hands are empty, not a ring or a bracelet, bare as God made them, and I wonder where the money's coming from. Still with that prim look she lifts a folded dollar bill out of the hollow at the center of her nubbled pink top. The jar went heavy in my hand. Really, I thought that was so cute.

Then everybody's luck begins to run out. Lengel comes in from haggling with a truck full of cabbages on the lot and is about to scuttle into that door marked MANAGER behind which he hides all day when the girls touch his eye. Lengel's pretty dreary, teaches Sunday school and the rest, but he doesn't miss that much. He comes over and says, "Girls, this isn't the beach."

Queenie blushes, though maybe it's just a brush of sunburn I was noticing for the first time, now that she was so close. "My mother asked me to pick up a jar of herring snacks." Her voice kind of startled me, the way voices do when you see the people first, coming out so flat and dumb yet kind of tony, too, the way it ticked over "pick up" and "snacks." All of a sudden I slid right down her voice into her living room. Her father and the other men were standing around in ice-cream coats and bow ties and the women were in sandals picking up herring snacks on toothpicks off a big glass plate and they were all holding drinks the color of water with olives and sprigs of mint in them. When my parents have somebody over they get lemonade and if it's a real racy affair Schlitz in tall glasses with "They'll Do It Every Time" cartoons stenciled on.

"That's all right," Lengel said. "But this isn't the beach." His repeating this struck me as funny, as if it had just occurred to him, and he had been thinking all these years the A & P was a great big dune and he was the head lifeguard. He didn't like my smiling — as I say he doesn't miss much — but he concentrates on giving the girls that sad Sunday-school-superintendent stare.

Queenie's blush is no sunburn now, and the plump one in plaid, that I liked better from the back — a really sweet can — pipes up, "We weren't doing any shopping. We just came in for the one thing."

"That makes no difference," Lengel tells her, and I could see from the way his eyes went that he hadn't noticed she was wearing a two-piece before. "We want you decently dressed when you come in here."

"We *are* decent," Queenie says suddenly, her lower lip pushing, getting sore now that she remembers her place, a place from which the crowd that runs the A & P must look pretty crummy. Fancy Herring Snacks flashed in her very blue eyes.

"Girls, I don't want to argue with you. After this come in here with your shoulders covered. It's our policy." He turns his back. That's policy for you. Policy is what the kingpins want. What the others want is juvenile delinquency.

All this while, the customers had been showing up with their carts but, you know, sheep, seeing a scene, they had all bunched up on Stokesie, who shook open a paper bag as gently as peeling a peach, not wanting to miss a word. I could feel in the silence everybody getting nervous, most of all Lengel, who asks me, "Sammy, have you rung up their purchase?"

I thought and said "No" but it wasn't about that I was thinking. I go through the punches, 4, 9, GROC, TOT — it's more complicated than you think, and after you do it often enough, it begins to make a little song, that you hear words to, in my case "Hello (*bing*) there, you (*gung*) hap-py *pee*-pul (*splat*)! — the *splat* being the drawer flying out. I uncrease the bill, tenderly as you may imagine, it just having come from between the two smoothest scoops of vanilla I had ever known were there, and pass a half and a penny into her narrow pink palm, and nestle the herrings in a bag and twist its neck and hand it over, all the time thinking.

The girls, and who'd blame them, are in a hurry to get out, so I say "I quit" to Lengel quick enough for them to hear, hoping they'll stop and watch me, their unsuspected hero. They keep right on going, into the electric eye; the door flies open and they flicker across the lot to their car, Queenie and Plaid and Big Tall Goony-Goony (not that as raw material she was so bad), leaving me with Lengel and a kink in his eyebrow.

"Did you say something, Sammy?"

"I said I quit."

"I thought you did."

"You didn't have to embarrass them."

"It was they who were embarrassing us."

I started to say something that came out "Fiddle-de-doo." It's a saying of my grandmother's, and I know she would have been pleased.

"I don't think you know what you're saying," Lengel said.

"I know you don't," I said. "But I do." I pull the bow at the back of my apron and start shrugging it off my shoulders. A couple customers that had been heading for my slot begin to knock against each other, like scared pigs in a chute.

Lengel sighs and begins to look very patient and old and gray. He's been a friend of my parents for years. "Sammy, you don't want to do this to your Mom and Dad," he tells me. It's true, I don't. But it seems to me that once you begin a gesture it's fatal not to go through with it. I fold the apron, "Sammy" stitched in red on the pocket, and put it on the counter, and drop the bow tie on top of it. The bow tie is theirs, if you've ever wondered. "You'll feel this for the rest of your life," Lengel says, and I know that's true, too, but remembering how he made that pretty girl blush makes me so scrunchy inside I punch the No Sale tab and the machine whirs "pee-pul" and the drawer splats out. One advantage to this scene taking place in summer, I can follow this up with a clean exit, there's no fumbling around getting your coat and galoshes, I just saunter into the electric eye in my white shirt that my mother ironed the night before, and the door heaves itself open, and outside the sunshine is skating around on the asphalt.

I look around for my girls, but they're gone, of course. There wasn't anybody but some young married screaming with her children about some candy they didn't get by the door of a powder-blue Falcon station wagon. Looking back in the big windows, over the bags of peat moss and aluminum lawn furniture stacked on the pavement, I could see Lengel in my place in the slot, checking the sheep through. His face was dark gray and his back stiff, as if he'd just had an injection of iron, and my stomach kind of fell as I felt how hard the world was going to be to me hereafter.

❚ We must see Sammy clearly — how did you show your audience the audience he is telling his story to?

Although this poem was written during the nineteenth century, it certainly is relevant to the world today. The poem's strength lies in the quality of mind and attitude that it reflects. The final sentence should be carefully controlled vocally to keep the last part of the stanza from overbalancing the important plea for fidelity.

Dover Beach
MATTHEW ARNOLD

The sea is calm tonight.
The tide is full, the moon lies fair
Upon the straits; — on the French coast the light
Gleams and is gone; the cliffs of England stand
Glimmering and vast, out in the tranquil bay.
Come to the window, sweet is the night-air!
Only, from the long line of spray
Where the sea meets the moon-blanched land,
Listen! you hear the grating roar
Of pebbles which the waves draw back, and fling,
At their return, up the high strand,
Begin, and cease, and then again begin,
With tremulous cadence slow, and bring
The eternal note of sadness in.

Sophocles long ago
Heard it on the Aegean, and it brought
Into his mind the turbid ebb and flow
Of human misery; we
Find also in the sound a thought,
Hearing it by this distant northern sea.

The Sea of Faith
Was once, too, at the full, and round earth's shore

Lay like the folds of a bright girdle furled.
But now I only hear
Its melancholy, long, withdrawing roar,
Retreating, to the breath
Of the night-wind, down the vast edges drear
And naked shingles of the world.

Ah, love, let us be true
To one another! for the world, which seems
To lie before us like a land of dreams,
So various, so beautiful, so new,
Hath really neither joy, nor love, nor light,
Nor certitude, nor peace, nor help for pain;
And we are here as on a darkling plain
Swept with confused alarms of struggle and flight,
Where ignorant armies clash by night.

▌ How did you vocally indicate the several shifts in locus?

Joan Didion gives us a portrait of Georgia O'Keeffe, one of the greatest painters of this century, who died in March 1986 at the age of 96. Didion is clearly the controlling voice in this excerpt, but she frequently quotes O'Keeffe both directly and indirectly. Be sure that your audience knows who is saying what.

FROM *The White Album*
JOAN DIDION

Georgia O'Keeffe

"Where I was born and where and how I have lived is unimportant," Georgia O'Keeffe told us in the book of paintings and words published in her ninetieth year on earth . . . "It is what I have done with where I have been that should be of interest."

. . . "Hardness" has not been in our century a quality much admired in women, nor in the past twenty years has it even been in official favor for me. When hardness surfaces in the very old we tend to transform it into "crustiness" or eccentricity, some tonic pepperiness to be indulged at a distance. On the evidence of her work and what she has said about it, Georgia O'Keeffe is neither "crusty" nor eccentric. She is simply hard, a straight shooter, a woman clean of received wisdom and open to what she sees. This is a woman who could early on dismiss most of her contemporaries as "dreamy" and would later single out one she liked as "a very poor painter." (And then add, apparently by way of softening the judgment: "I guess he wasn't a painter at all. He had no courage and I believe that to create one's own world in any of the arts takes courage.") This is a woman who in 1939 could advise her admirers that they were missing her point, that their appreciation of her famous flowers was merely sentimental. "When I paint a red hill," she observed coolly in a catalogue for an exhibition that year, "you say it is too bad that I don't always paint flowers. A flower touches almost everyone's heart. A red hill doesn't touch everyone's heart." This is a woman who could describe the genesis of one of her most well-known paintings — the "Cow's Skull: Red, White and Blue" owned by the Metropolitan — as an act of quite deliberate and derisive orneriness. "I thought of the city men I had been seeing in the East," she wrote. "They talked so often of writing the Great American Novel — the Great American Play — the Great American Poetry . . . So as I was painting my cow's head on blue I thought to myself, 'I'll make it an American painting. They will not think it great with the red stripes down the sides — Red, White and Blue — but they will notice it.'"

The city men. The men. They. The words crop up again and again as this astonishingly aggressive woman tells us what was on her mind when she was making her astonishingly aggressive paintings. It was those city men who stood accused of sentimentalizing her flowers: "I made you take time to look at what I saw and when you took time to really notice my flower you hung all your associations with flowers on my flower and you write about my flower as if I think and see what you think and see — and I don't." *And I don't.* Imagine those words spoken, and the sound you hear is *don't tread on me.* "The men" believed it impossible to paint New York, so Georgia O'Keeffe painted New York. "The men" didn't think much of her bright color, so she made it brighter. The men yearned toward Europe so she went to Texas, and then to New Mexico. The men talked about Cézanne, "long involved remarks about the 'plastic quality' of his form and color," and took one another's long involved remarks, in the view of this angelic rattlesnake in their midst, altogether too seriously. "I can paint one of those dismal-colored paintings like the men," the woman who regarded herself always as an outsider remembers thinking one day in 1922, and she did: a painting of a shed "all low-toned and dreary with the tree beside the door." She called this act of rancor "The Shanty" and hung it in her next show. "The men seemed to approve of it," she reported fifty-four years later, her contempt undimmed. "They seemed to think that maybe I was beginning to paint. That was my only low-toned dismal-colored painting."

▋ What have you done to keep the paragraphs complete within
themselves and distinct?

This poem is devastating in the cold simplicity of its literary style. The attitude of the persona is underscored by the word choice, the stark syntax,
and the stanza division counting off the three "places." Keep the quotations
within the unity of this attitude.

Her Story
NAOMI LONG MADGETT

They gave me the wrong name, in the first place.
They named me Grace and waited for a light and agile dancer.
But some trick of the genes mixed me up
And instead I turned out big and black and burly.

In the second place, I fashioned the wrong dreams.
I wanted to dress like Juliet and act
Before applauding audiences on Broadway.
I learned more about Shakespeare than he knew about himself.
But of course, all that was impossible.
"Talent, yes," they would tell me,
"But an actress has to look the part."
So I ended up waiting on tables in Harlem
And hearing uncouth men yell at me:
"Hey momma, you can cancel that hamburger
And come on up to 102."

In the third place, I tried the wrong solution.
The stuff I drank made me deathly sick
And someone called a doctor.
Next time I'll try a gun.

▋ How did you demonstrate the internal state of the speaker
prior to the first line?

In reply to an offer from the federal government to buy two million acres of his people's lands, Chief Seattle of the Suquamish Indians foresaw what few could have known in 1853. Indians still dominated more than half of North America, and the relocations and massacres were still to come. Yet Seattle sees the future clearly. His eloquent warning resonates today. Do not allow his voice to falter.

My People
CHIEF SEATTLE (OF THE SUQUAMISH INDIANS)

Yonder sky that has wept tears upon my people for centuries untold, and which to us appears changeless and eternal, may change. Today is fair. Tomorrow may be overcast with clouds. My words are like the stars that never change. Whatever Seattle says the great chief at Washington can rely upon with as much certainty as he can upon the return of the sun or the seasons. The White Chief says that Big Chief at Washington sends us greetings of friendship and goodwill. That is kind of him for we know he has little need of our friendship in return. His people are many. They are like the grass that covers vast prairies. My people are few. They resemble the scattering trees of a storm-swept plain. The great, and — I presume — good, White Chief sends us word that he wishes to buy our land but is willing to allow us enough to live comfortably. This indeed appears just, even gener-ous, for the Red Man no longer has rights that he need respect, and the offer may be wise also, as we are no longer in need of an extensive country. . . . I will not dwell on, nor mourn over, our untimely decay, nor reproach our paleface brothers with hastening it, as we too may have been somewhat to blame.

Youth is impulsive. When our young men grow angry at some real or imaginary wrong, and disfigure their faces with black paint, it denotes that their hearts are black, and then they are often cruel and relentless, and our old men and old women are unable to restrain them. Thus it has ever been. Thus it was when the white men first began to push our forefathers further westward. But let us hope that the hostilities between us may never return. We would have every-thing to lose and nothing to gain. Revenge by young men is consid-ered gain, even at the cost of their own lives, but old men who stay at home in times of war, and mothers who have sons to lose, know better.

Our good father at Washington — for I presume he is now our father as well as yours, since King George has moved his boundaries further north — our great good father, I say, sends us word that if we do as he desires he will protect us. His brave warriors will be to us a bristling wall of strength, and his wonderful ships of war will fill our harbors so that our ancient enemies far to the northward — the Hydas and Tsimpsians — will cease to frighten our women, children, and old men. Then in reality will he be our father and we his children. But can that ever be? Your God is not our God! Your God loves your people and hates mine. He folds his strong and protecting arms lovingly about the paleface and leads him by the hand as a father leads his infant son — but He has forsaken His red children — if they really are his. Our God, the Great Spirit, seems also to have forsaken us. Your God makes your people wax strong every day. Soon they will fill the land. Our people are ebbing away like a rapidly receding tide that will never return. The white man's God cannot love our people or He would protect them. They seem to be orphans who can look nowhere for help. How then can we be brothers? How can your God become our God and renew our prosperity and awaken in us dreams of returning greatness? If we have a common heavenly father He must be partial — for He came to his paleface children. We never saw Him. He gave you laws but He had no word for His red children whose teeming multitudes once filled this vast continent as stars fill the firmament. No; we are two distinct races with separate origins and separate destinies. There is little in common between us.

To us the ashes of our ancestors are sacred and their resting place is hallowed ground. You wander far from the graves of your ancestors and seemingly without regret. Your religion was written upon tables of stone by the iron finger of your God so that you could not forget. The Red Man could never comprehend nor remember it. Our religion is the traditions of our ancestors — the dreams of our old men, given them in solemn hours of night by the Great Spirit; and the visions of our sachems;[1] and it is written in the hearts of our people.

Your dead cease to love you and the land of their nativity as soon as they pass the portals of the tomb and wander way beyond the stars. They are soon forgotten and never return. Our dead never forget the beautiful world that gave them being.

Day and night cannot dwell together. The Red man has ever fled the approach of the White Man, as the morning mist flees before the morning sun. However, your proposition seems fair and I think that my people will accept it and will retire to the reservation you offer them. Then we will dwell apart in peace, for the words of the Great White Chief seem to be the words of nature speaking to my people out of dense darkness.

1. Indian chiefs.

It matters little where we pass the remnant of our days. They will not be many. A few more moons; a few more winters — and not one of the descendants of the mighty hosts that once moved over this broad land or lived in happy homes, protected by the Great Spirit, will remain to mourn over the graves of a people once more powerful and hopeful than yours. But why should I mourn at the untimely fate of my people? Tribe follows tribe, and nation follows nation, like the waves of the sea. It is the order of nature, and regret is useless. Your time of decay may be distant, but it will surely come, for even the White Man whose God walked and talked with him as friend with friend, cannot be exempt from the common destiny. We may be brothers after all. We will see.

We will ponder your proposition, and when we decide we will let you know. But should we accept it, I here and now make this condition that we will not be denied the privilege without molestation of visiting at any time the tombs of our ancestors, friends and children. Every part of this soil is sacred in the estimation of my people. Every hillside, every valley, every plain and grove, has been hallowed by some sad or happy event in days long vanished. . . . The very dust upon which you now stand responds more lovingly to their footsteps than to yours, because it is rich with the blood of our ancestors and our bare feet are conscious of the sympathetic touch. . . . Even the little children who lived here and rejoiced here for a brief season will love these somber solitudes and at eventide they greet shadowy returning spirits. And when the last Red Man shall have perished, and the memory of my tribe shall have become a myth among the White Men, these shores will swarm with the invisible dead of my tribe, and when your children's children think themselves alone in the field, the store, the shop, upon the highway, or in the silence of the pathless woods, they will not be alone. . . . At night when the streets of your cities and villages are silent and you think them deserted, they will throng with the returning hosts that once filled and still love this beautiful land. The White Man will never be alone.

Let him be just and deal kindly with my people, for the dead are not powerless. Dead, did I say? There is not death, only a change of worlds.

▌How did you show Chief Seattle's reluctant acceptance of the inevitable?

This small fragment of a Navajo ceremonial chant presents a real challenge to the interpreter. The repetition and the end-stopped lines are important for the quality of ritual and chant, but they should not be allowed to become monotonous. There is no need to attempt a musical accompaniment or tone, because the writing itself is so rich. Pay particular attention to the variety found in the middle of the lines where there are subtle word shifts. It will help to think of the first four lines as a cohesive unit; the "beauty" lines as a unit; and the last four lines as another phase of this prayer of purification. Remember the Indians' mystical kinship with the earth upon which they walk.

FROM *The Night Chant*
NAVAJO CEREMONIAL CHANT, TRANSLATED BY JOHN BIERHORST

In beauty may I walk
All day long may I walk.
Through the returning seasons may I walk.
On the trail marked with pollen may I walk.
With grasshoppers about my feet may I walk.
With dew about my feet may I walk.
With beauty may I walk.
With beauty before me, may I walk.
With beauty behind me, may I walk.
With beauty above me, may I walk.
With beauty below me, may I walk.
With beauty all around me, may I walk.
In old age wandering on a trail of beauty, lively, may I walk.
In old age wandering on a trail of beauty, living again, may I walk.
It is finished in beauty.
It is finished in beauty.

❚ Did your voice mark the differences in the repeated words? How did you avoid monotony?

William Least Heat Moon set out on the back roads and byways to discover something about himself and about America. His itinerary arose almost entirely by whim, but he often found unique people and learned subtle lessons, as in this segment from *Blue Highways*.

FROM *Blue Highways*
WILLIAM LEAST HEAT MOON

Had it not been raining hard that morning on the Livingston square, I never would have learned of Nameless, Tennessee. Waiting for the rain to ease, I lay on my bunk and read the atlas to pass time rather than to see where I might go. In Kentucky were towns with fine names like Boreing, Bear Wallow, Decoy, Subtle, Mud Lick, Mummie, Neon; Belcher was just down the road from Mouthcard, and Minnie only ten miles from Mousie.

I looked at Tennessee. Turtletown eight miles from Ducktown. And also: Peavine, Wheel, Milky Way, Love Joy, Dull, Weakly, Fly, Spot, Miser Station, Only, McBurg, Peeled Chestnut, Clouds, Topsy, Isoline. And the best of all, Nameless. The logic! I was heading east, and Nameless lay forty-five miles west. I decided to go anyway.

The rain stopped, but things looked saturated, even bricks. In Gainesboro, a hill town with a square of businesses around the Jackson County Courthouse, I stopped for directions and breakfast. There is one almost infallible way to find honest food at just prices in blue-highway America: count the wall calendars in a cafe.

> No calendar: Same as an interstate pit stop.
> One calendar: Preprocessed food assembled in New Jersey.
> Two calendars: Only if fish trophies present.
> Three calendars: Can't miss on the farm-boy breakfasts.
> Four calendars: Try the ho-made pie too.
> Five calendars: Keep it under your hat, or they'll franchise.

One time I found a six-calendar cafe in the Ozarks, which served fried chicken, peach pie, and chocolate malts, that left me searching for another ever since. I've never seen a seven-calendar place. But old-time travelers — road men in a day when cars had running boards and lunchroom windows said AIR COOLED in blue letters with icicles dripping from the tops — those travelers have told me the golden legends of seven-calendar cafes.

To the rider of back roads, nothing shows the tone, the voice of a small town more quickly than the breakfast grill or the five-thirty tavern. Much of what the people do and believe and share is evident then. The City Cafe in Gainesboro had three calendars that I could see from the walk. Inside were no interstate refugees with full bladders and empty tanks, no wild-eyed children just released from the glassy cell of a stationwagon backseat, no longhaul truckers talking in CB numbers. There were only townspeople wearing overalls, or catalog-order suits with five-and-dime ties, or uniforms. That is, here were farmers and mill hands, bank clerks, the dry goods merchant, a policeman, and chiropractor's receptionist. Because it was Saturday, there were also mothers and children.

I ordered my standard on-the-road breakfast: two eggs up, hashbrowns, tomato juice. The waitress, whose pale, almost translucent skin shifted hue in the gray light like a thin slice of mother of pearl, brought the food. Next to the eggs was a biscuit with a little yellow Smiley button stuck in it. She said, "You from the North?"

"I guess I am." A Missourian gets used to Southerners thinking him a Yankee, a Northerner considering him a cracker, a Westerner sneering at his effete Easternness, and the Easterner taking him for a cowhand.

"So whata you doin' in the mountains?"

"Talking to people. Taking some pictures. Looking mostly."

"Lookin' for what?"

"A three-calendar cafe that serves Smiley buttons on the biscuits."

"You needed a smile. Tell me really."

"I don't know. Actually, I'm looking for some jam to put on this biscuit now that you've brought one."

She came back with grape jelly. In a land of quince jelly, apple butter, apricot jam, blueberry preserves, pear conserves, and lemon marmalade, you always get grape jelly.

"Whata you lookin' for?"

Like anyone else, I'm embarrassed to eat in front of a watcher, particularly if I'm getting interviewed. "Why don't you have a cup of coffee?"

"Cain't right now. You gonna tell me?"

"I don't know how to describe it to you. Call it harmony."

She waited for something more. "Is that it?" Someone called her to the kitchen. I had managed almost to finish by the time she came back. She sat on the edge of the booth. "I started out in life not likin' anything, but then it grew on me. Maybe that'll happen to you." She watched me spread the jelly. "Saw your van." She watched me eat the biscuit. "You sleep in there?" I told her I did. "I'd love to do that, but I'd be scared spitless."

"I don't mind being scared spitless. Sometimes."

"I'd love to take off cross country. I like to look at different license plates. But I'd take a dog. You carry a dog?"

"No dogs, no cats, no budgie birds. It's a one-man campaign to show Americans a person can travel alone without a pet."

"Cain't travel without a dog!"

"I like to do things the hard way."

"Shoot! I'd take me a dog to talk to. And for protection."

"It isn't traveling to cross the country and talk to your pug instead of people along the way. Besides, being alone on the road makes you ready to meet someone when you stop. You get sociable traveling alone."

She looked out toward the van again. "Time I get the nerve to take a trip, gas'll cost five dollars a gallon."

"Could be. My rig might go the way of the steamboat." I remembered why I'd come to Gainesboro. "You know the way to Nameless?"

"Nameless? I've heard of Nameless. Better ask the amlance driver in the corner booth." She pinned the Smiley on my jacket. "Maybe I'll see you on the road somewhere. His name's Bob, by the way."

"The ambulance driver?"

"The Smiley. I always name my Smileys — otherwise they all look alike. I'd talk to him before you go."

"The Smiley?"

"The amlance driver."

And so I went looking for Nameless, Tennessee, with a Smiley button named Bob.

❚ What did you do in your performance to suggest the sincerity of the narrator's interest in the people in the City Cafe?

Bibliography

The following books have specific exercises on voice and articulation. Consult them for help with minor problems that need attention.

Berry, Cicely. *Voice and the Actor*. New York: Macmillan, 1973.
    Practical exercises from the voice director of the Royal Shakespeare Company.

Crannell, Kenneth. *Voice and Articulation: Developing Career Speech*. Belmont, Calif.: Wadsworth Publishing Company, 1986.
    Numerous useful exercises and an audio tape recording of important examples enrich this broad examination of the ways in which voice can suggest character.

Fairbanks, Grant. *Practical Voice Practice*. New York: Harper & Row, 1964.
    Aimed specifically at audibility, intelligibility, and flexibility. A book designed for the normal voice, with emphasis on minor problems in the above areas.

Heinberg, Paul. *Voice Training — For Speaking and Reading Aloud*. New York: The Ronald Press, 1964.
    Especially designed to provide an application of current scientific knowledge for the student of speech and drama.

Lessach, Arthur. *The Use and Training of the Human Voice*. 2nd ed. New York: Drama Book Specialists, 1967.
    This is a most effective book for students working with a knowledgeable instructor who has been trained in the Lessach method. Lessach divides

what he calls "vocal life" into three basic parts: consonant action, structural action, and tonal action. The method depends not on imitation but upon the development of the potential of each individual student's given voice.

Linklater, Kristin. *Freeing the Natural Voice.* New York: Drama Book Specialists, 1976.

Understanding the voice in human communication precedes a series of exercises to free, develop, and strengthen the instrument.

Machlin, Evangeline. *Speech for the Stage.* Rev. ed. New York: Theatre Arts Books, 1966.

A very serviceable book that makes use of the international phonetic alphabet and traditional approaches to the training of the voice for the stage. The approach is perhaps more imitative than innovative, but the book contains excellent breathing exercises, audition exercises, and warm-up exercises. It also includes a good section on speaking Shakespeare.

4

The Use of the Body in Oral Interpretation

O body swayed to music, O brightening glance,
How can we know the dancer from the dance?

W. B. Yeats, "Among School Children"

When you have decided on a piece of literature that interests you and is worth the time and effort you must spend in preparing for performance, your next responsibility is to work on understanding its elements — its logical meaning, its emotive overtones, and its qualities of literary craftsmanship. As we pointed out in Chapter 2, you should allow yourself to respond fully to all of the clues you find. You will become a part of the experience expressed in the writing, and it will become an integral part of you. Finally, when you feel sure of where the material is going and how it gets there, you can turn your attention to the most effective way of communicating the literature to the audience. It is at this point that control of the twofold instrument of body and voice becomes important. Just as a musician cannot give a satisfactory performance without having perfected the handling of his or her musical instrument, so an interpreter, who is both instrument and instrumentalist, cannot do justice to a selection without devoting attention to technique.

The term *technique* does not imply artificiality in the use of body and voice. In fact, the finer the technique is, the less apparent it is to the audience. Technique may be defined as style of performance. The style of performance in the art of interpretation must be unobtrusive if the interpreter is not to distract the audience from the material.

Overt attention to technique belongs in the rehearsal period and has no place in performance. Display of vocal or physical virtuosity as an end in itself has been outmoded since the decline of the "mechanical" school of elocution in the nineteenth century. Such display is considered in poor taste today, and it is interesting only to the degree that an exhibition of calisthenics or a recital of scales and arpeggios would be interesting. The interpreter develops and uses technique as a means of communicating the material; the material is not used as a vehicle for displaying technique.

You develop vocal and bodily technique by practicing, so that your muscles will respond to the demands made on them without apparent prompting or effort. During a performance you should concentrate on the material and on the response of the audience to that material. If you are adequately prepared, the muscles of your vocal mechanism and of your entire body will respond according to the habits you set up in rehearsal. As your skill increases through experience, this habitual response will become more dependable.

Since oral interpretation obviously involves the use of the voice, it would seem that the vocal mechanism should be of first importance. It is a mistake, however, to overlook or underestimate the subtle but very significant role of the body in oral interpretation. As a matter of fact, the body begins the process of communication even before the voice is heard. From the moment the audience becomes aware of your physical presence, you are arousing a response, establishing in your listeners what psychologists call a "set," or condition of mental readiness, toward what they are about to hear. It is true that you do not begin to communicate the *specific* material until you speak, but by your bodily actions you give intimations of a particular mental attitude toward yourself, the audience, and the material.

Although we will be touching briefly on separate areas of bodily action, such as posture, gesture, muscle tone, and empathy, it is important to remember that no bodily movement exists in isolation. Moreover, for a movement to be significant, it must be considered within a specific context. Sometimes what the body is communicating is in deliberate contradiction to what the words and thus the voice are saying. James Thurber, for example, relates chaotic events as if they are common occurrences in everyone's life. This incongruity can be a very useful technique for certain kinds of comedy. But unless it is evident in the writer's style, it can also interfere with what an unwary interpreter is trying to accomplish. When what we see contradicts what we hear, we tend to give greater weight to visual clues than to auditory clues. But when what we see underscores what we hear, the impact of the material being communicated is sharpened considerably.

An audience is quick to resent an overbearing or cocky attitude. It is equally quick to question the authority of a speaker who seems unsure of his or her ability. You will strike a happy medium when you are confident that you are adequately prepared, that your material is well chosen, and that your audience is capable of understanding and responding to that material. When you have doubts about any of these points, your uncertainty will be reflected in your physical bearing. The audience will sense your insecurity and will unconsciously share your discomfort. It is important, then, for you to avoid any mannerisms that may give an unfavorable impression, whether of virtuosity, arrogance, or lack of self-confidence.

Thus, through bodily carriage and physical actions, both of which are types of nonverbal communication, you establish in your audience definite attitudes toward yourself and your material. These attitudes are relevant to yet distinct from the specific content of that material. The body performs an even more important function in relation to the specific content. Your physical reaction to the experience in the literature, accompanying and, indeed, springing out of your mental and emotional response, is a vital factor in drawing a complete response from the audience.

Just as bodily action in all its aspects gives the audience clues about the interpreter, it is also of vital importance in suggesting character and reflecting the attitude of the author and/or the persona. We all have seen speakers whom we did not believe for a moment because something in what we saw contradicted what we heard. In drama, the way a character moves and the tone of his or her entire body often reveal as much as or more than the words he or she uses. The body and voice work together as you communicate your own thoughts in your introduction and transitions or convey those of the persona in the selection.

Bodily action may be defined as any movement of the muscles of the body. This movement may be a full gesture. It may merely be a relaxation or tension of the small muscles around the eyes or mouth, across the shoulders and back, or in the legs. It may be a combination of any or all of these movements. Bodily action includes the approach to and departure from the platform. It also includes movements of the head, arms, shoulders, hands, torso, and legs and changes in posture, facial expressions, and the muscle tone of the entire body. Modern interpreters have no desire to establish or call upon a set of rules for posture and gesture. They know that the test of bodily action is not conformity to technical rules. Rather, its effectiveness is proven in the ability to communicate the literature at hand. Bodily action is effective only when it is completely suited to the material and thus helps to elicit the desired response, when it is so unobtrusive as to go unnoticed except insofar as it contributes to that response, and when it is free of personal mannerisms that might distract the audience.

Posture

The basis of effective bodily action is good *posture,* which is primarily a matter of proper positional relations among the various parts of the body. Good posture is the arrangement of the bones and muscles that puts the body in its perfect natural alignment so that each unit does its job of supporting and controlling the bodily structure without undue tension or strain. When this arrangement is accomplished, the entire body is balanced, flexible, responsive, and coordinated. Good posture requires nothing more complicated than standing straight and easy from the ankle bone to the crown of the head, so that the various parts of the skeletal structure fall naturally into place.

Gesture

A *gesture* may be defined as any movement that helps to express or emphasize an idea or emotional response. In its most modern sense, gesture embraces the entire field of kinesics and includes both clearly discernible bodily movement and subtle changes in posture and muscle tone. Many people still think of gesture in its narrowest sense — as overt actions of the hands and arms and occasionally the head and shoulders. These parts of the body do not function as separate entities, however. Rather, they involve a "follow-through" that both affects and is affected by the degree of muscular tension in every other part of the body. It is impossible to treat gesture separately from an awareness of the body as an organic whole.

Still, the question of what to do with one's hands sometimes assumes undue importance in the mind of the beginning interpreter. Perhaps a few words on the traditional concept of gesture as hand and arm movements will help to clarify the more modern concept of gesture that includes all bodily action.

Unlike the readers trained in the theories and practices of the last century, when books on elocution and expression devoted several chapters to detailed study of gesture, modern interpreters are little concerned with hand and arm movements as a separate, specific part of interpretive training. Today, interpreters view such movements as an integral part of bodily action that grows out of a response to the material and that helps interpreters achieve complete communication. If an action does not help to communicate the material, it is not a gesture but only a distracting and extraneous movement violating the basic principle that no action by an interpreter should call attention to itself. This is not to say that hand and arm movements should not be used. It is to say that their use must be dictated by the demands of the material being presented.

Your use of hand and arm movements normally depends on two considerations. The first, as we have said, is your material. You should use whatever bodily action is necessary to make the meaning clear to your audience and to convey the emotional quality effectively. The second consideration is the personality of the interpreter. Some of us find it easier than others to respond physically. You should use whatever movement you wish in rehearsal until you can handle it effectively when you need it, but you should never let gestures as such become an issue when you are before an audience. In performance, when your concentration shifts from the material to the problem of what to do with your hands, the audience will be quick to sense your preoccupation.

However, a responsive body is such an important factor in the total process of communication that you would do well to work on gestures conscientiously during rehearsal periods. In the early phases of rehearsal, it is often helpful to use large, exaggerated actions or to move freely about the room, responding consciously and overtly to all the empathic cues and muscle imagery in the selection. This overt response during preparation is the basis of *muscle memory*, in which the muscles "remember" the big action, and muscle tone reflects this remembering even after the specific overt gesture is discarded or modified.

If, on the other hand, you have a tendency to "talk with your hands," you should use whatever movements make you feel at ease and help to communicate your material. It is important, however, to keep in mind both facets of this advice — "make you feel at ease" and "help to communicate." There is the danger that what makes you feel at ease may distract your audience and thus actually block communication.

Perhaps you have developed certain habitual physical actions that are not gestures at all in the sense that they do not help you to express an idea. You may be using a repetitious movement, such as a constant raising and lowering of one hand, a tilt of the head, or a shrug of the shoulders. Such personal mannerisms, called *autistic gestures* because they grow out of your own personality, direct attention to you and prevent the audience from concentrating on your material. Moreover, they can seriously interfere with the creation of a character or the persona in the literature.

Under ordinary circumstances, it is inadvisable for an interpreter to work before a mirror. By doing so you are likely to divorce bodily action from its proper function of communication. If, however, you suspect that you rely too heavily on a habitual pattern of movement, an occasional checkup before a large mirror will help call this fault to your attention.

Kinesics and Muscle Tone

The interaction between what the voice is saying and what the body is saying has recently become a fascinating area of research called *kinesics*. Some of the books in the bibliography at the end of this chapter give details on the extent of the research that continues to be of great value to the interpreter. Kinesics is sometimes popularly called body language or nonverbal or nonlinguistic communication.

We have already referred to muscle tone in our discussion, because it is impossible to talk about any effective bodily action without considering it. Muscle tone happens as a result of muscle memory, complete response to the material, and the interpreter's concentration on sharing that material with the audience. It is vital to the fulcrum and climax of "Dulce" (Chapter 2), for example. Usually we are not aware of muscle tone as a separate aspect of bodily action and need only to be reminded occasionally that it must not distract from or negate the other aspects of performance.

Muscle tone refers to the degree of tension or relaxation present in the entire body. It is extremely important to consider muscle tone when you are projecting material to an audience, because an audience responds to what it sees more strongly than to what it hears. Muscle tone lies at the heart of kinesics, and an awareness of its importance aids the interpreter in communicating the full sensory and attitudinal elements of the literature.

When one's posture is good, his or her body is in a state of controlled relaxation, with no undue muscular strain or tension. The properly poised body is flexible and responsive, and it moves with coordination and fluidity. Controlled relaxation is not to be confused with apathy or lack of physical energy. The interpreter who looks too tired, depressed, or bored to stand up straight communicates an unfortunate impression to the audience and draws an undesirable response because the listeners reflect in their own muscle tone this sense of weariness, depression, or boredom. Relaxation is an easing of tension; it is not total disintegration. The degree of relaxation is controlled in the interest of dignity and poise, and it is dictated by the requirements of the material being presented.

Although muscle tone should be dictated by the literature, it is often affected by the performer's mental and emotional state. It varies from obvious tension to assured, controlled relaxation in direct proportion to your own self-confidence and your confidence in the material and the audience. Any performance will carry with it a degree of excitement, which is translated into physical tension. The secret is to be able to channel that tension so that it becomes an asset instead of a hazard. "Butterflies" in your stomach are not a sign of fear but of excitement, which, properly understood and controlled, is communicated to the audience in terms of a vital, stimulating performance. Too frequently, however, the inexperienced performer attributes this tension to stage fright — and immediately sets up a fear pattern. If your material is acceptable and your preparation is adequate, then the "butterflies" are a good sign. They are the result of your personal involvement, which your performance needs in order to succeed.

Sense Imagery

Literature rich in universality and suggestion depends for much of its effectiveness on the skillful use of sense imagery. Images that appeal predominantly to the sense of sight are called *visual;* to the sense of hearing, *auditory;* to the sense of taste, *gustatory;* and to the sense of smell, *olfactory.* The sense of touch is appealed to in *tactual* (or tactile) imagery, which involves a sensation of physical contact, pressure, or texture, and in *thermal* imagery, which refers to the feelings of heat and cold.

There are two additional types of imagery that appeal directly to the muscles or motor sense. The first is *kinetic imagery,* a large, overt action of the muscles: running, jumping, sitting down, walking away. The second type is *kinesthetic imagery,* which refers to muscle tension and relaxation. It is closely related to muscle memory and resultant muscle tone, and is likely to be present in any particularly rich sense appeal. Clearly, from what we know of muscle tone, and, indeed, the whole area of kinesics, these actions are invariably accompanied by tension or relaxation. Rarely in literature do you find a kinetic action or motor image that does not clearly indicate how and why one ran or jumped or sat or walked. There is a difference between "I was terrified and I ran" and "I ran for the sheer joy of being young in summer."

How an action is performed is kinesthetic — the degree of body tension or relaxation that goes along with the kinetic, overt action. The kinesthetic is governed by the emotional state of the person performing the action and helps to communicate that emotional state to the audience. You should identify fully with the *how* and the *why* of the actions performed by the personae or characters in a selection. A kinesthetic response is also involved in our reactions to height and distance. It operates very strongly in Hopkins's "The Starlight Night" (Chapter 2), for instance. Let your whole body respond completely to these two contrasting phrases: "Right above my head there was a huge bumblebee"; "Far off on the horizon I could see a single gull flying high and then swooping low over the expanse of water." Your responses are kinesthetic as well as visual. There is no overt action involving the persona. But the emotional states differ, just as they do between "She sat primly waiting" and "She sat dozing in the sun." A kinesthetic image, unlike a kinetic one, often can stand alone.

Poets and prose writers alike use sense imagery not only to reveal their own attitudes, but also to create distinct and individual personalities for their personae. Robert Browning is a master of this technique, especially in his monologues, and Theodore Roethke uses it brilliantly in "Old Lady's Winter Words" at the end of this chapter. A playwright also may use sense imagery to tell us about a character's background and set of values. Look, for example, at the visual imagery Sondheim gives George in "Finishing the Hat" (Chapter 7).

Rarely does an image appeal to only one sense. In most good literature, certainly in all literature that is rich in suggestion, the images carry a complex of appeals. Besides the primary sense appeal of a word, phrase, or thought unit, there are usually additional or secondary appeals. When you examine a selection in detail, you become aware that imagery contributes strongly to the intrinsic factors — that it helps to produce unity and harmony, variety and contrast, balance and proportion, and rhythm. Perhaps a few examples will be useful here. In Wallace's "The Art of Love" (at the end of this chapter), note how the many images from the schoolroom suggest a richer meaning when applied to the speaker's life. Similarly, the complex sense imagery in Jones's "Mosquito" (also at the end of this chapter) holds the poem together as it provides essential harmony and contrast.

One of the most obvious methods of achieving unity through imagery is to use a single type of primary appeal throughout the unit, much as Singer so deftly does in "A Crown of Feathers" (at the end of this chapter) by focusing on the exotic, arcane, and mysterious in Akhsa's life.

Sometimes imagery displays very little unity of type but is held together by restrictions to a limited locale. This is true of the excerpt from Welty's "June Recital" (Chapter 5). Or the imagery may all be slanted toward one person or object, as in Faulkner's "Dry September" (Chapter 5); or it may focus on the parts of a series of details that relate to one object, place, or person. In the latter case, the effect is usually cumulative and must be handled so as to achieve the strongest ultimate impression. Charles Dickens uses this cumulative technique to describe a battle in *A Tale of Two Cities:*

> With a roar that sounded as if all the breath in France had been shaped into the detested word, the living sea rose, wave on wave, depth on depth, and overflowed the city to that point. Alarm-bells ringing, drums beating, the sea raging and thundering on its new beach, the attack began . . .
>
> Cannon, muskets, fire and smoke . . . Flashing weapons, blazing torches, smoking wagon-loads of wet straw, hard work at neighboring barricades in all directions, shrieks, volleys, execrations, bravery without stint, boom, smash and rattle, and the furious sounding of the living sea . . .

Dickens begins with the auditory appeal, to which he adds complexity that reaches its height in "cannon, muskets, fire and smoke."

Then he shifts to the visual and kinetic imagery of "flashing weapons," returning almost at once to the auditory appeal in "shrieks, volleys," which comes to a climax in "boom, smash and rattle." Finally, he blends all this into "the furious sounding of the living sea."

Thomas Wolfe's "The Golden World" gives the interpreter a complex problem in unity through imagery. The following sentence illustrates his use of cumulative technique.

> He knew the good male smell of his father's sitting room; of the smooth worn leather sofa, with the gaping horse-hair rent; of the blistered varnished wood upon the hearth; of the heated calf-skin bindings; of the flat moist plug of apple tobacco, stuck with a red flag; of woodsmoke and burnt leaves in October; of the brown tired autumn earth; of honey-suckle at night; of warm nasturtiums; of a clean ruddy farmer who comes weekly with printed butter, eggs and milk; of fat limp underdone bacon and of coffee; of a bakery-oven in the wind; of large deep-hued string beans smoking-hot and seasoned well with salt and butter; of a room of old pine boards in which books and carpets have been stored, long closed; of Concord grapes in their long white baskets.[1]

In this single sentence the imagery is predominantly olfactory, but within this unity of appeal there is a variety of place. The progression from interior to exterior and back to interior may prove troublesome unless the interpreter is careful to group the objects that appeal to the senses. The excerpt opens in the sitting room, where it remains through mention of the visual detail of "a red flag." Without warning or apparent motivation, the scene shifts to the outdoors, but the olfactory motif remains strong, and there is unity of appeal in the focus of attention on the earth and its produce. The "ruddy farmer" with his "butter, eggs and milk" sets up the train of thought that centers on the smell of food and calls up the rest of the images within the sentence. Included in these images is the "room of old pine boards in which books and carpets have been stored," an image that for the author belongs with these others, but to the interpreter may seem like an interpolation among the many references to food. The unifying factor here might best be classified as the author's presentation through a "stream of consciousness." To keep the transitions clear and acceptable, you should be careful to group the images by association of place or type of appeal, keeping in mind the importance of the primary olfactory appeal and the fact that the memories cluster around a single house. Do not forget, or allow your listeners to forget, that the sentence begins with "He knew the . . . smell of. . . ."

1. Thomas Wolfe, *Look Homeward Angel.*

Obviously, the type and vividness of the imagery should be in harmony with the total intention of the piece of literature: harmonious with the character and setting in a narrative and with the tastes and experiences of the intended audience in didactic writing and essays. Even the adjectives used to give the objects added richness should be highly appropriate: "heated calf-skin bindings" and "burnt leaves," for example, in the excerpt from "The Golden World." Books bound in watered silk would certainly not be harmonious with the "good male smell."

A skillful author is acutely aware, consciously or subconsciously, of the speed with which the senses tire. Everyone knows from experience that it is possible to become so accustomed to a smell, a sound, or a taste that the sensation loses its initial impact and may even pass into the realm of the subconscious and go unnoticed. Thus, as Thomas Wolfe does with his "red flag," an author suddenly will vary the appeal to allow readers to shift their response to another sense. When the writer returns to the original appeal, the readers' and listeners' responses are heightened because of this momentary relief. The same relieving function can be accomplished by contrast as well. Thus imagery makes a particularly rich contribution to both variety and contrast and is itself intensified by variation and contrast. It is one of the interpreter's tasks not to allow the variety to overshadow or violate the essential unity, but rather to use this variety to fulfill its purpose of relief.

Usually an author provides help with this problem. On close observation, you will discover that the author has not really abandoned the primary appeal, but has only allowed it to shift momentarily to a secondary position. There may also be a fairly consistent relationship between two types of imagery.

In the matter of balance and proportion, imagery is often used to weight a unit so that with this added vividness the section is comparable to a more detailed unit. In this case, imagery is usually combined with other factors as well — especially to heighten a climax or to sharpen a contrast.

In some literary selections imagery provides an interesting rhythm of logical content and emotional quality. Kinesthetic response is so much a part of emotional response that it cannot be ignored or underestimated; it is also basic to the implementation of empathy.

Empathy

One of the interpreter's most powerful tools is the control and use of *empathy*. Although the roots of the word are Greek, "empathy" is a term borrowed from modern psychology. It means literally a "feeling into" and it results from one's ability and willingness to project oneself intellectually and emotionally into a piece of literature or any other type of art. This emotional association enables an interpreter to identify thoroughly with and embody the mental and the emotional states of the speaker and characters in the selection. Such identification results in a corresponding physical response. The *interaction* of these emotional and physical responses, as they intensify each other, is the basis of empathy as it concerns the interpreter.

Every writer who deals with emotions uses words and phrases in such a way as to cause some mental disturbance, which may take the form of pleasure or pain, activity or repose. As an interpreter, you respond fully to these words and phrases. If you have not experienced precisely what the author is describing or creating, you can usually recall some parallel or approximate situation that has evoked a comparable response in you. As you react emotionally to the written material, your muscles tighten or relax, usually without a conscious effort on your part. This tightening or relaxing of muscles affects the tone of your entire body.

Try the following simple experiment to experience how this interaction actually works.

1. Divorce your mind from your immediate surroundings and recall some occasion or experience that made you feel happy and exhilarated. It does not matter in the least what the experience was, as long as it made you feel particularly pleased with yourself and with your world. Spend as long as you wish recapturing the circumstances and the accompanying response.

2. Next, turn your thoughts to a set of circumstances that once made you violently angry. Concentrate on every detail and allow yourself to become thoroughly resentful. This is your chance to say all the things you thought of after it was too late. Work yourself up into a state of complete irritation.

3. Now go back to the pleasant situation. Recapture the experience as completely as you can. As you allow your mood to change and the happy memory to take over, notice what is happening to your muscles.

4. Keeping your muscle tone exactly as it is, go back to the anger you felt before. Don't let a muscle tighten or change. It is clearly impossible to be as thoroughly angry as you were when your muscles were responding freely, although unconsciously.

Empathy works for the interpreter in three distinct steps: from the literature to the interpreter, from the interpreter to the audience, and from the audience back to the interpreter.

As we read a piece of literature, we relate to it actively. We all have had the experience of coming out of a movie or play or of finishing a book and being physically exhausted. We are not worn out because we have been uncomfortable but because we have participated so thoroughly that our muscles are tired. This participation, which combines intellect, emotions, and muscles, is the first step in empathy. It is partly what makes us choose a selection to read in the first place. You may lose this empathic response in the middle phases of preparation, while you are trying to determine climaxes, the fulcrum, the intrinsic factors, and all of the other elements involved in analysis. But when you get the material back together again and look forward to sharing it with an audience, the empathic response will come back, strengthened by your newly developed mastery over the parts that make up the whole. Thus, the first step in empathy is your own response to the stimulus provided by the literature. Without this response the second step is impossible.

The second step in empathy has to do with the audience's response to the interpreter's material. When you respond empathically to the selection, you give physical cues to the listeners. This is, of course, the whole concept of kinesics or nonverbal communication. The audience imitates your muscle tone, usually unconsciously; this physical imitation intensifies or inhibits their emotional involvement, just as your muscle tone intensified or inhibited your own emotional response in the exercise above. Have you ever noticed that simply because someone else is frowning, smiling, or yawning, you tend to frown and feel depressed or irritated, or to smile and feel happy, or to yawn and feel tired or bored?

Successful interpreters are aware of the value of empathy, even in the way they approach the platform. During your introduction you will use this element to help establish an emotional readiness in the audience. If the selection is brief and intense, like Dickinson's "Because I Could Not Stop for Death," you will find that the audience moves with you much more surely if you make full use of empathy. Their own mental and emotional states of readiness affect the tone of all their muscles. And the audience, by unconscious imitation of what it sees, will adopt the physical tone that you project. By imitating your physical tone, the audience puts itself into psychic readiness for the response you wish to get from your listeners.

The third step in empathy is the interpreter's ultimate reward: the audience sends back an empathic response through its concentration and its alternating tension and relaxation. Thus the cycle becomes complete from the printed page to the interpreter, out to the audience, and back to the interpreter.

Hints for Preparation

A study of mime is valuable to interpreters because it makes them acutely aware of how each separate muscle contributes to an overall impression. It demands subtle control and flexibility of the entire body working as a fluid unit.

So-called sensitivity sessions or awareness exercises are as valuable to interpreters as they are to actors. They involve the conscious recall of sensuous experience. Because interpreters should consider all of the stimuli received from the senses, strong concentration and a responsive body are indispensable during your preparation and rehearsal periods. By making yourself more open to the experience of the literature you are reading, you will enrich both your own pleasure and your audience's. Therefore, such exercises are helpful in achieving the first step in empathy.

A word of warning is advisable at this point. The muscular response is in itself a result of mental activity. The outward, physical signs are an indication of that inner activity, never a substitute for it. The mental and emotional response should come first; the muscular response should follow.

But richness of response is not enough for an interpreter. You must be able to channel and direct that response to your audience. A good rehearsal technique to help achieve this second step in empathy is to work occasionally with other people and attempt to create a mood in them without words — a sort of silent game of charades. You will develop an awareness of the way in which a response can be turned out to include other people, and you will sharpen and refine both your muscle memory and posture control.

After you have developed your own capacity to respond and have learned the all-important method of directing that response out for an audience to share, you should return to the material as it is written. Carefully and objectively evaluate how relevant your response is to the experience the author has written about. Then eliminate the areas of your own subjectivity that conflict with the clues in the writing. The author must always be the controlling factor.

Analyzing the Performance

Before you begin to examine your degree of success in making your voice and body work together to give your audience the selection you chose in its *aesthetic entirety,* go back and recheck the questions in the "Analyzing the Performance" section in Chapter 2. During this performance you will probably have focused your attention on some of the problems that occurred in your earlier performances. Where was the improvement you were seeking? Don't be discouraged if you are still encountering the same problems. Slight progress is still progress; take some heart from what you have achieved rather than becoming discouraged with what you haven't yet achieved. However slight your improvement, remember that the fullest performance of a piece of good literature is the result of slow and continuing self-monitoring, careful attention to the responses of the audience, and hard work.

Don't try to solve every problem in every rehearsal. Instead, concentrate on the trickiest or most difficult problem. Work on it at every rehearsal until it begins to jell. For example, if you are reading a story, be sure that you are absolutely clear about what the narrator sounds like and looks like before you get too involved in the characters in the story. Have you chosen a lyric poem? Make sure your voice and your body accurately reflect the structure of the poem. Are you giving each line the weight it needs to carry the fullest possible meaning, or are you rushing through the piece just to be sure that you get all the words in. Solving the major problems will give you the luxury of working on the minor difficulties. As you seem to be making progress with the larger dilemmas, gradually add others — but don't forget that the foundation is getting better and better.

Each selection demands a fresh start and perhaps a different point of attack from the last one. Do not allow yourself to perform only one kind of literature because you are most comfortable with it. Instead, experiment with many different kinds of selections. If you respect the literature and yourself as a performer, your audience will find something of value to see and hear.

Although the following questions relate directly to the chapters on voice development and the use of the body, they also apply to any performance you give.

Could you be heard? Could you be understood? (These are not always the same thing; why?)

Was your breath control satisfactory and comfortable? Did you find yourself running out of breath at places you had previously had under control? What happened in the lines just preceding these new problem areas?

Were you able to control and vary the pace to support the demands of your selection? Remember, audiences listen at a much slower rate than you can speak.

Were you careful to use pause effectively, being sure that you did not break the unity or destroy the harmony but made use of variety and contrast to achieve balance and proportion, to bring out the climaxes, and to suggest the fulcrum? Was your concentration steady during the pauses?

Was there a regional dialect or melody pattern that interfered with the audience's full enjoyment of the personae? Was monotone a problem?

Was your body communicating what your voice was communicating? Did your body and your voice complement each other? Did you remember that your performance begins the instant you leave your seat and continues until you return to it? The walk to the front of the room gives you a good opportunity to collect your thoughts for your introduction. Once on stage, take the time to get a good, satisfying (but inaudible) breath and to become comfortable behind the lectern. Get your body into easy alignment and focus your concentration on exactly what the persona is thinking immediately prior to the first words in your selection. When you are ready — and your audience is ready — begin.

Did your body respond to the imagery honestly without ignoring the intrinsic factors?

Did you notice any physical mannerisms that sometimes got in the way of what you were trying to communicate?

Did you handle the physical text unobtrusively?

These questions are also helpful in analyzing the performances of other readers. Remember to be descriptive. Select one striking moment in another's performance and see if you can describe *precisely* what it was that the performer did to achieve such distinction. Take the time to sketch verbally exactly what the performer's body was doing and exactly how the performer's voice behaved at that moment. Compare your responses with those of your classmates. Now, together, compare all of these descriptions with the actual text of the selection. Did the performance coincide with the selection? How? Did it veer away from what the author intended? Where? How? Why?

Finally, ask yourself where in the performance (whether your own or another's) did literature and the reader correlate most closely? Why? Before you begin your next performance, try to remember what you did to achieve such a richly rewarding blend. But above all, begin to work on your next performance. There is no time to rest on easy victories, nothing to learn without valiant effort.

Selections for Analysis and Oral Interpretation

All of the following selections have a strong suggestion of physical action. In preparing them for oral interpretation, let your muscles respond completely, taking time in some cases to work out a specific action, which you may or may not use in performance, to help you achieve the proper empathy. Since your voice and body must work together, many of the selections at the end of Chapter 3 also provide opportunities for bodily action, although they were chosen primarily because of their vocal demands.

Remember that each selection must be analyzed for organization, attitude, the elements of literary art, and suggested bodily action.

Be sure you understand all the allusions in this first selection. The action described is not that of the speaker, but kinesthetic imagery is very strong.

The Second Coming
WILLIAM BUTLER YEATS

Turning and turning in the widening gyre
The falcon cannot hear the falconer;
Things fall apart; the centre cannot hold;
Mere anarchy is loosed upon the world,
The blood-dimmed tide is loosed, and everywhere
The ceremony of innocence is drowned;
The best lack all conviction, while the worst
Are full of passionate intensity.

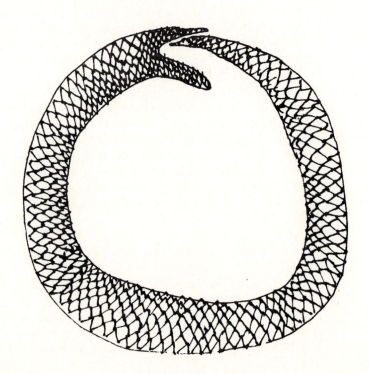

Surely some revelation is at hand;
Surely the Second Coming is at hand.
The Second Coming! Hardly are those words out
When a vast image out of *Spiritus Mundi*
Troubles my sight: somewhere in sands of the desert
A shape with lion body and the head of a man,
A gaze blank and pitiless as the sun,
Is moving its slow thighs, while all about it
Reel shadows of the indignant desert birds.
The darkness drops again; but now I know
That twenty centuries of stony sleep
Were vexed to nightmare by a rocking cradle,
And what rough beast, its hour come round at last,
Slouches towards Bethlehem to be born?

❚ What physical behavior did you use to show the persona's rise
in desperation and its troubled release?

Muscle tone and posture help to suggest the power and strength of the
Greek hero in the next selection. These qualities are more important than his
age. His memories of past actions and his hope for future ones are strongly
kinesthetic as he considers them, and they set up a clear rhythm of content.

Ulysses

ALFRED, LORD TENNYSON

It little profits that an idle king,
By this still hearth, among these barren crags,
Matched with an aged wife, I mete and dole
Unequal laws unto a savage race,
That hoard, and sleep, and feed, and know not me.
I cannot rest from travel; I will drink
Life to the lees. All times I have enjoyed
Greatly, have suffered greatly, both with those
That loved me, and alone; on shore, and when
Through scudding drifts the rainy Hyades
Vexed the dim sea. I am become a name;
For always roaming with a hungry heart
Much have I seen and known — cities of men,
And manners, climates, councils, governments,
Myself not least, but honored of them all, —
And drunk delight of battle with my peers,

Far on the ringing plains of windy Troy.
I am a part of all that I have met;
Yet all experience is an arch wherethrough
Gleams that untraveled world, whose margin fades
Forever and forever when I move.
How dull it is to pause, to make an end,
To rust unburnished, not to shine in use!
As though to breathe were life! Life piled on life
Were all too little, and of one to me
Little remains: but every hour is saved
From that eternal silence, something more,
A bringer of new things; and vile it were
For some three suns to store and hoard myself,
And this gray spirit yearning in desire
To follow knowledge, like a sinking star,
Beyond the utmost bound of human thought.
    This is my son, my own Telemachus,
To whom I leave the sceptre and the isle, —
Well-loved of me, discerning to fulfil
This labor, by slow prudence to make mild
A rugged people, and through soft degrees
Subdue them to the useful and the good.
Most blameless is he, centred in the sphere
Of common duties, decent not to fail
In offices of tenderness, and pay
Meet adoration to my household gods,
When I am gone. He works his work, I mine.
    There lies the port; the vessel puffs her sail;
There gloom the dark broad seas. My mariners,
Souls that have toiled, and wrought, and thought with me, —
That ever with a frolic welcome took
The thunder and the sunshine, and opposed
Free hearts, free foreheads, — you and I are old;
Old age hath yet his honor and his toil.
Death closes all; but something ere the end,
Some work of noble note, may yet be done,
Not unbecoming men that strove with Gods.
The lights begin to twinkle from the rocks;
The long day wanes; the slow moon climbs; the deep
Moans round with many voices. Come, my friends,
'Tis not too late to seek a newer world,
Push off, and sitting well in order smite
The sounding furrows; for my purpose holds
To sail beyond the sunset, and the baths

Of all the western stars, until I die.
It may be that the gulfs will wash us down;
It may be we shall touch the Happy Isles,
And see the great Achilles, whom we knew.
Though much is taken, much abides; and though
We are not now that strength which in old days
Moved earth and heaven, that which we are, we are;
One equal temper of heroic hearts,
Made weak by time and fate, but strong in will
To strive, to seek, to find, and not to yield.

▮ Your audience should feel themselves a part of Ulysses' audience. What did you do physically to demonstrate locus and
character?

This is the beginning of a long and splendid story by the Nobel laureate Isaac
Bashevis Singer. It is likely that the names and customs in the story will seem
bizarre or mysterious to you, but they are the *life* of Akhsa and the other
people who live in Krasnobród. And the narrator presides over it all with an
alluring, enigmatic profundity. There are several sections which, with a careful introduction, will serve as good units for class assignments.

FROM *A Crown of Feathers*
ISAAC BASHEVIS SINGER

Reb Naftali Holishitzer, the community leader in Krasnobród, was
left in his old age with no children. One daughter had died in
childbirth and the other in a cholera epidemic. A son had drowned
when he tried to cross the San River on horseback. Reb Naftali had
only one grandchild — a girl, Akhsa, an orphan. It was not the custom for a female to study at a yeshiva, because "the King's daughter
is all glorious within" and Jewish daughters are all the daughters of
kings. But Akhsa studied at home. She dazzled everyone with her
beauty, wisdom, and diligence. She had white skin and black hair;
her eyes were blue.

Reb Naftali managed an estate that had belonged to the Prince
Czartoryski. Since he owed Reb Naftali twenty thousand guldens,
the prince's property was a permanent pawn, and Reb Naftali had
built for himself a water mill and a brewery and had sown hundreds
of acres with hops. His wife, Nesha, came from a wealthy family in
Prague. They could afford to hire the finest tutors for Akhsa. One
taught her the Bible, another French, still another the pianoforte, and
a fourth dancing. She learned everything quickly. At eight, she was

playing chess with her grandfather. Reb Naftali didn't need to offer a dowry for her marriage, since she was heir to his entire fortune.

Matches were sought for her early, but her grandmother was hard to please. She would look at a boy proposed by the marriage brokers and say, "He has the shoulders of a fool," or, "He has the narrow forehead of an ignoramus."

One day Nesha died unexpectedly. Reb Naftali was in his late seventies and it was unthinkable that he remarry. Half his day he devoted to religion, the other half to business. He rose at daybreak and pored over the Talmud and the Commentaries and wrote letters to community elders. When a man was sick, Reb Naftali went to comfort him. Twice a week he visited the poorhouse with Akhsa, who carried a contribution of soup and groats herself. More than once, Akhsa, the pampered and scholarly, rolled up her sleeves and made beds there.

In the summer, after midday sleep, Reb Naftali ordered his britska harnessed and he rode around the fields and village with Akhsa. While they rode, he discussed business, and it was known that he listened to her advice just as he had listened to her grandmother's.

But there was one thing that Akhsa didn't have — a friend. Her grandmother had tried to find friends for her; she had even lowered her standards and invited girls from Krasnobród. But Akhsa had no patience with their chatter about clothes and household matters. Since the tutors were all men, Akhsa was kept away from them, except for lessons. Now her grandfather became her only companion. Reb Naftali had met famous noblemen in his lifetime. He had been to fairs in Warsaw, Kraków, Danzig, and Koenigsberg. He would sit for hours with Akhsa and tell her about rabbis and miracle workers, about the disciples of the false messiah Sabbatai Zevi, quarrels in the Sejm, the caprices of the Zamojskis, the Radziwills, and the Czartoryskis — their wives, lovers, courtiers. Sometimes Akhsa would cry out, "I wish you were my fiancé, not my grandfather!" and kiss his eyes and his white beard.

Reb Naftali would answer, "I'm not the only man in Poland. There are plenty like me, and young to boot."

"Where, Grandfather? Where?"

After her grandmother's death, Akhsa refused to rely on anyone else's judgment in the choice of a husband — not even her grandfather's. Just as her grandmother saw only bad, Reb Naftali saw only good. Akhsa demanded that the matchmakers allow her to meet her suitor, and Reb Naftali finally consented. The young pair would be brought together in a room, the door would be left open, and a deaf old woman servant would stand at the threshold to watch that the meeting be brief and without frivolity. As a rule, Akhsa stayed with the young man not more than a few minutes. Most of the suitors seemed dull and silly. Others tried to be clever and made undignified jokes. Akhsa dismissed them abruptly. How strange, but her grandmother still expressed her opinion. Once, Akhsa heard her say clearly, "He has the snout of a pig." Another time, she said, "He talks like the standard letter book."

Akhsa knew quite well that it was not her grandmother speaking. The dead don't return from the other world to comment on prospective fiancés. Just the same, it was her grandmother's voice, her style. Akhsa wanted to talk to her grandfather about it, but she was afraid he would think her crazy. Besides, her grandfather longed for his wife, and Akhsa didn't want to stir up his grief.

When Reb Naftali Holishitzer realized that his granddaughter was driving away the matchmakers, he was troubled. Akhsa was now past her eighteenth year. The people in Krasnobród had begun to gossip — she was demanding a knight on a white horse or the moon in heaven; she would stay a spinster. Reb Naftali decided not to give in to her whims any more but to marry her off. He went to a yeshiva and brought back with him a young man named Zemach, an orphan and a devout scholar. He was dark as a gypsy, small, with broad shoulders. His sidelocks were thick. He was nearsighted and studied eighteen hours a day. The moment he reached Krasnobród, he went to the study house and began to sway in front of an open volume of the Talmud. His sidelocks swayed, too. Students came to talk with him, and he spoke without lifting his gaze from the book. He seemed to know the Talmud by heart, since he caught everyone misquoting.

Akhsa demanded a meeting, but Reb Naftali replied that this was conduct befitting tailors and shoemakers, not a girl of good breeding. He warned Akhsa that if she drove Zemach away he would disinherit her. Since men and women were in separate rooms during the engagement party, Akhsa had no chance of seeing Zemach until the marriage contract was to be signed. She looked at him and heard her grandmother say, "They've sold you shoddy goods."

Her words were so clear it seemed to Akhsa that everyone should have heard them, but no one had. The girls and women crowded around her, congratulating her and praising her beauty, her dress, her jewelry. Her grandfather passed her the contract and a quill, and her grandmother cried out, "Don't sign!" She grabbed Akhsa's elbow and a blot formed on the paper.

Reb Naftali shouted, "What have you done!"

Akhsa tried to sign, but the pen fell from her hand. She burst into tears. "Grandfather, I can't."

"Akhsa, you shame me."

"Grandfather, forgive me." Akhsa covered her face with her hands. There was an outcry. Men hissed and women laughed and wept. Akhsa cried silently. They half led, half carried her to her room and put her on her bed.

Zemach exclaimed, "I don't want to be married to this shrew!"

He pushed through the crowd and ran to get a wagon back to the yeshiva. Reb Naftali went after him, trying to pacify him with words and money, but Zemach threw Reb Naftali's banknotes to the ground. Someone brought his wicker trunk from the inn where he had stayed. Before the wagon pulled away, Zemach cried out, "I don't forgive her, and God won't, either."

For days after that, Akhsa was ill. Reb Naftali Holishitzer, who had been successful all his life, was not accustomed to failure. He became sick; his face took on a yellow pallor. Women and girls tried to comfort Akhsa. Rabbis and elders came to visit Reb Naftali, but he got weaker as the days passed. After a while, Akhsa gained back her strength and left her sickbed. She went to her grandfather's room, bolting the door behind her. The maid who listened and spied through the keyhole reported that she had heard him say, "You are mad!"

Akhsa nursed her grandfather, brought him his medicine and bathed him with a sponge, but the old man developed an inflammation of the lungs. Blood ran from his nose. His urine stopped. Soon he died. He had written his will years before and left one-third of his estate to charity and the rest to Akhsa.

According to the law, one does not sit shivah in mourning after the death of a grandfather, but Akhsa went through the ceremony anyway. She sat on a low stool and read the book of Job. She ordered that no one be let in. She had shamed an orphan — a scholar — and caused the death of her grandfather. She became melancholy. Since she had read the story of Job before, she began to search in her grandfather's library for another book to read. To her amazement, she found a Bible translated into Polish — the New Testament as well as the Old. Akhsa knew it was a forbidden book, but she turned the pages anyway. Had her grandfather read it, Akhsa wondered. No, it couldn't be. She remembered that on the Gentile feast days, when holy icons and pictures were carried in processions near the house, she was not allowed to look out of the window. Her grandfather told her it was idolatry. She wondered if her grandmother had read this Bible. Among the pages she found some pressed cornflowers — a flower her grandmother had often picked. Grandmother came from Bohemia; it was said that her father had belonged to the Sabbatai Zevi sect. Akhsa recalled that Prince Czartoryski used to spend time with her grandmother when he visited the estate, and praised the way she spoke Polish. If she hadn't been a Jewish girl, he said, he would have married her — a great compliment.

That night Akhsa read the New Testament to the last page. It was difficult for her to accept that Jesus was God's only begotten son and that He rose from the grave, but she found this book more comforting to her tortured spirit than the castigating words of the prophets, who never mentioned the Kingdom of Heaven or the resurrection of the dead. All they promised was a good harvest for good deeds and starvation and plague for bad ones.

On the seventh night of shivah, Akhsa went to bed. The light was out and she was dozing when she heard footsteps that she recognized as her grandfather's. In the darkness, her grandfather's figure emerged: the light face, the white beard, the mild features, even the skullcap on his high forehead. He said in a quiet voice, "Akhsa, you have committed an injustice."

Akhsa began to cry. "Grandfather, what should I do?"

"Everything can be corrected."

"How?"

"Apologize to Zemach. Become his wife."

"Grandfather, I hate him."

"He is your destined one."

He lingered for a moment, and Akhsa could smell his snuff, which he used to mix with cloves and smelling salts. Then he vanished and an empty space remained in the darkness. She was too amazed to be frightened. She leaned against the headboard, and after some time she slept.

She woke with a start. She heard her grandmother's voice. This was not a murmuring like Grandfather's but the strong voice of a living person. "Akhsa, my daughter."

Akhsa burst into tears. "Grandmother, where are you?"

"I'm here."

"What should I do?"

"Whatever your heart desires."

"What, Grandmother?"

"Go to the priest. He will advise you."

Akhsa became numb. Fear constricted her throat. She managed to say, "You're not my grandmother. You're a demon."

"I am your grandmother. Do you remember how we went wading in the pond that summer night near the flat hill and you found a gulden in the water?"

"Yes, Grandmother."

"I could give you other proof. Be it known that the Gentiles are right. Jesus of Nazareth is the Son of God. He was born of the Holy Spirit as prophesied. The rebellious Jews refused to accept the truth and therefore they are punished. The Messiah will not come to them because He is here already."

"Grandmother, I'm afraid."

"Akhsa, don't listen!" her grandfather suddenly shouted into her right ear. "This isn't your grandmother. It's an evil spirit disguised to trick you. Don't give in to his blasphemies. He will drag you into perdition."

"Akhsa, that is not your grandfather but a goblin from behind the bathhouse," Grandmother interrupted. "Zemach is a ne'er-do-well, and vengeful to boot. He will torment you, and the children he begets will be vermin like him. Save yourself while there is time. God is with the Gentiles."

"Lilith! She-demon! Daughter of Ketev M'riri!" Grandfather growled.

"Liar!"

Grandfather became silent, but Grandmother continued to talk, although her voice faded. She said, "Your real grandfather learned the truth in Heaven and converted. They baptized him with heavenly water and he rests in Paradise. The saints are all bishops and cardinals. Those who remain stubborn are roasted in the fires of Gehenna. If you don't believe me, ask for a sign."

"What sign?"

"Unbutton your pillowcase, rip open the seams of the pillow, and there you will find a crown of feathers. No human hand could make a crown like this."

Her grandmother disappeared, and Akhsa fell into a heavy sleep. At dawn, she awoke and lit a candle. She remembered her grandmother's words, unbuttoned the pillowcase, and ripped open the pillow. What she saw was so extraordinary she could scarcely believe her eyes: down and feathers entwined into a crown, with little ornaments and complex designs no worldly master could have duplicated. On the top of the crown was a tiny cross. It was all so airy that Akhsa's breath made it flutter. Akhsa gasped. Whoever had made this crown — an angel or a demon — had done his work in darkness, in the inside of a pillow. She was beholding a miracle. She extinguished the candle and stretched out on the bed. For a long time she lay without any thoughts. Then she went back to sleep.

In the morning when she awoke, Akhsa thought she had had a dream, but on the night table she saw the crown of feathers. The sun made it sparkle with the colors of the rainbow. It looked as if it were set with the smallest of gems. She sat and contemplated the wonder. Then she put on a black dress and a black shawl and asked that the carriage be brought round for her. She rode to the house where Koscik, the priest, resided. The housekeeper answered her knock. The priest was nearing seventy and he knew Akhsa. He had often come to the estate to bless the peasants' bread at Easter time and to give rites to the dying and conduct weddings and funerals. One of Akhsa's teachers had borrowed a Latin-Polish dictionary from him. Whenever the priest visited, Akhsa's grandmother invited him to her parlor and they conversed over cake and vishniak.

The priest offered Akhsa a chair. She sat down and told him everything. He said, "Don't go back to the Jews. Come to us. We will see to it that your fortune remains intact."

"I forgot to take the crown. I want to have it with me."

"Yes, my daughter, go and bring it."

Akhsa went home, but a maid had cleaned her bedroom and dusted the night table; the crown had vanished. Akhsa searched in the garbage ditch, in the slops, but not a trace could she find.

Soon after that, the terrible news was abroad in Krasnobród that Akhsa had converted.

❚ How did your narrator physically demonstrate his easy control of the story?

This sardonic poem begins with unmistakable visual imagery on the part of the directly involved persona. It moves quickly into a complexity of sense imagery, returning to the visual in the thirteenth line and in the sixth line from the end, giving it rich variety within remarkable unity. There is no movement on the part of the persona. His attention, focused sharply on the mosquito, gives a strong sense of the kinesthetic. Work to transfer this feeling to your audience so that the mosquito is on their arms as well as on yours.

The Mosquito
RODNEY JONES

I see the mosquito kneeling on the soft underside of my arm,
        kneeling
Like a fruitpicker, kneeling like an old woman
With the proboscis of her prayer buried in the idea of God,
And I know we shall not speak with the aliens
And that peace will not happen in my life,
        not unless
It is in the burnt oil spreading across the surfaces of ponds,
        in the dark
Egg-rafts clotting and the wiggletails expiring like batteries.
Bring a little alcohol and a little balm
For these poppies planted by the Queen of Neptune.

In her photographs, she is bearded and spurred, embellished
           five hundred times,
Her modular legs crouching, her insufferable head unlocking
To lower the razor-edge of its tubes, and she is there
           in the afternoon
When the wind gives up the spirit of cleanliness
And there rises from the sound the brackish oyster and squid smell
           of creation.
Nights with her, I am loved for myself, for the succulent
Flange of my upper lip, the twin bellies of my eyelids.
She adores the easy, the soft. She picks the tenderest blossoms
           of insomnia.
Mornings while the jackhammer rips the pavement outside my
           window,
While the sanitation workers bang the cans against the big truck
           and shout to each other over the motor,
I watch her strut like an udder with my blood,
Imagining the luminous pick descending into Trotsky's skull
           and the eleven days
I waited for the cold chill, nightmare, and nightsweat of malaria,
Imagining the mating call in the vibrations of her wings,
And imagining, in the simple knot of her ganglia,
How she thrills to my life, how she sings for the harvest.

▌ Did your persona ever divert attention from the mosquito?
   Where? Why?

In recounting *One Writer's Beginnings*, Eudora Welty demonstrates how her
enduring themes and her commanding skill came into being. This memoir
allows the interpreter to enjoy both the immediacy of the scene and the
acuity of reflection. Young Eudora listens with her whole body — be sure
you tell the story the same way.

FROM *One Writer's Beginnings*
EUDORA WELTY

In that vanished time in small-town Jackson, most of the ladies I was
familiar with, the mothers of my friends in the neighborhood, were
busiest when they were sociable. In the afternoons there was regular
visiting up and down the little grid of residential streets. Everybody
had calling cards, even certain children; and newborn babies themselves were properly announced by sending out their tiny engraved
calling cards attached with a pink or blue bow to those of their parents. Graduation presents to high-school pupils were often "card

cases." On the hall table in every house the first thing you saw was a silver tray waiting to receive more calling cards on top of the stack already piled up like jackstraws; they were never thrown away.

My mother let none of this idling, as she saw it, pertain to her; she went her own way with or without her calling cards, and though she was fond of her friends and they were fond of her, she had little time for small talk. At first, I hadn't known what I'd missed.

When we at length bought our first automobile, one of our neighbors was often invited to go with us on the family Sunday afternoon ride. In Jackson it was counted an affront to the neighbors to start out for anywhere with an empty seat in the car. My mother sat in the back with her friend, and I'm told that as a small child I would ask to sit in the middle, and say as we started off, "Now *talk.*"

There was dialogue throughout the lady's accounts to my mother. "I said" . . . "He said" . . . "And I'm told she very plainly said" . . . "It was midnight before they finally heard, and what do you think it *was*?"

What I loved about her stories was that everything happened in *scenes.* I might not catch on to what the root of the trouble was in all that happened, but my ear told me it was dramatic. Often she said, "The crisis had come!"

This same lady was one of Mother's callers on the telephone who always talked a long time. I knew who it was when my mother would only reply, now and then, "Well, I declare," or "You don't say so," or "Surely not." She'd be standing at the wall telephone, listening against her will, and I'd sit on the stairs close by her. Our telephone had a little bar set into the handle which had to be pressed and held down to keep the connection open, and when her friend had said goodbye, my mother needed me to prize her fingers loose from the little bar; her grip had become paralyzed. "What did she say?" I asked.

"She wasn't *saying* a thing in this world," sighed my mother. "She was just ready to talk, that's all."

My mother was right. Years later, beginning with my story "Why I Live at the P.O.," I wrote reasonably often in the form of a monologue that takes possession of the speaker. How much more gets told besides!

This lady told everything in her sweet, marveling voice, and meant every word of it kindly. She enjoyed my company perhaps even more than my mother's. She invited me to catch her doodle-bugs; under the trees in her backyard were dozens of their holes. When you stuck a broom straw down one and called, "Doodlebug, doodlebug, your house is on fire and all your children are burning up," she believed this is why the doodlebug came running out of the hole. This was why I loved to call up her doodlebugs instead of ours.

My mother could never have told me her stories, and I think I knew why even then: my mother didn't believe them. But I could listen to this murmuring lady all day. She believed everything she heard, like the doodlebug. And so did I.

This was a day when ladies' and children's clothes were very often made at home. My mother cut out all the dresses and her little boys' rompers, and a sewing woman would come and spend the day upstairs in the sewing room fitting and stitching them all. This was Fannie. This old black sewing woman, along with her speed and dexterity, brought along a great provision of up-to-the-minute news. She spent her life going from family to family in town and worked right in its bosom, and nothing could stop her. My mother would try, while I stood being pinned up. "Fannie, I'd rather Eudora didn't hear that." "That" would be just what I was longing to hear, whatever it was. "I don't want her exposed to gossip" — as if gossip were measles and I could catch it. I did catch some of it but not enough. "Mrs. O'Neil's oldest daughter she had her wedding dress *tried on*, and all her fine underclothes featherstitched and ribbon run in and then —" "I think that will do, Fannie," said my mother. It was tantalizing never to be exposed long enough to hear the end.

Fannie was the worldliest old woman to be imagined. She could do whatever her hands were doing without having to stop talking; and she could speak in a wonderfully derogatory way with any number of pins stuck in her mouth. Her hands steadied me like claws as she stumped on her knees around me, tacking me together. The gist of her tale would be lost on me, but Fannie didn't bother about the ear she was telling it to; she just liked telling. She was like an author. If fact, for a good deal of what she said, I daresay she *was* the author.

Long before I wrote stories, I listened for stories. Listening *for* them is something more acute than listening *to* them. I suppose it's an early form of participation in what goes on. Listening children know stories are *there*. When their elders sit and begin, children are just waiting and hoping for one to come out, like a mouse from its hole.

It was taken entirely for granted that there wasn't any lying in our family, and I was advanced in adolescence before I realized that in plenty of homes where I played with schoolmates and went to their parties, children lied to their parents and parents lied to their children and to each other. It took me a long time to realize that these very same everyday lies, and the stratagems and jokes and tricks and dares that went with them, were in fact the basis of the *scenes* I so well loved to hear about and hoped for and treasured in the conversation of adults.

My instinct — the dramatic instinct — was to lead me, eventually, on the right track for a storyteller: the *scene* was full of hints, pointers, suggestions, and promises of things to find out and know about human beings. I had to grow up and learn to listen for the unspoken as well as the spoken — and to know a truth, I also had to recognize a lie.

▍ How and where did your muscles show us the remembered pleasure the persona so obviously relishes?

The style and vocabulary in this poem are disarmingly simple and harmonize well with the content. Unity is preserved despite the changes in locus within the school building. The *and* with which the last stanza opens ties together all that has gone before, and the two brief subjunctive sentences in the last line suggest both longing and regret.

The Art of Love
RONALD WALLACE

We get handwritten cards from the children:
Dear Parents, come visit our school —
our names painfully etched in crabbed script, the art
teacher's latest project. We say we would love
to come. We'll see Home Room, Art, and Music.
We promise to be there on time.

We've been talking a good deal these days about time.
About how when we were children
time was a kind of slow music,
a sure pulse of expectation, a school
in which, leisurely, we learned about love,
in which singing all day took no art.

The memory itself, we know, is all art.
It was never so happy as that at the time,
we remind ourselves, laughing, and love
wasn't easy, not even for children.
We remember those queasy afternoons after school:
the dark corridors of failure, of facing the music.

The first room we visit this time is Music.
An old upright piano, locked; art
work carved on the marred wooden school

desks; a metronome keeping the time
as we go through the motions of singing, the children
teaching us all of the songs that they love.

Valentines plaster the walls of the Art Room: Love
with its gaudy construction and fluff. No music
in these rough cuts and doilies the children
manufacture in the interests of "art."
It's getting late now, the time
moving faster, faster than it ever did in school.

But Home Room's the best thing in school,
they insist! We follow them out of love
through a motley of workbooks, torn papers, and time
tests, until memory turns up its old music
and everything blurs — Home Room, Music, and Art —
to the slow bobbing heads of the children.

And we know we would school ourselves in such music,
would cut out and paste up such love for all time,
would make a new start. Were we children. Had we the art.

▎ How did your performance demonstrate the silent partner of
the speaker?

This poem performs brilliantly, but be sure that you know *exactly* what the
relationship is between the speaker and the events. And don't throttle the
end — it will take care of itself.

The .38
TED JOANS

I hear the man downstairs slapping the hell out of his stupid wife
       again
I hear him push and shove her around the overcrowded room
I hear his wife scream and beg for mercy
I hear him tell her there is no mercy
I hear the blows as they land on her beautiful body
I hear glasses and pots and pans falling
I hear her fleeing from the room
I hear them running up the stairs
I hear her outside my door
I hear him coming toward her outside my door
I hear her banging on my door

I hear him bang her head on my door
I hear him trying to drag her away from my door
I hear her hands desperate on my doorknob
I hear the blows of her head against my door
I hear him drag her down the stairs
I hear her head bounce from step to step
I hear them again in their room
I hear a loud smack across her face (I guess)
I hear her groan — then
I hear the eerie silence
I hear him open the top drawer of his bureau (the .38 lives there)
I hear the fast beat of my heart
I hear the drops of perspiration fall from my brow
I hear him yell I warned you
I hear him say damn you I warned you and now it's too late

I hear the loud report of the thirty eight caliber revolver then
I hear it again and again the Smith and Wesson
I hear the bang bang bang of four death dealing bullets
I hear my heart beat faster and louder — then again
I hear the eerie silence
I hear him walk out of their overcrowded room
I hear him walk up the steps
I hear him come toward my door
I hear his hand on the doorknob
I hear the doorknob click
I hear the door slowly open
I hear him step into my room
I hear the click of the thirty eight before the firing pin hits the bullet
I hear the loud blast of the powder exploding in the chamber of
        the .38
I hear the heavy lead nose of the bullet swiftly cutting its way
        through the barrel of the .38
I hear it emerge into space from the .38
I hear the bullet of death flying toward my head the .38
I hear it coming faster than sound the .38
I hear it coming closer to my sweaty forehead the .38
I hear its weird whistle the .38
I hear it give off a steamlike noise when it cuts through my sweat
        the .38
I hear it singe my skin as it enters my head the .38 and
I hear death saying, *Hello, I'm here!*

▌ At what line did terror finally fill the speaker? What was your
  body *doing*?

There is no mistaking the strong kinetic and kinesthetic imagery throughout
this selection. Although the style may seem closer to prose than to poetry,
don't neglect the contribution of the lines as units of the thought progression.
The insistent *I* is varied sufficiently by the insertions of indirect discourse to
help control the pressure and rush of the bulk of the poem. The fulcrum is
clear and comes just in time for the persona and for us. The last long sentence
is gentle, and this contrast is helped considerably by the line lengths and
punctuation.

The Race

SHARON OLDS

When I got to the airport I rushed up to the desk
and they told me the flight was cancelled. The doctors had

said my father would not live through the night
and the flight was cancelled. A young man with a
dark blond mustache told me
another airline had a non-stop
leaving in seven minutes — see that
elevator over there well go
down to the first floor, make a right you'll
see a yellow bus, get off at the
second Pan Am terminal — I
ran, I who have no sense of direction
raced exactly where he'd told me, like a fish
slipping upstream deftly against the
flow of the river. I jumped off that bus with my
heavy bags and ran, the bags
wagged me from side to side as if to
prove I was under the claims of the material, I
ran up to a man with a white flower on his breast,
I who always go to the end of the line, I said
Help me. He looked at my ticket, he said make a
left and then a right go up the moving stairs and then
run. I raced up the moving stairs
two at a time, at the top I saw the
long hollow corridor and
then I took a deep breath, I said
goodbye to my body, goodbye to comfort, I
used my legs and heart as if I would
gladly use them up for this, to
touch him again in this life. I ran and the
big heavy dark bags
banged me, wheeled and swam around me like
planets in wild orbits — I have seen
pictures of women running down roads with their
belongings tied in black scarves
grasped in their fists, running under serious
gray historical skies — I blessed my
long legs he gave me, my strong
heart I abandoned to its own purpose, I
ran to Gate 17 and they were
just lifting the thick white
lozenge of the door to fit it into the
socket of the plane. Like the man who is not
too rich, I turned to the side and
slipped through the needle's eye, and then I
walked down the aisle toward my father. The jet was
full and people's hair was shining, they were

smiling, the interior of the plane was filled with a
mist of gold endorphin light,
I wept as people weep when they enter heaven,
in massive relief. We lifted up
gently from one tip of the continent and
did not stop until we set down lightly on the
other edge, I walked into his room and
watched his chest rise slowly and
sink again, all night
I watched him breathe.

▌ How did you show that your muscles remembered the effort
of the race?

Langston Hughes was able to condense and make vivid the history of his
race from its beginnings through the first quarter of the twentieth century in
this brief poem. The repetitions are, of course, a strong unifying factor, as
are the motifs. Be careful that they do not obscure the variety and progression. The pride and strength of the persona as he speaks in the first person
but also as a voice for an entire race will influence empathy and muscle tone.
Don't let the repetition at the beginning of lines become patterned. Allow
the verbs to provide the clues for handling them.

The Negro Speaks of Rivers
LANGSTON HUGHES

I've known rivers:
I've known rivers ancient as the world and older than the flow of
        human blood in human veins.
My soul has grown deep like the rivers.
I bathed in the Euphrates when dawns were young.
I built my hut near the Congo and it lulled me to sleep.
I looked upon the Nile and raised the pyramids above it.
I heard the singing of the Mississippi when Abe Lincoln went down
        to New Orleans, and I've seen its muddy bosom turn all
        golden in the sunset.

I've known rivers:
Ancient, dusky rivers.

My soul has grown deep like the rivers.

▌ What physical differences occurred in your persona before the
eighth line and before the tenth line? Why?

The old lady whose words we hear in this poem obviously once loved being alive and physically responsive. Be sure to emphasize her memory of the joy of her body. Note the inner strength and fire suggested in the two-line stanza. Rhythm of content reflects the rhythm of her life — as she remembers the past, is frozen in the present, and yearns for what is to come.

Old Lady's Winter Words
THEODORE ROETHKE

To seize, to seize, —
I know that dream.
Now my ardors sleep in a sleeve.
My eyes have forgotten.
Like the half-dead, I hug my last secrets.
O for some minstrel of what's to be,
A bird singing into the beyond,
The marrow of God, talking,
Full merry, a gleam
Gracious and bland,
On a bright stone.
Somewhere, among the ferns and birds,
The great swamps flash.
I would hold high converse
Where the winds gather,
And leap over my eye,
An old woman
Jumping in her shoes.
If only I could remember
The white grass bending away,
The doors swinging open,
The smells, the moment of hay, —
When I went to sea in a sigh,
In a boat of beautiful things.
The good day has gone:
The fair house, the high
Elm swinging around
With its deep shade, and birds.
I have listened close
For the thin sound in the windy chimney,
The fall of the last ash
From the dying ember.
I've become a sentry of small seeds,
Poking alone in my garden.
The stone walks, where are they?

Gone to bolster a road.
The shrunken soil
Has scampered away in a dry wind.
Once I was sweet with the light of myself,
A self-delighting creature,
Leaning over a rock,
My hair between me and the sun,
The waves rippling near me.
My feet remembered the earth,
The loam heaved me
That way and this.
My looks had a voice;
I was careless in growing.

If I were a young man,
I could roll in the dust of a fine rage.

The shadows are empty, the sliding externals.
The wind wanders around the house
On its way to the back pasture.
The cindery snow ticks over stubble.
My dust longs for the invisible.
I'm reminded to stay alive
By the dry rasp of the recurring inane,
The fine soot sifting through my south windows.
It is hard to care about corners,
And the sound of paper tearing.
I fall, more and more,
Into my own silences.
In the cold air,
The spirit
Hardens.

▌ Did your old lady have a clearly lived past *before* she began to
  speak? How did you demonstrate this to your audience?

Let your muscles respond to this famous speech on the seven ages of man. Remember the importance of muscle tone. Keep the progression firm and unified, but allow time for the physical and emotional transitions. The persona himself does not age, but he visualizes and empathizes.

FROM *As You Like It*

WILLIAM SHAKESPEARE

ACT II, SCENE 7

JAQUES: All the world's a stage,
And all the men and women merely players.
They have their exits and their entrances,
And one man in his time plays many parts,
His acts being seven ages. At first the infant,
Mewling and puking in the nurse's arms.
Then the whining school-boy, with his satchel
And shining morning face, creeping like snail
Unwillingly to school. And then the lover,
Sighing like furnace, with a woeful ballad
Made to his mistress' eyebrow. Then a soldier,
Full of strange oaths, and bearded like the pard,
Jealous in honor, sudden, and quick in quarrel,
Seeking the bubble reputation
Even in the cannon's mouth. And then the justice,
In fair round belly with good capon lin'd,
With eyes severe and beard of formal cut,
Full of wise saws and modern instances;
And so he plays his part. The sixth age shifts
Into the lean and slipper'd pantaloon,
With spectacles on nose and pouch on side,
His youthful hose, well sav'd, a world too wide
For his shrunk shank, and his big manly voice,
Turning again toward childish treble, pipes
And whistles in his sound. Last scene of all,
That ends this strange eventful history,
Is second childishness and mere oblivion,
Sans teeth, sans eyes, sans taste, sans everything.

▌ How did your Jaques incorporate the kinesthetic imagery in performance?

This is the first of two selections by Maya Angelou. They are very different in tone and content, but strikingly similar in spirit. The persona in this selection is a black woman who knows her identity and glories in it. It would be impossible to read this selection without responding to the kinesthetic imagery as well as the kinetic. Be careful, though, that you don't let the strong, deliberate swing of the last half of the stanzas become repetitious. Keep the close rhymes and short lines under control, but use them fully.

Phenominal Woman

MAYA ANGELOU

Pretty women wonder where my secret lies.
I'm not cute or built to suit a fashion model's size
But when I start to tell them,
They think I'm telling lies.
I say,
It's in the reach of my arms,
The span of my hips,
The stride of my step,
The curl of my lips.
I'm a woman
Phenominally.
Phenominal woman,
That's me.

I walk into a room
Just as cool as you please,
And to a man,
The fellows stand or
Fall down on their knees.
Then they swarm around me,
A hive of honey bees,
I say,
It's the fire in my eyes,
And the flash of my teeth,
The swing in my waist,
And the joy in my feet.
I'm a woman
Phenominally.
Phenominal woman,
That's me.

Men themselves have wondered
What they see in me.
They try so much

But they can't touch
My inner mystery.
When I try to show them
They say they still can't see.
I say,
It's the arch of my back,
The sun of my smile,
The ride of my breasts,
The grace of my style.
I'm a woman
Phenominally.
Phenominal woman,
That's me.

Now you understand
Just why my head's not bowed.
I don't shout or jump about
Or have to talk real loud.
When you see me passing
It ought to make you proud.
I say,
It's in the click of my heels,
The bend of my hair,
The palm of my hand,
The need for my care.
'Cause I'm a woman
Phenominally.
Phenominal woman,
That's me.

▌ This persona is neither shy nor dull. What forms did her spirit
take in performance? Why?

This memoir is probably as physical and spirited as Maya Angelou's early
life with her older brother, Bailey. Her fascination with everyone and everything in the Christian Methodist Episcopal Church in Stamps, Arkansas, has
not diminished with time. Keep those bodies alive!

FROM *I Know Why the Caged Bird Sings*
MAYA ANGELOU

In the Christian Methodist Episcopal Church the children's section
was on the right, cater-cornered from the pew that held those ominous women called the Mothers of the Church. In the young people's

section the benches were placed close together, and when a child's legs no longer comfortably fitted in the narrow space, it was an indication to the elders that that person could now move into the intermediate area (center church). Bailey and I were allowed to sit with the other children only when there were informal meetings, church socials or the like. But on the Sundays when Reverend Thomas preached, it was ordained that we occupy the first row, called the mourners' bench. I thought we were placed in front because Momma was proud of us, but Bailey assured me that she just wanted to keep her grandchildren under her thumb and eye.

Reverend Thomas took his text from Deuteronomy. And I was stretched between loathing his voice and wanting to listen to the sermon. Deuteronomy was my favorite book in the Bible. The laws were so absolute, so clearly set down, that I knew if a person truly wanted to avoid hell and brimstone, and being roasted forever in the devil's fire, all she had to do was memorize Deuteronomy and follow its teaching, word for word. I also liked the way the word rolled off the tongue.

Bailey and I sat alone on the front bench, the wooden slats pressing hard on our behinds and the backs of our thighs. I would have wriggled just a bit, but each time I looked over at Momma, she seemed to threaten, "Move and I'll tear you up," so, obedient to the unvoiced command, I sat still. The church ladies were warming up behind me with a few hallelujahs and Praise the Lords and Amens, and the preacher hadn't really moved into the meat of the sermon.

It was going to be a hot service.

On my way into church, I saw Sister Monroe, her open-faced gold crown glinting when she opened her mouth to return a neighborly greeting. She lived in the country and couldn't get to church every Sunday, so she made up for her absences by shouting so hard when she did make it that she shook the whole church. As soon as she took her seat, all the ushers would move to her side of the church because it took three women and sometimes a man or two to hold her.

Once when she hadn't been to church for a few months (she had taken off to have a child), she got the spirit and started shouting, throwing her arms around and jerking her body, so that the ushers went over to hold her down, but she tore herself away from them and ran up to the pulpit. She stood in front of the altar, shaking like a freshly caught trout. She screamed at Reverend Taylor. "Preach it. I say, preach it." Naturally he kept on preaching as if she wasn't standing there telling him what to do. Then she screamed an extremely fierce "I said, preach it" and stepped up on the altar. The Reverend kept on throwing out phrases like home-run balls and

Sister Monroe made a quick break and grasped for him. For just a second, everything and everyone in the church except Reverend Taylor and Sister Monroe hung loose like stockings on a washline. Then she caught the minister by the sleeve of his jacket and his coattail, then she rocked him from side to side.

I have to say this for our minister, he never stopped giving us the lesson. The usher board made its way to the pulpit, going up both aisles with a little more haste than is customarily seen in church. Truth to tell, they fairly ran to the minister's aid. Then two of the deacons, in their shiny Sunday suits, joined the ladies in white on the pulpit, and each time they pried Sister Monroe loose from the preacher he took another deep breath and kept on preaching, and Sister Monroe grabbed him in another place, and more firmly. Reverend Taylor was helping his rescuers as much as possible by jumping around when he got a chance. His voice at one point got so low it sounded like a roll of thunder, then Sister Monroe's "Preach it" cut through the roar, and we all wondered (I did, in any case) if it would ever end. Would they go on forever, or get tired out at last like a game of blindman's bluff that lasted too long, with nobody caring who was "it"?

I'll never know what might have happened, because magically the pandemonium spread. The spirit infused Deacon Jackson and Sister Willson, the chairman of the usher board, at the same time. Deacon Jackson, a tall, thin, quiet man, who was also a part-time Sunday school teacher, gave a scream like a falling tree, leaned back on thin air and punched Reverend Taylor on the arm. It must have hurt as much as it caught the Reverend unawares. There was a moment's break in the rolling sounds and Reverend Taylor jerked around surprised, and hauled off and punched Deacon Jackson. In the same second Sister Willson caught his tie, looped it over her fist a few times, and pressed down on him. There wasn't time to laugh or cry before all three of them were down on the floor behind the altar. Their legs spiked out like kindling wood.

Sister Monroe, who had been the cause of all the excitement, walked off the dais, cool and spent, and raised her flinty voice in the hymn, "I came to Jesus, as I was, worried, wound, and sad, I found in Him a resting place and He has made me glad."

The minister took advantage of already being on the floor and asked in a choky little voice if the church would kneel with him to offer a prayer of thanksgiving. He said we had been visited with a mighty spirit, and let the whole church say Amen.

On the next Sunday, he took his text from the eighteenth chapter of the Gospel according to St. Luke, and talked quietly but seriously about the Pharisees, who prayed in the streets so that the public would be impressed with their religious devotion. I doubt that anyone got the message — certainly not those to whom it was directed. The deacon board, however, did appropriate funds for him to buy a new suit. The other was a total loss.

▮ How did you keep the turmoil from getting out of control?
▮ Did you fully embody Sister Monroe?
▮ Did you take enough time for your audience to see all of it happen?

This is the second poem in Thomas Hardy's *Satires of Circumstance in Fifteen Glimpses.* Be sure we see how thrilling the preacher's voice is to his pupil. Don't let the poem become more than a "glimpse."

In Church

THOMAS HARDY

"And now to God the Father," he ends,
And his voice thrills up to the topmost tiles:
Each listener chokes as he bows and bends,
And emotion pervades the crowded aisles.
Then the preacher glides to the vestry-door,
And shuts it, and thinks he is seen no more.

The door swings softly ajar meanwhile,
And a pupil of his in the Bible class,
Who adores him as one without gloss or guile,
Sees her idol stand with a satisfied smile
And re-enact at the vestry-glass
Each pulpit gesture in deft dumb-show
That had moved the congregation so.

▮ Did you show us the pupil's discovery? Where? How?

Bibliography

Most communication and interpretation textbooks discuss the role of the body in oral communication. These books address more technical and specialized needs. Consult them with specific problems to answer.

Birdwhistle, Ray L. *Kinesics and Context: Essays on Body Motion and Communication.* Philadelphia: University of Pennsylvania Press, 1970.
> An expansion of one of the early basic studies in the relationship between kinesics and oral communication.

Blackmur, R. P. *Language as Gesture.* New York: Harcourt, Brace and Company, 1952.
> A detailed analysis of specific poems to illustrate the theory of poetry as language of gesture.

Burke, Kenneth. *The Philosophy of Literary Form: Studies in Symbolic Action.* Rev. ed. New York: Random House, Vintage Books, 1957.
> Essays on rhetoric and poetics, but basically a discussion of the theory of symbolic action.

Carlsöö, Sven. *How Man Moves.* London: Heinemann, 1975.
> Kinesiological methods and studies suggesting practical implications for performers in rehearsal.

Katz, Robert L. *Empathy: Its Nature and Uses.* New York: Macmillan, 1963.
> Emphasis on the dynamics of empathy and its social and aesthetic uses.

King, Nancy R. *A Movement Approach to Acting.* Englewood Cliffs, N.J.: Prentice-Hall, 1981.
> Program for movement training that begins with the performer's self-awareness and advances to difficult stage movement.

Klein, Maxine. *Time, Space, and Design for Actors.* Boston: Houghton Mifflin Company, 1975.
> Contains helpful theory and exercises for body relaxation, flexibility, and control.

Morris, Desmond, Peter Collett, Peter Marsh, and Marie O'Shaughnessy. *Gestures: Their Origins and Distributions.* New York: Stein and Day Publishers, 1979.
> An attempt to trace systematically the geographical range and antiquity of gesture.

Pisk, Litz. *The Actor and His Body.* London: George C. Harrap & Company, 1975.
> Contains basic movement exercises that help the performer discover a state of "equilibrium" or "freedom" so that performance becomes a reaction to a thought-feeling impulse rather than a matter of proscribed technique.

Vernon, John. *Poetry and the Body.* Urbana: University of Illinois Press, 1979.
> Based largely on R. P. Blackmur's *Language as Gesture,* this study extends the idea that the poetic experience is essentially a kinetic experience activated through the reader's imaginative participation.

II. The Interpretation of Prose

5 Some Aspects of Prose

No difference between man and beast is more important than syntax.

Herbert Read, English Prose Style

In Part I we discussed aspects of analysis that are common to all types of writing. We also showed how interpreters use the knowledge gained through analysis to communicate literature — with both their voices and their bodies. In Part II we are concerned specifically with prose. Parts III and IV deal with drama and poetry, respectively.

It is true that all types of literature have certain elements in common and that the basic principles of analysis and interpretation apply to all types. It is equally true that each literary form imposes special problems and requires various degrees of emphasis on one or more aspects of technique in preparation and presentation. For example, an oral interpreter uses the same basic approach to poetry as to any other type of material. But poetry also demands special attention to condensation, sound patterns, and whatever strictures of stanzaic form, meter, and rhyme the poet has imposed. Drama requires special emphasis on character, time, place, and situation — and on the relationship among these elements that sets up an essential conflict. One also should be aware of the dramatic form, which may be either prose or poetry. Prose, on the other hand, may be primarily nondramatic yet may contain passages calling for attention to character and setting. Thus, it presents problems similar to those found in drama. Or prose may be highly suggestive and come very close to poetry in its use of imagery.

Our division of material under the headings of prose, drama, and poetry, with smaller subdivisions, should be regarded as only a convenience. Our concern is not with literary labels, except insofar as these labels help us to analyze the material. Rather, we are interested in selecting suitable material and in completely understanding each piece of writing we wish to communicate to the listeners. Classification serves only as a starting point for detailed analysis.

It is your responsibility as an interpreter to discover the problems and advantages in each type of literature and then to go beyond this generalization to the specific, individual variations within a particular selection. Regardless of its form or type, each selection should be approached as an individual example. Before we consider various kinds of literature, we shall review some aspects of literary style that are found in all prose writing. Because subsequent chapters will be devoted to drama and poetry, we shall focus here on nondramatic prose.

Style

The word *style* comes from the Latin *stilus*, which simply meant a pointed instrument for writing. Each writer has a different way of using a writing instrument and thus may be thought of as having a distinctive style. At the end of the sixteenth century the word *style* came to mean a manner of writing or speaking.

George Bernard Shaw said, "He who has nothing to assert has no style." It is possible to suggest that style is the assertion of character. It is also the concrete, physical mode of written expression that appears on the page. Style embodies such technical considerations as overall organization of ideas; the steps in development of a central idea, as they are evident in major thought units (stanzas in poetry, acts and scenes in drama, and paragraphs in prose); the syntactical characteristics of the sentences within these major thought units; and choice of words and the interrelationship of words within a sentence. Because interpreters are interested in communicating the written symbols orally, they are concerned with additional aspects of style: the way the sentences can be broken up into speech phrases; the relationship of the sounds of the words as they are combined; and the location of stresses, which are necessary for clarity.

As British novelist Arnold Bennett said, "When a writer conceives an idea he conceives it in a form of words. That form of words is his style. . . ." Thus, one's style is shaped by the kind of person one is, by one's general philosophy of life, and by the culture and age in which one lives. For example, what one person refers to as a "charming old inn" can be a "broken-down dump" to another. Style is dictated by the author's attitudes toward the subject matter and toward the intended audience — the readers. Style is the heart of the intrinsic factor of harmony; it is basic in establishing the identity of the persona in a selection. It helps us to understand a character in drama and narrative prose, and it offers important clues to the handling of descriptive passages. Style is also a mode of performance. The interpreter's goal is to match the style of performance with the style of the writing.

Paragraphs

The first step in examining the style of a selection is to become aware of its general organization. The next step is to discover the organization and arrangement of the elements that make up the whole. In prose this process involves a consideration of the major thought units, the *paragraphs*.

Paragraph structure is important for the interpreter to understand, because each paragraph is a unit in the thought progression.

The length and complexity of the unit, and of the sentences that compose it, reflect both the author's approach to the thought and the pace at which the idea is developed. In general, short, simple sentences and paragraphs indicate a direct approach and suggest immediacy of experience. Long, complicated sentences and paragraphs suggest a more sophisticated and evaluative approach, perhaps an intellectualization of experience or a reflection on past experiences.

Writers indicate degrees of relationship and importance by what they put together in the paragraphs. For instance, several relevant examples of a key idea may appear in one paragraph. Alternatively, each example may have a separate paragraph, thus adding to its individual importance by setting it off from the others. A paragraph is a distinct subdivision of the main thought; it deals with a particular point and terminates only when that point has been developed. It usually has a slight climax of its own, where a logical point or emotional level emerges and prepares the way for others to follow. Paragraphs are large stepping stones to the main climax and the conclusion.

Sentences

The way an author handles the sentences within the paragraphs is of practical concern to the oral interpreter. Remember that your responsibility is to make each segment of the total meaning clear to the audience. In your analysis, you should pay attention to length and grammatical construction as clues to attitude and tone and as guides to the use of the techniques of pause, rate, emphasis, and inflection in your performance.

Take note of elementary syntactical distinctions such as simple, complex, and compound sentences. Also, consider sentence length, position of subordinate elements, order of words, and use of such effects as parallelism and balanced construction. The syntax of a sentence is a way of grouping the words to show their relationship and to suggest degrees of importance. For example, contrast the syntax in these two sentences: "All the marigolds and pinks in the bungalow gardens were bowed to earth with wetness" and "Drenched were the cold fuchsias." In the first sentence, the order is normal and easily leads to the completed thought. We get an extended view of numerous flower beds. In the second sentence, however, "drenched" is given strong emphasis by its uncommon position at the beginning of the sentence, and our focus is on the degree of wetness, which is intensified by "cold." "Drenched" is much wetter than "wetness."

The writer of the following excerpt is describing how he felt when landing his plane after a dangerous and fantastic flight. He is unable to reflect on the experience he has been through and cannot translate it through his intellect into an ordered pattern. The succession of short sentences that combine statements, questions, and an exclamation gives an almost breathless sense of the writer's emotional exhaustion and his inability to put his experience into words:

> Had I been afraid? I couldn't say. I had witnessed a strange sight. What strange sight? I couldn't say. The sky was blue and the sea was white. I felt I ought to tell someone about it since I was back from so far away! But I had no grip on what I had been through.[1]

Longer sentences can be more formal and probably need to be broken down into speech phrases when they are read aloud. Long modifying phrases and clauses (italicized in the examples below) present the interpreter with a special challenge. Try to determine the core of the sentence. Modifiers at the beginning of a sentence prepare readers for the main idea and orient them toward it, and you must build up to the key words of the thought. A sentence whose elements occur out of the normal order so that the meaning is held up until near the very end of the sentence is said to be of *periodic* construction. Because the periodic sentence delays the completion of meaning, it creates suspense. Because it breaks the usual sentence pattern and alters the normal stresses, it can be especially emphatic:

> *Wandering through clear chambers where the general effect made preferences almost as impossible as if they had been shocks, pausing at open doors where vistas were long and bland,* she would, *even if she had not already known,* have discovered for herself that Poynton was the record of a life.[2]

Modifiers in the middle of a sentence interrupt the main flow of the thought, even while explaining some elements within it. The meaning should be sustained, and the thread of the principal idea should be carried from one key word to another over the intervening material. At the same time, the contribution of those subordinate elements to the whole should not be nullified:

> The book in question, *which is at once a lasting contribution to English literature and a mere farrago of pretentious mediocrity,* was published about two months ago.[3]

1. Antoine de Saint Exupéry, *Wind, Sand and Stars.*
2. Henry James, *The Spoils of Poynton.* (Emphasis added.)
3. Virginia Woolf, *The Common Reader.* (Emphasis added.)

Modifiers at the end of a sentence continue the main idea, expanding or qualifying it, although the skeletal frame of the thought is already complete without them:

> I was at incredible pains in cutting down some of the largest trees for oars and masts, *wherein I was, however, much assisted by his Majesty's ship-carpenters, who helped me in smoothing them after I had done the rough work.*[4]

Sentences that contain parallelism and balanced construction provide another challenge for the oral interpreter. Each of the two sentences below logically divides into modifiers and main ideas, and each develops the main idea in a characteristic way. You should keep the parallel or coordinate elements equal in value at the same time you point out the connection or contrast between them. A compound sentence, which consists of two independent clauses connected by a conjunction, is an elementary example of syntactical parallelism. The clauses are related in grammatical construction because the ideas are closely connected and have equal value. The connective *and* (or sometimes a semicolon) is the signpost most often used for pointing out coordinations, as it does between parts of a compound subject or predicate. The parallelism may be a balanced construction, in which the parts are quite evenly set up against each other:

> No man is an island, entire of itself; every man is a piece of the continent, a part of the main.[5]

The parallelism here is easily demonstrated by lining up the parts:

| No man | is an island, | entire of itself; |
| every man | is a piece of the continent, | a part of the main. |

The parallelism also may be a series of elaborately wrought analogies and antitheses that are reflected in the form in which the sentence is cast, as in this example from Shakespeare's *Henry IV, Part I:*

> Harry, I do not only marvel where thou spendest thy time, but also how thou art accompanied; for though the camomile, the more it is trodden on the faster it grows, yet youth the more it is wasted the sooner it wears.

4. Jonathan Swift, *Gulliver's Travels.* (Emphasis added.)
5. John Donne, *Devotions, XVII.*

This sentence can be represented as follows:

Harry, I do	not only	marvel	where thou spendest thy time,
	but also		how thou art accompanied;
		for though	the camomile,
			the more it is trodden on
			the faster it grows,
	yet	youth	
			the more it is wasted
			the sooner it wears.

The important thing to remember is that at the syntactical level, parallelisms indicate parts of a sentence that are equal in value, although they may not be equal in length or number of syllables. The ideas balance each other and contribute to each other.

Too many sentences of similar construction or similar length can result in a monotonous style that fails to hold the reader's attention. Some textbooks fall victim to this error. Skillful writers vary both the length and structure of sentences and hold their readers' sustained attention by subtle shifts of emphasis and pattern. For instance, an uphill climb through three or four rather lengthy and difficult sentences may be broken by a short sentence, which serves as a plateau on which one can catch one's breath and reorient oneself to the view. Although variety and rhythm in style are controlled by the writer, you should be aware of stylistic changes in pace and should use them in holding the audience's attention and in emphasizing shifts in tone.

Speech Phrases

As we mentioned before, you probably need to break long, grammatically complex sentences into speech phrases when you read the material aloud. In this way you can ensure that the relationship of the clauses and phrases will be clear.

Speech phrases are often more important to the interpreter than to the writer. The relative lengths of units within the sentence as well as the location of stresses become integral parts of the sound pattern as the interpreter uses them. The division of a sentence into speech phrases is dictated by its punctuation and grammatical structure and by the need to make mood and idea clear to an audience.

Punctuation is the first guide, even though it is meant for the eye rather than the ear. A comma, for example, prevents the eye from running ahead and mistaking the sense of the sentence, but in oral reading a comma does not always demand a pause. A change of the pitch, tempo, or volume of your voice can often serve the same purpose less obtrusively than a pause.

Important clues are also given by semicolons, colons, parentheses, and dashes. A semicolon marks a turn of the thought or a definite separation between two aspects of the same thought, and it usually requires a slight pause to make the relationship clear to the listeners. Parentheses and dashes, in pairs, also mark off distinct speech phrases, which are often interpolative ideas across which the main thought of the sentence should be carried. (Long interpolations, of course, need to be further subdivided for convenience and clarity when reading aloud.) A single dash, or a colon, often marks the pause that occurs just before a summing-up and implies a reference to some previous portion of the sentence.

Because punctuation is inserted as a visual aid in silent reading, unfortunately it does not serve as an infallible or complete guide to follow when establishing speech phrases. In fact, punctuation alone is often inadequate for aural comprehension, and you may need to insert slight pauses for clarity. It is often necessary to use pauses to emphasize similar or contrasting ideas, as in the following example:

> The same cartoon humor that shows goats munching tin cans depicts ostriches swallowing alarm clocks, monkey wrenches, and cylinder heads.[6]

Although the punctuation is correct in this sentence, a pause between "cans" and "depicts" helps to balance the parallel ideas when the sentence is read aloud. The following single-sentence paragraph gives an even better example of the problem:

> There is an amusing belief among many country boys, for instance, that an owl has to turn his head to watch you and must watch you if you are near him, so that if you will only walk completely around him he will wring his own neck.[7]

If this sentence were read aloud without a pause or any attention to the author's punctuation, it would quickly lose an audience in a maze of clauses, and it would convey little of the idea intended. When it is read aloud, with each mark of punctuation reflected in a change of pitch, pace, or volume, the sentence becomes much clearer. The punctuation, however, does not take care of the parallel values in "that an owl has to turn his head to watch you and must watch you if you are near him," or of the suspension of thought from "so that" to "he will wring his own neck." Therefore, you need to break down these long units into shorter speech phrases. Be careful, of course, not to destroy the relationship between the parts and the whole.

6. Bergen Evans, *The Natural History of Nonsense.*

7. Ibid.

Balancing Sentences

Some sentences may seem much too long to sustain your audience's attention. The following two sentences (a paragraph from Lillian Hellman's *Pentimento,* a memoir in which she describes the life of her cousin Bethe after her arrival in New Orleans) are good examples:

> Bethe for a short time lived in the modest house on Prytania Street, sleeping on a cot in the dining room, rising at five o'clock to carry it to the back porch, to be the first to heat the water, to make the coffee, to roll and bake the German breakfast rolls that nobody liked. Then, to save the carfare, she walked the long distance to the end of Canal Street, where she carried shoe box stacks back and forth all day, for the German merchant who ran a mean store for sailors off the wharves.

Such sentences understandably cause anxiety; after all, there are a lot of *words* there. Take courage! Every sentence has a fulcrum, or balancing point. Recall our discussion of fulcrums in Chapter 2 and our discussion of speech phrases earlier in this chapter. Paragraphs, stanzas, poems, stories, and now sentences have fulcrums. At this point the action and language of the story, play, or poem pivot or balance. Sentences have their own point of balance, where the weight of the words in the first segment roughly equals the weight of the words in the second segment. Remember, there need not be exactly the same number of words or syllables in both components. As you know, one large adult can balance five or six small children on a seesaw. But the weight of sense in the two parts of a sentence should be equal.

In the first of these sentences, then, where would you place the fulcrum? A case can be made for one or two other places, but perhaps the most even balance for this sentence occurs if the fulcrum is placed after "Prytania Street." Thus, the first half of the sentence concerns Bethe's first weeks in New Orleans: "Bethe for a short time lived in the modest house on Prytania Street." The second half of the sentence describes Bethe's life in the house as a succession of activities: "sleeping on a cot in the dining room, rising at five o'clock to carry it to the back porch, to be the first to heat the water, to make the coffee, to roll and bake the German breakfast rolls that nobody liked."

If you consider these parts equal in substance (although they are unequal in numbers of syllables or the time they take to say), you realize that your performance must demonstrate their relationship in a vocal and physical way. We have to see and hear that, to Bethe, living in the house means completing all these tasks — and that's even before leaving for work! If you make each of the tasks in the second part more difficult or onerous because it follows and precedes its neighbors, the audience can have a fuller idea of what Bethe's life was like. You and they will understand why Hellman (who could also write very effective short sentences) chose to make this one so long.

Now consider the second sentence. This sentence, which describes a typical work day for the immigrant woman, has a much more typical structure than the first sentence. Where does the sentence logically and substantively divide? While some might place the fulcrum after "Then" (although as a critical and performance decision it seems eccentric), it is better to place the fulcrum after "Canal Street," nicely paralleling the fulcrum of the prior sentence. One part of the sentence then describes how Bethe got to work, and the other part tells what she did there. Thus the fulcrum clarifies the arrangement of Bethe's day and helps us see clearly the progress and purpose of the sentence.

Taken together, these two long sentences suggest the multitude of activity and the continual pressure Bethe found in New Orleans. If you perform them carefully, the audience, too, can become awed by Bethe's endurance.

Choice of Words

Any discussion of words as an aspect of style to some extent overlaps our earlier discussion of words as an aspect of content, for style and content are obviously inseparable. Nevertheless, the writer's choice of words is a vital part of style and deserves special attention.

We have already made a distinction between the denotations and the connotations of words. Now we should remind ourselves of another important aspect of literary style — the writer's use of allusions, similes, and metaphors. These three types of figures of speech are all means of comparing one thing to another; thus, they are instruments of connotative meaning. They are used in all types of writing, of course, but they are basic to description. They contribute primarily to harmony by intensifying theme or underscoring attitude. This is certainly the function of the simile in Welty's "June Recital" (the studio "decorated like the inside of a candy box") that sets the tone for the excerpt (reprinted at the end of this chapter).

The length of words is a practical concern for one who is reading aloud, but from the point of view of style, what is important is whether words are formal, informal, or even colloquial and whether they are unusual words or words that are common in everyday speech. In any case, the words should be evaluated in terms of the prevailing tone of the selection. The sentence from Woolf's *The Common Reader* that appeared earlier in this chapter is a delightful example of how word choice can shift within a single sentence to underscore attitude. Woolf begins with the straightforward, factual

"The book in question." This is also the tone of the closing phrase. In the middle of the sentence, however, is the almost classic academic reference to "a lasting contribution to English literature" and the cutting, deliberately elaborate "mere farrago of pretentious mediocrity." It is amusing to know that *farrago* means a hodgepodge and comes from a Latin word meaning mixed fodder for cattle. The author has given a deadly criticism indeed! Although it will not always be necessary for you to delve into the origins and derivations of words, you should be prepared to do so if this would be helpful in bringing out the complete meaning of a sentence.

Tone Color

The sounds of the words an author has chosen are especially important for interpreters, since one of their tasks is to translate the written symbols into sound symbols for their listeners. Writers who are concerned with appealing to the senses and emotions of their readers carefully establish harmony between what they are describing and the sounds of the words with which they choose to describe it. Of course it is the words, not the separate sounds, that carry the meaning; and it is the connotations of the words that influence the interpreter's pace, vocal quality, and all the rest of the elements of his or her vocal technique. There are, for instance, more factors affecting the way one would say *sleep, slap, slip,* and *slop* than merely the difference in the vowels. Nevertheless, certain combinations of sounds produce articulation problems that slow the pace or give a sharpness to separate words, while other combinations lend themselves to smooth linking and help to produce a flowing effect. The combination of sounds of vowels and consonants to achieve a particular effect is called *tone color*.

Read the following pair of examples aloud several times, fully realizing the imagery.

> The world was more wintry than he had expected. Hoarfrost lay white over the hard refrozen edges of things — the thatch that roofed the hovels, the ridges of mud, and the stones and rubbish in the lane.[8]

> The weather was airy and light; the stars came nightly into their appointed places; there were rills and cresses and kindling sticks, and fish for the catching in some of the streams.[9]

Now listen to how the sounds of the words in combination enhance and reinforce that imagery — and vice versa. There is a strong

8. Gladys Schmitt, *The Godforgotten* (New York: Harcourt Brace Jovanovich, Inc., 1972), p. 250.

9. Ibid., p. 301.

contrast in the syntactical structure of the two quotations that helps to set up a harmonious rhythm in each. These things are important when a skilled interpreter handles these brief descriptions of weather. They were put there by the author for you to use. Enjoy them!

Tone color is part of a writer's style: the sounds of words when they are put together influence not only the choice of words but also the way words are arranged in a sentence and, ultimately, the rhythm of the entire selection. It is your responsibility to make full use of tone color to help support the author's imagery. Moreover, tone color plays an important part in building empathy, since it underscores connotation and enriches suggestion. We shall return to a consideration of tone color in Chapter 9 when we discuss the sound patterns of poetry.

Prose Rhythm

Another important guide for the interpreter is the rhythm of a prose selection. All well-written prose has *rhythm* — not the formal, patterned rhythm of poetry, but a controlled flow of words that makes relationships clear and causes emphasis to fall on the important words.

We have already mentioned rhythm of content, which is established by the organization of the progression of thoughts and emotions. This type of rhythm depends on the placement of key words and phrases and of the major and minor climaxes, both logical and emotional, throughout the entire selection.

There is also a rhythm in *structure* that becomes evident when prose is read aloud. This prose rhythm is established by the length and grammatical construction of the sentences and speech phrases, and by the position of the stresses. As you group words into thought units and speech phrases, separating them with pauses of varying duration, you are creating cadences. A *cadence* is a flow of sound. Words that are grouped together form a flow of sound. A pause interrupts this flow, whether it is a terminal pause at the end of a sentence or a very brief pause to set off a speech phrase. Thus, length and frequency of pauses also become part of prose rhythm.

The rate at which the flows of sound are uttered and the number of syllables within the flows affect the rhythm pattern. A mechanical measurement of the cadences in prose usually is not necessary, although it may prove interesting and helpful. The interpreter whose ear is trained is aware of the existence and contribution of cadences.

The element of *stress* in prose results from a number of factors: the demands of proper pronunciation, the need for clarity, the development of contrast, or the combining of particular sounds. The sentences from *Pentimento* quoted earlier illustrate this. The use of numerous one-syllable words in sequence, for instance, may produce a sharp staccato rhythm, especially if the content is forceful in meaning and if the cadences established by the length of sentences and speech phrases are short. The brief excerpt from *Wind, Sand and Stars* near the beginning of this chapter provides an interesting illustration of this type of cadence.

A sensitive and attentive reader usually hears the various rhythmic devices of a prose selection without needing to count syllables or mark speech phrases and stresses. We have given detailed attention here to prose rhythm to emphasize the rhythmic basis in effective prose and to encourage you to use all of its elements as part of the aesthetic entirety that you will share with your audience.

Description

The form that writing takes may be classified roughly as dialogue, narration, or description. These types are not mutually exclusive. Within the dialogue that makes up a play, characters often sketch in needed background about themselves or about past events. Sometimes they use description as well. Poetry may be purely narrative, purely descriptive, or a combination of the two forms. Most narratives, whether poetry or prose, contain dialogue and revealing sections of description. It is important to be aware of the purpose that is served by such blending of the three forms. We shall discuss narration and dialogue more thoroughly in Chapters 6, 7, and 8 and concentrate here on description.

Descriptive writing appeals to the senses and explores the sensory qualities of people, places, things, and events. It engages us physically as well as emotionally, because it tells us how something looks, sounds, smells, or tastes. It may describe texture or pressure, heat or cold. It may show movement, energy, or light or may even convey a sense of bulkiness or weightlessness. In its rich appeals to the senses, descriptive writing is important in evoking empathic response. Interpreters should take care to use descriptive passages to ensure vividness and clarity and to help control and enrich suggestion.

When you examine a unit of descriptive writing, your first response will probably be subjective, and you will make associations from your own experience. This response should be followed by an objective analysis that enables you to communicate the experience that exists *within* the literature. Suppose, for example, that the subject is a storm at sea. You might never have known such an experience, and as you imagine it you know you would be terrified. The author, however, finds the storm exhilarating. Thus, you need to substitute the memory of another experience — one that had an exhilarating effect on you — in order to convey the emotion in the writing. Bring into your rehearsal the clues that the author has given you about persona and locus, as well as whatever elements of style are helpful. It is your task as an interpretative artist to embody the emotional experience within the framework of the writing.

In giving detailed consideration to each descriptive image, it is important to keep in mind the sense of the entire thought unit. Consider, for instance, the thermal implications of the word *hot*. When the word is used in a phrase like "hot bath after a cold walk," one has a natural tendency to let the accompanying suggestion of relaxation show in one's muscles, in the slower tempo of the words, and in a more relaxed vocal tone. If, on the other hand, the word is used in the context of "Ouch! That water is hot!" your muscles will become tense, the tempo of the words will quicken, and the force and tension of your voice will increase. In short, the image-bearing word or phrase should always be combined with the whole unit of thought.

Response to imagery has a definite effect on your muscle tone and consequently on the audience's empathic and emotional response. This is particularly true in the case of appeals to motor responses, but the attendant emotional associations the author has achieved through references to sights, sounds, tastes, and smells also make an empathic contribution.

After you have worked out the description through the various images, the next step is to consider what aspects of the imagery contribute most to the total context of the selection. How can you express particular images in such a way that they are a unifying force, and not a catalogue of separate items? In other words, which sense appeals contribute to unity and harmony, and which add variety and contrast within that unity? When the images are considered in relation to the whole, it is clear that some contribute more than others and should be stressed; those that provide variety within this unity may be played down.

Remember, seeing is believing. Your audience must rely on you to see what they are unable to see. Your description is their only means of understanding what the author wants them to see. Until you see it clearly, no audience will be able to see it reflected in your voice and body. The old elocutionists used to say, "Impression before expression." *See* what you are describing before telling your audience about it. Until and unless you do, the audience loses.

You may be tempted to overemphasize some especially vivid images, but you should remember that too much stress on descriptive detail may destroy the essential unity of the material. In your performance you should use the descriptive elements in the same way that you use every other aspect of content and form — subtly and unobtrusively. These elements are only part of the whole, and their importance is dictated by the author's larger purpose. You should always remember that the final step in preparation is to put the material back together so that all parts are coordinated. The final test of your performance is its honesty and the thoroughness of communication with your audience.

Types of Prose

Within the broad range of types of prose writing, there are numerous subdivisions that frequently overlap but that differ according to the author's purpose. We shall look briefly at some of these types as they relate to interpretation.

Factual Prose

The interpreter is not likely to be working extensively with strictly factual prose. Obviously, you would seldom choose to do a performance from an encyclopedia or a scientific work. Nevertheless, you may encounter passages or entire units in an essay that are technically factual and out of which the personal reflections of the author develop.

Factual prose, in the strictest definition of the term, is writing in which the author gives verifiable information. It states that something is so. The writer's personal comments are kept at a minimum. Unadulterated examples of this type of writing are probably found only in books on science and mathematics, where one is told, for instance, that "in an isosceles triangle the angles opposite the equal sides are themselves equal," or in an encyclopedia, which states on good authority that John Milton was born in England in 1608 and died in 1674. Objective journalistic reporting also may be considered factual when it limits itself to the simple formula of "who, where, when, what," and possibly "why."

In strictly factual material, the informative content and the logical development are of primary importance. There is no emotional content, since the author is concerned with fact, not response to fact. It is, of course, possible for a fact to be so startling or shocking that even the unadorned statement arouses an emotional response in the reader. However, any arousal of emotion is due to subjective conclusions and associations on the part of the reader. It does not lie in the fact or in the writer's purpose. The content of factual writing depends for effectiveness on authoritative statements, logical progression of proofs, and exact denotation of the words. In short, factual prose informs, defines, and explains. Facts need not be "sold" — only established. Anything that is demonstrated as true (and a fact is defined as something that is true) is accepted by the rational mind.

The interpreter is most likely to deal with prose that is factual in the sense that it makes use of facts to support or explain a thesis — that is, prose in which the author is concerned with the implication or interpretation of the facts. Sometimes the facts provide a touch of humor or satire; in other cases, the implied comment of the author is the desired end, and the factual content is merely a means of achieving that end. In other words, the presentation of the facts themselves may be the basic purpose of the writing, or the facts may merely be the framework for an expression of attitude. It is the interpreter's responsibility to discover how the author uses the information and to make sure that this same purpose is achieved when the material is communicated to the audience.

The Personal Essay

Personal essays offer a wide variety of material to interest an audience. Their content ranges from broad humor to philosophy, politics, and religion. Because they have a highly personal point of view, persona and locus are very important. The writer's personality and values are reflected in the facts and concrete objects that have been selected to set up associations. This is especially true in accounts of travel and in autobiographical sketches. The associations and connotations lead readers and listeners beyond the facts and the denotations of words and phrases.

For example, Jacques Barzun describes a certain mathematics teacher by saying, "He would put the chalk to his lips, make a noise like a straining gear box, and write out the correct result." We have no idea what the man looks like, and we do not need to. The depiction of his characteristic gesture of putting chalk to his lips calls forth in us a mental picture of bemused, pedantic concentration. The "noise like a straining gear box" suggests that he is more of a machine than a man, and when the gears start to move, out comes the answer!

Often, especially in humorous essays, an author chooses to write in the first person, whether or not the selection is in fact autobiographical. Certainly we are not expected to believe that James Thurber, for instance, actually experienced all the incidents he recorded in the first person! We are really not so concerned about the actual physical identity of the speaker as we are with the author's wit and sense of the ridiculous that has either exaggerated or played down the details of the incidents and ordered them for our enjoyment. We are often concerned with the age, sex, or social position of the speaker; but we care about these details as they relate to the speaker's situation and to the comments the author makes by implication or direct statement.

Sometimes essayists choose topics that seem impossible for a general audience. Not many people are vitally concerned about "the movement of water through aqueducts and siphons and pumps and forebays and afterbays and weirs and drains," but the novelist and essayist Joan Didion cares deeply about these topics. In "Holy Water" she describes a visit to the California State Water Projects Operations Control Center. For such a visit to mean something other than an odd place for an eccentric to visit, she must make her interest in water and drought have a broader appeal. The best personal essays make clear that what might seem like a peculiar individual concern is in fact remarkably close to a concern we all share — another aspect of the touchstones we mentioned in Chapter 1. Didion, in the first sentence of her essay, recognizes the problem her topic presents. "Some of us who live in arid parts of the world think about water with a reverence others might find excessive." Later, she states, "Not many people I know carry their end of the conversation when I want to talk about water deliveries . . ." But when, in the penultimate paragraph of the essay, she says, "Water is important to people who do not have it, and the same is true of control," we realize that she has, in fact, been talking about something that involves all of us. Needless to say it takes great skill on her part to keep us interested in the topic until we get to that conclusion, but such indirection is typical of one style of personal essay and permits the audience to become involved in a special way in the discovery of something personal about themselves.

A writer uses references for their universal appeal. References are also rooted in an author's background and experiences. They are selected very carefully. Scrutinize all expressions and references that seem to carry a comment, an evaluation, or a judgment. By understanding what all of the words mean and suggest, in themselves and in the total context, you can come to an understanding of who the author is and what the author is saying. Then you will be able to convey that attitude to an audience.

Journals, Diaries, Letters, Testimony, and Paraliterature

Journals and diaries often make excellent selections for performance, because they provide intimate glimpses into special moments in the lives of interesting personalities. Ostensibly, most diaries are written for the writer's private pleasure. They are likely to be less formal than essays, which are intended for public consumption. The organization of diaries often is dictated by highly subjective associations. A careful examination of the elements of style helps you to learn about the writer's personality and reveals attitudes and degrees of emotional involvement. When working with so personal a revelation as a diary or journal, it is important to find out as much as possible about the writer's life and times, since the motivation for recording certain details probably grew directly out of his or her relationship to this environment and the people in it.

One may say that in their writing diarists are speaking to themselves in their own voices. But there is an element of danger in this idea. You must have sufficient projection, both psychological and vocal, to hold your audience's attention and interest. One of the ways to achieve this delicate balance between private thoughts and public expression of them is to allow the writer to "think aloud" while you put thoughts in order or reread them aloud. This procedure helps you to remain actively engaged in organizing and expressing the entire entry.

In recent years a wealth of correspondence has been published. Much of the appeal of letters is undoubtedly the same as that of diaries and journals. Letters, however, present an added problem for the interpreter.

First, you need to distinguish whether they are public or private letters. Public letters may be handled very much as you would approach an oration or a public address. They are usually didactic, having been designed to persuade a large group of listeners or readers to a course of action or to the acceptance of an idea. The writer has selected details that have strong universal appeal and refer to matters with which the intended audience is easily familiar. The letter of St. Paul at the end of this chapter is an excellent example of a public letter; it is particularly interesting to examine for word choice and organization. Since the writer of a public letter is speaking to a specific audience, you may find it helpful to imagine that this particular audience and your own audience are identical. This approach helps to achieve directness. You may address your listeners in the person of the writer or, more probably, in the person of someone selected to present the letter to the intended audience.

Private letters are likely to involve a complex relationship between writer and recipient, and you need to find out as much as possible about both parties. The letter you are reading may be the reply to a letter received earlier by the writer; consequently, a chain of references may have to be investigated. The method of organization and the style of writing reflect both the purpose of the letter and the relationship between the writer and the person to whom the letter is addressed.

Sometimes you might be more interested in the reaction of the recipient than you are in the writer. In this case you might choose to read the letter as if you are the one to whom it is addressed. If this seems the more desirable approach, you must cope with a twofold problem: how to use the writer's style effectively and, at the same time, how to suggest the reaction of another person. Obviously, this approach is more useful when the relationship between the two people is clearly drawn or is so well known that the response is predictable. Letters are often used in this way within a play or narrative where the characters have been well established. The letter becomes virtually a part of the plot and motivation.

It is neither necessary nor desirable to try to re-create visually in performance the act of writing or the writer's physical details or immediate surroundings. Any strong suggestion of "pen-in-hand" action would slow down your presentation of the selection or strain the audience's willingness to believe. The interpreter's real concern is not how fast the writer wrote or with which hand or what type of pen. Rather, you should concentrate on what was written.

Increasingly, interpreters have found wonderful material for performance in collections of oral histories, testimony, depositions, and oral records, which are sometimes grouped under the general heading "paraliterature." This word suggests that in preparing such material an editor's skill is at least as important as the speaker's. But because the words began as speech, they carry with them an immediacy and a conviction that can be startling. In the past two decades, perhaps no one more that Studs Terkel has developed the art of oral history. In such works as *Hard Times, Division Street, Working,* and *The Good War,* Terkel, with his tape recorder, speaks with people from every level of society and in every possible occupation. He asks them to tell him what they have learned or discovered about their own lives, a special period, or an event. Then, with the skill of an artist, he splices together their words to make powerfully funny or poignant or telling testimony to the human condition. We see people whom we may easily know expressing something both unique and timeless. See "Terry Pickens" at the end of this chapter.

Terkel is not the only source for such materials. Oral history projects frequently flourish where archives are housed and can often be the source of impressive and moving material for performance. At the end of this chapter, for example, are selections in which two soldiers in the Revolutionary War tell what they discovered about themselves from fighting. Sometimes court records provide exciting exchanges between litigants in important cases; the *Congressional Record* will offer, on occasion, impressive speeches and exchanges between debating members of Congress. And do not neglect the various collections of memorabilia — letters, notes, journal entries, and reminiscences — that are assembled to mark historic events or to portray a locale or historic period. With care in selecting and attention to editing, such prose works can give vivid and powerful glimpses of the personalities who shaped our lives, either in great office or in unrecognized occupations. Because such material records the immediate voices of people struggling to make themselves understood, their communicative effectiveness and power are greatly enhanced. These records are too rich a source for interpreters to overlook.

Selections for Analysis and Oral Interpretation

In addition to the following excerpts, you will find some interesting descriptive passages in the selections in earlier chapters and within the narratives in Chapter 6.

The style here is as packed as the recital room. Pay particular attention to the shift in imagery as you reach the last paragraph.

FROM *June Recital*
EUDORA WELTY

The night of the recital was always clear and hot; everyone came. The prospective audience turned out in full oppression.

In the studio decorated like the inside of a candy box, with "material" scalloping the mantel shelf and doilies placed under every movable object, now thus made immovable, with streamers of white ribbons and nosegays of pink and white Maman Cochet roses and the last MacLain sweetpeas dividing and re-dividing the room, it was as hot as fire. No matter that this was the first night of June; no electric fans were to whir around while music played. The metronome, ceremoniously closed, stood on the piano like a vase. There was no piece of music anywhere in sight.

When the first unreasoning hush — there was the usual series — fell over the audience, the room seemed to shake with the agitation of palmetto and feather fans alone, plus the occasional involuntary tick of the metronome within its doors. There was the mixture together of agitation and decoration which could make every little forthcoming child turn pale with a kind of ultimate dizziness. Whoever might look up at the ceiling for surcease would be floundered within a paper design stemming out of the chandelier, as complicated and as unavailing as a cut-out paper snowflake.

Now Miss Eckhart came into the room all changed, with her dark hair pulled low on her brow, and gestured for silence. She was wear-

ing her recital dress which made her look larger and closer-to than she looked at any other times. It was an old dress: Miss Eckhart disregarded her own rules. People would forget that dress between times and then she would come out in it again, the untidy folds not quite spotlessly clean, gathered about her bosom and falling heavy as a coat to the sides; it was tawny crepe-back satin. There was a bodice of browning lace. It was as rich and hot and deep-looking as a furskin. The unexpected creamy flesh on her upper arms gave her a look of emerging from it.

Miss Eckhart, achieving silence, stood in the shadowy spot directly under the chandelier. Her feet, white-shod, shod by Mr. Sissum for good, rested in the chalk circle previously marked on the floor and now, she believed, perfectly erased. One hand, with its countable little muscles so hard and ready, its stained, blue nails, went to the other hand and they folded quite still, holding nothing, until they lost their force by lying on her breast and made a funny little house with peaks and gables. Standing near the piano but not near enough to help, she presided but not with her whole heart on guard against disaster; while disaster was what remained on the minds of the little girls. Starting with the youngest, she called them out.

So they played, and except Virgie, all played their worst. They shocked themselves. Parnell Moody burst into tears on schedule. But Miss Eckhart never seemed to notice or to care. How forgetful she seemed at exactly the moments she should have been agonized! You expected the whip, almost, for forgetting to repeat before the second ending, or for failing to count ten before you came around the curtain at all; and instead you received a strange smile. It was as though Miss Eckhart, at the last, were grateful to you for *anything*.

▌ Did you take the time to allow your narrator to experience each image without being rushed?
▌ How hot was the room?

In the following selection, Judith Martin offers some advice to graduating seniors. Her sentence structure, carefully chosen words, and elaborate parallels create a clear sense of personality. Remember, "proper" does not have to mean "stuffy."

FROM *Miss Manners'*® *Guide to Excruciatingly Correct Behavior*

JUDITH MARTIN

Graduations

Graduations are the perfect preparation for the laughable institution known on such occasions as Real Life or The World Out There. If you can sit quietly in the sun for two hours, listening to irrelevant platitudes with a respectful look on your face, and can survive with dignity the social mixture of your progenitors with your peers, life out there should hold no further terrors.

It is a mistake to think that graduations are held for the benefit of graduates, who therefore should be able to enjoy the celebrations as they choose or even boycott them. Graduations are held to mark the end of the sufferings of people who have been paying staggering tuition bills, nagging about homework until their own lives have no longer been worth living, or despairing that the efforts of their ancestors to achieve a modicum of civilization have been lost under their supervision.

The relief of these people on finding that one of society's most obvious goals has been achieved often borders on the hysterical.

Otherwise sensible and reserved parents will attempt to involve their graduating children in odd forms of exhibitionist behavior, and encourage younger siblings to do the same. They will create havoc by taking pictures at every possible moment, and when they are unable to accost strangers to find outlets for bragging, they will exchange such remarks with each other in unnaturally loud voices.

All this must be endured with grace by indulgent graduates. Not looking ashamed of one's parents, no matter where they demand to be shown, whom they insist on meeting, and what they cannot be prevented from saying, is a *rite de passage* certifying the maturity of the graduate.

He or she is not, however, permitted any unconventional behavior. Blue jeans that can be seen below academic robes, protest demonstrations against the school or any of its invited speakers, or any behavior — other than accepting prizes — that distinguishes one graduate from another cannot be tolerated. The graduation ceremony, in all its mesmerizing monotony, was carefully designed to fulfill the fantasies of families, not to enable the graduate to express his independence.

Even the allegedly private aspects, the proms and the parties, carry their family obligations. If you pose prettily beforehand and fabricate a comforting report afterward, it is possible that you and your peers will be allowed a small amount of private pleasure in between.

Satisfying one's family by going along with all their graduation expectations, no matter how silly or embarrassing, is not the graduate's only obligation. He or she also owes something to the educational institution, and that institution owes something to its older alumni — or if it doesn't, it isn't from lack of trying.

Alumni who are using graduations as the setting for their reunions are not always raucous and drunk. However, they are always caught in a mysterious time warp that leads to behavior that can be just as offensive.

Graduating seniors must listen with patient smiles to the questions and comments of alumni who have discovered that the school no longer has curfews, single-sex dormitories, or four years of required Biblical studies. That look will serve them well on job interviews and other such exasperating situations held Out There.

▌ Breath control is crucial to the sense of confidence this passage demands. Did you find yourself rushing? When? Why?

Moses Hall and Garret Watts were foot soldiers in the Revolutionary War. In the following selections they recount their wartime experiences for a federal pension board many years after the events had occurred. Note carefully how vivid these recollections are; be sure to make your readers feel their impact.

Moses Hall served in a troop that had just defeated a detachment of British soldiers and mercenaries (Tories).

FROM *The Revolution Remembered*

JOHN C. DANN, EDITOR

Moses Hall

The evening after our battle with the Tories, we having a considerable number of prisoners, I recollect a scene which made a lasting impression upon my mind. I was invited by some of my comrades to go and see some of the prisoners. We went to where six were standing together. Some discussion taking place, I heard some of our men cry out, "Remember Buford," and the prisoners were immediately hewed to pieces with broadswords. At first I bore the scene without any emotion, but upon a moment's reflection, I felt such horror as I never did before nor have since, and, returning to my quarters and throwing myself upon my blanket, I contemplated the cruelties of war until overcome and unmanned by a distressing gloom from which I was not relieved until commencing our march next morning before day by moonlight. I came to Tarleton's camp, which he had just abandoned leaving lively rail fires. Being on the left of the road as we marched along, I discovered lying upon the ground something with appearance of a man. Upon approaching him, he proved to be a youth about sixteen who, having come out to view the British through curiosity, for fear he might give information to our troops, they had run him through with a bayonet and left him for dead. Though able to speak, he was mortally wounded. The sight of this unoffending boy, butchered rather than be encumbered in the [illegible] on the march, I assume, relieved me of my distressful feelings for the slaughter of the Tories, and I desired nothing so much as the opportunity of participating in their destruction.

▌ What difficulties did your Hall undergo in retelling his story? Why? How did your audience notice this in your performance?

Garret Watts served in the Continental army under the generals de Kalb and Dickson; he recalls a vivid moment from a battle with British forces under Lord Cornwallis.

Garret Watts

The two armies came near each other at Sutton's about twelve or one o'clock in the night (this was in the year 1780). The pickets fired several rounds before day. I well remember everything that occurred the next morning: I remember that I was among the nearest to the enemy; that a man named John Summers was my file leader; that we had orders to wait for the word to commence firing; that the militia were in front and in a feeble condition at that time. They were fatigued. The weather was warm excessively. They had been fed a short time previously on molasses entirely. I can state on oath that I believe my gun was the first gun fired, notwithstanding the orders, for we were close to the enemy, who appeared to maneuver in contempt of us, and I fired without thinking except that I might prevent the man opposite from killing me. The discharge and loud roar soon became general from one end of the lines to the other. Amongst other things, I confess I was amongst the first that fled. The cause of that I cannot tell, except that everyone I saw was about to do the same. It was instantaneous. There was no effort to rally, no encouragement to fight. Officers and men joined in the flight. I threw away my gun, and, reflecting I might be punished for being found without arms, I picked up a drum, which gave forth such sounds when touched by the twigs I cast it away. When we had gone, we heard the roar of guns still, but we knew not why. Had we known, we might have returned. It was that portion of the army commanded by de Kalb fighting still. De Kalb was killed. General Dickson was wounded in the neck and a great many killed and wounded even on the first firing. After this defeat, many of the dispersed troops proceeded to Hillsboro in North Carolina. I obtained a furlough from General Dickson and had permission to return home a short time. This last tour was for the space of three months and truly laborious.

▌ How did your body behave when Watts admitted he was a deserter?

There is remarkable unity of focus in this selection. Notice how the descriptive details and the progress of time work together. The sentence structure is characteristic of Faulkner's style. Close attention to imagery and the relationship of descriptive words to each other will help untangle it.

FROM *Dry September*

WILLIAM FAULKNER

She was thirty-eight or thirty-nine. She lived in a small frame house with her invalid mother and a thin, sallow, unflagging aunt, where each morning between ten and eleven she would appear on the porch in a lace-trimmed boudoir cap, to sit swinging in the porch swing until noon. After dinner she lay down for a while, until the afternoon began to cool. Then, in one of the three or four new voile dresses which she had each summer, she would go downtown to spend the afternoon in the stores with the other ladies, where they would handle the goods and haggle over the prices in cold, immediate voices, without any intention of buying.

She was of comfortable people — not the best in Jefferson, but good people enough — and she was still on the slender side of ordinary looking, with a bright, faintly haggard manner and dress. When she was young she had had a slender, nervous body and a sort of hard vivacity which enabled her for a time to ride upon the crest of the town's social life as exemplified by the high school party and church social period of her contemporaries while still children enough to be unclassconscious.

She was the last to realize that she was losing ground; that those among whom she had been a little brighter and louder flame than any other were beginning to learn the pleasure of snobbery — male — and retaliation — female. That was when her face began to wear that bright, haggard look. She still carried it to parties on shadowy porticoes and summer lawns, like a mask or a flag, with that bafflement of furious repudiation of truth in her eyes. One evening at a party she heard a boy and two girls, all schoolmates, talking. She never accepted another invitation.

She watched the girls with whom she had grown up as they married and got homes and children, but no man ever called on her steadily until the children of the other girls had been calling her "aunty" for several years, the while their mothers told them in bright voices about how popular Aunt Minnie had been as a girl. Then the town began to see her driving on Sunday afternoons with the cashier in the bank. He was a widower of about forty — a high-colored man, smelling always faintly of the barber shop or of whisky. He owned the first automobile in town, a red runabout; Minnie had the first

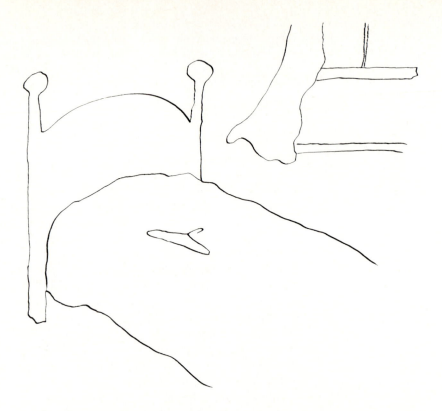

motoring bonnet and veil the town ever saw. Then the town began
to say: "Poor Minnie." "But she is old enough to take care of herself,"
others said. That was when she began to ask her old schoolmates
that their children call her "cousin" instead of "aunty."

It was twelve years now since she had been relegated into adul-
tery by public opinion, and eight years since the cashier had gone to
a Memphis bank, returning for one day each Christmas, which he
spent at an annual bachelors' party at a hunting club on the river.
From behind their curtains the neighbors would see the party pass,
and during the over-the-way Christmas day visiting they would tell
her about him, about how well he looked, and how they heard that
he was prospering in the city, watching with bright, secret eyes her
haggard, bright face. Usually by that hour there would be the scent
of whisky on her breath. It was supplied her by a youth, a clerk at
the soda fountain: "Sure; I buy it for the old gal. I reckon she's entitled
to a little fun."

Her mother kept to her room altogether now; the gaunt aunt ran
the house. Against that background Minnie's bright dresses, her idle
and empty days, had a quality of furious unreality. She went out in

the evenings only with women now, neighbors, to the moving pictures. Each afternoon she dressed in one of the new dresses and went downtown alone, where her young "cousins" were already strolling in the late afternoons with their delicate, silken heads and thin, awkward arms and conscious hips, clinging to one another or shrieking and giggling with paired boys in the soda fountain when she passed and went on along the serried store fronts, in the doors of which the sitting and lounging men did not even follow her with their eyes any more.

▌ Why does this narrator describe Miss Minnie as "thirty-eight or thirty-nine"? Doesn't he know?

The letters of St. Paul are noted for their arresting figures of speech and their organization. Some are straightforward and businesslike; others are distinctly poetic. The following letter has a marked lyric quality, due in part to the choice of words and images and in part to the rhythmic sentence structure. The text is that of the King James Bible.

FROM *The New Testament*
ST. PAUL

First Corinthians, Chapter 13

Though I speak with the tongues of men and of angels, and have not charity, I am become as sounding brass, or a tinkling cymbal. And though I have the gift of prophecy, and understand all mysteries, and all knowledge; and though I have all faith, so that I could remove mountains, and have not charity, I am nothing. And though I bestow all my goods to feed the poor, and though I give my body to be burned, and have not charity, it profiteth me nothing. Charity suffereth long, and is kind; charity envieth not; charity vaunteth not itself, is not puffed up; Doth not behave itself unseemly, seeketh not her own, is not easily provoked, thinketh no evil; Rejoiceth not in iniquity, but rejoiceth in the truth; Beareth all things, believeth all things, hopeth all things, endureth all things. Charity never faileth: but whether there be prophecies, they shall fail; whether there be tongues, they shall cease; whether there be knowledge, it shall vanish away. For we know in part, and we prophesy in part. But when that which is perfect is come, then that which is in part shall be done away. When I was a child, I spake as a child, I understood as a child, I thought as a child: but when I became a man, I put away childish things. For now we see through a glass, darkly; but then face to face:

now I know in part; but then shall I know even as also I am known. And now abideth faith, hope, charity, these three; but the greatest of these is charity.

▌ How did you convey the intensity of Paul's conviction in this
  letter?

This letter from the master novelist Henry James to Grace Norton is surely one of the most humanely considerate letters in the English language. The one long paragraph moves carefully through several concerns, but be sure that you are always aware of the persona's attitude toward Grace Norton. Imagine her sitting directly across from you; see her as you speak.

Letter to Grace Norton
HENRY JAMES

131 Mount Vernon St., Boston.
July 28th [1883].

My dear Grace,

Before the sufferings of others I am always utterly powerless, and your letter reveals such depths of suffering that I hardly know what to say to you. This indeed is not my last word — but it must be my first. You are not isolated, verily, in such states of feeling as this — that is, in the sense that you appear to make all the misery of all mankind your own; only I have a terrible sense that you give all and receive nothing — that there is no reciprocity in your sympathy — that you have all the affliction of it and none of the returns. However — I am determined not to speak to you except with the voice of stoicism. I don't know *why* we live — the gift of life comes to us from I don't know what source or for what purpose; but I believe we can go on living for the reason that (always of course up to a certain point) life is the most valuable thing we know anything about, and it is therefore presumptively a great mistake to surrender it while there is any yet left in the cup. In other words consciousness is an illimitable power, and though at times it may seem to be all consciousness of misery, yet in the way it propagates itself from wave to wave, so that we never cease to feel, and though at moments we appear to, try to, pray to, there is something that holds one in one's place, makes it a standpoint in the universe which it is probably good not to forsake. You are right in your consciousness that we are all echoes and reverberations of the *same*, and you are noble when your interest and pity as to everything that surrounds you, appears to have a sustaining and harmonizing power. Only don't, I beseech you, *gen-*

eralize too much in these sympathies and tendernesses — remember that every life is a special problem which is not yours but another's, and content yourself with the terrible algebra of your own. Don't melt too much into the universe, but be as solid and dense and fixed as you can. We all live together, and those of us who love and know, live so most. We help each other — even unconsciously, each in our own effort, we lighten the effort of others, we contribute to the sum of success, make it possible for others to live. Sorrow comes in great waves — no one can know that better than you — but it rolls over us, and though it may almost smother us it leaves us on the spot, and we know that if it is strong we are stronger, inasmuch as it passes and we remain. It wears us, uses us, but we wear it and use it in return; and it is blind, whereas we after a manner see. My dear Grace, you are passing though a darkness in which I myself in my ignorance see nothing but that you have been made wretchedly ill by it; but it is only a darkness, it is not an end, or *the* end. Don't think, don't feel, any more than you can help, don't conclude or decide — don't do anything but *wait*. Everything will pass, and serenity and *accepted* mysteries and disillusionments, and the tenderness of a few good people, and new opportunities and ever so much of life, in a word, will remain. You will do all sorts of things yet, and I will help you. The only thing is not to *melt* in the meanwhile. I insist upon the necessity of a sort of mechanical condensation — so that however fast the horse may run away there will, when he pulls up, be a somewhat agitated but perfectly identical G. N. left in the saddle. Try not to be ill — that is all; for in that there is a failure. You are marked out for success, and you must not fail. You have my tenderest affection and all my confidence. Ever your faithful friend —

Henry James

▌ Was your James clearly visualizing the grief-stricken Grace? How did your audience detect it?

Recipes aren't often performable, but Peter Feibleman's essay about *paella* (pronounced pī·ā·ə) will make your audience's mouths water. Lillian Hellman shared the writing (and eating) responsibilities for this collaboration. Be sure you know exactly how each ingredient tastes and looks and feels.

FROM *Eating Together*
LILLIAN HELLMAN AND PETER FEIBLEMAN

Of all the dishes in Spain, the most famous and the most messed with is something called *paella*. Lillian used to wince at the sight of *paella* till I made it for her outdoors at a picnic one day, and then she got so interested in the cooking that she forgot what she was eating and wound up liking it.

If fifty recipes for *gazpacho* are easy to come by, multiply that by ten for *paella* and you'll be missing some, since all it has to contain is rice, saffron and whatever looks cheap and fresh at the market. The dish is named after the *paellera*, the pan in which it's made, but an iron skillet will do just as well. If you like cooking outdoors, a *paella* can turn a picnic into a party.

The original dish came from a freshwater lagoon known as La Albufera, close to the city of Valencia on Spain's Levantine coast; it contained eels, green beans and snails and was eaten with small whole onions instead of bread. The dish you see on restaurant menus all over the world listed as *Paella Valenciana* is probably a concoction, and certainly a misnomer. Among the vast spectrum of *paellas*, the Valencian one is not high on the scale, for the Valencians, culinarily speaking, are a tightassed lot, given to rigid inhibitions about the mixing of meat and fish, fish and shellfish and meat with certain other meat. The polychromatic, dramatic-looking dish most people think of as *paella* is to be found around Alicante, and is worth the trouble you have to go through to find it.

The reason *paella* is easier to cook outdoors than indoors has to do with heat control: the pan is large and the flame on a stovetop is usually too limited in area. An electric stove can sometimes do the job if you like electric stoves (I don't) or if you're stuck with one, as Lillian is on the Vineyard. If you're cooking indoors and worst comes to worst, which it often does, you can always put the *paella* into the oven when you're ready to cook the rice.

What you want to do first is prepare things so that you can reach for them when you need them. Take some mussels, clams, shrimp and whitefish (or any combination thereof), and boil all of it in water for the required time — then remove it, save the water and peel the shrimp. Put the shrimp shells back into the same water and boil them for at least 30 minutes or longer. Then take the shells out, discard them and set that water aside.

Let's assume you're outdoors. If you have a barbecue handy use it. If you don't, use three stones to hold the pan up, then make a fire of wood sticks around them. The sticks should all point inward like spokes, up toward a central point where the fire will be hottest. Light it and wait. When it gets going, place the pan on top and splash a little olive oil into it.

As soon as the oil starts to smoke, add some chicken parts, giblets, pieces of pork and slices of sausage (exact amounts are given below). By now the fire ought to be licking at the entire surface of the bottom of the pan. When the meat is browned on all sides, lift it out, set it aside and replace it with thinly sliced onion. When the onion looks as if it had started to rust, add mashed garlic, tomatoes and (optionally) coarse salt.

What you now have is called a *sofrito*. Mush it all up together with a wooden spoon, take the pan off the flame for long enough to add some paprika, stir it again and put the pan back on. Add some crushed saffron, stir once more and put the meats back into the *sofrito*.

Stir all hell out of that.

About now you ought to check your fire. If it's low, push the partly burned sticks toward the center till the flames are high again.

Then add the rice.

At this point, if people don't gravitate toward the pan, attracted by the smell, you're doing something wrong. The odor should be aromatic, a combination of sea- and land-food, zesty and sharp, the kind of smell that has an immediate effect on the salivary glands and (from time to time) the gonads. Do not answer questions about what you're doing. Let people stand around, and keep doing it. See that somebody gives them a drink while you go on stirring for a couple of minutes until the rice has browned in the *sofrito*.

Now add the water you saved from the seafood and shrimp shells. It should be whitish, and you want twice as much water as rice. Fresh garden peas, squid rings and small artichokes can go in now if you happen to have any hanging around. One last stir, then kill the flames by pulling the last of the wood sticks out of the spoke formation — away from the pan — so that the pan sits on the hot embers. (If you're on a barbecue grill, mash the coals into one flat layer and lower the pan. If you're indoors, good luck.)

The rice is cooked, they say in Alicante, when the rice is cooked. What they mean is, look at it and taste it. Depending on what kind of rice you're using, after about 18 minutes it should be dark yellow and it should have risen almost to the top and sides of the pan. Chew a couple of grains. It shouldn't be too hard or too soft. When it's done, slide the last of the coals out from under the pan with a stick.

This is the time to insert the cooked clams, shrimp, mussels and whitefish — plus any other shellfish you've boiled, lobster or crawfish. You may garnish the finished *paella* with pimiento strips crisscrossed over the top, and you are now finished cooking. Wash your hands.

If you want to eat the *paella* the way they do at an Alicante outdoor family picnic, you and your friends will all be eating out of the pan you cooked in. It goes like this:

First, let people look at it. Seat them in a circle around the pan and give them each a spoon and a fork. Small wooden spoons are best, but any spoons will do. For every couple of people, set out a dish to be used as a sewer for shells and bones.

Next, take a small white plate and place it, upside down, in the very center of the *paella*, on top of the rice.

Now listen carefully. On top of that plate, place another plate, right side up. The second plate should contain a salad composed of lettuce, tomato and onions, with a plain oil and vinegar dressing.

Tell people to use their spoons and tell them to eat the *paella* up to the plate, stopping to pick up their forks and spear a piece of tomato or onion when they want from the salad at the center. By the time the salad is finished, the *paella* around it should be gone too.

Then lift both plates off and expose the final center portion, still warm, for anybody who wants seconds.

You should have a good time at your picnic. If you do, as Lillian says, do not thank me. Pay me.

▌ Did you allow enough time to make the process clear to your audience?
▌ Did you "have a good time at your picnic"?

Jane Tortillot kept a diary as she crossed the Great Plains from May to November 1862. On some days she was too busy to make any entries. When she did write, she gave a moving picture of the world of the wagon train; of her husband, Albert; of her life under extraordinarily difficult circumstances. To be sure, she suffered, but she didn't whine; keep her backbone strong!

FROM ***Women's Diaries of the Westward Journey***
LILLIAN SCHLISSEL, EDITOR

Jane Gould Tortillot

Friday, July 4   Today is the Fourth of July and here we are away off in the wilderness and can't even stay over a day to do any extra cooking. The men fired their guns. We wonder what the folks at home are doing and oh, how we wish we were there. Albert is not well today, so I drive. I have been in the habit of sleeping a while every forenoon, so naturally I was very sleepy driving. Went to sleep a multitude of times, to awaken with a start fancying we were running into gullies. After going a short distance we came in sight of a mail station, on the other side of the river there were several buildings. They are of adobe, I suppose. Nearly opposite on this side of the river we passed a little log hut which is used for a store. It was really a welcome sight after going four hundred miles without seeing a house of any kind. . . .

Saturday, July 5–Tuesday, July 8 . . .

Wednesday, July 9 . . .   We hear many stories of Indians depredations, but do not feel frightened yet. . . .

July 10 . . .

Friday, July 11 . . .   There was a little child run over by a wagon in Walker's train, who are just ahead of us. The child was injured quite seriously. . . . They sent for a German physician that belongs to our train, to see the child that was injured. He said he thought it would get better.

July 12–July 19 . . .

Sunday, July 20 . . .   The men had a ball-play towards night. Seemed to enjoy themselves very much, it seemed like old times.

Monday, July 21 . . .   Our men went to work this morning to building a raft. Worked hard all day. Half of the men in the water, too. . . .

Tuesday, July 22 . . .   Went to work this morning as early as possible to ferrying the wagons over. Had to take them apart and float the box and cover behind. The two boxes were fastened together by the rods, one before to tow in and the other to load. Worked till dark. We were the last but one to cross tonight. Got some of our groceries wet, some coffee, sugar dissolved.

July 24–July 25 . . .

Saturday, July 26 . . .   Annie McMillen had lagged behind, walking, when we stopped. The whole train had crossed the creek before they thought of her. The creek was so deep that it ran into the wagon boxes, so she could not wade. A man on horseback went over for her, and another man on a mule went to help her on. The mules refused to go clear across went where the water was very deep, threw the man off and almost trampled him, but he finally got out safe, only well wet and with the loss of a good hat, which is no trifling loss here.

Sunday, July 27 . . .

Monday, July 28 . . .   Came past a camp of thirty-six wagons who have been camped for some time here in the mountains. They have had their cattle stampeded four or five times. There was a woman died in this train yesterday. She left six children, one of them only two days old. Poor little thing, it had better have died with its mother. They made a good picket fence around the grave.

July 29–31, August 1–2 . . .

Sunday, August 3 . . .   We passed by the train I have just spoken of. They had just buried the babe of the woman who died days ago, and were just digging a grave for another woman that was run over by the cattle and wagons when they stampeded yesterday. She lived twenty-four hours, she gave birth to a child a short time before she died. The child was buried with her. She leaves a little two year old girl and a husband. They say he is nearly crazy with sorrow. . . .

August 4 . . .

Tuesday, August 5 . . .   Did not start very early. Waited for a train to pass. It seems today as if I *must* go home to fathers to see them all. I can't wait another minute. If I could only *hear* from them it would do some good, but I suppose I shall have to wait whether I am patient or not. . . .

August 6–9 . . .

Sunday, August 10   Traveled five or six miles when we came to Snake River. We stayed till two o'clock then traveled till about four or five, when *we* from the back end of the train saw those on ahead all get out their guns. In a short time the word came back that a train six miles on had been attacked by the Indians, and some killed and that was cause enough for the arming. In a short time were met by two men. They wanted us to go a short distance from the road and bring two dead men to their camp, five miles ahead.

Albert unloaded his little wagon and sent Gus back with them and about forty armed men from both trains, to get them. We learned that a train of eleven wagons had been plundered of all that was in them and the teams taken and the men killed. One was Mr. Bullwinkle who left us the 25th of last month, at the crossing of Green River. He went on with this Adams train. Was intending to wait for us but we had not overtaken him yet. He was shot eight times. His dog was shot four times before he would let them get to the wagon. They took all that he had in his wagon, except his trunks and books and papers. They broke open his trunks and took all that they contained. (He had six.) It is supposed that they took six thousand dollars from him, tore the cover from his wagon, it was oilcloth. He had four choice horses. They ran away when he was shot, the harnesses were found on the trail where it was cut from them when they went. It was a nice silver one. The Captain had a daughter shot and wounded severely. This happened yesterday. This

morning a part of their train and a part of the Kennedy train went in
pursuit of the stock. They were surrounded by Indians on ponies,
two killed, several wounded and two supposed to be killed. They
were never found. One of those killed was Capt. Adams' son, the
other was a young man in the Kennedy train. Those that we carried
to camp were those killed this morning. Mr. Bullwinkle and the two
others were buried before we got to the camp. There were one
hundred and fifty wagons there and thirty four of ours. Capt. Kennedy was severely wounded. Capt. Hunter of Iowa City train was
killed likewise by an Indian. We camped near Snake River. We could
not get George to ride after the news, he *would* walk and carry his
loaded pistol to help.

Monday, August 11 . . .   The two men we brought up were buried
early this morning with the other three, so they laid five men side by
side in this vast wilderness, killed by guns and arrows of the red
demons. The chief appeared yesterday in a suit of Mr. Bullwinkle's
on the battlefield. . . .

Tuesday, August 12   Capt. Adams' daughter died this morning from
the effects of her wound. Was buried in a box made of a wagon box.
Poor father and mother lost one son and one daughter, all of his
teams, clothing and four thousand dollars. Is left dependent on the
bounty of strangers. . . . In the evening we took in Mrs. Ellen Ives,
one of the ladies of the plundered train. Her husband goes in the
wagon just ahead of us. She was married the morning she started for
California. Not a very pleasant wedding tour. . . .

▌ How did you make your audience see the tensions building in
Jane at the end of July and the beginning of August?

Terry Pickens, fourteen, is a newsboy. Together with his brother Cliff (who
is twelve), he serves 111 customers, but Terry's route is more difficult. As he
says, "Cliff hasn't got any hills. Mine's all hills." Be sure we see Terry think
— he has become a very savvy young man. What question do you suppose
Terkel asked to get him started?

FROM *Working*
STUDS TERKEL

Terry Pickens

I've been having trouble collecting. I had one woman hid from me
once. I had another woman tell her kids to tell me she wasn't home.

He says, "Mom, newsboy." She says (whispers), "Tell him I'm not home." I could hear it from the door. I came back in half an hour and she paid me. She's not a deadbeat. They'll pay you if you get 'em. Sometimes you have to wait . . .

If I don't catch 'em at home, I get pretty mad. That means I gotta come back and come back and come back and come back until I catch 'em. Go around about nine o'clock at night and seven o'clock in the morning. This one guy owed me four dollars. He got real mad at me for comin' around at ten o'clock. Why'd I come around so late? He probably was mad 'cause I caught him home. But he paid me. I don't care whether he gets mad at me, just so I get paid.

I like to have money. It's nice to have money once in a while instead of being flat broke all the time. Most of my friends are usually flat broke. I spent $150 this summer. On nothing — candy, cokes, games of pool, games of pinball. We went to McDonald's a couple of times. I just bought anything I wanted. I wonder where the money went. I have nothing to show for it. I'm like a gambler, the more I have, the more I want to spend. That's just the way I am.

It's supposed to be such a great deal. The guy, when he came over and asked me if I wanted a route, he made it sound so great. Seven dollars a week for hardly any work at all. And then you find out the guy told you a bunch of bull. You mistrust the people. You mistrust your customers because they don't pay you sometimes.

Then you get mad at the people at the printing corporation. You're supposed to get fifty-seven papers. They'll send me forty-seven or else they'll send me sixty-seven. Sunday mornings they get mixed up. Cliff'll have ten or eleven extras and I'll be ten or eleven short. That happens all the time. The printers, I don't think they care. They make all these stupid mistakes at least once a week. I think they're half-asleep or something. I do my job, I don't see why they can't do theirs. I don't like my job any more than they do.

Sunday morning at three — that's when I get up. I stay up later so I'm tired. But the dark doesn't bother me. I run into things sometimes, though. Somebody's dog'll come out and about give you a heart attack. There's this one woman, she had two big German shepherds, great big old things, like three or four feet tall. One of 'em won't bite you. He'll just run up, charging, bark at you, and then he'll go away. The other one, I didn't know she had another one — when it bit me. This dog came around the bush. (Imitates barking.) When I turned around, he was at me. He bit me right there (indicates scar on leg). It was bleeding a little. I gave him a real dirty look.

He ran over to the other neighbor's lawn and tried to keep me from gettin' in there. I walked up and delivered the paper. I was about ready to beat the thing's head in or kill it. Or something with it. I was so mad. I called up that woman and she said the dog had all its shots and "I don't believe he bit you." I said, "Lady, he bit me." Her daughter started giving me the third degree. "What color was the dog?" "How big was it?" "Are you sure it was our yard and our dog?" Then they saw the dogs weren't in the pen.

First they told me they didn't think I needed any shots. Then they said they'd pay for the doctor. I never went to the doctor. It wasn't bleeding a whole lot. But I told her if I ever see that dog again, she's gonna have to get her papers from somebody else. Now they keep the dog penned up and it barks at me and everything. And I give it a dirty look.

There's a lot of dogs around here. I got this other dog, a little black one, it tried to bite me too. It lunged at me, ripped my pants, and missed me. (With the glee of W. C. Fields) I kicked it *good*. It still chases me. There are two black dogs. The other one I've kicked so many times that it just doesn't bother me any more. I've kicked his face in once when he was biting my leg. Now he just stays under the bushes and growls at me. I don't bother to give him a dirty look.

There were these two other dogs. They'd always run out in the street and chase me. I kicked them. They'd come back and I'd kick 'em again. I don't have any problems with 'em any more, because they got hit chasin' cars. They're both dead.

I don't like many of my customers, 'cause they'll cuss me if they don't get their papers just exactly in the right place. This one guy cussed me up and down for about fifteen minutes. I don't want to repeat what he called me. All the words, just up and down. He told me he drives past all those blank drugstores on his blank way home and he could stop off at one of 'em and get a blank newspaper. And I'm just a blank convenience.

I was so mad at him. I hated his guts. I felt like taking a lead pipe to him or something. But I kept my mouth shut, 'cause I didn't know if the press guy'd get mad at me and I'd lose my route. You see, this guy could help me or he could hurt me. So I kept my mouth shut.

A lot of customers are considerate but a lot of 'em aren't. Lot of 'em act like they're doing you such a favor taking the paper from you. It costs the same dime at a drugstore. Every time they want you to do something they threaten you: (imitates nasty, nasal voice) "Or I'll quit."

What I really can't stand: you'll be collecting and somebody'll come out and start telling you all their problems. "I'm going to visit my daughter today, yes, I am. She's twenty-two, you know." "Look here, I got all my sons home, see the army uniforms?" They'll stand for like half an hour. I got two or three like that, and they always got something to say to me. I'll have like two hours wasted listening to these people blabbin' before they pay me. Mmm, I don't know. Maybe they're lonely. But they've got a daughter and a son, why do they have to blab in my ear?

A lot of the younger customers have had routes and they know how hard it is, how mean people are. They'll be nicer to you. They tend to tip you more. And they don't blab all day long. They'll just pay you and smile at you. The younger people frequently offer me a coke or something.

Older people are afraid of me, a lot of them. The first three, four weeks — (muses) they seemed so afraid of me. They think I'm gonna rob 'em or something. It's funny. You wouldn't think it'd be like this in a small town, would you? They're afraid I'm gonna beat 'em up, take their money. They'd just reach through the door and give me the money. Now they know you so well, they invite you in and blab in your ear for half an hour. It's one or the other. I really don't know why they're afraid. I'm not old, so I wouldn't know how old people feel.

Once in a while I come home angry, most of the time just crabby. Sometimes kids steal the paper out of people's boxes. I lose my profits. It costs me a dime. The company isn't responsible, I am. The company wouldn't believe you probably that somebody stole the paper.

I don't see where being a newsboy and learning that people are pretty mean or that people don't have enough money to buy things with is gonna make you a better person or anything. If anything, it's gonna make a worse person out of you, 'cause you're not gonna like people that don't pay you. And you're not gonna like people who act like they're doing you a big favor paying you. Yeah, it sort of molds your character, but I don't think for the better. If anybody told me being a newsboy builds character, I'd know he was a liar.

I don't see where people get all this bull about the kid who's gonna be President and being a newsboy made a President out of him. It taught him how to handle his money and this bull. You know what it did? It taught him how to hate the people on his route. And the printers. And dogs.

❚ What did you do with your body and voice to let your audience see a fourteen-year-old boy eager to talk? What was his body doing?

Bibliography

Connolly, Cyril. *The Evening Colonnade*. New York: Harcourt Brace Jovanovich, 1975.
A variety of essays on literary subjects and personalities.

Cowley, Malcom. *And I Worked at the Writer's Trade: Chapters of Literary History, 1918–1978*. New York: Viking Press, 1978.
A consideration of the relationship of literary generations with interesting comments on changing themes and language.

Cowley, Malcom, ed. *Writers at Work: The "Paris Review" Interviews*. New York: Viking Press, 1961.
A collection of interviews on "How Writers Write." Sixteen interviews offer a range of styles and interests from E. M. Forster to Françoise Sagan.

Fiedler, Leslie, ed. *The Art of the Essay: Edited with Introduction, Notes and Exercise Questions*. New York: Thomas Y. Crowell Company, 1958.
An extensive collection of essays and travel accounts.

Gardner, John. *On Moral Fiction*. New York: Basic Books, 1978.
An examination of contemporary fiction measured against this outstanding novelist's premise that fiction is moral only when it attempts to share human values and efforts at human fulfillment.

Graves, Robert, and Alan Hodge. *The Reader over Your Shoulder*. 2nd ed. New York: Random House, 1971.
A practical discussion of the writer's responsibilities for clarity and the reader's need for precision.

Mallon, Thomas. *A Book of One's Own*. New York: Ticknor & Fields, 1984.
A highly readable collection excerpting famous diaries and journals — and more that ought to be famous. Useful bibliography.

Read, Herbert. *English Prose Style*. Boston: Beacon Press, 1952.
Still the most complete discussion of prose style per se. The approach is first from the standpoint of composition and then from that of rhetoric.

Thomas, Wright, and Stuart Gerry Brown. *Reading Prose: An Introduction to Critical Study*. New York: Oxford University Press, 1952.
An extensive collection of essays grouped thematically, with a brief section on experimental prose. The final section is a compact directive for developing a critical approach. The book has a helpful chronological index.

6 Narration

Well, you know or don't you kennet or haven't I
told you every telling has a taling and that's the
he and the she of it. Look, look, the dusk is
growing!

James Joyce, Finnegans Wake

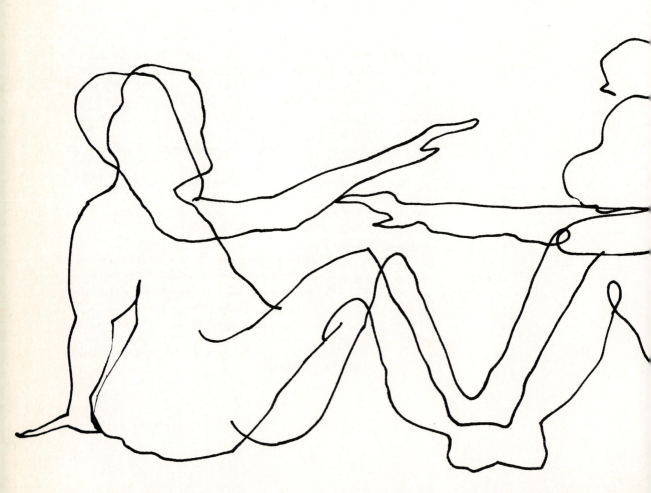

All of us tell stories every day, even if they are only about what happened to us yesterday or just a moment ago. We tell stories because they authenticate our lives and experiences and help us to make sense of who we are and what we are about. Good stories are good because the teller uses lively description to help listeners see what he or she has seen, because the teller is willing to step aside to let other characters speak, and because the teller summarizes the important intervening events or time. But always, at the center, is the storyteller — *telling* a tale.

Narration, then, is more than plot. Whether in prose or in verse, narration includes the *telling* (remember that active form) by a *narrator* of something that has happened (to the narrator or to someone else) or that might happen. Someone — obviously, the narrator — arranges and describes a series of events or incidents and thereby constructs a narration.

In the 1930s Gertrude Stein delivered some lectures at the University of Chicago about narration. In them she said:

> Narration is what anybody has to say in any way about anything that can happen has happened will happen in any way.
>
> That is what narrative is and so of course there always is narrative and anybody can stop listening to any way of telling anything. This undoubtedly can and does happen, even if it is exciting enough or has been.
>
> There we are.
>
> What do you tell and how do you tell it.
>
> If you tell it very well how do you tell it and if you do not tell it very well if you do not tell it well at all how do you tell it.
>
> This anybody knows since everybody is everybody and everybody is always one or many of them to always tell it.[1]

Stein knew what she was saying, since her method of saying it demonstrates what she says. You should read her comments carefully because they contain a special warning: "Anybody can stop listening." When you prepare narration for performance, you must answer five important questions:

1. What sort of person is telling this story?
2. Exactly what is going on here?
3. What sort of people is this story about?
4. What are they saying to each other?
5. Where is all of this taking place?

1. Gertrude Stein, *Narration* (Chicago: University of Chicago Press, 1969), pp. 31–32.

These five questions have many different kinds of answers and are frequently really clusters of questions, but if you are fully informed about each one of them, you will be well on your way to successful and engaging performances of narration.

Too often we read stories just to find out what happens, as if the words obstruct the facts or ideas or whatever might be conveyed by the story. The manner of telling the story, however, is just as important as the tale, for it reflects the unique personality of the narrator, shapes the tale, moves the event at the proper pace, and leads the reader to the planned conclusion. Along the way occur all the details that make this telling of the events unique. If you read rapidly, you may skip these vital clues, which are in fact the verbal fingerprints of the teller. So it's wisest to begin our analysis with strategies for answering the first question, "What sort of person is telling the story?"

Point of View

Every story has a storyteller, a person who selects what we see and hear, the perspective from which we view the action, the details on which we linger, and how long it takes us to traverse time. Every story is shaped by its narrator, who establishes a *point of view*, a way to experience the world from a particular vantage point. Every narrator sets for us — by the position from which the action is viewed *and* by his or her unique personality — a characteristic way of showing and telling. This characteristic way of telling a story tells us about the narrator, too.

When we attend a film, everything we see has been selected by the eye of the camera. Although we might want desperately to see the woman's reaction to the man's proposal, we see only what the camera shows us. We watch the scene as long as the camera wants us to watch it, at the distance from which the camera wants us to see it, and lit in the manner the camera allows. Similarly, the narrator in a story selects and organizes what we see and hear, telling us what we must know or allowing us to overhear characters carrying on dialogue from which we draw our own conclusions. Storytellers have different attitudes and manners. Objective, clinical, cut-and-dried, black-and-white news stories look and feel different from stories that jump around in time and locale and are full of vivid happenings with improbable people doing impossible things. In all cases, though, the events are related according to the vision of the eye that both sees and speaks. At the center of a story, shaping, controlling, refining, and guiding us through the narrative, is what Henry James calls the "central intelligence." Your first task as an interpreter is to communicate the narrator.

First-Person Narrators

Two brief passages demonstrate how palpable and present that central intelligence can be. The first is from *The Odyssey*:

> Tell me, Muse, of the man of many ways, who was driven far journeys, after he had sacked Troy's sacred citadel. Many were they whose cities he saw, whose minds he learned of, many the pains he suffered in his spirit on the wide sea, struggling for his own life and the homecoming of his companions.[2]

We know by the second syllable that the story is being told by a specific somebody. "Tell *me*, Muse," the narrator says. The invocation of the Muse and the simplicity and confidence of the words further suggest that the narrator is awed by the hero and his journey. Only if he is inspired by the gods can he convey the story of the "god-like Odysseus." The narrator also seems to be at some distance from the events, though they still impress him. These first few lines summarize the ordeal that is revealed in the story ahead, and the majesty in the words gives emotional impact to the beginning of this great tale.

Now look at the first paragraph of John Updike's "A & P" (the entire story can be found at the end of Chapter 3):

> In walks these three girls in nothing but bathing suits. I'm in the third checkout slot, with my back to the door, so I don't see them until they're over by the bread. The one that caught my eye first was the one in the plaid green two-piece. She was a chunky kid, with a good tan and a sweet broad soft-looking can with those two crescents of white just under it, where the sun never seems to hit, at the top of the back of her legs. I stood there with my hand on a box of HiHo crackers trying to remember if I rang it up or not. I ring it up again and the customer starts giving me hell. She's one of these cash-register-watchers, a witch about fifty with rouge on her cheekbones and no eyebrows, and I know it made her day to trip me up. She's been watching cash registers for fifty years and probably never seen a mistake before.

Here we meet Sammy, a boy with his eye on three girls. How else is he identified here? What — precisely — is he doing? Where is he doing it? How is it going to get him into trouble before the paragraph

2. Homer, *The Odyssey*, trans. Richmond Lattimore (New York: Harper and Row, 1967), p. 27.

is over? He is clearly interested in the girls and in their bathing suits, and he takes time from his tasks to describe the cut and color of one costume and the effect the suit has on the girl wearing it. But is his mind on his work? What is Sammy's attitude toward the people he meets during his job? He addresses us as if we were his friends. The vivid impression these girls make is marked for both Sammy and us by the use of the present tense in the first sentence. What happens to tense as the paragraph progresses?

We are located quickly in the familiar world of the A & P: we recognize the grocery store, know about lanes and checkers and cash-register-watchers, and we may even have purchased HiHo crackers. We know the landscape; we're on Sammy's side, ready to hear about what happens to these three girls.

Sammy is surely not the disembodied voice of Homer and he is surely not Updike, the author. The persona, Sammy, is simply the teller of a tale vivid enough to him to be worth telling to us; his language makes us his peers. When interpreting this story, you should create a Sammy to whom all of this story has happened and who, as he recalls it so vividly, needs to tell us about it.

Both of these stories exemplify *first-person narration*. They are told by different kinds of narrators, and yet each narrator takes an active and lively part in telling something that happened to him.

In *first-person narration*, the person telling the story speaks directly to the reader as "I," although he or she is also the "eye" of the story. Sometimes the "I" is physically identified, as we saw in the excerpt from Updike's story; in other cases, as with the narrator of Homer's epic, the "I" is not physically identified, although he or she definitely demonstrates a characteristic personality. The narrator may observe from either afar or quite near the events, may participate in the actions described or merely report what occurs, or may report and evaluate as well. But whatever the degree of physical presence in the story, the narrator remains very much at the center of things, and the narrator's personality shapes and colors everything we see and hear.

The kind of first-person narration that is presented in "A & P" and in Betts's "The Ugliest Pilgrim" at the end of this chapter gives us all the vitality of a teller who lives through the tale. Just as all of us have memories with conviction because of our actual experiences, first-person narrators are peculiarly convinced of their own vision. They *know* it, because it happened to them. And like most people who live through experiences that they want to talk about later, first-person narrators are incapable of complete objectivity. They shape events to favor themselves and to prove their antagonists unreasonable, unattractive, and irresponsible. Such qualities do not make first-person narrators less interesting people; on the contrary, the foibles, idiosyncracies, and peculiar diction and vision of these narrators may present a special challenge to the interpreter (see, for example, Bell's "The Naked Lady" at the end of this chapter). Only by assuming the personality of the narrator can the interpreter develop a believable response to the material. In this way the narrator, revealed in the way the story is told, becomes a full-blooded character, unquestionably the most important character you will be expected to present. An interpreter must move as the narrator moves, must sound as the narrator sounds. You must find within your body and your voice sufficient similarities to the body and voice of the storyteller to convince the audience that they are listening to a story told by someone to whom all of this actually happened.

First-person narrators, then, may be either central participants in the action of the story or observers. Each posture presents both benefits and liabilities to interpreters and their audiences. If you are telling a first-person story with an actively involved narrator, you obviously have immediate access to many of the events; you know precisely what is going on inside one of the major characters. But you are also restricted to that person's perception of the events, and you may find yourself the victim of some fancy elaboration of the truth. If you are telling a first-person story in which your narrator is chiefly observing the events, you get a much less subjective (although not entirely objective) picture of what is happening, but you do not get the inner concerns of any of the major characters. As an example, consider an automobile accident. Obviously, the driver of the car knew exactly what *he* was doing and thinking when the truck pulled out in front of him, but he could not see (and could not know) about the truck driver's fears about being late or the little puppy that jumped into the trucker's vision and caused the truck to swerve and collide with the car. Someone watching from the streetcorner may have seen many of these events happen, more or less clearly, but wouldn't know about any of the internal concerns of the participants. In either case, though, the narrator remains at the center of the story, and when we hear the words of the characters we hear them and see them *through* the voice of the narrator.

Obviously, not all narrators are first-person observers or even participants. Authors rarely write in the *second-person voice* (although Damon Runyon's colorful tales about New York's underworld are noteworthy exceptions, as is much travel literature), because it tends to limit the number and kind of activities in which the narrator engages and it restricts the range of response from readers.

Third-Person Narrators

Third-person narration is probably the most familiar to you. For most beginning interpreters, this form of narration may be the most difficult narrative posture of all, chiefly because the narrator seems to fade from existence or to resemble some sort of disembodied voice or uninflected reporter simply stating facts. Nothing could be further from the truth, for these narrators are lively and full-blooded, although discovering the ways in which they make their presence known requires careful scrutiny, a keenly deductive mind, and a spirited imagination.

There are many different forms of third-person narrators, and any extended study of narration will require you to become familiar with all of them. (The bibliography at the end of this chapter lists many books that can help you learn further.) For our purposes, we divide third-person narrators into two broadly inclusive groups: *objective observers* and *omniscient observers*. Generally, objective observers simply recount the events, incidents, dialogue, and activity that could be related by any reasonable individual present at the scene. *Omniscient observers* — and omniscience may be limited to only one character — have all of these powers as well as access to the internal life of a character or characters. Although these narrators *can* tell us about the inner fears and hopes, concerns, past, and future of a character who interests them, they do not *have* to tell us. Furthermore, they choose the time to tell us such internal details. In both kinds of third-person narration, though, careful examination of diction, grammar, and syntax will help reveal the narrators' personalities. Note which kinds of events they dwell on and which they pass over. Inspect the relationship they establish with the characters in their tales. Some careful deductions will begin to flesh out the personality who is telling a particular tale and whom you must communicate to your audience.

Look at the opening of Eudora Welty's *Losing Battles:*

When the rooster crowed, the moon had still not left the world but was going down on flushed cheek, one day short of the full. A long thin cloud crossed it slowly, drawing itself out like a name being called. The air changed, as if a mile or so away a wooden door had swung open, and a smell, more of warmth than wet, from a river at low stage, moved upward into the clay hills that stood in darkness.

Then a house appeared on its ridge, like an old man's silver watch pulled once more out of its pocket. A dog leaped up from where he'd lain like a stone and began barking for today as if he meant never to stop.

Then a baby bolted naked out of the house. She monkey-climbed down the steps and ran open-armed into the yard, knocking at the walls of flowers still colorless as faces, tagging in turn the four big trees that marked off the corners of the yard, tagging the gatepost, the well-piece, the birdhouse, the bell post, a log seat, a rope swing, and then, rounding the house, she used all her strength to push over a crate that let a stream of white Plymouth Rocks loose on the world. The chickens rushed ahead of the baby, running frantic, and behind the baby came a girl in a petticoat. A wide circle of curl-papers, paler than the streak of dawn, bounced around her head, but she ran on confident tiptoe as though she believed no eye could see her. She caught the baby and carried her back inside, the baby with her little legs still running like a windmill.

The distant point of the ridge, like the tongue of a calf, put its red lick on the sky. Mists, voids, patches of woods and naked clay, flickered like live ashes, pink and blue. A mirror that hung within the porch on the house wall began to flicker as at the striking of kitchen matches. Suddenly two chinaberry trees at the foot of the yard lit up, like roosters astrut with golden tails. Caterpillar nets shone in the pecan tree. A swollen shadow bulked underneath it, familiar in shape as Noah's Ark — a school bus.

Then as if something came sliding out of the sky, the whole tin roof of the house ran with new blue. The posts along the porch softly bloomed downward, as if chalk marks were being drawn, one more time, down a still misty slate. The house was revealed as if standing there from pure memory against a now moonless sky. For the length of a breath, everything stayed shadowless, as under a lifting hand, and then a passage showed, running through the house, right through the middle of it, and at the head of the passage, in the center of the front gallery, a figure was revealed, a very old lady seated in a rocking chair with head cocked, as though wild to be seen.

Then Sunday light raced over the farm as fast as the chickens were flying. Immediately the first straight shaft of heat, solid as a hickory stick, was laid on the ridge.

Miss Beulah Renfro came out of the passage at a trot and cried in the voice of alarm which was her voice of praise, "Granny! Up, dressed, and waiting for 'em! All by yourself! Why didn't you holler?"

There is no "I" in this account of dawn in the rural South, but there is a very strong "eye." Even though the speaker is an omniscient observer and even though this account is in the past tense, there is a sense of immediacy about it. A very distinct personality emerges as each sentence reveals not only the illuminated details of the farm but also the character of the storyteller.

The passage is rich in imagery and metaphor. Faced with the task of preparing and performing this text, the interpreter should ask what sort of person is seeing this scene and describing it. What do the metaphors tell about the character of the narrator? The moon is going down "on flushed cheek." As the sun creeps nearer to the top of the ridge, the farmhouse appears "like an old man's silver watch pulled once more out of its pocket." The dog has been lying "like a stone." The naked baby "monkey-climbs" down the steps. The narrator knows that the chickens let loose in the new light are Plymouth Rocks. The curl-papers in the girl's hair are "paler than the streak of dawn." The baby's legs are "running like a windmill." The point of the ridge is "like the tongue of a calf." The mirror on the porch wall begins to flicker "as at the striking of kitchen matches." The shadows of the porch posts are like "chalk marks . . . being drawn." The heat that comes with Sunday's first light is "solid as a hickory stick."

The images used by the storyteller to give poetic radiance to the details in the story belong to what kind of person? Does the speaker seem to be a stranger in these parts or a part of the world of the story? Do the images and metaphors reflect the world of the story, or do they seem literary or sophisticated when compared with the setting and the characters?

If the language is beautiful and evocative, the metaphors are indeed plain. The narrator seems to know the locale; the images used as figures of comparison are homely and a part of the world of the story. The heat is not oppressive, not like a slab. It is solid like a hickory stick, an object that belongs to the people of the story as well as to the narrator, just like the bulky school bus and the shadows like chalk on slate. These metaphors all suggest the air of "country school" that hangs about the dawn in the rural South even on a Sunday. The narrator does not stand aloof from the characters and events in the story but seems rather to be a member of their community, one whose vision of this morning light is infused with affection for the land and its people.

Sometimes a film begins with shots that set the scene and give a sense of atmosphere before the main characters are introduced. Similarly, this narrator glides smoothly over the landmarks of the farm, as light glides, and then illuminates at last the character who is to be the central figure in the novel: the old lady seated in the rocker. Granny, whose birthday celebration is the occasion of the novel, has been up and dressed long before dawn. She was sitting there from the first word of the description but is not mentioned until the sun is fully up, and its light, as well as the narrator's eye, reveals her.

We see, then, that third-person narration (like first-person narration) has both advantages and disadvantages. *Objective observers* clearly are for some the most reliable of storytellers, because all they tell is what has verifiably occurred. This "just the facts, nothing but the facts" approach can allow an audience to deduce relationships and attitudes and temperament for themselves. At the same time, this form of narration tends to be less gripping and can be difficult to sustain over a long tale. *Omniscient observers* — in all of the many forms this narrative type takes — ideally provide us with access to the past, future, and internal life of characters who command central positions in the story. However, like all the other narrators, omniscient observers can withhold information at crucial times, and their interest in a given character may inhibit or even preclude equal interest in another character. Both kinds of third-person narrators, however, are real people. A narrator does not have to appear as a character in a story to breathe, sympathize, or grieve. Personality cannot help but emerge in all the little details that give away the concerns of the soul. Certainly, clear attitudes, reflected in the words the narrator selects, the images the narrator chooses, the angle of vision the narrator employs, and of course the incidents themselves selected for narration, are all integral parts of the sensibility telling the tale. Interpreters need to be keenly aware of all of the details that reveal personality and character, even if the narrator never speaks from the personal point of view.

Samuel Beckett also begins a novel (*The Lost Ones*) with the dawning of a day. However, his narrator says, "The sun rose, having no alternative, on the nothing new." Compare that personality with the sensibility in Welty's novel. What a contrast! What a bleak vision of the coming of a tired light into a desolate space! We can communicate narration only when we communicate the narrator.

Action and Plot

Once you understand who is telling a story, you need to understand precisely what is going on, how the narrative moves and where it is going. You should ask of every story, "What is its action?" *Action* is the sequence of visible or discernible physical happenings, the movement that courses through events. How is the action of a story different from its plot? *Plot* is the term used to describe the scheme or plan or design of the action. Plot orders action and arranges it in a pattern. The plot may involve psychological or physical action, and it may turn when one of the characters undergoes a change that affects the outcome of the story.

The *crisis* of a narrative is the turning point of the action. Like the fulcrum in a poem, the crisis serves as the "point of no return"; it is that point after which there can be only one possible resolution.

Conflict is essential in narrative; it causes action and plot. As you know, most works of literature involve people facing problems. (We rarely find much interest in people who are happy, at peace, and have nothing to do.) In both comedy and tragedy characters face obstacles: comic characters tend to overcome their problems, while tragic characters succumb to them. But there are always some obstacles, some types of conflict. They may be internal and psychological, or external and social. Frequently, external and internal conflicts are combined, one accenting the other or causing the other. Characters may fight city hall, nature, their in-laws, society, massive machines, repressive traditions, or even an idea whose time has come.

Conflict need not be completely explained nor absolutely real; there need not even be an absolute logic in the design of the events. But each element must obey the rules the story sets up for itself. Meaning arises from the way in which the tale is true to itself. Just as the characters in Archibald Marshall's "The Detective" can speak without proper punctuation and still be very proper Englishmen, and just as Baucis and Philemon can become intertwined trees in Ovid's *Metamorphoses* (both selections appear at the end of this chapter), characters do what they must to live in the particular world of the work they inhabit. If narratives — indeed, if any works of art — can be said to obey rules at all, they obey the rules they set for themselves.

Character

At this point in our analysis, we have discovered who is telling the story and the general action (as ordered in the plot) of the tale itself. Now we must discover what sort of people this story is about, the third of the crucial questions we mentioned earlier. Without a narrator, of course, there would be no action; without action, the characters would have nothing to do — indeed, there would be no characters, since we understand characters by examining what they do, what they say, and what others say about them. First and last, it is the people we encounter — the characters — who grasp us most when we read, who help us understand who *we* are.

Narrative discovers character through action. We learn about people from what others — including the narrator — say about them. And we learn about character from the manner in which the narrator supplies all this information. (Setting, too, affects people and personality; we shall discuss this below.) Most often, personality, habit, and response motivate a character's reaction to the forces that shape a story.

A third-person narrator may tell us all we need to know about a character's appearance, behavior, speech, or thoughts. To consolidate these clues we must add material from our own lives and experiences. Be sure to understand exactly why characters refer to each other in the manner they do. If Clara calls George a "bonehead," be sure you know what George calls her and why she considers George in such a light before you take her word as truth. And remember that unreliable narrators (first-person narrators) can sometimes change the truth of an event to suit their preferences.

Characters whom you confront may be simple (like those who populate Marshall's "The Detective"). Depth and development of character are not requirements for successful stories. Little Red Riding Hood just wants to get to her grandmother's house, and the tortoise beats the hare chiefly because he doesn't stop to munch a carrot. Not much more is needed, since the situation itself or the attitude of the storyteller to the events is what interests us.

Fuller characters — those that E. M. Forster calls "round characters" — require an internal life that both corresponds to and illumines the external make-up of the character. Sometimes the physical lives of the characters predominate; sometimes the psychological components are primary. Most often, both aspects together sketch the outlines of the character — as happens with Tony/Tommy in Malamud's "The Prison" at the end of this chapter. Whatever component is emphasized, in performance the characters must be totalities. Only for purposes of analysis can we separate their components. As in life, so in narrative: the character is greater than the sum of his or her attributes.

Dialogue

The fourth question to answer is "What are they saying to each other?" Almost every narrator at some point allows the characters to speak for themselves, providing the audience immediate access to the scene of the story, affording variety through distinctive personalities and speech rhythms, and emphasizing vividness in characterization. Although it may be useful and convenient for the writer, dialogue can cause trouble for the interpreter.

Dialogue may be in the form of either direct or indirect discourse. *Direct discourse* is the verbatim recording of the words the character is speaking. It is usually marked by quotation marks, although you cannot always depend on authors to use them. Dialogue tags like "she said" are not much help either, for they do not always precede or follow a speech. Direct discourse introduces in the place of narration the total presence of a character, as if the narrator has momentarily stepped aside to allow the character to assume fully the telling of the tale. The richness of the story is enhanced immeasureably by the presence of the character's voice and perspective. Direct discourse depends on the interchange of question, response, and opinion. Characters speak because they wish to be heard, if only by themselves. Audiences should always be aware of who is speaking and who is listening and the listener's effect on the speaker.

On the other hand, *indirect discourse* is a reporting of the words the characters spoke and depends on an articulated or assumed "that." For example, in "she admitted she would eat the turtle," only the first two words are unquestionably pure narration. The remainder blends both the narrator's reporting and the character's declaration. Thus the interpreter must make clear who is speaking by suggesting the personality of the character through the skillful use of body, voice, and the appropriate mental and physical attitude.

Indirect discourse blends the presence of the narrator with the presence of the character, so that narrator and character are seen and heard from simultaneously. The degree to which the narrator adopts the language, diction, and sentiments of the character is the ratio of the blend of narrator and character that the audience sees and hears. A remembered remark, for example, would carry less of the character's attitude than a reiterated demand would, although in both cases both narrator and character appear. Narrators commonly use indirect discourse in either simple grammatical sentences like "He said that . . ." or in more complex forms such as "She remembered having heard him say that . . ."

Examine this sentence from Flannery O'Connor's "Greenleaf":

"I thank God for ever thang," said Mr. Greenleaf.

Now compare it with these two sentences:

Mr. Greenleaf said that he thanked God for ever thang.

Then Greenleaf acknowledged divine providence.

O'Connor's sentence clearly demonstrates direct discourse: from the opening quotation marks the character fully assumes the line, and the narrator does not reappear until the end of the sentence. The second sentence blends the character and the narrator; but since the narrator has clearly adopted the characteristic diction and figures of speech of the character ("ever thang"), this sentence may demonstrate the character's attitude more than the narrator's. Finally, the last sentence has a narrator who has retained only the character's idea and has transformed it into his or her own language — language that is much more sophisticated than the character. In performance this would be seen as a narrator who dominates, but does not obliterate, the character. Sometimes, when indirect discourse implies subsequent activity ("He finally decided that he'd leave the kitchen and see for himself"), there is a clear appeal to a character's muscle response. The narrator can both describe this appeal and suggest it by mentally projecting the decision and its result. In each of these cases, though, remember that your decisions on how to perform a line rest on stylistic as well as literal clues, since style reveals background, attitudes, and the degree of mental or emotional tension of the moment.

Understanding the differences between these two kinds of narration can help you understand the various technical ways in which an interpreter can persuade an audience to believe that they are seeing before them not a student in a class but a character in a story. To achieve such belief, you must solve the technical problems that arise from performing dialogue. We discuss some of the techniques here. Also examine Chapter 8, particularly the section "Embodying Characters." Techniques for creating character are useful in narration as well as drama.

First, remember that characters are persons with bodies and voices. Read the story carefully to find all of the clues the narrator gives about the characters in the story. Note carefully the kinds of language the characters use, the kinds of things others say to and about the characters. Then begin to observe — very carefully — the world around you. Have you ever seen thirteen-year-old boys coming home from school? How do they carry themselves? How does a thoughtful boy hold his head? What does a rambunctious boy do with his arms and legs? Your own age and gender are immaterial at this point. When you have some physical clues about these boys, you are beginning to prepare to perform Roth's "The Conversion of the Jews," which appears at the end of this chapter. But you have only *just* begun. Now start listening carefully. How do boys this age talk? Has the voice changed? Or is it in that horrible no man's land between soprano and baritone, where it hits most of the notes in the scale? Begin to play with your voice. See if you can make yourself sound that age. Your first efforts will probably make you want to consider changing stories, but keep your courage and stay with it. Now add your body to the voice. It ought to feel out of place, since you are not thirteen, possibly not male. How can your body resemble the boys you observed? With a voice and body that begin to sound and look like something, it is often easier to undertake the biggest problem in creating characters.

You have established some external characteristics for the audience, but these will simply be externals until you provide the personality that sparks the voice and body to life. Are you thinking about these people in the worlds that they inhabit? Have you examined the part they play in the action of the tale?

Of course, no character exists apart from a story. That is why you should know as much as possible about the persons you are performing. Review the whole story and glean whatever clues you can from the information given, remembering that this overall view places the characters in proper perspective. Determine the character's gender, age, and maturity. Then define the personal characteristics that distinguish the character's attitude, degree of emotional intensity, and any peculiar or significant personal traits. Be sure to notice explicit descriptions about how a speech is said or what state of mind has prompted it, for narrative writing is uniquely able to stop action and examine motivation. Don't miss the implicit clues contained in the style of the speech, in the narrator's understanding of and sympathy with the character, and in the way in which the character's position is presented to the audience. Finally, remember that however bizarre these characters may seem to you, they are real in their own worlds, and you should create them to live there on their terms, not within your world. In "Conversion of the Jews," for example, you should discover why the boys are concerned about Rabbi Binder. Be sure you understand why they act the way they do. Is your Ozzie making serious efforts to figure out what Rabbi Binder is arguing? Here concentration will become increasingly important, since only if you commit yourself to the character's life can your audience fully perceive the character's goals. Once you have completed this process for one speaking character, repeat it for all the major characters in the passage you are reading.

When you speak the words of a character's dialogue, re-create in your mind the person who is being addressed; see that person vividly in front of you, established at a position slightly above and beyond the audience. This technique permits the audience to sit in the middle of the tension that ties the characters together and that prompts them to speak; it also protects any particular audience member from feeling directly addressed. Your mental and vocal projection should therefore be strong enough to carry slightly beyond the last row. When you resume the words of the narrator and describe or summarize, you will be able to speak directly to your audience and to establish rapport with them. If several characters speak in rapid succession, establish a place (a point of focus) for each of them, once again slightly above and beyond the audience. (You may wish to consult Chapter 8, particularly the section called "Physical Focus," for a further discussion of the ways to solve this kind of problem.)

Remember that dialogue has different levels of intensity; not every word is intended to be either engraved in marble or carelessly thrown away. Seek the degree of forcefulness that suggests the character's emotional and psychological state at the moment of speaking; casual comments can be delivered with less power than pleas for freedom are. This does not mean that your *mental* focus can be relaxed. When a character speaks — even such a line as "Close the door, please" — the speaker should be totally in character. People ask for the butter more often than they scream for help. The key is spontaneity, since it acknowledges the other characters and motivates responses. Similarly, you do not need to shout a speech, although it may have been shouted within the literature, if you have the proper

level of intensity and can suggest distance by your combined mental
and vocal projection.

Although you may feel at this point that there isn't anything else
you can learn about a story, much remains to be understood. We
mentioned that characters live in their own worlds. Because we need
to know not only what and why they act, but also *where* they act, we
must examine the role setting plays in narration.

Setting

Setting is a matter not only of locale but also of style. Narrators can
see the world through all kinds of spectacles, but where they allow
their characters to interact and where they permit them to speak is
as much a matter of the tale as it is a choice of the teller. If the maiden
aunt pours her tea "each afternoon as the sun strikes four against the
walnut bureau," we can see not only the aunt's habitual tea but also
her residence; the narrator acknowledges her ritual by permitting the
sun to toll its time as solemnly as a clock. Dylan Thomas weaves
another kind of world in one of the stories from *Quite Early One
Morning:*

> I was born in a large Welsh town at the beginning of the Great War —
> an ugly, lovely town (or so it was and is to me), crawling by a long and
> splendid curving shore where truant boys and sandfield boys and old
> men from nowhere, beach-combed, idled and paddled, watched the
> dock-bound ships or the ships steaming away into wonder and India,
> magic and China, countries bright with oranges and loud with lions;
> threw stones into the sea for the barking outcast dogs; made castles and
> forts and harbours and race tracks in the sand; and on Saturday summer
> afternoons listened to the brass band, watched the Punch and Judy, or
> hung about on the fringes of the crowd to hear the fierce religious speak-
> ers who shouted at the sea, as though it were wicked and wrong to roll
> in and out like that, whitehorsed and full of fishes.[3]

What an abundance of things to see and hear and smell and
touch and taste! And the rush of activity — presented in one massive,
breathless sentence — surrounds the reader utterly. Notice how
Thomas couples the items in the catalog: the town is ugly and lovely;
boys and old men idle and paddle and beachcomb; the sea that licks
that splendid shore carries men to wonder and magic; brass bands
and summers; puppet plays and town prophets; charging and pulling
seas finally full of nothing scarier than fishes: what a wonderful,
breathless world!

3. Dylan Thomas, *Quite Early One Morning* (New York: New Directions, 1954).

To interpret the story, you need to capture that world. Develop a keen visual and physical sense, so that in performance the whirling scene is all around you and your audience. Don't begin until you do. Let your audience see the shore and the boys, and then (as in an aerial shot in a film) move to the ships, the stones, and continue on through the town. A gesture might locate those most important places as they pass before you; let that palpable, living world motivate your description. Put Thomas's world there, in front of you. Tell your listeners about it!

Although not every scene is as boisterous as this one, every scene affects the characters and at the same time locates the action. Travel and adventure stories, in particular, use place as a crucial element in the telling of the tale, since landscape, climate, and time of day inevitably affect the characters. Biographies and autobiographies, histories and historical fiction all depend on an audience's acceptance of the vividness of the period, a sense that life was lived fully. Even the most fantastic story uses setting as an element to persuade an audience of the internal reality of the world of the tale, affecting the characters in obvious or subtle, superficial or profound ways.

Cutting and Excerpting

Only rarely do interpreters discover a poem or a story or a play that fits exactly all of the many requirements that performers impose on texts: the right length, the right balance of characters, the right distribution of lines and action, the right level of challenge. Consequently, interpreters have to take on works that, in one way or another, do not measure up to the performance or time requirements imposed by the occasion or assignment. They must cut or excerpt the text.

As we have stressed, interpretation seeks to communicate a work of literary art in its intellectual, aesthetic, and emotional entirety. This does not necessarily mean that one must perform every syllable of a work; indeed, the *essence* of an entire piece of literature can successfully be conveyed through performance of only a selection from it. There is a crucial distinction between excerpting a segment from a longer work and cutting, or abridging, a work in an attempt to encompass the entire work in a short amount of time. You should be aware of problems and dangers in both methods.

In *excerpting* from a longer work, the interpreter chooses a scene or passage that, when taken on its own, displays a totality of action, theme, or character development. Claire Morrill's "Miss Lizzie" (Chapter 2) offers several episodes that can be successfully excerpted, as does Isaac Bashevis Singer's "A Crown of Feathers" (Chapter 4). In each of these selections various brief segments seem to be relatively complete. In excerpting a segment, you should supply — in a brief introduction or in transitional comments — all the information necessary for the audience to understand fully what happens in the story. The segment itself should remain uncut; that is, you do not need to make interlinear or internal cuts, since the range or length of the segment itself conforms to the various requirements imposed by the particular performance situation. A long chapter that boasts a particularly attractive opening scene and a vivid conclusion might tempt an interpreter to splice the two sections together. However, the splicing itself can dangerously impair the delicate rhythms established by the author. Why not admit frankly that you are presenting two scenes from the same chapter? Perform the whole compelling opening; then, in your own words, fill in the transition with whatever information is necessary for the audience to understand the conclusion, which then can be performed as written by the author. This method has at least three special benefits. First, you can more accurately suggest the intellectual, aesthetic, and emotional entirety of the complete work, since you have not tampered with the internal tempo or development of the segments. Second, you can deal with the smaller segments more effectively in short periods of rehearsal time. Finally, since the segments themselves are more easily manageable, you have a better chance of capturing your audience's attention and appreciation. Best of all, of course, is the fact that excerpting allows you to select scenes from any work of literature that you want: the entirety of *Moby Dick* is impossible to perform, but there are numerous crucial scenes within the book that can be presented rewardingly.

Cutting differs from excerpting in that it imposes on diverse or unrelated words, lines, or scenes a false consecutiveness or immediate relationship that was not intended by the author. Some interpreters refuse to eliminate anything from what they perform, because they do not wish to impose on the work a pattern or scheme that violates its integrity. For other interpreters, cutting presents no particular problem. A performance may be restricted by time, by financial or physical resources, or sometimes by the intent of the performance. In spite of these limitations, you should approach the task of cutting literature with respect and concern for its essence, because the life of the work is what interests you; that life is what you seek to communicate in performance.

You should be fully aware of all of the problems that cutting can create. Of course, cutting a character who has one or two lines, such as a maid or an attendant lord whose chief responsibility is to announce an arrival or present a prop, usually does not impair the excitement of the scene; but be sure that the arriving character or the prop is not central to the scene itself.

Tempo and rhythm should be regarded with utmost caution when you are considering cutting. Look at the passage from Toni Morrison's *Sula* at the end of this chapter. Hannah repeats "Plum" and "Mamma" at crucial places. However tempting it may seem, avoid altering the delicate rhythm Morrison worked so hard to achieve. Let the story remain undamaged.

A cutting that may be small or seem insignificant can strongly affect the sense of the story. Consider Malamud's "The Prison," where the performer — already undertaking the narrator, the central character Tony/Tommy, his wife Rosa, and the little girl — is confronted for only a moment by the little girl's mother, who appears very briefly at the very end of the tale. It would be easy to cut her line; it is tempting, too, since cutting it would eliminate another character to suggest. However, what she says ("You little thief, this time you'll get your hands burned good") tells us quickly and fully what drove the little girl to steal and why she ignored the central character's warnings. Cutting the mother would drastically violate the achievement of the story.

So the interpreter alters a text with care and tact. We are not saying that you should never cut; we are saying that sensitive and experienced interpreters undertake cutting with great caution. If they can avoid cutting, they do. Think carefully and completely about what you are about to do, since cutting must not be some immediate response at an instant when it seems you'll never master the line. Judge honestly what you will gain and what you will lose if you eliminate a line or a few sentences. First of all, see if you can keep the selection whole and provide a transitional bridge between two or three segments that interest you most. Before actually removing any word or line, try to find another way to solve the problems that the line presents. You may be surprised at how your imagination, stretched by the richness of the story, conceives new ways to include all of the narrative's elements. If, however, there is no other, more discreet way to overcome the restrictions imposed by time or circumstance, cut only the minimum, and only what *must* be cut. Since virtually any limitation can be accommodated by excerpting, try to solve your dilemma by selecting segments to perform that are entire in and of themselves, thereby avoiding any internal cutting. Most works can be excerpted; few survive when they are cut internally.

Analyzing the Performance

Before we concentrate on how successfully you performed narration and prose, recheck the questions in the "Analyzing the Performance" sections in Chapters 2 and 4. Recall the problems that cropped up in your earlier readings. Have you improved your ability to concentrate? Have you paid clear and consistent attention to variety and contrast? Has your voice contributed to the unity and harmony of the selection? Has your body become more responsive to the imagery, particularly the kinesthetic images of your selection?

Such questions will never disappear from your performance analysis because whatever literature you select will challenge you in new and exciting ways. Don't allow yourself to become discouraged if some aspect of your performance seems to resist improvement. Sometimes skill requires considerably more effort than may be apparent. No one is instantly proficient at playing tennis or the violin. Constant, careful, and consistent concentration and commitment will produce the kinds of results you anticipate. One further thought about progress: be sure to listen carefully to and watch closely every other performer you can. You can always learn something instructive. At the same time, don't measure your own progress against others in your class. Better to gauge your developing prowess against the fine difficulty of the works you choose to perform. The most significant development in performance comes from valiant efforts with literature that causes you to reach slightly beyond your grasp. Nothing is gained by repeating the easy.

If you have not yet begun to experiment, why not begin? If you have performed only verse thus far, now is the time to try prose. Have you been concentrating on contemporary literature? Try a passage from one of the classic authors. Have you attempted personae whose gender is opposite to yours? What about characters of different ages and background and dialects? The function of any class in oral interpretation is not to confirm you in your ability to perform melancholy young women disappointed in love or brash and joking punks who always crack up audiences. Rather, oral interpretation asks that you experience the human condition in all its manifestations. Keep exploring yourself and your performance possibilities.

Now, together we can explore some common problems in performing prose. Again, try to respond to the questions as honestly as you can.

Did your analysis of the style of the writer suggest physical and vocal analogues to the literature? How did your compound-complex sentences look and sound?

Did your body and voice manifest the personality apparent in the speaker's word choice? Were you consistent?

Did you balance each sentence, locating the precise point for the most efficient placement of the fulcrum?

Did you control your physical and vocal resources to shape each sentence (and each paragraph) to the shape of the thought?

Were you attentive to parallel structure? Did you carefully attend to each speech phrase?

Did you allow your body and voice to reflect the fullest possible engagement with the tone color?

Did you carefully construct an internal and external life for your narrator? Was your audience always certain who was in charge? Did you permit the narrator to relinquish dominance during passages of scene and discourse?

Were your characters as full-blooded as those of the narrator? Did your narrator blend into the characters in the passage? Why?

Did you center the narrator's interest on the action and plot? Were your body and voice in control of the events?

Did the dialogue passages seem spontaneous and unforced? Was your audience certain who was speaking?

Did you excerpt without internal cutting?

These questions can also help you focus on the performance of others. In your classroom discussion, try to describe as precisely as possible at least two or three of the following concerns:

1. the nature of the narrator you *saw* and *heard:* his or her age and attitude toward events, characters, setting, and the audience to whom the tale is told

2. the relationships between the narrator and the characters, as demonstrated by the performer

3. the internal and external lives of the narrator and characters, as demonstrated by the performer

4. performance behavior that gave life to personalities in the story

5. facility in the management of dialogue, as demonstrated by the performer

6. the immediacy of the tale being told, as shown in the performance

When differences of opinion arise, return to the literature being performed. Your job as critic is to describe what you saw and heard and then to compare that performance with the text you know. Possibly you have performed the same passage yourself and thus know some of the problems more thoroughly than your classmates. Still, keep your attention directed to what happened in the performance you *saw* and *heard,* not what might have happened or what didn't happen. It isn't very helpful to say to a performer, "I didn't see any anger in Rosa's response to Tommy." Rather, try to describe exactly what you did see and hear; for example, "I saw a Rosa who seemed very calm and relaxed; your rate and volume were very easygoing." When you

combine your responses with those of other audience members —
and with the performer — you are ready to re-examine the story to
find those clues that suggest precisely how Rosa ought to sound and
behave.

Performing takes courage. If you want to improve, it helps to feel
secure enough with your fellow students to experiment. Such freedom is difficult to achieve if you expect to get "torn apart" each time
you perform. Discussion of a performance permits everyone to learn
if everyone listens carefully and everyone thinks for a moment before
speaking. Any given performance is a step on the route to the best
possible performance. If you genuinely want to be helped by your
classmates, be genuinely helpful in what you say to them.

In Chapter 11, "The Group Performance of Literature," we describe the technique of Chamber Theatre, which is the staging of
narrative. You may wish to examine this chapter for further ideas
about dealing with narration. Although that chapter focuses on
groups, many of the techniques it describes may spark your imagination with solutions that a solo performer can use. If you remember
that your primary responsibility is to tell the audience a story — the
tale that the author conceived and the narrator relates — your performance of narration will enlighten both you and your audience.
You will discover the rare pleasure of having told it very well, very
well indeed.

Selections for Analysis and Oral Interpretation

Since the narrator in this story understands Tommy's frustration much better
than the character himself does, the audience receives a rich and complex
picture of the young man's entrapment, his grim existence, and his future.
Pay careful attention to the ways in which Malamud's language indicates
shifts in the closeness of narrator and central character.

The Prison
BERNARD MALAMUD

Though he tried not to think of it, at twenty-nine Tommy Castelli's
life was a screaming bore. It wasn't just Rosa or the store they tended
for profits counted in pennies, or the unendurably slow hours and
endless drivel that went with selling candy, cigarettes, and soda
water; it was this sick-in-the-stomach feeling of being trapped in old
mistakes, even some he had made before Rosa changed Tony into
Tommy. He had been as Tony a kid of many dreams and schemes,

especially getting out of this tenement-crowded, kid-squawking neighborhood, with its lousy poverty, but everything had fouled up against him before he could. When he was sixteen he quit the vocational school where they were making him into a shoemaker, and began to hang out with the gray-hatted, thick-soled-shoe boys, who had the spare time and the mazuma and showed it in fat wonderful rolls down in the cellar clubs to all who would look, and everybody did, popeyed. They were the ones who had bought the silver caffe espresso urn and later the television, and they arranged the pizza parties and had the girls down; but it was getting in with them and their cars, leading to the holdup of a liquor store, that had started all the present trouble. Lucky for him the coal-and-ice man who was their landlord knew the leader in the district, and they arranged something so nobody bothered him after that. Then before he knew what was going on — he had been frightened sick by the whole mess — there was his father cooking up a deal with Rosa Agnello's old man that Tony would marry her and the father-in-law would, out of his savings, open a candy store for him to make an honest living. He wouldn't spit on a candy store, and Rosa was too plain and lank a chick for his personal taste, so he beat it off to Texas and bummed around in too much space, and when he came back everybody said it was for Rosa and the candy store, and it was all arranged again and he, without saying no, was in it.

That was how he had landed on Prince Street in the Village, working from eight in the morning to almost midnight every day, except for an hour off each afternoon when he went upstairs to sleep, and on Tuesdays, when the store was closed and he slept some more and went at night alone to the movies. He was too tired always for schemes now, but once he tried to make a little cash on the side by secretly taking in punchboards some syndicate was distributing in the neighborhood, on which he collected a nice cut and in this way saved fifty-five bucks that Rosa didn't know about; but then the syndicate was written up by a newspaper, and the punchboards all disappeared. Another time, when Rosa was at her mother's house, he took a chance and let them put in a slot machine that could guarantee a nice piece of change if he kept it long enough. He knew of course he couldn't hide it from her, so when she came and screamed when she saw it, he was ready and patient, for once not yelling back when she yelled, and he explained it was not the same as gambling because anybody who played it got a roll of mints every time he put in a nickel. Also the machine would supply them a few extra dollars cash they could use to buy television so he could see the fights without going to a bar; but Rosa wouldn't let up screaming, and later her father came in shouting that he was a criminal and chopped the machine apart with a plumber's hammer. The next day the cops raided for slot machines and gave out summonses wherever they found them, and though Tommy's place was practically the only candy store in the neighborhood that didn't have one, he felt bad about the machine for a long time.

Mornings had been his best time of day because Rosa stayed upstairs cleaning, and since few people came into the store till noon, he could sit around alone, a toothpick in his teeth, looking over the *News* and *Mirror* on the fountain counter, or maybe gab with one of the old cellar-club guys who had happened to come by for a pack of butts, about a horse that was running that day or how the numbers were paying lately; or just sit there, drinking coffee and thinking how far away he could get on the fifty-five he had stashed away in the cellar. Generally the mornings were this way, but after the slot machine, usually the whole day stank and he along with it. Time rotted in him, and all he could think of the whole morning, was going to sleep in the afternoon, and he would wake up with the sour remembrance of the long night in the store ahead of him, while everybody else was doing as he damn pleased. He cursed the candy store and Rosa, and cursed, from its beginning, his unhappy life.

It was on one of these bad mornings that a ten-year-old girl from around the block came in and asked for two rolls of colored tissue paper, one red and one yellow. He wanted to tell her to go to hell and stop bothering, but instead went with bad grace to the rear, where Rosa, whose bright idea it was to keep the stuff, had put it. He went from force of habit, for the girl had been coming in every Monday since the summer for the same thing, because her rock-faced mother, who looked as if she arranged her own widowhood, took care of some small kids after school and gave them the paper to cut out dolls and such things. The girl, whose name he didn't know, resembled her mother, except her features were not quite so sharp and she had very light skin with dark eyes; but she was a plain kid and would be more so at twenty. He had noticed, when he went to get the paper, that she always hung back as if afraid to go where it was dark, though he kept the comics there and most of the other kids had to be slapped away from them; and that when he brought her the tissue paper her skin seemed to grow whiter and her eyes shone. She always handed him two hot dimes and went out without glancing back.

It happened that Rosa, who trusted nobody, had just hung a mirror on the back wall, and as Tommy opened the drawer to get the girl her paper this Monday morning that he felt so bad, he looked up and saw in the glass something that made it seem as if he were dreaming. The girl had disappeared, but he saw a white hand reach into the candy case for a chocolate bar and for another, then she came forth from behind the counter and stood there, innocently waiting for him. He felt at first like grabbing her by the neck and socking till she threw up, but he had been caught, as he sometimes was, by this thought of how his Uncle Dom, years ago before he went away, used to take with him Tony alone of all the kids, when he went crabbing to Sheepshead Bay. Once they went at night and threw the baited wire traps into the water and after a while pulled them up and they had this green lobster in one, and just then this fat-faced cop came along and said they had to throw it back unless it was nine inches. Dom said it was nine inches, but the cop said not to be a wise guy so Dom measured it and it was ten, and they laughed about that lobster all night. Then he remembered how he had felt after Dom was gone, and tears filled his eyes. He found himself thinking about the way his life had turned out, and then about this girl, moved that she was so young and a thief. He felt he ought to do something for her, warn her to cut it out before she got trapped and fouled up her life before it got started. His urge to do this was strong, but when he went forward she looked up frightened because he had taken so long. The fear in her eyes bothered him and he didn't say anything. She thrust out the dimes, grabbed at the tissue rolls and ran out of the store.

He had to sit down. He kept trying to make the desire to speak to her go away, but it came back stronger than ever. He asked himself what difference does it make if she swipes candy — so she swipes it; and the role of reformer was strange and distasteful to him, yet he could not convince himself that what he felt he must do was unimportant. But he worried he would not know what to say to her. Always he had trouble speaking right, stumbled over words, especially in new situations. He was afraid he would sound like a jerk and she would not take him seriously. He had to tell her in a sure way so that even if it scared her, she would understand he had done it to set her straight. He mentioned her to no one but often thought about her, always looking around whenever he went outside to raise the awning or wash the window, to see if any of the girls playing in the street was her, but they never were. The following Monday, an hour after opening the store he had smoked a full pack of butts. He thought he had found what he wanted to say but was afraid for some reason she wouldn't come in, or if she did, this time she would be afraid to take the candy. He wasn't sure he wanted that to happen until he had said what he had to say. But at about eleven, while he was reading the *News,* she appeared, asking for the tissue paper, her eyes shining so he had to look away. He knew she meant to steal. Going to the rear he slowly opened the drawer, keeping his head lowered as he sneaked a look into the glass and saw her slide behind the counter. His heart beat hard and his feet felt nailed to the floor. He tried to remember what he had intended to do, but his mind was like a dark, empty room so he let her, in the end, slip away and stood tongue-tied, the dimes burning his palm.

Afterwards, he told himself that he hadn't spoken to her because it was while she still had the candy on her, and she would have been scared worse than he wanted. When he went upstairs, instead of sleeping, he sat at the kitchen window, looking out into the back yard. He blamed himself for being too soft, too chicken, but then he thought, no there was a better way to do it. He would do it indirectly, slip her a hint he knew, and he was pretty sure that would stop her. Sometime after, he would explain to her why it was good she had stopped. So next time he cleaned out this candy platter she helped herself from, thinking she might get wise he was on to her, but she seemed not to, only hesitated with her hand before she took two candy bars from the next plate and dropped them into the black patent leather purse she always had with her. The time after that he cleaned out the whole top shelf, and still she was not suspicious, and reached down to the next and took something different. One Monday he put some loose change, nickels and dimes, on the candy plate, but she left them there, only taking the candy, which bothered him a little. Rosa asked him what he was mooning about so much and why was he eating chocolate lately. He didn't answer her, and she began to look suspiciously at the women who came in, not excluding the little girls; and he would have been glad to rap her in the teeth, but it didn't matter as long as she didn't know what he had on his mind. At the same time he figured he would have to do something sure soon, or it would get harder for the girl to stop her stealing. He had to be strong about it. Then he thought of a plan that satisfied him. He would leave two bars on the plate and put in the wrapper of one a note she could read when she was alone. He tried out on paper many messages to her, and the one that seemed best he cleanly printed on a strip of cardboard and slipped it under the wrapper of one chocolate bar. It said, "Don't do this any more or you will suffer your whole life." He puzzled whether to sign it A Friend or Your Friend and finally chose Your Friend.

This was Friday, and he could not hold his impatience for Monday. But on Monday she did not appear. He waited for a long time, until Rosa came down, then he had to go up and the girl still hadn't come. He was greatly disappointed because she had never failed to come before. He lay on the bed, his shoes on, staring at the ceiling. He felt hurt, the sucker she had played him for and was now finished with because she probably had another on her hook. The more he thought about it the worse he felt. He worked up a splitting headache that kept him from sleeping, then he suddenly slept and woke without it. But he had awaked depressed, saddened. He thought about Dom getting out of jail and going away God knows where. He wondered whether he would ever meet up with him somewhere, if he took the fifty-five bucks and left. Then he remembered Dom was a pretty old guy now, and he might not know him if they did meet. He thought about life. You never really got what you wanted. No matter how hard you tried you made mistakes and couldn't get past them. You could never see the sky outside or the ocean because you were in a prison, except nobody called it a prison, and if you did they didn't know what you were talking about, or they said they didn't. A pall settled on him. He lay motionless, without thought or sympathy for himself or anybody.

But when he finally went downstairs, ironically amused that Rosa had allowed him so long a time off without bitching, there were people in the store and he could hear her screeching. Shoving his way through the crowd he saw in one sickening look that she had caught the girl with the candy bars and was shaking her so hard the kid's head bounced back and forth like a balloon on a stick. With a curse he tore her away from the girl, whose sickly face showed the depth of her fright.

"Whatsamatter," he shouted at Rosa, "you want her blood?"

"She's a thief," cried Rosa.

"Shut your face."

To stop her yowling he slapped her across her mouth, but it was a harder crack than he had intended. Rosa fell back with a gasp. She did not cry but looked around dazedly at everybody, and tried to smile, and everybody there could see her teeth were flecked with blood.

"Go home," Tommy ordered the girl, but then there was a movement near the door and her mother came into the store.

"What happened?" she said.

"She stole my candy," Rosa cried.

"I let her take it," said Tommy.

Rosa stared at him as if she had been hit again, then with mouth distorted began to sob.

"One was for you, Mother," said the girl.

Her mother socked her hard across the ear. "You little thief, this time you'll get your hands burned good."

She pawed at the girl, grabbed her arm and yanked it. The girl, like a grotesque dancer, half-ran, half-fell forward, but at the door she managed to turn her white face and thrust out at him her red tongue.

▮ How did you embody the relationship between the narrator
and Tommy?

▮ How much of Tommy did we see during indirect discourse?

Violet, the narrator of this story, is a woman of substantial courage and
determination. You do not have to share her beliefs to recognize that she is
a survivor with a healthy disrespect for the world she inhabits. Remember
that she never forgets her facial disfigurement.

FROM *The Ugliest Pilgrim*

DORIS BETTS

I sit in the bus station, nipping chocolate peel off a Mounds candy
bar with my teeth, then pasting the coconut filling to the roof of my
mouth. The lump will dissolve there slowly and seep into me the way
dew seeps into flowers.

I like to separate flavors that way. Always I lick the salt off cracker
tops before taking my first bite.

Somebody sees me with my suitcase, paper sack, and a ticket in
my lap. "You going someplace, Violet?"

Stupid. People in Spruce Pine are dumb and, since I look dumb,
say dumb things to me. I turn up my face as if to count those dead
flies piled under the light bulb. He walks away — a fat man, could
be anybody. I stick out my tongue at his back; the candy oozes down.
If I could stop swallowing, it would drip into my lung and I could
breathe vanilla.

Whoever it was, he won't glance back. People in Spruce Pine
don't like to look at me, full face.

A Greyhound bus pulls in, blows air; the driver stands by the
door. He's black-headed, maybe part Cherokee, with heavy shoulders but a weak chest. He thinks well of himself — I can tell that.
I open my notebook and copy his name off the metal plate so I can
call him by it when he drives me home again. And next week,
won't Mr. Wallace Weatherman be surprised to see how well I'm
looking!

I choose the front seat behind Mr. Weatherman, settle my bag
with the hat in it, then open the lined composition book again. Maybe
it's half full of writing. Even the empty pages toward the back have
one repeated entry, high, printed off Mama's torn catechism:
GLORIFY GOD AND ENJOY HIM FOREVER.

I finish Mr. Weatherman off in my book while he's running his
motor and getting us onto the highway. His nose is too broad, his
dark eyes too skimpy — nothing in his face I want — but the hair is

nice. I write that down, "Black hair?" I'd want it to curl, though, and be soft as a baby's.

Two others are on the bus, a nigger soldier and an old woman whose jaw sticks out like a shelf. There grow, on the backs of her hands, more veins than skin. One fat blue vessel, curling from wrist to knuckle, would be good; so on one page I draw a sample hand and let blood wind across it like a river. I write at the bottom: "Praise God, it is started. May 29, 1969," and turn to a new sheet. The paper's lumpy and I flip back to the thick envelope stuck there with adhesive tape. I can't lose that.

We're driving now at the best speed Mr. Weatherman can make on these winding roads. On my side there is nothing out the bus window but granite rock, jagged and wet in patches. The old lady and the nigger can see red rhododendron on the slope of Roan Mountain. I'd like to own a tight dress that flower color, and breasts to go under it. I write in my notebook, very small, the word "breasts," and turn quickly to another page. AND ENJOY HIM FOREVER.

The soldier bends as if to tie his shoes, but instead zips open a canvas bag and sticks both hands inside. When finally he sits back, one hand is clenched around something hard. He catches me watching. He yawns and scratches his ribs, but the right fist sets very lightly on his knee, and when I turn he drinks something out of its cup and throws his head quickly back like a bird or a chicken. You'd think I could smell it, big as my nose is.

Across the aisle the old lady says, "You going far?" She shows me a set of tan, artificial teeth.

"Oklahoma."

"I never been there. I hear the trees give out." She pauses so I can ask politely where she's headed. "I'm going to Nashville," she finally says. "The country-music capital of the world. My son lives there and works in the cellophane plant."

I draw in my notebook a box and two arrows. I crisscross the box.

"He's got three children not old enough to be in school yet."

I sit very still, adding new boxes, drawing baseballs in some, looking busy for fear she might bring out their pictures from her big straw pocketbook. The funny thing is she's looking past my head, though there's nothing out that window but rock wall sliding by. I mumble, "It's hot in here."

Angrily she says, "I had eight children myself."

My pencil flies to get the boxes stacked, eight-deep, in a pyramid. "Hope you have a nice visit."

"It's not a visit. I maybe will move." She is hypnotized by the stone and the furry moss in its cracks. Her eyes used to be green. Maybe, when young, she was red-haired and Irish. If she'll stop

talking, I want to think about trying green eyes with that Cherokee
hair. Her lids droop; she looks drowsy. "I am right tired of children,"
she says and lays her head back on the white rag they button on
these seats.

Now that her eyes are covered, I can study that face — china
white, and worn thin as tissue so light comes between her bones and
shines through her whole head. I picture the light going around and
around her skull, like water spinning in a jar. If I could wait to be
eighty, even my face might grind down and look softer. But I'm
ready, in case the Preacher mentions that. Did Elisha make Naaman
bear into old age his leprosy? Didn't Jesus heal the withered hand,
even on Sunday, without waiting for the work week to start? And
put back the ear of Malchus with a touch? As soon as Job had learned
enough, did his boils fall away?

Lord, I have learned enough.

The old lady sleeps while we roll downhill and up again; then
we turn so my side of the bus looks over the valley and its thickety
woods where, as a girl, I pulled armloads of galax, fern, laurel, and
hemlock to have some spending money. I spent it for magazines full
of women with permanent waves. Behind us, the nigger shuffles a
deck of cards and deals to himself by fives. Draw poker — I could
beat him. My papa showed me, long winter days and nights snowed
in on the mountain. He said poker would teach me arithmetic. It
taught me there are four ways to make a royal flush and, with two
players, it's an even chance one of them holds a pair on the deal.
And when you try to draw from a pair to four of a kind, discard the
kicker; it helps your odds.

The soldier deals smoothly, using his left hand only with his
thumb on top. Papa was good at that. He looks up and sees my
whole face with its scar, but he keeps his eyes level as if he has seen
worse things; and his left hand drops cards evenly and in rhythm.
Like a turtle, laying eggs.

I close my eyes and the riffle of his deck rests me to the next main
stop where I write in my notebook: "Praise God for Johnson City,
Tennessee, and all the state to come. I am on my way."

At Kingsport, Mr. Weatherman calls rest stop and I go straight
through the terminal to the ladies' toilet and look hard at my face in
the mirror. I must remember to start the Preacher on the scar first of
all — the only thing about me that's even on both sides.

Lord! I am so ugly!

Maybe the Preacher will claim he can't heal ugliness. And I'm
going to spread my palms by my ears and show him — this is a
crippled face! An infirmity! Would he do for a kidney or liver what

he withholds from a face? The Preacher once stuttered, I read someplace, and God bothered with that. Why not me? When the Preacher
labors to heal the sick in his Tulsa auditorium, he asks us at home to
lay our fingers on the television screen and pray for God's healing.
He puts forth his own ten fingers and we match them, pad to pad,
on that glass. I have tried that, Lord, and the Power was too filtered
and thinned down for me.

I touch my hand now to this cold mirror glass, and cover all but
my pimpled chin, or wide nose, or a single red-brown eye. And
nothing's too bad by itself. But when they're put together?

I've seen the Preacher wrap his hot, blessed hands on a club foot
and cry out "HEAL!" in his funny way that sounds like the word
"Hell" broken into two pieces. Will he not cry out, too, when he sees
this poor, clubbed face? I will be to him as Goliath was to David, a
need so giant it will drive God to action.

I comb out my pine-needle hair. I think I would like blond curls
and Irish eyes, and I want my mouth so large it will never be done
with kissing.

The old lady comes in the toilet and catches me pinching my bent
face. She jerks back once, looks sad, then pets me with her twiggy
hand. "Listen, honey," she says, "I had looks once. It don't amount
to much."

I push right past. Good people have nearly turned me against
you, Lord. They open their mouths for the milk of human kindness
and boiling oil spews out.

So I'm half running through the terminal and into the café, and
I take the first stool and call down the counter, "Tuna-fish sandwich,"
quick. Living in the mountains, I eat fish every chance I get and
wonder what the sea is like. Then I see I've sat down by the nigger
soldier. I do not want to meet his gaze, since he's a wonder to me,
too. We don't have many black men in the mountains. Mostly they
live east in Carolina, on the flatland, and pick cotton and tobacco
instead of apples. They seem to me like foreigners. He's absently
shuffling cards the way some men twiddle thumbs. On the stool
beyond him is a paratrooper, white, and they're talking about what
a bitch the army is. Being sent to the same camp has made them
friends already.

I roll a dill-pickle slice through my mouth — a wheel, a bitter
wheel. Then I start on the sandwich and it's chicken by mistake when
I've got chickens all over my back yard.

"Don't bother with the beer," says the black one. "I've got better
on the bus." They come to some agreement and deal out cards on
the counter.

It's just too much for me. I lean over behind the nigger's back and say to the paratrooper, "I wouldn't play with him." Neither one moves. "He's a mechanic." They look at each other, not at me. "It's a way to cheat on the deal."

The paratrooper sways backward on his stool and stares around out of eyes so blue that I want them, right away, and maybe his pale blond hair. I swallow a crusty half-chewed bite. "One-handed grip; the mechanic's grip. It's the middle finger. He can second-deal and bottom-deal. He can buckle the top card with his thumb and peep."

"I be damn," says the paratrooper.

The nigger spins around and bares his teeth at me, but it's half a grin. "Lady, you want to play?"

I slid my dishes back. "I get mad if I'm cheated."

"And mean when you're mad." He laughs a laugh so deep it makes me retaste that bittersweet chocolate off the candy bar. He offers the deck to cut, so I pull out the center and restack it three ways. A little air blows through his upper teeth. "I'm Grady Fliggins and they call me Flick."

The paratrooper reaches a hand down the counter to shake mine. "Monty Harrill. From near to Raleigh."

"And I'm Violet Karl. Spruce Pine. I'd rather play five-card stud."

By the time the bus rolls on, we've moved to its wider back seat playing serious cards with a fifty-cent ante. My money's sparse, but I'm good and the deck is clean. The old lady settles into my front seat, stiffer than plaster. Sometimes she throws back a hurt look.

Monty, the paratrooper, plays soft. But Flick's so good he doesn't even need to cheat, though I watch him close. He drops out quick when his cards are bad; he makes me bid high to see what he's got; and the few times he bluffs, I'm fooled. He's no talker. Monty, on the other hand, says often, "Whose play is it?" till I know that's his clue phrase for a pair. He lifts his cards close to his nose and gets quiet when planning to bluff. And he'd rather use wild cards but we won't. Ah, but he's pretty, though!

After we've swapped a little money, mostly the paratrooper's, Flick pours us a drink in some cups he stole in Kingsport and asks, "Where'd you learn to play?"

I tell him about growing up on a mountain, high, with Mama dead, and shuffling cards by a kerosene lamp with my papa. When I passed fifteen, we'd drink together, too. Applejack or a beer he made from potato peel.

"And where you headed now?" Monty's windburned in a funny pattern, with pale goggle circles that start high on his cheeks. Maybe it's something paratroopers wear.

"It's a pilgrimage." They lean back with their drinks. "I'm going to see this preacher in Tulsa, the one that heals, and I'm coming home pretty. Isn't that healing?" Their still faces make me nervous. "I'll even trade if he says. . . . I'll take somebody else's weak eyes or deaf ears. I could stand limping a little."

The nigger shakes his black head, snickering.

"I tried to get to Charlotte when he was down there with his eight-pole canvas cathedral tent that seats nearly fifteen thousand people, but I didn't have money then. Now what's so funny?" I think for a minute I am going to have to take out my notebook, and unglue the envelope and read them all the Scripture I have looked up on why I should be healed. Monty looks sad for me, though, and that's worse. "Let the Lord twist loose my foot or give me a cough, so long as I'm healed of my looks while I'm still young enough —" I stop and tip up my plastic cup. Young enough for you, blue-eyed boy, and your brothers.

"Listen," says Flick in a high voice. "Let me go with you and be there for that swapping." He winks one speckled eye.

"I'll not take black skin, no offense." He's offended, though, and lurches across the moving bus and falls into a far seat. "Well, you as much as said you'd swap it off!" I call. "What's wrong if I don't want it any more than you?"

Monty slides closer. "You're not much to look at," he grants, sweeping me up and down till I nearly glow blue from his eyes. Shaking his head, "And what now? Thirty?"

"Twenty-eight. His drink and his cards, and I hurt Flick's feelings. I didn't mean that." I'm scared, too. Maybe, unlike Job, I haven't learned enough. Who ought to be expert in hurt feelings? Me, that's who.

"And you live by yourself?"

I start to say "No, there's men falling all over each other going in and out my door." He sees my face, don't he? It makes me call, "Flick? I'm sorry." Not one movement. "Yes. By myself." Five years now, since Papa had heart failure and fell off the high back porch and rolled downhill in the gravel till the hobblebushes stopped him. I found him past sunset, cut from the rocks but not much blood showing. And what there was, dark, and already jellied.

Monty looks at me carefully before making up his mind to say, "That preacher's a fake. You ever see a doctor agree to what he's done?"

"Might be." I'm smiling. I tongue out the last liquor in my cup. I've thought of all that, but it may be what I believe is stronger than him faking. That he'll be electrified by my trust, the way a magnet can get charged against its will. He might be a lunatic or a dope fiend, and it still not matter.

Monty says, "Flick, you plan to give us another drink?"

"No." He acts like he's going to sleep.

"I just wouldn't count on that preacher too much." Monty cleans his nails with a matchbook corner and sometimes gives me an uneasy look. "Things are mean and ugly in this world — I mean *act* ugly, do ugly, be ugly."

He's wrong. When I leave my house, I can walk for miles and everything's beautiful. Even the rattlesnakes have grace. I don't mind his worried looks since I'm writing in my notebook how we met and my winnings — a good sign, to earn money on a trip. I like the way army barbers trim his hair. I wish I could touch it.

"Took one furlough in your mountains. Pretty country. Maybe hard to live in? Makes you feel little." He looks toward Flick and says softer, "Makes you feel like the night sky does. So many stars."

"Some of them big as daisies." It's easy to live in, though. Some mornings a deer and I scare up each other in the brush, and his heart stops, and mine stops. Everything stops till he plunges away. The next pulsebeat nearly knocks you down. "Monty, doesn't your hair get lighter in the summers? That might be a good color hair to ask for in Tulsa. Then I could turn colors like the leaves. Spell your last name for me."

He does, and says I sure am funny. Then he spells Grady Fliggins and I write that, too. He's curious about my book, so I flip through and offer to read him parts. Even with his eyes shut, Flick is listening. I read them about my papa's face, a chunky block face, not much different from the Preacher's square one. After Papa died, I wrote that to slow down how fast I was forgetting him. I tell Monty parts of my lists: that you can get yellow dye out of gopherwood and Noah built his ark from that, and maybe it stained the water. That a cow eating snakeroot might give poison milk. I pass him a pressed maypop flower I'm carrying to Tulsa, because the crown of thorns and the crucifixion nails grow in its center, and each piece of the bloom stands for one of the apostles.

"It's a mollypop vine," says Flick out of one corner of his mouth. "And it makes a green ball that pops when you step on it." He stretches. "Deal you some blackjack?"

For no reason, Monty says, "We oughtn't to let her go."

We play blackjack till supper stop and I write in my book, "Praise God for Knoxville and two new friends." I've not had many friends. At school in the valley, I sat in the back rows, reading, a hand spread on my face. I was smart, too; but if you let that show, you had to stand for the class and present different things.

When the driver cuts out the lights, the soldiers give me a whole seat, and a duffelbag for a pillow. I hear them whispering, first about women, then about me; but after a while I don't hear that anymore.

By the time we hit Nashville, the old lady makes the bus wait while she begs me to stop with her. "Harvey won't mind. He's a good boy." She will not even look at Monty and Flick. "You can wash and change clothes and catch a new bus tomorrow."

"I'm in a hurry. Thank you." I have picked a lot of galax to pay for this trip.

"A girl alone. A girl that maybe feels she's got to prove something?" The skin on her neck shivers. "Some people might take advantage."

Maybe when I ride home under my new face, that will be some risk. I shake my head, and as she gets off she whispers something to Mr. Weatherman about looking after me. It's wasted, though, because a new driver takes his place and he looks nearly as bad as I do — oily-faced and toad-shaped, with eyeballs a dingy color and streaked with blood. He's the flatlands driver, I guess, because he leans back and drops one warty hand on the wheel and we go so fast and steady you can hardly tell it.

Since Flick is the tops in cards and we're tired of that, it's Monty's turn to brag on his motorcycle. He talks all across Tennessee till I think I could ride one by hearsay alone, that my wrist knows by itself how far to roll the throttle in. It's a Norton and he rides it in Scrambles and Enduro events, in his leathers, with spare parts and tools glued all over him with black electrician's tape.

"So this bastard tells me, 'Zip up your jacket because when I run over you I want some traction.'"

Flick is playing solitaire. "You couldn't get me on one of them killing things."

"One day I'm coming through Spruce Pine, flat out, throw Violet up behind me! We're going to lean all the way through them mountains. Sliding the right foot and then sliding the left." Monty lays his head back on the seat beside me, rolls it, watches. "How you like that? Take you through creeks and ditches like you was on a skateboard. You can just holler and hang on."

Lots of women have, I bet.

"The Norton's got the best front forks of anybody. It'll nearly roll up a tree trunk and ride down the other side." He demonstrates on the back seat. I keep writing. These are new things, two-stroke and

four-stroke, picking your line on a curve, Milwaukee iron. It will all come back to me in the winters, when I reread these pages.

Flick says he rode on a Harley once. "Turned over and got drug. No more."

They argue about what he should have done instead of turning over. Finally Monty drifts off to sleep, his head leaning at me slowly, so I look down on his crisp, light hair. I pat it as easy as a cat would, and it tickles my palm. I'd almost ask them in Tulsa to make me a man if I could have hair like his, and a beard, and feel so different in so many places.

He slides closer in his sleep. One eyebrow wrinkles against my shoulder. Looking our way, Flick smokes a cigarette, then reads some magazine he keeps rolled in his belt. Monty makes a deep noise against my arm as if, while he slept, his throat had cleared itself. I shift and his whole head is on my shoulder now. Its weight makes me breathe shallow.

I rest my eyes. If I should turn, his hair would barely touch my cheek, the scarred one, like a shoebrush. I do turn and it does. For miles he sleeps that way and I almost sleep. Once, when we take a long curve, he rolls against me, and one of his hands drifts up and then drops in my lap. Just there, where the creases are.

I would not want God's Power to turn me, after all, into a man. His breath is so warm. Everywhere, my skin is singing. Praise God for that.

▌ When did your Violet shift her interest from the Preacher to Flick and Monty? Why? How did your audience see it happen?

The cheerful storyteller in this tale may surprise you, but nothing seems to disturb him seriously. Be sure you render the bodies and voices of the narrator and Monroe carefully. Let their adventures arise inevitably out of their lives. And take your time — a good story needs room to stretch out.

The Naked Lady

MADISON SMARTT BELL

This is a thing that happened before Monroe started maken the heads, while he was still maken the naked ladies.

Monroe went to the college and it made him crazy for a while like it has done to many a one.

He about lost his mind on this college girl he had. She was just a little old bit of a thing and she talked like she had bugs in her mouth and she was just nothen but trouble. I never would of messed with her myself.

When she thown him over we had us a party to take his mind off it. Monroe had these rooms in a empty mill down by the railroad yard. He used to make his scultures there and we was both liven there too at the time.

We spent all the money on whiskey and beer and everbody we known come over. When it got late Monroe appeared to drop a stitch and went to thowin bottles at the walls. This caused some people to leave but some other ones stayed on to help him I think.

I had a bad case of drunk myself. A little before sunrise I crawled off and didn't wake up till up in the afternoon. I had a sweat from sleepin with clothes on. First thing I seen when I opened my eyes was this big old rat setten on the floor side the mattress. He had a look on his face like he was wonderen would it be safe if he come over and took a bite out of my leg.

It was the worst rats in that place you ever saw. I never saw nothin to match em for bold. If you chunked somethin at em they would just back off a ways and look at you mean. Monroe had him this tin sink which was full of plaster from the scultures and ever night these old rats would mess in it. In the mornin you could see they had left tracks goen places you wouldnt of believed somethin would go.

We had this twenty two pistol we used to shoot em up with but it wasnt a whole lot of good. You could hit one of these rats square with a twenty two and he would go off with it in him and just get meaner. About the only way to kill one was if you hit him spang in the head and that needs you to be a better shot than I am most of the time.

We did try a box of them exploden twenty twos like what that boy shot the president with. They would take a rat apart if you hit him but if you didnt they would bounce around the room and bust up the scultures and so on.

It happened I had put this pistol in my pocket before I went to bed so Monroe couldnt get up to nothin silly with it. I taken it out slow and thew down on this rat that was looken me over. Hit him in the hindquarter and he went off and clamb a pipe with one leg draggen.

I sat up and saw the fluorescents was on in the next room thew the door. When I went in there Monroe was messen around one of his sculture stands.

Did you get one, he said.

Winged him, I said.

That aint worth much, Monroe said. He off somewhere now plotten your doom.

I believe the noise hurt my head more'n the slug hurt that rat, I said. Is it any whiskey left that you know of.

Let me know if you find some, Monroe said. So I went to looken around. The place was nothin but trash and it was glass all over the floor.

I might of felt worse some time but I dont just remember when it was, I said.

They's coffee, Monroe said.

I went in the other room and found a half of a pint of Heaven Hill between the mattress and the wall where I must of hid it before I tapped out. Pretty slick for drunk as I was. I taken it in to the coffee pot and mixed half and half with some milk in it for the sake of my stomach.

Leave me some, Monroe said. I hadnt said a word, he must of smelt it. He tipped the bottle and took half what was left.

The hell, I said. What you maken anyway?

Naked lady, Monroe said.

I taken a look and it was this shape of a woman setten on a mess of clay. Monroe made a number of these things at the time. Some he kept and the rest he thown out. Never could tell the difference myself.

Thats all right, I said.

No it aint, Monroe said. Soon's I made her mouth she started in asken me for stuff. She wants new clothes and she wants a new car and she wants some jewry and a pair of Italian shoes.

And if I make her that stuff, Monroe said, I know she's just goen to take it out looken for some other fool. I'll set here all day maken stuff I dont care for and she'll be out just riden and riden.

Dont make her no clothes and she cant leave, I said.

She'll whine if I do that, Monroe said. The whole time you was asleep she been fussen about our relationship.

You know the worst thing, Monroe said. If I just even thought about maken another naked lady I know she would purely raise hell.

Why dont you just make her a naked man and forget it, I said.

Why dont I do this? Monroe said. He whopped the naked lady with his fist and she turned into a flat clay pancake, which Monroe put in a plastic bag to keep soft. He could hit a good lick when he wanted. I hear this is common among scultures.

Dont you feel like doen somethin, Monroe said.

I aint got the least dime, I said.

I got a couple dollars, he said. Lets go see if it might be any gas in the truck.

They was some. We had this old truck that wasnt too bad except it was slow to start. When we once got it goen we drove over to this pool hall in Antioch where nobody didnt know us. We stayed awhile and taught some fellers that was there how to play rotation and five in the side and some other games that Monroe was good at. When this was over with we had money and I thought we might go over to the Ringside and watch the fights. This was a bar with a ring in the middle so you could set there and drink and watch people get hurt.

We got in early enough to take seats right under the ropes. They was an exhibition but it wasnt much and Monroe started in on this little girl that was setten by herself at the next table.

Hey there Juicy Fruit, he said, come on over here and get somethin real good.

I wouldnt, I told him, haven just thought of what was obvious. Then this big old hairy thing came out from the back and sat down at her table. I known him from a poster out front. He was champion of some kind of karate and had come all the way up from Atlanta just to beat somebody to death and I didnt think he would care if it was Monroe. I got Monroe out of there. I was some annoyed with him because I would have admired to see them fights if I could do it without bein in one myself.

So Monroe said he wanted to hear music and we went some places where they had that. He kept after the girls but they wasnt any trouble beyond what we could handle. After while these places closed and we found us a little railroad bar down on Lower Broad.

It wasnt nobody there but the pitifulest band you ever heard and six bikers, the big fat ugly kind. They wasnt the Hell's Angels but I believe they would have done until some come along. I would of left if it was just me.

Monroe played pool with one and lost. It wouldnt of happened if he hadnt been drunk. He did have a better eye than me which may be why he is a sculture and I am a second rate pool player.

How come all the fat boys in this joint got on black leather jackets? Monroe hollered out. Could that be a new way to lose weight?

The one he had played with come bellyen over. These boys like to look you up and down beforehand to see if you might faint. But Monroe hooked this one side of the head and he went down like a steer in the slaughterhouse. This didnt make me as happy as it might of because it was five of em left and the one that was down I thought apt to get up shortly.

I shoved Monroe out the door and told him to go start the truck. The band had done left already. I thown a chair and I thown some other stuff that was layen around and I ducked out myself.

The truck wasnt started yet and they was close behind. It was this old four ten I had under the seat that somebody had sawed a foot off the barrel. I taken it and shot the sidewalk in front of these boys. The pattern was wide on account of the barrel bein short like it was and I believe some of it must of hit all of em. It was a pump and took three shells and I kept two back in case I needed em for serious. But Monroe got the truck goen and we left out of there.

I was some mad at Monroe. Never said a word to him till he parked outside the mill. It was a nice moon up and thowin shadows in the cab when the headlights went out. I turned the shotgun across the seat and laid it into Monroe's ribs.

What you up to? he said.

You might want to die, I said, but I dont believe I want to go with you. I pumped the gun to where you could hear the shell fallen in the chamber.

If that's what you want just tell me now and I'll save us both some trouble.

It aint what I want, Monroe said.

I taken the gun off him.

I dont know what I do want, Monroe said.

Go up ther and make a naked lady and you feel better, I told him.

He was messen with clay when I went to sleep but that aint what he done. He set up a mirror and done a head of himself instead. I taken a look at the thing in the mornin and it was a fair likeness. It looked like it was thinkin about all the foolish things Monroe had got up to in his life so far.

That same day he done one of me that was so real it even looked like it had a hangover. Ugly too but that aint Monroe's fault.

He is makin money with it now.

How we finally fixed them rats was we brought on a snake. Monroe was the one to have the idea. It was a good-sized one and when it had just et a rat it was as big around as your arm. It didnt eat more than about one a week but it appeared to cause the rest of em to lay low.

You might say it was as bad to have snakes around as rats but at least it was only one of the snake.

The only thing was when it turned cold the old snake wanted to get in the bed with you. Snakes aint naturally warm like we are and this is how come people think they are slimy which is not the truth when you once get used to one.

This old snake just comes and goes when the spirit moves him. I aint seen him in a while but I expect he must be still around.

▌ In your performance, what were the chief physical differences between the narrator and Monroe? What were the vocal differences?

From the Eighth Book of Ovid's *The Metamorphoses* (as translated by the American poet Rolfe Humphries) comes this tale of an old couple able to stay together even after death. Be sure you understand why Lelex (the narrator) tells this tale. Trust the line length to help you balance these long sentences.

FROM **The Metamorphoses**
OVID

The Story of Baucis and Philemon

                    An oak-tree stands
Beside a linden, in the Phrygian hills.
There's a low wall around them. I have seen
The place myself; a prince once sent me there
To land ruled by his father. Not far off

A great marsh lies, once habitable land,
But now a playground full of coots and divers.
Jupiter came here, once upon a time,
Disguised as mortal man, and Mercury,
His son, came with him, having laid aside
Both wand and wings. They tried a thousand houses,
Looking for rest; they found a thousand houses
Shut in their face. But one at last received them,
A humble cottage, thatched with straw and reeds.
A good old woman, Baucis, and her husband,
A good old man, Philemon, used to live there.
They had married young, they had grown old together
In the same cottage; they were very poor,
But faced their poverty with cheerful spirit
And made its burden light by not complaining.
It would do you little good to ask for servants
Or masters in that household, for the couple
Were all the house; both gave and followed orders.
So, when the gods came to this little cottage,
Ducking their heads to enter, the old man
Pulled out a rustic bench for them to rest on,
As Baucis spread a homespun cover for it.
And then she poked the ashes around a little,
Still warm from last night's fire, and got them going
With leaves and bark, and blew at them a little,
Without much breath to spare, and added kindling,
The wood split fine, and the dry twigs, made smaller
By breaking them over the knee, and put them under
A copper kettle, and then she took the cabbage
Her man had brought from the well-watered garden,
And stripped the outer leaves off. And Philemon
Reached up, with a forked stick, for the side of bacon,
That hung below the smoky beam, and cut it,
Saved up so long, a fair-sized chunk, and dumped it
In the boiling water. They made conversation
To keep the time from being too long, and brought
A couch with willow frame and feet, and on it
They put a sedge-grass mattress, and above it
Such drapery as they had, and did not use
Except on great occasions. Even so,
It was pretty worn, it had only cost a little
When purchased new, but it went well enough
With a willow couch. And so the gods reclined.
Baucis, her skirts tucked up, was setting the table

With trembling hands. One table-leg was wobbly;
A piece of shell fixed that. She scoured the table,
Made level now, with a handful of green mint,
Put on the olives, black or green, and cherries
Preserved in dregs of wine, endive and radish,
And cottage cheese, and eggs, turned over lightly
In the warm ash, with shells unbroken. The dishes,
Of course, were earthenware, and the mixing-bowl
For wine was the same silver, and the goblets
Were beech, the inside coated with yellow wax.
No time at all, and the warm food was ready,
And wine brought out, of no particular vintage,
And pretty soon they had to clear the table
For the second course: here there were nuts and figs
And dates and plums and apples in wide baskets —
Remember how apples smell? — and purple grapes
Fresh from the vines, and a white honeycomb
As centerpiece, and all around the table
Shone kindly faces, nothing mean or poor
Or skimpy in good will.
                              The mixing-bowl,
As often as it was drained, kept filling up
All by itself, and the wine was never lower.
And this was strange, and scared them when they saw it.
They raised their hands and prayed, a little shaky —
"Forgive us, please, our lack of preparation,
Our meagre fare!" They had one goose, a guardian,
Watchdog, he might be called, of their estate,
And now decided they had better kill him
To make their offering better. But the goose
Was swift of wing, too swift for slow old people
To catch, and they were weary from the effort,
And could not catch the bird, who fled for refuge,
Or so it seemed, to the presence of the strangers.
"Don't kill him," said the gods, and then continued:
"We are gods, you know: this wicked neighborhood
Will pay as it deserves to; do not worry,
You will not be hurt, but leave the house, come with us,
Both of you, to the mountain-top!" Obeying,
With staff and cane, they made the long climb, slowly
And painfully, and rested, where a bowman
Could reach the top with a long shot, looked down,
Saw water everywhere, only their cottage
Standing above the flood. And while they wondered

And wept a little for their neighbors' trouble,
The house they used to live in, the poor quarters
Small for the two of them, became a temple:
Forked wooden props turned into marble columns;
The thatch grew brighter yellow; the roof was golden;
The doors were gates, most wonderfully carved;
The floor that used to be of earth was marble.
Jupiter, calm and grave, was speaking to them:
"You are good people, worthy of each other,
Good man, good wife — ask us for any favor,
And you shall have it." And they hesitated,
Asked, "Could we talk it over, just a little?"
And talked together, apart, and then Philemon
Spoke for them both: "What we would like to be
Is to be priests of yours, and guard the temple,
And since we have spent our happy years together,
May one hour take us both away; let neither
Outlive the other, that I may never see
The burial of my wife, nor she perform
That office for me." And the prayer was granted.
As long as life was given, they watched the temple,
And one day, as they stood before the portals,
Both very old, talking the old days over,
Each saw the other put forth leaves, Philemon
Watched Baucis changing, Baucis watched Philemon,
And as the foliage spread, they still had time
To say "Farewell, my dear!" and the bark closed over
Sealing their mouths. And even to this day
The peasants in that district show the stranger
The two trees close together, and the union
Of oak and linden in one. The ones who told me
The story, sober ancients, were no liars,
Why should they be? And my own eyes have seen
The garlands people bring there; I brought new ones,
Myself, and said a verse: *The gods look after*
Good people still, and cherishers are cherished.

▌ What happened to *your* body and voice when the narrator
described the transformation?

This passage from the novel *Sula* is powerful and moving. Pay close attention to its moment-by-moment build-ups. The language is vivid, and the subject is shocking. It will require a total commitment from the interpreter.

FROM **Sula**
TONI MORRISON

So late one night in 1921, Eva got up from her bed and put on her clothes. Hoisting herself up on her crutches, she was amazed to find that she could still manage them, although the pain in her armpits was severe. She practiced a few steps around the room, and then opened the door. Slowly, she manipulated herself down the long flights of stairs, two crutches under her left arm, the right hand grasping the banister. The sound of her foot booming in comparison to the delicate pat of the crutch tip. On each landing she stopped for breath. Annoyed at her physical condition, she closed her eyes and removed the crutches from under her arms to relieve the unaccustomed pressure. At the foot of the stairs she redistributed her weight between the crutches and swooped on through the front room, to the dining room, to the kitchen, swinging and swooping like a giant heron, so graceful sailing about in its own habitat but awkward and comical when it folded its wings and tried to walk. With a swing and a swoop she arrived at Plum's door and pushed it open with the tip of one crutch. He was lying in bed barely visible in the light coming from a single bulb. Eva swung over to the bed and propped her crutches at its foot. She sat down and gathered Plum into her arms. He woke, but only slightly.

"Hey, man. Hey. You holdin' me, Mamma?" His voice was drowsy and amused. He chuckled as though he had heard some private joke. Eva held him closer and began to rock. Back and forth she rocked him, her eyes wandering around his room. There in the corner was a half-eaten store-bought cherry pie. Balled-up candy wrappers and empty pop bottles peeped from under the dresser. On the floor by her foot was a glass of strawberry crush and a *Liberty* magazine. Rocking, rocking, listening to Plum's occasional chuckles, Eva let her memory spin, loop and fall. Plum in the tub that time as she leaned over him. He reached up and dripped water into her bosom and laughed. She was angry, but not too, and laughed with him.

"Mamma, you so purty. You so purty, Mamma."

Eva lifted her tongue to the edge of her lip to stop the tears from running into her mouth. Rocking, rocking. Later she laid him down and looked at him a long time. Suddenly she was thirsty and reached for the glass of strawberry crush. She put it to her lips and discovered it was blood-tainted water and threw it to the floor. Plum woke up and said, "Hey, Mamma, whyn't you go on back to bed? I'm all right. Didn't I tell you? I'm all right. Go on, now."

"I'm going, Plum," she said. She shifted her weight and pulled her crutches toward her. Swinging and swooping, she left his room. She dragged herself to the kitchen and made grating noises.

Plum on the rim of a warm light sleep was still chuckling. Mamma. She sure was somethin'. He felt twilight. Now there seemed to be some kind of wet light traveling over his legs and stomach with a deeply attractive smell. It wound itself — this wet light — all about him, splashing and running into his skin. He opened his eyes and saw what he imagined was the great wing of an eagle pouring a wet lightness over him. Some kind of baptism, some kind of blessing, he thought. Everything is going to be all right, it said. Knowing that it was so he closed his eyes and sank back into the bright hole of sleep.

Eva stepped back from the bed and let the crutches rest under her arms. She rolled a bit of newspaper into a tight stick about six inches long, lit it and threw it onto the bed where the kerosene-soaked Plum lay in snug delight. Quickly, as the *whoosh* of flames engulfed him, she shut the door and made her slow and painful journey back to the top of the house.

Just as she got to the third landing she could hear Hannah and some child's voice. She swung along, not even listening to the voices of alarm and the cries of the deweys. By the time she got to her bed someone was bounding up the stairs after her. Hannah opened the door. "Plum! Plum! He's burning, Mamma! We can't even open the door! Mamma!"

Eva looked into Hannah's eyes. "Is? My baby? Burning?" The two women did not speak, for the eyes of each were enough for the other. Then Hannah closed hers and ran toward the voices of neighbors calling for water.

▌ Did your audience see what it cost Eva to make her move? How?

Here is the beginning of possibly the most famous story ever told. An enormously challenging narrator presides here: how does he or she know all this? Be sure we get all the appropriate scope and resonance. Don't forget to see and hear each step in the creation process.

Genesis I: 1–16

THE TORAH

When God began to create the heaven and the earth — the earth being unformed and void, with darkness over the surface of the deep and a wind from God sweeping over the water — God said, "Let there be light"; and there was light. God saw that the light was good, and God separated the light from the darkness. God called the light Day, and the darkness He called Night. And there was evening and there was morning, a first day.

God said, "Let there be an expanse in the midst of the water, that it may separate water from water." God made the expanse, and it separated the water which was below the expanse from the water which was above the expanse. And it was so. God called the expanse Sky. And there was evening and there was morning, a second day.

God said, "Let the water below the sky be gathered into one area, that the dry land may appear." And it was so. God called the dry land Earth, and the gathering of waters He called Seas. And God saw that this was good. And God said, "Let the earth sprout vegetation: seed-bearing plants, fruit trees of every kind on earth that bear fruit with the seed in it." And it was so. The earth brought forth vegetation: seed-bearing plants of every kind, and trees of every kind bearing fruit with the seed in it. And God saw that this was good. And there was evening and there was morning, a third day.

God said, "Let there be lights in the expanse of the sky to separate day from night; they shall serve as signs for the set times — the days and the years; and they shall serve as lights in the expanse of the sky to shine upon the earth." And it was so. God made the two great lights, the greater light to dominate the day and the lesser light to dominate the night, and the stars. And God set them in the expanse of the sky to shine upon the earth, to dominate the day and the night, and to separate light from darkness. And God saw that this was good. And there was evening and there was morning, a fourth day.

God said, "Let the waters bring forth swarms of living creatures, and birds that fly above the earth across the expanse of the sky." God created the great sea monsters, and all the living creatures of every kind that creep, which the waters brought forth in swarms; and all the winged birds of every kind. And God saw that this was good.

God blessed them, saying, "Be fertile and increase, fill the waters in the seas, and let the birds increase on the earth." And there was evening and there was morning, a fifth day.

God said, "Let the earth bring forth every kind of living creature: cattle, creeping things, and wild beasts of every kind." And it was so. God made wild beasts of every kind and cattle of every kind, and all kinds of creeping things of the earth. And God saw that this was good. And God said, "Let us make man in our image, after our likeness. They shall rule the fish of the sea, the birds of the sky, the cattle, the whole earth, and all the creeping things that creep on earth." And God created man in His image, in the image of God He created him; male and female He created them. God blessed them and God said to them, "Be fertile and increase, fill the earth and master it; and rule the fish of the sea, the birds of the sky, and all the living things that creep on earth."

God said, "See, I give you every seed-bearing plant that is upon all the earth, and every tree that has seed-bearing fruit; they shall be yours for food. And to all the animals on land, to all the birds of the sky, and to everything that creeps on earth, in which there is the breath of life, [I give] all the green plants for food." And it was so. And God saw all that He had made, and found it very good. And there was evening and there was morning, the sixth day.

❚ Each repetition carries a richer, newer meaning. How did you convey these subtle distinctions to your audience?

This simple story is sheer nonsense and wonderful fun if you succumb to the spirit of its irrepressible narrator. What seems like eccentric punctuation in fact is a splendid performance clue.

The Detective
ARCHIBALD MARSHALL

Once there was a detective who was good at finding out crimes, and one day a gentleman came to him and said somebody has just tried to murder my rich aunt, do you think you could find out for me who it was?

And the detective said well I might, but why not let sleeping dogs lie?

And he said well when she comes to she may think that I did it because of her money, and it will be rather awkward for me.

So the detective said yes I can quite see that, and I will find out for you who it was and you can go back to your wife and your three little girls and tell them not to worry, and you needn't be late for breakfast any more.

And he said how do you know I have a wife and three little girls and that I was late for breakfast?

And the detective said oh that is quite easy, you have three spots of marmalade on your face where they kissed you good morning, and if your wife had been dead you would be wearing a black tie instead of a blue one with red anchors on it, and you must have been late for breakfast because your little girls had finished theirs or they would have left egg or porridge or bacon on your face but not marmalade.

So he said well it is very wonderful, and the detective said oh that is nothing to what I can find out if I like, did the man who tried to murder your rich aunt leave any finger-prints or things like that behind him?

And he said well he did leave a photograph of himself with his name and address on it, I suppose it fell out of his pocket.

The detective said well that might be of some help if everything else fails, now I had better see your rich aunt and then I shall have something more to go on.

And he said oh you can't do that, she hasn't come to yet.

But the detective said oh that doesn't matter, and he took him to see his rich aunt, and she was lying in a bed with a pink eider-down on it.

So when the detective had looked all round the room, especially on the toilet-table, he said I am glad I came here, it is quite easy now and by the time your rich aunt comes to I shall be able to tell you who tried to murder her.

So the next morning the gentleman went to him again, and he said my rich aunt has come to now, and she wants to know who tried to murder her, if you have found out I shall be glad if you will tell me because she thinks I tried to do it because of her money.

And the detective said oh yes, I have found out who it was, I told you it would be quite easy, you know that shop Bigg and Bolt in the High Street?

And he said he did.

And the detective said well if you go there you will find a man serving in the shop with black hair rather rough, and if a policeman goes with you he can take him to prison because he is the one.

And he said it is very wonderful, how did you find out?

And the detective said oh it was quite easy, that pink eider-down was a new one and it had the name of that shop on it, and I knew the man who had sold it to your rich aunt would want to see what it looked like on her bed, and his hair was rough because he brushed it with your rich aunt's hairbrush before he went away, I found a black hair on it and hers is more mouse-coloured.

Well the gentleman asked a policeman to go with him, but they were all ladies serving in that shop and their hair was more lemon-coloured, and they said they hadn't stocked pink eider-downs for a long time and if his rich aunt's eider-down looked new perhaps she had laid it by. And Mr Bigg who was quite bald said he was sorry somebody had tried to murder the gentleman's rich aunt because she had been a good customer, and if it had been anybody in his shop he would have spoken about it but it must have been somebody else. And Mr Bolt said so too, and his hair was red so it couldn't have been him either.

So the policeman didn't take up anybody there and the gentleman went back to the detective and he said look here you must have made a mistake about this.

And the detective said well I did, I have been looking at that hair through a microscope and it belongs to a black spaniel, and if your rich aunt keeps one I expect she brushes it with her own hairbrush sometimes.

And he said well she does keep a black spaniel called Fido, and perhaps she does brush it sometimes with her own hairbrush, her habits were always rather dirty.

And the detective said why didn't you tell me that, it would have made all the difference, if you keep things back I'm afraid I can't go on any more for you.

So the gentleman said don't you think it would be worth while to try that man who left the photograph of himself behind, with his name and address on it?

And the detective said well you can do that if you like, it isn't the sort of clue I care about myself, it is too easy, but if anybody ever tries to murder your rich aunt again you can come to me and perhaps I shall have better luck next time.

So the gentleman gave the photograph to the police and they had the man sent to prison, and the gentleman's rich aunt was pleased with him for finding out who had tried to murder her, and she said she would leave him all her money because he hadn't tried to do it himself.

▌ How did you distinguish among the speakers?
▌ What posture did your narrator adopt? Why?

Since so much of Philip Roth's story below begins during a scene, the narrator emerges only gradually as the tale unfolds. Don't be tempted to skimp on preparation, for the narrator's complex understanding of Ozzie's dilemma is central to the total effect of the story. Ozzie and Itzie are two full-blooded twelve-year-old boys who are radically different yet remarkably similar.

FROM *The Conversion of the Jews*
PHILIP ROTH

"You're a real one for opening your mouth in the first place," Itzie said. "What do you open your mouth all the time for?"

"I didn't bring it up, Itz, I didn't," Ozzie said.

"What do you care about Jesus Christ for anyway?"

"I didn't bring up Jesus Christ. He did. I didn't even know what he was talking about. Jesus is historical, he kept saying. Jesus is historical." Ozzie mimicked the monumental voice of Rabbi Binder.

"Jesus was a person that lived like you and me," Ozzie continued. "That's what Binder said — "

"Yeah? . . . So what! What do I give two cents whether he lived or not. And what do you gotta open your mouth!" Itzie Lieberman favored closed-mouthedness, especially when it came to Ozzie Freedman's questions. Mrs. Freedman had to see Rabbi Binder twice before about Ozzie's questions and this Wednesday at four-thirty would be the third time. Itzie preferred to keep *his* mother in the kitchen; he settled for behind-the-back subtleties such as gestures, faces, snarls and other less delicate barnyard noises.

"He was a real person, Jesus, but he wasn't like God, and we don't believe he is God." Slowly, Ozzie was explaining Rabbi Binder's position to Itzie, who had been absent from Hebrew School the previous afternoon.

"The Catholics," Itzie said helpfully, "they believe in Jesus Christ, that he's God." Itzie Lieberman used "the Catholics" in its broadest sense — to include the Protestants.

Ozzie received Itzie's remark with a tiny head bob, as though it were a footnote, and went on. "His mother was Mary, and his father probably was Joseph," Ozzie said. "But the New Testament says his real father was God."

"His *real* father?"

"Yeah," Ozzie said, "that's the big thing, his father's supposed to be God."

"Bull."

"That's what Rabbi Binder says, that it's impossible — "

"Sure it's impossible. That stuff's all bull. To have a baby you gotta get laid," Itzie theologized. "Mary hadda get laid."

"That's what Binder says: 'The only way a woman can have a baby is to have intercourse with a man.'"

"He said *that*, Ozz?" For a moment it appeared that Itzie had put the theological question aside. "He said that, intercourse?" A little curled smile shaped itself in the lower half of Itzie's face like a pink mustache. "What you guys do, Ozz, you laugh or something?"

"I raised my hand."

"Yeah? Whatja say?"

"That's when I asked the question."

Itzie's face lit up. "Whatja ask about — intercourse?"

"No, I asked the question about God, how if He could create the heaven and earth in six days, and make all the animals and the fish and the light in six days — the light especially, that's what always gets me, that He could make the light. Making fish and animals, that's pretty good — "

"That's damn good." Itzie's appreciation was honest but unimaginative: it was as though God had just pitched a one-hitter.

"But making light . . . I mean when you think about it, it's really something," Ozzie said. "Anyway, I asked Binder if He could make all that in six days, and He could *pick* the six days he wanted right out of nowhere, why couldn't He let a woman have a baby without having intercourse."

"You said intercourse, Ozz, to Binder?"

"Yeah."

"Right in class?"

"Yeah."

Itzie smacked the side of his head.

"I mean, no kidding around," Ozzie said, "that'd really be nothing. After all that other stuff, that'd practically be nothing."

Itzie considered a moment. "What'd Binder say?"

"He started all over again explaining how Jesus was historical and how he lived like you and me but he wasn't God. So I said I under*stood* that. What I wanted to know was different."

What Ozzie wanted to know was always different. The first time he had wanted to know how Rabbi Binder could call the Jews "The Chosen People" if the Declaration of Independence claimed all men to be created equal. Rabbi Binder tried to distinguish for him between political equality and spiritual legitimacy, but what Ozzie wanted to know, he insisted vehemently, was different. That was the first time his mother had to come.

Then there was the plane crash. Fifty-eight people had been killed in a plane crash at La Guardia. In studying a casualty list in the newspaper his mother had discovered among the list of those dead eight Jewish names (his grandmother had nine but she counted

Miller as a Jewish name); because of the eight she said the plane crash was "a tragedy." During free-discussion time on Wednesday Ozzie had brought to Rabbi Binder's attention this matter of "some of his relations" always picking out the Jewish names. Rabbi Binder had begun to explain cultural unity and some other things when Ozzie stood up at his seat and said that what he wanted to know was different. Rabbi Binder insisted that he sit down and it was then that Ozzie shouted that he wished all fifty-eight were Jews. That was the second time his mother came.

"And he kept explaining about Jesus being historical, and so I kept asking him. No kidding, Itz, he was trying to make me look stupid."

"So what he finally do?"

"Finally he starts screaming that I was deliberately simple-minded and a wise guy, and that my mother had to come, and this was the last time. And that I'd never get bar-mitzvahed if he could help it. Then, Itz, then he starts talking in that voice like a statue, real slow and deep, and he says that I better think over what I said about the Lord. He told me to go to his office and think it over." Ozzie leaned his body towards Itzie. "Itz, I thought it over for a solid hour, and now I'm convinced God could do it."

Ozzie had planned to confess his latest transgression to his mother as soon as she came home from work. But it was a Friday night in November and already dark, and when Mrs. Freedman came through the door she tossed off her coat, kissed Ozzie quickly on the face, and went to the kitchen table to light the three yellow candles, two for the Sabbath and one for Ozzie's father.

When his mother lit the candles she would move her two arms slowly towards her, dragging them through the air, as though per-suading people whose minds were half made up. And her eyes would get glassy with tears. Even when his father was alive Ozzie remembered that her eyes had gotten glassy, so it didn't have any-thing to do with his dying. It had something to do with lighting the candles.

As she touched the flaming match to the unlit wick of a Sabbath candle, the phone rang, and Ozzie, standing only a foot from it, plucked it off the receiver and held it muffled to his chest. When his mother lit candles Ozzie felt there should be no noise; even breathing, if you could manage it, should be softened. Ozzie pressed the phone to his breast and watched his mother dragging whatever she was dragging, and he felt his own eyes get glassy. His mother was a round, tired, gray-haired penguin of a woman whose gray skin had begun to feel the tug of gravity and the weight of her own history. Even when she was dressed up she didn't look like a chosen person. But when she lit candles she looked like something better; like a woman who knew momentarily that God could do anything.

After a few mysterious minutes she was finished. Ozzie hung up the phone and walked to the kitchen table where she was beginning to lay the two places for the four-course Sabbath meal. He told her that she would have to see Rabbi Binder next Wednesday at four-thirty, and then he told her why. For the first time in their life together she hit Ozzie across the face with her hand.

All through the chopped liver and chicken soup part of the dinner Ozzie cried; he didn't have any appetite for the rest.

On Wednesday, in the largest of the three basement classrooms of the synagogue, Rabbi Marvin Binder, a tall, handsome, broad-shouldered man of thirty with thick strong-fibered black hair, removed his watch from his pocket and saw that it was four o'clock. At the rear of the room Yakov Blotnik, the seventy-one-year-old custodian, slowly polished the large window, mumbling to himself, unaware that it was four o'clock or six o'clock, Monday or Wednesday. To most of the students Yakov Blotnik's mumbling, along with his brown curly beard, scythe nose, and two heel-trailing black cats, made of him an object of wonder, a foreigner, a relic, towards whom they were alternately fearful and disrespectful. To Ozzie the mumbling had always seemed a monotonous, curious prayer; what made it curious was that old Blotnik had been mumbling so steadily for so many years. Ozzie suspected he had memorized the prayers and forgotten all about God.

"It is now free-discussion time," Rabbi Binder said. "Feel free to talk about any Jewish matter at all — religion, family, politics, sports — "

There was silence. It was a gusty, clouded November afternoon and it did not seem as though there ever was or could be a thing called baseball. So nobody this week said a word about that hero from the past, Hank Greenberg — which limited free discussion considerably.

And the soul-battering Ozzie Freedman had just received from Rabbi Binder had imposed its limitation. When it was Ozzie's turn to read aloud from the Hebrew book the rabbi had asked him petulantly why he didn't read more rapidly. He was showing no progress. Ozzie said he could read faster but that if he did he was sure not to understand what he was reading. Nevertheless, at the rabbi's repeated suggestion Ozzie tried, and showed a great talent, but in the midst of a long passage he stopped short and said he didn't understand a word he was reading, and started in again at a drag-footed pace. Then came the soul-battering.

Consequently when free-discussion time rolled around none of the students felt too free. The rabbi's invitation was answered only by the mumbling of feeble old Blotnik.

"Isn't there anything at all you would like to discuss?" Rabbi Binder asked again, looking at his watch. "No questions or comments?"

There was a small grumble from the third row. The rabbi requested that Ozzie rise and give the rest of the class the advantage of his thought.

Ozzie rose. "I forget it now," he said, and sat down in his place.

Rabbi Binder advanced a seat towards Ozzie and poised himself on the edge of the desk. It was Itzie's desk and the rabbi's frame only a dagger's-length away from his face snapped him to sitting attention.

"Stand up again, Oscar," Rabbi Binder said calmly, "and try to assemble your thoughts."

Ozzie stood up. All his classmates turned in their seats and watched as he gave an unconvincing scratch to his forehead.

"I can't assemble any," he announced, and plunked himself down.

"Stand up!" Rabbi Binder advanced from Itzie's desk to the one directly in front of Ozzie; when the rabbinical back was turned Itzie gave it five-fingers off the tip of his nose, causing a small titter in the room. Rabbi Binder was too absorbed in squelching Ozzie's nonsense once and for all to bother with titters. "Stand up, Oscar. What's your question about?"

Ozzie pulled a word out of the air. It was the handiest word. "Religion."

"Oh, now you remember?"

"Yes."

"What is it?"

Trapped, Ozzie blurted the first thing that came to him. "Why can't He make anything He wants to make!"

As Rabbi Binder prepared an answer, a final answer, Itzie, ten feet behind him, raised one finger on his left hand, gestured it meaningfully towards the rabbi's back, and brought the house down.

Binder twisted quickly to see what had happened and in the midst of the commotion Ozzie shouted into the rabbi's back what he couldn't have shouted to his face. It was a loud, toneless sound that had the timbre of something stored inside for about six days.

"You don't know! You don't know anything about God!"

The rabbi spun back towards Ozzie. "What?"

"You don't know — you don't — "

"Apologize, Oscar, apologize!" It was a threat.

"You don't — "

Rabbi Binder's hand flicked out at Ozzie's cheek. Perhaps it had only been meant to clamp the boy's mouth shut, but Ozzie ducked and the palm caught him squarely on the nose.

The blood came in a short, red spurt on to Ozzie's shirt front.

The next moment was all confusion. Ozzie screamed, "You bastard, you bastard!" and broke for the classroom door. Rabbi Binder lurched a step backwards, as though his own blood had started flowing violently in the opposite direction, then gave a clumsy lurch forward and bolted out the door after Ozzie. The class followed after the rabbi's huge blue-suited back, and before old Blotnik could turn from his window, the room was empty and everyone was headed full speed up the three flights leading to the roof.

▎ Ozzie is serious and intelligent, but he isn't solemn. How did you demonstrate to your audience his continued efforts to understand?

Bibliography

Allot, Miriam. *Novelists on the Novel*. London: Routledge and Kegan Paul, 1959.

A good source book in which novelists of all periods write about the problems of writing fiction.

Bakhtin, M. M. *The Dialogic Imagination: Four Essays*. Ed. Michael Holquist. Trans. Caryl Emerson and Michael Holquist. Austin: University of Texas Press, 1981.

An important study that provides new insights into the peculiar use of language in the novel as well as the various ways in which time and space intersect in various forms of the novel.

Bentley, Phyllis. *Some Observation on the Art of Narrative*. New York: Macmillan Company, 1947.

Extensive treatment of summary, description, and scene. A standard reference work for analysis of narratives.

Booth, Wayne C. *The Rhetoric of Fiction*. 2nd ed. Chicago: University of Chicago Press, 1983.

The expanded second edition of this classic in criticism of prose fiction extends and clarifies concepts explored in the first edition.

Chatman, Seymour. *Story and Discourse: Narrative Structure in Fiction and Film*. Ithaca, N.Y.: Cornell University Press, 1978.

An exploration of narrative in fiction and film written after and heavily influenced by Genette's work with narrative. A further attempt to determine the "deep structures" of narrative as particularized in the "surface structures" of fiction and film.

Cohn, Dorritt. *Transparent Minds: Narrative Modes for Presenting Consciousness*. Princeton, N.J.: Princeton University Press, 1978.
Thoughtful examination of three fundamental options a narrator has for presenting a character's consciousness in first- and third-person narrative.

Forster, E. M. *Aspects of the Novel*. New York: Harcourt, Brace and Company, 1927.
A splendidly readable, enormously practical book that clearly explains the implications of theoretical problems facing novelists.

Genette, Gerard. *Narrative Discourse*. Trans. Jane E. Lewin. Ithaca, N.Y.: Cornell University Press, 1980.
An impressive categorization of the functions and effects of narrative techniques that deserves close scrutiny.

James, Henry. *The Art of Fiction*. New York: Oxford University Press, 1948.
A classic work by an author who was himself a master in the field of fiction.

Kawin, Bruce F. *The Mind of the Novel: Reflexive Fiction and the Ineffable*. Princeton, N.J.: Princeton University Press, 1982.
An exploration of the underlying voice in first-person fiction as it is revealed apart from the conscious projection of an image of self by the narrator.

Lanser, Susan Snaider. *The Narrative Act: Point of View in Prose Fiction*. Princeton, N.J.: Princeton University Press, 1981.
An analysis of point of view grounded in speech act theory that examines the narrator's *status* in relation to the speech act, *contact* with the audience, and *stance* with regard to the narrated word.

Moffett, James, and Kenneth R. McElheney. *Points of View: An Anthology of Short Stories*. New York: New American Library, 1966.
Anthology arranged according to variations in point of view. A brief introduction precedes each of the eleven classifications, and the stories richly reward performance.

Nabokov, Vladimir. *Lectures on Literature*. Ed. Fredson Bowers. New York: Harcourt Brace Jovanovich, 1980.
Special attention to plot structure and action in the works of Austen, Dickens, Flaubert, Stevenson, Proust, Kafka, and Joyce.

Pratt, Mary Louise. *Toward a Speech Act Theory of Literary Discourse*. Bloomington: Indiana University Press, 1981.
This study refutes the distinction between literary and nonliterary uses of language, arguing that literature is a speech act that is best analyzed in terms of the speaker's attempt to control the focus of the reader.

Raban, Jonathan. *The Technique of Modern Fiction: Essays in Practical Criticism.* South Bend, Ind.: University of Notre Dame Press, 1969.

An excellent and very readable study dealing with fifteen aspects of fictional technique, illustrating each topic with a long extract from a contemporary novel or short story. Elements of narrative, character, style, and language are examined in works of modern fiction.

Robbe-Grillet, Alain. *For a New Novel: Essays of Fiction.* Trans. Richard Howard. New York: Grove Press, 1965.

Robbe-Grillet has had a lasting impact on contemporary fiction, and in this collection he records his own precise notions about the novel. He replies to his critics and attacks Sartre and the social realists. He also discusses specific works of Camus, Beckett, Raymond Roussel, Italo Svevo, and others.

Stevick, Phillip, ed. *The Theory of the Novel.* New York: Free Press, 1967.

A collection of excerpts by noted authors and critics from books, essays, and the introductions to novels on topics ranging from "Point of View" to "Narrative Technique."

Thompson, David W., and Virginia Fredricks. *Oral Interpretation of Fiction: A Dramatic Approach.* Minneapolis: Burgess Publishing Company, 1964.

A solid brief text stressing a "dramatistic" approach to oral interpretation, based on the theory that "the total symbolic action in literature and in the reader's oral interpretation of it can be discovered only from exploring all the interacting relationships of Scene-Role-Gesture."

III. The Interpretation of Drama

7

The Solo Performance of Drama

Imitations produce pain or pleasure, not because they are mistaken for realities, but because they bring realities to mind.

Samuel Johnson, Preface to The Plays of William Shakespeare

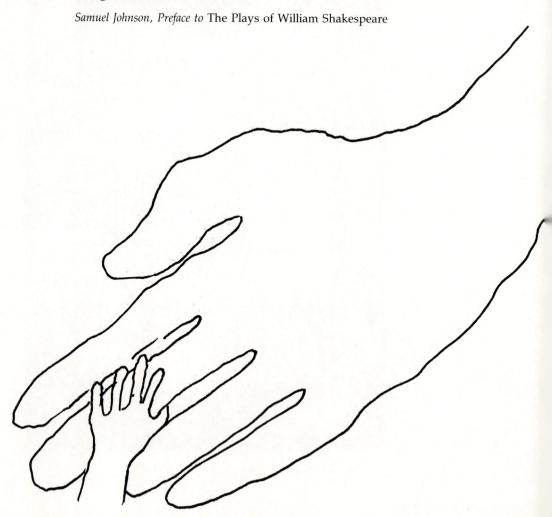

Audiences enjoy watching plays in part because drama is more interesting than life. Like real life, dramatic life has a beginning, a middle, and an end (or, in terms of the play, a point to which the audience must be brought); but unlike real life, dramatic life consists of selected events, each of which takes place for a discernible reason. In even the most convoluted play, everything that happens on stage is subordinate to the central action. That action involves a conflict among two or more forces, and the excitement of the conflict arises from the equality of the matched contestants. Thus, in order to understand drama, at different points one studies people, conflict, life, and choices, because people in conflict making choices about their lives is the essence of drama.

But drama is also *play* in the sense of make-believe, game, and ritual. The actress playing Juliet pretends to die, speaking iambic pentameter, while the audience willingly suspends disbelief. To help create the illusion that the events the audience observes are happening for the first time, the characters must seem to live in the world each play creates. This means that the actors must speak and move as they do not because of their rehearsals or the audience but because this is the way real people lead their lives. As you interpret drama, you too must create a completely convincing illusion.

Compare the characters in a play with opponents in a game who attempt to achieve their opposite goals in spite of all efforts to deter them. Characters in plays pursue goals that range from a complete reversal of their current lives to a strict maintenance of the status quo. A major character appears on stage when something or someone there can affect that character's progress toward his or her goal; and no character ought to leave the stage until it is clear that that opportunity has passed or that another opportunity is more attractive. In some plays, the game ends when the main character achieves his or her goal (as often happens in a comedy); in other plays, the game ends when the goal is achieved too late for it to matter anymore (as often happens in a tragedy). Some contemporary dramas (like Beckett's *Waiting for Godot* or *Endgame*) appear never to finish; or they finish when the main characters realize that they will always be striving, that for them the game is never over. Perhaps it is best to say that the game of a play ends when the characters have exhausted their resources and there is nothing left to contest.

Western drama, which began in the religious celebrations of ancient Greece, still includes rituals, and sometimes the rituals are so widely accepted that they become rules or conventions. For example, performers in a play speak, performers in a musical or opera sing, and performers in a ballet dance. Each form has its own rules, and each performance and production must be true to the form as well as to its story. Like a game, every play follows its own set of rules. Even the most experimental play by the most determined iconoclast follows rules. When the eighteenth-century critic Samuel Johnson said that "the drama's patrons give," he meant that, for the drama to exist, the audience must be sufficiently pleased not to leave the theatre before the play is over.

Whether you perform drama in a classroom, on a podium, or in an auditorium; whether or not you use a lectern; and whether or not you decide to carry a manuscript, you create about yourself and inhabit the world of the play. Today we can see drama performed at almost any place or time. Like play of other kinds, however, drama is always performed in a place that both performer and audience acknowledge as the playing space. Actors appearing on stage are expected to fill that space with their energy, concentration, and commitment and to sketch the boundary within which they exist. Around them the audience constructs the frame of seeing. The audience attends to that space diligently, not wanting to miss a thing, and so long as they are not misled, they accept the world the performer suggests.

A great deal of concentration and commitment is also required for the solo performance of drama. No audience will ever accept the reality of the world of the play unless the interpreter believes in the characters and setting and, through concentration, communicates that belief to the audience. Concentration allows you to supplant temporarily all the details of personal life with the intricate truth of the characters' lives; commitment enables you to accept the world of the play (and the rules of that world) as your own.

Of course, concentration and commitment alone are not enough: the interpreter should communicate the drama through body and voice. Unlike the actor, the interpeter works alone in a playing space that is reduced to the boundaries sketched by one body and one voice. You will succeed only by training your body and voice to bring the world of the play to life. In Chapters 3 and 4 we discussed the use of voice and body in interpretation; review these chapters as preparation for the performance of drama.

We have said that performing drama also requires (at different stages) a study of life, of conflict, and of people. If you have studied people, you can create believable characters who could live in their real world; if you have carefully scrutinized the nature of their conflict, you will recognize how the tensions shift in the play and how its goals are achieved, abandoned, or revised; if you have studied life, you can create the world of a particular play — a world that your audience will understand and that, together with your audience, you can populate, decorate, and illuminate.

Finally, the performance of literature requires that you make choices on such matters as how to say a word and where to stress a point. Drama is no exception. Each choice you make measures your sensitivity, acuity, and accuracy as an interpreter. Each choice testifies to the work done — or ignored. No performer is ever more important than the play, and no play is ever more important than the performer. With proper preparation, the right choice will appear; if you're constantly wondering when you should gesture, perhaps you haven't really finished your homework. Keep these responsibilities in mind as you read the next few sections and remember as you proceed that you have something unique to offer an audience in your performance.

The Purpose of Solo Performance

Since the process of performing drama may seem formidable, beginning interpreters frequently have a question that they are reluctant to ask in class: "What is to be gained by one person's doing something that was clearly written to be done by a group?" If you are harboring such a doubt, the next few paragraphs should be very helpful for you.

Performing drama requires considerable coordination of all the skills that are used in performing other genres, and as in any art based on skills, mastering the basic skills requires considerable practice. The skills of the solo performer of drama are also the skills used to perform poetry and prose.

In part, the solo performance gives you a unique way of knowing the play. Actors speak of "knowing" their lines, dancers of "knowing" the steps, typists of "knowing" the keyboard; what they mean is that they have acquired a special understanding of what they are studying. An interpreter is somewhat like an actor, because the interpreter communicates the play with body and mind and emotional make-up. Unlike an actor, however, the interpreter takes on *all* the characters. An interpreter's knowledge will encompass more than an actor's knowledge, since the interpreter's task is to communicate the *entirety* of the play.

An audience benefits from a solo performance because it sees the play from a unique perspective: the shifting focus of the speaking character. A person watching a staged production may be distracted from the point that the actors and the director want to emphasize. But in your solo performance no one can upstage you; no one moves on your line; no one covers you. The audience sees how individual forces acting upon each other make the play what it is. Your audience also takes part in the play's creation, since they must imaginatively provide the spectacle that you suggest.

Even the play benefits from a solo performance because it has a unique embodiment — you. You take on the entire play: your vision informs the audience without the difficulties that can accompany a staged performance. Only the play and the interpreter and the audience exist. If taken seriously by serious students, solo performance is one exciting way of experiencing the world of drama.

Acting and Interpretation

Another important question that students ask is "What is the difference between acting and interpretation?" In recent years, few issues for performance theorists have raised more passions. Some people argued that any sort of movement automatically makes interpreters into actors (although, of course, eyes blink and mouths move). Others have said that interpreters use books when they perform, and actors don't. Still others have said that actors perform plays, and interpreters perform stories and poems. Each of these qualifications has met reasonable questions ("If actors use a book in rehearsal, are they interpreters?" or "What happens when an actor reads a story?"). Obviously, many theorists have felt the need to define the limits of what an interpreter does, although distinguishing between these two forms of performance became more difficult when students taking courses in both acting and interpretation would use techniques learned in one course when performing in the other.

Interpretation is marked by emphasizing the text and minimizing physical activity, some theorists argue, while they agree that interpretation and acting are more similar than different. Since similarities between the two forms abound, differences may be less important — but they are no less keenly felt. Both acting and interpretation begin with a script that is carefully studied and thoroughly understood. Actors tend to limit themselves to plays, and usually to one character; interpreters perform all types of literature. Both kinds of performers must have supple, responsive bodies that can communicate fine degrees of emotion and activity to audiences; both must have voices distinguished by clear diction, adequate volume, and sufficient flexibility. Both rehearse their materials by basing their performance choices on their own experiences as well as close study of the text. Little wonder confusion arises, especially since actors often become interpreters, and interpreters become actors.

Nevertheless, there are distinct differences between acting and interpretation. The interpreter of drama is charged with becoming *all* of the characters in a scene, and, more importantly, of communicating the *whole* of the scene. The interpreter must communicate not just one character, but the sum of all the characters. This whole adds up to more than the sum of its parts if the drama is to be conveyed in its intellectual, emotional, and aesthetic entirety.

Standing alone in performance, your body creates the frame from within which half of the scene is played. The other half exists at the end of a character's line of tension with an opponent, just out beyond the far edge of the audience. The character speaks. The audience sees him demand the knife from the deranged woman, who clearly refuses to give it up. The tension arising from their conflict crackles along a line that *parallels* the sight lines of the audience, who find themselves in the middle of the excitement without analyzing how it is happening.

Actors, on the other hand, completely memorize their lines and ask the audience to believe that they are actually the people to whom the events happen. Each actor portrays only one character at a time; this portrayal is aided by other members of the cast, scenery, costume, make-up, and properties. The scene is *onstage* and exists around the players, while the audience watches, its sight lines *perpendicular* to the lines of tension that excite the staged production. Each actor is one element in the total work, one part of the whole. Each is surrounded by the reality of the play, though that reality may penetrate or include the audience as well as the stage. Every actor is, of course, conscious of the audience — sensing their responses, waiting for their laughs, and taking care to project in order to be heard in the last row of the balcony.

Briefly, then, an interpreter shares the actor's commitment to a faithful creation of the play, but from a different perspective. You are all of the characters in the scene and each individual character, one at a time. As you speak, you create an illusion of the simultaneous presence of all of the characters in the scene by letting them really and honestly respond and listen to one another. You share with actors the ability to *react* as well as to *act*. Your body and voice create the performance frame. Though this frame is smaller than the stage, everything you do and say takes on greater significance, and the power of every gesture is magnified. Each lifted eyebrow fills more of the total picture than an actor or actress can manage. Together, the interpreter and the audience create the world of the drama; together they are living in it, jointly committed to its conclusion.

Structural Elements of a Play

Plays are organized on the principles of unity and probability, and their basic ingredient is conflict. The ways in which conflict is presented, developed, and resolved vary widely. In general, however, the opening scenes of a play are devoted to exposition through action and dialogue. Then comes the challenge that introduces the inciting or exciting force. There may be several such units as the play develops. The primary challenge that is touched on in the exposition may be reintroduced and intensified by developing action or relationships so that it becomes more acute. This is usually followed by moves and countermoves among the characters who are most involved, thus producing a tightening of conflict and what is often termed the *rising action*. The rising action comes to a point of decision in the crisis. The *crisis* is that moment of limitation that directs the action to its final outcome. The crisis makes inevitable and brings about the *climax*, the culmination of all the elements of the conflict. This is followed by the *denouement* or *resolution*, or, in tragedy, the inevitable catastrophe.

The events of most dramas follow some variation of this general form; in the changes and alterations each drama achieves its unique pattern of emotional build-ups, intensity, and pace. These bare events or occurrences should not be confused with plot. As we discuss in Chapter 6, plot cannot be separated from the characters. We call *plot* all that which the characters say and do, and we know about characters from what they say and do and from what others say about and do to them. Chekhov's *The Three Sisters*, some people say, is about three women who don't go to Moscow, and it is true that the sisters never reach that goal. Still, this description shows very little understanding of what the sisters *do* reach, or how they get it, or what it costs, or what happens along the way.

When you are studying a play during your rehearsal period, proceed carefully with each speech, being sure that everything that is happening onstage is clear to you and that you understand everything that is being said. Sometimes a small stage map helps to clarify where everyone is; sometimes you might want to develop a close, literal paraphrase of a difficult speech. Remember that the paraphrase is not an end but one means of understanding the speech itself. Don't proceed to the next speech until you are sure that you understand what the speaker is saying and doing and what everyone else onstage (or about to come onstage) is doing. Are all the others listening to the speaking character? What is on their minds? What are they *not* saying? What is the speaker thinking? What is the speaker doing? What is the speaker trying to hide? Where is everyone looking? What should an audience know about the movement onstage?

The narrator in a work of prose or poetry guides both the audience and the interpreter, helping to clarify and focus everyone's attention on important detail, to organize the perception of events, and to orchestrate the rhythms of characters and action. Dramatists sometimes also provide guides who act like narrators — the Singer in Brecht's *Caucasian Chalk Circle* (Chapter 11) is a fine example. Narrators help keep interpreters in touch with the what, how, and why of the story's action; but playwrights generally have the characters give out information.

Since explicit clues about what is happening, and particularly what the characters are thinking, are not always provided in the drama, be on the lookout for implicit or even concealed clues in a given scene, speech, line, or word. Interpreters must discover how the scheme of events figures in the total work, for each scene may have a crisis and a climax just as the entire play does.

Let us examine a scene together to find some of these explicit and hidden clues about character. Perhaps our discussion of a scene from *The Three Sisters*, a play about time filled with the minutiae of life, will resolve some questions. Much of the action doesn't seem to get anybody anywhere. But Chekhov recognized what we all know: only rarely do lives change because of drastic or melodramatic events. More often changes "just happen" without our direction — as we drink coffee, turn the page of a newspaper, stroll along a walkway overlooking the water.

In the following scene, almost at the end of the play, Irina, the youngest sister, converses with her new fiancé, the Baron Tuzenbach. For three and one-half acts the Baron has carefully courted Irina, who has quietly rejected all his tenuous but persistent offers and has been pained by his declarations because she has dreamed of marrying a Prince Charming who would come to rescue her on a white horse. Time has pulled that dream apart; Irina has grown up and settled for the Baron, perhaps as the last hope to get her out of the small town where her culture and achievements are "like a sixth finger." Settling for the Baron has cost quite a high price, too, for he is painfully ugly. But his devotion to her never flags, and he even challenges a rival to a duel. As the scene begins, the Baron is about to leave for the duel; he may die because of it (and thereby destroy even this fragment of Irina's dream), but he will not tell her of that future.

[*Enter* **IRINA** *and* **TUZENBACH**, **TUZENBACH** *wearing a straw hat;* **KULYGIN** *crosses the stage, calling "Aa-oo, Masha! Aa-oo!"*]

TUZENBACH: That seems to be the only man in town who's glad the officers are leaving.

IRINA: It's understandable. [*Pause*] Our town is going to be empty now.

TUZENBACH: Dear, I'll be back shortly.

IRINA: Where are you going?

TUZENBACH: I must go into town . . . to see my comrades off.

IRINA: That's not true. . . . Nikolai, why are you so distracted today?
[*Pause*] What happened yesterday near the theater?

TUZENBACH [*with a gesture of impatience*]:   I'll come back in an hour and
be with you again. [*Kisses her hands.*] My beloved. . . . [*Looks into her
face.*] It's five years now that I have loved you, and I still can't get
used to it, and you seem always more beautiful to me. What lovely,
wonderful hair! What eyes! Tomorrow I shall carry you off, we'll
work, and be rich, and my dreams will come true. You shall be happy.
There is only one thing, only one: you do not love me!

IRINA: That is not within my power! I'll be your wife, faithful and obedient, but it's not love, I can't help it! [*Weeps.*] I have never in my life
been in love. Oh, how I have dreamed of love, dreamed of it for a
long time now, day and night, but my soul is like a fine piano that
is locked, and the key lost. [*Pause*] You look troubled.

TUZENBACH: I haven't slept all night. There is nothing in my life so
terrible as to frighten me, only that lost key racks my soul and will
not let me sleep. . . . Tell me something. . . . [*Pause*] Tell me something. . . .

IRINA: What? What shall I say? What?

TUZENBACH: Something.

IRINA: Don't! Don't! [*Pause*]

TUZENBACH: What trifles, what silly little things in life will suddenly, for
no reason at all, take on meaning. You laugh at them just as you've
always done, consider them trivial, and yet you go on, and you feel
that you haven't the power to stop. Oh, let's not talk about that! I
feel elated, I see these fir trees, these maples and birches, as if for the
first time, and they all gaze at me with curiosity and expectation.
What beautiful trees, and, in fact, how beautiful life ought to be with
them! [*A shout of: "Aa-oo! Yoo-hoo!"*] I must go, it's time. . . . There's
a tree that's dead, but it goes on swaying in the wind with the others.
So it seems to me that if I die, I'll still have a part in life, one way or
another. Good-bye, my darling. . . . [*Kisses her hands.*] The papers
you gave me are on my table, under the calendar.

IRINA: I am coming with you.

TUZENBACH [*alarmed*]:   No, no! [*Quickly goes, then stops in the avenue.*]
Irina!

IRINA: What?

TUZENBACH [*not knowing what to say*]:   I didn't have any coffee this morning. Ask them to make me some. [*Quickly goes out.*]

[**IRINA** *stands lost in thought, then goes to the back of the stage and sits down
in the swing.*]

On a first reading, there does not seem to be very much happening here at all: man and woman enter, talk about love, happiness, a

piano, some trees, and man runs off. All that is true. Lest we miss something complex or subtle, it would be wise to reread the scene carefully, speech by speech, to see what, indeed, is happening.

The Baron enters with Irina. He had renounced his aristocracy to join the army, and now he has even renounced the army — he wants to join Irina and work for their future together. Although Irina has accepted this comically ugly man whom her sister recommended to her, can you imagine her mixed feelings when she gave up her dream of a dashing hero gloriously whisking her off? Seeing Kulygin, the cuckolded husband of Irina's sister Masha, the Baron gently acknowledges another unfortunate man's devotion in spite of defiance and infidelity. Irina is neither so generous nor perceptive. Irina and the Baron stand onstage together, silent. Each contemplates marriage: both the failed marriage of Masha and Kulygin, which was unsuccessful as much because the partners did not understand each other as because they were not really in love, and their own imminent marriage, on only slightly firmer ground. They continue silent. Do they touch? The text does not tell us.

Irina breaks the pause with "Our town is going to be empty now." This statement reinforces her family's further isolation, and reminds us how far we have come from the opening scene, when the family excitedly entertained the newly arrived battery commander. Time presses. Tuzenbach looks at his watch (he must not be late for the duel in which he is to be killed) and reassures Irina that he will return shortly. Anxious and distracted, he stumbles through his half-lie about saying good-bye to friends. Irina senses his fear, knows he isn't telling her the truth, and gently encourages him to confide in her.

Time presses. This silent Tuzenbach — agonized because he displeases and worries the woman he never dreamed would say yes — reminds us of the earlier, silent Tuzenbach, who is awed by Irina's beauty. Impatiently he ignores the repeated question with a repeated assurance. He kisses her hand and looks directly into her eyes to repeat the love he has declared so often in the past. (Remember what he looks like now, how his looks are a silent reminder to her of what her dreams have come to.) Exclaiming over her beautiful eyes and hair, he begins to sketch their future; but notice carefully what he says and how he says it: "Tomorrow I shall carry you off, we'll work, and be rich, and my dreams will come true. You shall be happy."

Consider those personal pronouns carefully: Baron Tuzenbach wants to be sure that *he* fulfills Irina's dreams by taking her away, as a knight on a charger rescues a damsel in distress. The kingdom he offers her is the simple life of working together and being rich together, as if one inevitably followed the other, as if work were as simple as saying it. When all of this occurs, Tuzenbach assures, then *"my"* dreams of five years will all be true. But will they? Will Irina love him? Will she love this ugly man as he loves her? Tuzenbach knows she doesn't love him, and fears that more than his imminent death. He assures her that *she'll* be happy. And he admits that fear: she doesn't love him.

Irina's honest answer does not intend cruelty, although it must have ravaged the Baron, particularly when he is about to duel with a rival for her love. She agrees to be a wife, but it must be with open eyes and without pretenses, for dreams have evaporated. And with those dreams so changed in front of her, she begins to cry about what has become of her ambitions. At last she is passionate about something she *isn't*; her "soul is like a fine piano that is locked, and the key lost." And again they stand, silent. What has she said about their future to this man who adores her, who will soon die? Has he not countless reasons to look worried?

More time passes. Tuzenbach admits that he does not shirk the future, even death; only death without her love tortures him, terrifies him. He is willing not to be the pianist on the expensive piano of her soul; he will settle with being the key, if only she will let him. In some concealed, bravely disguised misery, they stand silent. Time passes. Now he begs her to speak to him.

The conflict that both joins them and sets them apart emerges more obviously. Begging some assurance that he is valued or even respected, Tuzenbach is at his most vulnerable. The only cover is Irina's insipid "What? What shall I say? What?" She isn't being coy or heartless. She doesn't know his future, knows only of their future together that she doesn't love him, can't love him, and mustn't pretend to love him. On the verge of tears and almost numb, he offers one word in isolation; but he gets the response a mother might give a distraught child. Surely the hero going off to battle needs something else from his beloved, but he asks for that which Irina does not have and cannot give. They stand together, silent again. Time presses.

Tuzenbach's only complaining lines appear here when he speaks of how "trifles" (like duels) and "silly little things" (like phrases uttered without thinking — even by a woman who has told him that it does not lie in her power to love him) come to matter in his life. It takes a moment for Tuzenbach's admirable optimism to assert itself. But on reflection he admits that he is curiously happy. He has waited for Irina, and she has agreed; looking around him he sees the trees that enchanted him in the first and second act (and that will be cut down as soon as the curtain falls): "What beautiful trees, and, in fact, how beautiful life ought to be with them!" With the special clarity of the condemned, he values any world that can make them both so miserable as it rewards them. The subjunctive mood used in the second half of the line qualifies his future, just as he suddenly stiffens when he hears the call from the duel, a hello that means good-bye. Death waits for them all — it is only a matter of time. But he still will not succumb; even the dead, dried-up tree partakes somehow of life with the others, is moved as they move, and so Tuzenbach knows that he will live some kind of life after the duel. At last he takes her hand and kisses it.

Irina knows that this emotional farewell is not typical and moves to protect the man. She is alarmed by everyone's refusal to share with her the mystery of what has happened. How much can she do if no one will help her protect him? It is her future, of course, but it is also *his*! She will go with him. Tuzenbach, alarmed, refuses to consider it and moves, now, to join those trees both living and dead with whom he has linked himself. He cannot let her know what will happen; she mustn't be hurt. Abruptly he stops, turning once more to glimpse her eyes and her hair (that charm against confusion) and calls out for her. He wants to say "Good-bye," and "I love you," and "I'm doing this for you," and "Please just tell me that you love me." And Irina, alone, unsure, afraid, confused, echoes what she said before: "What?" — as much an answer as a question about his needs and her ability to fill them. What more can either say? He requests some coffee, and in the last moment onstage finds himself caught between saying everything and nothing. Refusing to collapse, he gets one more glimpse. Just as he is about to break, he dashes off. She stands alone. Time passes.

These apparently patternless events actually disguise careful plotting of speech, incident, and silence. Each of these components furthers the action of the play. Tuzenbach must repeat his love to Irina and then somehow prepare her for the future that might not include him. Irina must make clear to Tuzenbach just what her agreement to marry him does and does not include. Neither can leave the stage until these objectives are fulfilled, and the conflict arises from the unresolvable tasks both characters undertake. Through their language, the characters convey their limitations and the degree to which they are willing to expose themselves: Tuzenbach speaks almost constantly. In dismay Irina responds briefly until her one long speech during which Tuzenbach learns the futility of his hopes. He moves toward her, away from her, finally runs off; she tolerates, accepts, endures.

And then they are silent. Admittedly, characters must speak in order for an audience to achieve the fullest possible understanding of their lives. But in drama some of the most moving moments are silent ones. Do not presume that nothing happens during a pause.

A great deal happens, which even words cannot convey. Chekhov places five pauses in this brief scene, all at moments when nothing that the characters can say demonstrates their agony as effectively as their momentary speechlessness. "What shall I say?" Irina asks, as if to admit that even together she and Tuzenbach are more than ever apart and alone.

In patterning this scene, Chekhov creates a telling rhythm with long speeches that allow for prolonged self-disclosure (Tuzenbach on Irina's beauty, Irina on her inability to love Tuzenbach, Tuzenbach on the trees) set against brief questions and answers. Midscene the impasse between the two characters is clearest, and the language breaks down almost completely. It is possible, therefore, to detect rich and poignant resources for performance when you understand clearly when and how to look for them.

In this scene we saw two characters engaged in a great deal of inner conflict — turmoil displayed through activity, silences, bursts of speech, stillnesses. We have seen their unity tightened by their concern for each other, made poignant by the distance that still separates them. This brief excerpt is not Chekhov's entire play, of course. It is only a fragment through which the characters progress as they attempt to achieve their goals. These particular moments are possible only because the stage frees the characters to be alone; offstage all the other characters pursue their own goals. Irina and Tuzenbach are not the only characters in the play; their drama is only part of Chekhov's drama; they contribute their lives to the world that the play describes. Still, a play is a composite of such moments, orchestrated perceptions designed by the playwright for a specific end.

Working a Scene

Knowing how and where to look for clues to understand a character only begins the interpreter's preparation. Using these techniques you need to answer countless questions about a scene to be sure that you fully understand the shape of the action onstage and can therefore draft a performance that will communicate the scene to your audience.

Let us look briefly at a scene from a different kind of play to see if by charting the action one can determine the nature of the characters and their unique relationship. Try to answer the questions that are asked as the discussion proceeds, and be sure to take the time to incorporate all of your discoveries into the performance preparation.

These scenes occur in the beginning of Edward Albee's *Who's Afraid of Virginia Woolf?* George is a forty-six-year-old associate professor of history; his fifty-two-year-old wife, Martha, is the daughter of the president of the college. It is after two in the morning, and husband and wife have just returned from a party given by the president to welcome new faculty. At the party Martha has met a new biology professor and his wife and has invited them home for a nightcap. George, exhausted and more harassed than usual by his boisterous wife, has complained about their guests' tardiness. Martha retorts:

MARTHA [*after a moment's consideration*]:   You make me puke!

GEORGE: What?

MARTHA: Uh . . . you make me puke!

GEORGE [*thinks about it . . . then . . .*]:   That wasn't a very nice thing to say, Martha.

MARTHA: That wasn't *what*?

GEORGE: . . . a very nice thing to say.

MARTHA: I like your anger. I think that's what I like about you most . . . your anger. You're such a . . . such a simp! You don't even have the . . . the what? . . .

GEORGE: . . . guts? . . .

MARTHA: PHRASEMAKER! [*Pause . . . then they both laugh.*] Hey, put some more ice in my drink, will you? You never put any ice in my drink. Why is that, hunh?

GEORGE [*takes her drink*]:   I always put ice in your drink. You eat it, that's all. It's that habit you have . . . chewing your ice cubes . . . like a cocker spaniel. You'll crack your big teeth.

MARTHA: THEY'RE MY BIG TEETH!

GEORGE: Some of them . . . some of them.

MARTHA: I've got more teeth than you've got.

GEORGE: Two more.

MARTHA: Well, two more's a lot more.

GEORGE: I suppose it is. I suppose it's pretty remarkable . . . considering how old you are.

MARTHA: YOU CUT THAT OUT! [*Pause.*] You're not so young yourself.

GEORGE [*with boyish pleasure . . . a chant*]:   I'm six years younger than you are . . . I always have been and I always will be.

MARTHA [*glumly*]:   Well . . . you're going bald.

GEORGE: So are you. [*Pause . . . they both laugh.*] Hello, honey.

MARTHA: Hello. C'mon over here and give your Mommy a big sloppy kiss.

GEORGE: . . . oh, now. . . .

MARTHA: I WANT A BIG SLOPPY KISS!

GEORGE [*preoccupied*]:   I don't *want* to kiss you, Martha. Where *are* these people? Where are these *people* you invited over?

MARTHA: They stayed on to talk to Daddy. . . . They'll be here. . . . *Why* don't you want to kiss me?

GEORGE [*too matter-of-fact*]:   Well, dear, if I kissed you I'd get all excited . . . I'd get beside myself, and I'd take you, by force, right here on

the living room rug, and then our little guests would walk in, and
. . . well, just think what your father would say about *that.*

MARTHA: You pig!

GEORGE [*haughtily*]:   Oink! Oink!

MARTHA: Ha, ha, ha, HA! Make me another drink . . . lover.

GEORGE [*taking her glass*]:   My God, you can swill it down, can't you?

MARTHA [*imitating a tiny child*]:   I'm firsty.

GEORGE: Jesus!

MARTHA [*swinging around*]:   Look, sweetheart, I can drink you under any
goddamn table you want . . . so don't worry about me!

GEORGE: Martha, I gave you the prize years ago. . . . There isn't an
abomination award going that you. . . .

MARTHA: I swear . . . if you existed I'd divorce you. . . .

GEORGE: Well, just stay on your feet, that's all. . . . These people are
your guests, you know, and. . . .

MARTHA: I can't even see you . . . I haven't been able to see you for
years. . . .

GEORGE: . . . if you pass out, or throw up, or something . . .

MARTHA: . . . I mean, you're a blank, a cipher . . .

GEORGE: . . . and try to keep your clothes on, too. There aren't many
more sickening sights than you with a couple of drinks in you and
your skirt up over your head, you know. . . .

MARTHA: . . . a zero . . .

GEORGE: . . . your *heads,* I should say. . . .

[*The front doorbell chimes.*]

MARTHA: Party! Party!

GEORGE [*murderously*]:   I'm really looking forward to this, Martha. . . .

MARTHA [*same*]:   Go answer the door.

GEORGE [*not moving*]:   You answer it.

MARTHA: Get to that door, you. [*He does not move.*] I'll fix you, you. . . .

GEORGE [*fake-spits*]:   . . . to you. . . .

[*Door chime again.*]

MARTHA [*shouting . . . to the door*]:   C'MON IN! [*To* **GEORGE**, *between her
teeth.*] I said, get over there!

GEORGE [*moves a little toward the door, smiling slightly*]:   All right, love . . .
whatever love wants. [*Stops.*] Just don't start on the bit, that's all.

MARTHA: The bit? The bit? What kind of language is that? What are you
talking about?

GEORGE: The bit. Just don't start in on the bit.

MARTHA: You imitating one of your students, for God's sake? What are
you trying to do? WHAT BIT?

GEORGE: Just don't start in on the bit about the kid, that's all.

MARTHA: What do you take me for?

GEORGE: Much too much.

MARTHA [*really angered*]:   Yeah? Well, I'll start in on the kid if I want to.

GEORGE: Just leave the kid out of this.

MARTHA [*threatening*]:   He's mine as much as he is yours. I'll talk about him if I want to.

GEORGE: I'd advise against it, Martha.

MARTHA: Well, good for you. [*Knock.*] C'mon in. Get over there and open the door!

GEORGE: You've been advised.

MARTHA: Yeah . . . sure. Get over there!

GEORGE [*moving toward the door*]:   All right, love . . . whatever love wants. Isn't it nice the way some people have manners, though, even in this day and age? Isn't it nice that some people won't just come breaking into other people's houses even if they *do* hear some sub-human monster yowling at 'em from inside . . . ?

MARTHA: SCREW YOU!

[*Simultaneously with* **MARTHA**'s *last remark,* **GEORGE** *flings open the front door.* **HONEY** *and* **NICK** *are framed in the entrance.*]

This scene certainly does not depict a typical academic couple at home. In order to understand the play completely, you should determine exactly what happens in the scene, and then determine how this action arises from the characters' needs and goals. Albee's stage directions greatly aid analysis, as does his curious use of ellipsis marks to indicate both pause and thought at the same time.

Martha's insult is repeated as the scene begins. George's response is not a rejoinder but a mild reprimand, which in turn elicits from Martha first mock surprise and then increased vituperation and disgust. She begins to phrase another insult, when George himself supplies the word she lacks. She then accuses (not castigates) him. They pause and laugh *together*. The pattern thus described in these nine brief lines is then immediately repeated, after a suddenly soothed Martha again is provoked by George's taunting her about her age. Can you detect where the difference between them is bridged and then opened again?

Martha puts on the role of "Mommy," but George refuses to play this game. He also refuses to be infuriated by her insults and becomes disgusted by her drinking. The violent Martha reappears; George challenges this Martha; and the battle resumes until the doorbell rings announcing their guests. There is a contest of wills about answering the door, and in the middle of the fury George cautions Martha, who is too angry to heed his advice, not to "start in on the bit about the kid." Martha, in no temper to accept orders from George, refuses and receives further warnings. All the while the guests are waiting outside the door.

We can begin by analyzing this scene together. You will develop your own method by a process of trial and error as you gain experience with different kinds of plays. The first steps in analyzing character should always be taken in terms of the entire play. Follow carefully the patterns of action and inaction, silence and speech. What do George and Martha say? In what circumstances do they say it? How does what they say further the development of their goals?

Understanding the physical activity that occurs during the scene enables us to understand the changes in persona that constantly occur in George and Martha. Where does Martha drop one role and assume another? There are several such points before the front doorbell chimes. Where does George shift his role? How frequently does this occur? Who changes personality more often? How are George and Martha different by the last line of this scene? Keeping in mind this rough sketch of the ground to be covered, go back to the beginning and determine how to approach these moments most efficiently.

Once you know the content of the scene, you should consider the relationship of the characters to the setting in which they live. Different people respond in different ways to a particular environment. A knowledge of period customs and costumes is often necessary to understand and appreciate a character. Albee has set this scene "in the living room of a house on campus of a small New England college." It is not difficult to believe that George and Martha are sloppy housekeepers; moreover, they have lived here for over twenty years, and the accumulations of their lives fill this home. Books probably abound; are they all neatly shelved? Now ask the further questions that your answers imply. You can probably imagine fairly accurately the rest of their world. Might the ashtrays be full? Are the glasses empty and sweating on the table? Is it likely that George has suddenly taken out the vacuum and begun to tidy up? What are they wearing? Does what you know about Martha suggest a smart, chic woman, svelte and haughtily fashionable? Might her clothes be tighter, smaller, younger looking than she is? Why? Does George look like an illustration from *Gentlemen's Quarterly*? Why?

Consider the differences between them. How do they compare, contrast, and balance in terms of temperament, maturity, and cultural background? The variety and contrast of the play as a whole is achieved by pitting remarkable differences against each other and by comparing the tiny differences that loom larger when so many other things are similar. George appears willing to submit to Martha's abuse, but doesn't he taunt her, too? Both delight in word play; each is able to learn new rules as quickly as the other changes the game. Such interdependence arises out of years of practice, as well as out of some fundamental unity, something that they share. Look at George and Martha again from this perspective. It has been said that married couples tend to resemble each other after many years; is there no way in which this is true for George and Martha? Do their similarities outnumber or outweigh their differences? Why have they been together for so long? They fight viciously, so conflict obviously exists. In this scene, apart from the couple's obvious physical differences, what are the chief points of opposition between them? How do these different temperaments appear in the lines? Is either partner obliterated by the other? Why?

Answer these preliminary questions before you proceed with any detailed analysis of this scene. Every scene requires such close examination because the lives of the characters are both internal and external, as your life is. Your room may look immaculate or messy, you may have a favorite item of apparel, a manner of talking or habit of smoking, but you are surely not just the woman with the southern accent who wears scarves or the man in the bomber jacket who smokes Tareytons. Characters are much more than their appearance.

Focusing attention on one character at a time (and starting with the person who has the most lines), apply the now-familiar process of understanding logical content, giving careful attention to climaxes and focal points, style and rhythm, and the denotative and connotative richness of all the words. Once you are sure of the content, you are ready to study the fusion of external and internal activity that makes a character appear to be alive.

Look closely at Martha. Albee describes her as "a large, boisterous woman, 52, looking somewhat younger. Ample but not fleshy." All external clues should be taken into consideration here, so Martha must also be capable of rapid changes in personality: she is a braying woman, a Mommy, a tiny child, a vituperative wife, a shouting harridan. How do these changes occur in Martha? Where do these shifts take place? What do they arise from? Why does shared laughter accelerate the change? Does Martha need to move out of her chair? Why? Is there any difference among the kinds of anger Martha shows? All of these outward characteristics are just that — outward. When you know what must be seen by the audience, you can clarify better both what internal life gives rise to these elements and how these responses affect other characters.

Now apply the same kinds of questions to George, whom Albee tellingly describes as "her husband, 46. Thin; hair going gray." Not much to build on there, one might think. But there is a great deal here, for George is six years younger than Martha, and he taunts her with this fact. He is described as "her husband," an adjunct to her, rather than a man or a history professor or a "failure," though he is all of these things, too. His physical spareness — borne out in his lines and perhaps even in his volume — contrasts with her abundance. His mildness is not passivity, since he is capable both of succumbing to her commands and annoying her, of submitting as well as dominating. Can you point to moments when he does each? Is there any way in which "giving in" can be considered a victory? Does "submission" mean a loss of dignity? Is it ever easier to do something than to fight about it? Martha calls George "a blank, a cipher" and moments later "a zero"; is he? Are they unequally matched? George opens the door at the end of the scene, as Martha has ordered — why? He is clearly the more physically active of the two in this scene; does this movement parallel another kind of flexibility, his submissiveness, or both?

The interpreter of drama should follow much the same method of characterization as a conscientious actor does. You need to know how a character looks, lives, thinks, and behaves long before the play or the scene takes place. The playwright does not always give this complete information, and you may need to depend on your knowledge of human nature to supply the omitted details. Try to develop an ability to observe life, and then go behind the exterior manifestations to discover the motivations. You are dealing with human actions and reactions, and the more you know of your fellow creatures, the more easily you can understand and communicate to the audience the complexities of the characters in the play.

With the physical, psychological, and emotional background filled in, the interpreter can begin to study the sources of the incidents in the play. From examining this segment can you project what George and Martha were doing immediately prior to their entrance? Did George enjoy his father-in-law's party? Did he remember the young biology professor? Why did George and Martha go to the party? Why did Martha remember the biology professor? Why did they leave the party? Why do you suppose Martha put off telling her husband about the late guests? Did George expect any of this? Are they both prepared for what happens in the scene?

All characters, in drama as well as in life, represent at least the sum of their past experiences. All people behave in response to pressures and needs of a given situation on the basis of the events of their past. Psychologists have taught us how much of adult human behavior and personality is really a response, a *reaction*, both to the world as it was learned in childhood and also to the primal relationship of parent and child. Such substance renders much of the excitement of this scene, and many of its difficulties as well. How do George and Martha live with each other? Why have they put up with all this abuse for so long? They are not a couple who would refuse to consider divorce from any religious scruple. Martha mentions divorce, surely not for the first time. Can you fight over something you don't care about? The first act is called "Fun and Games," and both characters change considerably, even during this scene; how do they know when a new game is being played? George appears to submit to Martha; does Martha ever give in to George? How do they "weigh out" in the match between them? They certainly laugh a great deal

— together and separately; does one person's laughter ridicule or scorn the other? When George cautions Martha not to "start in on the bit about the kid," is it a threat, a taunt, or a caution? Does he expect Martha to obey him? Does the reaction of either partner surprise the other? Why?

You should answer all of these questions — and countless others — and then incorporate the answers into your performance. Some words of caution are due here, now that so much information has been gathered and so much work has been done. Beginning interpreters often become so enamored of a favorite character in a play or a scene that the rest of the characters never appear. Continue careful analysis of each character, studying each as an individual and evaluating his or her relationship to every other individual. Remember that your responsibility is to the scene as a whole, to the play as Albee wrote it. Balance your own observations with the play's truth, keeping in mind that while the audience wants to see and hear you (which will happen in any case), they also want to see and hear Albee's play.

Now try to put the speeches together. Are you listening to George? Has Martha faded from the picture? Does Martha expect what George will say next? What is so funny about "PHRASEMAKER," which elicits their first laugh together? Why are italics, capitalized words, and ellipses used in the dialogue? Who uses them? Why? Go over the first nine speeches. Is Martha's voluptuousness clearly suggested to the audience? Does George appear as a "simp"? Is it after 2:00 A.M.? Does this couple want guests? Try the scene again, being sure to keep *where* George and Martha are vividly in mind, particularly the glasses and ashtrays all over the room. Once more, take the first nine speeches. What are these people thinking about that they aren't showing us? When Martha tells George that he makes her puke, what does he think about? Why does he pause? And why does he answer in the way he does? As you proceed through the rest of the scene, try not to become discouraged. It takes work to perform, but if you are conscientious, you will feel, see, and hear progress. No one can minimize the importance or the difficulty of the "putting-together" step in rehearsal.

Rhythm

As your characters begin to jell, some of the most exciting moments in rehearsal occur. It is now apparent where the scene is going. The tempo of the play emerges. As the rhythms of the individuals' speeches become more and more obvious, the ways in which speeches work off each other become more apparent and important.

The rhythm of a play is extremely interesting and somewhat complex. First, at the stylistic level there is the individual speech rhythm of each character. Second, in terms of both content and form, there are important fluctuations in emotional tension. Third, there is the inevitable alternation between activity and passivity. We demonstrated this alternation in the scene from *The Three Sisters*. Of course, no part of a good play is ever really passive inasmuch as a play depends on action for development. Some scenes or portions of scenes may consist primarily of exposition and may serve the same purpose as transitional units in narrative. They may clarify cause and effect, present necessary relationships, allow the playwright to plead a case through one of the characters, or provide the needed suspense in preparation for a climax. This alternation between active and passive elements affects the tempo at which the various scenes and speeches move. It also determines the speed with which they build toward minor climaxes and finally toward the main climax, whether in terms of action or character development or both. In a well-written play, these transitional, static scenes are used sparingly and present nothing that does not bear on the ultimate outcome of the action. The playwright's arrangement of these scenes probably is governed by the same principles that influence the writer of narrative prose: how much the audience must know about background and where added background material can be most effectively inserted. The playwright also takes into account the need for relaxation from tension and intense activity and channels the audience's concentration into another area, which is different in kind if not in degree.

As is apparent in *Who's Afraid of Virginia Woolf?* and *The Three Sisters*, changes in rhythm are caused by changes of content, as well as by stylistic, linguistic, grammatical, or syntactical changes. The words Chekhov uses range from spare to elaborate, but each word exists because at that particular moment with those people, at that point in their lives, only that combination of words expresses the complexity of their characters. Albee allows George and Martha to complete each other's lines, but he achieves their characteristic attitudes through techniques that include careful management of punctuation and pause. The patterning of silences in order to achieve a specific tempo appears often in contemporary drama. Harold Pinter, in particular, has elevated the pause to a dramatic force that can be both menacing and pitiful, ominous and poetic.

Style

Dialogue style includes what a character omits as well as what he or she says; playwrights don't leave characters speechless because they can't think of anything for them to say. In discovering the elements of dialogue style, interpreters learn about another part of a character's life. The language a character uses indicates a great deal about background and attitude. The arrangement of ideas gives a clue to the person's clarity of thinking and is likely to reflect intensity of emotion. The length of the thought units also may reveal much about a character's personality, forcefulness, and authority, as well as the degree of psychological tension. Read Pinter's *Betrayal* (Chapter 8) with this aspect of character development in mind.

Style is an interesting consideration in contemporary drama. In Ionesco's *The Bald Soprano*, part of which appears at the end of this chapter, the language is deliberately reduced to its lowest level of suggestion to help achieve the dehumanization of the characters. Other contemporary plays also present similar stylistic problems for the interpreter. At the heart of absurdist drama is the human inability to communicate with one's fellows and even to put into words the frustrations and fears of one's own mind. Thus, you should examine motivation and character interaction differently from the way you approach those elements in a traditional play. The motivation for both speech and action often is confined to the character's own mind and is formed by a sense of isolation from the world or by acceptance of the belief that people, the world, life, love, and death are equally absurd. The dialogue often takes the form of extremely long near-monologues or soliloquies. These are difficult for an interpreter to sustain, not only because they are subjectively motivated but also because they are highly repetitive. This aspect of repetition is used as a device for anticlimax in the structure of many contemporary plays. Likewise, the action is often either violent and almost stylized or statically impotent. When you are interpreting, the shifts in your muscle tone should be swift and sharp. Thorough analysis and considerable patience are necessary to make such scenes credible and dramatic, but they provide extraordinary rewards to the solo performer.

Scenography

When you go to the theatre, you are likely to see costumed performers on a carefully lighted stage that probably has properties and set pieces to suggest the period and social status of the world of the play. When done most elaborately, these technical achievements can astonish an audience: watch a three-masted ship in full sail explode into flames under a starry sky while seventy-eight choristers and six principals in seventeenth-century Venetian costume sing lustily. The spectacle will amaze you. Setting tends to be easily achieved by dramatists, since they can put whatever information is necessary into stage directions and descriptions that precede or come between the scenes. Renaissance dramatists evoke setting within the speeches of the characters; contemporary dramatists specify lighting, setting, and costume; George Bernard Shaw provides voluminous and minute description for almost every second. In whatever period, drama always has been partly spectacle.

A solo performer appears in street clothes, possibly behind a lectern, probably carrying a book or a script. How can this interpreter hope to compete with the visually pleasing sets and costumes that surround actors? Carefully consider what you are doing. The technical resources that create visual statements in realistic dramas do not exist for the solo interpreter. But such resources aren't any more necessary to the interpreter than they were to Shakespeare or Sophocles. And while spectacle is part of drama, it need not be the spectacle fact of a staged production. Some realistic dramas of the late nineteenth and early twentieth centuries attempted to convince the audience of the reality of stage activity by featuring objects and details of real life (real bacon frying in a real cast-iron skillet over a real fire built on real sod). Proponents of these outlandish experiments (the real sod, after all, rested on a stage floor and was lit by stage lights) forget that belief is not as much a matter of what goes on in front of the audience's eyes as it is a matter of what goes on inside the audience's minds, for there illusion is made real. Absolutely crucial stage directions and descriptions can always be given by the performer (not the characters) before the performance begins. Audiences do not expect one performer to be eighty-four performers, nor do they expect the lavish spectacle of the stage. Your listeners assist in creating the scenographic elements in the performance with their imaginations, and they can do this quite well when their imaginations are carefully guided. For the scene to exist within the space filled by the audience, the space that surrounds the performer should resemble the space that surrounds the audience; all of it is set, lit, and costumed in the combined imaginations of audience and performer.

Sometimes, of course, the interpreter is called upon to describe some intensely interpersonal activity that one person simply cannot duplicate — a pie fight, swordplay resulting in death, a wrestling match, a kiss. Or the interpreter is presented with some vast or intricate set piece or design requirement. Under such circumstances it is far wiser to describe the action as the playwright describes it in the stage directions than to attempt somehow to manage it in performance.

In Shaw's *Candida*, for example, nearly a thousand words of stage directions precede the rise of the curtain on Act I. Some of this infor-

tiously. In drama, perhaps more than in any other genre, the key is not to take anything for granted: thorough rehearsal of a three-minute segment is infinitely preferable to the same time devoted to a five-minute scene. Next, don't expect it all to happen instantly. You know how long you took on your earlier performances; allot yourself at least half again as much time to work up this performance. Last, remember our opening comments about drama as "play." If you have rehearsed carefully, you have every reason to enjoy what you are doing. If you have studied the scene carefully, you have no reason to be surprised.

Perhaps the most difficult thing about interpreting drama, aside from the purely mechanical or technical problems of suggesting character and action, is keeping the numerous threads of character development and reaction separated and yet related. This demands careful preparation and a high degree of concentration during performance. The interpreter must check carefully, especially during preparation, to avoid presenting a mere series of character sketches, each complete in itself but unrelated to the others. Besides having a thorough knowledge of each character, you should have a constant awareness of relationships and of progressions in these relationships. As the actor must learn to *hear* the speeches of other characters, the interpreter must learn to *have heard*, to be sure each character is responding to what has gone before. All the characters must stay "in scene" and be ready to pick up the progression as they speak.

Thus the interpreter needs to select for each character enough significant physical and vocal details so that the listeners can themselves fill in the outline to make a three-dimensional, believable person. It is impractical and even dangerous to offer specific directions for achieving this final communication of character, because each personality in each play presents its own slightly different problems. Some suggestions for handling mechanical details — and they are suggestions only — are given in the next chapter. For the moment, however, it is enough to be aware that the interpreter needs to spend considerable time and effort perfecting control of voice and body, and should exert extreme care in performance to remain unobtrusive.

mation is of immediate interest to the audience, but a great dea
is aimed primarily at establishing the background out of whic
characters have come and against which they develop. Consequ
in giving the stage directions, the interpreter could omit from
formance the detailed information (using it, of course, in prepa
as a guide to plot motivation and character development). Sir
scene is not going to be presented scenographically to the aud
the interpreter, by selecting the important details, can ena
listeners to focus on essential background information. On th
hand, the audience needs the description of the sphinx from
Caesar and Cleopatra (at the end of this chapter), although mos
specific description of the characters might well be omitted.

Scenography is responsible for more than lavish sets, co
and lights. Period manners, social customs, and economic co
all are communicated to an audience and all affect the ch
Writers of narratives can and do often remind their reader
physical and psychological impact of surroundings on chara
terpreters of drama constantly should scrutinize the world
attempting to suggest to be sure that the telltale parts clearl
in their performance. Tuzenbach keenly feels the impa
birches as he and Irina stand in front of the house; Geor
feels once again the messiness of his house as it is to be vi
the first time by the new arrivals.

Place can establish a motive, motivate an action, describ
limit alternatives, impede the achievement of a goal. Prop
various details of the sets may also play an important p
action; the river separating Simon and Grusha in Brecht's
Chalk Circle (Chapter 11) intensifies the poignancy of their
Antony and Cleopatra (at the end of this chapter), Cleopatra
asp to die. Shakespeare stresses the snake's presence, and
image of a woman with an asp at her breast was a
Elizabethan icon. But no interpreter ought to reject this sc
because of the inability to recruit a snake. If, as Cleopatra, y
you are holding the asp and show your audience that yo
will believe. (We shall discuss the management of prop
fully in Chapter 8.)

Putting It Together

If the list of responsibilities and problems you are likely t
in performing drama seems daunting, one or two word
agement may help. First, the solo performance *can* be
rewarding performances occur when serious students wo

Selections for Analysis and Oral Interpretation

This scene opens the second act of *Fifth of July*. Shirley, fourteen, is the somewhat precocious and self-dramatizing niece of Jed's lover, Ken. All have assembled at the Talley farm near Lebanon, Missouri, for a celebration presided over by Sally, the aunt of Ken and the great-aunt of Shirley. Jed — an almost silent listener — is essential for Shirley to achieve her effect. Don't let either character become outlandish.

FROM *Fifth of July*

LANFORD WILSON

The porch. **JED** *is sitting in the sunshine, referring back and forth between two books, trying to compose a letter on a legal-size yellow pad. A bell tolls in the distance, fifteen seconds between each deep, heavy stroke.*

SHIRLEY *enters. She enjoys being alone with* **JED** *for a moment. She looks out over the garden, quite forgetting that* **JED** *does not see her there. She notices the bell.*

SHIRLEY: Oh! Listen!

JED: (*Jumps a foot*) Oh, God.

SHIRLEY: "Ask not for whom the bell tolls . . . "

JED: It tolls for Harley Campbell.

SHIRLEY: Who?

JED: Your Aunt Sally went to the funeral. They ring the bell before the service and after the service.

SHIRLEY: Oh. Oh, God, now it sounds horrible. Oh, God, that's mournful.

JED: If the man made more than a hundred thousand a year and left a widow, they ring it all during the service as well.

SHIRLEY: We, of course, are the first. (*He looks at her, not understanding*) To arise this morning.

JED: You're the last.

SHIRLEY: Last?

JED: You're up in time for brunch. . . .

SHIRLEY: Gwen is up?

JED: Yeah. And on the phone.

SHIRLEY: Uncle Kenny's up?

JED: Yeah, Sally and I had breakfast at seven, I drove her to church, woke up Ken, and we made an herbal anti-fungus concoction guaranteed to fail, and sprayed thirty-five phlox plants. With Wes's, uh . . . supervision.

SHIRLEY: (*Adjusts*) Oh. Yes . . . I slept . . . fitfully. I tossed, I . . .

JED: Turned?

SHIRLEY: I had this really weird dream. I was being chased by a deer. All through the woods, over bridges, this huge deer. What does a dream like that mean?

JED: Did he have antlers?

SHIRLEY: I don't remember. Why? (**JED** *goes back to his books*)

JED: If you happen to dream about seven fat cows and seven lean cows, I know what that one means.

SHIRLEY: I would never dream of a cow.

JED: Not a feisty young heifer? Jumping fences, trying to get into the corn?

SHIRLEY: Oh, please. I certainly hope you don't think of me like that! I am not a common cow! I am a . . . flower, Jed. Slowly and frighteningly opening her petals onto the spring morning. A trimu-a-timulus, a timu —

JED: What? A mimulus? You're probably a mimulus.

SHIRLEY: What's a mimulus?

JED: Mimulus is a wild flower. Pinkish-yellow, the monkey flower, they call —

SHIRLEY: No, not that one. Not a monkey flower! I am a . . .

JED: What?

SHIRLEY: Well, not — I don't know. And it's important, too. But . . . I can *see* it. A nearly white, small, single . . .

JED: What about an apple blossom? The first tree of spring to —

SHIRLEY: No, oh, God, no. And grow into an apple? A fat, hard, red, bloated, tasteless apple? For some crone to bake in a pie for her ditchdigger husband to eat without even knowing it? Oh, God. Never. I'm more than likely the daughter of an Indian chief. My mother was very broad-minded and very promiscuous.

JED: So I've heard.

SHIRLEY: (*Thinks*) I am a blossom that opens for one day only . . . and I fall. I am not pollinated. It's too early for the bees. They don't find me. And I fade. Dropping my petals one by — what kind of flower is that? (*She thinks a moment*) A wild rose?

JED: No, you wouldn't flower till May at the earliest. There'd be bees lined up around the block.

SHIRLEY: Well, *what?* God. Daisies are when? (*He shakes his head*) Peony?

JED: There are some anemones . . . that bloom very early.

SHIRLEY: An anemone . . .

JED: The original ones are from Greece, so they're all claimed by heroes who fell in battle and their blood seeped into the ground and anemones sprang up, but I think they've found one or two

somewhere else that haven't been claimed yet. I have a picture of them somewhere.

SHIRLEY: Could you find it?

JED: It's around; I'll look it up.

SHIRLEY: (*Hand on sleeve*) Jed. Thank you. This is, you know, very important to me.

JED: (*Mock seriousness*) Shirley. It's important to us all.

SHIRLEY: I know.

JED: We don't dwell on it because we try to spare you the pressure of all our expectations. We multitudes.

SHIRLEY: I know. But don't. Don't spare me. It makes me strong.

❚ How did you show the audience the seriousness underlying Shirley's humor and the humor underlying Jed's seriousness?

Here is a beautiful illustration of the way in which the text and the interpreter are fused into a single visual image. This is the speech of the maid in Ionesco's classic absurdist drama *The Bald Soprano*. How might you achieve this visual effect in performance? Would you consider projecting a slide of the speech onto the body of the interpreter? What is the value for the audience of featuring the text in this way? Why is it interesting to be able to *read* Ionesco's words and hear them at the same time? How does this project the play's special interest in language, cliché, and the relationship between what we *say* and what we *are*?

FROM *The Bald Soprano*

EUGENE IONESCO

Elizabeth
and Donald
are now far
too happy to
be able to
hear me So
I can tell
you   a
s e c r e t
Elizabeth is not
Elizabeth and Donald is not
Donald And I'll prove it to you
The child Donald talked of is not
Elizabeth's daughter not the same
child at all Donald's little girl has
one red eye and one white eye just
like Elizabeth's little girl But whereas
it's the right eye of Donald's child
that's red and the left eye that's
white it's the left eye of Elizabeth's
child that's red and the right eye
that's white Consequently the
whole fabric of Donald's argu-
mentation falls to the ground
when it encounters this
final obstacle which anni-
hilates his entire theory In
spite of the extraordinary
coincidence which would
appear incontrovertible evidence to the contrary as
Donald and Elizabeth are not
after all the parents of the same
child they are not in fact Donald
and Elizabeth Donald may well
believe he is Donald Elizabeth may
well think she is Elizabeth Donald
may well believe her to be Elizabeth
Elizabeth may well think him to be
Donald they are both grievously
deceived But who is the real Donald?
Which is the real Elizabeth? Who
can possibly be interested in prolonging
this misunderstanding? I haven't the

She takes several steps towards the door, then returns and addresses the audience again.

slightest idea Let us make no attempt to find out Let us leave things strictly alone My   real   name   is   Sherlock   Holmes

She goes out.

■ The performer's body is crucial here, of course. How can your body suggest the shape of the printed page?

Following are excerpts from three plays about Cleopatra. Each picture of this notorious queen reflects the changing world as she ages, as well as the attitudes and concerns about the age in which the play was written. The most recent of the plays — Shaw's *Caesar and Cleopatra* — also paints the youngest image of the queen. This Cleopatra is a frightened and superstitious little girl. Julius Caesar is an old campaigner at the twilight of his career. Wandering away from his army, he comes upon and addresses a sphinx, who responds in the voice of a girl. Caesar can only believe he is dreaming.

FROM *Caesar and Cleopatra, Act I*
GEORGE BERNARD SHAW

CAESAR [*to himself*]   What a dream! What a magnificent dream! Only let me not wake, and I will conquer ten continents to pay for dreaming it out to the end. [*He climbs to the Sphinx's flank, and presently reappears to her on the pedestal, stepping round its right shoulder*].

CLEOPATRA.   Take care. That's right. Now sit down: you may have its other paw. [*She seats herself comfortably on its left paw*]. It is very powerful and will protect us; but [*shivering, and with plaintive loneliness*] it would not take any notice of me or keep me company. I am glad you have come: I was very lonely. Did you happen to see a white cat anywhere?

CAESAR [*sitting slowly down on the right paw in extreme wonderment*]   Have you lost one?

CLEOPATRA.   Yes: the sacred white cat: is it not dreadful? I brought him here to sacrifice him to the Sphinx; but when we got a little way from the city a black cat called him, and he jumped out of my arms and ran away to it. Do you think that the black cat can have been my great-great-great-grandmother?

CAESAR [*staring at her*]   Your great-great-great-grandmother! Well, why not? Nothing would surprise me on this night of nights.

CLEOPATRA.   I think it must have been. My great-grandmother's great-grandmother was a black kitten of the sacred white cat; and the river Nile made her his seventh wife. That is why my hair is so wavy. And I always want to be let do as I like, no matter whether it is the will of the gods or not: that is because my blood is made with Nile water.

CAESAR.   What are you doing here at this time of night? Do you live here?

CLEOPATRA.   Of course not: I am the Queen; and I shall live in the palace at Alexandria when I have killed my brother, who drove me out of it. When I am old enough I shall do just what I like. I shall be able to poison the slaves and see them wriggle, and pretend to Ftatateeta[1] that she is going to be put into the fiery furnace.

CAESAR.   Hm! Meanwhile why are you not at home and in bed?

CLEOPATRA.   Because the Romans are coming to eat us all. You are not at home and in bed either.

CAESAR [*with conviction*]   Yes I am. I live in a tent; and I am now in that tent, fast asleep and dreaming. Do you suppose that I believe you are real, you impossible little dream witch?

CLEOPATRA [*giggling and leaning trustfully towards him*]   You are a funny old gentleman. I like you.

CAESAR.   Ah, that spoils the dream. Why don't you dream that I am young?

CLEOPATRA.   I wish you were; only I think I should be more afraid of you. I like men, especially young men with round strong arms; but I am afraid of them. You are old and rather thin and stringy; but you have a nice voice; and I like to have somebody to talk to, though I think you are a little mad. It is the moon that makes you talk to yourself in that silly way.

CAESAR.   What! you heard that, did you? I was saying my prayers to the great Sphinx.

CLEOPATRA.   But this isn't the great Sphinx.

CAESAR   [*much disappointed, looking up at the statue*] What!

CLEOPATRA.   This is only a dear little kitten of a Sphinx. Why, the great Sphinx is so big that it has a temple between its paws. This is my pet Sphinx. Tell me: do you think the Romans have any sorcerers who could take us away from the Sphinx by magic?

CAESAR.   Why? Are you afraid of the Romans?

CLEOPATRA [*very seriously*]   Oh, they would eat us if they caught us. They are barbarians. Their chief is called Julius Caesar. His father was a tiger and his mother a burning mountain; and his nose is like an elephant's trunk. [*Caesar involuntarily rubs his nose*]. They all have long noses, and ivory tusks, and little tails, and seven arms with a hundred arrows in each; and they live on human flesh.

CAESAR.   Would you like me to shew you a real Roman?

CLEOPATRA [*terrified*)   No. You are frightening me.

CAESAR.   No matter: this is only a dream —

---

1. Cleopatra's imperious maid.

CLEOPATRA [*excitedly*]   It is not a dream: it is not a dream. See, see. [*She plucks a pin from her hair and jabs it repeatedly into his arm*].

CAESAR.   Ffff — Stop. [*Wrathfully*] How dare you?

CLEOPATRA [*abashed*]   You said you were dreaming. [*Whimpering*] I only wanted to shew you —

CAESAR [*gently*]   Come, come: don't cry. A queen mustn't cry. [*He rubs his arm, wondering at the reality of the smart*]. Am I awake? [*He strikes his hand against the Sphinx to test its solidity. It feels so real that he begins to be alarmed, and says perplexedly*] Yes, I — [*quite panicstricken*] no: impossible: madness, madness! [*Desperately*] Back to camp — to camp. [*He rises to spring down from the pedestal*].

CLEOPATRA [*flinging her arms in terror round him*]   No: you shan't leave me. No, no, no: don't go. I'm afraid — afraid of the Romans.

CAESAR [*as the conviction that he is really awake forces itself on him*] Cleopatra: can you see my face well?

CLEOPATRA.   Yes. It is so white in the moonlight.

CAESAR.   Are you sure it is the moonlight that makes me look whiter than an Egyptian? [*Grimly*] Do you notice that I have a rather long nose?

CLEOPATRA [*recoiling, paralysed by a terrible suspicion*]   Oh!

CAESAR.   It is a Roman nose, Cleopatra.

CLEOPATRA.   Ah! [*With a piercing scream she springs up; darts round the left shoulder of the Sphinx; scrambles down to the sand; and falls on her knees in frantic supplication, shrieking*] Bite him in two, Sphinx: bite him in two. I meant to sacrifice the white cat — I did indeed — I [*Caesar, who has slipped down from the pedestal, touches her on the shoulder*] — Ah! [*She buries her head in her arms*].

CAESAR.   Cleopatra: shall I teach you a way to prevent Caesar from eating you?

CLEOPATRA [*clinging to him piteously*]   Oh do, do, do. I will steal Ftatateeta's jewels and give them to you. I will make the river Nile water your lands twice a year.

CAESAR.   Peace, peace, my child. Your gods are afraid of the Romans: you see the Sphinx dare not bite me, nor prevent me carrying you off to Julius Caesar.

CLEOPATRA [*in pleading murmurings*]   You won't, you won't. You said you wouldn't.

CAESAR.   Caesar never eats women.

CLEOPATRA [*springing up full of hope*]   What!

CAESAR [*impressively*]   But he eats girls [*she relapses*] and cats. Now you are a silly little girl; and you are descended from the black kitten. You are both a girl and a cat.

CLEOPATRA [*trembling*]   And will he eat me?

CAESAR.   Yes; unless you make him believe that you are a woman.

CLEOPATRA.   Oh, you must get a sorcerer to make a woman of me. Are you a sorcerer?

CAESAR.   Perhaps. But it will take a long time; and this very night you must stand face to face with Caesar in the palace of your fathers.

CLEOPATRA.   No, no. I daren't.

CAESAR.   Whatever dread may be in your soul — however terrible Caesar may be to you — you must confront him as a brave woman and a great queen; and you must feel no fear. If your hand shakes: if your voice quavers; then — night and death! [*She moans*]. But if he thinks you worthy to rule, he will set you on the throne by his side and make you the real ruler of Egypt.

▌ How did you demonstrate Caesar's growing interest in Cleopatra?

▌ How did your Cleopatra exhibit the potential for greatness Caesar detects?

Caesar now is dead. Cleopatra is many years older and loves Antony. For political reasons, however, Antony has married a distinguished Roman matron. In the following brief segment from *All for Love*, John Dryden presents Octavia, the recent bride of Antony, confronting Cleopatra, the one woman her husband will love beyond his destruction. Notice how differently these two characters speak of the same man — and how different this Cleopatra is from Shaw's portrayal of her at an earlier age. Be sure your performance demonstrates the differences between Octavia and Cleopatra. (Cleopatra's servant Alexas speaks first.)

FROM *All for Love, Act III*

JOHN DRYDEN

Alexas manet.

Enter **CLEOPATRA, CHARMION, IRAS,** [*and*] *train.*

ALEX.   O madam, I have seen what blasts my eyes!
Octavia's here!

CLEO.   Peace with that raven's note.
I know it too; and now am in
the pangs of death.

ALEX.   You are no more a queen;
Egypt is lost.

CLEO.   What tell'st thou me of Egypt?
My life, my soul is lost! Octavia has him! —

O fatal name to Cleopatra's love!
My kisses, my embraces now are hers;
While I — But thou hast seen my rival; speak,
Does she deserve this blessing? Is she fair?
Bright as a goddess? And is all perfection
Confined to her? It is. Poor I was made
Of that coarse matter, which, when he was finished,
The gods threw by, for rubbish.

ALEX.   She's indeed a very miracle.

CLEO.   Death to my hopes, a miracle!

ALEX. (*bowing*).   A miracle;
I mean of goodness; for in beauty, madam,
You make all wonders cease.

CLEO.   I was too rash:
Take this in part of recompense. But, oh!

(*Giving a ring.*)

I fear thou flatter'st me.

CHAR.   She comes! she's here!

IRAS.   Fly, madam, Caesar's sister!

CLEO.   Were she the sister of the thund'rer Jove,
And bore her brother's lightning in her eyes,
Thus would I face my rival.

Meets **OCTAVIA** *with* **VENTIDIUS. OCTAVIA** *bears up to her. Their trains come up on either side.*

OCTAV.   I need not ask if you are Cleopatra;
Your haughty carriage —

CLEO.   Shows I am a queen:
Nor need I ask you who you are.

OCTAV.   A Roman:
A name that makes and can unmake a queen.

CLEO.   Your lord, the man who serves me, is a Roman.

OCTAV.   He was a Roman, till he lost that name,
To be a slave in Egypt; but I come
To free him thence.

CLEO.   Peace, peace, my lover's Juno.
When he grew weary of that household clog,
He chose my easier bonds.

OCTAV.   I wonder not
Your bonds are easy; you have long been practised
In that lascivious art: he's not the first
For whom you spread your snares: let Caesar witness.

CLEO. I loved not Caesar; 'twas but gratitude
I paid his love. The worst your malice can,
Is but to say the greatest of mankind
Has been my slave. The next, but far above him
In my esteem, is he whom law calls yours,
But whom his love made mine.

OCTAV. (*coming up close to her*).   I would view nearer
That face which has so long usurped my right,
To find th' inevitable charms that catch
Mankind so sure, that ruined my dear lord.

CLEO. Oh, you do well to search; for had you known
But half these charms, you had not lost his heart.

OCTAV. Far be their knowledge from a Roman lady,
Far from a modest wife! Shame of our sex,
Dost thou not blush to own those black endearments
That make sin pleasing?

CLEO.   You may blush, who want 'em.
If bounteous nature, if indulgent heav'n
Have giv'n me charms to please the bravest man,
Should I not thank 'em? Should I be ashamed,
And not be proud? I am, that he has loved me;
And, when I love not him, heav'n change this face
For one like that.

OCTAV.   Thou lov'st him not so well.

CLEO. I love him better, and deserve him more.

OCTAV.   You do not — cannot: you have been his ruin.
Who made him cheap at Rome, but Cleopatra?
Who made him scorned abroad, but Cleopatra?
At Actium, who betrayed him? Cleopatra.
Who made his children orphans, and poor me
A wretched widow? only Cleopatra.

CLEO.   Yet she who loves him best is Cleopatra.
If you have suffered, I have suffered more.
You bear the specious title of a wife,
To gild your cause, and draw the pitying world
To favor it: the world contemns poor me,
For I have lost my honor, lost my fame,
And stained the glory of my royal house,
And all to bear the branded name of mistress.
There wants but life, and that too I would lose
For him I love.

OCTAV.   Be't so, then; take thy wish.

Exit cum suis.

CLEO.   And 'tis my wish,
Now he is lost for whom alone I lived.
My sight grows dim, and every object dances,
And swims before me, in the maze of death.
My spirits, while they were opposed, kept up;
They could not sink beneath a rival's scorn:
But now she's gone, they faint.
ALEX.   Mine have had leisure
To recollect their strength, and furnish counsel,
To ruin her, who else must ruin you.
CLEO.   Vain promiser!
Lead me, my Charmion; nay, your hand too, Iras:
My grief has weight enough to sink you both.
Conduct me to some solitary chamber,
And draw the curtains round;
Then leave me to myself, to take alone
My fill of grief
        There I till death will his unkindness weep;
        As harmless infants moan themselves asleep.

Exeunt.

❚ Both women genuinely love the same man. How did you
  demonstrate their equal degree of affection but distinctively
  different methods of showing it?

Shakespeare, the earliest of the three playwrights, gives the final picture of
Cleopatra. Antony has committed an ignominious suicide, and Cleopatra
has been captured by Roman forces but bargains for time — enough time to
conclude her own life. The women who have served her remain faithful to
their deaths. Through the magic of some of Shakespeare's most shimmering
poetry, Cleopatra embodies fidelity even beyond the grave. For her, at least,
this death is the richest victory.

FROM *Antony and Cleopatra, Act V, Scene II*
WILLIAM SHAKESPEARE

[*Enter* **IRAS** *with a robe, crown, etc.*]

CLEO.   Give me my robe, put on my crown, I have
281 Immortal longings in me. Now no more
The juice of Egypt's grape shall moist this lip.
Yare, yare, good Iras; quick. Methinks I hear
Antony call; I see him rouse himself

285   To praise my noble act. I hear him mock
The luck of Caesar, which the gods give men
To excuse their after wrath. Husband, I come!
Now to that name my courage prove my title!
I am fire and air; my other elements
290   I give to baser life. So, have you done?
Come then, and take the last warmth of my lips.
Farewell, kind Charmian, Iras, long farewell.

[Kisses them. Iras falls and dies.]

Have I the aspic in my lips? Dost fall?
If thou and nature can so gently part,
295   The stroke of death is as a lover's pinch,
Which hurts, and is desir'd. Dost thou lie still?
If thus thou vanishest, thou tell'st the world
It is not worth leave-taking.
CHAR.   Dissolve, thick cloud, and rain, that I may say
The gods themselves do weep!
CLEO.   This proves me base.
301   If she first meet the curled Antony,
He'll make demand of her, and spend that kiss
Which is my heaven to have. Come, thou mortal wretch,

[To an asp, which she applies to her breast.]

With thy sharp teeth this knot intrinsicate
305   Of life at once untie. Poor venomous fool,
Be angry, and dispatch. O, couldst thou speak,
That I might hear thee call great Caesar ass
Unpolicied!
CHAR.   O eastern star!
CLEO.   Peace, peace!
309   Dost thou not see my baby at my breast,
That sucks the nurse asleep?
CHAR.   O, break! O, break!
CLEO.   As sweet as balm, as soft as air, as gentle —
O Antony! — Nay, I will take thee too:

[Applying another asp to her arm.]

What should I stay —   *Dies.*

---

287. **their:** i.e. the gods'.   288. **title:** right.   289. **other elements:** i.e. earth and water.
290. **baser:** i.e. mortal.   293. **aspic:** asp.   298. **leave-taking:** taking leave of.
302. **make . . . her:** i.e. ask her for news of me.   **spend:** i.e. reward her with.
303. **mortal wretch:** deadly creature.   304. **intrinsicate:** intricate.
308. **Unpolicied:** outdone in craftiness (in the contest with Cleopatra).
313. **What:** why.

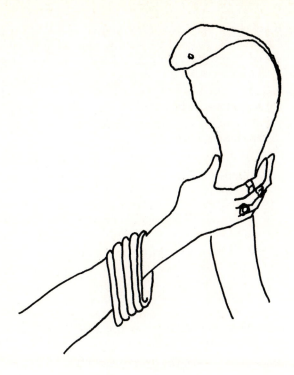

CHAR.   In this [vile] world? So fare thee well!
315   Now boast thee, death, in thy possession lies
A lass unparallel'd. Downy windows, close,
And golden Phoebus never be beheld
Of eyes again so royal! Your crown's [awry],
319   I'll mend it, and then play —

▍With so much going on in this scene, it is easy to get flustered
or rushed. Did you give your audience time to see Cleopatra's
transformation?
▍How did you create the voice and body of "a lass unparallel'd"?

Bibliography

Bentley, Eric. *The Playwright as Thinker: A Study of Drama in Modern Times.* New York: Reynal and Hitchcock, 1946.
An important work of dramatic criticism that has influenced the thinking of critics and dramatists for over forty years.

316. **windows:** eyelids.

Bentley, Eric. *The Life of the Drama*. New York: Atheneum, 1965.
A brilliant and readable survey of the drama from Aeschylus to Shakespeare, and from Moliere to Samuel Beckett. This is an interesting and valuable collection of essays.

Boleslavsky, Richard. *Acting: The First Six Lessons*. New York: Theatre Arts Books, 1949.
A delightful, sound book on the basic principles of observation and character analysis.

Cohen, Robert. *Acting Power*. Palo Alto, Calif.: Mayfield Publishing Company, 1978.
A serviceable book that focuses primarily on training the actor's mind rather than the voice and body, with an emphasis on aligning the actor's consciousness of situation, character, style, and theatricality. Includes helpful exercises.

Corrigan, Robert W. *The Context and Craft of Drama: An Anthology of Critical Essays on the Nature of Drama and Theatre*. San Francisco: Chandler Publishing Company, 1964.
A collection of contemporary dramatic criticism presented in two divisions. Context includes discussions of the nature, language, structure, and criticism of drama; craft discusses the role of the playwright, actors, director, designer, and critic.

Dukore, B. F. *Dramatic Theory and Criticism: The Greeks to Grotowski*. New York: Holt, Rinehart and Winston, 1974.
Collects the major documents in dramatic theory.

Freytag, Gustav. *Technique of the Drama*. Trans. E. J. MacEwan. Chicago: Griggs, 1895. Reprinted by the Scholarly Press, 1972.
A useful constructionist approach to the analysis of drama; dated but still substantial.

Gassner, John. *Form and Idea in Modern Theatre*. New York: Holt, Rinehart and Winston, 1956.
Considerations of dramatic structure and style within a historical development.

George, Kathleen. *Rhythm in Drama*. Pittsburgh: University of Pittsburgh Press, 1980.
Defining rhythm as the processes through which perceivers are moved by drama, the author explores the ways in which rhythm is manifested in language, attitude, gesture, interaction among characters, staging, and set design. Her discussions are illustrated with the plays of Sophocles, Shakespeare, Chekhov, Ibsen, Beckett, Albee, and Pinter.

Grotowski, Jerzy. *Towards a Poor Theatre*. New York: Simon and Schuster, 1970.
The author is the founder of the Polish Laboratory Theatre and for over a decade has been a leader in the contemporary theatre movement around the world. Novel theories and methods.

Joseph, B. L. *Acting Shakespeare*. New York: Theatre Arts Books, 1960.
  Problems in creating characters in verse dramas, with particular attention
  to Shakespeare.

Magarshack, David. *Stanislavsky on the Art of the Stage*. New York: Hill
  and Wang, 1961.
  A translation of this famous classic with an introductory essay on the
  Stanislavsky system.

McGaw, Charles. *Acting Is Believing: A Basic Method for Beginners*. 2nd
  ed. New York: Holt, Rinehart and Winston, 1966.
  Clear, practical statement on basic theories and techniques of acting.
  Exercises from well-known plays and two complete plays for analysis
  and practice.

Nicoll, Allardyce. *The Theatre and Dramatic Theory*. New York: Barnes
  and Noble, 1962.
  Succinct discussion of the practical implications of the theoretical debates
  about the theatre, its function, and its form.

Styan, J. L. *Chekhov in Performance*. Cambridge: Cambridge University
  Press, 1971.
  A moment-by-moment discursive analysis of the four great Chekhov
  plays in performance, by a masterful critic who understands literature
  and performance.

———. *The Elements of the Drama*. Cambridge: Cambridge University
  Press, 1960.
  An introduction to the drama with a very strong emphasis on perform-
  ance. The book includes close textual analysis of works of Shakespeare,
  Ibsen, Chekhov, Wilde, Shaw, Strindberg, Pirandello, Anouilh, Sartre,
  Eliot, and others.

Wiles, Timothy J. *The Theatre Event: Modern Theories of Performance*.
  Chicago: University of Chicago Press, 1980.
  Explication and comparison of the theories of Stanislavsky, Grotowski,
  Brecht, and Artaud, particularly with regard to the relationship between
  actors, director, and audience in the theatre event.

8

Technique in Drama

Technique is a test of a man's sincerity.

Ezra Pound

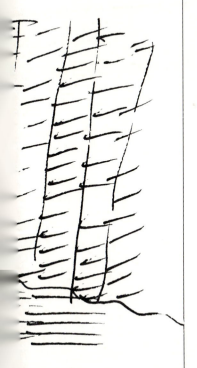

P erforming drama obviously demands great skill. Actors or interpreters need to understand and respond emotionally, mentally, and physically to the aesthetic entirety of a play. Unlike actors, who embody characters with lives independent of the audience, an interpreter, employing selectivity and suggestion, creates a life that emanates from the performer and includes the audience. Interpreter and audience together create the scene. The interpreter's skillful use of body and voice persuades the audience to believe that the characters jointly created move about the world jointly designed, costumed, and lit.

To achieve this goal, interpreters must solve the technical problems of solo performance. This chapter suggests several ways to deal with some of these problems, but suggestions are not rules. You should develop your own individual method of handling the problems posed by each new scene. However, keep in mind one unbreakable rule: interpreters must communicate the total achievement of the playwright, whether they are performing the entire play or only a single scene. All the technical achievements of the interpreter should be directed to that end.

Technique in Interpretation

An interpreter spends a great deal of time and effort in disciplining voice and body to respond without hesitation to the dictates of a scene. As we saw in Chapter 7, you often may have to go over and over a difficult speech or exchange or scene, working it out the way a dancer perfects a complicated step. Only such in-depth rehearsal can bring your resources to the point where you communicate the scene rather than embellish or exhibit it. Of course, none of these rehearsal devices is apparent to an audience; you have worked them out so thoroughly before performance that your audience's attention is focused strictly on the material you are presenting.

Technique is the *most economical management of a performer's resources*. Every work of art demands some technique that has been acquired and refined in a unique way by each artist. Although one artist's technique differs from another's, there are always some fundamental similarities. What is achieved must be more than just a demonstration of technique. Technical mastery of body and voice allows the interpreter to communicate to the audience all the discoveries made during the rehearsal process.

Beginning actors often have some common misunderstandings about technique that have led to countless misconceptions about per-

formance, interpretation, and acting. Some actors feel that a technically proficient actor is a hollow performer who substitutes a supple
body and resonant voice for the character's life. On the other hand,
performers committed to technical proficiency retort that the internal-
reality performer merely grunts and stumbles in a display of personal
anguish that also has nothing to do with the character's life. Both
extremes typify selfish performers, whether they are actors or interpreters. Without the ability to project and refine gesture, internal
commitment to the reality of the play is worthless. Without internal
commitment, technical mastery simply shows — with striking clarity
— how empty the interpreter really is. As you become more familiar
with the performance of drama, it will become more and more apparent to you that certain kinds of gestures or vocal habits impress the
audience. You will be developing a bag of tricks. Tricks are not
technique. Tricks deceive in order to puzzle or amuse. Technique
refines, clarifies. Skill in execution and economy in performance present the selection instead of the performer.

Control

Some beginning performers erroneously believe that an interpreter
should not respond emotionally to a scene during performance or
rehearsal. Make no mistake — the intensity of the interpreter's response is as great as the actor's. Controlling the outward manifestations of an emotion is not suppressing it. You well know that when
you have to "hold your tongue," or when you must accept an invitation you do not look forward to fulfilling, you do not eliminate emotional involvement. Both audience and interpreter have as their goal
the fullest possible life for the scene or the play; but interpreters
always remember that the characters, the action, the author's intentions, and their own personal preferences should all be directed to
the life of the play. None is an end in itself.

Misunderstanding the interpreter's role has led to other problems. Some people have even claimed that interpreters are so concerned with control that the scenes they present are pale and lifeless.
You should be able to manage your emotional commitment as you
do the other components of your performing instrument, remembering of course that *you* manage *them,* and not the other way around.
The principle of *aesthetic distance* does not require lessened intensity
in commitment or in execution; it requires greater control over the
intensity.

This concept may be the single most difficult principle for performers to understand. Yet it is the one principle that, if ignored,
leads to the most trouble in performance. Control in a scene is like

paying taxes: if you give less than required, you get into trouble; if you give more, you are either foolish or careless. Interpreters in control of a scene spend just enough resources to be sure that the audience fully experiences the life of the drama. As performers, they may not be experiencing precisely the same emotions as the audience is; but as characters, they are suggesting the emotional fullness of the role. Interpreters should not confuse their personal response to a character's plight (from the examples in Chapter 7, sorrow at Irina's loss, or anger with Martha) with the intention of the character; and they should channel the character's intention into the scene's intention. By controlling their personal response to the scene, interpreters allow the audience to fulfill its part in the experience. An audience can then focus on the life of the scene and not on the personal travails and traumas of the interpreter as a performer. Excessive displays display only excess.

Memorizing Lines

Happily, we are now past the days when interpreters were told that memorizing means acting. Constant repetition of a scene or a passage allows the performer to become so familiar with the emotional and intellectual progress of the speech that the words become inevitable parts of the character, as they should be. It is not necessary to memorize a scene — and surely it would be extraordinarily difficult to memorize an entire play. Still, there are times when memorizing may be useful.

When a scene features two or three characters whose rapid, short dialogue prevents graceful consultation with the text (as in Hugh Leonard's *Da*), memorizing allows the pace of the scene to continue unabated. Sometimes transitions between characters are intricate and one character may interrupt the speaker with one or two words; in this case it is far easier to memorize the lines surrounding the interruptions to ensure that the audience has the benefit of your full-front placement and projection in clarifying the change in character. A particularly involved gesture demanded by the scene may prohibit consulting a text. In this case, you should be fully aware of the lines as you move from the lectern; if you move tentatively away from the text, you can make your audience nervous. Generally speaking, it is more graceful to pick up the lines that you don't know by glancing at the text while you are speaking lines that you *do* know. Your rehearsal will have been extensive enough so that a key word or phrase triggers the rest of the line in your mind. Memorizing can help you enormously, because it allows you to spend your resources directly with the audience. If you are tied to the text, with your face forever buried in paper, no audience will ever see the life of the characters. Even exemplary vocal projection suffers when it is directed to the floor.

However, memorizing carries with it some problems of its own that should be avoided. The most dangerous pitfall is a *set-speech* attitude: the type of delivery made by children who have had their "piece" drummed into them for the grade-school pageant and say all the words as rapidly as they can — and with very little sense of what they are saying. This lifelessness shows that the performer has memorized the text — but little more. Words mean things, ideas, hopes, and actions; words communicate to audiences and disclose the world that lives within the playwright. When a performer simply rattles off words, all the audience perceives is the rattling off of words.

Perhaps the best method to understand the needs of a scene is to ask whether the scene can be presented most fully if it is completely memorized, is memorized in small or large part, or is presented entirely from the text. Think carefully and keep this question as your guide: "During this scene what does the audience need to *see*?"

Setting the Scene

When people attend a play they receive programs with the characters' names, actors' names, setting and time, act divisions, and program notes. The interpreter, on the other hand, is responsible for presenting all of these elements. But the burden isn't so grim as it may sound.

The audience probably knows your name already, so your concern should be with the characters who appear in your scene. Be sure that whatever information you give is restricted to what is needed in the scene you are performing. The *Dramatis Personae* usually lists whatever additional information an audience should know, although if you begin the play after the opening curtain, it is helpful to tell your audience what has happened prior to the first line of your scene. You might also take the time at the beginning to indicate the arrival of any characters who will appear during the scene.

As you are standing at the lectern, remember that the picture you present to the audience is the general *frame* of your performance; the audience focuses its attention within this frame. Moreover, you are flexible, and the lectern is defined, rigid, and strict. If you plan to move about the lectern, you might extend the frame by delivering the necessary opening comments from the side of the lectern. As the scene begins, you will not need to repeat each character's name, since the characterizations you present, coupled with your placement of characters out front, should clarify that matter sufficiently for the audience.

When stage directions appear important, they can be incorporated into the performance by the interpreter (*not* by the characters), who presents whatever necessary material should be communicated directly to the audience — as a narrator does with summary in a story. You may want to give some indication of time and locale, if they are not made clear by the lines of the play and are crucial to understanding of the scene. If there is a rapid passage of time between two or three scenes you have selected to perform, relay this fact to the audience at the least obtrusive moment during your performance, usually at the end of one scene or just prior to an important segment. Once again the question that must be answered is this: "Is the performance fuller with this information supplied explicitly rather than understood implicitly?"

Sometimes it is necessary to provide scenographic information that is crucial to an understanding of the scene. In George Bernard Shaw's *Caesar and Cleopatra,* for instance, the audience should know that the set of the first act requires a sphinx. In some scenes, the lines of the play can themselves set the scene much more effectively than any explanation by the performer. It is not necessary for an audience to know minor details when the broadest outline can allow them both to follow the playwright's requirements and to complete the details in their imaginations.

Entrances and exits during the course of a scene may occasionally cause some difficulty. If a character's exit occurs at the close of a speech and indicates the completion of a key scene, the interpreter may simply turn away from the scene established. If there are elaborate activities accompanying the departure, the performer (*not* the character) may describe the action: "She pauses a moment, slipping on the long white gloves, gently grasping the parasol in her left hand, and turning ever so delicately toward the French doors, where she finds herself moments later as the curtain falls." If the audience's attention should remain with the character or characters onstage, you can adjust the description to reflect the departing character's activity while allowing the remaining characters to resume the scene. If a character enters mid-scene — or later — you may have to give that identification with a two- or three-word description. You will want to place such an entrance according to the world you and your audience have created ("She enters from the porch"), rather than from some stage-setting location ("She enters up left"); the world of the play is not on the stage but includes your audience.

When a character enters or departs during another character's speech, careful handling of placement of character and focus can indicate to the audience that someone has either entered or left the

room. You can welcome an arriving character or bid farewell to a
departing character with a slight rise in mental and vocal projection,
reaching over the greater distance. (Try these techniques with Lady
Capulet's departure in *Romeo and Juliet* or the approach of Da in *Da*
— both at the end of this chapter.) The best guide to keep in mind
remains the answer to this question: "How can my audience best
understand the activity of this scene without losing attention on the
scene itself?" The best playwrights have done a great deal of the
homework for you.

Moreover, audiences come to your performance prepared to believe what they see; they want to believe, and they want to participate
in the creation of the world of the scene, provided you let them in
on the scene and do not give them false clues or misdirect their
attention. Present your suggestions with economy; your physical
presence restricts the frame within which the audience follows the
speaking character, and your opportunity to create the scene arises
chiefly through the shifting focus of the speaking character. If you
remember these guidelines, your responsibilities are clear, and you
can make difficult judgments with greater confidence and skill.

Properties

Properties can cause many types of problems for performers. If you
use real properties, be sure that all the characters who appear in the
scene use the *same* prop, or you will be asking your audience to
permit and dismiss reality without regard for the play's requirements.

Sometimes, however, it is necessary to present a mimed prop. If
anything, mimed props should be treated more carefully than real
properties, since the performer carefully establishes, nurtures, and
concludes their existence. The danger is that the scene might become
a scene about a prop rather than a scene in which the prop helps
the characters in their attempt to reach a goal. It is important to
use the imaginary prop insofar as it touches the characters' lives
and the purpose of the scene.

In the potion scene in *Romeo and Juliet*, Juliet has a vial. Stage
tradition suggests that she lift it high for the audience to see, just as
she shows a dagger later in the same speech. An interpreter with a
text at a sloping lectern faces some problems in trying to juggle book,
bottle, and knife. The energy used in finding and mastering the props
would be better spent in rehearsing the scene and attempting to convey Juliet's dilemma. By barely sketching the gesture of holding a vial
in hand, you can convey the mixture of fear and anticipation with
which Juliet regards the liquid. If you project the muscle response

that accompanies that tension, you will further create the power that piece of glass has over Juliet; this, after all, is the point of the scene. When, a few lines later, Juliet picks up the dagger, you can establish the presence of the knife by a similar gesture, slightly to the right or left of wherever you have placed the vial. As your body remembers what your muscles did in picking up the dagger, you can persuade the audience that Juliet is considering hefting the dagger. If you have suggested the action economically, the only performance action the audience may in fact see is the opening of a hand. They will imagine that Juliet has considered and rejected the dagger and has returned to the vial to complete the scene. Perhaps at the end you will have Juliet raise her hand and touch her lips with her fingers, almost in a farewell kiss.

The interpreter should be careful not to fall into the trap of too-explicit gestures, shuttling imaginary properties from hand to hand, plucking others from mid-air and laying them down on nothingness. Even though a scene may need a lot of tension, and the fullest response requires some physical activity, the interpreter should guard against overt representations or mimetic gestures. They often cause more trouble than they are worth and require effort that should be used more effectively elsewhere. Remember that your goal is to enable the audience to see the scene in their minds and feel it in their muscles; Juliet's agony of decision is the point of the scene; the properties are secondary. *Suggestion* keeps you from plucking at the air; *empathy* allows the audience to feel what the characters feel; *controlled intensity* pinpoints the conflict, increasing the density of the scene's power.

Embodying Characters

The interpreter must feel in the muscles the physical lives of the characters in the scene if the audience is to respond. It is sometimes helpful to go through the entire selection and develop a physical technique for one character at a time, concentrating wholly on those speeches and actions as if you were going to act that part — and only that part — on the stage. In making this type of study, you will use the other characters merely as line feeders until you feel that the main character is clearly and lastingly instilled in your mind, muscles, and voice. Then, one by one, allow the other characters to emerge with their individualities, progressions, and interrelationships. You may find it helpful to "walk" the main character, and the others in their turn — to rehearse relevant business exactly as if you were going to do it with properties and scenery. All this is an invaluable aid to timing, pace, and muscle tension, as well as to the motivation of changes in thought, the means for suggesting the character to your audience. Since this suggested procedure is time-consuming, you should select for your classroom assignment a brief scene with relatively few characters, so that you may prepare thoroughly. After the habits of preparation are set, the process becomes less puzzling, because you know what you are looking for and where to find it.

After the characters are "set," the next step is vocal and physical selectivity. It is here that the paths of actor and interpreter of drama separate. The interpreter, like the actor, has created an explicit character with individual mental, emotional, physical, and vocal traits. The interpreter now decides which vocal elements — such as tempo, rhythm, inflection, range, and quality — will most accurately and swiftly suggest each character to the audience. The interpreter now depends primarily on posture, muscle tone, and kinesthetic response to suggest physical characteristics whenever they aid communication.

The time spent in rehearsing the actual business is by no means lost, however, because the *memory* of it will add to the vitality, pace, and general effectiveness of the performance. This principle of muscle memory is sometimes referred to as the *theory of remembered action.* Muscle memory affects the reader's empathy and aids in suggesting hurry or leisure, activity or passivity, tension or relaxation as the scenes progress. In this way climaxes are built more effectively.

To test the effectiveness of this theory of muscle memory, read the following scene from Ibsen's *Hedda Gabler* aloud, ignoring the stage directions for the moment. Of course, it is necessary to consider this scene in the context of the entire play before complete character development can emerge. Nevertheless this excerpt as it stands will serve our purpose as an illustration.

BRACK: No. But you will have to answer the question: Why did you give Eilert Lövborg the pistol? And what conclusions will people draw from the fact that you did give it to him?

HEDDA (*Lets her head sink*):   That is true. I did not think of that.

BRACK: Well, fortunately, there is no danger, so long as I say nothing.

HEDDA (*Looks up at him*):   So I am in your power, Judge Brack. You have me at your beck and call, from this time forward.

BRACK (*Whispers softly*):   Dearest Hedda — believe me — I shall not abuse my advantage.

HEDDA: I am in your power none the less. Subject to your will and your demands. A slave, a slave then! (*Rises impetuously.*) No, I cannot endure the thought of that! Never!

BRACK (*Looks half-mockingly at her*):   People generally get used to the inevitable.

HEDDA (*Returns his look*):   Yes, perhaps. (*She crosses to the writing table.*)

After analyzing the elements of content and style and the relationship of the characters so that you are certain of their interplay, go through the excerpt again, and follow the directions for action that Ibsen has given. Start perhaps with Brack, since he does not change his position. Assume that he is standing, leaning against a chair. Get the feeling in your muscles of one who leans on a chair, perfectly in control of the situation. Let Brack look down at Hedda, who is seated. He will probably straighten slightly and shift his focus as she rises. Act out the excerpt exactly as you would if you were rehearsing his lines for the stage. Next, take Hedda from a sitting position, through the drooping of her head and the upward look that follows, her sudden rising, and her cross to the table. Repeat as often as necessary to perfect the timing. You will note that it is easier to vary pace and inflection, as well as muscle tone and emotional tension, when the action accompanies the words. Now, applying the theory of muscle memory, reread the scene without making the overt physical movements for either character. You will be able to retain the vocal variety as well as the physical variety for a strong degree of suggested activity.

When the interpreter selects for each character enough significant physical and vocal details, the listeners themselves can fill in the outline to make a three-dimensional, believable person.

Building Bodies and Voices of Characters

As an interpreter you are not being asked to represent the characters; rather, you suggest them to an audience so that, together, you and the audience create the life of the character. Suggestion does not diminish your responsibility to give a full performance; nor does it alter the need for real people — not shadows — to speak the lines.

All characters have bodies. Sometimes they are buried to their necks, sometimes they are chained to garbage cans, sometimes they appear odd or marvelously strange or fiendishly elusive; but in performance, they all have bodies. The performer's body should be sufficiently flexible to suggest a number of characters without worrying about false wigs, noses, or humps.

The first worry for most interpreters is the matter of gender: can a male performer ever persuade an audience that he is really Irina or Martha? How can a female ever convince an audience that she is Caesar? An interpreter can suggest either sex quite satisfactorily, because audiences want to believe. You are not asking them to believe you are physically a particular character; you are asking them to imagine a character who behaves and thinks in the fashion you are presenting and who happens to be a male or a female. Like age and infirmity, gender is finally a matter of characterization; neither age, infirmity, nor gender alone is sufficient to create a character.

Faced with the problem of performing a character of the opposite sex, the interpreter first should determine precisely the size and shape of the character. Not all women look like Cleopatra; not all men look like Mark Antony. Try to find real people who seem to you to look like the character. See how they carry themselves; watch them walk. Be on the lookout for people who may provide you with the perfect telltale gesture to clarify a goal or finish a scene. Note in particular what happens to a person's hips, thighs, shoulders, and hands as the person moves, walks, and sits. As movement takes place, what happens to the center of gravity? Actors sometimes find animals that resemble their characters and watch them carefully. Use any technique you need, but be sure that you are fully aware of how the body moves.

Now look at what you have to work with — yourself. Where do you carry your weight? Are there any similarities between the ways you and your characters move that you can use? Some men may find that the way they sit is not at all unlike the way Martha sits; some women may find that they make certain motions that resemble the way in which Tuzenbach looks back to Irina. You probably will develop many of the character's gestures and motions from observation and from trying different things with your own body. Use a full-length mirror. And practice alone, because you can concentrate better on the way you know you want to look.

Women who want to perform male characters have found that, generally speaking, straightening their shoulders, increasing the feel of weight in their forearms and hands, and broadening their stance gets them moving in the right direction. Not all male characters will require all of these elements; some will require none. These simply are ways to start the trial-and-error process. Men who want to perform female characters have found that, generally speaking, narrowing their base of support, lightening the weight in their hands, forearms, and upper legs, and drawing in their shoulders will help them begin to suggest some female characters. Once again, this is simply one way to begin the process.

Once you have developed a character's body, you must put some clothes on it. Your own clothes may restrict movement in ways that period costume does not, and vice versa. If you intend, for example, to perform a scene from *All for Love* (Chapter 7) in jeans, you need to know how Octavia's body can be suggested by yours, how her movement can be suggested by yours. Costumes restrict physical activity and enforce specific kinds of postures: because of his girth and sloppy demeanor, Falstaff would not be able to stand at attention very successfully. Corsets, skirts, and swords all hamper agility and restrict freedom of gesture.

When you are costumed in what you will wear in the performance — in what you see the character wearing — move, stand, sit, and jump in the body of the character. Note how your body moves through the passages in the scene, trying any particularly active movements several times. Does the restricted frame of the lectern inhibit any activity? How does your costumed body feel in that frame?

Finally, see what voice emerges from the body you have made and dressed. Try not to force wide variations in pitch, range, or volume. Does this newly costumed body create a voice by itself? Without imposing any preconceptions on the voices, try the central lines for each body you have created. Run the scene entirely as the character you have created, moving as the character might in a staged version. How does it feel and sound? Don't expect instant success; you will need to practice. Work through the scene again, this time without saying a word. Do you remember what differences the voice made? What the body felt like? How the voice and the body together arose from the situation? Listen to people whose voices sound like your characters, and try those voices out on the new bodies. You have begun to build characters, and that is the beginning of building a scene.

Sometimes characters with physical infirmities pose special problems. The best way to deal with these characters is to examine how the infirmity affects their living in the scene. Although some octogenarians are lively and spry, others are feeble. How do their bodies differ *specifically:* is it simply that they gesture more slowly and deliberately? Or is the character arthritic, showing pain with each movement? Remember that habit creates character: Tiresias in Sophocles' *Oedipus the King* at the end of this chapter is well accustomed to his blindness, and his infirmity doesn't hinder him from recognizing how little he has to fear from his tragically deluded king.

Interpreters should be careful not to impose stock physical attributes on the characters they are depicting. It is true that some old people have voices that crack piteously, but not all old voices crack; it is true that age bends some men and women, but you know old people who are erect and vigorous. Be sure that the character's infirmity arises from the text, that you do not impose it in an excess of zeal for characterization.

Your attention to specific detail is the key to effective depiction of characters. Each moment and each movement should clarify a new bit of information for the audience. Each must contribute something different to the picture the audience is assembling and to which they are adding their own discoveries as well. Each movement arises out of the prior moment, leads into the following moment, and suggests the complexity that makes a character a vital human being. Bodies and characters are never divorced, they never cease their intricate dance of information.

Physical Contact

Physical contact is difficult for the solo performer to achieve, but it is not nearly so difficult for the audience to believe in its happening. Audiences want to believe the scene, and they will fill in generously, as everyone does at movies that ask us to believe that flickering shadows are real people. Interpersonal activity is almost impossible to convey, because anything that requires repeated, flesh-on-flesh contact cannot be duplicated successfully by one person. If there is a swordfight, or a boxing match, or a pistol whipping, or even several punches that motivate the plot or initiate crucial character development, it is wisest to narrate the conflict, allowing the imagination of the audience to stage the scene more fully than any solo performer can manage.

Sometimes, though, scenes that appear to be intensely physical on first or second reading are in fact marvelous opportunities for the solo performer to stretch the possibilities of the craft and challenge technical facility. The key to detecting these scenes is to remember that what the audience always sees is the speaking character: as the line shifts, so does the speaking character. Ask this question: "How does the activity immediately *touch* the speaking character?" Utilizing the speaking character as the recipient or initiator of the action, consider the scene again. What can the speaking character do that will suggest activity on the part of the silent characters? Such behavior is called *reflexive physical activity,* because it suggests activity on the part of someone other than the speaker. For example, suppose a silent character picks up a vase to throw at the speaking character; if the speaking character keeps focus on the silent character and on the vase, increasing the tension, excitement, and volume, the audience will believe that something they can't see is causing the character's increased concern. When the silent character finally lets the object fly, the speaker can dodge the vase as it narrowly misses him, or, if it finds its mark, can quickly grasp his forehead to cover the blood, and then complete the speech, still suffering from the blow.

It is impossible to formulate general rules that can be applied to all types of physical contact scenes; each instance presents its own problems, and each interpreter is at a different level of technical proficiency. Once again we can provide some questions to help you determine some workable solutions to try in rehearsal. The first question is "How explicit must I be in order for the audience to believe the action?" Your answer should not be in terms of how much action you can get away with, but in terms of how little you need to use. Remember that technique is the economical management of your *resources*, and audience belief is one of them.

The second question is "Will the technique I have chosen call the audience's attention to a trick or to me and away from the scene?" If you move, bend, and sway as the text permits, you will determine that what the audience sees is the movement of the scene and the character — not the clever or not-so-clever jumping around of the performer. Go to both extremes during your rehearsal. Stage the scene fully, and find out what the lives of the characters feel like. Then eliminate all activity so that your muscles remember, and you can clear away all the unnecessarily distracting movements. Somewhere between these two extremes you will discover the form that most fully communicates the total scene — all its elements in proper proportion — to an audience anxious to fulfill its part in the creation.

Interplay of Characters

After you have discovered a body and a voice for each character in your scene and have decided how to cope with their physical contact, something else remains. You want them to appear to listen to each other. Obviously, you cannot listen as one character while you speak as another. Interpreters of drama develop the ability to pick up a speech midway into a train of thought, to "have heard," which requires split-second response and complete control of the characters. You are not going to become split personalities but rather compound ones, each with a sharp focus on what is happening, where it is happening, and how what is happening affects everyone else. All of this effort is necessary, because drama arises from the interplay of the characters whose goals engage each other, either because they share these goals or oppose them. You do not want your audience to feel that they are watching a number of people speaking from a series of disconnected islands.

It is now time to repeat some of the questions that you asked at the very beginning of your preparation. When the bodies of the characters have been assembled, ask yourself again: "Why are these people continuing to talk to each other?" "What keeps them onstage dealing with each other?" "What does this character hope to gain by continuing his attention to that character?" Relationships are built through the sequences of speeches; as each character speaks, the other listens carefully and joins the dialogue without a pause when the first stops speaking.

Characters interacting in this way seem to be together on the same stage, carrying on their conversations, creating the tension that is the heartbeat of the *scene*, the interpreter's real goal. When characters at last begin to live in the scene, they *lean into* the action. This does not mean that they incline their bodies forward over the reading stand, although they may do that. Leaning into the scene is the way to demonstrate their need to get at the object of their discussion, there, in front of them; it embodies their intention to connect with another character, to whom they speak with earnest conviction. If the character who is being addressed moves, the speaking character follows, always keeping the person in focus and clearly as the object of the speech. And then, instantly, without any gap in which one character is dropped and another assumed, the audience sees the next speaking character.

Picking Up Cues

In the matter of picking up cues, the solo performance of drama is at its most artificial, the problems for the performer are the greatest, and the potential liabilities the most dangerous. Poor planning is frequently responsible for most problems here, and lack of foresight or enough rehearsal can destroy all the effort that has been made. The trick with transitions is to remember to focus the audience's attention on what *is* there (the speaking character) and not to distract them with what isn't there. There are no empty spaces in life — and there should be no empty spaces in the scene either. You are laboring to achieve the totality of the scene, and lapses break or kill the continuity.

When the audience is constantly seeing character, they do not have the time to see the machinery of the interpreter's efforts; they do not have the time to see you groping for lines or pausing to think about what comes next. Maintaining the forcefulness of the scene requires some attention to what the body is doing during the transitions. Try to be sure that whatever posture the character may be in at the conclusion of a line is not so extreme as to require the next character to make any extravagant movement. This does not mean that characters cannot move. It means that eccentric postures should be adjusted and resolved by the time the line is concluded, so that the performer is in a posture that is neutral enough to conclude one character and begin the next fluently. Without the need for any excessive or radical alteration in posture, the interpreter can shift the focus to the new character and begin the line effortlessly, and the audience will not be jolted.

Thorough rehearsal will make these transitions come more readily to the performer. Vocal and physical changes will occur so rapidly that an audience will not have time for a lapse in belief. Begin your rehearsal well in advance of the performance, so that there is time to evolve the habits of each character and to develop ease in assuming characters. Many brief practice sessions are far superior to one long session, for the interpreter must live with the characters in order to get to know them.

Physical Focus

The action of the scene should move along a line that stretches from the performer through the audience to the opposing character or characters, who exist just above and beyond the listeners' heads. This arrangement places the audience at the center of the interaction, with the interpreter providing the constant source of information and activity within the scene. Characters who are being addressed live at some distance from the speaker who addresses them; this distance should be bridged by the performer's intensity and commitment. The audience will support and enhance the tension among the characters, but only if they have something to go on, some cue to sustain the excitement and direction of the scene. The source of this cue should be the performer facing them. The physical focus of the scene should exist out front. Resist any temptation to place other characters on stage, to your right or left, leaving you in profile. Not only would the audience be denied the cues that your face and body can give them, but their attention also would be drawn away from what is in front of them. Keep the characters talking to other characters, and be sure that all the characters exist out front.

When the interpreter needs to distinguish between different heights or eye levels for the characters, the difference should not be even slightly exaggerated, because the audience can grossly distort the intended angle of placement. You usually can make sufficient distinction with your eyes, and you need never substantially alter the horizontal angle of your head.

A word of analogy might be helpful. When you see *Gone with the Wind* on the screen, in their final scene together you see Rhett Butler and Scarlett O'Hara confront each other for the last time in front of the staircase. You know that they are talking to each other, but there in front of you at one moment is a tight closeup of Clark Gable speaking directly to *you*; then, in turn, there is a similar closeup of Vivien

Leigh's face as she talks directly to *you*. Of course both performers are speaking directly to the camera, and if you had seen the segment on the stage, there would have been no camera — only the two actors speaking to each other directly. In the film, the camera is interposed between the characters; because the camera is there, so are you. You can see in their eyes and their mouths all of the tension of that moment.

Much the same phenomenon occurs in the solo performance of drama, except that instead of interposing the camera between the characters, the performer allows the audience the fullest view. We accept this convention because our experience with watching films and television renders it perfectly natural for two people who in fact are talking to each other to appear to be addressing the audience. If you keep in mind the analogy between the placement of the camera and that point where the audience enters the excitement of the scene, your initial fears about audience belief may be calmed. But remember that the performers in the film were so skillful that they made you believe that their characters were talking to each other. What the camera does is help us to see more — and differently — than we could ever see on a stage.

If the action of a scene is elaborate, you can use an explanatory narrative technique to describe it. If the action is important primarily for its revelation of an attitude or an emotional state, then the audience should be made aware of the cause rather than the action itself. The action, after all, is the outward manifestation of the interior response, and this gives the interpreter an important clue to the way action should be handled. It is not so much *what* the characters do as *how* they do it that reveals what they are thinking and feeling. If, for example, a character sinks dejectedly into a chair, it is not the process of sitting down that is important; it is the dejection that is emphasized by the action. Dejection shows itself in the muscle tone of the interpreter's entire body, in the pace of speech, in vocal quality, and in other ways. In rehearsal, the staged scene should certainly be practiced in detail, and the act of sitting should be synchronized with the speech so that voice and body are saying the same thing. In performance, however, your sinking into a set-piece chair would pull the scene up on stage instead of keeping it out front. It would be thoroughly impractical and cause needless complications, because you would need a chair to sink into and you need to get up in time to deliver the other characters' lines. Such activity draws attention to what isn't there at the expense of what is. Continue standing throughout the scene, and suggest a particular attitude not by an overt bodily activity but by empathy, muscle tone, and whatever aspects of focal technique are appropriate.

Angle of Placement

Onstage, actors move from place to place, and we watch them and follow them as they move. Part of the spectacle of a play is formed by the interesting and artful management of moving bodies. Understandably, interpreters cannot show such compositions in their performances, since they are alone. Through careful character placement, however, they can imply the movement of characters and suggest to the audience something of the essential movement of the play. After all, spatial relationships among characters contribute to their motivations and their lives.

Furthermore, interpeters can clarify the speaker's position by directing comments to specific locales. Too often, however, the angle of character placement is substituted for characterization; it is merely a tool to assist characterization. Placement of characters comes among the last of the responsibilities the interpreter need face.

There are at least two popular methods used to place characters out front. The easiest one is to locate a point for each character that is slightly above and slightly beyond the audience, and to address all of the character's lines to that point. When these points are placed reasonably close together — not so far apart that they require a large turn of the head — an interpreter can locate five or six characters very neatly. This method assures that a specific character always looks in the same direction, no matter who the listener is. The interpreter's eyes are not glued to one spot, since several people can be addressed in succession by a slight eye movement within the area that has been indicated for a particular character. An audience always knows that a particular character's comments are addressed to a particular area; by retaining for each character's speeches the same relative position, the beginning interpreter can become accustomed to a nearly automatic pickup of focus and muscle tone that is set for each character.

Another method, which is much more difficult and should not be attempted unless you are willing to spend hours in practicing its execution, uses the stage picture for its foundation. Picture a scene in which Arnold addresses Betty: he directs his comments to the imagined Betty. Then he has a line to Conrad, and he turns slightly to address these words to the imagined Conrad. When you become Betty in performance, you, too, address your comments to Conrad to the same place that Arnold looked when he spoke to Conrad, the difference between Arnold and Betty being distinguished by different characterization and different physical and vocal quality. Your goal is to make the audience believe that Arnold and Betty and Conrad are behind them, all in a kind of proximity to each other that permits movement on the characters' part and allows the speaking character to address the other characters as individuals.

Whatever method you choose, be sure that the important characters are in the center of the audience and that less important characters are grouped accordingly, only slightly to either side of that center line. If you place characters too far apart, you will constantly be moving your head back and forth. The extra time spend on transitions will allow the audience to pick up on the artificialities of the performing method, and they will focus their attention on what is *not* there, rather than what *is*.

The method you adopt must be the one that you feel gives the audience the clearest, least ambiguous information. The audience should always know who is speaking. Whatever the method, any reasonable activity can occur within a given speech, provided that the activity is begun and concluded by the interpreter's focusing at the agreed-upon character point and that the speech remains addressed to characters within the play.

The interpreter generally does not have any direct audience contact during the passages in which characters talk to characters. But when you present any narrative material or explanation, you can establish audience contact since you are delivering that material as yourself. Characters themselves occasionally speak directly to the audience in a soliloquy or an aside. In any case, avoid addressing your words to a single member of the audience, because that person might become uneasy under the constant gaze of the performer. Also, as an interpreter, you do not need to be thrown off your performance by connecting with individual expressions in the audience.

This does not mean that the audience will be ignored in your performance. You are engaged in this performance for them, and they are actively involved in creating characters and places and ideas with your guidance. If you are constantly in character, giving your listeners new information, alive and fully aware of the excitement of your scene, they will be with you, enthralled, absorbed, and perhaps as exhausted as you are by the conclusion.

The Reading Stand

For many people, the reading stand or lectern[1] is one of the hallmarks of the interpreter. It can be used or ignored. There are a number of reasons for using a lectern. It holds the script very nicely and liberates the performer's hands and arms for gesture. If the lectern is used, however, it should not be ignored, and the text not consulted. Its use

---

1. A *lectern* is a reading stand; it should not be confused with a *podium,* which is an elevated platform that one stands on.

allows for greater freedom and flexibility in suggestion, since it allows for easy transitions from character to character and can serve as a table, a bar, a counter, a ledge, a tray, or any other necessary stage piece to support the performer's body.

There is an aesthetic element to the lectern: it provides a frame for the performance. An interpreter appears before the audience as a person with a book. Around this person the audience unconsciously creates a frame, since any performer is a presentational object. The performer is then responsible for filling the frame with the life of the play — with becoming the impulse that triggers the audience to share the experience of the play. Thus framed, the performer is given, in the audience's mind, an immediate restriction of movement; of course, movement to and from the lectern is allowed. But like many restrictions, this one carries with it a certain kind of freedom: the freedom that allows suggestion to assist the audience in creating the world of the play. In a staged production, an actor must compete for the audience's attention with set and costume and all the other actors; dramatic gestures must be sufficiently grand to fill a large space. Because they are restricted, interpreters can use substantially more refined, more economical activity than actors. Thus they become capable of more variety, subtlety, and nuance in their physical world, since they can achieve the same effect with less, and since the audience itself is cooperating.

There is one other practical matter about lecterns that should be mentioned: unfortunately, they can obliterate carefully planned gestures and obscure delicate muscle memory. Rehearse with one, if at all possible.

Cutting and Excerpting

In Chapter 6 we discussed some of the most responsible techniques to employ if you are faced with a need for excerpting, and every interpreter is sooner or later confronted by this delicate task. The safest, most conservative rule regarding cutting and excerpting remains: the less, the better. Since each text is unique and every performer and performance situation varies from every other, we cannot establish any set rules for excerpting. But we are quick to recognize that drama frequently requires some kind of condensation, particularly for a solo interpreter.

Because time limitations can cause problems, it is wisest to excerpt a segment from a longer work that adequately fills the time limit without any internal cutting. You are able to benefit from the carefully constructed rhythmic patterns of the play; the intricate, involved structure that sometimes hides itself at first glance emerges during your rehearsal process. Moreover, as you build the scene, you will have all the benefits of the author's craft on your side. If your segment should occur midway in the play, you can describe to the audience what has happened just prior to the scene; if subsequent events are important for an understanding of your passage, you can relate them after you have finished. If you start at the very beginning of a play, your audience can join the performance as if they are watching a staged production, since your performance will present all the required information. All the dramatic selections reprinted here are such excerpts.

Sometimes, though, it is necessary to cut the material, and you must be extremely careful how you do this. Often a performer's reflexive physical activity can suggest an action that has been performed: a speaking character is allowed to continue speaking, while the performer nods to an imaginary butler and mimes the action of picking up a letter from a proferred tray. If this is the butler's only appearance and his only line, the audience will scarcely miss him; if, however, your play is one in which "the butler did it," cutting his appearance here would deprive your audience of crucial information. Before cutting anything, try conscientiously to include everything; most often you will be surprised at how unnecessary any cutting is. Only extraordinary circumstances should require you to cut more than a few words. If these circumstances do arise, at all costs avoid interlinear cutting, since it defeats your purpose, misrepresents the play, and confuses the audience. Keep the speech whole.

Analyzing the Performance

Begin your analysis with an update and a review. By now you should be familiar with the performance problems that habitually plague you. Have you spent sufficient time on rehearsal? Have you been maintaining concentration? Have you made substantial and serious efforts to transform the literary analysis into performance behavior? Is your body responding more flexibly? Has your voice continued to demonstrate the tone color and vocal variety that marks successful interpretation? As we have said, these questions will never disappear. They will shift focus and degree, of course, with each selection you prepare and each performance you deliver, but the fundamental concerns of interpretation remain the same for beginning students as for veterans.

Performing drama affords another opportunity to broaden your experiences. Drama presents special problems in creating character, managing dialogue, and demonstrating action. These problems, of course, also appear when performing narration, and some types of poetry — particularly confessional poems — require similar effort for the construction of character. Thus, the skills you develop in these performances rest on the skills you have already established, and they will also be useful when you confront the special problems of performing poetry.

Try to respond, then, to the following questions about your performance of drama not simply in terms of this genre's unique concerns, but in terms of the *process* you undertake in performing any literary selection. While these questions may seem specifically related to drama, they intimately involve your development as an interpreter of all kinds of literature.

Was your commitment to the scene total? Did your audience see only character during the time of the performance? When did the interpreter emerge? Why? Was it planned?

Did you carefully analyze the structure of your scene, taking time to establish clearly all the principal components of the action?

Did your close analytical reading disclose hidden clues about characters?

How did you find appropriate bodies and voices for the people in your scene? Gestures?

How was silence used in your scene? Did your characters fill the silences with their personalities? Did the speaker watch carefully for responses from the silent characters?

Did you stage the scene for yourself during rehearsal? Did you carefully imagine and define the settings and properties filling the world of the scene? Did you dress these characters appropriately?

Did your movement through the scene clarify the reason each character speaks and why the character chooses the language used? Did you need a paraphrase to understand the intellectual component of the scene?

Were properties necessary? Were they kept alive? Did you *economically* suggest stage movement? Did your audience always know where the characters were, in addition to who was speaking? How did you solve the scenographic requirements of the play?

Were you sensitive to the rhythm of the speeches? Did you allow each character a distinctive vocal timbre?

Were you in control? Were you too much in control? Have you begun to develop a method for rehearsal? Did memorization intrude? Ought memorization to have been used?

Were your muscles remembering the bodies you created in rehearsal? Did you make clear why each character remains onstage?

Did you pick up your cues?

Did you place the action of the scene directly out front? Did you keep the characters distinct?

If you used a lectern, was it part of the performance or part of the woodwork? Did you make your physical text part of the performance?

Did you cut your scene internally? Was it living when you finished?

These questions can also focus your reponses to the performances of others in your class. Keeping in mind that your chief responsibility is to be descriptive, try to make sure that you say *precisely* what you saw and heard and, most important, that what you say is precisely what you mean. If there is some possibility of misunderstanding, take the time to clarify before proceeding. For example, if you say, "I thought the performer seemed out of breath, gasping and choking," when in fact you mean you thought a *character* in the scene demonstrated this behavior, do not be surprised if the interpreter is puzzled. Using clear, shared language includes understanding shared goals: in laboratory sessions a performer might work on a special problem (dialect, for example, or physical debility in a character) and, in his or her attention to this concern, might slight other responsibilities (character placement or volume). Know what the performer is working on; if you don't know or it isn't apparent, ask. As you know, performers like very much to talk about what they do.

Acknowledging that there are many responsibilities for a performer, as well as fulfilling each of these responsibilities with equal distinction, is a rare — a very rare — achievement. But because something remains to be done does not mean that nothing has been done. Much may have been omitted from a performance in which much else has been included.

Finally, discussing performance can become an enormously humanizing concern, if performer and audience are both primarily concerned with understanding. For criticism to be useful, it must be humane. This doesn't mean it cannot be specific or sharp or blunt, as the case warrants. It means that the goal for the critic ought to be the goal for the performer: the fullest possible communication of a work of literature. Whatever diverts attention from that goal isn't really worth our time.

Selections for Analysis and Oral Interpretation

Stephen Sondheim won a Pulitzer Prize for *Sunday in the Park with George,* a musical exploring the responsibilities of artists by examining the life of the French pointillist painter Georges Seurat. George's girlfriend has left him because he has been obsessed with his work and has neglected their relationship. Now she is looking for him. In this song George makes clear that what caused the problem will always remain. Sondheim also composed particularly ravishing music for these lyrics, but everything you need for performing is in the words he wrote. Show us how George thinks. Trust Sondheim's line length.

FROM ***Sunday in the Park with George***
STEPHEN SONDHEIM

Finishing the Hat

Yes, she looks for me — good.
Let her look for me to tell me why she left me —
As I always knew she would.
I had thought she understood
They have never understood,
And no reason that they should.
But if anybody could . . .

Finishing the hat,
How you have to finish the hat.
How you watch the rest of the world
From a window
While you finish the hat.

Mapping out a sky,
What you feel like, planning a sky.
What you feel when voices that come
Through the window
Go
Until they distance and die,
Until there's nothing but sky.

And how you're always turning back too late
From the grass or the stick
Or the dog or the light,
How the kind of woman willing to wait's
Not the kind that you want to find waiting

To return you to the night,
Dizzy from the height,
Coming from the hat,
Studying the hat,
Entering the world of the hat,
Reaching through the world of the hat
Like a window,
Back to this one from that.

Studying a face,
Stepping back to look at a face
Leaves a little space in the way like a window,
But to see —
It's the only way to see.

And when the woman that you wanted goes,
You can say to yourself, "Well, I give what I give."
But the woman who won't wait for you knows
That, however you live,
There's a part of you always standing by,
Mapping out the sky,
Finishing a hat . . .
Starting on a hat . . .
Finishing a hat . . .
Look, I made a hat . . .
Where there never was a hat . . .

▌ Did you find the fulcrum of George's speech? Did your audience see it?
▌ What do the last five lines mean?

The beginning of this famous scene, with its entrances and exits, requires
some care to keep the abrupt stage directions from interrupting the dialogue.
Juliet's speech, with its problem of properties and her loss of consciousness
at the end, has been discussed within this chapter. Watch the build-up of
hysteria toward the end of the speech and the resultant problem of balancing
the climactic "This do I drink to thee." Juliet is always *thinking*.

FROM *Romeo and Juliet*
WILLIAM SHAKESPEARE

ACT IV, SCENE 3

(*Enter* JULIET *and* NURSE.)

JULIET: Ay, those attires are best; but, gentle nurse,
I pray thee, leave me to myself to-night;
For I have need of many orisons
To move the heavens to smile upon my state,
Which, well thou know'st, is cross and full of sin.

(*Enter* **LADY CAPULET**.)

LADY CAPULET: What, are you busy, ho? Need you my help?
JULIET: No, Madame; we have cull'd such necessaries
As are behoveful for our state to-morrow.
So please you, let me now be left alone,
And let the nurse this night sit up with you;
For, I am sure, you have your hands full all,
In this so sudden business.
LADY CAPULET: Good-night.
Get thee to bed, and rest; for thou hast need.

(*Exeunt* **LADY CAPULET** *and* **NURSE**.)

JULIET: Farewell! God knows when we shall meet again.
I have a faint cold fear thrills through my veins,
That almost freezes up the heat of life.
I'll call them back again to comfort me.
Nurse! What should she do here?
My dismal scene I needs must act alone.
Come, vial.
What if this mixture do not work at all?
Shall I be married then to-morrow morning?
No, no; this shall forbid it. Lie thou there. (*Laying down her dagger.*)
What if it be poison, which the friar
Subtly hath minist'red to have me dead,
Lest in this marriage he should be dishonour'd
Because he married me before to Romeo?
I fear it is; and yet, methinks, it should not,
For he hath still been tried a holy man.
How if, when I am laid into the tomb,
I wake before the time that Romeo
Come to redeem me? There's a fearful point!
Shall I not then be stifled in the vault,
To whose foul mouth no healthsome air breathes in,
And there die strangled ere my Romeo comes?
Or, if I live, is it not very like
The horrible conceit of death and night,
Together with the terror of the place, —
As in a vault, an ancient receptacle,

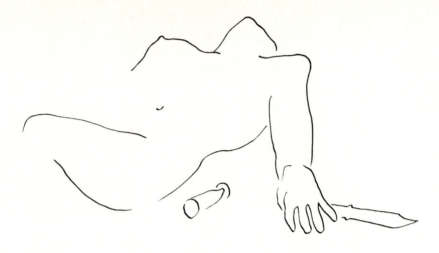

Where, for this many hundred years, the bones
Of all my buried ancestors are pack'd;
Where bloody Tybalt, yet but green in earth,
Lies fest'ring in his shroud; where, as they say,
At some hours in the night spirits resort; —
Alack, alack, is it not like that I,
So early waking, — what with loathsome smells,
And shrieks like mandrakes' torn out of the earth,
That living mortals, hearing them, run mad; —
O, if I wake, shall I not be distraught,
Environed with all these hideous fears,
And madly play with my forefathers' joints,
And pluck the mangled Tybalt from his shroud,
And, in this rage, with some great kinsman's bone
As with a club, dash out my desperate brains?
O, look! methinks I see my cousin's ghost
Seeking out Romeo, that did spit his body
Upon a rapier's point. Stay, Tybalt, stay!
Romeo, I come! This do I drink to thee.

(*She falls upon her bed, within the curtains.*)

▌ What kind of a mother was your Lady Capulet?
▌ What caused Juliet finally to drink the potion? Did your audi-
    ence see that, too?

Charlie, the central character of Hugh Leonard's *Da*, sees himself as a young lad determined to grow up as fast as possible, and he hopes the "Yellow Peril" will help him. He does not take his father, "Da," into consideration, however. This scene features a flashback that allows the adult Charlie to remember his young self, his friend Oliver, Da, and Mary, the Yellow Peril. Keep three things in mind: the young and the adult Charlies are similar in significant ways; Charlie and Da converse naturally, although Da is dead when Charlie recalls these events; and, finally, the dialect resides more in the words than in any extravagant variations in pronunciation.

FROM *Da*

HUGH LEONARD

CHARLIE. (*To* **DA.**) We all dreamed, privately and sweatily, about committing dark deeds with the Yellow Peril. Dark was the word, for if you were seen with her, nice girls would shun you and tell their mothers, and their mothers would tell yours: the Yellow Peril was the enemy of mothers. And the fellows would jeer at you for your beggarman's lust — you with your fine words of settling for nothing less than Veronica Lake. We always kept our sexual sights impossibly high: it preserved us from the stigma of attempt and failure on the one hand, and success and mortal sin on the other. The Yellow Peril never winked, smiled or flirted: the sure sign of an activist. We avoided her, and yet she was a comfort to us. It was like having a trusty flintlock handy in case of necessity. (**YOUNG CHARLIE** *and* **OLIVER** *both look at* **MARY.**)

YOUNG CHARLIE.   They say she's mustard.

OLIVER.   Oh, yes. Red-hot-you-know.

YOUNG CHARLIE.   And she has a fine-looking pair.

OLIVER.   Of legs-you-mean?

YOUNG CHARLIE.   Well, yeah: them, too.

OLIVER.   Oh, Ho-ho-ho. Oh, now. Joll-y good. (**MARY** *looks up from her book as* **OLIVER** *raises his voice: a calm direct look, neither friendly nor hostile.*)

YOUNG CHARLIE.   She's looking. (*To* **MARY,** *bravely.*) 'Evening.

OLIVER. (*Embarrassed.*)   Don't.

YOUNG CHARLIE.   Why?

OLIVER.   We'll get ourselves a bad name. Where was I? Yes . . . I was telling you about Maria Montez in "Cobra Woman." Now there's a fine figure of a —

YOUNG CHARLIE.   They say she'd let you. All you have to do is ask.

OLIVER.   Maria Montez? Is that a fact?

YOUNG CHARLIE. (*Pointing.*)   Her.

OLIVER.   Ah, yes: but who is that hard up for it?

CHARLIE.   I was.

OLIVER.   I mean, who wants to demean himself?

CHARLIE.   I did.

YOUNG CHARLIE.   God, I wouldn't touch her in a fit. I'm only —

OLIVER.   And she would make a holy show of you, you know, like she done with the man who tried to interfere with her in the Picture House.

YOUNG CHARLIE.   When?

OLIVER.   I think it was a Bette Davis. The man sat down next to her and as soon as the big picture came on the screen he started tampering with her in some way. And she never said a word, only got up and dragged him to the manager by his wigger-wagger.

YOUNG CHARLIE.   (*Stunned.*)   She never.

OLIVER.   True as God. He felt very small. I can tell you.

YOUNG CHARLIE.   Still, if she minded she can't be all that fast.

OLIVER.   Oh-I-don't-know. If she wasn't fast she'd have dragged him by something else.

(YOUNG CHARLIE *looks at* MARY *in awe.*)

CHARLIE.   Lust tied granny-knots in my insides. I wanted the Yellow Peril like I wanted no girl before or no woman since. What was worse, I was wearing my new suit for the first time and I had to do it now, now or never, before the newness wore off.

OLIVER. (*Who has been talking.*)   So will we trot up to the billiard hall?

YOUNG CHARLIE.   You go.

OLIVER.   Me?

YOUNG CHARLIE.   I'll follow you. (*He looks almost tragically at* OLIVER. *Pause. Then* OLIVER *stares from him to* MARY.)

OLIVER.   Her?

YOUNG CHARLIE. (*Agonised.*)   Go on.

OLIVER.   Ho-ho-ho-ho. Oh, now. (*Dismay.*) You wouldn't.

YOUNG CHARLIE.   Olly . . . fizz off.

OLIVER.   But you don't want to chance your arm with her; she'd *let* you. (*Then.*) Where will you take her?

YOUNG CHARLIE.   I dunno; down the back.

OLIVER.   I'll see you, then.

YOUNG CHARLIE.   Yeah.

OLIVER.   I suppose you know you'll destroy your good suit.

YOUNG CHARLIE.   Will you go on. See you. (OLIVER *does not move. Hostility forms on his face.*)

OLIVER.   I was the one you came out with-you-know. (YOUNG CHARLIE *waits for him to go.*) They say it's very disappointing-you-know, very over-rated. (*Pause. Angrily.*) Well, don't salute me in the town when you see me, because you won't be saluted back. (*He goes.* **YOUNG CHARLIE** *goes towards the bench. He stops, suddenly panic-stricken.* **CHARLIE** *has by now moved out of the kitchen area.*)

CHARLIE.   Do you want a hand? (*Still looking at* **MARY,** **YOUNG CHARLIE** *motions to him to be quiet.*) If they think you're afraid of them they attack you. You said yourself, all you have to do is ask.

YOUNG CHARLIE.   Dry up, will you. (**MARY** *looks at him.*)

CHARLIE.   Now . . . quick!

YOUNG CHARLIE.   'Evening.

MARY.   You said that.

CHARLIE.   Sit. (**YOUNG CHARLIE** *sits beside her. What follows is ritual, laconic and fast.*)

MARY.   Didn't ask you to sit down.

YOUNG CHARLIE.   Free country.

MARY.   Nothing doing for you here.

YOUNG CHARLIE.   Never said there was.

MARY.   Ought to have gone off with that friend of yours.

YOUNG CHARLIE.   Who ought?

MARY.   You ought.

YOUNG CHARLIE.   What for?

MARY.   Nothing doing for you here.

YOUNG CHARLIE.   Never said there was.

(*Pause. Phase Two in conversation.*)

MARY.   What's your name, anyway?

YOUNG CHARLIE.   Bruce.

MARY. (*A sceptical grin.*)   Yeah?

YOUNG CHARLIE.   It is. (*He crosses his eyes and thumbs his nose at* **CHARLIE** *by way of defiance.*)

MARY.   Bruce?

YOUNG CHARLIE.   Mm.

MARY.   Nice name.

YOUNG CHARLIE. (*Pointing off.*)   He's Oliver.

MARY.   That so?

YOUNG CHARLIE.   He's from the town.

MARY.   Where *you* from?

YOUNG CHARLIE.   Trinity College.

MARY.   That right?

YOUNG CHARLIE.   English Literature.

MARY.   Must be hard.

YOUNG CHARLIE.   Bits of it.

(*She goes back to her reading. A lull. End of Phase Two.*)

CHARLIE.   Ask her.

YOUNG CHARLIE.   She's not on.

CHARLIE.   Ask. (*Instead,* **YOUNG CHARLIE** *clamps his arm heavily around* **MARY.** *She does not look up from her magazine during the following.*)

MARY.   Wouldn't Edward G. Robinson put you in mind of a monkey?

YOUNG CHARLIE.   Let's see. Do you know, he does.

MARY.   One of them baboons.

YOUNG CHARLIE.   Yes. Yes, yes, yes, yes. (*At each "yes" he slaps her vigorously on the knee. She stares as if mesmerized at his hand as it bounces up and down and finally comes to rest on her knee in an iron grip. As she returns to her magazine he begins to massage her kneecap.*)

CHARLIE. (*Staring.*)   You insidious devil, you.

MARY.   It doesn't screw off.

YOUNG CHARLIE.   What?

MARY.   Me leg. (*His other hand now slides under her armpit, intent on touching her breast. He is unaware that he is kneading and pinching her handbag, which is tucked under her arm. She watches this hand, fascinated.*)

CHARLIE.   I think you're getting her money all excited.

MARY. (*Having returned to her reading.*)   You needn't think there's anything doing for you here.

YOUNG CHARLIE.   I don't.

MARY.   Dunno what you take me for . . . sort of person who'd sit here and be felt with people passing. If you won't stop I'll have to go down the back. (*She looks at him directly for the first time.*) If you won't stop.

YOUNG CHARLIE. (*Not stopping; hoarsely.*)   All right.

MARY. (*Looking off.*)   Wait till that old fella goes past.

YOUNG CHARLIE.   Who?

MARY.   Him. (*Fondling his knee.*) Not that you're getting anything.

YOUNG CHARLIE. (*Dazed with lust.*)   I know.

CHARLIE.   My silver-tongue eloquence had claimed its helpless victim. Defloration stared me in the face. My virginhood swung by a frayed thread. Then . . . !

DA. (*Off.*)

"Oh, says your oul' one to my oul' one:
Will you come to the Waxie Dargle?
And says my oul' one to your oul' one:
Sure I haven't got a farthing."

(**YOUNG CHARLIE**'s *kneading and rubbing comes to a halt. As* **DA** *walks on at a good stiff pace, he tries to extract his hand from under* **MARY**'s *armpit but she holds it fast. Passing.*) More power. (*He walks a few more paces, stops, turns and stares.*) Jesus, Mary and Joseph.

YOUNG CHARLIE.   (*His voice cracking.*) Hello.

MARY.   Don't talk to him. (**DA** *looks at* **MARY**'s *hand on* **YOUNG CHARLIE**'s *knee.* **YOUNG CHARLIE** *removes her hand; she replaces it.*)

DA.   Sure the whole world is going mad.

MARY.   Don't answer him. (**DA** *sits next to her.*)

DA.   The whist drive was cancelled, bad scran to it. Only four tables. Says I: "I'm at the loss of me tram fare down, but I won't be at the loss of it back, for I'll walk." (*He looks at* **YOUNG CHARLIE**'s *hand flapping helplessly.*) I dunno. I dunno what to say.

MARY.   He'll go away. Don't mind him.

CHARLIE.   If my hand was free I'd have slashed my wrists.

DA.   Oh, the young ones that's going nowadays would eat you. I dunno.

MARY.   He doesn't know much.

DA. He knows too shaggin' much. (*To* **YOUNG CHARLIE.**) If your mother was here and seen the antrumartins of you, there'd be blood spilt.

MARY. Much she'd care.

DA. Much who'd care.

MARY. Me ma.

YOUNG CHARLIE. He's talking to me.

DA. Certainly I'm talking to him, who else? That's my young lad you're trick-acting with.

MARY. (*To* **YOUNG CHARLIE.**) Is he your —

DA. Oh, that's Charlie.

MARY. Who?

YOUNG CHARLIE. Bruce is me middle name.

DA. That's Charles Patrick.

YOUNG CHARLIE. Oh, thanks.

DA. (*To* **MARY.**) You mind me, now. What is it they call you?

MARY. (*A little cowed.*) Mary Tate.

YOUNG CHARLIE. Leave her alone.

DA. You hold your interference. From where?

MARY. Glasthule . . . the Dwellin's. (**DA** *makes a violent gesture, gets up, walks away, turns and points at her dramatically.*)

DA. Your mother was one of the Hannigans of Sallynoggin. Did you know that?

MARY. Yes.

DA. And your uncle Dinny and me was comrades the time of the Troubles. And you had a sister that died of consumption above in Loughlinstown.

MARY. Me sister Peg.

DA. And another one in England.

MARY. Josie.

DA. Don't I know the whole seed and breed of yous! (*To* **YOUNG CHARLIE.**) Sure this is a grand girl. (*He nudges* **YOUNG CHARLIE** *off the bench and sits down next to* **MARY.**) Tell me, child, is there news of your father itself?

MARY. (*Her face clouding.*) No.

DA. That's hard lines.

MARY. (*Bitterly.*) We don't *want* news of him. Let him stay wherever he is — we can manage without him. He didn't give a curse about us then, and we don't give a curse about him now.

DA. There's some queer people walking the ways of the world.

MARY. Blast him. (**DA** *talks to her. She listens, nods, wipes her eyes.*)

CHARLIE. And before my eyes you turned the Yellow Peril into Mary Tate of Glasthule, with a father who had sailed off to look for work in Scotland five years before, and had there decided that one could live more cheaply than seven. The last thing I'd wanted that evening was a person. (**DA** *rises, about to go.*)

DA. (*To* **YOUNG CHARLIE.**)   You mind your manners and treat her right, do you hear me. (*To* **MARY.**) Don't take any impudence from him. Home by eleven, Charlie.

YOUNG CHARLIE.   Yes, Da.

DA.   'Bye-'bye, so. Mind yourselves.

MARY.   'Bye . . . (*They watch until he is out of sight.*) Your old fellow is great gas.

YOUNG CHARLIE. (*Sourly.*)   Oh, yeah. A whole bloody gasometer.

MARY. (*Pause, then.*)   Well, will we go down the back?

YOUNG CHARLIE.   Uh . . . down the back . . . yeah.

MARY.   He's gone, he won't see us. (*Affectionately, mocking.*) Bruce!

YOUNG CHARLIE.   The thing is, I promised Oliver I'd see him in the billiard hall.

MARY.   Oh, yeah?

YOUNG CHARLIE.   Maybe some evening next week, if you're around, we can —

MARY.   Mm . . . sure.

YOUNG CHARLIE.   Oliver's holding a table for us. Got to run. Well . . . see you.

MARY.   Suppose you will. (*As he goes.*) Y'ought to wrap yourself in cotton wool. (*Chanting.*) Daddy's little baby! . . . Daddy's little b — (*She stops and begins to cry, then goes off.*)

CHARLIE.   I stayed away from the sea front for a long time after that.

▮ How did you show the shifts in time?
▮ What role did silence play in this scene?

This play explores the slow denouement of at least three relationships in a complex series of nine scenes that begin in 1977 and recede in time to 1968. Midway through the play Robert and Emma — husband and wife — vacation in Venice, but their sojourn cannot be relaxing for either. Pinter uses *"Pause"* and *"Silence"* more eloquently than other modern dramatists, and you must scrupulously follow his directions. Be sure, however, that these pauses are filled with concentration.

FROM *Betrayal, Scene Five*

HAROLD PINTER

HOTEL ROOM. VENICE. 1973. SUMMER.

EMMA: *on bed reading.* **ROBERT** *at window looking out. She looks up at him, then back at the book.*

EMMA: It's Torcello tomorrow, isn't it?

ROBERT: What?

EMMA: We're going to Torcello tomorrow, aren't we?

ROBERT: Yes. That's right.

EMMA: That'll be lovely.

ROBERT: Mmn.

EMMA: I can't wait.

Pause

ROBERT: Book good?

EMMA: Mmn. Yes.

ROBERT: What is it?

EMMA: This new book. This man Spinks.

ROBERT: Oh that. Jerry was telling me about it.

EMMA: Jerry? Was he?

ROBERT: He was telling me about it at lunch last week.

EMMA: Really? Does he like it?

ROBERT: Spinks is his boy. He discovered him.

EMMA: Oh. I didn't know that.

ROBERT: Unsolicited manuscript.

Pause

You think it's good, do you?

EMMA: Yes, I do. I'm enjoying it.

ROBERT: Jerry thinks it's good too. You should have lunch with us one day and chat about it.

EMMA: Is that absolutely necessary?

Pause

It's not as good as all that.

ROBERT: You mean it's not good enough for you to have lunch with Jerry and me and chat about it?

EMMA: What the hell are you talking about?

ROBERT: I must read it again myself, now it's in hard covers.

EMMA: Again?

ROBERT: Jerry wanted us to publish it.

EMMA: Oh, really?

ROBERT: Well, naturally. Anyway, I turned it down.

EMMA: Why?

ROBERT: Oh . . . not much more to say on that subject, really, is there?

EMMA: What do you consider the subject to be?

ROBERT: Betrayal.

EMMA: No, it isn't.

ROBERT: Isn't it? What is it then?

EMMA: I haven't finished it yet. I'll let you know.

ROBERT: Well, do let me know.

Pause

Of course, I could be thinking of the wrong book.

Silence

By the way, I went into American Express yesterday.

She looks up.

EMMA: Oh?

ROBERT: Yes. I went to cash some travellers cheques. You get a much better rate there, you see, than you do in an hotel.

EMMA: Oh, do you?

ROBERT: Oh yes. Anyway, there was a letter there for you. They asked me if you were any relation and I said yes. So they asked me if I wanted to take it. I mean, they gave it to me. But I said no, I would leave it. Did you get it?

EMMA: Yes.

ROBERT: I suppose you popped in when you were out shopping yesterday evening?

EMMA: That's right.

ROBERT: Oh well, I'm glad you got it.

Pause

To be honest, I was amazed that they suggested I take it. It could never happen in England. But these Italians . . . so free and easy. I mean, just because my name is Downs and your name is Downs doesn't mean that we're the Mr and Mrs Downs that they, in their laughing Mediterranean way, assume we are. We could be, and in fact are vastly more likely to be, total strangers. So let's say I, whom they laughingly assume to be your husband, had taken the letter, having declared myself to be your husband but in truth being a total stranger, and opened it, and read it, out of nothing more than idle curiosity, and then thrown it in a canal, you would never have received it and would have been deprived of your legal right to open your own mail, and all this because of Venetian je m'en foutisme. I've a good mind to write to the Doge of Venice about it.

Pause

That's what stopped me taking it, by the way, and bringing it to you, the thought that I could very easily be a total stranger.

Pause

What they of course did not know, and had no way of knowing, was that I am your husband.

EMMA: Pretty inefficient bunch.

ROBERT: Only in a laughing Mediterranean way.

Pause

EMMA: It was from Jerry.

ROBERT: Yes, I recognised the handwriting.

Pause

How is he?

EMMA: Okay.

ROBERT: Good. And Judith?

EMMA: Fine.

Pause

ROBERT: What about the kids?

EMMA: I don't think he mentioned them.

ROBERT: They're probably all right, then. If they were ill or something he'd have probably mentioned it.

Pause

Any other news?

EMMA: No.

Silence

ROBERT: Are you looking forward to Torcello?

Pause

How many times have we been to Torcello? Twice. I remember how you loved it, the first time I took you there. You fell in love with it. That was about ten years ago, wasn't it? About . . . six months after we were married. Yes. Do you remember? I wonder if you'll like it as much tomorrow.

Pause

What do you think of Jerry as a letter writer?

She laughs shortly.

You're trembling. Are you cold?

EMMA: No.

ROBERT: He used to write to me at one time. Long letters about Ford Madox Ford. I used to write to him too, come to think of it. Long letters about . . . oh, W. B. Yeats, I suppose. That was the time when we were both editors of poetry magazines. Him at Cambridge, me at Oxford. Did you know that? We were bright young men. And close friends. Well, we still are close friends. All that was long before I met you. Long before he met you. I've been trying to remember when I introduced him to you. I simply can't remember. I take it I *did* introduce him to you? Yes. But when? Can you remember?

EMMA: No.

ROBERT: You can't?

EMMA: No.

ROBERT: How odd.

Pause

He wasn't best man at our wedding, was he?

EMMA: You know he was.

ROBERT: Ah, yes. Well, that's probably when I introduced him to you.

Pause

Was there any message for me, in his letter?

Pause

I mean in the line of business, to do with the world of publishing. Has he discovered any new and original talent? He's quite talented at uncovering talent, old Jerry.

EMMA: No message.

ROBERT: No message. Not even his love?

Silence

EMMA: We're lovers.

ROBERT: Ah. Yes. I thought it might be something like that, something along those lines.

EMMA: When?

ROBERT: What?

EMMA: When did you think?

ROBERT: Yesterday. Only yesterday. When I saw his handwriting on the letter. Before yesterday I was quite ignorant.

EMMA: Ah.

Pause

I'm sorry.

ROBERT: *Sorry?*

Silence

Where does it . . . take place? Must be a bit awkward. I mean we've got two kids, he's got two kids, not to mention a wife . . .

EMMA: We have a flat.

ROBERT: Ah. I see.

Pause

Nice?

Pause

A flat. It's quite well established then, your . . . uh . . . affair?

EMMA: Yes.

ROBERT: How long?

EMMA: Some time.

ROBERT: Yes, but how long exactly?

EMMA: Five years.

ROBERT: *Five years?*

Pause

Ned is one year old.

Pause

Did you hear what I said?

EMMA: Yes. He's your son. Jerry was in America. For two months.

Silence

ROBERT: Did he write to you from America?

EMMA: Of course. And I wrote to him.

ROBERT: Did you tell him that Ned had been conceived?

EMMA: Not by letter.

ROBERT: But when you did tell him, was he happy to know I was to be a father?

Pause

I've always liked Jerry. To be honest, I've always liked him rather more than I've liked you. Maybe I should have had an affair with him myself.

Silence

Tell me, are you looking forward to our trip to Torcello?

▌ How did you demonstrate that Robert knows of the affair as the scene begins?

▌ How did you prepare your audience for Emma's confession?

Oedipus, king of Thebes, who once answered the riddle of the Sphinx and thus destroyed its power, has been visited by the elders and townsmen begging him to deliver them once again from famine and pestilence. He tells them that he has sent his brother-in-law, Creon, to the oracle to find out what he might do to save the state. When Creon returns, he reveals that the oracle has said the curse will not be lifted until the murderer of King Laius, who held the throne before Oedipus, is found and driven from Thebes. Oedipus has issued a proclamation to carry out this task. Moreover, he has sent for the blind prophet Tiresias in the hope that he can help identify the murderer through his powers of divination. Oedipus stands on the steps of his palace surrounded by his citizens, waiting for the arrival of the revered man.

FROM *Oedipus the King*

SOPHOCLES

(*Enter* TIRESIAS, *led by a* BOY.)

OEDIPUS: You know all things in heaven and earth, Tiresias:
Things you may speak of openly, and secrets
Holy and not to be revealed. You know,
Blind though you are, the plague that ruins Thebes.
And you, great prophet, you alone can save us.
Phoebus has sent an answer to our question,
An answer that the messengers may have told you,
Saying there was no cure for our condition
Until we found the killers of King Laius
And banished them or had them put to death.
Therefore, Tiresias, do not begrudge your skill
In the voice of birds or other prophecy,
But save yourself, save me, save the whole city,
Save everything that the pestilence defiles.
We are at your mercy, and man's noblest task
Is to use all his powers in helping others.
TIRESIAS: How dreadful a thing, how dreadful a thing is wisdom,
When to be wise is useless! This I knew
But I forgot, or else I would never have come.
OEDIPUS: What is the matter? Why are you so troubled?
TIRESIAS: Oedipus, let me go home. Then you will bear
Your burden, and I mine, more easily.
OEDIPUS: Custom entitles us to hear your message.
By being silent you harm your native land.
TIRESIAS: You do not know when, and when not to speak.
Silence will save me from the same misfortune.

OEDIPUS: If you can be of help, then all of us
Kneel and implore you not to turn away.
TIRESIAS: None of you know the truth, but I will never
Reveal my sorrow — not to call it yours.
OEDIPUS: What are you saying? You know and will not speak?
You mean to betray us and destroy the city?
TIRESIAS: I refuse to pain you. I refuse to pain myself.
It is useless to ask me. I will tell you nothing.
OEDIPUS: You utter scoundrel! You would enrage a stone!
Is there no limit to your stubbornness?
TIRESIAS: You blame my anger and forget your own.
OEDIPUS: No one could help being angry when he heard
How you dishonor and ignore the state.
TIRESIAS: What is to come will come, though I keep silent.
OEDIPUS: If it must come, your duty is to speak.
TIRESIAS: I will say no more. Rage to your heart's content.
OEDIPUS: Rage? Yes, I will rage! I will spare you nothing.
In the plot against King Laius, I have no doubt
That you were an accomplice, yes, almost
The actual killer. If you had not been blind,
I would have said that you alone were guilty.
TIRESIAS: Then listen to my command! Obey the edict
That you yourself proclaimed and never speak,
From this day on, to me or any Theban.
You are the sinner who pollutes our land.
OEDIPUS: Have you no shame? How do you hope to escape
The consequence of such an accusation?
TIRESIAS: I have escaped. My strength is the living truth.
OEDIPUS: This is no prophecy. Who taught you this?
TIRESIAS: You did. You forced me to speak against my will.
OEDIPUS: Repeat your slander. Let me learn it better.
TIRESIAS: Are you trying to tempt me into saying more?
I have spoken already. Have you not understood?
OEDIPUS: No, not entirely. Give your speech again.
TIRESIAS: I say you are the killer, you yourself.
OEDIPUS: Twice the same insult! You will pay for it.
TIRESIAS: Shall I say more to make you still more angry?
OEDIPUS: Say what you want to. It will make no sense.
TIRESIAS: You are living in shame with those most dear to you,
As yet in ignorance of your dreadful fate.
OEDIPUS: Do you suppose that you can always use
Language like that and not be punished for it?
TIRESIAS: Yes. I am safe, if truth has any strength.

OEDIPUS: Truth can save anyone excepting you,
You with no eyes, no hearing, and no brains!
TIRESIAS: Poor fool! You taunt me, but you soon will hear
The self-same insults heaped upon your head.
OEDIPUS: You live in endless night. What can you do
To me or anyone else who sees the day?
TIRESIAS: Nothing. I have no hand in your destruction.
For that, Apollo needs no help from me.
OEDIPUS: Apollo! Is this your trick, or is it Creon's?
TIRESIAS: Creon is guiltless. The evil is in you.
OEDIPUS: How great is the envy roused by wealth, by kingship,
By the subtle skill that triumphs over others
In life's hard struggle! Creon, who has been
For years my trusted friend, has stealthily
Crept in upon me to seize my power,
The unsought gift the city freely gave me.
Anxious to overthrow me, he has bribed
This scheming mountebank, this fraud, this trickster,
Blind in his art and in everything but money!
Your art of prophecy! When have you shown it?
Not when the watch-dog of the gods was here,
Chanting her riddle. Why did you say nothing,
When you might have saved the city? Yet her puzzle
Could not be solved by the first passer-by.
A prophet's skill was needed, and you proved
That you had no such skill, either in birds
Or any other means the gods have given.
But I came, I, the ignorant Oedipus,
And silenced her. I had no birds to help me.
I used my brains. And it is I you now
Are trying to destroy in the hope of standing
Close beside Creon's throne. You will regret
This zeal of yours to purify the land,
You and your fellow-plotter. You seem old;
Otherwise you would pay for your presumption.
CHORUS: Sir, it appears to us that both of you
Have spoken in anger. Anger serves no purpose.
Rather we should consider in what way
We best can carry out the god's command.
TIRESIAS: Kind though you are, I have a right to answer
Equal to yours. In that I too am king.
I serve Apollo. I do not acknowledge
You as my lord or Creon as my patron.

You have seen fit to taunt me with my blindness.
Therefore I tell you this: you have your eyesight
And cannot see the sin of your existence,
Cannot see where you live or whom you live with,
Are ignorant of your parents, bring disgrace
Upon your kindred in the world below
And here on earth. And soon the double lash
Of your mother's and father's curse will drive you headlong
Out of the country, blinded, with your cries
Heard everywhere, echoed by every hill
In all Cithaeron. Then you will have learned
The meaning of your marriage, learned in what harbor,
After so fair a voyage, you were shipwrecked.
And other horrors you could never dream of
Will teach you who you are, will drag you down
To the level of your children. Heap your insults
On Creon and my message if you choose to.
Still no one ever will endure the weight
Of greater misery than will fall on you.

OEDIPUS: Am I supposed to endure such talk as this,
Such talk from him? Go, curse you, go! Be quick!

TIRESIAS: Except for your summons I would never have come.

OEDIPUS: And I would never have sent for you so soon
If I had known you would prove to be a fool.

TIRESIAS: Yes. I have proved a fool — in your opinion,
And yet your parents thought that I was wise.

OEDIPUS: What parents? Wait! Who was my father? Tell me!

TIRESIAS: Today will see your birth and your destruction.

OEDIPUS: You cannot speak unless you speak in riddles!

TIRESIAS: And yet how brilliant you are in solving them!

OEDIPUS: You sneer at me for what has made me great.

TIRESIAS: The same good fortune that has ruined you.

OEDIPUS: If I have saved the city, nothing else matters.

TIRESIAS: In that case I will go. Boy, take me home.

OEDIPUS: Yes, let him take you. Here, you are in the way.
Once you are gone, you will give no further trouble.

TIRESIAS: I will not go before I have said my say,
Indifferent to your black looks. You cannot harm me.
And I say this: the man whom you have sought,
Whom you have threatened, whom you have proclaimed
The killer of King Laius — he is here.
Now thought an alien, he shall prove to be
A native Theban, to his deep dismay.

Now he has eyesight, now his wealth is great;
But he shall make his way to foreign soil
Blinded, in beggary, groping with a stick.
In his own household he shall be shown to be
The father of his children — and their brother,
Son to the woman who bore him — and her husband,
The killer and the bedfellow of his father.
Go and consider this; and if you find
That I have been mistaken, you can say
That I have lost my skill in prophecy.

(*Exeunt* **OEDIPUS** *and* **TIRESIAS**.)

▌ When did your Oedipus get seriously worried? What happened
to him during Tiresias' final speech? How did your audience
see that in Tiresias' face and body?

Bibliography

Consult the bibliography at the end of Chapter 7 for several sources
that can help you develop your technical prowess in performance.

IV. The Interpretation of Poetry

9
The Language of Poetry

If I read a book and it makes my whole body so
cold no fire can ever warm me, I know that it is
poetry. If I feel physically as if the top of my
head were taken off, I know that it is poetry.
Is there any other way?

Emily Dickinson

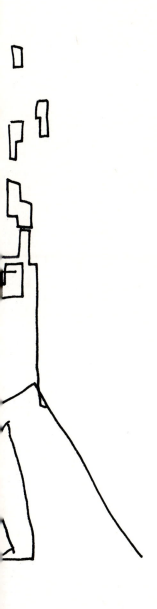

Broadly speaking, poetry differs from prose in its compactness, in the emotional weight of its content, and in the importance of its sound pattern. In poetry, perhaps more than in any other kind of literature, the content and the form are combined to achieve the total effect. They are inseparable elements and intensify each other. A poet's ear is attuned to the sounds of words as a composer's is to tone and to the effect of tone sequences; the poet tests words for sound as well as for denotation and connotation. Consequently, one may say that poetry is the particular province of the oral interpreter, because it reaches its ultimate objective only when it is read aloud.

The high degree of emotion in poetry requires that you make full use of all the sense imagery, which is usually more abundant in poetry than in other types of writing. Complete response to this imagery affects posture and muscle tone and helps draw an appropriate empathic response from the listeners. The principle of empathy lies at the very heart of poetry, since emotion produces and is in turn intensified by physical response. Because poetry is so condensed, an audience profits considerably from the trained interpreter's knowledge and control of vocal quality, inflection, force, and timing that help to clarify the meaning and add richness to the associational values of the words.

The structure of poetry, examined in detail in Chapter 10, has its traditional requisite of rhythm, which is based on an effective combination of sounds and silences and of light and heavier stresses. This pattern of sound and stress can be fully realized and appreciated only when it strikes the ear. Poetry demands the utmost vocal flexibility and control, and it is your responsibility to keep the content and the sound pattern in harmonious balance so that neither obscures the other. The audience's response to a poem is influenced by this harmony, and the total effect of the poem is achieved only when content and structure are perfectly coordinated. Nevertheless, both content and structure present some individual problems that should be considered separately during the process of objective analysis.

Poetic Content

In previous chapters, logical content (what a piece of writing *says*) and emotive content (what causes the reader's pleasure or pain, relaxation or tension) often have been considered separately, although they actually can never be divorced in either prose or poetry. As we have noted, emotive content may be found even in predominantly factual prose, where it is not an end in itself but rather a means of reinforcing or making more vivid the idea being developed. Descriptive prose has an accompanying emotive response that intensifies and adds effectiveness to the actual description. In drama, a high degree of emotive response may grow out of conflict and character reactions.

In poetry, the logical content and the emotive content are blended so completely that it is nearly impossible to tell where one ends and the other begins. Poetry is characterized by the greatest possible condensation. It leaves much unsaid. Because poets must give readers enough clues to guide their responses, they select every word with the utmost care. This principle of selectivity operates, of course, in other forms of writing, but in poetry each word must carry specific denotative and rich connotative meanings and make a harmonious contribution to the sound pattern as well. It is partly by this process of careful selectivity that condensation is achieved. The condensation, in turn, sharpens the emotional impact and allows the poem to move on several levels simultaneously.

Since poets are intent on emotive response, they use organization and whatever aspects of progression, character suggestion, and description they find effective in implementing and establishing that emotion. The experiences they wish to share may call up responses as pleasant and delicate as those from E. E. Cummings's "Spring is like a perhaps hand" (Chapter 10), or as disturbing as those from Emily Dickinson's "I Felt a Funeral," which we looked at in Chapters 1 and 2.

It may be necessary, therefore, to reconsider the established concept of content, or what the author has said. Obviously, a poet must have something to say and must say it so that the audience understands. This does not mean that a poem must be as immediately clear and factual as an essay or a newspaper article. If the poet had wished simply to inform, he or she would have put the idea into a prose essay or article — that is, a form that lends itself more easily to developing a purely logical idea. But a poet intends to communicate something beyond fact or opinion. Indeed, much poetry does not require an opinion at all; it asks the reader merely to accept an attitude. One does not have to accept this attitude as a philosophy of life, but merely to grant the poet the right to hold it. Enjoying poetry is like enjoying music or any other form of art, because a degree of cooperation from the perceiver is required.

Some people distrust poetry, because they think it does not say anything. They would insist that all literature must present information, an answer to some problem of living, or a logical explanation of some phenomenon. They are so accustomed to reading for information that they fall into the trap of message hunting.

Poetry is a record of *experience to be shared*. This does not mean that the experience needs to be explained, nor does it always mean totality of experience. A poem may give us only a segment of an experience. Poets may certainly write of facts, but they interpret these facts in the wider areas of human life. A poem may be motivated by an idea, but if the idea were the whole concern, the poet would not need the additional suggestion and richness of sound that are characteristic of poetry. Rather, poetry is usually concerned with an emotional or aesthetic response to an idea. Even in didactic poetry, where the idea may be of first importance, provoking emotive response is the force behind the idea. Sometimes the poet's intention is primarily to give readers aesthetic pleasure; a poem may merely create a mood, or it may recapture the effects of a specific emotion — love, hate, joy, or fear. In any case, poetry goes beyond the confines of strictly logical content. The success of a poem should be judged in terms of what the poet has chosen to do, not what the reader thinks should have been done.

Archibald MacLeish says in his "Ars Poetica":

A poem should not mean
But be.

This statement implies that a poem must be a complete, harmonious entity — that it not *only* "means" something, but also has an existence beyond purely logical meaning. When you accept the fact that poetry is not only *what* it means but *how* it means (to borrow a phrase from John Ciardi), you are ready to let the poet and the poem begin their communication with you.

The first step in understanding and evaluating a poem is to read the entire work to get a general idea of what it says. This first step may be less objective, less purely "intellectual" with poetry than it is with much prose or drama. Your initial response to a poem may not be in terms of idea or logical content at all, but rather in terms of pleasure or pain, excitement or repose — in short, of emotive content. Read the poem aloud several times and permit yourself the luxury of a completely subjective response before beginning an objective analysis. Give full play to the sound and to the harmony between content and form. Instead of working on the poem, let the poem work on you. Enjoyment is a good starting point for appreciation, even if the reason for liking the poem cannot be put into words immediately.

Do not be discouraged if you find only a very simple, obvious meaning in a poem and someone else finds a great deal of implication. As your experience with life and poetry increases, you will be better able to enrich the core of meaning with appropriate associations. Above all, be careful not to get so preoccupied with reading between the lines that you lose sight of the lines themselves.

Poetry has been classified by types according to innumerable systems. Some are based on content, some on structure, and some on combinations of both elements. Many of the classifications overlap, and you will find differences of opinion about the proper category in which certain poems should be placed. The interpreter is not concerned with technical names and categories, except as they provide handles for grasping the material. However, it will be helpful to consider briefly some of the more common classifications in order to point out their advantages and special problems. You will, of course, always go beyond these generalizations to the special qualities of the individual selection.

For our purposes, poetry may be classified under three major headings: narrative, lyric, and dramatic. These distinctions are based largely on a consideration of the persona — the speaker in the poem. This consideration is important to you as a guide to your relation to the audience. You should know who is speaking in the poem, to whom the person is speaking, and whether the experience is being revealed directly (as in a narrative poem), is overheard (as in a dramatic poem), or is the personal utterance of a single speaker (as in a lyric poem). The discussion of persona and locus in Chapter 2 is very relevant to an understanding of poetry.

Narrative Poetry

Narrative poetry tells a story or relates a series of events that lead up to a climax. In this respect, narrative poetry resembles narrative prose, and many of the steps of analysis discussed in Chapter 6 are applicable here. It is necessary to discover the key situations, their focal points, and their relationship to the main climax. You should give attention to the establishment of time and place, the development of characters, and the relationships between characters, as these elements further the plot of the narrative. Setting, situation, and physical and psychological traits of character — and the interdependence of these factors — must also be considered. The persona is the narrator. Narrative poetry often includes dialogue, and you already should know how to handle this element, just as you deal with dialogue in narrative prose. Also, as in narrative prose, there are descriptive passages in narrative poetry where imagery is used to reinforce setting or effect transitions between key situations.

When you elect to present a narrative poem, you accept a twofold responsibility. You should, first of all, take the role of a storyteller;

that is, the progression of events should be your primary concern. Analyze the content carefully to become thoroughly aware of all the aspects of organization. Remember that you are telling a story in poetry, and that you should use the aspects of poetry to implement the story and enhance its movement and emotional impact.

If it is necessary to cut a long narrative poem, you may follow the same procedure used in cutting narrative prose, but you should be very careful not to violate the poem's structural pattern. That is, if absolutely necessary, you may cut complete sections but not lines or parts of lines within stanzas. For example, the tag "he said" might be eliminated from a sentence of prose, but cutting it out of a line of poetry would destroy the pulse of the line and break the sound pattern.

One of the oldest types of narrative poetry is the *popular ballad,* a form that began before the advent of printing. It is a folk product, and its author is always anonymous. Over the centuries, many poets have adopted some of the characteristics of the popular ballad, which is a short, swift, stark narrative, simple in plot and metrical structure. The language is unadorned, and the characters are basically types rather than individuals. Ballads usually have refrains, which may help to implement the plot but which often are primarily rhythmic. Refrains should be handled carefully so that they do not break the progress of the story but still serve their purpose of repetition. The narrator is completely objective and interjects little, if any, comment on the events being related. The modern interpreter needs a strong sense of performance to give these stark and often bloody stories the gusto to make them convincing.

Even modernized versions of the old ballads retain traces of dialect or archaic words and spellings. The extent to which the modern interpreter uses dialect depends partly on personal ability to make it convincing. Even more important, the interpreter should be sensitive to the listeners' backgrounds and their willingness and ability to follow dialect without finding it an annoying barrier to understanding. The safest thing to do is to give just a *suggestion* of dialect, pronouncing the words as they are written in order to preserve the rhythm and rhyme, but concentrating on overall flavor and lilt rather than on individual sounds. The ballad should have an easy flow of sound, but it also should tell a fast-moving and exciting story.

The second important type of narrative poetry is the *metrical tale,* which is like a full-length novel or short story in verse. It may be a medieval tale such as Chaucer's *Canterbury Tales* or a more modern product like Keats's "The Eve of St. Agnes," Masefield's "Dauber," or Frost's "The Death of the Hired Man." In any case, the process of analyzing its content and organization is comparable to that used for the short story. As in "The Eve of St. Agnes," the characters may be romanticized types who exhibit very little complexity; or they may be completely realized individuals, like Mary, Warren, and Silas in "The Death of the Hired Man." Descriptions of the setting are likely to be fairly explicit, and the relationship between the characters and the setting is important. Moreover, the persona expresses personal attitudes and sympathies from time to time, while still retaining the position of observer.

The third type of narrative poetry is the *epic*. An epic is characterized by its extreme length, by its elevated tone, and especially by the type of events it relates. An epic centers on a hero of superhuman proportions, both morally and physically, whose exploits are of great significance to a tribe, race, or nation. *The Aeneid*, an art epic, and *Beowulf*, a folk epic, are examples of this type of narrative poetry. Another kind of epic concerns humanity's battle with the forces of evil and the struggle for a divine victory; John Milton's *Paradise Lost* is a prime example. The mock epic, exemplified by Alexander Pope's "The Rape of the Lock," applies the grand epic scope and manner to trivial circumstances with amusing satirical effect.

The style of an epic is lofty, the language is highly poetic and exalted, and the sentences are usually complex and elaborate, with numerous clauses and inversions. You can use these aspects of style to help suggest the scope of the episodes and the heroic proportions of the participants. Epics are not written about common people in everyday situations. They involve whole nations and heroes who are larger than life, and they should be given their proper dimension in performance.

Lyric Poetry

The *lyric* is most typically a short poem, though it may be a long, sustained emotional utterance. It is a strongly unified form of poetry, for all aspects of content are shaped toward the emotional focal point. A lyric poem has been compared to a flash of lightning that illuminates some object with a moment of vividness, in this case emotional vividness. Lyric poets usually give little, if any, account of what leads up to or follows the emotional experience, since their concern is with *sharing* the experience, not *explaining* it. You, however, may find that sketching in some relevant background in your own mind enhances appreciation and helps set the appropriate mood. The high degree of association and the intensity of emotion make it imperative for an interpreter to be in complete control of techniques before even beginning to read the poem to an audience, because the extreme condensation of a lyric poem allows no time to warm up or to find an equilibrium. Thus, the introduction is exceptionally important.

The persona in a lyric poem is usually a single speaker whose primary purpose is to share an emotional experience. Whether or not the speaker and the poet are the same is a matter of debate among contemporary critics. The differences of opinion grow in part out of a semantic problem. For our purposes, we shall assume that the poet is speaking in a "pure" lyric, remembering that poets, like the rest of us, have varying moods and attitudes and complex and many-sided personalities. When we discuss the dramatic lyric, we shall address the problem of someone who thinks and feels like the poet but who is a clearly distinguishable character. It might be helpful to point out, however, that we are not concerned in a lyric with the physical being of the poet; rather, we are dealing with the *emotional* and *psychological personality* as it is revealed in the particular poem.

Most lyric poetry must be read more slowly than other forms of writing, partly because it contains much imagery, which is less easy to assimilate than a story line, and partly because a swiftly paced reading does not permit the sound pattern to make its full contribution to both music and emotion. The audience should have time to hear the words, re-create the images, and set up the response. Lyric poetry requires less directness in presentation than narrative writing, but you should be careful not to withdraw completely from the audience and read as though you are lost in the clouds. On the other hand, direct eye contact with the members of the audience may inhibit their response and make them self-conscious. The happy mean is to adopt an attitude of *sharing* the experience. Although you are aware of the power to stimulate the listeners' emotions, you know that emotions cannot be compelled. Your goal is to bring the audience into the poem, not to thrust the poem at them. The process is sharing — not explaining.

The emotion that characterizes lyric poetry is often expressed in terms of reflection or description. Thus, the *reflective lyric*, as its name suggests, is the persona's emotional response through recall and reflection or contemplation. This element of an emotional experience remembered is important to the interpreter, because it gives a clue to the degree of activity — or, more precisely, the absence of physical activity — in the poem. Angelou's "I Almost Remember" (Chapter 10) is an excellent example of a reflective lyric.

The *elegy* is a lyric that expresses grief, usually at the death of an individual. In Greek verse, the elegy had a definite structural form, but it was brought over into English poetry not as a form but as a type of emotional expression. Thus, an elegy may assume any conventional metrical pattern or may even be written in free verse.

Usually, however, there is a formality of language and structure that lends dignity to the expression of grief and harmonizes with the solemn mystery of death and the sense of personal loss. W. H. Auden's "In Memory of W. B. Yeats" is an elegy that uses a combination of structural patterns that change as the tones of the separate sections change.

Like the elegy, the *ode* was a recognized lyrical form in Greek verse. Designed to be accompanied by music and a highly stylized dance, it consisted of three movements, two of which had identical music and dance patterns. But although these Greek structures have been imitated in English verse, the term *ode* has come to be applied to any sustained lyric utterance of exalted theme, often in commemoration of some important event or experience. An ode, then, is a dignified, relatively long lyric poem, which is formal in language and formal, though not necessarily strictly regular, in structure. In general tone, the ode is more contemplative than active and suggests a restraint of movement similar to that expressed by a reflective lyric. By no means does it suggest complete passivity, for a sense of movement in the particularly strong kinesthetic imagery accompanies response to an exalted theme.

Perhaps the most familiar type of lyric is the *sonnet*. This poetic form is interesting to the interpreter for several reasons. In the first place, its form is widely used, and the greatest challenge it presents to both poet and interpreter lies in this fixed form.

A sonnet is a fourteen-line poem, written predominantly in iambic meter, with five feet to the line. It has, moreover, a prescribed rhyme scheme. The two most common types of sonnet are the Petrarchan and the Shakespearean, which differ primarily in the arrangement of their rhyme sounds. The distinction between them is important, but it need not concern the interpreter except as it gives certain guides to the organization of content and to the intricacy of the sound pattern.

Both in content and in structure, the Petrarchan sonnet is very strictly organized. The first four lines introduce the subject, and the next four develop it. In a true Petrarchan sonnet, each of these quatrains completes a unit of thought, and the sentences are allowed to run on past the line ends. The next three lines introduce a new but related theme, and the last three lines bring the observation to its conclusion. The rhyme scheme, which is *abba, abba, cdc, cdc,* or *cdcdcd,* reinforces the division of content. A true Petrarchan sonnet is somewhat rare in English, however, as most poets have chosen to vary the strict form.

The Shakespearean sonnet follows the same principle of organization through the first eight lines; it departs from this pattern by devoting the last six lines to the conclusion, with the focal point occurring in the final two lines. There is also greater flexibility in the rhyme scheme of the Shakespearean sonnet: *abab, cdcd, efef, gg*. This variation in rhyme pattern concerns the interpreter, because it corresponds to the divisions of the content and helps bring the poem to a firm close by introducing a rhyming couplet for the last two lines.

When analyzing poetry that follows such traditional restrictions of organization and structure, you should also give particular attention to the way the sonnet form augments the emotion being expressed. The sonnet's prescribed principles of organization of content will help you in analyzing this type of poem, so be sure to preserve the sonnet's balance and proportion.

If a lyric is to achieve its purpose, you should respond to it completely. Only through your complete response will your audience be moved. This does not mean that you should become carried away by emotions. In the earliest phases of preparation, you may indulge in complete subjectivity, but in performance your task is to *share* the *experience* in the poem — not to display personal sensitivity. This sharing requires intelligent control of techniques. The more your listeners are moved by the material and are unaware of your presence, the more successful your performance will be.

Dramatic Poetry

Many contemporary critics take the position that all poetry is dramatic because it, in itself, is an action concerning a person or persons and because it contains a distinct development or revelation. This approach to poetry can prove very helpful. Nevertheless, in line with our early classifications of literature, our discussion of dramatic poetry concerns works that center on a character who is in conflict with internal or external forces, whose development is revealed without a third-person narrator. There are four types of dramatic poetry: *dramatic narrative, dramatic lyric, dramatic monologue,* and *soliloquy.* Although these terms are often used interchangeably, the four types vary slightly in emphasis on character and situation. Knowing the differences among them may help you in making analyses and in deciding on the degree of characterization that is necessary for performance. In each case, the persona is an identifiable character who speaks directly to an audience, or thinks aloud, or talks to other characters involved in a dramatic situation. Physical setting and historical period are often important considerations.

A *dramatic narrative* is a poem in which the incidents or series of incidents are related by a participant who is affected by the events described. Lord Byron's "The Prisoner of Chillon" is a dramatic narrative. It opens with Bonivard's brief description of his present physical state. The purposes of this unit are to establish the flashback technique that reveals the plot and to indicate the point of view that gives the incidents greater vividness. After the introductory statement, Bonivard begins to draw the story out of the past. His attention is on the story, and his own reactions to events are used primarily as transitions from one key situation to the next. Thus you may assume that the personality of Bonivard is in reality a device for revealing the plot and is not a motivating force for the plot's progression. Therefore, one need suggest only enough of the prisoner's broken health and spirit to make the plot credible and prepare for the closing phrase:

>   — even I
> Regain'd my freedom with a sigh.

The *dramatic lyric*, like any other type of lyric poetry, is a reflection of the poet's subjective responses, thoughts, and aspirations. It is dramatic because the poet reveals these thoughts and emotions through the words of an appropriate character, so that there is added force and vividness to the expression. Tennyson's "Ulysses" (Chapter 4) falls into the general classification of dramatic lyric, although it also shares some of the characteristics of a dramatic monologue. You need to emphasize in your suggestion of character those qualities that make the speaker an appropriate exponent of the philosophy being expressed. Ulysses' essential qualities, for instance, are his mental vigor, maturity, and wisdom, and his authority and leadership. It is unwise to take too literally his phrase "you and I are old," because he turns immediately to the belief that

> Old age hath yet his honor and his toil,

which he reinforces with

>   . . . but something ere the end,
> Some work of noble note, may yet be done,
> Not unbecoming men that strove with Gods.

The poem closes on the positive note that Ulysses is still

>   . . . strong in will
> To strive, to seek, to find, and not to yield.

The *dramatic monologue* is spoken by a single character who is not the poet. The persona directly addresses other characters, who are also affected by the incidents taking place and who help motivate the persona's reactions and train of thought. The other characters do not speak, but they are developed as personalities, or at least as forces that act on the speaker. Browning's "My Last Duchess" (Chapter 10) is an excellent example of this type of dramatic poetry. The Duke's ideas reflect his time and his attitude toward himself and others. He is not acting as an appropriate mouthpiece for the poet's subjective response, but is created outside the poet and speaks for himself. In your perform- ance, you should give the audience a clear, three-dimensional picture of the Duke so that they understand his thoughts and feelings.

The *soliloquy* is also spoken by a single character. The unique aspect of this form is that no other characters are being addressed. Since the speaker in a soliloquy is alone, the degree of directness is likely to be less pronounced. However, as in Browning's "Soliloquy of the Spanish Cloister" at the end of this chapter, the speaker may receive direct and immediate motivations from some exterior source. Although the monk is speaking only to himself, Brother Lawrence's actions direct his thoughts.

Figurative Language

Poetry is, as we have said, a highly condensed form of expression. The poet has neither the time within the poem nor the inclination for literal explanations and logical expositions. Although poetry may seem to communicate less directly than prose, it actually makes a *more* direct appeal; it does not talk about something but attempts to present the essence of that something. Poetry does this by reaching readers at as many points of contact as possible — striking at them through senses, emotions, intellect, and imagination, and calling forth a blended response that gives new insight into experience. Hence, the poet uses exact words that carry with them not only pre- cise denotations but, perhaps more important, the right connotations as well.

The words the poet uses do not define a concept so much as they *expand* it in the reader's consciousness, as a pebble tossed into a pool sends over-widening circles rippling out from the point of surface contact. The implications of the words take the reader beyond the narrow confines of exact definition into the area of suggested meaning. In examining a poet's choice of words, then, you should remember that just as a poem not only means something but *is* something beyond meaning, so the words that compose it go beyond fact and information.

In spite of good intentions, many people never learn to read poetry so that it has meaning for them or for others. This failure often stems from the reader's inability to untangle certain complexities that are present in all but the most direct poetic expression. One of the most common of these complexities is the use of figurative language.

Allusions

A poet often achieves condensation and emotional impact by using references, or *allusions,* that embody a wealth of implication. These allusions may contribute materially to the logical meaning of the poem, but they are likely to be most valuable for the associations they set up by implied comparison. Very often they are references to mythical or historical persons or places, although with the passing of the classical tradition, their associational value may be lessened for the reader today. Still, a reader can recognize them easily as allusions and knows that they are explained in an encyclopedia or other appropriate reference book.

In some poetry, however, connotative literary allusions may prove more difficult, since they may involve the deliberate echo of a phrase or line from another poem in order to reinforce mood or emotion by inviting comparison or ironic contrast. A poem that uses implied reference to other literary works is Marcia Lee Masters's "The Heart's Place," in which the references to the modern poet in Rome, full of memories of Shelley and Keats, add rich irony to her purchase of the nightingale and recall the Romantic escapism in Keats's "To a Nightingale." A literary allusion says something directly, in its context. Hearing literary echoes brings an added level of understanding and a more complex response — it strengthens the poem's impact.

How does an interpreter deal with allusions? Obviously, you are not going to explain the references to the audience, to stand between poem and audience as a sort of collection of footnotes. However, you are concerned with the quality of your own understanding and response, for you cannot share the poem with your audience if you have not assimilated it first yourself. The more thoroughly you understand the allusions, the more fully you will appreciate the poet's purpose in using them — and the more intelligently you can use them in communicating the whole intent of the poem to others. You must, therefore, be familiar enough with the allusions to understand the type of response they are intended to arouse or reinforce. By integrating them into the poem as it stands, as a self-contained whole, you can use them as a means of drawing the proper empathic response from the audience.

Figures of Speech

Three of the most common figures of speech — *simile, metaphor,* and *analogy* — are all based on comparing one thing to another. These

comparisons appeal to our senses and our motor responses. Therefore, they depend on sense imagery, which is discussed at some
length in Chapters 4 and 5.

A *simile* is easily recognized, because it makes an explicit comparison, generally using the words *like* or *as.* It compares two objects of
common nature or the particular qualities of one thing to the general
qualities of another. Keats uses simile to compare Autumn's activity
to that of a gleaner:

> And sometimes like a gleaner thou dost keep
> Steady thy laden head across a brook.

A *metaphor* states that something *is* something else; the comparison is based on some related but not identical factor. It establishes a
relationship between two elements that may be dissimilar in their
basic components and yet have attributes in common, such as "Your
eyes are stars." Sometimes a metaphor expresses a synthesis of
thought and feeling so subtle and complex that it becomes an organic
or structural part of an entire poem. Indeed, critics often use the term
metaphor or *metaphorical* to describe writing that goes beyond fact and
obvious relationships.

An *analogy* is an extended metaphor and may serve to implement
an entire poem. In Francis Thompson's "The Hound of Heaven," for
example, God's pursuit of the human soul is compared to a hound's
pursuit in the hunt; the poem ends with the final triumph of the
pursuer over the pursued. This particular poem, as it happens, is also
especially rich in similes and metaphors within the analogy.

These three types of figurative language, all means of making
comparisons, are important for several reasons. First, of course, you
should understand what they are and how they function in order to
find the total meaning of the poem. More particularly, you need to
be aware not only of the objects being compared but of the attributes
of those objects that make their comparison acceptable. Finally, you
should use your knowledge of sense imagery and empathy to make
the comparisons work effectively for the audience.

Two other figures of speech — *metonymy* and *synecdoche* — carry
associational values that are somewhat different from those of the
three figures mentioned above. *Metonymy* is the use of one word for
another that it suggests, such as "a good table" for "good food."
Synecdoche is the use of a part for a whole, such as "sail" for "boat."
The technical difference between these two figures is of minor importance for our discussion here, and they are not likely to present you
with any very real difficulties once you are aware of their function.
Metonymy and synecdoche are useful whenever they suggest certain
characteristics emphasized by the part that is chosen for the whole.

For example, "sail" is a more picturesque word than "boat" and could be used to imply majesty, in which case you would wish to make use of the visual and kinesthetic imagery that would be called up by tall sails against the sky rather than by a tugboat or a coal barge.

But your major concern is not with putting a name to what the poet did or classifying a figure of speech. You are always concerned with understanding why that figure was used, what it is intended to convey, and what it demands when the material is presented to an audience. The poet achieves concreteness and vividness of suggestion by using figures that indicate or imply a comparison or an association. They must be understood for what they are and for the purpose they serve before you can proceed with the job of doing justice to the poetry.

In addition to these five figures of speech, two others directly affect the interpreter's communication. They are personification and apostrophe.

Personification is the attributing of human qualities to an abstract or inanimate object. This figure of speech is closely related to simile, metaphor, and analogy — the "comparison" figures — because the poet treats an inanimate object or abstraction as if it were a person, thus giving it definite human characteristics. Keats, for example, uses personification throughout "To Autumn" (see page 364). In the second line, he calls Autumn the "close bosom-friend of the maturing sun." In the second stanza, the personification is most vivid, where Autumn is depicted as "sitting careless on a granary floor," and "on a half-reaped furrow sound asleep," and "by a cider-press" watching "the last oozings hours by hours."

You will find personification a great aid in visualizing poetry. It is easier to re-create a person than an abstraction. Moreover, this device allows for more kinetic and kinesthetic imagery. You should not overlook the animate quality this figure of speech provides.

Frequently, personification is combined with the figure of speech known as *apostrophe* — direct address to an abstraction or to an absent or inanimate object. "To Autumn" consistently uses a combination of personification and apostrophe. The opening line, "Season of mists and mellow fruitfulness," might be taken merely as a reflective thought about the season, if considered by itself. On close examination, however, it is evident that the poet becomes more direct in his approach to the season as the poem progresses, and there can be no doubt about the directness of address in the opening lines of the final stanza:

Where are the songs of Spring? Ay, where are they?
Think not of them, thou hast thy music too . . .

An awareness of apostrophe will help you keep the unity of a poem, as well as bring out variety. You will add vitality to the words and thus enhance the effect of the imagery. You should remember, however, that apostrophe is not as direct as an address to an actual person from whom a reply is expected. Even so, the complex train of imagery that develops out of the personification and apostrophe in the two lines just quoted is worth noting.

Thus, figurative language enables a writer to express an abstract idea in concrete terms, to make it more vivid and more readily grasped by comparing it or relating it to a concrete object or a specific quality. Through figures of speech, poets may bring together things that are not ordinarily seen in relation to one another and thus open the way to new insights. Clearly, then, sense imagery and figurative language, or literary imagery, are interdependent, and the motor responses to literary and sensory imagery are inseparably tied to emotional response and empathy.

Imagery was discussed in Chapter 4 in terms of the primary and secondary strength of the appeals and its contribution to the intrinsic factors. The primary appeal was fairly easy to isolate in the excerpts used as examples of descriptive prose. In poetry, however, the appeals are often so blended and many sided that this separation is not possible. Even when the primary appeal in individual units is immediately identifiable, the secondary appeals assume an almost equal importance in the total effect. Frequently a particular type of imagery, such as kinesthetic, or a combination of types, is used in a secondary position throughout a poem and provides an important clue to unity and empathy.

Sensory Appeals

Many poems depend almost completely on sensory appeals for their final achievement. If so, you should accept and use all the clues the writer has provided. Keats's "To Autumn" involves many sensory appeals. One of the characteristics of Keats's writing is its strong sensory quality, and his skill in blending and even combining words to intensify the appeal to the senses makes this poem one of his most famous.

The chief purpose of "To Autumn" is to record the sights, sounds, smells, and rich textures of the season. This poem makes no other significant comment about life, except perhaps to imply that satisfaction can be found in inevitable change:

Where are the songs of Spring? Ay, where are they?
Think not of them, thou hast thy music too . . .

The poet devotes his entire attention to a series of descriptions of autumn, and the poem (which we quote in its entirety) lays claim to emotional response through the pleasure this season gives to the senses.

To Autumn

JOHN KEATS

Season of mists and mellow fruitfulness,
   Close bosom-friend of the maturing sun;
Conspiring with him how to load and bless
   With fruit the vines that round the thatch-eaves run;
To bend with apples the mossed cottage-trees,
   And fill all fruit with ripeness to the core;
     To swell the gourd, and plump the hazel shells
   With a sweet kernel; to set budding more,
And still more, later flowers for the bees,
Until they think warm days will never cease,
     For Summer has o'er-brimmed their clammy cells.

Who hath not seen thee oft amid thy store?
   Sometimes whoever seeks abroad may find
Thee sitting careless on a granary floor,
   Thy hair soft-lifted by the winnowing wind;
Or on a half-reaped furrow sound asleep,
   Drowsed with the fume of poppies, while thy hook
     Spares the next swath and all its twinèd flowers:
And sometimes like a gleaner thou dost keep
   Steady thy laden head across a brook;
   Or by a cider-press, with patient look,
     Thou watchest the last oozings hours by hours.

Where are the songs of Spring? Ay, where are they?
   Think not of them, thou hast thy music too, —
While barrèd clouds bloom the soft-dying day,
   And touch the stubble-plains with rosy hue;
Then in a wailful choir the small gnats mourn
   Among the river sallows, borne aloft
     Or sinking as the light wind lives or dies;
And full-grown lambs loud bleat from hilly bourn;
   Hedge-crickets sing; and now with treble soft
   The red-breast whistles from a garden-croft
     And gathering swallows twitter in the skies.

The opening lines have a characteristic complexity of appeals. Since the title is "To Autumn," the "season of mists" has a strong thermal appeal that combines at once the warmth of the sun and the coolness of the mists. "Mellow fruitfulness" carries with it olfactory, gustatory, visual, and kinesthetic appeal, as well as a continuation of thermal and a possibility of tactual appeal. The second line brings in a still stronger thermal appeal. The effect is one of warmth, and it enhances the feeling of drowsiness and almost static heaviness that recurs in each stanza. The next three lines contain all of these previous appeals to sensory perception, but with kinetic appeals added — in fact, with special appeal to kinetic and kinesthetic response: "load with fruit," "vines that run," "to bend with apples."

Because the appeals are so complex and so closely interwoven, it is almost impossible, and probably unnecessary, to decide which is the primary appeal within a unit of thought. The strength of the appeals shifts from one type to another almost within a single word. Indeed, the first five lines include every type of imagery except auditory, and even that is suggested later in the stanza by "the bees."

As the poem progresses, the visual and auditory appeals become increasingly important. The second stanza indicates the poet's concern with the visual by its opening question, "Who hath not seen thee . . . ?" The third stanza is strongly auditory, with its references to "songs" and "music." Within this framework, the sensory appeals remain complex. You will find that the imagery acts not only as a guide to making the descriptions vivid, but also contributes significantly to the unity, harmony, and variety of the poem. Attention to the kinesthetic imagery and the kinetic imagery, both of which are made more vivid through personification, will help to keep this poem from becoming merely a lush combination of beautiful sounds. Awareness of the shift to visual and then to auditory imagery in the second and third stanzas will help to unravel the complicated sentences and keep the poem moving.

Stanzas

Paragraphs are the major organizational signposts in the progress of thought in prose writing. A stanza often serves the same purpose in poetry. In blank verse and free verse, the stanzas or unit divisions (if they exist) are often of irregular length, and they are dictated by the amount of attention the author wishes to devote to each unit of content. Hence, they may be considered in the same light as prose paragraphs as far as progression of content is concerned. In other types of poetry, however, the poet usually limits the stanzas to a specific length and condenses or expands each unit of thought to coincide with this structural restriction. Nevertheless, even in the most tightly structured poetry, a stanza usually operates as a major thought unit, and this entity is intensified if a formal rhyme scheme is used.

Stanley Kunitz's poem "Open the Gates" (at the end of this chapter) progresses chronologically and in giant steps from one four-line stanza to the next. John Ciardi, on the other hand, allows his two seventeen-line stanzas to move smoothly and flowingly on either side of the two-line fulcrum stanza in "As I Would Wish You Birds" (Chapter 10). Theodore Roethke uses a similar method of setting off the persona's flash of intense anger in "Old Lady's Winter Words" (Chapter 4), although his other stanzas are not as regular in length as Ciardi's. It must not be assumed that these poets just forgot to follow the form they started out with.

You will find considerable help in achieving variety as well as rhythm of content if you carefully consider stanzaic divisions. These separate units of thought should not be allowed to break off from each other, and the transitions from stanza to stanza should be kept clear so that the audience receives a unified experience. Transitions in poetry are often abrupt and implied rather than stated explicitly. They may be transitions of time or place, of course; but often, as in "To Autumn," they simply move us into another aspect of the same subject or provide a subtle shift in mood. In any case, the order of the stanzas is not an accident, and the stanza breaks are in reality links. In "Soliloquy of the Spanish Cloister," for example, some of the stanzas are linked by the monk's observations of some action by Brother Lawrence as he moves about in his garden, while others are connected only by the monk's stream of consciousness as he muses on his "heart's abhorrence" and his daily contacts with Brother Lawrence.

Poetic Syntax

The stanzas of a poem provide the main divisions of organization and content. Within the stanzas, sentences are minor units of thought progression. In poetry the syntax of the sentence is sometimes more complicated than it is in prose. This is due in part to the weight of suggestion within the condensation that is characteristic of poetry.

Poets often achieve this condensation by using long, involved sentences that contain numerous dependent clauses and descriptive phrases. These clauses and phrases are not always adjacent to the words they modify. Consequently some care in analysis and in performance may be required to keep the thread of thought from becoming hopelessly entangled and the poem from seeming to consist merely of unrelated sets of words.

Perhaps the first approach to an involved sentence is simply to recast it in normal order, identifying the subject, the verb, and the object, if any, and arranging the clauses and phrases to modify the appropriate parts of the sentence. You should not, however, insist that poetry display the same clarity and syntactical precision as factual prose. Often parts of speech are omitted, and references are implied rather than stated. Normal word order is frequently changed for emotional effect, for heightening of sound qualities, or both.

The opening sentence of Hopkins's "The Windhover" (which is completely reprinted at the end of this chapter) is an excellent example of this ellipsis or omission of words.

> I CAUGHT this morning morning's minion, kingdom of daylight's
>   dauphin, dapple-dawn-drawn Falcon, in his riding
>   Of the rolling level underneath him steady air, and striding
> High there, how he rung upon the rein of a wimpling wing
> In his ecstasy! then off, off forth on swing,
>   As a skate's heel sweeps smooth on a bow-bend: the hurl and gliding
>   Rebuffed the big wind.

The sentence, which whirls on for five and one-half lines, begins reasonably enough with the simple "I caught" (meaning "caught sight of" rather than "captured"). The capitalization of "caught" is the poet's and adds a sense of surprise and wonder to the sight. The adverbial phrase "this morning" tells us when the event took place. After this comes the object of the sentence, the windhover, which the poet calls "minion," "dauphin," and "Falcon," and we are told what the bird was doing. He was riding and striding, and "he rung upon the rein of a wimpling wing" — that is, he flew upward in spirals by folding or "pleating" or tipping one wing. And then he was off as smoothly as an ice skate cuts a curve, and "the hurl and gliding rebuffed" (snubbed, refused to consider) "the big wind." This, then, is the syntactical skeleton of the sentence.

The next step is to attempt to find the proper relationship of the rest of the words that modify and flesh out this syntactical skeleton in our own minds. We need to add some connectives and phrases to compensate for Hopkins's elliptical quality. In the process we shall obviously destroy much of the beauty of the sound, but that, too, may help to prove our point. The sentence might now read: This morning I caught (sight of) morning's minion (in his) kingdom of (which he is) daylight's dauphin (and) dapple-dawn-drawn Falcon, in his riding of the rolling level (which was) underneath him (and which was) steady air and (when he was) striding high there (you should have seen) how he rung upon the rein of a wimpling wing in his ecstasy (and) then (he was) off, off forth on a swing as (smoothly as) a skate's heel sweeps on a bow-bend (and) the hurl and gliding rebuffed the big wind.

Admittedly, this is an extremely awkward sentence, plodding heavily from one detail to the next. We have lost all the "hurl and gliding," the sense of lift and freedom, and much of the beauty of the sound combinations. Harmony has almost completely disappeared. The insertion of "and" after the exclamation point defeats the poet's own ecstasy at the sight. The substitution of "and" for the colon before the last clause robs it of its conclusive value by making it just one more item rather than a culmination of several. Now that you understand where the thought is going and how it gets there, you must go back to the sentence as the poet wrote it. With your control of pace and pauses, and the poet's remarkable imagery and tone color, your audience will have no difficulty in catching the totality of the poem's experience.

Tone Color

In addition to connotative values and sensory appeals, another important factor in poetry is the choice and arrangement of words. A poet strives for the perfect union of sense and sound and is acutely aware of the contribution that each makes to the other. This attention to the sounds of words separately and in combination is called *tone color*. It was discussed briefly in Chapter 5 in the section on descriptive prose, but it is so basic to the sound pattern of poetry that it requires some added consideration here.

Tone color is the combination of vowels and consonants to help achieve a particular effect. Clearly, poets do not simply scramble together assorted vowels and consonants. They must, of course, use words. But the choice of a word and its position in relation to other words is partially dictated by the way the sounds go together. Cummings's poem "Spring is like a perhaps hand" (Chapter 10) owes part of its effectiveness to tone color. The two words "perhaps hand" are characteristic of his remarkable freedom with syntax, using "perhaps" as an adjective to modify "hand." The connotation is helped, however, by juxtaposing "haps" and "hand," both of which must be said carefully to pronounce the aspirate *h* and the vowel *a*. The *p* and *s* of "haps" slow the rate, and a slight pause is necessary before the *h* of "hand." This is a subtle effect, but to be aware of its importance one need only consider what a difference it would make if the line read, "Spring is perhaps like a hand." This arrangement drastically changes the meaning, rhythm, and sound values.

The general term *tone color* embraces onomatopoeia and allitera-tion, assonance and consonance.

Onomatopoeia is the use of words whose sounds suggest or rein-force their meaning: for example, "hiss," "thud," "crack," and "bub-ble." *Alliteration* is the repetition of identical or nearly identical sounds at the beginnings of two or more words in a line or phrase. The phrase *"morning morning's minion"* in "The Windhover" is a classic example, and there are many other alliterative combinations in the poem. Many poets use alliteration that is more widely spaced and operates throughout a large unit or even through an entire brief poem. Dylan Thomas does this most effectively in "In My Craft or Sullen Art" (at the end of this chapter), for example.

The use of identical or closely approximated vowels within words is called *assonance;* the close repetition of identical or approximate consonants within or at the ends of words is called *consonance.* These two techniques are also found throughout "The Windhover": asso-nance in the repeated *o*'s and consonance very strong in the *n* sounds of "morning morning's minion," and both assonance and consonance in "minion," "dauphin," and "Falcon" in the long first line.

Tone color performs several functions in poetry. The amount and richness of it vary with the poem's purpose. The more marked the aesthetic and emotional effect desired, the richer and more complex the tone color is likely to be. One of the most important uses of tone color is to enrich the emotional content. Most authorities agree that it is nearly impossible to divorce the connotation of a word from its sound. Even in everyday conversation, words are colored and their meanings intensified or depreciated by the elongation or shortening of the vowel sounds and by the softening or sharpening of the con-sonants. This coloring or intensification through sound is even more marked in poetry, when a word is used with others to strengthen the associational values. Thus, tone color makes an important contribu-tion to suggestion.

Tone color is also important in implementing sense imagery and intensifying empathy. "To Autumn" offers a particularly good example. The opening lines, or indeed any lines chosen at random, provide unmistakable proof of Keats's concern with sounds:

> *Season of mists and mellow fruitfulness,*
> *Close bosom-friend of the maturing sun.*

Within these lines, the consonants *s, m, n,* and *l* predominate, skill-fully combined with rich "oo" and "u" sounds, while the lighter vowels in "mists," "mell," "ness," and "friend" keep the effect from becoming monotonous. With such a strong hint from the poet in the opening lines, the interpreter should pay particular attention to the combination of sounds in the rest of the poem. It will become clear that they vary as the content varies, but in every case, sound, connotation, and sense imagery reinforce each other.

Another extremely important function of tone color is to provide for change of tempo and give clues to variation in vocal quality. Certain combinations of vowels and consonants allow and even encourage the reader to speak more rapidly or slowly than other combinations do. A skilled poet is aware of variety of tempo and probably has used it in the poem. You should look for it and use it, too. Of course, variations in tempo also depend on the content, both emotional and logical, and on the type of imagery they augment.

The last stanza of "To Autumn" contains an excellent example of the use of tone color to provide variety of tempo and vocal quality. The short speech phrases in the form of the questions

Where are the songs of Spring? Ay, where are they?

help to achieve needed variety after the rich, slow sounds of

Thou watchest the last oozings hours by hours.

which closed the preceding stanza. "Think not of them" is likewise light and almost crisp in its sound and its implication of dismissal. Immediately, however, the tempo slows again with "thou hast thy music too," and even more in the next line with "barrèd clouds bloom." The pace picks up slightly on "touched the stubble-plains" but immediately slows again on "rosy hue." This alternation continues throughout the entire stanza. The contrast between "lambs loud bleat from hilly bourn" and the following "hedge-crickets sing" is particularly effective. Attention to subtle changes indicated by the sounds will allow you to make the most of the needed variety. And certainly ease or difficulty in articulating any specific series of words is a factor in control and variety of pace and vocal quality.

Tone color usually does not make a major contribution to unity except within small units or stanzas. An entire poem that is richly laden with the same sound combinations would be extremely difficult to handle. But tone color is certainly basic to harmony and is valuable in achieving variety and contrast. Its primary function is supportive, and it should be used in its proper relationship with all the other elements you discover in analysis.

Tone color is another of the elements that make poetry so satisfying to and, in turn, so dependent on the artist-interpreter. Obviously, there is no way to appreciate tone color or permit it to achieve its purpose except to give the words their sounds. To use tone color fully, you should be sure to enunciate clearly and form all sounds properly. The poet had a purpose in combining the sounds as they are, and you should accept the responsibility of reproducing them accurately as they were put down.

Titles

An important but sometimes overlooked clue to the meaning of a poem is found in its title. Hopkins identifies his "morning's minion" in the title "The Windhover" and thus helps us to untangle the analogy. Browning tells us that his monk is alone and speaking in a soliloquy. Roethke clearly identifies the persona in "Old Lady's Winter Words." Another equally effective title is "To His Coy Mistress": "Coy" is a very important word; she is not, obviously, completely reluctant or unalterably opposed — she is being "coy." Poets choose their titles with great care to help us in deciding what a poem is about as well as to guide us in the way we are to take it.

Sometimes poets give us even more help by introducing the poem with an epigraph, as Hopkins does with the words "To Christ Our Lord," just beneath the title of "The Windhover." These brief quotations, frequently from literature or folk sayings, may establish the theme of the poem. Do not ignore them, even if you must translate them from a foreign language.

Admittedly, some poets do not use titles. Then the elements of style within the poem itself reveal the meaning. The poet's choice of words and figures of speech and the way these elements are combined into phrases, line units, sentences, and stanzas should be carefully considered. Method of organization and the resultant balance and proportion give valuable clues to the weight attached to the various phases of thought development. The sound pattern supporting the content often indicates the degree of seriousness and dignity inherent in the attitude. We will give this aspect more attention in Chapter 10; now, however, if you look at the last three lines of each stanza of John Donne's "Go and Catch a Falling Star" (Chapter 10), you will be convinced that this is *not* a poem of tragic love, a fact that is indicated as well in the opening lines with their abrupt and impossible commands.

What, then, is the secret of a poem's effectiveness? It is impossible to answer that question satisfactorily. We know only that the poet has somehow expressed and lifted out of time a transient moment — a universal moment — that may not, cannot be prolonged. The blending of logical and emotional qualities is certainly one of the important factors, but it is not the whole answer. Nor will we find the *whole* answer even after the most careful analysis. An objective study of the component parts enables you to make the best possible use of the poet's technique as a guide to performance. But the essence of a poem is not quantitative; its whole is more than the sum of its parts. The poem must be put back together after each step in analysis so that it will finally emerge as a complete entity — from its title or first words to its conclusion.

It is extremely important to be willing to let the poet lead the way. You must examine every word of the poem in its relationship to every other word and let each operate as it must within the whole — not as you wish it did. If there is a line or phrase that does not fit into your concept of the poem, you should reconsider your analysis. You should share with your audience the poet's or persona's attitudes toward love, death, childhood, or the passing years — not your own attitude. If you do not like the philosophy being expressed, you should find another selection. You are responsible for the totality of the poem as the poet has written it.

Selections for Analysis and Oral Interpretation

Let the full richness of the sounds come through to increase the lift and sweep of this poem. The dedication will help you to understand the poet's attitude. The two stresses in the eleventh line were put there by the poet, as were the two words in capital letters. The poem shifts to direct address to Christ ("my chevalier") in the second stanza. We have been prepared for this by the epigraph.

The Windhover
GERARD MANLEY HOPKINS

To Christ our Lord

I CAUGHT this morning morning's minion, kingdom of daylight's
        dauphin, dapple-dawn-drawn Falcon, in his riding
    Of the rolling level underneath him steady air, and striding
High there, how he rung upon the rein of a wimpling wing
In his ecstasy! then off, off forth on swing,
    As a skate's heel sweeps smooth on a bow-bend: the hurl and
        gliding
    Rebuffed the big wind. My heart in hiding
Stirred for a bird, — the achieve of, the mastery of the thing!

Brute beauty and valour and act, oh, air, pride, plume, here
   Buckle! AND the fire that breaks from thee then, a billion
Times told lovelier, more dangerous, O my chevalier!

   No wonder of it: sheér plód makes plough down sillion
Shine, and blue-bleak embers, ah my dear,
   Fall, gall themselves, and gash gold-vermilion.

▌ What does "Buckle!" in the ninth line mean? How did you
demonstrate all those levels to your audience?

This seventeenth-century poem is a famous example of the use of hyperbole.
The rhyme reinforces the sophisticated light touch.

To His Coy Mistress
ANDREW MARVELL

Had we but world enough, and time,
This coyness, lady, were no crime.
We would sit down, and think which way
To walk, and pass our long love's day.
Thou by the Indian Ganges' side
Should'st rubies find: I by the tide
Of Humber would complain. I would
Love you ten years before the Flood,
And you should, if you please, refuse
Till the conversion of the Jews.
My vegetable love should grow
Vaster than empires, and more slow.
An hundred years should go to praise
Thine eyes, and on thy forehead gaze:
Two hundred to adore each breast:
But thirty thousand to the rest;
An age at least to every part,
And the last age should show your heart.
For, lady, you deserve this state,
Nor would I love at lower rate.
   But at my back I always hear
Time's winged chariot hurrying near:
And yonder all before us lie
Deserts of vast eternity.
Thy beauty shall no more be found;
Nor, in thy marble vault, shall sound

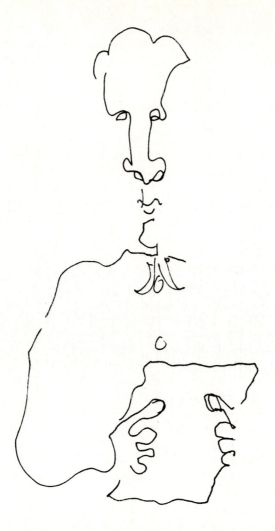

My echoing song: then worms shall try
That long-preserved virginity,
And your quaint honour turn to dust,
And into ashes all my lust.
The grave's a fine and private place,
But none, I think, do there embrace.
   Now, therefore, while the youthful hue
Sits on thy skin like morning dew,
And while thy willing soul transpires
At every pore with instant fires,

Now let us sport us while we may;
And now, like amorous birds of prey,
Rather at once our Time devour,
Than languish in his slow-chapt power.
Let us roll all our strength and all
Our sweetness up into one ball,
And tear our pleasures with rough strife
Through the iron gates of life.
Thus, though we cannot make our sun
Stand still, yet we will make him run.

■ How did you keep the mistress alive during your performance?
How coy was she? Is she the only coy one we see?

This long, loosely constructed sentence requires careful attention to progression as you move through the numerous *and*'s into new but closely related minor thought units. The fulcrum begins seven lines from the end, so an awareness of balance and proportion is important.

Nikki-Rosa

NIKKI GIOVANNI

childhood remembrances are always a drag
if you're Black
you always remember things like living in Woodlawn
with no inside toilet
and if you become famous or something
they never talk about how happy you were to have
your mother
all to yourself and
how good the water felt when you got your bath
from one of those
big tubs that folk in chicago barbecue in
and somehow when you talk about home
it never gets across how much you
understood their feelings
as the whole family attended meetings about Hollydale
and even though you remember
your biographers never understand
your father's pain as he sells his stock
and another dream goes
And though you're poor it isn't poverty that

concerns you
and though they fought a lot
it isn't your father's drinking that makes any difference
but only that everybody is together and you
and your sister have happy birthdays and very good
Christmasses
and I really hope no white person ever has cause
to write about me
because they never understand
Black love is Black wealth and they'll
probably talk about my hard childhood
and never understand that
all the while I was quite happy.

▌ What prompted your persona to speak? Did your audience see those memories?

The reversed organization of content in the second stanza of this poem should be coordinated carefully with the opening stanza to allow this "credo" to come full circle. Pay close attention to the kinesthetic imagery, the slight alteration of the repeated lines, and the parallel grammatical structure.

In My Craft or Sullen Art

DYLAN THOMAS

In my craft or sullen art
Exercised in the still night
When only the moon rages
And the lovers lie abed
With all their griefs in their arms,
I labour by singing light
Not for ambition or bread
Or the strut and trade of charms
On the ivory stages
But for the common wages
Of their most secret heart.

Not for the proud man apart
From the raging moon I write
On these spindrift pages
Nor for the towering dead
With their nightingales and psalms

But for the lovers, their arms
Round the griefs of the ages,
Who pay no praise or wages
Nor heed my craft or art.

▌ Why did your speaker write for "lovers" who pay him no
heed?

This poem moves on several levels. The line lengths contribute to the directness and intimacy of the style. The near-rhymes are interesting and help
capture the regret and gentle irony that the persona shares with us.

The Heart's Place
MARCIA LEE MASTERS

Having just come from Rome
Where I had seen Keats' rooms
Close to the Spanish Stairs —
Where I was told the nightingale still sang
As if poor Keats were there,
Blood bursting into stars;

And having looked at Shelley's grave,
The heart's place!
Locked into time beneath the tall Italian trees,
And felt the spell of stones,
And timeless things:
The azure sound of twilight birds —
Those seashells of the sky!
I had to find when I reached Paris
A nightingale.

And so, upon a rainy day in Paris,
When parks and prisons swirled in their own mists,
I went to buy my bird.
I passed the children on their rainy bikes,
Not caring where they went, like dandelions,
And couples in a trance of love,
Hips fat or lean
Pressed close as hothouse roses
Tied in a long-stemmed box.

Upon a shabby street down at the mart,
A street still marking time with curios,
Fine lamps, and paintings, and exotic gems,
I found my bird.
He was so hushed and frail and dark
There in his cage,
That no one knew at first he was a nightingale.
I did not barter,
Simply took him back to my hotel.

It was a fitful night: rain drowsed,
Then trampled through the chestnut trees.
Then suddenly, at three o'clock
Those castanets of heaven shook.

Rachmaninoff in crystal!

Mountains and skies all tumble,
As they are now:
Love, escape, and terror
Loosed from a diamond throat.

When morning came, my bird was almost dead
Inside his frightened cage —
I had to let him go —
His wings still shedding shadows,
His eyes like wounded stones.

And now, a world away, I think of him,
The mystery, the anguish, and the art
That drove him almost blinded back
(For where else would he fly?)
Into the forest's heart.

▌ What happened to the persona's muscles when the nightingale
  sang? How did this confirm a choice suggested earlier?

The title indicates much about the direction this poem is going to take. The references to everyday objects are particularly apt. Persona and locus are established by the title and opening lines. This is a very compact contemporary elegy.

A Woman Mourned by Daughters

ADRIENNE RICH

Now, not a tear begun,
we sit here in your kitchen,
spent, you see, already.
You are swollen till you strain
this house and the whole sky.
You, whom we so often
succeeded in ignoring!
You are puffed up in death
like a corpse pulled from the sea;
we groan beneath your weight.
And yet you were a leaf,
a straw blown on the bed,
you had long since become
crisp as a dead insect.
What is it, if not you,
that settles on us now
like satin you pulled down
over our bridal heads?
What rises in our throats
like food you prodded in?
Nothing could be enough.
You breathe upon us now
through solid assertions
of yourself: teaspoons, goblets,
seas of carpet, a forest
of old plants to be watered,
an old man in an adjoining
room to be touched and fed.
And all this universe
dares us to lay a finger
anywhere, save exactly
as you would wish it done.

▌ How did your body and voice communicate the poem's stillness? its emotional intensity?

The persona in this poem is clearly Stevens himself. Pay close attention to the shifts from his ruminating to his direct address to the silent and unidentified Ramon Fernandez, whose presence keeps us and Stevens in the realm of reality within the well-established locus. Find the persona's key thoughts, remembering that he, as a poet, is also a maker of songs and shares our common "rage for order" in the universe around us. Use the tone color and the widely scattered rhymes when they occur for their valuable contribution to the sound pattern.

The Idea of Order at Key West
WALLACE STEVENS

She sang beyond the genius of the sea.
The water never formed to mind or voice,
Like a body wholly body, fluttering
Its empty sleeves; and yet its mimic motion
Made constant cry, caused constantly a cry,
That was not ours although we understood,
Inhuman, of the veritable ocean.

The sea was not a mask. No more was she.
The song and water were not medleyed sound
Even if what she sang was what she heard,
Since what she sang was uttered word by word.
It may be that in all her phrases stirred
The grinding water and the gasping wind;
But it was she and not the sea we heard.

For she was the maker of the song she sang.
The ever-hooded, tragic-gestured sea
Was merely a place by which she walked to sing.
Whose spirit is this? we said, because we knew
It was the spirit that we sought and knew
That we should ask this often as she sang.

If it was only the dark voice of the sea
That rose, or even colored by many waves;
If it was only the outer voice of sky
And cloud, of the sunken coral water-walled,
However clear, it would have been deep air,
The heaving speech of air, a summer sound
Repeated in a summer without end
And sound alone. But it was more than that,
More even than her voice, and ours, among

The meaningless plungings of water and the wind,
Theatrical distances, bronze shadows heaped
On high horizons, mountainous atmospheres
Of sky and sea.
                        It was her voice that made
The sky acutest at its vanishing.
She measured to the hour its solitude.
She was the single artificer of the world
In which she sang. And when she sang, the sea,
Whatever self it had, became the self
That was her song, for she was the maker. Then we,
As we beheld her striding there alone,
Knew that there never was a world for her
Except the one she sang and, singing, made.

Ramon Fernandez, tell me, if you know,
Why, when the singing ended and we turned
Toward the town, tell why the glassy lights,
The lights in the fishing boats at anchor there,
As the night descended, tilting in the air,
Mastered the night and portioned out the sea,
Fixing emblazoned zones and fiery poles,
Arranging, deepening, enchanting night.

Oh! Blessed rage for order, pale Ramon,
The maker's rage to order words of the sea,
Words of the fragrant portals, dimly-starred,
And of ourselves and of our origins,
In ghostlier demarcations, keener sounds.

▌ Did your audience see you hearing her song? How?

> Don't be deceived by the simplicity of vocabulary and structure in this poem. Use the line lengths exactly as the poet has. The short sentences in the first and last stanzas set off the climaxes. Use them to stop the rush of the action, but remember that they relate strongly to the speaker, her brother, and/or "the man." Decide who is the major character, but don't neglect the others.

Power
CORRINE HALES

No one we knew had ever stopped a train.
Hardly daring to breathe, I waited

Belly-down with my brother
In a dry ditch
Watching through the green thickness
Of grass and willows.
Stuffed with crumpled newspapers,
The shirt and pants looked real enough
Stretched out across the rails. I felt my heart
Beating against the cool ground,
And the terrible long screech of the train's
Braking began. We had done it.

Then it was in front of us —
A hundred iron wheels tearing like time
Into red flannel and denim, shredding the child
We had made — until it finally stopped.

My brother jabbed at me,
Pointed down the tracks. A man
Had climbed out of the engine, was running
In our direction, waving his arms,
Screaming that he would kill us —
Whoever we were.
Then, very close to the spot
Where we hid, he stomped and cursed
As the rags and papers scattered
Over the gravel from our joke.

I tried to remember which of us
That red shirt had belonged to,
But morning seemed too long ago, and the man
Was falling, sobbing, to his knees.
I couldn't stop watching.
My brother lay next to me,
His hands covering his ears,
His face pressed tight to the ground.

▌ Did your audience see and hear why the persona "couldn't
  stop watching" while her brother's face was "pressed tight to
  the ground"?

The strength of the words and images, combined with the starkness and near-brutality of syntax, help to keep this brief poem moving fiercely and swiftly to its conclusion.

Open the Gates
STANLEY KUNITZ

Within the city of the burning cloud,
Dragging my life behind me in a sack,
Naked I prowl, scourged by the black
Temptation of the blood grown proud.

Here at the monumental door,
Carved with the curious legend of my youth,
I brandish the great bone of my death,
Beat once therewith and beat no more.

The hinges groan: a rush of forms
Shivers my name, wrenched out of me.
I stand on the terrible threshold, and I see
The end and the beginning in each other's arms.

▌ Did your audience see the persona's discovery? How?

This elegy for a little girl contains some interesting problems of balance and proportion. Look carefully at the structure of the three middle stanzas. Keep the speaker and his attitude clear.

Bells for John Whiteside's Daughter
JOHN CROWE RANSOM

There was such speed in her little body,
And such lightness in her footfall,
It is no wonder her brown study
Astonishes us all.

Her wars were bruited in our high window.
We looked among orchard trees and beyond,
Where she took arms against her shadow,
Or harried unto the pond

The lazy geese, like a snow cloud
Dripping their snow on the green grass,
Tricking and stopping, sleepy and proud,
Who cried in goose, Alas,

For the tireless heart within the little
Lady with rod that made them rise
From their noon apple-dreams, and scuttle
Goose-fashion under the skies!

But now go the bells, and we are ready;
In one house we are sternly stopped
To say we are vexed at her brown study,
Lying so primly propped.

■ Do the memories dispel the gloom of the setting? Why? Where did you leave your audience?

This poem presents a character study not only of the monk who is speaking, but of Brother Lawrence as well. Remember that the poem is a soliloquy, which indicates that the speaker is alone. Evidently, however, Brother Lawrence is moving within sight of the speaker, and his actions provide the motivations for the swift changes of thought. Notice how spiteful the monk who follows the letter of the law feels toward the man who lives by the spirit. The structure of the poem helps to underscore this feeling.

Soliloquy of the Spanish Cloister
ROBERT BROWNING

Gr-r-r — there go, my heart's abhorrence!
    Water your damned flower-pots, do!
If hate killed men, Brother Lawrence,
    God's blood, would not mine kill you!
What? Your myrtle-bush wants trimming?
    Oh, that rose has prior claims —
Needs its leaden vase filled brimming?
    Hell dry you up with its flames!

At the meal we sit together:
10   *Salve tibi.* I must hear
Wise talk of the kind of weather,
    Sort of season, time of year:
Not a plenteous cork-crop: scarcely
    Dare we hope oak-galls, I doubt:
What's the Latin name for "parsley"?
    What's the Greek name for Swine's Snout?

Whew! We'll have our platter burnished,
    Laid with care on our own shelf!
With a fire-new spoon we're furnished,
20   And a goblet for ourself,
Rinsed like something sacrificial
    Ere 'tis fit to touch our chaps —
Marked with L for our initial
    (He-he! There his lily snaps!)

10 *Salve tibi:* Hail.

Saint, forsooth! while brown Dolores
　　Squats outside the Convent bank
With Sanchicha, telling stories,
　　Steeping tresses in the tank,
Blue-black, lustrous, thick like horse-hairs,
30　　— Can't I see his dead eye glow,
Bright as 'twere a Barbary corsair's?
　　(That is, if he'd let it show!)

When he finishes refection,
　　Knife and fork he never lays
Cross-wise, to my recollection,
　　As do I, in Jesu's praise.
I the Trinity illustrate,
　　Drinking watered orange-pulp
In three sips the Arian frustrate;
40　　While he drains his at one gulp.

Oh, those melons! If he's able
　　We're to have a feast! so nice!
One goes to the Abbot's table,
　　All of us get each a slice.
How go on your flowers? None double?
　　Not one fruit-sort can you spy?
Strange! — And I, too, at such trouble
　　Keep them close-nipped on the sly!

There's a great text in Galatians,
50　　Once you trip on it, entails
Twenty-nine distinct damnations,
　　One sure, if another fails:
If I trip him just a-dying,
　　Sure of heaven as sure can be,
Spin him round and send him flying
　　Off to hell, a Manichee!

Or, my scrofulous French novel
　　On gray paper with blunt type!
Simply glance at it, you grovel
60　　Hand and foot in Belial's gripe:

39 *Arian:* The Arian heresy held that Christ was created by God, and was inferior to Him in nature
and dignity.
56 *Manichee:* A sect that combined Persian and Christian beliefs.

If I double down its pages
   At the woeful sixteenth print,
When he waters his greengages,
   Ope a sieve and slip it in't?

Or there's Satan! One might venture
   Pledge one's soul to him, yet leave
Such a flaw in the indenture
   As he'd miss till, past retrieve,
Blasted lay that rose-acacia
70   We're so proud of! *Hy, Zy, Hine* . . .
'St, there's Vespers! *Plena gratia,*
   Ave, Virgo! G-r-r-r — you swine!

  ▌ How did locus and reflexive physical activity operate in your
    performance?

70 *Hy, Zy, Hine:* This series of sounds has caused considerable dissension among critics. It may
be the beginning of a curse on Brother Lawrence.
71–72 *Plena gratia, Ave, Virgo!:* Full of grace, Hail, Virgin!

James Dickey captures the sterility and chill of the hospital remarkably well
as he underscores the isolation that it imposes on those who leave a loved
one there and return to the outdoor world. (You might want to compare this
poem with Sharon Olds's "The Race" in Chapter 4.) The word choice is
excellent, even when it seems, deliberately, not poetic. Don't neglect the
subtle tone color. The kinetic, kinesthetic, and auditory imagery make an
excellent contrast to the hospital room. Watch the stanza divisions.

The Hospital Window

JAMES DICKEY

I have just come down from my father.
Higher and higher he lies
Above me in a blue light
Shed by a tinted window.
I drop through six white floors
And then step out onto pavement.

Still feeling my father ascend,
I start to cross the firm street,
My shoulder blades shining with all
The glass the huge building can raise.
Now I must turn round and face it,
And know his one pane from the others.

Each window possesses the sun
As though it burned there on a wick.
I wave, like a man catching fire.
All the deep-dyed windowpanes flash,
And, behind them, all the white rooms
They turn to the color of Heaven.

Ceremoniously, gravely, and weakly,
Dozens of pale hands are waving
Back, from inside their flames.
Yet one pure pane among these
Is the bright, erased blankness of nothing.
I know that my father is there,

In the shape of his death still living.
The traffic increases around me
Like a madness called down on my head.
The horns blast at me like shotguns,
And drivers lean out, driven crazy —
But now my propped-up father

Lifts his arm out of stillness at last.
The light from the window strikes me
And I turn as blue as a soul,
As the moment when I was born.
I am not afraid for my father —
Look! He is grinning; he is not

Afraid for my life, either,
As the wild engines stand at my knees
Shredding their gears and roaring,
And I hold each car in its place
For miles, inciting its horn
To blow down the walls of the world

That the dying may float without fear
In the bold blue gaze of my father.
Slowly I move to the sidewalk
With my pin-tingling hand half-dead
At the end of my bloodless arm.
I carry it off in amazement,

High, still higher, still waving,
My recognized face fully mortal,
Yet not; not at all, in the pale,

Drained, otherworldly, stricken,
Created hue of stained glass.
I have just come down from my father.

   ❚ How did you make your audience see and hear what caused
     your persona to stop the traffic?

This soft-spoken poem is completely devoid of sentimentality. The negation
is underscored by the simple word choice and by the conversational relationship of thought units and line lengths in the first four stanzas. Pay particular
attention to the single-line stanzas.

Preface to a Twenty Volume Suicide Note
IMAMU AMIRI BARAKA

Lately, I've become accustomed to the way
The ground opens up and envelops me
Each time I go out to walk the dog.
Or the broad edged silly music the wind
Makes when I run for a bus —

Things have come to that.

And now, each night I count the stars,
And each night I get the same number.
And when they will not come to be counted
I count the holes they leave.

Nobody sings anymore.

And then last night, I tiptoed up
To my daughter's room and heard her
Talking to someone, and when I opened
The door, there was no one there . . .
Only she on her knees,
Peeking into her own cupped hands.

   ❚ How did your persona feel when he glimpsed his daughter?
     How did you demonstrate this attitude to your audience?

Bibliography

Consult the bibliography at the end of Chapter 10 for several sources
on the structure and other technical aspects of poetry.

10 The Structure of Poetry

What I like to do is to treat words as a craftsman
does his wood or stone or what-have-you, to hew,
carve, mould, coil, polish and plane them into
patterns, sequences, sculptures, fugues of sound . . .

Dylan Thomas

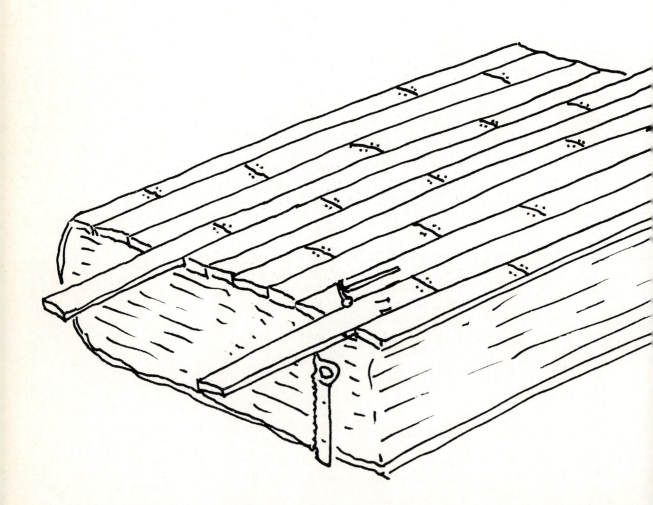

Language in poetry is carried to the highest degree of order. This order is apparent in the condensation and organization of the content and in the close interaction of content and form. It is even more apparent in the discipline that poetic structure places on the writer and, consequently, on the interpreter. In successful poetry, structure and content are in perfect harmony, and in an evaluation of the whole, neither may be considered without the other. Poetry depends for its full meaning on the perfect blend of sound and sense.

The study of the structure of poetry is called *prosody*. The term *structure* is used in different ways by different critics, but it is generally taken to mean the way the component parts of a piece of literature are formed into a whole. Structure includes all of the elements of the language of poetry that we have been discussing: sense imagery, paradoxes, allusions, and other literary imagery. In this chapter, however, we shall use the term to apply specifically to devices that produce the sound pattern in a poem. Obviously, this includes a careful consideration of tone color, which was discussed in Chapter 9, because this element is part style, or language, and part sound patterning.

In this discussion we shall focus on stanzaic form — composition and length of lines; rhythm as established by both stress and flow of sound; and rhyme. These are the bases of the sound pattern on which much of a poem's effectiveness depends. These component parts of the sound pattern depend in a very special way on the skill of the interpreter, because they can be thoroughly appreciated and allowed to fulfill their function only when the poem is read aloud.

Since the late nineteenth century, critics have found it convenient to make a distinction between conventional or traditional types of poetry, such as the sonnet, and free verse. The structure of *conventional poetry* is based on a clearly discernible pattern of light and heavier stresses, grouped into a traditional system of metrical feet, and on a fixed pattern of stanza and line length. The same pattern, with only slight variation, usually recurs from stanza to stanza, in both length of lines and arrangement of stresses within those lines. Moreover, the number of lines per stanza is usually consistent. Within this fixed structural framework, however, there may be numerous variations both in stress pattern and in the location of pauses in a line to keep the fall of the words from becoming monotonous. Finally, conventional poetry — with the notable exception of blank verse — has the added element of rhyme, with the corresponding sounds in the line-end positions arranged in an easily perceived pattern called the *rhyme scheme*.

Blank verse is a special type of conventional poetry. It is unrhymed and has no recurring stanza pattern because the stanzas are divided according to the development of the thought and are irregular in length. Blank verse does have a definitely prescribed line length of five metrical feet, and a prescribed prevailing foot — the *iamb*. Blank verse is of particular interest to interpreters because it is so often used in material that is inherently attractive to an audience. Because of the absence of rhyme and the lack of restriction on stanzaic structure in blank verse, skillful poets use this form effectively with narrative and dramatic materials. Shakespeare, an acknowledged master of blank verse in poetic drama, used it to wed nobility of utterance to acceptable rhythms of speech. Poets as diverse as Robert Browning and Robert Frost have used it to sustain the dramatic quality of long poems and to achieve the difficult feats of making poetry sound like conversation and conversation like poetry.

Free verse is often considered to be a recent addition to the realm of poetry. The term is modern, and the genre has developed during the last hundred years or so, though it is possible to find earlier examples of free verse. Free verse is a term adopted from the French *vers libre*. *Vers* in French refers to a "line" of poetry; hence, *vers libre* actually means a "free line." It is the varying lengths of the lines and the arrangement of stresses within them that gives the surest indication that a poem is in free verse.

Free verse differs in many ways from traditional poetry. If a free-verse poem is divided into stanza units at all, they are often irregular in length, although a free-verse poem *may* have quite regular stanzaic division. The free-verse line may vary in length from a single syllable to fifty or more — if the poet needs to use such a long line and can bring it off successfully. Free verse often is not rhymed, though the poet may choose to introduce rhyme in order to achieve some special effect, as T. S. Eliot frequently does. Free verse exhibits no significant pattern of metrical feet, and its rhythm is based on cadence rather than meter.

Successful free verse is not, as the term might suggest, completely lacking in form and discipline. There must be a discoverable rhythmic basis. Sometimes it can be found in the number of syllables in the speech phrases within the lines, or in the number of heavier stresses within those speech phrases. Sometimes it can be discovered by analyzing the number of heavier stresses per line regardless of their relative positioning with lighter stresses. The important point is to find out what the poet has done and then see how it works with the content to produce a successful whole.

The strict dichotomy between conventional verse and free verse is becoming much less important in contemporary poetry. Most poets today work *from* rather than *within* strict metrical patterns, so that we often find an interesting combination of the two modes within a single poem. The traditional lines establish a certain expectation for us; when, a few lines later, we find the insertion of free verse, and that expectation is denied, variety and contrast are underscored. Or, on the other hand, a strictly regular line may surprise us with its steady beat and help point up a climax. Stanley Kunitz's poem "Open the Gates" (Chapter 9) contains an interesting example of this effect. William Van O'Connor, speaking of T. S. Eliot's prosody, quotes the poet when he says, "Even in the 'freest' of free verse there should lurk the ghost of some simple meter 'which should advance menacingly as we doze, and withdraw as we arouse.'"[1] And Robert Frost once remarked that writing what some people called free verse was like playing tennis with the net down. Thus contemporary free verse could more accurately be labeled "freed verse." You should make a careful study to find out how freed it is from traditional patterns and how this freedom is coordinated with the content to produce the total effect of the poem.

The Stanza

As we saw in Chapter 9, a stanza of poetry is roughly comparable to a paragraph in prose, in that it is often a major unit of thought. As such, it is an important factor in the organization. But a stanza also may be a unit of sound, just as a line of poetry is not only a line of print but also a unit of sound, and a word is not only a symbol for meaning but a sound or combination of sounds as well. The stanzaic structure may contribute significantly to the poem's pattern of sound. The recurrence of the same stanza pattern throughout, together with the poet's skill in making thought units coincide with the stanzas, may divide the poem into nearly identical units of sound when the poem is read aloud. We tend to separate major divisions in thought by appropriate use of pause and to establish terminations by both pause and vocal inflection.

How stanzaic length contributes to the sound pattern of a poem varies considerably in importance from one selection to another. In general, shorter stanzas and a tighter rhyme scheme produce a more apparent sound effect. For example, a poem written entirely in two-line stanzas sets up a very close pattern of sounds and silences, especially if each pair of lines completes a thought division. This is an important aspect of structural unity but might seriously threaten the variety unless the poet has been very skillful. In blank verse, on the

---

1. William Van O'Connor, *Sense and Sensibility in Modern Poetry* (Chicago: University of Chicago Press, 1948), p. 58.

other hand, the contribution of stanzaic structure to sound pattern is almost negligible, partly because of the absence of rhyme, but primarily because the stanzas are of unequal length and may run to a hundred lines or more.

In contemporary poetry of regular stanza pattern, the thought units are frequently not identical with the stanzas but run on from one to another. There may be a comma or another punctuation mark that does not indicate a full stop — or, indeed, there may be no punctuation at all — at the end of the last line of a stanza. This pattern appears throughout Cruz's poem "Today Is a Day of Great Joy" at the end of this chapter. This type of punctuation serves as a warning that the thought is unfinished and that the break imposed by the stanza pattern is a suspended break. The poet has chosen the stanzaic pattern as a discipline but has reserved the right to take liberties within it whenever it seems justified by the overall purpose.

Stanza length and composition can be strong factors in the unity, harmony, and rhythm of both content and structure. Variety and contrast are also served by this aspect of structure. A change in stanzaic pattern is sometimes used to emphasize the fulcrum or the climax, as it does in Ciardi's "As I Would Wish You Birds" and in Alice Walker's untitled poem at the end of this chapter.

You should be aware of whatever contribution the stanza length makes to the sound pattern adopted by the poet. In evaluating the importance of stanza length, you must take your cue from the poet. When the poet has made a point of adhering to brief, regular stanzas, or has emphasized stanza divisions by repetition, you should assume that this strict discipline serves a definite purpose. On the other hand, when the stanzas are long or irregular in length, you may assume that the stanzas function primarily as a means of organizing the logical or emotional content.

The Line

The three main types of prosody, which all are based on the composition of the individual lines within stanzas, are usually designated as *metrical* or *foot prosody, stress prosody,* and *syllabic prosody.* We shall discuss metrical or foot prosody first, since it is the most familiar and, at least until the last few decades, has been the most commonly used in poetry written in English.

Foot Prosody

Poetry is generally characterized in part by a high degree of regularity in the pattern of structural rhythm. The structural rhythm of conventional poetry is based on meter. *Meter* is the pattern set up by a reasonably regular recurrence of an identifiable combination of light and heavier stresses within a line. This pattern is discovered through *scansion*, the division of the poetic line into metrical feet. A *metrical foot* is a grouping of light and heavier stresses into a unit. The groupings, which were named centuries ago, are useful primarily for making the metrical pattern graphic, as the stresses are marked and grouped within the poetic lines. The most common feet in English poetry are these:

1. the *iamb* — an unstressed syllable followed by a stressed syllable (˘ ′)[2]:

$$\breve{}\quad ′\qquad \breve{}\quad ′\qquad \breve{}\quad ′\qquad \breve{}\quad ′\qquad \breve{}\quad ′$$
When I/ have fears/ that I/ may cease/ to be

2. the *anapest* — two unstressed syllables followed by a stressed syllable (˘ ˘ ′):

$$\breve{}\ \breve{}\ ′\quad \breve{}\quad \breve{}\ \breve{}\ ′\quad \breve{}\quad \breve{}\ \breve{}\ ′\quad \breve{}\ \breve{}\ ′$$
Of my dar/ ling — my dar/ ling — my life/ and my bride

3. the *trochee* — a stressed syllable followed by an unstressed syllable (′ ˘):

$$′\ \breve{}\qquad ′\ \breve{}\qquad ′\quad \breve{}\qquad ′\quad \breve{}$$
Tell me/ not in/ mournful/ numbers

4. the *dactyl* — a stressed syllable followed by two unstressed syllables (′ ˘ ˘):

$$′\quad \breve{}\quad \breve{}\qquad ′\quad \breve{}\quad \breve{}$$
Cannon to/ right of them

5. the *spondee* — two heavy stresses (′ ′), usually used in combination with other types of feet:

$$′\quad ′\qquad \breve{}\quad ′\qquad \breve{}\quad ′\qquad \breve{}\quad ′$$
Beat once/ therewith/ and beat/ no more.

6. the *pyrrhic* — two light stresses (˘ ˘), also usually found within another basic pattern:

$$\breve{}\quad ′\quad \breve{}\ \breve{}\quad \breve{}\ ′\quad \breve{}\ \breve{}\quad \breve{}\ ′\quad \breve{}\ ′$$
The end/ and the/ begin/ ning in/ each oth/ er's arms.

There are some other combinations, such as the *amphibrach* (˘ ′ ˘) and the *amphimacer* (′ ˘ ′), but the six types above are the most common.

---

2. (′) indicates a stressed syllable; (˘) is an unstressed syllable. A line (/) is used here to mark off the feet.

A line is classified according to its prevalent foot as *iambic, anapestic, trochaic,* or *dactylic;* and according to the number of feet it contains as a *monometer* (one foot), *dimeter* (two), *trimeter* (three), *tetrameter* (four), *pentameter* (five), *hexameter* (six), and so on. Thus, a line of five iambic feet is spoken of as an *iambic pentameter*.

In almost all conventional poetry, one type of metrical foot prevails. In English poetry, the iamb (˘′) is the most common foot, due in part to our pronunciation. It is often varied by the trochee (′˘), its reversed counterpart. The next most common is probably the anapest (˘˘′), and then the dactyl (′˘˘). The spondee (′′) and pyrrhic (˘˘) are used primarily for variation within a framework of the other more common patterns. Certain harmonies are sometimes achieved most successfully by strict consistency in meter, or by approximate consistency (as in the combination of iamb and anapest), but most poets make effective use of variations in the prevalent measure, since variety in unity is the keystone of all art.

A detail that may clarify the process of scanning a conventional poem is relative stress. Not all stressed syllables receive the same degree or value of stress when the poem is read aloud. The following line might be scanned as a regular iambic pentameter:

$$\breve{}\;\;\prime\quad\breve{}\;\;\prime\quad\breve{}\;\;\prime\quad\breve{}\;\;\prime\quad\breve{}\;\;\prime$$
Not mar / ble, nor / the gild / ed mon / uments

However, in an oral reading, the relative values of the stresses would be something like this, where (′) indicates a heavy stress, (ˋ) a lighter one, and (˘) no discernible stress:

$$\grave{}\;\;\prime\quad\breve{}\;\;\grave{}\quad\breve{}\;\;\prime\quad\breve{}\;\;\prime\quad\breve{}\;\;\grave{}$$
Not mar / ble, nor / the gild / ed mon / uments

A most interesting study can be made of the relative values of stresses, but for our purposes we shall use only two degrees, lighter and heavier; that is, a syllable receives a lighter or heavier stress than the syllables on either side of it.

How do you begin to scan a poem? Stress in poetry, as in prose, results from the demands of proper pronunciation and of the total meaning, mood, and purpose of the literature. It is simplest to start with the words of more than one syllable, putting the stress where it must fall for pronunciation. *Marble* is of course pronounced *márble*, not *marblé*. If unsure of syllabication, the interpreter should check a dictionary. It is imperative that every syllable is accounted for.

The next step cannot be undertaken until the poem has been at least partially analyzed and you are familiar not only with what it says but how it means what it says. You should note key words that must be emphasized for clarity and general comprehension. The attitude of the speaker is an important consideration here. This step is followed by a careful look at words that create mood or contribute sharply to needed variety and contrast. For instance, when a new type of sense imagery is introduced, it may need to be emphasized slightly so it will serve its purpose for later lines. You scan a poem the way it must be read to achieve its total effect. The purpose for scanning is to find what the poet has actually done, not to make the lines fit a preconceived pattern.

After these first two steps, you may discover that a *fairly* regular pattern of light and heavier stresses in traditional feet is beginning to emerge. Complete the pattern by filling in whatever syllables have not yet been assigned a degree of stress to conform as nearly as is practical to the predominant type of foot. If no such pattern emerges, examine the poem further to determine whether or not you are dealing with stress prosody. Perhaps the poet has used syllabic prosody. This will be easy to determine, since you have already marked the stresses. You should look to line lengths, speech phrases, and the number of stresses within them for structural unity.

The relative degree of stress is a matter you must work out for yourself from an understanding of the poem, for there is no one "right" way of reading a poem that can be imposed. Not to submerge meaning in meter, not to lose sight of pattern in an attempt to communicate expressively: these are the twin channel markers you should watch in steering your course. The poet always leads the way. Find out what the poet has done with meter, if that is the basis of rhythm in the poem, but be sure to allow the necessary variations. If poets can best achieve the rhythmic effects they want by following a regular meter very closely, they will keep to that meter; if they can achieve them by departing from a regular meter, they will do that.

Stress Prosody

Stress prosody finds its rhythmic base in the number of stresses *per line*, regardless of their position in relation to each other. Thus it is often impossible, or at least impractical, to try to group the lighter and heavier stresses into traditional metrical feet. The number of syllables in a line may vary widely, but the number of stresses per line remains consistent or varies only occasionally for a specific effect. This concept of rhythm is important in understanding cadences of poetry and in determining the effectiveness of stresses within flows of sound. Dylan Thomas makes excellent use of a nearly consistent number of stresses per line in "In My Craft or Sullen Art" (Chapter 9).

Syllabic Prosody

Syllabic prosody is somewhat less common in English, although it is the basis of French prosody. Since the turn of this century, many poets have used syllabic prosody most effectively in combination with foot or stress prosody. Syllabic prosody measures flow of sound rather than stresses and depends quite simply on the number of syllables per line. Thomas combines this technique with a consistency of stresses in "In My Craft or Sullen Art," and all but three lines contain seven syllables. Incidentally, two of those three lines are used to terminate stanzas.

Stanley Kunitz's lyric "Open the Gates" is an excellent example of how at least two of the three systems work within a single contemporary poem.

Open the Gates

STANLEY KUNITZ

1 Within/ the ci/ ty of/ the burn/ ing cloud,

2 Dragging/ my life/ behind/ me in/ a sack,

3 Naked/ I prowl,/ scourged by/ the black

4 Tempta/ tion of/ the blood/ grown proud.

5 Here at/ the mon/ ument/ al door,

6 Carved with the/ curious/ legend of/ my youth,

7 I brand/ ish the great/ bone of/ my death,

8 Beat once/ therewith/ and beat/ no more.

9 The hing/ es groan:/ a rush/ of forms

10 Shivers/ my name,/ wrenched out/ of me.

11 I stand/ on the ter/ rible thresh/ old, and/ I see

12 The end/ and the/ beginning/ in each oth/ er's arms.

Admittedly, there is more than one way to group the light and heavy stresses into traditional feet, particularly in lines 6, 11, and 12. This is a problem that may plague a prosodist, but our concern is basically with the relative positioning of the stresses within the line.

For us, the grouping of stresses into traditional feet is largely a convenient way of clarifying the pattern. The scansion reveals that the meter is *basically* iambic with a great many variations. As a matter

of fact, Kunitz uses each of the other five common types of feet at
least twice. The only purely iambic line is line 9, which immediately
follows the fulcrum.

From our preliminary marking, then, we discover that the first
two lines and the last two lines of "Open the Gates" have five feet;
the others have four feet. The four pentameter lines all have a pyrrhic
foot, however, so that the stresses per line are consistently four,
except for line 8, which is the fulcrum, and line 10, which contains
the emotional climax; in these lines, spondees add a fifth stress. Thus,
despite the greater length of the opening and closing lines, unity of
stress is carefully preserved.

Some interesting details immediately become apparent. For instance, line 6 contains eleven syllables and yet contains only four
heavier stresses, as does the nine-syllable line that follows it. These
two lines immediately preceding the fulcrum are the only ones with
an uneven number of syllables.

An examination of the scansion of this brief poem assures us that
there is more to poetic rhythm than a "da-dá da-dá" alternation of light
and heavy stresses. Stanley Kunitz has achieved remarkable variety
within unity. See also the chart of this poem later in this chapter.

The Interpreter's Use of Line Lengths

Early in our discussion of the three types of prosody, we mentioned
the importance of the line as a structural unit. A line of poetry, it
should be remembered, is not just a line of print. It is a unit of sound
as well as a minor unit of thought. Because it functions as both sound
and sense, it is important to consider in some detail the twofold
discipline that poets have imposed on themselves — and consequently on their interpreters — with specific line lengths.

Poets who write conventional poetry consistently divide the stanzas into lines whose length is prescribed by or appropriate to the
form of stanza they are using. They combine this measure with a
more or less regular arrangement of stresses, and perhaps with
rhyme at the line ends, to achieve the pattern of sound. Obviously,
then, the line units should not be ignored. After all, poets have put
the content into units of a specific length. You may assume that they
had some reason for selecting this particular line length, or at least
that, having selected it, they made some effort to fit their thought
units — which also become sound units when the poem is read aloud
— into that pattern.

Blank verse presents us with the greatest temptation to ignore
line length, partly because the line ends do not have the added rein-
forcement of rhyme. Yet one of the accepted requisites of the best
blank verse is that there must be an opportunity to establish the line

length when the poem is read aloud. The degree or value of the pause will vary, but the line length should be given special consideration, since it is one of the components of the rhythmic pattern. The extent to which the poet is able to conform to this discipline, while achieving variety within it, is one standard for measuring excellence of achievement. On the other hand, you should remember that verse is written in sentences as well as in lines, and that the line should not be emphasized at the expense of sentences and overall sense. Not only would a drop of the voice or a distinct pause at the end of every line produce monotony; it also would distort the sense (since we are accustomed to consider a marked pause as signifying the completion of a thought) and would cancel out one of the chief advantages of the blank verse line — its approximation of the rhythms of conversational speech.

A writer of free verse often uses long sentences, so that the flow of sense may be technically uninterrupted for an entire unit (T. S. Eliot does this in most of his poems). One may certainly assume, then, that since the poet may arrange these sentences in lines as long or as short as desired, there is a reason for the line division used. Some critics contend that a line of free verse ends where it is convenient to take a breath — that it is written with the scope of a breath in mind. We may invert this statement and say that for the interpreter's practical purposes, it is convenient to take a breath where the free verse line ends. It is logical, too, because the breath comes at a division of the thought, or at a point where the poet wishes to reinforce feeling or establish a relationship or progression. There is an excellent example of such subtle progression in Eliot's "Journey of the Magi" (at the end of this chapter). In the last stanza we find these lines:

All this was a long time ago, I remember,
And I would do it again, but set down
This set down
This: . . .

When the lines are read aloud, their arrangement gives a far different effect from what it would be if the words were arranged as follows:

All this was a long time ago,
I remember, and I would do it again,
But set down this, set down this:

To realize the full contribution of line length to rhythm and to content, then, you must make a pause *of some kind* at the end of each line of poetry.

It should be remembered that pauses vary greatly in duration. The line end as a line end (that is, apart from punctuation, sentence construction, and overall meaning) does not require a terminal pause of the kind used to end a sentence. Indeed, if the sentence or speech phrase runs over into the next line — a device technically known as *enjambment*[3] — there is no *obvious* hesitation. Nevertheless, the line length imposes a sense of the boundaries or "shape" of the poem; this shape is marked by the eye in silent reading and is carried over into the voice in oral interpretation, though not to the point where the physical pattern of the poem obtrudes into the listener's consciousness at the expense of meaning, sound, and feeling.

Thus the length, force, and terminal effect of the line-end pauses vary — from a barely perceptible pause, or a slight drawing out or suspension of the terminal vowel sound, to a semistop or "breath pause," to a full pause at the end of the sentence or thought unit. Accordingly, you should be alert to make the most of these opportunities for variety in treating line lengths by the use of pauses and voice inflections at the line ends. In a caution to poets, Ezra Pound once wrote: "Don't make each line stop dead at the end, and then begin every next line with a heave. Let the beginning of the next line catch the rise of the rhythm wave, unless you want a definite longish pause." Interpreters, too, can apply this advice to their own art.

Line length, especially in free verse, will be considered further in the following discussion of cadence. For the moment, however, we shall merely acknowledge the importance of line length and give poets credit for being able to fit their thoughts into whatever restrictions of structure they have set for themselves. Obviously, the audience should not be made aware of the length of each line, any more than of any other single aspect of the material. Each element makes its contribution to the whole and should be blended with and properly related to all of the other elements.

Cadences

Analyzing cadences is a way of making graphic the length and stress composition of the separate flows of sound within a poem. This process brings together considerations of syllabic prosody (the number of syllables in each line) and stress prosody (the number rather than location of stresses in each line).

A *cadence*, as the term is used here, is simply an uninterrupted flow of sound. Pauses of varying duration and prominence break the

3. From the French *enjambment*, meaning "straddling": that is to say, one leg of the thought on either side of the line end.

flow and thus establish new cadences. Since the syllable is the smallest functional unit of sound, cadences are measured by the number of syllables they contain.

When we mentioned syllabic and stress prosody earlier, we were concerned only with the line as a unit of measure. In analyzing cadences, we are concerned again with the line, but we shall also give attention to the way the individual lines may be divided into speech phrases when the poem is read aloud and to the length of entire sentences, whether or not they continue past the line end.

We touched on these matters of sentence length and speech phrases within sentences when we examined prose style. Here we shall apply the same approach to poetic style. Analyzing the length and composition of speech phrases and sentences is important in studying prose rhythm, and it is absolutely essential in examining poetic rhythm. This is partly because of the importance of line lengths in poetic structure. It is also because cadences are part of the essential sound pattern on which all poetry depends and because they should be coordinated with all the other sound factors.

A *primary cadence* is the number of syllables in an entire sentence. *Secondary cadences* refer both to line lengths and to the speech phrases within the lines. It is, of course, immediately obvious that merely counting syllables does not give us the total picture. This is simply a way of getting at one of the basic elements of poetic rhythm, especially in contemporary poetry. Cadences should always be considered in relation to two other elements that exist within them. The first of these is the number and arrangement of stresses, especially within lines. This consideration, of course, overlaps scansion in conventional poetry, and it is considerably important in free verse even when a clear, consistent metrical pattern cannot be established. The second element is partly a matter of tone color and has to do with the length or duration of the sounds within syllables. Thus, a duration pattern as well as a stress pattern is at work within the syllables in secondary cadence. We shall not go into detail here on the aspect of duration, because you are already familiar with tone color and its effect on tempo and quality.

There can be no question about the length of the primary cadences in a given poem. A primary cadence is the number of syllables in the sentence, from its beginning to its end as marked by terminal punctuation. The number of syllables in each line is also immediately evident. The lengths of the speech phrases, however, are somewhat more subjectively determined, since not all interpreters would pause at precisely the same places. Sometimes there can be no doubt about the need for a pause, and hence for establishing a cadence — for example, when the poet has inserted appropriate punctuation. Beyond these restrictions, however, you may make your own decisions about pauses, as you are guided by the requirements of content (both logical and emotive), by the relationship of phrases and clauses to the terms they modify and to the complete sentence, and by opportunities for conveying variety and contrast within unity and for communicating imagery and tone color. These pauses, however slight, will break the line into speech phrases.

Meter is, of course, the basis of the rhythmic structure in foot prosody, but a consideration of the cadences as well may open up unsuspected possibilities for variety and harmony. Frequently, poets achieve a large part of their rhythm by manipulating the cadences within a strict pattern of scansion. This is one of the important attributes of successful blank verse. Tennyson uses cadences most effectively, for instance, in "Ulysses" (Chapter 4), in which many of the lines are broken near the middle either by terminal punctuation or by a colon or semicolon. This provides variety, of course, without breaking the unity of the iambic pentameter line. Such a significant pause within a line is called a *caesura*. In numerous other lines, a balanced syntax or the need to point a comparative phrase may cause the interpreter to insert a somewhat less distinct pause, which nevertheless interrupts the flow of sound within the line as a unit.

Primary cadences — that is, complete sentences — usually tell us more by their relation to each other than by their specific lengths. In Eliot's "Journey of the Magi," where most of the primary cadences are long and cover several lines, the final sentence forms an interesting contrast and brings the poem to a firm close. Edna St. Vincent Millay's "Sonnet XXX," at the end of this chapter, is another good example.

The line-length cadences are probably the most fundamental in poetry, since all types of prosody take the line as a basic measure. Keeping this in mind, we can look at speech phrases *within* the separate lines, knowing that even an enjambment line has some kind of pause, however unobtrusive, at its end. In extremely long lines (as in Walt Whitman's poems), these speech phrases often provide the surest basis for the rhythm.

Since analyzing cadences brings together syllabic prosody and stress prosody, you also should be aware of any consistency in the number of stresses per secondary cadence. The number of stresses in the primary cadences is not likely to help much if the sentences are long and overflow the line.

In Kunitz's "Open the Gates," which is an interesting example of carefully controlled variation from traditional metrics, the cadences contribute to unity and harmony as well as to variety and contrast. Counting the syllables and major stresses within lines and speech phrases and noting the sentence lengths, we discover the following pattern:

	Secondary Cadences				Syllables per Primary Cadence
Line No.	Syllables per Line	Stresses per Line	Syllables per Speech Phrase	Stresses per Speech Phrase	
1	10	4	10	4	36
2	10	4	7-3	3-1	
3	8	4	4-1-3	2-1-1	
4	8	4	3-3-2	1-1-2	
5	8	4	1-7	1-3	36
6	11	4	1-7-3	1-2-1	
7	9	4	9	4	
8	8	5	4-4	3-2	FULCRUM
9	8	4	4-4	2-2	16
10	8	5	4-4	2-3	CLIMAX
11	12	4	9-3	3-1	24
12	12	4	2-5-5	1-1-2	

As usual, the primary cadences tell us less by their specific length than they do by their relation to each other. Although they are of minor significance in this poem, the primary cadences are obviously a unifying factor in the first two stanzas. Furthermore, the change from the established thirty-six syllables to sixteen syllables helps set off the climax.

Looking at the secondary cadences, we notice that lines of identical length are used in pairs or in threes, except for the two center lines. These two are neatly bracketed by eight-syllable lines and serve as a steadying force in the middle of the poem. The stresses per line are a strong unifying force, with the added stress in lines 8 and 10 providing contrast to reinforce the fulcrum.

The speech phrases provide needed variety within this unity. They too, however, tend to cluster; three predominate near the opening, varied by units of seven, four, one, and two. The one-and-seven combination is apparent in line 5, and one and seven and three in line 6. The even four-and-four division in lines 8, 9, and 10, mentioned in relation to scansion, helps reinforce the emotional weight of the content.

Further analysis reveals even more subtle effects in this remarkable poem. Perhaps we have proved well enough that the line-length and speech-phrase cadences and their stresses are important in the pattern of a successful poem — and that such analysis is basic in discovering the rhythmic elements of free verse.

Why have we bothered to make a chart of it? Because this is the simplest way to clarify what you have to work with. A careful analysis of the cadences and stresses in a poem will convince you that conventional poetry does not need to be read like a nursery rhyme, and that the discipline inherent in free verse is a safeguard against the danger of reading this type of poetry as if it were prose. Free verse, properly written, is probably the most demanding type of poetry to read aloud, and interpreters who choose it should be prepared to analyze its structure painstakingly. Such analysis will greatly increase your own artistic ability as well as your appreciation of the poet's artistic achievement.

Clearly, no audience could be expected to appreciate the subtlety of this rhythmic pattern for itself when the poem is read aloud. Indeed, it would be most unfortunate if you called attention to the pattern. Nevertheless, you should understand what the poet has done in order to communicate the total effect.

Rhyme

Rhyme is closely allied with line length, since it most commonly occurs at the line ends. The lines may contain internal rhymes as well. Rhyme, unlike rhythm and cadence, is not an essential element of poetry. But when it is used, it is important because it reinforces rhythm, cadence, pattern, and tone color.

Although corresponding sounds strike the mind's ear in a silent reading, they emerge for complete appreciation only when a poem is read aloud. Like a chime of music, rhyme is satisfying and pleasing to hear; it gives intellectual pleasure through the delights of repetition and anticipation. But the purpose of rhyme is not to decorate a poem but rather to bind it more closely together. For one thing, it unifies the pattern of sound. It reinforces the stanza pattern by establishing a recurring rhyme scheme. It emphasizes the line lengths by creating an expectation of repeated sounds at regular intervals. On the other hand, experienced poets and interpreters know that rhyme, if used unwisely, can shatter rather than intensify the unity of a poem. Therefore, when they use rhyme, they exhibit great care and variety in handling it. An interpreter who bears down hard on every rhyme makes the physical shape of the poem block out all of its other qualities. If a poem is read in this way, the audience will have the sensation of being taken for a ride on a rocking horse, instead of on a winged Pegasus.

Rhyme is the exact correspondence of both final vowel and consonant sounds (*love – dove*); *assonance* is the correspondence of vowel sounds only, regardless of the final consonant sounds (*place – brave*). There are many kinds of rhyme. In *half rhymes* (*pavement – gravely, river – weather*) only half of a two-syllable word rhymes with another. In *double rhymes*, the two final syllables correspond (*crying – flying, arrayed – afraid*). There are even *triple rhymes* (*din – afore – pinafore*), though these are usually too jingling and ingenious for anything but humorous verse. And there is *approximate rhyme* or *rhyme by consonance:* most commonly, the final consonant sounds are identical, but the vowel sounds are not (*rock – luck*). If used carefully, rhyme can be a strong way to reinforce tone color.

A rhyme scheme is indicated in prosodic analysis by letters that stand for the terminal rhyme sounds; *a* represents the sound of the first line and of every line corresponding to it; *b* stands for the next terminal sound and its corresponding lines; and so on. The rhyme scheme in this stanza from Percy Bysshe Shelley's "Adonais" would be marked as follows:

Most musical of mourners, weep anew!	*a*
Not all to that bright station dared to climb;	*b*
And happier they their happiness who knew,	*a*
Whose tapers yet burn through that night of time	*b*
In which suns perished; others more sublime,	*b*
Struck by the envious wrath of man or God,	*c*
Have sunk, extinct in their refulgent prime;	*b*
And some yet live, treading the thorny road,	*c*
Which leads, through toil and hate, to Fame's serene abode.	*c*

This gives a rhyme scheme designated by the letters *ababbcbcc*.

Rhyme plays an important part in poetry. It can cause some trouble for an interpreter, especially if the pattern is very strict and the form the poet has adopted is too rigid for effective oral reading. When this is true, you should attempt to compensate by giving close attention to every opportunity for variety in using pauses and inflection at line ends. Particular attention to tone color within lines can bring some of the interior words to a prominence that challenges the strength of the rhyming words. Emphasis on imagery also adds variety.

As we have said, the problem of rhyme does not arise in blank verse. But its very absence here affects interpreters. On one hand, you are released from one of the disciplines you often should consider in interpreting poetry; on the other hand, you are deprived of a significant means of communicating structural unity. For these reasons, you should pay particular attention to other elements in the sound pattern of blank verse: alliteration, harsh or euphonious vowel and consonant combinations, the echoing of mood or sense in sound. The surest guide to structural unity in blank verse is found in the prevalent iambic meter and in the consistent line length.

Writers of free verse may or may not use rhyme. They may use it consistently throughout a poem, but this technique is unusual. Sometimes rhyme appears, if it appears at all, only in brief units of the poem. When these units appear, you should carefully examine their contribution to content, for the poet will have used rhyme consciously. It will not be part of a conventional pattern, but will come out of a subjective decision to use rhyme at that particular point. The sounds of the rhymes and the length of the lines containing the rhymes are very important for intensifying certain aspects of the content.

Contemporary poets are very sophisticated in their use of rhymes and near-rhymes. "Open the Gates" provides us with an excellent example of this use. On reading the poem aloud, one finds rhyming sounds woven intricately throughout the poem. The terminal rhymes are identical and are therefore satisfying; the only exceptions are the paradoxical rhyme of "youth" and "death" immediately preceding the fulcrum, and the slight variance between "forms" and "arms" in the last stanza. Moreover, the identity of the rhymes is emphasized because all but three of the lines are wholly or partially end-stopped by punctuation. Of the three enjambment lines, the first is the inescapable, harsh rhyme of "black" and "sack." The other two are found in the last stanza, one the softening "forms," the other the softening "see."

An additional aspect of line-end sounds is not strictly a matter of rhyme, but it is worthy of the interpreter's attention. This is the use of masculine and feminine line endings. A *masculine* line ending has a discernible stress. All of the line endings in "Open the Gates," for example, are masculine. A *feminine* line end terminates on a lighter stress. Sometimes feminine endings are used to weaken or soften the line end, especially when they are combined with enjambment. Modern poets, like T. S. Eliot, frequently use feminine line ends to reinforce a feeling of instability. Maya Angelou's "I Almost Remember," at the end of this chapter, uses a mixture of masculine and feminine line ends to help sustain the feeling of uneasiness and depression. They are effective psychologically, because the added light stress negates our expectations.

Careful, detailed analysis of the structure of a poem gives you a sure basis for understanding the poet's techniques. Poetry is an art, but it is also a kind of science, and the intricacies of a successful poem are amazing. Once you have discovered the aspects of structure that the poet has used, you should carefully relate them to content. You should then evaluate both content and structure in the light of the touchstones for judging every piece of literature: the extrinsic factors of universality, individuality, and suggestion; the intrinsic factors of unity and harmony, variety and contrast, balance and proportion, and rhythm. Finally, when you present a selection, remember that no single aspect of structure should be exhibited for its own sake; it should be skillfully blended with every other aspect to communicate the aesthetic wholeness of the poem.

Analyzing the Performance

Poetry's condensation provides special challenges to interpreters, and your understanding of the language and structure of poetry is constantly tested in rehearsal and performance. Of course, we do not mean that we are no longer interested in the basic problems of every kind of performance: efficient management of the vocal and physical resources and careful attention to communicating the intellectual, emotional, and aesthetic entirety of the work. But poetry brings more complex uses of sound and sense than many kinds of narration or drama do. The interpreter must be particularly careful not to allow concentration to lapse and not to allow the communicative thrust of the performance to fade. Poetry performances in which the interpeter seems chiefly interested in musing over the lines for himself or herself and the one or two people seated closest are really still in rehearsal.

With the information you have obtained from Chapters 9 and 10, then, and an informed and observant perspective, use the following questions to analyze the performance you gave. As before, any questions you ask of yourself can as well be asked of other performances you see. Keep the poem at the center of your discussion and analysis and treat it with respect. Remember, it was alive before you met it and will be around long after all of us have gone.

Did you let the poet lead the way?

Was your audience responsive to what the poet meant and especially to *how* it was meant?

Did you use your empathic response fully so that the audience responded empathically as well?

Did you carefully preserve the unity of the poem? Did you keep all the other instrinsic factors working fully within it?

Was the persona clear? Was the locus clear?

Did you take full advantage of all of the sound patterns? Did you use the poem's rhythm, or did it use you? Did you clarify the relationship between the lines and the cadences? Did you demonstrate the interaction of rhyme and tone color?

Did your brief introduction prepare the audience for the mood and attitude of the poem? Did you spend more time introducing than performing?

Were you able to blend aspects from the previous chapters applicable to this selection and keep them in their proper relationship to create the "whole" poem?

Did your audience hear the poem as a totality? Were they primarily interested in and aware of you as performer?

How did the poem change for you after your analysis? How has it changed for you after your rehearsals and performance?

What problems still plague you as a performer? What progress have you made in defining them? in solving them? in eliminating them?

For the performances you saw, how did the interpreter suggest the complex language and structure of poetry? Specifically, how did the poem you saw and heard compare with the one you read on the page?

Selections for Analysis and Oral Interpretation

It is interesting to compare the structure and syntax of these two Roethke poems. They offer sharply contrasting physical responses. This first poem is held at a fairly steady level and builds to the final triumph a child would feel at having undivided attention. Keep the poem unified without sacrificing the excitement of the separate thought units within the single primary cadence.

Child on Top of a Greenhouse
THEODORE ROETHKE

The wind billowing out the seat of my britches,
My feet crackling splinters of glass and dried putty,
The half-grown chrysanthemums staring up like accusers,
Up through the streaked glass, flashing with sunlight,
A few white clouds all rushing eastward,
A line of elms plunging and tossing like horses,
And everyone, everyone pointing up and shouting.

▌ How did you use reflexive physical activity in your performance?

This villanelle uses a highly restrictive structure. Let the stanzaic structure help keep the cadences from becoming abrupt. Make full use of the remarkable tone color, especially the assonance.

For Roethke all of life was a waking toward the sleep of death. His affirmation of life is reminiscent of Dylan Thomas's.

The Waking
THEODORE ROETHKE

I wake to sleep, and take my waking slow.
I feel my fate in what I cannot fear.
I learn by going where I have to go.

We think by feeling. What is there to know?
I hear my being dance from ear to ear.
I wake to sleep, and take my waking slow.

Of those so close beside me, which are you?
God bless the Ground! I shall walk softly there,
And learn by going where I have to go.

Light takes the Tree; but who can tell us how?
The lowly worm climbs up a winding stair;
I wake to sleep, and take my waking slow.

Great Nature has another thing to do
To you and me; so take the lively air,
And, lovely, learn by going where to go.

This shaking keeps me steady. I should know.
What falls away is always. And is near.
I wake to sleep, and take my waking slow.
I learn by going where I have to go.

■ How did you distinguish among the different levels of meaning in the repeated lines?

The stanzaic structure is interesting here. There is also a good deal of ellipsis. Be sure you understand the seemingly simple allusions as they are used to reflect attitude. The line lengths as units of thought are particularly important; use them as the poet has.

As I Would Wish You Birds

JOHN CIARDI

Today — because I must not lie to you —
there are no birds but such as I wish
for. There is only my wish to wish you
birds. Catbirds with spatula tails up
jaunty. Jays, gawky as dressed-up toughs.
Humming birds, their toy engines going.
Turkeys with Savonarola heads. Bitchy
Peacocks. The rabble of Hens in their
stinking harems — these three (and
Ostriches and Dodos) a sadness to think
about. But then Gulls — ultimate bird
everywhere everything pure wing and wind
are, there over every strut, flutter, cheep,
coo. At Dover over the pigeon-cliffs.
At Boston over the sparrows. Off tropics
where the lyre-tails and the green-
irridescent heads flash. And gone again.

You never see Gulls in aviaries. Gulls are
distance. Who can put distance in a cage?

Today — and I could never lie to you —
there is no distance equal to what I wish
for. There is only my wish to wish you
a distance full of birds, a thronged air
lifting above us far, lifting us, the sun
bursting in cloud chambers, a choir there
pouring light years of song, its wings
flashing. See this with me. Close your eyes
and see what air can do with more birds in it
than anything but imagination can put there.
There are not enough birds in the eyes we
open. There are too many hens, turkeys, and
that peacock seen always on someone else's
lawn, the air above it wasted unused, songless.
Birds cannot be seen in fact. Not enough

of them at once, not now nor any day. But think
with me what might be, but close your eyes and see.

∎ How did you show *your* audience the persona's audience?
∎ Does the relationship between persona and audience change?
   How?

In this poem the line-length cadences are not only important for structural
rhythm but provide clues to emotional content and connotations. The first
five lines are quoted from a famous sermon. Notice how skillfully Eliot moves
into his own comment. The quote should not be set off too obviously from
the rest of the stanza. Eliot uses capital letters for spiritual birth and death
as opposed to physical birth and death.

Journey of the Magi
T. S. ELIOT

'A cold coming we had of it,
Just the worst time of the year
For a journey, and such a long journey:
The ways deep and the weather sharp,
The very dead of winter.'
And the camels galled, sore-footed, refractory,
Lying down in the melting snow.
There were times we regretted
The summer palaces on slopes, the terraces,
And the silken girls bringing sherbet.
Then the camel men cursing and grumbling
And running away, and wanting their liquor and women,
And the night-fires going out, and the lack of shelters,
And the cities hostile and the towns unfriendly
And the villages dirty and charging high prices:
A hard time we had of it.
At the end we preferred to travel all night,
Sleeping in snatches,
With the voices singing in our ears, saying
That this was all folly.

   Then at dawn we came down to a temperate valley,
Wet, below the snow line, smelling of vegetation;
With a running stream and a water-mill beating the darkness,
And three trees on a low sky,
And an old white horse galloped away in the meadow.
Then we came to a tavern with vine-leaves over the lintel,

Six hands at an open door dicing for pieces of silver,
And feet kicking the empty wine-skins.
But there was no information, and so we continued
And arrived at evening, not a moment too soon
Finding the place; it was (you may say) satisfactory.

   All this was a long time ago, I remember,
And I would do it again, but set down
This set down
This: were we led all that way for
Birth or Death? There was a Birth, certainly,
We had evidence and no doubt. I had seen birth and death,
But had thought they were different; this Birth was
Hard and bitter agony for us, like Death, our death.
We returned to our places, these Kingdoms,
But no longer at ease here, in the old dispensation,
With an alien people clutching their gods.
I should be glad of another death.

   ❚ Was your persona "glad of another death" as the poem began?
     How did your audience know?

James Wright's gift for simple eloquence is unmatched among contemporary American poets. Restraint and sincerity characterize the achievement in this lyric.

A Blessing
JAMES WRIGHT

Just off the highway to Rochester, Minnesota,
Twilight bounds softly forth on the grass.
And the eyes of those two Indian ponies
Darken with kindness.
They have come gladly out of the willows
To welcome my friend and me.
We step over the barbed wire into the pasture
Where they have been grazing all day, alone.
They ripple tensely, they can hardly contain their happiness
That we have come.
They bow shyly as wet swans. They love each other.
There is no loneliness like theirs.
At home once more,
They begin munching the young tufts of spring in the darkness.
I would like to hold the slenderer one in my arms,

For she has walked over to me
And nuzzled my left hand.
She is black and white,
Her mane falls wild on her forehead,
And the light breeze moves me to caress her long ear
That is delicate as the skin over a girl's wrist.
Suddenly I realize
That if I stepped out of my body I would break
Into blossom.

▌ What happened to your body and voice four lines from the
    end? Why?

Much of the wit in this poem is underscored by the rhymes and occasional feminine line ends. Use the structure confidently.

Go and Catch a Falling Star

JOHN DONNE

Go and catch a falling star,
    Get with child a mandrake root,
Tell me where all past years are,
    Or who cleft the devil's foot,
Teach me to hear mermaids singing,
Or to keep off envy's stinging,
        And find
        What wind
Serves to advance an honest mind.

If thou beest born to strange sights,
    Things invisible to see,
Ride ten thousand days and nights,
    Till age snow white hairs on thee,
Thou, when thou return'st, wilt tell me
All strange wonders that befell thee,
        And swear
        No where
Lives a woman true, and fair.

If thou find'st one, let me know,
    Such a pilgrimage were sweet;
Yet do not, I would not go,
    Though at next door we might meet;
Though she were true when you met her,
And last till you write your letter,
        Yet she
        Will be
False, ere I come, to two or three.

▌ How did your persona change between the stanza breaks? Why?

Trust this poet completely, and use his line lengths exactly as he has put them down. He uses capital letters for a shade of emphasis. Keep the thought suspended across the parentheses, which make a sort of "subpoem" in themselves. The kinesthetic imagery is important.

Spring is like a perhaps hand
E. E. CUMMINGS

Spring is like a perhaps hand
(which comes carefully
out of Nowhere) arranging
a window, into which people look (while
people stare
arranging and changing placing
carefully there a strange
thing and a known thing here) and

changing everything carefully

spring is like a perhaps
Hand in a window
(carefully to
and fro moving New and
Old things, while
people stare carefully
moving a perhaps
fraction of flower here placing
an inch of air there) and

without breaking anything.

▮ How did your body and voice capture the *perhap*ses? Were they all the same?

Speech-phrase cadences provide much of the basic rhythm in this selection. Use the line units and stanza divisions exactly as they are, but be careful to retain the overall progress. This poem requires enormous energy — there is nothing placid or still here.

FROM Song of Myself
WALT WHITMAN

A child said *What is the grass?* fetching it to me with full hands;
How could I answer the child? I do not know what it is anymore
            than he.

I guess it must be the flag of my disposition, out of hopeful green
    stuff woven.

Or I guess it is the handkerchief of the Lord,
A scented gift and remembrancer designedly dropt,
Bearing the owner's name some way in the corners, that we may see
    and remark, and say *Whose?*

Or I guess the grass is itself a child, the produced babe of the
    vegetation.

Or I guess it is a uniform hieroglyphic,
And it means, Sprouting alike in broad zones and narrow zones,
Growing among black folks as among white,
Kanuck, Tuckahoe, Congressman, Cuff, I give them the same, I
    receive them the same.

And now it seems to me the beautiful uncut hair of graves.

Tenderly will I use you curling grass,
It may be you transpire from the breasts of young men,
It may be if I had known them I would have loved them,
It may be you are from old people, or from some offspring taken
    soon out of their mothers' laps,
And here you are the mothers' laps.

This grass is very dark to be from the white heads of old mothers,
Darker than the colorless beards of old men,
Dark to come from under the faint red roofs of mouths.

O I perceive after all so many uttering tongues,
And I perceive that they do not come from the roofs of mouths for
    nothing.

I wish I could translate the hints about the dead young men and
    women,
And the hints about old men and mothers, and the offspring taken
    soon out of their laps.

What do you think has become of the young and old men?
And what do you think has become of the women and children?

They are alive and well somewhere,
The smallest sprout shows there is really no death,
And if ever there was it led forward life, and does not wait at the
    end to arrest it,
And ceas'd the moment life appear'd.

All goes onward and outward, nothing collapses,
And to die is different from what any one supposed, and luckier.

▌ How did you embody the logic of the poem's progress?

Parodies should be read with almost exaggerated seriousness. The fun lies
in the awareness on the part of the interpreter, the poet, and the audience
of the characteristic style of the one being parodied.

Jack and Jill
CHARLES BATTEL LOOMIS

(As Walt Whitman Might Have Written It)

I celebrate the personality of Jack!
I love his dirty hands, his tangled hair, his locomotion blundering.
Each wart upon his hands I sing,
Paeans I chant to his hulking shoulder blades.
Also Jill!
Her I celebrate.
I, Walt, of unbridled thought and tongue,
Whoop her up!
What's the matter with Jill!
Oh, she's all right!
Who's all right?
Jill.
Her golden hair, her sun-struck face, her hard and reddened hands;
So, too, her feet, hefty, shambling.
I see them in the evening, when the sun empurples the horizon, and

through the darkening forest aisles are heard the sounds of
    myriad creatures of the night.
I see them climb the steep ascent in quest of water for their mother.
Oh, speaking of her, I could celebrate the old lady if I had time.
She is simply immense!

But Jack and Jill are walking up the hill.
(I didn't mean that rhyme.)
I must watch them.
I love to watch their walk,
And wonder as I watch;
He, stoop-shouldered, clumsy, hide-bound,
Yet lusty,
Bearing his share of the 1-lb. bucket as though it were a
    paperweight.
She, erect, standing, her head uplifting,
Holding, but bearing not the bucket.
They have reached the spring.
They have filled the bucket.
Have you heard the "Old Oaken Bucket"?
I will sing it: —

Of what countless patches is the bed-quilt of life composed!
Here is a piece of lace. A babe is born.
The father is happy, the mother is happy.
Next black crêpe. The beldame "shuffles off this mortal coil."
Now brocaded satin with orange blossoms,
Mendelssohn's "Wedding March," an old shoe missile,
A hospital in ▶ A broken carriage window, the bride in the Bellevue* sleeping.
Manhattan Here's a large piece of black cloth!
"Have you any last words to say?"
"No."
"Sheriff, do your work!"
Thus it is: from "grave to gay, from lively to severe."

I mourn the downfall of my Jack and Jill.
I see them descending, obstacles not heeding.
I see them pitching headlong, the water from the pail outpouring,
    a noise from the leathern lungs out-belching.
The shadows of the night descend on Jack, recumbent, bellowing,
    his pate with gore besmeared.
I love his cowardice, because it is an attribute, just like
Job's patience or Solomon's wisdom, and I love attributes.
Whoop!!!

▌How was your performance a celebration?
▌What role did your audience play?

This sonnet contains some difficulties in the denotation and connotation of words and in the involved sentence structure. Remember that a sonnet requires certain organization of content. Variety in unity is apparent in the structure.

Sonnet 29
WILLIAM SHAKESPEARE

When, in disgrace with Fortune and men's eyes,
I all alone beweep my outcast state,
And trouble deaf heaven with my bootless cries,
And look upon myself and curse my fate,
Wishing me like to one more rich in hope,
Featured like him, like him with friends possess'd,
Desiring this man's art, and that man's scope,
With what I most enjoy contented least;
Yet in these thoughts myself almost despising,
Haply I think on thee; and then my state,
Like to the lark at break of day arising
From sullen earth, sings hymns at heaven's gate;
    For thy sweet love rememb'red such wealth brings
    That then I scorn to change my state with kings.

▌Was your persona sufficiently "low" for your audience to see and hear the change in mood?

This famous sonnet uses a different but equally conventional rhyme scheme and division of content.

On His Blindness
JOHN MILTON

When I consider how my light is spent
Ere half my days, in this dark world and wide,
And that one talent which is death to hide
Lodged with me useless, though my soul more bent
To serve therewith my Maker, and present
My true account, lest he returning chide,

"Doth God exact day-labor, light denied?"
I fondly ask. But Patience, to prevent
That murmur, soon replies: "God doth not need
Either man's work or his own gifts: who best
Bears his mild yoke, they serve him best. His state
Is kingly: thousands at his bidding speed,
And post o'er land and ocean without rest;
They also serve who only stand and wait."

▌ How did your body and voice convey the persona's certainty?

Be sure you embody the Duke's character. He is moved alternately by guilt
and regret and admiration and contempt. And don't ignore the poem's tight
structure — those rhymed couplets are not simply accidental and suggest
some of the restrictions inherent in the Ferrara of the poem.

My Last Duchess
ROBERT BROWNING

Ferrara

That's my last Duchess painted on the wall,
Looking as if she were alive. I call
That piece a wonder, now: Frà Pandolf's hands
Worked busily a day, and there she stands.
Will't please you sit and look at her? I said
"Frà Pandolf" by design, for never read
Strangers like you that pictured countenance,
The depth and passion of its earnest glance,
But to myself they turned (since none puts by
The curtain I have drawn for you, but I)
And seemed as they would ask me, if they durst,
How such a glance came there; so, not the first
Are you to turn and ask thus. Sir, 'twas not
Her husband's presence only, called that spot
Of joy into the Duchess' cheek: perhaps
Frà Pandolf chanced to say, "Her mantle laps
Over my lady's wrist too much," or "Paint
Must never hope to reproduce the faint
Half-flush that dies along her throat:" such stuff
Was courtesy, she thought, and cause enough
For calling up that spot of joy. She had

A heart — how shall I say? — too soon made glad,
Too easily impressed: she liked whate'er
She looked on, and her looks went everywhere.
Sir, 'twas all one! My favour at her breast,
The dropping of the daylight in the West,
The bough of cherries some officious fool
Broke in the orchard for her, the white mule
She rode with round the terrace — all and each
Would draw from her alike the approving speech.
Or blush, at least. She thanked men, — good! but thanked
Somehow — I know not how — as if she ranked
My gift of a nine-hundred-years-old name
With anybody's gift. Who'd stoop to blame
This sort of trifling? Even had you skill
In speech — (which I have not) — to make your will
Quite clear to such an one, and say, "Just this
Or that in you disgusts me; here you miss,
Or there exceed the mark" — and if she let
Herself be lessoned so, nor plainly set
Her wits to yours, forsooth, and made excuse,
— E'en then would be some stooping; and I choose
Never to stoop. Oh sir, she smiled, no doubt,
Whene'er I passed her; but who passed without
Much the same smile? This grew; I gave commands;
Then all smiles stopped together. There she stands
As if alive. Will't please you rise? We'll meet
The company below, then. I repeat,
The Count your master's known munificence
Is ample warrant that no just pretence
Of mine for dowry will be disallowed;
Though his fair daughter's self, as I avowed
At starting, is my object. Nay, we'll go
Together down, sir. Notice Neptune, though,
Taming a sea-horse, thought a rarity,
Which Claus of Innsbruck cast in bronze for me!

❙ How did you sketch the world of the Duke's palace?
❙ How did you keep the Count's emissary present and lively?

The author of "Phenominal Woman" (Chapter 4) gives us quite a different experience in the following poem. Use her line lengths precisely as she has put them down, and you will find they often provide highly suggestive ambiguity. The tone color allows for excellent variety of pace.

I Almost Remember

MAYA ANGELOU

I almost remember
   smiling some
years past
   even combing the ceiling
with the teeth of a laugh
(longer ago than the smile).
Open night news-eyed I watch
channels of hunger
    written on children's faces
    bursting bellies balloon
in the air of my day room.

There was a smile, I recall
now jelled in
a never yester glow. Even a laugh
that tickled the tits of
heaven
(older than the smile).
In graphs, afraid, I see the black
brown hands and
white thin yellowed fingers.

Slip slipping from the
ledge of life. Forgotten by
all but hatred.
Ignored
by all but disdain.

On late evenings when
quiet inhabits my garden
when grass sleeps and
streets are only paths for silent
mist.

    I seem to remember
        Smiling.

▮ How did your persona's memories fade and brighten?

Hyperbole in the selection of allusions sets the cavalier tone of this love poem. The rhymes help as well, especially in the closing couplet.

Since There's No Help
MICHAEL DRAYTON

Since there's no help, come let us kiss and part.
Nay, I have done; you get no more of me,
And I am glad, yea, glad with all my heart,
That thus so cleanly I myself can free;
Shake hands for ever, cancel all our vows,
And when we meet at any time again,
Be it not seen in either of our brows
That we one jot of former love retain.
Now at the last gasp of Love's latest breath,
When, his pulse failing, Passion speechless lies,
When Faith is kneeling by his bed of death,
And Innocence is closing up his eyes,
Now if thou wouldst, when all have given him over,
From death to life thou mightst him yet recover.

▮ How strongly did your persona want to separate? Was that apparent from the first line? How?

The two long sentences in this poem must not be allowed to become repetitious in their tight syntax. The fulcrum begins in the ninth line and moves slowly to the climax in the last half line. Use the two short cadences in the last line with enough strength to balance the "negative" aspects of the other thirteen lines.

Sonnet XXX
EDNA ST. VINCENT MILLAY

Love is not all; it is not meat nor drink
Nor slumber nor a roof against the rain,
Nor yet a floating spar to men that sink
And rise and sink and rise and sink again;
Love can not fill the thickened lung with breath,

Nor clean the blood, nor set the fractured bone;
Yet many a man is making friends with death
Even as I speak, for lack of love alone.
It well may be that in a difficult hour,
Pinned down by pain and moaning for release,
Or nagged by want past resolution's power,
I might be driven to sell your love for peace,
Or trade the memory of this night for food.
It well may be. I do not think I would.

▌ How did you demonstrate the thought processes of the
persona?
▌ What was happening in the pause between the two sentences
in the last line?

The long suspended sentence that makes up this poem must be carefully sustained without allowing the variety to break the build. Notice how skillfully the one-line stanzas are used as fulcrum and climax. The poem is full of energy and empathy, especially after the fulcrum. Remember what we have said about poets breaking their lines where they want in order to achieve subtle effects. Allow Cruz his privilege.

Today Is a Day of Great Joy
VICTOR HERNANDEZ CRUZ

when they stop poems
in the mail & clap
their hands & dance to
them
when women become pregnant
by the side of poems
the strongest sounds making
the river go along

it is a great day

as poems fall down to
movie crowds in restaurants
in bars

when poems start to
knock down walls to

choke politicians
when poems scream &
begin to break the air

that is the time of
true poets that is
the time of greatness

a true poet aiming
poems & watching things
fall to the ground

it is a great day.

▌ How vivid was your persona's desire?
▌ How poignant are the repeated lines?

This poem is so perfectly structured that it gives the interpreter everything
one could ask for. The single long sentence of the first two stanzas makes
the background of the persona remarkably clear. Make full use of the change
of style at the fulcrum. Be meticulous about the punctuation and line lengths.
Don't slight the faint suggestions of rhyme. Keep the repetitions well within
the unity of each stanza as they build to the final single word. Don't overlook
the change from "your" to "our" in the last stanza. Although the poem
requires superb aesthetic control, it rewards you accordingly.

FROM *Horses Make a Landscape
Look More Beautiful*

ALICE WALKER

for two who
slipped away
almost
entirely:
my "part" Cherokee
great-grandmother
Tallulah
(Grandmama Lula)
on my mother's side
about whom
only one

agreed-upon
thing
is known:
her hair was so long
she could sit on it;

and my white (Anglo-Irish?)
great-great-grandfather
on my father's side;
nameless
(Walker, perhaps?),
whose only remembered act
is that he raped
a child:
my great-great-grandmother,
who bore his son,
my great-grandfather,
when she was eleven.

Rest in peace.
The meaning of your lives
is still
unfolding.

Rest in peace.
In me
the meaning of your lives
is still
unfolding.

Rest in peace, in me.
The meaning of your lives
is still
unfolding.

Rest. In me
the meaning of your lives
is still
unfolding.

Rest. In Peace
in me
the meaning

of our lives
is still
unfolding.

Rest.

▌ How did you chart the prayer's progress for your audience?

Bibliography

Bodkin, Maud. *Archetypal Patterns in Poetry.* New York: Oxford University Press, 1963.
  Poetry analyzed in terms of Jung's theory of the collective unconscious. Psychological studies in imagination.

Brooks, Cleanth. *The Well Wrought Urn.* New York: Harcourt, Brace and World, 1947.
  Based on the theory of poetry as dramatic discourse and on the organic relationship of art and meaning in poetry. Essays on specific poems.

Brooks, Cleanth, and Robert Penn Warren. *Understanding Poetry.* 4th ed. New York: Holt, Rinehart and Winston, 1973.
  A good introductory book. An anthology with critical discussions and commentaries on representative poems.

Ciardi, John. *How Does a Poem Mean?* Boston: Houghton Mifflin Company, 1959.
  An excellent discussion of reading poetry, with particularly good examples. Covers many aspects of content and structure.

Crane, R. S. *The Languages of Criticism and the Structure of Poetry.* Toronto: University of Toronto Press, 1953.
  A scholarly discussion on the complexities of poetic criticism.

Davie, Donald. *Articulate Energy: An Enquiry into the Syntax of English Poetry.* London: Routledge and Kegan Paul, 1955.
  A somewhat specialized but stimulating examination of syntactical manipulations in a variety of poems.

Deutsch, Babette. *Poetry Handbook: A Dictionary of Terms.* New York: Funk and Wagnalls, 1957.
  A complete, concise sourcebook of poetic terminology.

Dickey, James. *Babel to Byzantium.* New York: Farrar, Straus & Giroux, 1968.
  A series of brief essays and criticisms about the work of a wide variety of modern poets.

Eliot, T. S. *On Poetry and Poets*. New ed. New York: Farrar, Straus and Company, 1957.
Essays on poetry, poetic drama, and poetic criticism, with chapters on specific poets from Virgil to Yeats.

Empson, William. *Seven Types of Ambiguity*. 3rd ed. London: Chatto and Windus, 1956.
A scholarly consideration of imaginative language as it functions to convey several meanings simultaneously.

Frye, Northrop. *The Well-Tempered Critic*. Bloomington: Indiana University Press, 1963.
A refreshing re-evaluation of some traditional and contemporary modes of criticism.

Fussell, Paul, Jr. *Poetic Meter and Poetic Form*. New York: Random House, 1965.
A clear discussion of the elements of prosody.

Geiger, Don. *The Dramatic Impulse in Modern Poetics*. Baton Rouge: Louisiana State University Press, 1967.
An important book for its intelligent and readable consideration of the problem of persona, written by a poet and teacher of interpretation.

Gibbons, Reginald, ed. *The Poet's Work*. Boston: Houghton Mifflin Company, 1979.
Twenty poets, including Lorca, Stevens, Schwartz, Moore, Thomas, Williams, Auden, and Levertov, have written separate chapters on their methods and aims. Includes a selective bibliography on poets (such as Eliot) who have extensively written elsewhere on this subject.

Hollander, John. *Modern Poetry: Essays in Criticism*. New York: Oxford University Press, 1968.
Twenty-five essays by established critics arranged chronologically to highlight changes in critical approaches from 1913 to 1968.

Hackleman, Wauneta, ed. *The Study and Writing of Poetry: American Women Poets Discuss Their Craft*. Troy, N.Y.: Whitson Publishing Company, 1983.
Brief, readable essays by fifty women poets discussing abstract and organic forms of poetry and poetic technique, illustrated with examples from their own work and with poetry of their contemporaries.

McAuley, James. *Versification: A Short Introduction*. Ann Arbor: Michigan State University Press, 1966.
Discussion of stress, meter, and speed as they apply to rhythm in poetry.

Nemerov, Howard, ed. *Poets on Poetry*. New York: Basic Books, 1966.
Nineteen essays by poets on their own work. Contributors include Conrad Aiken, Marianne Moore, Richard Eberhart, John Berryman, May Swenson, Richard Wilbur, and James Dickey.

Nims, John F. *Western Wind*. 2nd ed. New York: Random House, 1983.
  A refreshing discussion of how a poem works, with attention to and
  selections from numerous poets.

Ostroff, Anthony, ed. *The Contemporary Poet as Artist and Critic: Eight
  Symposia*. Boston: Little, Brown and Company, 1964.
  A collection of twenty-four essays on eight contemporary poems and the
  responses of the poets themselves. The poets include Wilbur, Roethke,
  Kunitz, Lowell, Ransom, Eberhart, Auden, and Shapiro.

Preminger, Alex, Frank J. Warnke, and O. B. Hardison, Jr., eds.
  Princeton Encyclopedia of Poetry and Poetics. Enl. ed. Princeton, N.J.:
  Princeton University Press, 1974.
  Comprehensive yet lucid treatment of all aspects of poetry by noted
  scholars. A bibliography of primary sources for further study accom-
  panies each entry. A valuable reference tool.

Ransom, John Crowe. *The World's Body*. Baton Rouge: Louisiana State
  University Press, 1963.
  A fine collection of fifteen essays, primarily on Ransom's own theory of
  poetry. The book offers a lucid explanation of the obscurity of contemporary verse.

Sebeok, Thomas A., ed. *Style in Language*. New York: John Wiley and
  Sons, 1960.
  Numerous essays dealing with linguistic and psychological approaches
  to literature, with special attention to modern theories of prosody.

Shapiro, Karl. *A Bibliography of Modern Prosody*. Baltimore: Johns Hopkins University Press, 1948.
  A valuable sourcebook for detailed study of critical and practical discussions of poetic techniques.

Smith, Barbara Herrnstein. *Poetic Closure: A Study of How Poems Ends*.
  Chicago: University of Chicago Press, 1968.
  A superb and lucid study of the behavior of poems. The book sees
  closure as "a function of the perception of structure." It draws on illustrations from all of the related arts.

Spender, Stephen. *The Making of a Poem*. New York: W. W. Norton
  and Company, 1962.
  A collection of readable and penetrating essays on various aspects of the
  contemporary literary situation, with a comparative look at the Roman-
  tics. Also includes discussions of novels and autobiographies.

Thompson, John. *The Founding of English Metre*. New York: Columbia
  University Press, 1961.
  Historical survey of the basic meters and variations in English poetry.

Wimsatt, W. K., Jr. *The Verbal Icon: Studies in the Meaning of Poetry*.
  New York: Farrar, Straus and Company, 1954.
  One of the classics of modern criticism, with particular attention to some
  of the fallacies of poetic criticism.

Wright, George T. *The Poet in the Poem: The Personae of Eliot, Yeats and Pound*. Berkeley and Los Angeles: University of California Press, 1960.
    Excellent discussion of Eliot, Yeats, and Pound, plus a sound, provocative analysis of poetry in general.

V. Group Performance

11 The Group Performance of Literature

You must habit yourself to the dazzle of the light
  and of every moment in your life.

Long have you timidly waded holding a plank by the shore
Now I will you to be a bold swimmer
To jump off in the midst of the sea, rise again, nod to
  me, shout, and laughingly dash with your hair.

Walt Whitman, "Song of Myself"

Clearly, this book has been written primarily for the solo interpreter. Nevertheless, group performance methods often help individuals to find solutions to their own performance problems. Of course, there are fundamental differences between solo and group performances, but there is a great deal of common ground. Unfortunately, group performance in the past too often meant that a collection of relatively like-minded solo interpreters had agreed to attack the same text at the same time and place, although not necessarily in the same manner. Today, happily, groups successfully tackle everything from *Paradise Lost* to the wits of the Algonquin round table.

This current vogue is not surprising, since some form of group performance of literature has existed since the rhapsodists read plays in relays in ancient Greece. Only in the past forty years — and particularly in the last twenty years — has this area of oral interpretation really exploded. Many reasons for the popularity of group performance undoubtedly exist. Known now as *Readers Theatre* (or *reader's theater*), *Chamber Theatre*, *mixed-media*, or *compiled scripts*, some form of group performance has become a common and exciting part of the experience of oral interpretation. With the professional theatre's concurrent interest in plays that feature presentational techniques, interpreters find more and more opportunities to expand the borders of their art. Contemporary plays freely range through several levels of consciousness, stop time to examine character motivation, frankly admit the illusion of the theatre, present a single character performed by several different performers to demonstrate the facets or sides of the character, or assign one performer many characters to portray with little outward differentiation. Many innovative techniques born in interpretation productions, transplanted and refined in theatrical settings, flourish and produce dramatic events centering on the staging of narrative (such as the Royal Shakespeare Company's monumental *Nicholas Nickelby*) or on collections of poems, letters, and memoirs (such as *Belle of Amherst*, a program celebrating Emily Dickinson).

Such crossbreeding has obliterated whatever line formerly separated "theatre performances" and "interp performances" and has encouraged many of the innovative developments that make group performance so attractive. Just as theatre events began to feature interpretation's experimental techniques, interpreters discovered ways for groups to solve literary problems with theatrical techniques. And as more interpreters explored group performance, scenography and staging became more elaborate, greater flexibility arose in developing performance analogues for literary constructs, and the range of literature selected for performance broadened. The presence of

435

several performers permitted — even demanded — greater physical and vocal variety. Frankly presentational performances capitalized on localized settings. More bodies and voices meant more opportunities (and more potential pitfalls) for interpreters to take on literary problems a solo performer might understandably avoid — such as large group scenes, multiple attitudes, several scenes occurring simultaneously at the same or different locales. This new flexibility has enabled interpreters to delve into aspects of literature that they previously were unable to explore: long passages or scenes with many characters; entire novellas; carefully abridged longer works; nonfiction works; experimental plays; concrete poetry; texts that demand multiple media or that were not conceived with performance in mind.

The indispensable principles remain the same: a group's analysis and rehearsal begin with and return to the intentions and range of the text. A group performance requires the same techniques as an individual performance: suggestion, character placement, frontal focus, well-trained bodies and voices. The interpreter's respect for the audience's proper function in the creation of the work never changes.

Understandably, with the changes that group performance underwent came dangers: an urge to provide a "good show" might sacrifice the intricacies of the text. Sometimes a director might channel a group's energies to exploring one aspect of the literature at the expense of others. Like any other kind of performance, group performance should present the text through the bodies and voices of the performers to an audience that joins with the performers to create the whole of the literary selection. A performance that is interested only in demonstrating the cleverness of the director or the versatility of the performer actually becomes a demonstration of egoism.

Readers Theatre

Readers Theatre and *Chamber Theatre* are two terms used to describe group performance events. For some they have relatively unrestricted meanings; for others *Readers Theatre* refers to any group interpretation event, and *Chamber Theatre* refers specifically to the staging of narrative. In its broadest and simplest definition, Readers Theatre is a performance by a group of interpreters seeking to explore, to embody, and in special ways, to *feature* a given literary text. This convention of performance, with a long history rooted in the presentational modes of the ancient Greeks, is used today as an exciting and flexible method to explore drama, fiction, nonfiction, and poetry.

There is no recipe for a Readers Theatre production any more than there is a recipe for solo performance. Our purpose here is to suggest the breadth of the possibilities each director can examine and indicate what has already been done. Readers Theatre — like any group performance of literature — has developed because people have tried different ways to achieve the same goal. The future for Readers Theatre is particularly exciting, since so many performance conventions have been adopted by theatrical directors and since our contemporary notions about Readers Theatre are flexible and accommodating.

Readers Theatre does have certain characteristics and criteria. One of the most obvious conventions of the Greek theatre, for example, figures prominently in most contemporary productions of Readers Theatre: the presentational, rather than the representational, reality of the performance. For the Greeks, the role of the actor was similar to the role of the priest — the actor symbolized the actions of the gods and the great mortals. During the ritual of the performance, the audience believed in the *re-enactment* of the story or play, rather than in its immediate illusion of reality. No Greek actually endured the travails of Oedipus; Medea was not meant to be like the woman next door. The telling of the tale became the central issue: how beautifully the dance embodied the emotional dilemma of those colossal characters, how richly the cadences of the verse, with the delicate harmonies of the music, suggested the experiences of those great beings. The grace and power of the telling were enormously important, because the story itself generally was very well known to the audience.

If you were to attend a play about the last days of Abraham Lincoln, your major concern would not be to know how things turn out, although you may become fearful and excited when Lincoln decides to attend the theatre one night in April. Rather, you would be interested in the character of the man himself, how we see him today, how his intellectual and emotional gifts have affected our lives. You would, perhaps, admire his efforts, regret his follies, pity his mistakes, understand his limitations; but at the end you would be inspired by his example and sacrifice. Your attention would focus on how the story is told rather than on any of its events. Just as you might be curious about the way a playwright would tell the story of Lincoln, the Greeks were interested in how the young playwright Euripides handled a tale previously told by Aeschylus.

This interest in presentation, in the manner of the telling and hence in the text itself, still primarily influences contemporary experiments in Readers Theatre. For one thing, there is no "fourth wall," or illusion of eavesdropping, in Readers Theatre, as there is in most

realistic drama. The action is all turned outward, because the performers frankly admit that the audience has come to see and hear a
text. The performing space is a playing space from which you project
the text, not unlike the space you describe for yourself when you
begin a solo performance.

In the Greek theatre this space was called the *orkastra* and was
often occupied by the chorus, since they were the ones who interpreted and reflected on the action by commenting about it to the
audience. Because the Greek theatres were enormous and had no
amplifiers the actors wore masks with enormous features that not
only revealed to even the most distant spectators the inner states of
the characters but also projected their voices.

Shakespeare also used the stage as a projection space. Many of
his characters talk in soliloquy directly to the playgoers, thus allowing
them to participate in the characters' inner workings and motivations.
Hamlet tells the audience what he's thinking and, quite openly in
front of them, upbraids himself for what he sees as his cowardice.

These presentational conventions have also been used by many
modern dramatists, including Bertolt Brecht and Thornton Wilder.
(See the Singer's interpretation of the internal life of Grusha and
Simon in Brecht's *Caucasian Chalk Circle* at the end of this chapter.)
The Readers Theatre would open up and project frankly out front a
scene that a traditional theatrical convention might play as closed or
onstage. When two characters, for example, George and Martha in
Albee's *Who's Afraid of Virginia Woolf?*, talk to each other, traditional
staging allows them to play to and with one another in a closed space
that they both occupy and in which the audience observes them. The
line representing their tension is perpendicular to the sight lines of
the audience. George moves toward Martha with a drink, facing her
and expecting her to reach for the drink. Compare this with a Readers
Theatre presentation of the same scene, in which George and Martha
stand several feet apart and "look at" each other out front: that is,
each sees the other directly in front, above, and slightly beyond the
audience, as shown on the following page.

When George approaches Martha, he would take his step directly
toward the audience. Martha would see him approaching as if he
were entering from the audience and would reach out there for the
drink he carries.

What makes this open form so rewarding is the way it allows
audience members to examine multiple levels by placing them in the
middle of the activity, participating intimately in what is going on
between the characters. Furthermore, it reveals secrets that a staged
performance simply could not disclose. When George approaches
Martha with the drink, he offers to continue her inebriation,

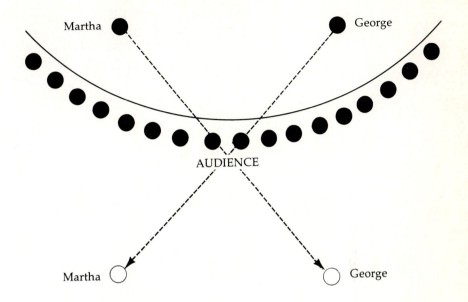

perpetuating her way of life. As we see her reach for this sustenance, we see that both of them have had to participate together in "this sewer of a marriage" in order for it to have lasted so long. The image in front of us — Martha reaching out for help, George offering the alcoholic solution — is an icon of the play itself, foreshadowing what will happen and symbolizing what is wrong with George and Martha. Readers Theatre features this element of the text by frankly placing it out front.

Some technical problems arise in this form of performance, but these can be solved by a little careful thinking. George and Martha cannot be so close together on stage that it seems odd for them not to address each other. They cannot enter the same physical relationship that they would display in a staged production; nor can they intimately relate to a background of props and scenery as they might in a staged production. The formality of the convention prohibits such kinds of behavior, even as it allows other kinds. George advances forward rather than sideways. If he and Martha were close together, they might legitimately be expected to turn and talk to each other. If addressing another character out front instead of directly seems uncomfortable to you, think about the last time you had your hair cut. When the barber or stylist asked you about length and shaping, you probably looked at yourself in the mirror, responding to the reflected questioner, who answered your questions by looking at your *reflection*, not at you.

The scene should be projected from a *playing space* or a *performance area* neutral enough to suggest a locale that belongs neither to audience nor to characters. In order for us to accept the convention, the angles of vision need to cross one another. If George and Martha were to see one another like this

they would not appear to be in the same scene; they would not intersect. Moreover, this point of intersection must occur within the audience, for there the action clashes. If the intersection of each angle were to occur onstage, as in

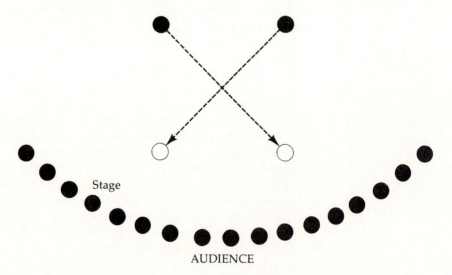

the scene would still be closed, and it would seem extremely odd for the characters not to turn toward one another and play the scene in that closed space they both obviously occupy.

For the convention to be accepted, the tension of each character reaching for the other must pierce the "wall" that separates audience from character. Only then can the audience participate in the internal processes of each of the characters.

Readers Theatre enables a selection of literature to be presented so that performers — and the audience — share new insights into the text. To do this, the interpreter should keep responsibly and responsively in touch with the literature. In opening up the work, we must remain open to it.

Chamber Theatre

Chamber Theatre is a rewarding method for a group to perform narrative fiction. Robert Breen, the scholar who is most responsible for the innovation and development of Chamber Theatre, defines it as "a technique for dramatizing the point of view of narrative fiction." We have discussed how, in narrative fiction, point of view manifests the relationships among the narrator and the characters and events of the story. As you know, simply discovering the point of view does not solve all performance problems, of course, but it does provide the center of focus for a group wishing to demonstrate to an audience how a *specific* tale is related by a *specific* narrator. Moreover, Chamber Theatre embodies in concrete form the relationships between *that* narrator and *those* characters in *that* setting. Since the action of the novel unfolds with the immediacy of drama, the audience can see and hear the impact of the events on the characters; and since the narrator is retained, the governing central intelligence of the fiction so conditions the audience's view of the world that they listen to and watch exactly what — and *only* what — the narrator wants them to hear and see.

A Chamber Theatre production of a novel or a story may boast all of the scenographic resources of a staged production of a play. Performers may be costumed, may appear without scripts of any kind, may represent one or several characters at one time, and may even focus on each other rather than out front. In all cases, narrators are present and highly visible onstage, *at the center of the action.* The narrators are not on the periphery watching the activity, unless they have momentarily stepped aside to let a scene between the characters play uninterrupted. Narrators are *not* like the avuncular and observant Stage Manager in Thornton Wilder's *Our Town.* Staged narrators participate in the action, organize it, unify it, just as they do in the novel. The heart of Chamber Theatre remains the careful and intelligent use of the narrator, because the narrator is responsible for moving the story along in terms of action and pace. The narrator also governs the selectivity of the story by indicating where the audience should look and by conditioning the listeners' responses to the characters and the action.

The intriguing theoretical and aesthetic values of Chamber Theatre can best be understood after you look at a segment of a story from a practical point of view. One of the very first elements to consider in the development of a Chamber Theatre production for the stage is the preparation of the script. Numerous choices are presented to the director/adapter. In grappling with the problems these choices present, we can examine some important features of this technique.

Read the following scene from Nathanael West's *Miss Lonelyhearts*, a novel about a man in his middle thirties who is the author of an advice column in the New York *Post-Dispatch*. He is haunted by his troubled correspondents and plagued by moral and religious doubts. Miss Lonelyhearts (he is never given any other name in the novel) takes Mary Shrike, the wife of his editor, out for dinner. Although they share considerable intimacy, they are not having an affair.

She came out of the closet wearing a black lace slip and began to fix her hair in front of the dressing table. Miss Lonelyhearts bent down to kiss the back of her neck.

"Now, now," she said, acting kittenish, "you'll muss me."

He took a drink from the whiskey bottle, then made her a highball. When he brought it to her, she gave him a kiss, a little peck of reward.

"Where'll we eat?" she asked. "Let's go where we can dance. I want to be gay."

They took a cab to a place called El Gaucho. When they entered, the orchestra was playing a Cuban rhumba. A waiter dressed as a South-American cowboy led them to a table. Mary immediately went Spanish and her movements became languorous and full of abandon.

But the romantic atmosphere only heightened his feeling of icy fatness. He tried to fight it by telling himself that it was childish. What had happened to his great understanding heart? Guitars, bright shawls, exotic foods, outlandish costumes — all these things were part of the business of dreams. He had learned not to laugh at the advertisements offering to teach writing, cartooning, engineering, to add inches to the biceps and to develop the bust. He should therefore realize that the people who came to El Gaucho were the same as those who wanted to write and live the life of an artist, wanted to be an engineer and wear leather puttees, wanted to develop a grip that would impress the boss, wanted to cushion Raoul's head on their swollen breasts. They were the same people as those who wrote to Miss Lonelyhearts for help.

But his irritation was too profound for him to soothe it in this way. For the time being, dreams left him cold, no matter how humble they were.

"I like this place," Mary said. "It's a little fakey, I know, but it's gay and I so want to be gay."

She thanked him by offering herself in a series of formal, impersonal gestures. She was wearing a tight, shiny dress that was like glass-covered steel and there was something cleanly mechanical in her pantomime.

"Why do you want to be gay?"

"Every one wants to be gay — unless they're sick."

Was he sick? In a great cold wave, the readers of his column crashed over the music, over the bright shawls and picturesque waiters, over her shining body. To save himself, he asked to see the medal. Like a little girl helping an old man to cross the street, she leaned over for him to look into the neck of her dress. But before he had a chance to see anything, a waiter came up to the table.

"The way to be gay is to make other people gay," Miss Lonelyhearts said. "Sleep with me and I'll be one gay dog."

The defeat in his voice made it easy for her to ignore his request and her mind sagged with his: "I've had a tough time," she said. "From the beginning, I've had a tough time. When I was a child, I saw my mother die. She had cancer of the breast and the pain was terrible. She died leaning over a table."

"Sleep with me," he said.

"No, let's dance."

"I don't want to. Tell me about your mother."

"She died leaning over a table. The pain was so terrible that she climbed out of bed to die."

Mary leaned over to show how her mother had died and he made another attempt to see the medal. He saw that there was a runner on it, but was unable to read the inscription.

"My father was very cruel to her," she continued. "He was a portrait painter, a man of genius, but . . ."

He stopped listening and tried to bring his great understanding heart into action again. Parents are also part of the business of dreams. My father was a Russian prince, my father was a Piute Indian chief, my father was an Australian sheep baron, my father lost all his money in Wall Street, my father was a portrait painter. People like Mary were unable to do without such tales. They told them because they wanted to talk about something besides clothing or business or the movies, because they wanted to talk about something poetic.

When she had finished her story, he said, "You poor kid," and leaned over for another look at the medal. She bent to help him and pulled out the neck of her dress with her fingers. This time he was able to read the inscription: "Awarded by the Boston Latin School for first place in the 100 yd. dash."

It was a small victory, yet it greatly increased his fatigue and he was glad when she suggested leaving.

The first "character" to consider is the narrator, who governs all our responses to Miss Lonelyhearts, the hero of the story. Many of Nathanael West's narrators have characteristic and complex ways of telling their stories: the language of *Miss Lonelyhearts,* for example, is often as vivid and brutal as are its characters. Full of human misery presented in relentless progression, the novel moves swiftly and painfully to its final moments. The narrator does not spare us from suffering or unpleasantness. His metaphors throughout the novel are blunt, nightmarish, and disturbing, even though they are based on the everyday objects that swarm about the characters. Miss Lonelyhearts receives letters that are "stamped from the dough of suffering with a heart-shaped cookie knife," and we can see the pathetic, funny, and painfully mundane worlds their writers inhabit. The air in a little park smells "as though it had been artificially heated," and we detect the rancid oil and dense closeness of cheap rooms. The shadow of a lamppost pierced him "like a spear," and "the gray sky looked as if it had been rubbed with a soiled eraser." We see how ineffectual Miss Lonelyhearts is in relieving the pain suffered by the people who expect aid from him and how their expectations smudge even the daylight.

So, at the center of this novel is a narrator who speaks strong and vivid poetry. To eliminate such a person from the drama and let only the characters occupy the stage would render only part of the work, and an interpreter is interested in the fullest possible performance of the literature. As we see in the passage quoted above, the narrator is responsible for pointing us carefully into the interior life of Miss Lonelyhearts himself; through the narrator we are privy to the tortured mind and spirit that seek to counsel the troubled world.

Let's get back to the scene itself: "She came out of the closet wearing a black lace slip and began to fix her hair in front of the dressing table." This stage direction describes simply and directly what Mary Shrike is doing, and yet the description itself indicates a deliberate move on her part. She is wearing *only* a slip. Why would a woman do that? Let us assign the line to the narrator, who is sure to point up that detail; perhaps he will even speak to both the audience and Miss Lonelyhearts, who needs to know that he is deliberately being tempted by Mary Shrike's display. Perhaps Miss Lonelyhearts does not know quite how to respond. He is, in a sense, impotent and is caught over and over again in the web of other people's problems. Since Miss Lonelyhearts is unsure, let the narrator tell him what to do: the line "Miss Lonelyhearts bent down to kiss the back of her neck" is spoken directly to Miss Lonelyhearts so that he knows what to do and so that the audience will not miss the closeness of his relationship with Mary.

"Now, now . . . you'll muss me" is obviously Mary's response to the kiss. She is, as you recall, at her dressing table, preening and admiring herself. Since "acting kittenish" is a qualification of Mary's behavior, as well as another effort on her part to tantalize Miss Lonelyhearts, Mary could take the entire line: " 'Now, now,' she said, acting kittenish, 'you'll muss me.' " Thus she has a second level in the performance: there is a Mary who is in the scene, reacting and responding on the surface in the public way Miss Lonelyhearts sees; and there is a Mary who is inside watching herself, describing her own motivation and superficiality. The next short paragraph gives another simple stage direction. There might be some value, though, in providing for the audience both the action that is performed by the characters and the narrator's description of it. "When he brought it to her, she gave him a kiss, a little peck of reward." But isn't "a little peck of reward" Miss Lonelyheart's attitude toward the kiss? If we allow him to say so, we can see the part of him that corresponds to the second, interior side of Mary. In revealing these various aspects, the director and adapter of a Chamber Theatre production can amplify and expand on the numerous levels of the text, clarifying what the author's artistry has achieved.

There is even a further possibility in the exchange between Mary and Miss Lonelyhearts. Since scenes in the novel shift fluently from speakeasy to bedroom, from Shrike's apartment to the office, to the little park, even from wakefulness to sleep, the staging requires a mobility that realistic or detailed scenography would prohibit. The space of the novel itself is more psychological than physical, as it depicts the tortured interior world of Miss Lonelyhearts. Miss Lonelyhearts moves about his world as through a void, being caught here or there by the disturbing troubles of his correspondents. If there are only a few set pieces and specific scenes are suggested by neutral properties, then the void of Miss Lonelyhearts's world can be demonstrated without the problems of sixteen full sets with attendant decorations.

Such flexibility itself leads to some interesting choices, since it becomes the physical or performance analogue for the literary construction that is our imagined world of Miss Lonelyhearts. Throughout the novel we read the letters — full texts of pleas from "Sick-of-it-all" or "Desperate" or "Harold S." or "Broad Shoulders" — but Miss Lonelyhearts actually meets only one of the correspondents during the story. Still, since he doesn't have bodies for them in fact, his tortured consciousness creates real people. He *sees* them everywhere; they have a palpable reality for him. How can he be sure that the woman he passes on the street is not the woman who left her husband because he had contracted tuberculosis and she couldn't stand the smell of death?

Marvelously, Chamber Theatre can create these ghosts: the interpreter playing Miss Lonelyhearts can confront *living* letters — real people who pursue him and invade his consciousness at strategic points throughout the action. One may haunt him during the scene with Mary Shrike. The set is minimal, so why not let "Sick-of-it-all" or "Disillusioned-with-Tubercular-Husband" hold Mary's mirror for her? And do you even need an actual glass? Try using just the empty oval mirror frame, so that when Miss Lonelyhearts crosses the room to hand Mary her drink, as he bends over to kiss her neck, he sees into the mirror, and there, where there ought to be the face of Mary Shrike, he sees the haunting face of one of the correspondents he cannot escape. Staring at that face and thinking, "Will I never be free?" he could hear Mary Shrike's words — echoed by the face in the glass — "Where'll we eat? Let's go where we can dance. I want to be gay."

The novel has begun to become as immediate as a play: you have given it the simultaneity of drama, since more than one thing is happening at once. Of course the serial perception of the novel is not lost, since the narrator sustains the importance of the progress through the fiction; but in Chamber Theatre we see both the question and the answer at the same time. Miss Lonelyhearts is caught vividly between the forces that will destroy him: the decadence and emptiness of Mary Shrike and her world and the pain and privation of the world of "Sick-of-it-all." What an irony it is for Miss Lonelyhearts to seek escape in Mary Shrike's mirror, only to find there the face of the very specter he most wants to avoid!

After Mary says, "I want to be gay," the action speeds up and, as if in a film, we jump to the cab and then to the entrance of El Gaucho. Such a rapid transition requires the stage to be as flexible and dynamic as the screen. There is no scenery to move around, happily; at the center there is the one who describes the setting — the narrator, who can cross-fade or dissolve a scene by saying a few words, or by merely walking in front of it. You can let the narrator suspend or protract time; and using this person's special relationship with the audience, you can have the narrator cross down toward the audience, summarizing with the line, "They took a cab to a place called El Gaucho." Mary and Miss Lonelyhearts need do no more than get up and turn arm-in-arm to face what has now become the entrance to the restaurant. If the narrator slips a white towel over an arm and prepares to function as one of the minor service characters, Miss Lonelyhearts himself can observe, after he hears the music, "When they entered, the orchestra was playing a Cuban rhumba." Then the narrator could lead the two characters around the stage back to the seats center, saying, "A waiter dressed as a South-American cowboy led them to a table." Mary, caught up in the atmosphere and again conscious of the effect of her actions, could say, "Mary immediately went Spanish and her movements became languorous and full of abandon."

Mary's comment, spoken about herself, might sound awkward to a beginning performer. You might be troubled by the fact that characters speak about themselves in the third person or in the past tense, but you should remember that all of the performers on the stage are telling the story and showing the story to the audience. A slight alienation effect — very much like the one created in the Epic Theatre of Brecht or in the Japanese Noh drama — is created when characters are allowed to perceive themselves as participants in a scene. This distancing can have aesthetic value as well: it may serve to bring us even closer to the characters, since it reminds us that they lead only fictional lives. And such third-person talk is really not so foreign to everyday lives. Perhaps you have heard a woman cautioning her child, "Mommy doesn't want her little girl to get too near the hot stove."

As Mary plunges into the ambience of El Gaucho, Miss Lonelyhearts becomes troubled and pulls into himself. While this internalization would be hidden from an audience at a play, the narrator (who has dropped the waiter persona), privy to the workings of Miss Lonelyhearts's heart, reports what an audience needs to know: "But the romantic atmosphere only heightened his feeling of icy fatness." It would be ludicrous to stage this moment with the narrator and characters far apart physically. The closer they are to each other temperamentally, the closer their placement on the stage should be, and the more they will share in the same experience. In this way you can achieve on stage the performance analogue of West's fiction.

Have the narrator speak the line "But the romantic . . . fatness" directly to Miss Lonelyhearts, who, in turn, can respond directly to the narrator with, "He tried to fight it by telling himself that it was childish." This interchange is a good opportunity for Miss Lonelyhearts to tell his response physically *to himself* as if he were the narrator, who functions throughout the novel as Miss Lonelyhearts's alter ego. The result is really a dialogue scene. It takes place on the stage, which for the moment becomes Miss Lonelyhearts's mind. Both performers should play to each other, listening and responding to each other.

NARRATOR: What had happened to his great understanding heart?
MISS L.:   Guitars, bright shawls, exotic foods, outlandish costumes — all these things were part of the business of dreams.
NARRATOR: He had learned not to laugh at the advertisements offering to teach writing, cartooning, engineering, to add inches to the biceps and to develop the bust.

MISS L.: He should therefore realize that the people who came to El
Gaucho were the same as those who wanted to write and live the life
of an artist,

NARRATOR: wanted to be an engineer and wear leather puttees,

MISS L.: wanted to develop a grip that would impress the boss,

NARRATOR: wanted to cushion Raoul's head on their swollen breasts.

MISS L.: They were the same people as those who wrote to Miss Lonelyhearts for help.

NARRATOR: But his irritation was too profound for him to soothe it in
this way.

MISS L.: For the time being, dreams left him cold, no matter how humble
they were.

At this point, Mary stops this internal scene by intruding the
external world of the nightclub, "I like this place." Now try to adapt
the rest of the scene. When does the narrator step in to advance the
action? Is there more internal dialogue? ("Was he sick?") What happens when you get to the paragraph in which suffering voices seem
to invade Miss Lonelyhearts's heart with "My father was a Russian
Prince," "my father lost all his money in Wall Street," and so on? Can
you use those other specters again?

Each of the narrative forms we examined in Chapter 6 — a third-
person narrator who is objective, or a first-person narrator who is a
character in a story — has its own opportunities for demonstration.
Interestingly, Hugh Leonard's *Da* (Chapter 8) uses Chamber Theatre
techniques, and the method in which two actors play the same
character at different times can frequently be used in a first-person
story to demonstrate how changes have worked on a character. Any
narration — prose or verse, fiction or nonfiction — can benefit from
the scrutiny that Chamber Theatre affords.

What Chamber Theatre tells us about the nature of the relationships in narration should not be separated from its entertainment or
performance value. Like all forms of interpretation, Chamber Theatre
should be based on a clear understanding of the principles involved in
the mode of presentation, a careful analysis of the author's achievement, and a high degree of artistic integrity and flexibility. Chamber
Theatre does not make plays out of stories. It presents fiction *as it was
written*, with the narration making point of view as vividly physical as it
is focal. Summary, scene, and description all perform their usual functions, and literary style becomes physical in the performance itself. For
Chamber Theatre to serve the narrative, the interpreter undertakes all
of these responsibilities in the spirit of experiment and inquiry, attempting at all times to embody on a stage what the author has conceived on the page. The transformation of the story thus becomes an
endless process of discovery in which all of the skills you have learned
contribute to the fullest performance of the text.

Group Performance of Compiled Scripts

With an increasing interest in the group performance of nonfiction texts came experiments to combine fiction and nonfiction in full-length programs. Essays, reportage, impressions, memoirs, travel literature, diaries, oral histories, and testimony all offer interesting opportunities for group performance and can be approached by a group using the methods of Chamber Theatre or Readers Theatre. By mixing materials from different genres and supplementing them with slides, film, television, tapes, or other media, interpreters use tools of the electronic era to examine the various levels of life in a text.

The techniques used in Readers Theatre and Chamber Theatre are flexible enough to be adapted to the performance of such compiled scripts, but the interpreter should keep several key responsibilities in mind. First, the shape of the entire program should reflect the intention of the works involved; too often the performer can lose sight of the whole when closely engaged with each segment. Second, whatever nonliterary material is used should contribute to the entire program, rather than appearing for its own sake. Film and sound effects can be very enriching, but the goal should not simply be a travelogue or a slide show, and the film should not distract from the literature or become the show. The works of literature themselves are the key; when they are juxtaposed in a program, they should illuminate each other, and their relationship should be clear to the audience. Be certain that the combination of texts contributes to the full sense of the entire program, as do all of the other elements — performers, media, selections. Third, compiled scripts should be constructed with a clear beginning, middle, and end. Their components should be cohesive, and although they may not be of the same mode or genre, they should still contribute in some apparent way to the progress of the entire program. Combining a series of smaller pieces can lead to either coalescence or diffusion — to a totality that is greater than the sum of the parts, or to simply a string of parts. When you are tempted by the possibilities of multimedia presentations, remember that it is best to present seamlessly meshed components offering the fullest possible examination of the multiple levels of the work. If you cannot achieve this combination, it is better to examine *some* of the levels clearly and precisely than all of the levels (or even most of the levels) muddily or incompletely.

Suggestions for program possibilities are endless. The requirements of each performance opportunity will restrict your choices and will suggest new and sometimes widely different concepts. If the faithful communication of text always remains your guideline, with each selection you will begin an exciting and thoroughly uncharted experiment.

Current interest in nonfiction, journals, letters, diaries, magazines, and newspapers as sources for group performance has probably resulted from a desire for new types of material and from the fact that these texts are fairly flexible. To celebrate a particular date, such as the founding of a town or a school, a group of performers could combine audio, visual, or physical representations with selections from several area or national newspapers and magazines, thereby suggesting what was happening in the rest of the world at that particular time. A group also could celebrate the variety and impact of a particular publication by presenting selections that represent the publication's characteristic quality or attitude. (See Appendix B for a discussion of a production of the *New York Times*.) Groups have commonly celebrated events or anniversaries by combining original documents, diaries, letters, and dispatches with journal accounts that have appeared in various places and relate to the commemorated event.

There are great opportunities for research in such programs, apart from the obvious searches through archives and back issues of serial publications. Such presentations also encourage nonperformers to experience the rewards of performing and can lead to powerful converts to oral interpretation. The visual reconstruction of certain events can be reinforced with photographs and reprinted etchings and illuminations. Commercial art often characterizes a time or an event — posters, handbills, advertisements, and catalogs give an excellent impression of what life was like during a particular time. If you select an event in the not-too-distant past, you can also use audio and video recordings. A production about Chautauqua, New York (see Appendix C), might feature the advertisements and announcements that heralded the annual opening; typical speeches and performances; photographs or sketches (published and private); songs from original presentations; and descriptions of people who used Chautauqua as a base for their national activities. Through costume, slide, film, sound, and performance, a group can evoke the earnest yet brash approach of the era in its attempt to popularize and democratize "culture."

Fanny Burney's late-eighteenth-century diaries and letters can tie together an examination of the world in which she traveled and of the people she knew. In depicting that rare woman who was accepted as an equal in exclusively male circles, a performance could examine her peculiar impact on the literary and political titans of her day, giving as well substantial attention to her characteristic contributions to English literature.

Joan Didion's extended essay "Slouching Towards Bethlehem," which describes in a cinematic series of sixty-three incidents and scenes the social atmosphere of San Francisco's Haight-Ashbury district in 1967, could be supplemented with contemporaneous videotape, film, slides, newspaper accounts, political speeches, music, and commercial advertisements. Such material, if arranged as carefully as the essay is, could further demonstrate Didion's view of the atomization of American culture in the late sixties and her pervading sense that, as Yeats said in "The Second Coming" (Chapter 4), "the centre cannot hold."

Or comb the several works about the American experience in Vietnam. Any of the oral histories of the soldiers who served there (such as Al Santoli's *Everything We Had* — see the excerpt at the end of this chapter — or Wallace Terry's *Bloods*), or the histories of the people who made the decisions about involving American personnel (such as Stanley Karnow's *Vietnam*), or the reportage filed on the scene (such as Michael Herr's *Dispatches*), or the attitudes about U.S. involvement offered by an articulate officer (such as Philip Caputo's *A Rumor of War*), or the effects of the war at home (as in C. D. B. Bryan's *Friendly Fire*) offer numerous powerful passages for performance. Combined with video and film clips from television news reports or press conferences, with newspaper headlines and music of the period, and perhaps with clips from films that examine the experience (such as Francis Ford Coppola's *Apocalypse Now*) and the testimony of the many Vietnamese who now live in America, an interpreter could shape a stirring and powerful production. Indeed, any major historical event, for example, the Holocaust, the civil rights struggles, the Depression, or the Civil War, offers countless opportunities to examine and understand. Terrible events, when carefully scrutinized, reveal human beings in the acts of heroism and cowardice that are the stuff of great literature. To share such truth with an audience can be both ennobling and entertaining, in the richest sense of the word.

The most valuable tools for the director-adapter to use in this form of script composition are imagination and tact when drawing relationships between events and texts. Keep your mind open to possible inclusions and remember that an artfully structured program that allows the greatest flexibility and achieves the maximum impact has at its center substantial literature that is worth performing. The ultimate goal is to perform the literature as fully as possible, while simultaneously suggesting what the event, time, or publication was like. Performing the individual components does not differ significantly in responsibility from any other type of group performance. Chamber Theatre techniques work just as richly with nonfiction narrative as they do with fiction; bodies and voices can suggest the nonverbal and visual elements as well as they do in Readers Theatre or Chamber Theatre productions.

Other Kinds of Literature

We have described some of the techniques that are used in Readers Theatre and Chamber Theatre and have discussed some of the ways in which compiled scripts are prepared. The current interest in the group performance of literature is not limited to these methods, however, and a great deal of excitement and many discoveries can be generated when a group attempts to perform materials that are not usually associated with performance, such as concrete poetry, filmscripts, courtroom transcripts, and even comic books. Naturally, these sources should conform to the original criteria for selecting performance material; but the new challenges each form creates offer experienced students new ways to understand literature. Appendix B includes descriptions of programs that are built in rather traditional ways around fiction and poetry on the one hand and nonfiction and media on the other. The principles used in each of these programs are also applicable to the material presented here.

Concrete poetry can be defined broadly as a verbal work in which visual, tactile, or iconographic representation carries at least as much weight as any of the denotative and connotative meanings of the words. Sometimes concrete poems are printed in patterns, which themselves tell stories about the "text" of the poem; sometimes they are not reproducible as print on paper but rather appear as pictures or forms or sculpture or even, appropriately enough, castings in concrete. Once again the *form* of the poem means something that is tangible and realizable in three dimensions.

When you decide to perform a sonnet, you take into consideration the fact that the poem is composed of fourteen lines of iambic pentameter that follow a particular rhyme scheme and obey certain formal strictures regarding octave and sestet. All of these elements are parts of the poem's *form*, and your performance attempts to correspond to that form, insofar as your body and your voice are able. Of course all poetry — all literature — has form. Concrete poetry asks you to present in your performance, as fully as your bodies and voices can, a form that corresponds to the form of the work. Because group performance allows much greater flexibility in the creation of that form, concrete poetry allows groups to experiment with the sounds and attitudes of the work by using the combined voices and bodies to suggest — in three dimensions — the full size and shape of the poem. Mary Ellen Solt's "Forsythia" and

Reinhard Döhl's "Apfel" (both at the end of this chapter) are both enormously challenging and a great deal of fun. Most of your experience thus far will not have prepared you for this kind of experimentation unless you are willing to stretch your understanding of performance. But the interpreter who at least attempts that stretch will perform more traditional literatures in a much broader world. Not everyone masters every form instantly, but all responsible artists try to discover ways to refine their art and techniques.

Initially it would seem that to perform a filmscript would come easily to interpreters. Filmscripts are, after all, plays put on film; and interpreters perform plays all the time. Even a cursory study of literate scripts, however, indicates how very different a good film is from a play, although the outward similarities of dialogue remain obvious. Rather, a better analogy can be made between fiction and film — that of a narrator and the eye of a camera. If you are particularly impressed by a filmscript, why not try to perform it by casting a performer as the camera and allowing that interpreter to perform all of the camera directions? The performer would operate much as a narrator would in a work of narrative fiction. You could develop the cinematic sense by continuing the analogy when the camera, in its role as eye, displays carefully to the audience what it wants them to see. Since characters in film exist only insofar as the camera sees or hears them, why not show them similarly in the production? The camera can show characters, indicating carefully what the audience is to see; perhaps the camera could even assist a character in performing actions an audience should see, and then, as it turns its eye to someone else, let the *performer* resume normal behavior. The tension that is created between the illusion of what the camera shows and what is seen after the camera leaves can give another level of the tale. Or you can continue the tension of the scene among the characters and wait for them to break as the scene concludes.

One of the more playful elements of group performance can combine both of these concepts — try a comic book! Of course *very* few comic books have the literary substance to carry more than a bit of experimentation, but it can be an interesting and broadening change to ask a group to attempt to stage each frame of the comic book as a concrete poem, incorporating what a performance of concrete poetry teaches about form and what a performance of a filmscript teaches about episodic, or momentary, scenes. A great deal of information can be packed into such moments, with all of the economy and precision the group can muster. In addition, the group should maintain the ironic seriousness, as well as the broad comedy that words like *pow* or *wam* or *booooom* carry with them. Good training, then, can be flexible, broadening, and fun.

Some Concluding Cautions

The suggestions we have given should not be taken as the only ways to perform these materials; nor are these the only materials that can be performed. We are quick to caution students who want to under-take group performance that there are many difficulties in performing these materials. (Not the least of these difficulties may befall the direc-tor who fails to secure the permission of the copyright holder. Appen-dix A discusses this and provides some tips about directing group performances.) Everything printed — and even that which is not printed — is fair game for the sensitive, serious, and tactful inter-preter. If you have understood and followed the touchstones we pre-sented at the beginning of the book, you will be able to present literature and performances that are interesting to your audiences.

We are convinced that the students who enjoy and learn from solo performance can develop deeper, richer, different kinds of knowledge from working with each other in group performances. If the texts remain the center of your attention and interest, the kinds of knowledge you derive from group performance will enormously expand the limits of the literature. There is no one method of per-formance that is always best for all kinds of literature with all casts. Most good literature responds in different ways to the pressure put upon it by different performance techniques, yielding quite diverse and surprising discoveries under each different test. When a group probes a text with imagination and flexibility, the potential rewards are limitless.

Analyzing the Performance

Admitting that a group performance differs from a solo performance suggests that the criteria for evaluating the two kinds of performance must be different. This suggestion is both true and insufficient. Group performances are made up of several individual performers, and many of their responsibilities are not radically different from those we have discussed thus far. Each performer must understand the language of the text, must carefully attend to the tone, color, and imagery of the text, and must be able to be seen and heard without difficulty. In short, each performer must suggest the intellectual, emotional, and aesthetic entirety of that segment of the whole work that is his or her specific charge.

In a group performance, however, each individual executes these responsibilities in concert with other interpreters, under the direction of still another interpreter whose general vision and principal concern remains the work as a whole. The audience responds to the contributions of several individuals. Analyzing such performances often requires a preliminary sorting out of responsibilities and an attempt to understand, first of all, what was conceived before judging what was achieved.

This procedure does not greatly differ from the familiar process of analysis we have examined throughout this book — describing what was seen and heard and comparing that description with the text itself. In analyzing a group performance, however, some special questions arise that can apply to performances of narration, lyric poetry, dramatic prose, or any combination of these types. First, however, be sure that you are familiar with the specific kinds of questions that the efficient management of body and voice bring to mind (see Chapters 2 and 4). If you are unsure about problems in performing prose and narration, consult Chapter 6; if the performance analysis of drama still puzzles you, see Chapter 8; techniques for discussing the performance of poetry appear in Chapter 10. These questions all provide the foundation upon which we can build some questions for group performance.

How did the presentational nature of the Readers Theatre form, exhibit, or display the nature of the text? How was the literature the center of the production?

Did the various interpreters vocally and physically demonstrate significantly different aspects of the literature?

How did the individual performers contribute to the total impression of the event? Did they detract from the aesthetic entirety? How?

What dimensions of the text(s) seemed most fully demonstrated in performance? What dimensions needed to be clearer? Give specific examples.

How well did the individual performers project themselves into the audience? Was there sufficient opportunity for the audience to participate in the creation of the work?

Was the overall concept both clear and responsive to the text(s) performed?

In a Chamber Theatre performance of a story (or stories), was the narrator central or incidental to the action? How was the narrative presence demonstrated in performance? What dimensions were emphasized by the group? What dimensions were ignored or lost?

Was the distribution of dialogue lines appropriate to the characters? What was demonstrated when the characters spoke narrative lines? Were there clear and apparent reasons in the story?

How did the scenography clarify and refine the goals of the story? What functions did members of the group serve in making these goals clear during performance?

How did this adaptation of the story explore dimensions or levels a solo performer could not?

In a compiled script, did the components individually and collectively advance the progress and intention of the entire program? Did each component clearly and significantly contribute to a newer, fuller understanding of the topic? Was the beginning concise? Did the development cover all the major aspects? Was the climax clearly presented? Did the conclusion permit the audience to understand the full implications of the works and the topic?

Did any nonliterary material clearly serve the texts? Were the media used effectively? How did the media used clarify those dimensions of the work(s) inaccessible to the performers?

Was there sufficient variety in the selections and modes of performance to sustain the audience's interest? Did the components appropriately contrast tempo, rhythm, attitude, and persona?

Finally, what did you see and hear from the group that you could not have seen and heard from an individual? How did this enrich your understanding and appreciation of the material performed? How did the vividness of collected bodies and voices demonstrate the intentions of the literature?

Obviously, you can develop further questions that respond more accurately to any specific presentation. Remember that as the number of performers increases, the number of potential problems a director can face increases as well. Many experienced directors would say that the problems increase geometrically. Most of these same directors, however, would add that the rewards increase at the same rate, and that the realms of literature open to group performance almost always make the possibility of staging an attractive option. In that "almost" is all of the attraction and danger of the experience.

Selections for Analysis and Oral Interpretation

This astonishing tale combines many prominent themes in black folklore, including flying Africans, disappearing slaves, and magic hoes. The story testifies powerfully to the enduring value of *telling*, since those who could not fly kept the dream alive. Why not stage this story with the audience in the tale taking all the roles the storyteller devises?

The People Could Fly
Retold by VIRGINIA HAMILTON

They say the people could fly. Say that long ago in Africa, some of the people knew magic. And they would walk up on the air like climbin up on a gate. And they flew like blackbirds over the fields. Black, shiny wings flappin against the blue up there.

Then, many of the people were captured for Slavery. The ones that could fly shed their wings. They couldn't take their wings across the water on the slave ships. Too crowded, don't you know.

The folks were full of misery, then. Got sick with the up and down of the sea. So they forgot about flyin when they could no longer breathe the sweet scent of Africa.

Say the people who could fly kept their power, although they shed their wings. They kept their secret magic in the land of slavery. They looked the same as the other people from Africa who had been coming over, who had dark skin. Say you couldn't tell anymore one who could fly from one who couldn't.

One such who could was an old man, call him Toby. And standin tall, yet afraid, was a young woman who once had wings. Call her Sarah. Now Sarah carried a babe tied to her back. She trembled to be so hard worked and scorned.

The slaves labored in the fields from sunup to sundown. The owner of the slaves callin himself their Master. Say he was a hard lump of clay. A hard, glinty coal. A hard rock pile, wouldn't be moved. His Overseer on horseback pointed out the slaves who were slowin down. So the one called Driver cracked his whip over the slow ones to make them move faster. That whip was a slice-open cut of pain. So they did move faster. Had to.

Sarah hoed and chopped the row as the babe on her back slept.

Say the child grew hungry. That babe started up bawling too loud. Sarah couldn't stop to feed it. Couldn't stop to soothe and quiet it down. She let it cry. She didn't want to. She had no heart to croon to it.

"Keep that thing quiet," called the Overseer. He pointed his finger at the babe. The woman scrunched low. The Driver cracked his whip across the babe anyhow. The babe hollered like any hurt child, and the woman fell to the earth.

The old man that was there, Toby, came and helped her to her feet.

"I must go soon," she told him.

"Soon," he said.

Sarah couldn't stand up straight any longer. She was too weak. The sun burned her face. The babe cried and cried, "Pity me, oh, pity me," say it sounded like. Sarah was so sad and starvin, she sat down in the row.

"Get up, you black cow," called the Overseer. He pointed his hand, and the Driver's whip snarled around Sarah's legs. Her sack dress tore into rags. Her legs bled onto the earth. She couldn't get up.

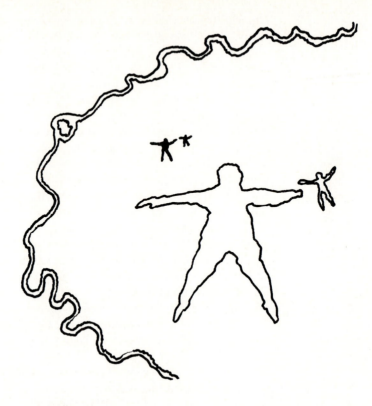

Toby was there where there was no one to help her and the babe.

"Now, before it's too late," panted Sarah. "Now, Father!"

"Yes, Daughter, the time is come," Toby answered. "Go, as you know how to go!"

He raised his arms, holding them out to her. "*Kum . . . yali, kum buba tambe,*" and more magic words, said so quickly, they sounded like whispers and sighs.

The young woman lifted one foot on the air. Then the other. She flew clumsily at first, with the child now held tightly in her arms. Then she felt the magic, the African mystery. Say she rose just as free as a bird. As light as a feather.

The Overseer rode after her, hollerin. Sarah flew over the fences. She flew over the woods. Tall trees could not snag her. Nor could the Overseer. She flew like an eagle now, until she was gone from sight. No one dared speak about it. Couldn't believe it. But it was, because they that was there saw that it was.

Say the next day was dead hot in the fields. A young man slave fell from the heat. The Driver come and whipped him. Toby come over and spoke words to the fallen one. The words of ancient Africa once heard are never remembered completely. The young man forgot them as soon as he heard them. They went way inside him. He got up and rolled over on the air. He rode it awhile. And he flew away.

Another and another fell from the heat. Toby was there. He cried out to the fallen and reached his arms out to them. *"Kum kunka yali, kum . . . tambe!"* Whispers and sighs. And they too rose on the air. They rode the hot breezes. The ones flyin were black and shinin sticks, wheelin above the head of the Overseer. They crossed the rows, the fields, the fences, the streams, and were away.

"Seize the old man!" cried the Overseer. "I heard him say the magic *words.* Seize him!"

The one callin himself Master come runnin. The Driver got his whip ready to curl around old Toby and tie him up. The slaveowner took his hip gun from its place. He meant to kill old, black Toby.

But Toby just laughed. Say he threw back his head and said, "Hee, hee! Don't you know who I am? Don't you know some of us in this field?" He said it to their faces. "We are ones who fly!"

And he sighed the ancient words that were a dark promise. He said them all around to the others in the field under the whip, ". . . *buba yali . . . buba tambe. . . ."*

There was a great outcryin. The bent backs straighted up. Old and young who were called slaves and could fly joined hands. Say like they would ring-sing. But they didn't shuffle in a circle. They didn't sing. They rose on the air. They flew in a flock that was black against the heavenly blue. Black crows or black shadows. It didn't matter, they went so high. Way above the plantation, way over the slavery land. Say they flew away to *Free-dom.*

And the old man, old Toby, flew behind them, takin care of them. He wasn't cryin. He wasn't laughin. He was the seer. His gaze fell on the plantation where the slaves who could not fly waited.

"Take us with you!" Their looks spoke it but they were afraid to shout it. Toby couldn't take them with him. Hadn't the time to teach them to fly. They must wait for a chance to run.

"Goodie-bye!" The old man called Toby spoke to them, poor souls! And he was flyin gone.

So they say. The Overseer told it. The one called Master said it was a lie, a trick of the light. The Driver kept his mouth shut.

The slaves who could not fly told about the people who could fly to their children. When they were free. When they sat close before the fire in the free land, they told it. They did so love firelight and *Free-dom,* and tellin.

They say that the children of the ones who could not fly told their children. And now, me, I have told it to you.

▌ How did you keep alive the overpowering tension and fear when the Master, Overseer, and Driver were present?

This tale — familiar although told in quite a startling way — is drawn from Anne Sexton's *Transformations*. Once again, the audience in the work occupies a central position. Be sure to personify the curiously contemporary narrator. Can you determine the fulcrum? Why is it where it is?

Cinderella

ANNE SEXTON

You always read about it:
the plumber with twelve children
who wins the Irish Sweepstakes.
From toilets to riches.
That story.

Or the nursemaid,
some luscious sweet from Denmark
who captures the oldest son's heart.
From diapers to Dior.
That story.

Or a milkman who serves the wealthy,
eggs, cream, butter, yogurt, milk,
the white truck like an ambulance
who goes into real estate
and makes a pile.
From homogenized to martinis at lunch.

Or the charwoman
who is on the bus when it cracks up
and collects enough from the insurance.
From mops to Bonwit Teller.
That story.

Once
the wife of a rich man was on her deathbed
and she said to her daughter Cinderella:
Be devout. Be good. Then I will smile
down from heaven in the seam of a cloud.
The man took another wife who had
two daughters, pretty enough
but with hearts like blackjacks.
Cinderella was their maid.
She slept on the sooty hearth each night
and walked around looking like Al Jolson.
Her father brought presents home from town,

jewels and gowns for the other women
but the twig of a tree for Cinderella.
She planted that twig on her mother's grave
and it grew to a tree where a white dove sat.
Whenever she wished for anything the dove
would drop it like an egg upon the ground.
The bird is important, my dears, so heed him.

Next came the ball, as you all know.
It was a marriage market.
The prince was looking for a wife.
All but Cinderella were preparing
and gussying up for the big event.
Cinderella begged to go too.
Her stepmother threw a dish of lentils
into the cinders and said: Pick them
up in an hour and you shall go.
The white dove brought all his friends;
all the warm wings of the fatherland came,
and picked up the lentils in a jiffy.
No, Cinderella, said the stepmother,
you have no clothes and cannot dance.
That's the way with stepmothers.

Cinderella went to the tree at the grave
and cried forth like a gospel singer:
Mama! Mama! My turtledove,
send me to the prince's ball!
The bird dropped down a golden dress
and delicate little gold slippers.
Rather a large package for a simple bird.
So she went. Which is no surprise.
Her stepmother and sisters didn't
recognize her without her cinder face
and the prince took her hand on the spot
and danced with no other the whole day.

As nightfall came she thought she'd better
get home. The prince walked her home
and she disappeared into the pigeon house
and although the prince took an axe and broke
it open she was gone. Back to her cinders.
These events repeated themselves for three days.
However on the third day the prince
covered the palace steps with cobbler's wax

and Cinderella's gold shoe stuck upon it.
Now he would find whom the shoe fit
and find his strange dancing girl for keeps.
He went to their house and the two sisters
were delighted because they had lovely feet.
The eldest went into a room to try the slipper on
but her big toe got in the way so she simply
sliced it off and put on the slipper.
The prince rode away with her until the white dove
told him to look at the blood pouring forth.
That is the way with amputations.
They don't just heal up like a wish.
The other sister cut off her heel
but the blood told as blood will.
The prince was getting tired.
He began to feel like a shoe salesman.
But he gave it one last try.
This time Cinderella fit into the shoe
like a love letter into its envelope.

At the wedding ceremony
the two sisters came to curry favor
and the white dove pecked their eyes out.
Two hollow spots were left
like soup spoons.

Cinderella and the prince
lived, they say, happily ever after,
like two dolls in a museum case
never bothered by diapers or dust,
never arguing over the timing of an egg,
never telling the same story twice,
never getting a middle-aged spread,
their darling smiles pasted on for eternity.
Regular Bobbsey Twins.
That story.

▎ Is the narrator's body in the same world as the characters'
  bodies? Did your audience see that?

A garbage collector who muses on his life in Omar Khayyám stanzas? The resilient irony of this speaker — even his blood type is negative — rescues what could be a sentimental deluge. See what happens when a group takes on the shapes, shadows, and spectres who variously confront the speaker. Keep the poem whole!

B Negative

X. J. KENNEDY

M/60/5 FT 4/W PROT

You know it's April by the falling-off
In coughdrop boxes — fewer people cough —
   By daisies' first white eyeballs in the grass
And every dawn more underthings cast off.

Though plumtrees stretch recovered boughs to us
And doubledecked in green, the downtown bus,
   Love in one season — so your stab-pole tells —
Beds down, and buds, and is deciduous.

Now set down burlap bag. In pigeon talk
The wobbling pigeon flutes on the sidewalk,
   Struts on the breeze and clicks leisurely wings
As if the corn he ate grew on a stalk.

So plump he topples where he tries to stand,
He pecks my shoelaces, come to demand
   Another sack, another fifteen cents,
And yet — who else will eat out of my hand?

It used to be that when I laid my head
And body with it down by you in bed
   You did not turn from me nor fall to sleep
But turn to fall between my arms instead

And now I lay bifocals down. My feet
Forget the twist that brought me to your street.
   I can't make out your face for steamed-up glass
Nor quite call back your outline on the sheet.

I know how, bent to a movie magazine,
The hobo's head lights up, and from its screen
   Imagined bosoms in slow motion bloom
And no director interrupts the scene:

I used to purchase in the Automat
A cup of soup and fan it with my hat
    Until a stern voice from the changebooth crashed
Like nickels: *Gentlemen do not do that.*

Spring has no household, no abiding heat,
Pokes forth no bud from branches of concrete,
    Nothing to touch you, nothing you can touch —
The snow, at least, keeps track of people's feet.

The springer spaniel and the buoyant hare
Seem half at home reclining in mid-air
    But Lord, the times I've leaped the way they do
And looked round for a foothold — in despair.

The subway a little cheaper than a room,
I browse the *News* — or so the guards assume —
    And there half-waking, tucked in funny sheets,
I hurtle within my mile-a-minute womb.

Down streets that wake up earlier than wheels
The routed spirit flees on dusty heels
    And in the soft fire of a muscatel
Sits up, puts forth its fingertips, and feels —

Down streets so deep the sun can't vault their walls,
Where one-night wives make periodic calls,
    Where cat steals stone where rat makes off with child
And lyre and lute lie down under three balls,

Down blocks in sequence, fact by separate fact,
The human integers add and subtract
    Till in a cubic room in some hotel
You wake one day to find yourself abstract.

And turn a knob and hear a voice: *Insist
On Jiffy Blades, they're tender to the wrist* —
    Then static, then a squawk as if your hand
Had shut some human windpipe with a twist.

I know how, lurking under trees by dark,
Poor loony stranglers out to make their mark
    Reach forth shy hands to touch a woman's hair —
I pick up after them in Central Park.

▐ How did your group's voices demonstrate the sounds that fill this persona?

▐ This speaker is very active: could you stage the poem with a chorus and a single reader?

This excerpt suggests the torturous internal life of a soldier in Vietnam. It seems as if several different forces are battling within James Bombard's mind. Why not personify each of these agents and let them together demonstrate the war within this soldier that mirrors the war surrounding him?

FROM *Everything We Had*

AL SANTOLI

James Bombard
Rifle Platoon Leader
101st Airborne Division
Phan Rang
December 1967 – February 1968

I can remember sitting at McCord Air Base before I went to Vietnam with a friend of mine, Hunter Shotwell, he and his wife. He was a West Pointer and had been to Vietnam before the build-up as an adviser. He was from Massachusetts. He had a beautiful wife and a little child, it was beautiful. I said to him, "Hunter, why are you going back? You're going to get out of the Army." He wanted to be a lawyer. He wanted to set his life in motion. And he said, "I'm going back because I am a soldier." I said, "But you're leaving the military." He said, "But I believe in the nation and I believe that this is my duty. I went to West Point. I am leaving, but I must shoulder the responsibility of leadership." Hunter was a patrician and from a good family. Hunter and I and his wife proceeded to have a few beers and we were pretty mellow when we left together that day. We had served together in the 82nd, we were very close. He had been a hockey player and I was a hockey player, and we had a lot to talk about. He represented everything that was good about the country, the future of the country — it was bright, he was bright, he was handsome. He was everything that our generation stood for.

Right after the Tet offensive I found out that Hunter Shotwell had been killed. And I couldn't help but feel that had been such a loss, such a waste. I had seen other people killed, I had experienced the loss of many friends closer than Hunter was to me, guys I was in the field with . . . But somehow his death to me was the most significant, the most moving. Somehow I saw that he had served, he had shouldered his responsibility and yet he had done it again. The nation shouldn't have asked him to do it again. He represented to me what was good and right in the nation. And he was destroyed. I thought of his little child and his wife, what that did to them. And with that death and many like his, with each death a little bit of the fiber of what was good in this country was being destroyed. That's what bothered me.

I didn't see Hunter Shotwell get killed, but I felt like I had. There were many people close to us in the field who were killed. Doc Brown. I remember Doc Brown was a medic who always read philosophy and never took a bath and would always tell everybody to clean up and wash for infection: "Do as I say, not as I do." He would read Saint Thomas and he was a confirmed atheist and he would philosophize. But in the field he was tremendously skilled as a medic and also very daring, and he was killed the day I was wounded. He was moving to a man and he was wounded and killed. Here was a man who was an intellectual, a philosopher, a thinker, and he was there. Probably not agreeing with what was happening. But somehow, again, the good was being destroyed.

I think we lost a lot more in Vietnam than the troops we lost. We really didn't lose too many battles. When we met the enemy we usually won. What did we win? We lost more than we won, especially the aftermath of the war. Having served in Vietnam, having served in the infantry, having been wounded, feeling the bullet rip into your flesh, the shrapnel tear the flesh from your bones and the blood run down your leg, and feeling like you're gonna piss in your pants and it's the blood running down your leg. To put your hand on your chest and to come away with your hand red with your own blood, and to feel it running out of your eyes and out of your mouth, and seeing it spurt out of your guts, realizing you were dying . . .

I had been hit the second time by a direct hit from a mortar. I was ripped open from the top of my head to the tip of my toes. I had forty-five holes in me and I was bleeding everywhere. I can remember saying to myself, "My God, I'm dying." And at that split second, I was calm. Completely, completely at peace with myself.

▌ Remember that this is the recounting of one human being. Did your group maintain his integrity?

Simon and Grusha pledged themselves to each other before Simon went to war. Grusha rescues the Governor's abandoned infant, Michael, and together they begin an uncertain, event-filled life. And now, of course, Simon returns. Keep the Singer close to the two — and don't forget the river that separates them. Their poignant formality increases the tension in the scene.

FROM ***The Caucasian Chalk Circle, Section III***

BERTOLT BRECHT

MICHAEL *runs away. The children run after him.* **GRUSHA** *laughs, following them with her eyes. On looking back, she sees* **SIMON SHASHAVA** *standing on the opposite bank. He wears a shabby uniform.*

GRUSHA: Simon!

SIMON: Is that Grusha Vashnadze?

GRUSHA: Simon!

SIMON (*formally*): A good morning to the young lady. I hope she is well.

GRUSHA (*getting up gaily and bowing low*): A good morning to the soldier. God be thanked he has returned in good health.

SIMON: They found better fish, so they didn't eat me, said the haddock.

GRUSHA: Courage, said the kitchen boy. Good luck, said the hero.

SIMON: How are things here? Was the winter bearable? The neighbor considerate?

GRUSHA: The winter was a trifle rough, the neighbor as usual, Simon.

SIMON: May one ask if a certain person still dips her toes in the water when rinsing the linen?

GRUSHA: The answer is no. Because of the eyes in the bushes.

SIMON: The young lady is speaking of soldiers. Here stands a paymaster.

GRUSHA: A job worth twenty piasters?

SIMON: And lodgings.

GRUSHA (*with tears in her eyes*): Behind the barracks under the date trees.

SIMON: Yes, there. A certain person has kept her eyes open.

GRUSHA: She has, Simon.

SIMON: And has not forgotten? (**GRUSHA** *shakes her head.*) So the door is still on its hinges as they say? (**GRUSHA** *looks at him in silence and shakes her head again.*) What's this? Is anything not as it should be?

GRUSHA: Simon Shashava, I can never return to Nuka. Something has happened.

SIMON: What can have happened?

GRUSHA: For one thing, I knocked an Ironshirt down.

SIMON: Grusha Vashnadze must have had her reasons for that.

GRUSHA: Simon Shashava, I am no longer called what I used to be called.

SIMON (*after a pause*): I do not understand.

GRUSHA: When do women change their names, Simon? Let me explain. Nothing stands between us. Everything is just as it was. You must believe that.

SIMON: Nothing stands between us and yet there's something?

GRUSHA: How can I explain it so fast and with the stream between us? Couldn't you cross the bridge there?

SIMON: Maybe it's no longer necessary.

GRUSHA: It is very necessary. Come over on this side, Simon, Quick!

SIMON: Does the young lady wish to say someone has come too late?

GRUSHA *looks up at him in despair, her face streaming with tears.* **SIMON** *stares before him. He picks up a piece of wood and starts cutting it.*

SINGER:

So many words are said, so many left unsaid.
The soldier has come.
Where he comes from, he does not say.
Hear what he thought and did not say:
"The battle began, gray at dawn, grew bloody at noon.
The first man fell in front of me, the second behind me, the
        third at my side.
I trod on the first, left the second behind, the third was run
        through by the captain.
One of my brothers died by steel, the other by smoke.
My neck caught fire, my hands froze in my gloves, my toes in
        my socks.
I fed on aspen buds, I drank maple juice, I slept on stone,
        in water."

SIMON: I see a cap in the grass. Is there a little one already?

GRUSHA: There is, Simon. There's no keeping *that* from you. But please don't worry, it is not mine.

SIMON: When the wind once starts to blow, they say, it blows through every cranny. The wife need say no more. (**GRUSHA** *looks into her lap and is silent.*)

SINGER:

There was yearning but there was no waiting.
The oath is broken. Neither could say why.
Hear what she thought but did not say:
"While you fought in the battle, soldier,

The bloody battle, the bitter battle
I found a helpless infant
I had not the heart to destroy him
I had to care for a creature that was lost
I had to stoop for breadcrumbs on the floor
I had to break myself for that which was not mine
That which was other people's.
Someone must help!
For the little tree needs water
The lamb loses its way when the shepherd is asleep
And its cry is unheard!"

SIMON: Give me back the cross I gave you. Better still, throw it in the stream. (*He turns to go.*)

GRUSHA (*getting up*): Simon Shashava, don't go away! He isn't mine! He isn't mine! (*She hears the children calling.*) What's the matter, children?

VOICES: Soldiers! And they're taking Michael away!

GRUSHA *stands aghast as two* **IRONSHIRTS,** *with* **MICHAEL** *between them, come toward her.*

ONE OF THE IRONSHIRTS: Are you Grusha? (*She nods.*) Is this your child?

GRUSHA: Yes. (**SIMON** *goes.*) Simon!

IRONSHIRT: We have orders, in the name of the law, to take this child, found in your custody, back to the city. It is suspected that the child is Michael Abashwili, son and heir of the late Governor Georgi Abashwili, and his wife, Natella Abashwili. Here is the document and the seal. (*They lead the* **CHILD** *away.*)

GRUSHA (*running after them, shouting*): Leave him here. Please! He's mine!

▮ How did your group underline the physical separation between the characters?

▮ Did your Singer sing?

The following three poems owe at least as much to their typographic layout as to their words. They require flexible bodies and voices. In Roger McGough's poem, be sure your group physically shows the line separating the couple. Play tennis with the words.

40 – Love

ROGER McGOUGH

middle	aged
couple	playing
ten	nis
when	the
game	ends
and	they
go	home
the	net
will	still
be	be
tween	them

▋ How did your group let the audience see the net and hear the rackets?

Note how the stems of the forsythia in this poem telegraph a kind of code. Can a chorus of voices suggest that sound?

Forsythia

MARY ELLEN SOLT

FORSYTHIA

How did your bodies and voices suggest the delicacy of the forsythia? How can this delicacy also "insist action"?

Reinhard Döhl offers an elusive intruder in his apple. Consider the apple as a symbol in Western mythology before you plan your group performance.

Apfel

REINHARD DÖHL

▌ Did your audience meet the surprise visitor the way the silent reader does? How?

The distinctive power of Ntozake Shange's verse arises from the flexibility of her language and the commitment of her experiences. If you take time to find the music the characters mention, you will see how, as in good jazz, the rhythms of the lines correspond to and take off from their musical models. Bodies inextricably linked to voices characterize this passage.

FROM *For Colored Girls Who Have Considered Suicide/When the Rainbow Is Enuf*

NTOZAKE SHANGE

The Dells singing "Stay" comes in and all of the ladies except the lady in blue join in and sing along.

LADY IN BLUE:
you gave it up in a buick?
LADY IN YELLOW:
yeh, and honey, it was wonderful.
LADY IN GREEN:
we used to do it all up in the dark
in the corners. . .
LADY IN BLUE:
some niggah sweating all over you.
LADY IN RED:
it was good!
LADY IN BLUE:
i never did like to grind.
LADY IN YELLOW:
what other kind of dances are there?
LADY IN BLUE:
mambo, bomba, merengue

when i waz sixteen i ran off to the south bronx
cuz i waz gonna meet up wit willie colon
& dance all the time
            mamba bomba merengue
LADY IN YELLOW:
do you speak spanish?
LADY IN BLUE:
olà
my papa thot he was puerto rican & we wda been
cept we waz just reglar niggahs wit hints of spanish
so off i made it to this 36 hour marathon dance
con salsa con ricardo
'suggggggggggar' ray on southern blvd
next door to this fotografi place

jammed wit burial weddin & communion relics
next door to la real ideal genuine spanish barber
            up up up up up stairs & stairs & lotsa hallway
wit my colored new jersey self
didn't know what anybody waz saying
cept if dancin waz proof of origin
                i was jibarita herself that nite
& the next day
i kept smilin & right on steppin
if he cd lead i waz ready to dance
if he cdnt lead
i caught this attitude
                i'd seen rosa do
& wd not be bothered
i waz twirlin hippin givin much quik feet
& bein a mute cute colored puerto rican
til saturday afternoon when the disc-jockey say
'SORRY FOLKS WILLIE COLON AINT GONNA MAKE IT TODAY'

& alla my niggah temper came outta control
& i wdnt dance wit nobody
& i talked english loud
& i love you more than i waz mad
un huh uh huh
more than more than

when i discovered archie shepp & subtle blues
doncha know i wore out the magic of juju
heroically resistin being possessed

ooooooooooooooh the sounds
sneakin in under age to slug's
to stare ata real 'artiste'
& every word outta imamu's mouth waz gospel
& if jesus cdnt play a horn like shepp
waznt no need for colored folks to bear no cross as all

& poem is my thank-you for music
& i love you more than poem
more than aureliano buendia loved macondo
more than hector lavoe loved himself
more than the lady loved gardenias
more than celia loves cuba or graciela loves el son
more than the flamingoes shoo-do-n-doo-wah love bein pretty

oyè négro
te amo mas que   te amo mas que
when you play
yr flute
EVERYONE (*very softly*):
te amo mas que   te amo mas que

LADY IN RED:
without any assistance or guidance from you
i have loved you assiduously for 8 months 2 wks & a day
i have been stood up four times
i've left 7 packages on yr doorstep
forty poems 2 plants & 3 handmade notecards i left
town so i cd send to you have been no help to me
on my job
you call at 3:00 in the mornin on weekdays
so i cd drive 27½ miles cross the bay before i go to work
charmin charmin
but you are of no assistance
i want you to know
this waz an experiment
to see how selfish i cd be
if i wd really carry on to snare a possible lover
if i waz capable of debasin my self for the love of another
if i cd stand not being wanted

when i wanted to be wanted
& i cannot
so
with no further assistance & no guidance from you
i am endin this affair

this note is attached to a plant
i've been waterin since the day i met you
you may water it
yr damn self
LADY IN ORANGE:
i dont wanna write
in english or spanish
i wanna sing   make you dance
like the bata   dance   scream
twitch hips wit me cuz
i done forgot all abt words
aint got no definitions
i wanna whirl
            with you

Music starts, "Che Che Cole" by Willie Colon. Everyone starts to dance.

our whole body
wrapped like a ripe mango
ramblin whippin thru space
on the corner in the park
where the rug useta be
let willie colon take you out
swing your head
push your leg to the moon with me

i'm on the lower east side
in new york city
and i can't   i can't
talk witchu no more
LADY IN YELLOW:
we gotta dance to keep from crying
LADY IN BROWN:
we gotta dance to keep from dying
LADY IN RED:
so come on
LADY IN BROWN:
come on

LADY IN PURPLE:
come on
LADY IN ORANGE:
hold yr head like it was ruby sapphire
i'm a poet
who writes in english
come to share the worlds witchu
EVERYONE:
come to share our worlds witchu
we come here to be dancin
       to be dancin
     to be dancin
   baya

There is a sudden light change, all of the ladies react as if they had been struck in the face. The lady in green and the lady in yellow run out up left, the lady in orange runs out the left volm, the lady in brown runs out up right.

▌ How did your group permit interaction during individual speeches? Why did they do it the way they did?

This eerie, spellbinding tale depends on rhyme and meter for many of its effects. It stages beautifully if you allow Rossetti's language full measure *and* if the performers playing Laura and Lizzie closely attend to the tone color and imagery. Keep the Goblins alive — they are no harmless mirage to these women. Where is the narrator throughout the torture scene?

Goblin Market
CHRISTINA GEORGINA ROSSETTI

Morning and evening
Maids heard the goblins cry:
"Come buy our orchard fruits,
Come buy, come buy:
Apples and quinces,
Lemons and oranges,
Plump unpecked cherries,
Melons and raspberries,
Bloom-down-cheeked peaches,
Swart-headed mulberries,
Wild free-born cranberries,
Crab-apples, dewberries,
Pine-apples, blackberries,

Apricots, strawberries; —
All ripe together
In summer weather, —
Morns that pass by,
Fair eves that fly;
Come buy, come buy;
Our grapes fresh from the vine,
Pomegranates full and fine,
Dates and sharp bullaces,
Rare pears and greengages,
Damsons and bilberries,
Taste them and try:
Currants and gooseberries,
Bright-fire-like barberries,
Figs to fill your mouth,
Citrons from the South,
Sweet to tongue and sound to eye;
Come buy, come buy."

Evening by evening
Among the brookside rushes,
Laura bowed her head to hear,
Lizzie veiled her blushes:
Crouching close together
In the cooling weather,
With clasping arms and cautioning lips,
With tingling cheeks and fingertips.
"Lie close," Laura said,
Pricking up her golden head:
"We must not look at goblin men,
We must not buy their fruits:
Who knows upon what soil they fed
Their hungry thirsty roots?"
"Come buy," call the goblins
Hobbling down the glen.
"Oh," cried Lizzie, "Laura, Laura,
You should not peep at goblin men."
Lizzie covered up her eyes,
Covered close lest they should look;
Laura reared her glossy head,
And whispered like the restless brook:
"Look, Lizzie, look, Lizzie,
Down the glen tramp little men.
One hauls a basket,

One bears a plate,
One lugs a golden dish
Of many pounds' weight.
How fair the vine must grow
Whose grapes are so luscious;
How warm the wind must blow
Through those fruit bushes."
"No," said Lizzie: "No, no, no;
Their offers should not charm us,
Their evil gifts would harm us."
She thrust a dimpled finger
In each ear, shut eyes and ran:
Curious Laura chose to linger
Wondering at each merchant man.
One had a cat's face,
One whisked a tail,
One tramped at a rat's pace,
One crawled like a snail,
One like a wombat prowled obtuse and furry,
One like a ratel tumbled hurry skurry.
She heard a voice like voice of doves
Cooing all together:
They sounded kind and full of loves
In the pleasant weather.

Laura stretched her gleaming neck
Like a rush-imbedded swan,
Like a lily from the beck,
Like a moonlit poplar branch,
Like a vessel at the launch
When its last restraint is gone.

Backwards up the mossy glen
Turned and trooped the goblin men,
With their shrill repeated cry,
"Come buy, come buy."
When they reached where Laura was
They stood stock still upon the moss,
Leering at each other,
Brother with queer brother;
Signalling each other,
Brother with sly brother.
One set his basket down,
One reared his plate;

One began to weave a crown
Of tendrils, leaves, and rough nuts brown
(Men sell not such in any town);
One heaved the golden weight
Of dish and fruit to offer her:
"Come buy, come buy," was still their cry.
Laura stared but did not stir,
Longed but had no money.
The whisk-tailed merchant bade her taste
In tones as smooth as honey,
The cat-faced purr'd,
The rat-paced spoke a word
Of welcome, and the snail-paced even was heard;
One parrot-voiced and jolly
Cried "Pretty Goblin" still for "Pretty Polly";
One whistled like a bird.

But sweet-tooth Laura spoke in haste:
"Good Folk, I have no coin;
To take were to purloin:
I have no copper in my purse,
I have no silver either,
And all my gold is on the furze
That shakes in windy weather
Above the rusty heather."
"You have much gold upon your head,"
They answered all together:
"Buy from us with a golden curl."
She clipped a precious golden lock,
She dropped a tear more rare than pearl,
Then sucked their fruit globes fair or red.
Sweeter than honey from the rock,
Stronger than man-rejoicing wine,
Clearer than water flowed that juice;
She never tasted such before,
How should it cloy with length of use?
She sucked and sucked and sucked the more
Fruits which that unknown orchard bore;
She sucked until her lips were sore;
Then flung the emptied rinds away
But gathered up one kernel stone,
And knew not was it night or day
As she turned home alone.

Lizzie met her at the gate
Full of wise upbraidings:
"Dear, you should not stay so late,
Twilight is not good for maidens;
Should not loiter in the glen
In the haunts of goblin men.
Do you not remember Jeanie,
How she met them in the moonlight,
Took their gifts both choice and many,
Ate their fruits and wore their flowers
Plucked from bowers
When summer ripens at all hours?
But ever in the noonlight
She pined and pined away;
Sought them by night and day,
Found them no more, but dwindled and grew grey;
Then fell with the first snow,
While to this day no grass will grow
Where she lies low:
I planted daisies there a year ago
That never blow.
You should not loiter so."
"Nay, hush," said Laura:
"Nay, hush, my sister:
I ate and ate my fill,
Yet my mouth waters still:
To-morrow night I will
Buy more;" and kissed her.
"Have done with sorrow;
I'll bring you plums to-morrow
Fresh on their mother twigs,
Cherries worth getting;
You cannot think what figs
My teeth have met in,
What melons icy-cold
Piled on a dish of gold
Too huge for me to hold,
What peaches with a velvet nap,
Pellucid grapes without one seed:
Odorous indeed must be the mead
Whereon they grow, and pure the wave they drink
With lilies at the brink,
And sugar-sweet their sap."

Golden head by golden head,
Like two pigeons in one nest
Folded in each other's wings,
They lay down in their curtained bed:
Like two blossoms on one stem,
Like two flakes of new-fall'n snow,
Like two wands of ivory
Tipped with gold for awful kings.
Moon and stars gazed in at them,
Wind sang to them lullaby,
Lumbering owls forebore to fly,
Once discerning even one goblin
Racing, whisking, tumbling, hobbling —
Let alone the herds
That used to tramp along the glen,
In groups or single,
Of brisk fruit-merchant men.

Till Lizzie urged, "O Laura, come;
I hear the fruit-call, but I dare not look:
You should not loiter longer at this brook:
Come with me home.
The stars rise, the moon bends her arc,
Each glow-worm winks her spark,
Let us get home before the night grows dark:
For clouds may gather
Though this is summer weather,
Put out the lights and drench us through;
Then if we lost our way what should we do?"

Laura turned cold as stone
To find her sister heard that cry alone,
That goblin cry,
"Come buy our fruits, come buy."
Must she then buy no more such dainty fruit?
Must she no more such succous pasture find,
Gone deaf and blind?
Her tree of life drooped from the root:
She said not one word in her heart's sore ache:
But peering thro' the dimness, nought discerning,
Trudged home, her pitcher dripping all the way;
So crept to bed, and lay
Silent till Lizzie slept;
Then sat up in a passionate yearning,

And gnashed her teeth for baulked desire, and wept
As if her heart would break.

Day after day, night after night,
Laura kept watch in vain
In sullen silence of exceeding pain.
She never caught again the goblin cry,
"Come buy, come buy;" —
She never spied the goblin men
Hawking their fruits along the glen:
But when the noon waxed bright
Her hair grew thin and grey;
She dwindled, as the fair full moon doth turn
To swift decay and burn
Her fire away.

One day remembering her kernel-stone
She set it by a wall that faced the south;
Dewed it with tears, hoped for a root,
Watched for a waxing shoot,
But there came none.
It never saw the sun,
It never felt the trickling moisture run:
While with sunk eyes and faded mouth
She dreamed of melons, as a traveller sees
False waves in desert drouth
With shade of leaf-crowned trees,
And burns the thirstier in the sandful breeze.

She no more swept the house,
Tended the fowls or cows,
Fetched honey, kneaded cakes of wheat,
Brought water from the brook:
But sat down listless in the chimney-nook
And would not eat.

Tender Lizzie could not bear
To watch her sister's cankerous care,
Yet not to share.
She night and morning
Caught the goblins' cry:
"Come buy our orchard fruits,
Come buy, come buy:" —
Beside the brook, along the glen,

She heard the tramp of goblin men,
The voice and stir
Poor Laura could not hear;
Longed to buy fruit to comfort her,
But feared to pay too dear.
She thought of Jeanie in her grave,
Who should have been a bride;
But who for joys brides hope to have
Fell sick and died
In her gay prime,
In earliest winter time,
With the first glazing rime,
With the first snow-fall of crisp winter time.

Till Laura dwindling
Seemed knocking at Death's door.
Then Lizzie weighed no more
Better and worse;
But put a silver penny in her purse,
Kissed Laura, crossed the heath with clumps of furze
At twilight, halted by the brook:
And for the first time in her life
Began to listen and look.

Laughed every goblin
When they spied her peeping:
Came towards her hobbling,
Flying, running, leaping,
Puffing and blowing,
Chuckling, clapping, crowing,
Clucking and gobbling,
Mopping and mowing,
Full of airs and graces,
Pulling wry faces,
Demure grimaces
Cat-like and rat-like,
Ratel- and wombat-like,
Snail-paced in a hurry,
Parrot-voiced and whistler,
Helter skelter, hurry skurry,
Chattering like magpies,
Fluttering like pigeons,
Gliding like fishes, —
Hugged her and kissed her:

Squeezed and caressed her:
Stretched up their dishes,
Panniers, and plates:
"Look at our apples
Russet and dun,
Bob at our cherries,
Bite at our peaches,
Citrons and dates,
Grapes for the asking,
Pears red with basking
Out in the sun,
Plums on their twigs;
Pluck them and suck them, —
Pomegranates, figs."

"Good folk," said Lizzie,
Mindful of Jeanie:
"Give me much and many:"
Held out her apron,
Tossed them her penny.
"Nay, take a seat with us,
Honour and eat with us,"
They answered grinning:
"Our feast is but beginning.
Night yet is early,
Warm and dew-pearly,
Wakeful and starry:
Such fruits as these
No man can carry;
Half their bloom would fly,
Half their dew would dry,
Half their flavour would pass by.
Sit down and feast with us,
Be welcome guest with us,
Cheer you and rest with us." —
"Thank you," said Lizzie: "But one waits
At home alone for me:
So without further parleying,
If you will not sell me any
Of your fruits though much and many,
Give me back my silver penny
I tossed you for a fee." —
They began to scratch their pates,
No longer wagging, purring,

But visibly demurring,
Grunting and snarling.
One called her proud,
Cross-grained, uncivil;
Their tones waxed loud,
Their looks were evil.
Lashing their tails
They trod and hustled her,
Elbowed and jostled her,
Clawed with their nails,
Barking, mewing, hissing, mocking,
Tore her gown and soiled her stocking,
Twitched her hair out by the roots,
Stamped upon her tender feet,
Held her hands and squeezed their fruits
Against her mouth to make her eat.

White and golden Lizzie stood,
Like a lily in a flood, —
Like a rock of blue-veined stone
Lashed by tides obstreperously, —
Like a beacon left alone
In a hoary roaring sea,
Sending up a golden fire, —
Like a fruit-crowned orange-tree
White with blossoms honey-sweet
Sore beset by wasp and bee, —
Like a royal virgin town
Topped with gilded dome and spire
Close beleaguered by a fleet
Mad to tug her standard down.

One may lead a horse to water,
Twenty cannot make him drink.
Though the goblins cuffed and caught her,
Coaxed and fought her,
Bullied and besought her,
Scratched her, pinched her black as ink,
Kicked and knocked her,
Mauled and mocked her,
Lizzie uttered not a word;
Would not open lip from lip
Lest they should cram a mouthful in:
But laughed in heart to feel the drip
Of juice that syruped all her face,

And lodged in dimples of her chin,
And streaked her neck which quaked like curd.
At last the evil people,
Worn out by her resistance,
Flung back her penny, kicked their fruit
Along whichever road they took,
Not leaving root or stone or shoot;
Some writhed into the ground,
Some dived into the brook
With ring and ripple,
Some scudded on the gale without a sound,
Some vanished in the distance.

In a smart, ache, tingle,
Lizzie went her way;
Knew not was it night or day;
Sprang up the bank, tore thro' the furze,
Threaded copse and dingle,
And heard her penny jingle
Bouncing in her purse, —
Its bounce was music to her ear.
She ran and ran
As if she feared some goblin man
Dogged her with gibe or curse
Or something worse:
But not one goblin skurried after,
Nor was she pricked by fear;
The kind heart made her windy-paced
That urged her home quite out of breath with haste
And inward laughter.

She cried, "Laura," up the garden,
"Did you miss me?
Come and kiss me.
Never mind my bruises,
Hug me, kiss me, suck my juices
Squeezed from goblin fruits for you,
Goblin pulp and goblin dew.
Eat me, drink me, love me;
Laura, make much of me;
For your sake I have braved the glen
And had to do with goblin merchant men."

Laura started from her chair,
Flung her arms up in the air,

Clutched her hair:
"Lizzie, Lizzie, have you tasted
For my sake the fruit forbidden?
Must your light like mine be hidden,
Your young life like mine be wasted,
Undone in mine undoing,
And ruined in my ruin,
Thirsty, cankered, goblin-ridden?" —
She clung about her sister,
Kissed and kissed and kissed her:
Tears once again
Refreshed her shrunken eyes,
Dropping like rain
After long sultry drouth;
Shaking with aguish fear, and pain,
She kissed and kissed her with a hungry mouth.

Her lips began to scorch,
That juice was wormwood to her tongue,
She loathed the feast:
Writhing as one possessed she leaped and sung,
Rent all her robe, and wrung
Her hands in lamentable haste,
And beat her breast.
Her locks streamed like the torch
Borne by a racer at full speed,
Or like the mane of horses in their flight,
Or like an eagle when she stems the light
Straight toward the sun,
Or like a caged thing freed,
Or like a flying flag when armies run.

Swift fire spread through her veins, knocked at her heart,
Met the fire smouldering there
And overbore its lesser flame;
She gorged on bitterness without a name:
Ah fool, to choose such part
Of soul-consuming care!
Sense failed in the mortal strife:
Like the watch-tower of a town
Which an earthquake shatters down,
Like a lightning-stricken mast,
Like a wind-uprooted tree
Spun about,

Like a foam-topped waterspout
Cast down headlong in the sea,
She fell at last;
Pleasure past and anguish past,
Is it death or is it life?

Life out of death.
That night long Lizzie watched by her,
Counted her pulse's flagging stir,
Felt for her breath,
Held water to her lips, and cooled her face
With tears and fanning leaves.
But when the first birds chirped about their eaves
And early reapers plodded to the place
Of golden sheaves,
And dew-wet grass
Bowed in the morning winds so brisk to pass,
And new buds with new day
Opened of cup-like lilies on the stream,
Laura awoke as from a dream,
Laughed in the innocent old way,
Hugged Lizzie but not twice or thrice;
Her gleaming locks showed not one thread of grey,
Her breath was sweet as May,
And light danced in her eyes.

Days, weeks, months, years
Afterwards, when both were wives
With children of their own;
Their mother-hearts beset with fears,
Their lives bound up in tender lives;
Laura would call the little ones
And tell them of her early prime,
Those pleasant days long gone
Of not-returning time:
Would talk about the haunted glen,
The wicked quaint fruit-merchant men,
Their fruits like honey to the throat
But poison in the blood
(Men sell not such in any town):
Would tell them how her sister stood
In deadly peril to do her good,
And win the fiery antidote:
Then joining hands to little hands

Would bid them cling together, —
"For there is no friend like a sister
In calm or stormy weather;
To cheer one on the tedious way,
To fetch one if one goes astray,
To lift one if one totters down,
To strengthen whilst one stands."

▌ How did your group suggest the opulence of the opening? the
terror of the climax? the internal and external characteristics of
Lizzie and Laura?

Bibliography

Breen, Robert S. *Chamber Theatre*. Evanston, Ill.: William Caxton,
1986.
    Provocative and illuminating discussions of the scope and practice of
    staging prose fiction that are written by the scholar who is most respon-
    sible for its success.

Coger, Leslie Irene, and Melvin R. White. *Readers Theatre Handbook:
A Dramatic Approach to Literature*. Rev. ed. Glenview, Ill.: Scott,
Foresman and Company, 1973.
    Readers Theatre as a "theatre of the mind." Among the earliest works,
    this pioneering book features scripts, discussions, and illustrations of
    practical solutions to problems.

Kleinau, Marion L., and Janet Larsen McHughes. *Theatres for Literature*. Sherman Oaks, Calif.: Alfred Publishing Company, 1980.
    A substantial discussion of the theory and practice of Readers Theatre,
    Chamber Theatre, and other group performance events, featuring prac-
    tical advice and stimulating theoretical questions. An excellent all-round
    book.

Long, Beverly Whitaker, Lee Hudson, and Phillis Rienstra Jeffrey.
Group Performance of Literature. Englewood Cliffs, N.J.: Prentice-
Hall, 1977.
    Some theoretical discussion precedes a substantial collection of script
    suggestions, fragments, and reports of productions, which are illustrated
    and amplified by their original directors.

Maclay, Joanna H. *Readers Theatre: Toward a Grammar of Practice*. New
York: Random House, 1971.
    Among the earliest efforts to develop a theoretical foundation for staging
    literature, this book asks provocative questions and supplies substantial
    practical suggestions.

McHughes, J. L. "The Poesis of Space: Prosodic Structures in Concrete Poetry." *Quarterly Journal of Speech*, 63 (1977), 168–179.
A discussion arguing that space is the axis from which the poem emerges. This and the article by Francine Merritt have provided considerable support to the growing interest in the performance of concrete poetry.

Merritt, Francine. "Concrete Poetry — Verbivocovisual." *Speech Teacher*, 18 (1969), 109–114.
Chiefly a series of definitions and examples of ten different kinds of concrete poems.

Provenmire, E. Kingsley. *Choral Speaking and the Verse Choir*. New York: A. S. Barnes, 1975.
The most recent addition to the study of this form of group interpretation, with many practical suggestions and examples.

APPENDIX A

Some Notes on Directing the Group Performance

In this book we have repeatedly stressed our interest in the solo performance of drama, but we recognize that sometimes a group performance piques the interest of an individual student, who proceeds to undertake a production with not much more support than conviction and good intentions. Many good textbooks on stage directing and directing group performance events appear in the bibliography at the end of Chapter 11. Any student contemplating a group production should examine these works carefully.

Group performance demands a substantial commitment in terms of analysis, rehearsal, spectacle, and staging. No one should undertake group work in the belief that it is going to be an easy way to mount a performance. The potential rewards are considerable and, make no mistake, very different from the rewards of solo performance. The general comments that follow are directed to interpreters who are beginning work in group performance. As you develop expertise and begin to trust yourself and your choice of literature, you will undoubtedly acquire your own method of proceeding. The following suggestions are not rules; they are ways in which group performances have been developed. Use them as a source of good advice, not as recipes or rigid regulations.

The director's first responsibility is to prepare the script for performance. This task is an imposing one. You may avoid considerable grief if you take the time to prepare a script that allows for innovation during rehearsal but provides the individual performers with the foundation to begin their explorations. Even if you choose a play whose script requires very little reworking, you still need to clarify your concepts. If you value your own particular focus on the work, do not simply duplicate someone else's script for your production. Or find a story, a poem, a novel, an essay, or even a filmscript — or a collection of these — that speaks fully and intricately to an audience. Use the touchstones for selecting literature with which you are by now very familiar, and which you can present fully in terms of cast, staging, scenography, and rehearsal time.

Let us say that you choose to explore one of the stories that appear in this text, Bernard Malamud's "The Prison" (Chapter 6). You begin a seemingly endless series of questions for yourself and for everyone who touches the production, questions that do not end until well after the final performance. Do you fully understand everything that is going on in the story? Read it again, and then again, to be sure. Look at other stories by Malamud. How can you cast the story with the people who are available? (If yours is a group of 11 nine-year-olds, you probably can't.) Do you have enough time to prepare the story? Remember, *too* much time to rehearse rarely occurs, although time spent unprofitably frequently hampers even the best intentions. Will you be able to respond to the scenographic demands the story makes? This doesn't mean you must build a candy store, but you should be able to suggest to the audience the atmosphere of the store, its inhabitants, and their lives.

Reread the story again. What is it about this story that interests you? Do you visualize any particular image that suggests what the audience might see? Can you detect any pictures in the words; are any stage pictures apparent in the levels of the story? Have you any ideas — even vague ones — of how a specific scene or a sentence or even a phrase may sound or look to an audience? You don't have to stage the entire work in your mind, but you should have some idea of what you hope the final performance will resemble. Reread the story again. Do you still want to spend all the time and effort on this work? If you are still convinced of your choice at this point, proceed to the preparation of a *working* script.

Next you must solve the issue of permissions. Performance outside of class — whether for public audiences or other classmates, regardless of whether an admission fee is charged — requires permission from the copyright holder. Although the work you select may be in the public domain, even older works (such as the plays of Shakespeare) exist in several different editions, each the product of an editor who holds the copyright on the work. Rather than risk any legal unpleasantness, write a letter well ahead of time to the publisher(s) of the work(s) you are presenting, stating performance dates and the nature of your production plans for each work you are using. You may wish to enclose a copy of the script you have prepared. Only when you receive the permission of the copyright holder are you legally (and ethically) free to show your work to the public. Because you have chosen Malamud's "The Prison," contact the copyright holder, Farrar, Strauss and Giroux, Inc.

Since you are working with fiction, and since this story features a narrator who is sympathetic toward the central character, you will use the technique of Chamber Theatre for your presentation. As discussed in Chapter 11, this technique encourages the full staging of prose fiction while retaining the narrator. Now you should examine the story from the perspectives of the audience and of the director, using the analytical principles discussed in Chapters 2, 5, and 6, as well as the technical suggestions given in Chapter 11. Always keep in mind that many of your decisions will be adjusted or even discarded when rehearsal comes, and some things that you think ought to work stupendously will have to be changed.

At this point, you should make some firm decisions about the degree to which you wish to commit your resources — time, money, and personnel — toward the visual statement you expect the performance to make. Typically, this decision will be based on the amount of time and money you budget and on the degree to which crucial action, properties, and scenes must be enacted. One perfectly splendid item of setting or costume can carry an entire scene if it is used properly. Don't waste time, money, and effort trying to dress an army battalion in complete costumes when helmets alone might suffice admirably. Cooperative audiences can create finer settings than any designer or technician could. Slides and filmclips can suggest a Boeing 747 in flight; one period chair can suggest an entire English great house library. Once you have determined what properties and settings you do need, arrange to make them available as soon into the rehearsal period as you can, because the longer the performers work with them, the more confident they will appear to the audience. Decide how large a playing space you will need and what configuration best represents the story. Obviously, this decision will be influenced enormously by what is available, but do not allow yourself to be lulled into accepting a proscenium stage when other opportunities might suggest the locales of the story better and might enable fuller interaction among the narrator, characters, and audience.

Several business problems emerge. Do you plan to have an audience? Have you obtained permission from the author and the publisher to work with this story? Has the publisher responded to your request for permission? If not, write again. How many performances do you intend to give? Programs, tickets, ushers, advertising, house management, and similar other details can quickly grow into major dilemmas if ignored. Can you count on someone reliable to assist in any of this? Enlist that person now.

Even though you have not begun to audition potential performers, you have made tremendous progress toward your goal. Avoid performing and directing simultaneously, since both tasks will suffer. Both are difficult enough alone. When you audition performers for your production, you will doubtless have ideas about how each of the characters should behave; possibly you will have a specific person in mind for a particular part. Allow each person who is auditioning sufficient time to make an impression and to develop within the character, but if a performer is unsuitable, do not waste that person's — and your own — time. If there is no possible way for the seven-foot-tall basketball player to play a little girl, don't expect him or ask him to work on that character. Generally speaking, you should cast the strongest performer as the narrator, since, as we discovered in Chapter 6, the narrator carries the heaviest burden by being responsible for moving along the action of the story. If the strongest performer is also the most experienced, so much the better, for the narrator must fulfill the task of storyteller. As you know, part of the tale is the telling. Be sure that the performers whom you have tentatively selected look and sound appropriate together; unless you wish to achieve some comic or outlandish effect, be sure that they are able to operate as an ensemble. For many directors, casting a production is the most difficult job, but if you have done your homework, you know what you need. Take the time you need to make sure you have what you want, but make the choice as soon as you can.

Now put cast and tentative script together. Many directors ask the performers to read through the script several times before staging, to be sure that everyone fully understands the characters. Describe to the cast why you chose the particular story, what you see in it, and how you hope the production will look and sound when you are finished. See what the story does under the close pressure of the group's attention to it. Watch what happens to interactions, to the lines, to the characters, as the performers begin to feel their bodies and their voices. Be patient, attentive, and clearsighted: watch what is being presented, and respond to the performers with suggestions. Answer their questions frankly. A performer needs to understand the perspective of the director, but as you very well know, a performer also wants room to create. Don't crowd the performers with too many details too soon. They need a little freedom to get used to new ways of walking, talking, seeing, and thinking. Give them time.

Slowly the story will begin to come alive, sometimes through only a sentence or a phrase, in brief moments. Work out a rehearsal schedule that uses each performer's time economically. Groups should not have to wait while you rehearse individuals. Be patient and open to new ideas from everyone associated with the project. A gesture suggested by a performer may be clearer than the one you had in mind. Does the distribution of lines exactly demonstrate the relationship between narrator and character? Serious and responsible interpreters will begin by asking questions and end by helping. In this process of creating, everyone involved comes to know the story at its fullest. If this stage of rehearsal is conducted in the proper manner, it can be a profoundly rewarding and exciting experience.

What progress has been made on the technical problems and the business problems? The production should be on its feet now; if you will not be using books, they should be disappearing at this point. Certain moments should be emerging as clear and stable. Each rehearsal will show more and more such moments, but do not allow the story to become glib or easy. Inexperienced performers might want to relax now, to simply say the words without remembering what the words carry. Be patient about problems and clear and precise about ways to solve difficulties. At this point in rehearsal, no performer wants (or needs) to hear, "Something's wrong with that line; try it another way." Specify what you expect; be prepared to let the performer work on it, too.

As the performance date approaches, integrate the technical elements as soon as they are available. Sound and film cues should be rehearsed as often as possible to enable the people responsible for their operation to understand how their contribution enhances the entire presentation. Also, the performers have to know what is going on around and behind them so that they can cooperate with it. In performance the flexibility of people must accommodate the inflexibility of the machines. Knowing what is supposed to happen creates an indispensable awareness should something unforeseen occur during a performance. It frequently makes sense to rehearse only the technical elements, including lights, tapes, film, and set or property changes. Don't cut corners or time at this point in the rehearsal period: be sure that every item that must be obtained or action that must be performed is clear and set and ready.

The technical and scenographic elements are ready. The performers have studied, analyzed, and rehearsed. The script probably looks somewhat different from what you originally intended, but somehow more accurate than you imagined. There will be a final series of run-throughs before an audience of sympathetic students or friends or colleagues. Performers need to know how an audience may respond, where to expect a laugh they never dreamed they would get. Each rehearsal should be followed by brief discussions with performers, technical people, and assistants to answer questions that have come up during the rehearsal and to suggest ways to solve new problems. These conferences should be used as ways for the group to solve problems as well as a time for you to improve the production.

Each performance ought to be a learning experience for you: take notes and discover the story under the pressure of performance with an audience. This production probably will not capture everything you know to be in the story; nor will it represent everything this group of people is capable of doing. But you have begun.

APPENDIX B

Building and Presenting a Program

Throughout this text, we have attempted to keep a balance between the demands for detailed literary analysis and the techniques necessary to communicate the literature to an audience. In this discussion of program building we assume that the interpreter has thoroughly analyzed the literature and that physical and vocal techniques are under control. If you can't perform a selection properly, why not choose another topic better suited to your resources?

Some aspects of building a sustained and well-integrated program should be mentioned here. Although we have not focused on training the professional recitalist, there can be considerable pleasure and satisfaction gained from presenting a program or lecture recital to an audience outside the classroom. Much of the discussion that follows can also be applied to the longer class performance, such as a final reading, or to the increasingly popular reading hours being offered on many campuses. After all, the techniques used in performance are dictated by the demands of the *material* rather than by the length or circumstances of the presentation.

The difference between a program and a lecture recital is primarily one of proportion and degree. A *program* uses a minimum of transitional material and focuses almost entirely on the various works of literature themselves. A *lecture recital*, by contrast, has a strong central unity; critics' opinions and historical data are used as transitions, and the selections are arranged to illustrate whatever technical or thematic development the speaker has chosen. The lecture recital emphasizes evaluation as much as appreciation, but it should not simply use the literature to endorse a position or assume a posture that is inconsistent with the integrity of the writing.

A number of performance possibilities come to mind. Suppose you want to examine the scope and variety of Robert Browning's work. You plan to include letters, short poems, and selections from *The Ring and the Book,* from the verse play *Pippa Passes,* and from the unsuccessful play *Stafford.* If you also include critical comments and references to Browning's early Romanticism and his position as one of the great Victorian writers, you will be giving a lecture recital. On the other hand, a program on Browning would be less concerned with the range of his writing or the direction of its development than with selections an audience would enjoy as pieces of literature. As we said earlier, the difference between a program and a lecture recital is largely one of degree. Here, we focus on the program for individuals and groups, since the lecture recital appeals to a more specialized audience and is much less practical for the beginning interpreter.

Condensations of novels and plays are probably too ambitious for most beginning interpreters. For this discussion we shall build programs of varied selections, referring to material in the text as well as to selections you can find in your library, and featuring group performances of both fiction and poetry and nonfiction.

Selecting Material

The first consideration in selecting the material you will present is its literary worth. Do not read something you consider to be inferior because you think your audience will not accept anything more difficult to understand. It is your job to present the selection so well that it does not seem difficult. The second consideration is permission to use the material. Reread the advice about copyright in Appendix A if you are in doubt.

You might be asked to do a special program for a particular group or occasion. Perhaps the group is following a particular course of study — contemporary theatre, the Old Testament, human relations, ecology, or any one of a number of areas of interest — and they want you to add a new dimension or an introductory or concluding unit. Of course, you should select material that is appropriate. The time of year may influence your selection. For a Christmas program, for example, you might want to include both an old favorite (Truman Capote's *A Christmas Memory*) and a less well-known piece (say, Ogden Nash's witty "Epstein, Spare That Yule Log"). A spring luncheon could feature Eudora Welty's "Lily Daw and the Three Ladies." February offers the opportunity to read love poems, love letters, and love scenes from plays. Since this month also celebrates the birthdays of two famous Americans, it also offers the opportunity to present historical material, patriotic selections, or perhaps a scene from Arthur Miller's *The Crucible* or Gore Vidal's *Lincoln*. Selections from Walt Whitman's journals and his poem "When Lilacs Last in the Dooryard Bloom'd" are particularly appropriate for a program on Lincoln. In short, almost any topic of human interest can become the focal point of a program. The range of possibilities is limited only by the interpreter's skill and imagination.

Unifying the Program: A Traditional Method

Whatever the occasion, your program should have a unifying theme that is dictated by what you know about your audience, the time of year, the purpose of the organization you are reading for, and many other factors. The program should cohere. Indeed, of utmost importance are the intrinsic factors of unity and harmony, variety and contrast, balance and proportion, rhythm of emotional impact, and focus of interest.

Working toward a unified program is important, but it may not be the most important factor in your selection decision. Often it is more practical to begin with what you like to read and can get ready and then to see what thematic unity your preferences offer. For example, suppose you already have prepared Robert Frost's "Wild Grapes." This poem is about many things, all operating within a harmonious unity: memory of childhood, a young girl and her brother, an experience with nature, wisdom, letting go with the hands but not with the heart, and so on. Any one of these topics could become your unifying theme. If you choose memories of childhood for your program topic, you might wish to include Theodore Roethke's "Child on Top of a Greenhouse," a selection from Eudora Welty's *One Writer's Beginnings,* a selection from Garrison Keillor's *Lake Wobegon Days,* some of Lillian Hellman's *An Unfinished Woman,* part of James Joyce's *Portrait of the Artist as a Young Man,* or a selection from John Knowles's *A Separate Peace.* Mark Twain's writing evokes warm memories for many people. Roethke's poems are rich in memories of his childhood in Michigan, and Gwendolyn Brooks's *Annie Allen* and *A Street in Bronzeville* contain many examples of a black girl's memories, as do the poems of Nikki Giovanni and Sonia Sanchez. Walt Whitman's "A Child Went Forth" and A. E. Housman's "When I Was One-and-twenty" could be used, as could selections from the poetry of William Wordsworth. And don't forget Hugh Leonard's *Da* and *A Life.* The list of available material is practically endless; the interpreter needs only time and interest.

You might decide to set the theme with Jaques's speech from Shakespeare's *As You Like It,* moving from infancy and childhood to maturity and old age. You could close with Roethke's "Old Lady's Winter Words" and use Stanley Kunitz's "I Dreamed that I Was Old" and Tennyson's "Ulysses" or "Tithonus" with the sequence. Edith Sitwell's poem "Colonel Fantock" and D. H. Lawrence's short story "The Lovely Lady" would add interesting variety, as would units from Edgar Lee Masters's *Spoon River Anthology,* or scenes from such widely divergent plays as Henrik Ibsen's *A Doll's House,* George Bernard Shaw's *Caesar and Cleopatra,* or Shakespeare's *King Lear.* There are innumerable variations on the theme of youth and age. The readings might have a strongly humorous tone or a rhythm that combines the gently humorous and the deeply moving.

Interesting programs can be arranged around people and places, rural and urban life, regional American literature, descriptive and dramatic writing about foreign places, or the letters, travel accounts, and diaries of famous people.

The works of one particular author may serve as a unifying device. Concentrate on the treatment of a theme, such as Shakespeare's kings; or on a method of revealing character, as through Browning's monologues or Ann Beattie's remarkable short stories. You could show some developmental trend, beginning with an author's early works and concluding with the later ones.

Following is a description of a unified, well-illustrated performance treating the works of D. H. Lawrence. The program, which was presented at a D. H. Lawrence festival, combined Lawrence's fiction and nonfiction with books and letters that were written about him by other people. The eight readers held their manuscripts and sat on stools of various heights; a general wash of warm light illuminated the stage. The four women wore simple white blouses and long, full denim skirts in vivid colors; the four men wore khaki trousers, solid-color sports shirts, and corduroy jackets.

To begin, an introductory montage was followed by autobiographical material and selections from *Sons and Lovers.* The next section included some of Lawrence's letters dealing with his mother's illness and death and closed with two short poems he wrote in her memory.

A short biographical paragraph formed a bridge to Lawrence's meeting with Frieda Weekley. His poem "Fröhleichnam," followed by four excerpts from letters, led to "The Song of the Man Who Has Come Through." The next section took up the couple's travels that eventually took them to Sicily. Lawrence's letters introduced his famous poem "Snake" and a section from *Sea and Sardinia,* and one of Frieda's letters led into Mabel Dodge's account of her invitation for the Lawrences to visit New Mexico. The first act of the performance ended with the Lawrences' acceptance and their later postponement of the trip.

The second act began with the Lawrences' arrival in Taos and included some humor — from Frieda's and Lawrence's letters to friends, from Mabel Dodge's comments, and from the poet Dorothy Brett. A fragment of the play *Altitude* was used; since much of this work's humor depends on the pointless, amusing activity of breakfast preparations when the cook fails to appear, the group decided to stage, rather than read, this segment. The performers simply put down their books, moved their stools to suggest a stove and a grouping around a table, and began the play. When the play ends abruptly, since Mabel Dodge never finished it, the readers moved rapidly to replace the stools and retrieve their books, resuming with the Lawrences' move to Lobo Ranch and the long winter that followed. Dorothy Brett's account, Lawrence's poem "Mountain Lion," his letters, and his essays "Taos," "New Mexico," and "Indians and an Englishman" followed. A segment from one of Lawrence's letters told enough about his declining health to form a bridge to Frieda's letter about his death, which was interspersed with brief sections from Lawrence's "The Ship of Death." The program concluded with the poem "Bavarian Gentians."

This program's unity and variety — both in type of writing and in range of mood and feeling — suggest how rhythms of the emotional impact should be carefully considered in order to make the entire performance move smoothly and without monotony. Don't be afraid of variety: use materials from various sources, interspersing them for contrast and illumination.

Using Multiple Readers, Different Types of Literature, and Multimedia

Using more than one reader for a program often helps to solve the problems of short preparation time and inexperience. Moreover, two or more interpreters add variety and thus increase the program's audience appeal. This is not to suggest that several people can simply read whatever they happen to have handy. There must be some central unity. The several readers should rehearse together so that transitions are clear and the material is arranged to provide variety and contrast, rhythm of emotional impact, and effective use of climactic selections.

There are great opportunities for experimentation in program building with groups. Much literature combines well with dance and music, which either can serve as accompaniments to the reading or can be inserted at various places in the program to underscore, sustain, or alter mood. Electronic media strike instant and effective responses in an audience but be sure to eliminate any potential technical glitches. Visual art can also be used. For example, William Blake and E. E. Cummings were both artists of some distinction as well as poets, and some of their drawings and paintings might well be combined with their writing for an interesting program. The drawings and prose writings in Gerard Manley Hopkins's *Notebooks* might be skillfully combined with his poetry to provide an unusual and enlightening program. Or you could combine Vaslav Nijinsky's intriguing diaries with dance, adding film clips of Nureyev or Baryshnikov performing some of the ballets that Nijinsky created and enriching the entire presentation with excerpts from Igor Stravinsky's music.

There are practically endless possibilities for using various combinations of readers and combinations of other art forms with all types of literature. Combine Readers Theatre and Chamber Theatre with the performance of single readers when the material seems suitable for the techniques. You should be careful, however, not to let variety overpower unity. Also, be sure that the literature itself is not obscured by too many sound effects or visual distractions.

Suppose you decide to work with the *New York Times*.[1] After examining several issues, you detect the newspaper's characteristic attitudes towards advertisements, politics, presentation, and news. Remember, any publication frankly seeks readership, and the performance analogue for such frankness is an equally frank frontal placement and focus — bodies and voices creating the presentational equivalent to the newspaper. Such placement frees the bodies and voices to suggest the pictures, drawings, and graphics. In rehearsal, try to achieve an ensemble that can display all the levels of the work as well as its impact as a whole.

What does the *New York Times* represent? It holds a position as the "paper of record" in the United States, offering pre-eminent news reporting, widely respected editorials, broadly distributed features, an immediately recognizable logo, and a particular style of presentation.

What should a performance represent? Since there is no need to limit oneself to any single issue of the paper, select from among the finest of the editorials, op-ed articles, obituaries, sports stories, fashion news reports, lifestyle and social information, the television-film-theatre-dance-music reviews, the Sunday *New York Times Magazine* articles, the book reviews and interviews with authors, the advertisements, the personal columns, and the job offerings. Your selection, of course, will be based on the needs and interests of the audience, so you may wish to slant your presentation toward a particular period or event, if you maintain an accurate reflection of the typical components of an issue. Should you include selections from the books written about the *Times* (Gay Talese's *The Power and the Glory*, Harrison Salisbury's *Without Fear or Favor*, or Daniel Halberstam's *The Powers That Be*)? It all depends on what you intend this performance to demonstrate.

1. Julian Kaufman contributed generously to many of these ideas.

Look at the visual responsibilities. What are the characteristic graphic elements used in the *Times*? How can these be suggested in performance by bodies and voices? Your rehearsals will begin in experimentation, so don't restrict yourself in terms of the visual elements. Sometimes the group can represent the visual element better than slides or set pieces could.

Consider what could happen with the front page in a group production. The front page of the *Times* is characterized by several different but related factors. First, the chief stories of the day all begin (but never end) on the front page. On occasion, a feature story or a research story also begins on the front page — but it, too, never ends there. The front page also includes — in extremely small print — one- or two-line advertisements at the bottom of some columns, the weather forecast, and price and publication information. Usually there is one large three- or four-column photograph, often illustrating the major story of the day. Sometimes a small chart or a symbol tied to the text of a story that appears elsewhere appears above the fold to the left of center. The most important stories appear in the columns that begin at the top of the page; stories of lesser importance begin below the fold. Several stories about the same event are clustered, usually to the upper right or the upper left. The front page also features variations in print size, from the most prominent headline to the smallest classified advertisement. The largest print on the page is the Gothic type masthead — *The New York Times.*

How can the bodies and voices of the performers suggest the world of that page? Obviously, if the news stories are going to be performed, they will require all the attention normally given the performance of nonfiction. But since the stories are separate, why not give one story to each performer? When a news figure is quoted, let the performer suggest the figure as fully as possible, and let the stories continue simultaneously. At first everyone talking at once may seem cacophonous, but the blurt of all the news is one of the distinctive features of the paper's front page. And, before the stories begin, the group can suggest the elaborate archaic type of the masthead by singing the words *The New York Times* like a madrigal. Perhaps the large picture could be frozen into space by three or four of the performers; or a slide of the performers in an identical posture could be projected on a screen in back. Although the performers start together with the stories skipping along, they will stop at random, as their contents are continued elsewhere and new stories take their place. How can you suggest the newer, less important news? Could those tiny want ads be whispered?

Similar questions need to be answered for all the parts of the paper you intend to perform. The attitudes of the editorials tend to be dignified, except for an occasional whimsical salute to a change of season, but the attitudes of the letters and op-ed page offer real potential for characterization, and the masthead can be elaborate, stately, and refined. Photos can duplicate fashion news, but might not bodies and voices better suggest fashion's attitudes? Try to achieve the peculiar attitude of the recipes: knowledgeable, clear-sighted, with an extraordinarily well-equipped kitchen that could be the domain of the chef of a great French restaurant. Can you convey the intriguing, sometimes cryptic, world that lies behind the terse abbreviations of want ads or personal advertisements? Surely there are several opportunities for characterization among these. Capture the appeal each advertisement makes, through postures and voice. Plan each of the components carefully.

When compiling the parts — putting the paper together, as it were — be careful to watch the amount of time you spend on each "page." Work for balance and continuity by trying to achieve the feeling of the page turning. The arrangement of the pieces depends on changes of tempo in the stories, on the sizes of the advertisements you encounter, on how thick a paper you want to present, and on the degree to which you want to embody pictorial elements or to represent them with slides.

Whatever choices you make, the performance should build to a climax — something that the paper never does, but that an audience must see. Your decision to perform a newspaper imposes a structure that the paper itself does not necessarily follow. But it always moves along. Your performance should convey to the audience all that is involved in reading the *New York Times.*

Of course, a newspaper is not the only kind of publication that would benefit from such an effort. The *New York Review of Books,* for example, offers interesting reviews and articles, distinctive advertisements and David Levine graphics, and irrepressible personal announcements. The *Dial,* a magazine of poetry, fiction, and criticism, which was published during the twenties and provided an early forum for many outstanding contemporary authors, would be an equally interesting publication to perform, since its visual statement deftly supported the verbal substances of the work.

Perhaps the most obvious choice among magazines would be the *New Yorker:* its unsurpassed collection of nonfiction, poetry, light fiction, articles, and humor, with renowned cartoons and the unmistakably bemused hauteur of Eustace Tilley, the magazine's monocled symbol, provide a wonderfully varied forum for a performance. This program might include other works from typical *New Yorker* writers, or passages about the magazine from Brendan Gill's *Here at the New Yorker,* or segments from the memoirs and autobiographies of some of its most famous staffers. A collection of *New Yorker* pieces, including Janet Flanner's "Letter from Paris" (collected as *Paris Was Yesterday*), might provide the foundation for another program. Whatever you choose, you should determine the attitude that makes the publication unique, and you should develop the corresponding physical and vocal behaviors.

The important thing to remember is that the performance as a whole should have both unity and variety. It should have an introductory unit, a climax (usually the longest selection and the one that most clearly exemplifies your theme), and a conclusion. When you have selected and arranged your material, look at the whole program and check it against each of the intrinsic factors. Keep the introduction short. The audience came to hear the program, not a long preamble. Your introductory remarks bridge the mood and train of thought you wish to establish. The transitions between selections should allow the listeners a few seconds to complete their emotional response to the preceding selection and should lead them economically into the mood of the one that follows.

Adapting to the Audience

It is impossible to know exactly what the interests of your audience are, unless the group has a special purpose. It is possible, however, to make some generalizations. The gender of the members of the audience makes less difference than their age, which is probably the most important factor to consider in audience adaptation. In general, a young audience of either sex is more open to experimental material and to a wider range of subject matter. An audience of elderly people usually wants to see and hear traditional, familiar material. While you might understandably avoid material about old age, illness, or death, do not ignore Maryann Hartman's work. In a group with a wide age spread, there should be something for everyone; but if you are in doubt about the suitability of a selection for even a segment of the audience, it is better to omit that selection than to risk offending anyone.

Children make a wonderful audience. They like material about people, animals, nature, and anything they can visualize, whether real or imaginary. They like poetry with a clear rhythm and a rhyme. You should choose selections that are short, and you should handle the transitions carefully, in order to connect what the children know with what the literature says. Stories, of course, are great favorites, and children enjoy having the characters made vivid by more explicit vocal and physical characterization than would be appropriate for a mature audience. Don't limit yourself to children's literature exclusively. Children are young in experience but they are sensitive and intelligent; they might enjoy the sounds and basic references in Hopkins's "The Starlight Night" or "Pied Beauty," Lewis Carroll's "Jabberwocky," and Walter de la Mare's "The Listeners."

You should in no way sacrifice your own standards of literary value to audience expectation. There are dozens of ways to write about any subject. Your audience is interested first in the substance of your material and second in how that material is presented.

You should be aware of the audience's image of you. An audience that has asked you to present a program expects you to be skilled and intelligent and to have something interesting to say. They expect you to be well prepared and can be very critical if your performance is not polished. They have invited you because they think of you as an artist: you can do something they cannot do as well.

Timing

You should be careful not to let your program run past its allotted time by more than one or two minutes. Listeners often become ill at ease and distracted if the program runs long. It is better to leave an audience wishing for more than to risk their sigh of relief and hurried exit.

Time your selections and transitions several times during your preparation. You will find that you consume more time as you progress. It is probably safe to add at least ten minutes per hour to your early reading time; audience response and your own increased control of the selections will tend to slow your pace in final performance. If you are sharing a program with other readers or with musicians, find out how much time you have been allotted and stick to it *precisely*.

A program of varied selections is particularly difficult to time, because it may be lengthened by applause between selections. This is, of course, a phenomenon no performer wishes to prevent. Nevertheless, enthusiastic applause can add ten minutes or more to a fifty-minute program of fairly short selections. Be sure to consider this in your planning. In general, applause permits the audience to complete their response to what you have just given them. Accept it graciously and with poise.

In some instances, applause is inappropriate. If you sense that this is the situation, a moment's pause after each selection and before the next transition can be helpful. Do not prolong the pause so that your audience thinks you are waiting for applause. This sense of timing will develop as your experience increases. Applause might break a mood that you are trying to establish, especially if you are using a number of short selections. In this case, you might indicate in your transition that you will be using a group of short poems that touch on one aspect of your theme. Hold your performance dimension for a brief pause after each piece, and then move directly into the next selection or brief transition. When you finish the group of poems, drop your directness slightly and allow the audience to show its appreciation before you move into the next unit. Your audience will be sensitive to your wishes and will take your cues easily.

Whenever you do a program, remember that in your role of interpreter it is your duty and privilege to *share* a piece of interesting literature with your audience. Remember that your art and your technique should serve the author's intentions. Planning and preparing a performance takes time and energy. Even so, the experience of sharing good literature with an audience is always rewarding and exciting.

APPENDIX C

A Brief History of Theories of Interpretation

From earliest times, the spoken word has attracted audiences and influenced their thinking. The history of public speaking has been traced by numerous authorities, who have shown that its thread has been unbroken from the fourth century B.C. to the present. The theatre enjoys a similarly clear history. Oral interpretation, too, even though its genesis and growth as a distinct art may be less easy to define, has a long lineage of its own.[1]

The art of interpretation probably had its beginnings with the rhapsodies of ancient Greece, when poets gathered to read their works in public competition. However, the emergence of interpretation as a field of study in its own right was delayed, because for a long time it was confused with oratory and rhetoric. In the eighteenth and nineteenth centuries, actors and ministers were given extensive training in what was, in reality, interpretation. It is enough to sketch the outlines very lightly here, in order to note the development of certain theories and to see where we now stand in relation to those theories.

American colleges were already giving some attention to the oral interpretation of literature at the beginning of the nineteenth century. As early as 1806, when John Quincy Adams assumed the chair of Rhetoric and Oratory, Harvard, which from its founding had carried on the medieval tradition of "declamations" and "disputations," was offering a few courses that included the interpretative approach to literary materials. As the century progressed, more and more colleges offered specific courses in spoken English — courses that carried such titles as "Declamation and Composition," "Declamation," "Elements of Orthoepy and Elocution," or simply "Elocution."

---

1. *Performance of Literature in Historical Perspectives,* edited by David W. Thompson (Landham, Md.: University Press of America, 1983), illustrates "five continuing concerns of the field of interpretation, namely language, culture, teaching, theory, and entertainment." The product of eight years of research by six editors and thirty-three prominent scholars, this well-organized, copiously annotated compendium offers invaluable assistance to those interested in further scholarly investigation.

The word *elocutio* (Latin *eloqui, elocutus,* "to speak out") originally referred to effective literary or oratorical style. Between 1650 and 1750, however, a shift in connotation took place, and the term *elocution* was applied to the manner of oral delivery rather than to the written style of a composititon. *Pronuntiatio,* which had meant primarily the management of voice and body, gradually took on our modern meaning of pronunciation as the correct phonation of individual words. By 1750, then, these shifts in meaning had taken place, and the term *elocution* had come to connote a considerable degree of emphasis on delivery. By this time, also, a renewed interest in reading aloud and in oratory had developed, especially in England, where an important group of writer-speakers known as the English Elocutionists had come into being. Outstanding among them were Thomas Sheridan (1719–1788) and John Walker (1732–1807), whose books and lectures had great bearing on the development in America of what we now call interpretation.

Thomas Sheridan, father of the famous dramatist Richard Brinsley Sheridan and himself an actor, published his *Course of Lectures on Elocution* in 1763. This book came out strongly against artificialities and stressed the method of natural conversation in the oral presentation of literature. Sheridan thus became known as the leader of the "natural school." His thesis was that elocution should follow the laws of nature. He held that body and voice are natural phenomena and are therefore subject to the laws of nature. He pointed out that nature gives to the passions and emotions certain tones, looks, and gestures which are perceived through the ear and the eye. Therefore, he contended, the elocutionist should reproduce these tones, looks, and gestures as nearly as possible in presenting literature orally to an audience. Basically, this theory is sound.

As often happens in the application of a theory, however, Sheridan became trapped in his efforts to be specific, and he began to evolve a system of markings and cues for the discovery and reproduction of these "natural" tones and gestures. By the end of his career, he had become the exponent of a method that, judged by modern standards, was much more mechanical than natural. Nevertheless, the term "natural school" has persisted to the present day.

The other famous English Elocutionist, John Walker, published his *Elements of Elocution* in 1781. He, too, professed to take his cues from nature. However, he could not (or at least did not) resist the urge to set down specific rules and markings for the slightest variations of vocal tempo, inflection, and force, and for the various aspects of gesture. These markings caught the public fancy, because they were more concrete than anything that had been offered before. (It is always so much easier to be told exactly how to do something than to put one's own intelligence to work to solve each individual problem as it arises!) Walker must be given credit for stating clearly that these markings were intended as aids toward the satisfactory projection of the material at hand; and perhaps he is not to be held wholly responsible for the fact that future generations placed more emphasis on the markings and other mechanical devices than on the projection of material. Walker and his imitators, then, established what has been called the "mechanical school" — in seeming opposition to Sheridan's "natural school." Thus began a schism that is only now disappearing.

Two other names must be mentioned in connection with the English Elocutionists of the eighteenth century. Although they were less prolific and influential than Sheridan and Walker, John Mason (1706–1763) and James Burgh (1714–1775) both wrote books that enjoyed considerable popularity. Mason's *An Essay on Elocution or Pronunciation* (1748), the first book to include the word *elocution* in its title, put heavy emphasis on the "right" management of the voice.

James Burgh was primarily a political philosopher whose interest in speech probably grew out of his political activities. In his book *The Art of Speaking* (1762), he discussed with some vehemence the rules for expressing "the principal Passions and Humors." This volume, which contained an anthology of readings, with the passions and humors carefully documented, was based on the theory that nature had given every passion its proper physical expression and that only by careful attention to the physical features, such as the eye, can the proper passion be projected.

To summarize, the closing years of the eighteenth century saw an increased interest in the use of voice and body in the oral presentation of literature. Sheridan had set up a "natural school," purportedly based on the "laws of nature"; Walker had established a "mechanical school," based in fact on the same premises but more preoccupied with markings and charts. It is understandable that the followers of these men tended to emphasize their differences rather than their similarities, and that some degree of confusion and dissension resulted.

In the nineteenth century, two names stand out above all others in the history of interpretation. The first is that of an American, James Rush (1786–1869), a medical doctor turned speech teacher and lecturer. Rush confined himself almost entirely to the study of vocal projection. He believed that the management of the voice is in reality not an art but a science, and he went to great lengths to develop an appropriate vocabulary for that science. Indeed, much of his terminology has become standard among modern teachers of speech. He also went to great lengths in the title of his book, published in

1827: *The Philosophy of the Human Voice: Embracing its Physiological History: Together with a System of Principles by Which Criticism in the Art of Elocution May be Rendered Intelligible, and Instruction, Definite and Comprehensive, to Which Is Added a Brief Analysis of Song and Recitative.*

Rush developed elaborate charts and markings for pitch, force, abruptness, quality, and time. He was convinced that rules could be developed to govern the analysis of vocal technique, although he was careful to point out that the practice of these rules must be accompanied by concentration on the literature being read. This last bit of advice, however, was often forgotten by his more zealous and less discriminating followers; as a result, attention was focused even more sharply on markings and symbols. Nevertheless, Rush's use of appropriate scientific method and vocabulary and his studies of the mechanisms of the human voice were valuable contributions to the field of speech.

The second significant name in nineteenth-century interpretation is François Delsarte (1811–1871). About the time Rush's method was making its way in America, Delsarte was delivering lectures in France on elocution and calisthenics. He left no writings, but so strong was his influence that many of his students recorded his philosophy and system in great detail. The Delsarte system concerned itself entirely with bodily action, and it became an accepted complement to Dr. Rush's treatises on vocal management. Delsarte based his system on a philosophy of the interrelation of the human soul, mind, and body, and on a complicated and highly mystical concept of a corresponding triune relationship throughout the entire universe. Despite this philosophical premise, the system became mechanical in the extreme.

Delsarte, like Walker and Rush, suffered somewhat at the hands of his followers. One example of the perversion of a basically sound but inadequately expressed theory — that gestures must spring from the heart — was the notion that all gestures must start from the breastbone and sweep out in a graceful curve. This misconception persisted for generations. Although Delsarte's system in practice took on mechanical aspects that had some unfortunate results, modern teachers of speech have been greatly influenced by his concept of mind, soul (heart or emotions), and body working together.

Thus, almost simultaneously, Rush in America was setting up a scientific approach to vocal technique and Delsarte in France was teaching a philosophical approach to bodily action. Although both men were originally concerned with the artistic projection of materials, the people they influenced often concentrated on the techniques rather than on the reasons for the techniques. In this way, the mechanical school, well established under the aegis of Walker's disciples, became even more firmly entrenched.

Near the close of the nineteenth century, the natural school received new impetus under the leadership of Samuel Silas Curry (1847–1921). His first book, *The Province of Expression*, published in Boston in 1891, was based on the major premise that the mind, in order to express an idea, must actively hold that idea and thus dictate the appropriate means of expression. This theory he summed up in the admonition "Think the thought!" It is understandable that such a phrase would catch the fancy of those who read his books and heard of his teachings — and equally understandable that it would lead to oversimplification, to the extent that Curry's fundamentally sound theory came to be popularized as "Think the thought and all things else will be added unto you." As a result, many teachers began to assert that the training of voice and body consists of wholly artificial and mechanical procedures, and that comprehension of thought and active concentration on that thought will ensure adequate projection of any material to an audience.

Admittedly, this idea came as a relief to those who had become weary of the exhibitionism that prevailed among the second- and third-generation advocates of the mechanical method. In an attempt to break more completely with the earlier artificialities, teachers even began to shy away from the term *elocution*, with all its connotations, and to adopt instead Curry's term *expression*. Thus, lessons in "elocution" became lessons in "expression."

One of the most interesting and influential teachers in America at the close of the century was Charles Wesley Emerson (1837–1908), founder of the Emerson College of Oratory, now Emerson College in Boston. His *Evolution of Expression* (1905) stressed vocal technique and gymnastics for their therapeutic value as well as for their contribution to the techniques of communicating literature.

By the end of the nineteenth century, then, three distinct groups had emerged: one militantly carried on the traditions of the mechanical school; another distrusted mechanics, relied on the natural method, and developed in the direction of "think-the-thought"; and a third was composed of a few independents who found some values in each camp and attempted to blend the two approaches.

Out of the Victorian interest in earnest self-improvement and edification arose emporiums for the dispersal of culture: for example, the Lyceum Movement, and, more prominently, the Chautauqua Institution. The latter was begun in the mid-nineteenth century as a Sunday-school teachers' summer camp and still thrives as a lively cultural center. At its most influential time, Chautauqua established nationwide book clubs and correspondence schools; great readers, speakers, and artists performed on its lecture platforms. Chautauqua was not an isolated phenomenon. From across the country came the call for performers and a full complement of touring guest artists and readers, who covered the country with uplifting readings and speeches, lectures, and programs. Famous readers or lecturers — Charles Dickens, for example, and Wendell Phillips — were paid considerable sums for their personal appearances. These professionals catered to the call for living performers. Periodicals and publications like the *Voice* and *Werner's Magazine* carried testimonials for products like voice balm, scripts with appropriate and elaborate markings, annotated transcriptions of how famous performers read famous speeches — all responding to the needs of amateur elocutionists in remote towns and villages.

By the beginning of the twentieth century, a number of colleges were offering courses in elocution or expression, but most students did not include speech in their program of studies unless they were preparing themselves for the ministry, politics, or law. Most of those who wished to do "platform work" as "readers" enrolled in private schools or studios. There they worked under teachers often three or four times removed from the originators of basically sound theories, and received instruction that, having filtered through several personalities, was strongly flavored by the individual teacher's own taste and understanding.

The first three decades of the twentieth century were the era of the private, highly specialized school or studio of speech. Each had its own staff of teachers, most of whom had been trained by the head of that particular school. Each had its own course of study and its own special emphasis. And each prided itself on its independence and its difference from the others. Consequently, there was no common philosophy or methodology. Each school emphasized its individuality, rather than working with the others toward solidarity and a unity of purpose among all teachers in the field.

Many people who studied at these schools returned to their homes, framed their certificates and hung them on their walls, and opened their own studios, where they taught to the best of their ability what they had learned. Their students, in turn, acquired certificates and went out to spread the gospel as they understood it. Thus, of the thousands of teachers who were conducting classes and giving private lessons, very few had had an opportunity to receive sound training under the great leaders. As a result, the original principles and practices were continually watered down. Not only were teachers often imperfectly prepared, but they worked in comparative isolation, without professional associations and strong university departments of speech to serve as centers for the exchange of ideas. The better informed and more progressive teachers who studied under Curry and his contemporaries grew with the entire educational system to become the outstanding men and women in the field of speech as a whole and in the more specialized area of interpretation. Others, however, continued to teach specific gesture, highly obtrusive vocal technique, and the use of materials of questionable literary merit, thus perpetuating to our own day not only the more regrettable excesses and misconceptions in vogue in the early years of the century but also a confusion in terminology and in standards of performance.

An important link between the theorists and teachers of the nineteenth century and the present is *Principles of Vocal Expression* (1897), by William B. Chamberlain (1847–1903) and Solomon H. Clark (1861–1927). This book, acknowledging a deep indebtedness to Curry, stressed the interaction of mind and body and the control of "instincts" by reason. Clark made a more important contribution in his *Interpretation of the Printed Page* (1913), which helped to turn the attention of teachers and students from the mechanical techniques to the appreciation and analysis of the literature itself. His concept of "impression" as distinct from and prerequisite to "expression" became the basis of *The Art of Interpretative Speech,* by Charles H. Woolbert and Severina E. Nelson, published in 1929.

Another popular book of the early twentieth century was *Natural Drills in Expression with Selections* (1909). The author, Arthur Edward Phillips (1867–1932), reflects much of Chamberlain's interest in paraphrase and tone drills, and the book was used extensively for many years in schools and colleges.

With the advance of the twentieth century, departments of speech grew in stature in colleges and universities and became fully accepted members of the academic family. Many private schools also moved with the times, some of them burgeoning into degree-granting colleges. Speech training, freed from the cultist studio, flourished under the stimulating crosswinds of professional associations and the spur of more homogeneous standards. Ideas were pooled, theories argued, heritages re-evaluated. Interpretation emerged from the strait jacket of the "reading" (which was not a reading at all, but a virtuoso exhibition of memory and technique), and reoriented itself to the printed page.

The fourth decade of this century was one of transition and stabilization. Interest in history and research increased, as described by Mary Margaret Robb in *Oral Interpretation of Literature in American Colleges and Universities* (1947) and the establishment of doctoral programs in the field.

Cornelius Carman Cunningham, Gertrude Johnson, Wayland Maxwell Parrish, Solomon Henry Clark, and Maud May Babcock published texts that had an important effect on the whole area of study. Although these books differ somewhat in emphasis, all firmly insist on the primacy of the literature and the importance of the demands it makes. The present generation of interpreters and teachers is deeply indebted to these authors for their ability to come to grips with critical and aesthetic principles and to formulate standards that apply to both analysis and performance.

Today there are three general approaches to interpretation, each of which has prominent theorists and vigorous adherents, and each of which has contributed substantially to the status of the field. For some people, the art of interpretation is seen chiefly as a communicative act between performers and audience, with possibilities for concomitant empirical research. For others, interpretation is a way to study literature, in which textual analysis is only a part and performance acts as the individual's embodiment of knowing. Still others view oral interpretation as a performing act in which the performer's instrument is trained to suggest the range and scope of the literature. These schools are very flexible. This book has drawn from all three theories but depends for its position most fully on the latter two. And our history indicates that modern interpreters agree on a great deal more than they differ about.

Modern interpreters believe in training both voice and body. They know that the voice should be flexible and strong and the articulation should be clear if they are to do justice to the material they have chosen. They know, too, that the body should be trained to respond in harmony with the voice. They are no longer afraid of the word *technique*, because they understand what it is and what they must do with it.

They also believe in carefully analyzing the material and actively concentrating on it when they present it to an audience. In a sense, they revert to the classical tradition of rhetoric in an insistence on the importance of understanding the elements of literary craftsmanship in the selection to be interpreted. They are concerned with the author's art — how the whole is shaped out of its parts.

Happily, differences still exist in degrees of emphasis on one or another aspect of the field. However, the isolationism and long list of "thou-shalt-nots" that characterized oral interpretation in the early part of the century no longer prevail. Modern interpreters open their minds to the aesthetician, the literary critic, the linguist, the psychologist, the philosopher, the anthropologist, and the folklorist.[2]

2. *Literature in Performance*, a journal of literary and performing art sponsored by the Interpretation Division of the Speech Communication Association, has since 1980 provided probing scholarship, wide-ranging research, and stimulating reviews that draw on this ever-widening circle of influence.

They realize that the more they know about related studies, the more they learn about literature. They are no longer afraid to experiment, because they know precisely where their first dependence lies — on the works of literature they have chosen. Excellent books present a strong rhetorical approach, a dramatistic approach, or a primary emphasis on applied and theoretical literary criticism. Aware of the complexity of good literature, contemporary interpreters are eager to bring to it whatever is needed for its full comprehension and appreciation, whether for their own or an audience's enjoyment.

ACKNOWLEDGMENTS

Albee, Edward. Edward Albee, excerpted from *Who's Afraid of Virginia Woolf?* Copyright © 1962 Edward Albee. Reprinted with the permission of Atheneum Publishers, Inc.

American Heritage Dictionary. © 1980 by Houghton Mifflin Company. Reprinted by permission from *The American Heritage Dictionary of the English Language, New College Edition.*

Angelou, Maya. "Phenominal Woman." From *And Still I Rise,* by Maya Angelou. Copyright © 1978 by Maya Angelou. Reprinted by permission of Random House, Inc. From *I Know Why the Caged Bird Sings,* by Maya Angelou. Copyright © 1969 by Maya Angelou. Reprinted by permission of Random House, Inc. "I Almost Remember." From *Oh Pray My Wings Are Gonna Fit Me Well,* by Maya Angelou. Copyright © 1975 by Maya Angelou. Reprinted by permission of Random House, Inc.

Auden, W. H. "Leap Before You Look," from *W. H. Auden: Collected Poems,* ed. Edward Mendelson. Reprinted by permission of Random House, Inc., and Faber and Faber Ltd.

Baraka, Imamu Amiri. "Preface to a Twenty Volume Suicide Note." Reprinted by permission of The Sterling Lord Agency, Inc. Copyright © 1961 by LeRoi Jones.

Bell, Madison Smartt. "The Naked Lady" © 1984 by Madison Smartt Bell. Reprinted by permission of John Farquarson, Ltd.

Betts, Doris. From "The Ugliest Pilgrim." Reprinted by permission of Russell & Volkening, Inc. as agents for the author. Copyright © 1973 by Doris Betts.

Bierhorst, John. Excerpt from "The Night Chant" from *Four Masterworks of American Indian Literature* by John Bierhorst. Copyright © 1974 by John Bierhorst. Reprinted by permission of Farrar, Straus and Giroux, Inc.

Bowen, Elizabeth. From *The Little Girls,* by Elizabeth Bowen. Copyright © 1963 by Elizabeth Bowen. Reprinted by permission of Random House, Inc.

Brecht, Bertolt. From *The Caucasian Chalk Circle* by Bertolt Brecht. Reprinted by permission of the University of Minnesota Press.

Cameron, Peter. "Homework." Reprinted by permission; © 1984 Peter Cameron. Originally appeared in *The New Yorker.*

Capote, Truman. From "A Christmas Memory." Copyright © 1956 by Truman Capote. Reprinted from *Selected Writings of Truman Capote,* by permission of Random House, Inc. Originally appeared in *Mademoiselle.*

Chekov, Anton. From *The Three Sisters.* From *Chekov: The Major Plays,* translated by Ann Dunnigan. Reprinted by arrangement with New American Library, New York, New York.

Ciardi, John. "As I Would Wish You Birds." Copyright © 1962 by John Ciardi. From *In Fact* by John Ciardi (Rutgers University Press). Reprinted by permission of the author.

Cruz, Victor Hernandez. From *Today Is a Day of Great Joy,* by Victor Hernandez Cruz. Reprinted by permission of the author.

Cummings, E. E. "Spring is like a perhaps hand" is reprinted from *TULIPS & CHIM-NEYS* by E. E. Cummings by permission of Liveright Publishing Corporation. Copyright 1923, 1925 by E. E. Cummings and renewed 1951, 1953 by E. E. Cummings. Copyright © 1973, 1976 by The Trustees for the E. E. Cummings Trust. Copyright © 1973, 1976 by George James Firmage.

Dann, John C. From *The Revolution Remembered*, ed. John C. Dann. Copyright © 1980 by The University of Chicago. All rights reserved.

Dickey, James. "The Hospital Window." Copyright © 1962 by James Dickey. Reprinted from *Drowning With Others* by permission of Wesleyan University Press. "The Hospital Window" first appeared in *Poetry*.

Dickinson, Emily. "Because I Could Not Stop for Death" and "I Felt a Funeral." Reprinted by permission of the trustees of Amherst College and the publishers from *The Poems of Emily Dickinson*, edited by Thomas H. Johnson, Cambridge, Massachusetts: The Belknap Press of Harvard University Press, Copyright © 1951, 1955 by the President and Fellows of Harvard College.

Didion, Joan. *The White Album*, "Georgia O'Keeffe." Copyright © 1979 by Joan Didion. Reprinted by permission of Simon & Schuster, Inc.

Döhl, Reinhard. "Apfel." Reprinted by permission of the author.

Dryden, John. From *All for Love* in *British Dramatists from Dryden to Sheridan* (George H. Nettleton and Arthur E. Case, Editors). Revised by George Winchester Stone, Jr. Copyright © 1969 Houghton Mifflin Company. Used with permission.

Eliot, T. S. "Journey of the Magi." From *Collected Poems 1909–1962* by T. S. Eliot, copyright © 1936 by Harcourt Brace Jovanovich, Inc.; copyright © 1963, 1964 by T. S. Eliot. Reprinted by permission of the publisher.

Faulkner, William. From *Dry September*. Copyright 1930 and renewed 1958 by William Faulkner. Reprinted from *Collected Stories of William Faulkner* by permission of Random House, Inc.

Frost, Robert. "Wild Grapes." From *The Poetry of Robert Frost* edited by Edward Connery Lathem. Copyright 1923, © 1969 by Holt, Rinehart and Winston. Copyright 1951 by Robert Frost. Reprinted by permission of Henry Holt and Co., Inc.

Giovanni, Nikki. "Nikki-Rosa" from *Black Feeling, Black Talk, Black Judgement* by Nikki Giovanni. Copyright © 1968, 1970 by Nikki Giovanni. By permission of William Morrow & Company.

Hales, Corrine. "Power," by Corinne Hales, in *New Voices 1979–1983*, ed. May Swenson. Reprinted by permission of the Academy of American Poets.

Hamilton, Virginia. From *The People Could Fly: American Black Folktales*, by Virginia Hamilton. Copyright © 1985 by Virginia Hamilton. Reprinted by permission of Alfred A. Knopf, Inc.

Hellman, Lillian, and Peter Feibleman. From *Eating Together: Recollections & Recipes* by Lillian Hellman and Peter Feibleman. Copyright © 1984 by Left Leg, Inc. and Frog Jump Inc.

Hoyt, Helen. "The Sense of Death" from *The Home Book of Modern Verse*, edited by Burton E. Stevenson. Reprinted by permission of The Trustee for the Burton E. Stevenson Endowment for Children.

Hughes, Langston. "The Negro Speaks of Rivers." Copyright 1926 by Alfred A. Knopf, Inc. and renewed 1954 by Langston Hughes. Reprinted from *Selected Poems of Langston Hughes*, by permission of Alfred A. Knopf, Inc.

Ionesco, Eugene. From *The Bald Soprano (The Bald Prima Donna)* by Eugene Ionesco, translated by Donald Watson, courtesy of John Calder (Publishers) Ltd., London. Reprinted by permission of Grove Press, Inc. Copyright © 1958 by Grove Press, Inc.

Joans, Ted. "The .38." From *Black Pow-Wow, Jazz Poems* by Ted Joans. Copyright © 1969 by Ted Joans. All rights reserved. Reprinted by permission of Gunther Stuhlmann, Author's Representative.

Jones, Rodney. "The Mosquito." Reprinted by permission of The Atlantic Monthly Press. From *The Unborn*, copyright © 1985 by Rodney Jones.

Keillor, Garrison. From *Lake Wobegon Days*, by Garrison Keillor. Copyright © Garrison Keillor, 1985. Reprinted by permission of Viking Penguin, Inc.

Kennedy, X. J. "B Negative." Reprinted from *Cross Ties* by X. J. Kennedy, © 1985 X. J. Kennedy. Reprinted by permission of the University of Georgia Press.

Kunitz, Stanley. "Open the Gates." From *Selected Poems 1928–1958* by Stanley Kunitz Copyright 1944 by Stanley Kunitz. By permission of Little, Brown and Company, in association with The Atlantic Monthly Press.

Leonard, Hugh. Hugh Leonard, excerpted from *Da.* Copyright © 1973, 1978 Hugh Leonard. Reprinted with the permission of Atheneum Publishers, Inc.

MacLeish, Archibald. From "Ars Poetica" by Archibald MacLeish in *New and Collected Poems 1917–1976*. Copyright © 1976 by Archibald MacLeish. Reprinted by permission of Houghton Mifflin Company.

Madgett, Naomi Long. "Her Story" from *Star by Star* by Naomi Long Madgett, Detroit, Harlo, 1965, Evenill, 1970. With permission of the author.

Malamud, Bernard. "The Prison" from *The Magic Barrel* by Bernard Malamud. Copyright © 1950, renewed 1978 by Bernard Malamud. Reprinted by permission of Farrar, Straus and Giroux, Inc.

Martin, Judith. Judith Martin, "Graduations" from *Miss Manners' Guide to Excruciatingly Correct Behavior*. Copyright © 1982 United Feature Syndicate, Inc. Reprinted with the permission of Atheneum Publishers, Inc.

Masters, Marcia Lee. "The Heart's Place" reprinted by permission of the author.

McGough, Roger. "40 – Love" from *After the Merrymaking* by Roger McGough. Reprinted by permission of A. D. Peters & Co., Ltd., and Jonathan Cape Ltd.

Millay, Edna St. Vincent. "Sonnet XXX." From *Collected Poems*, Harper & Row. Copyright 1931, 1958 by Edna St. Vincent Millay and Norma Millay Ellis.

Moon, William Least Heat. From *Blue Highways: A Journey Into America* by William Least Heat Moon. Copyright © 1982 by William Least Heat Moon. By permission of Little, Brown and Company, in association with The Atlantic Monthly Press.

Morrill, Claire. "Miss Lizzie." From *A Taos Mosaic, Portrait of a New Mexico Village.* Albuquerque: University of New Mexico Press, 1973. Copyright held by author. Used by permission of the author.

Morrison, Toni. From *Sula,* by Toni Morrison. Copyright © 1973 by Toni Morrison. Reprinted by permission of Alfred A. Knopf, Inc.

Olds, Sharon. "The Race." Reprinted by permission; © 1985 Sharon Olds. Originally appeared in *The New Yorker.*

Ovid. "The Story of Baucis and Philemon." From *The Metamorphoses,* translated by Rolfe Humphries. Reprinted by permission of the Indiana University Press.

Pinter, Harold. From *Betrayal,* by Harold Pinter. Reprinted by permission of Grove Press, Inc. and Methuen & Co. Ltd.

Ransom, John Crowe. "Bells for John Whiteside's Daughter." Copyright 1924 by Alfred A. Knopf, Inc. and renewed 1952 by John Crowe Ransom. Reprinted from *Selected Poems, Third Edition, Revised and Enlarged,* by John Crowe Ransom, by permission of Alfred A. Knopf, Inc.

Rich, Adrienne. "A Woman Mourned by Daughters" is reprinted from THE FACT OF A DOORFRAME, *Poems Selected and New 1950–1984,* by Adrienne Rich, by permission of W. W. Norton & Company, Inc. Copyright © 1984 by Adrienne Rich. Copyright © 1975, 1978 by W. W. Norton & Company, Inc. Copyright © 1981 by Adrienne Rich.

Roethke, Theodore. "Child on Top of a Greenhouse" copyright 1946 by Editorial Publications, Inc. "The Waking" and "Old Lady's Winter Words" copyright 1948, 1952 by Theodore Roethke. All from *The Collected Poems of Theodore Roethke* and reprinted by permission of Doubleday & Company, Inc.

Roth, Philip. From "The Conversion of the Jews" in *Goodbye Columbus and Five Short Stories* by Philip Roth. Copyright © 1959 by Philip Roth. Reprinted by permission of Houghton Mifflin Company.

Santoli, Al. From *Everything We Had,* by Albert Santoli. Copyright © 1981 by Albert Santoli and Vietnam Veterans of America. Reprinted by permission of Random House, Inc.

Schlissel, Lillian. From *Women's Diaries of the Westward Journey,* ed. Lillian Schlissel. Reprinted by permission of Gertrude Tortillot Bradley.

Sexton, Anne. "Ringing the Bells." From *To Bedlam and Part Way Back* by Anne Sexton. Copyright © 1960 by Anne Sexton. Reprinted by permission of Houghton Mifflin Company. "Cinderella." From *Transformations* by Anne Sexton. Copyright © 1971 by Anne Sexton. Reprinted by permission of Houghton Mifflin Company.

Shakespeare, William. All selections from Neilson/Hill: *Complete Plays and Poems of William Shakespeare.* Copyright © 1942 by William Allan Neilson and Charles Jarvis Hill, renewed 1969 by Caroline Steiner and Margaret N. Helburn. Used by permission of Houghton Mifflin Company.

Shange, Ntozake. Reprinted with permission of Macmillan Publishing Company from *For Colored Girls Who Have Considered Suicide/When the Rainbow Is Enuf* by Ntozake Shange. Copyright © 1975, 1976, 1977 by Ntozake Shange.

Shaw, George Bernard. Excerpt from *Caesar and Cleopatra,* reprinted by permission of The Society of Authors on behalf of the Bernard Shaw Estate.

Sherman, Deborah. "Dulce." Reprinted by permission of the author.

Singer, Isaac Bashevis. Excerpt from "A Crown of Feathers" from *A Crown of Feathers* by Isaac Bashevis Singer. Copyright © 1972, 1973 by Isaac Bashevis Singer. Originally appeared in *The New Yorker.* Reprinted by permission of Farrar, Straus and Giroux, Inc.

Solt, Mary Ellen. "Forsythia" from *Concrete Poetry: A World View,* by Mary Ellen Solt. Reprinted by permission of Indiana University Press.

Sondheim, Stephen. Music and lyrics by Stephen Sondheim (from *Sunday in the Park with George*). Copyright © 1973, 1985 Rilting Music, Inc. & Revelation Music Publishing Corp., Suite 2110, 1270 Avenue of the Americas, New York, NY 10020. International Copyright Secured. Made in U.S.A. All rights reserved. A Tommy Valando Publication.

Sophocles. From *Three Theban Plays by Sophocles: Antigone, Oedipus the King, and Oedipus at Colonus,* translated by Theodore Howard Banks. Copyright 1956 by Theodore Howard Banks; renewed 1984 by Marian C. Banks. Reprinted by permission of Oxford University Press, Inc.

Stevens, Wallace. "The Idea of Order at Key West." Copyright 1936 by Wallace Stevens and renewed 1964 by Holly Stevens. Reprinted from *The Collected Poems of Wallace Stevens* by permission of Alfred A. Knopf, Inc.

Terkel, Studs. From *Working: People Talk About What They Do All Day and How They Feel About What They Do,* by Studs Terkel. Copyright © 1972, 1974 by Studs Terkel. Reprinted by permission of Pantheon Books, a Division of Random House, Inc.

Thomas, Dylan. "In My Craft or Sullen Art." Dylan Thomas, *Poems of Dylan Thomas.* Copyright 1946 by New Directions Publishing Corporation. Reprinted by permission of New Directions and David Higham Associates Ltd.

The Torah. From Genesis. This material is copyrighted by and used through the courtesy of The Jewish Publication Society.

Updike, John. "A & P." Copyright © 1962 by John Updike. Reprinted from *Pigeon Feathers and Other Stories,* by John Updike, by permission of Alfred A. Knopf, Inc.

Wallace, Ronald. "The Art of Love" by Ronald Wallace. Reprinted by permission of the author. Originally appeared in *The Atlantic Monthly;* subsequently in *Tunes for Bears to Dance To* (University of Pittsburgh Press, 1983).

Walker, Alice. Untitled dedicatory poem from *Horses Make a Landscape Look More Beautiful* by Alice Walker. Copyright © 1984 Alice Walker. Reprinted by permission of Harcourt Brace Jovanovich, Inc.

Welty, Eudora. Reprinted by permission of the publishers from *One Writer's Beginnings,* by Eudora Welty, Cambridge, Mass.: Harvard University Press, Copyright © 1983, 1984 by Eudora Welty. From *Losing Battles,* by Eudora Welty. Copyright © 1970 by Eudora Welty. Reprinted by permission of Random House, Inc. From "June Recital." Copyright 1947, 1975 by Eudora Welty. Abridged from her volume *The Golden Apples* by permission of Harcourt Brace Jovanovich, Inc.

West, Nathanael. Nathanael West, *Miss Lonelyhearts & The Day of The Locust.* Copyright © 1960 by Laura Perelman. Reprinted by permission of New Directions Publishing Corporation.

Wilson, Lanford. Excerpt from *5th of July* by Lanford Wilson. Copyright © 1979 by Lanford Wilson. Reprinted by permission of Hill and Wang, a division of Farrar, Straus and Giroux, Inc.

Wright, James. "A Blessing." Copyright © 1961 by James Wright. Reprinted from *The Branch Will Not Break* by permission of Wesleyan University Press. "A Blessing" first appeared in *Poetry*.

Yeats, William Butler. "The Second Coming." Reprinted with permission of Macmillan Publishing Company from *Collected Poems* by William Butler Yeats. Copyright 1924 by Macmillan Publishing Company, renewed 1952 by Bertha Georgie Yeats; and by permission of Michael B. Yeats and Macmillan, London Ltd. Reprinted with permission of Macmillan Publishing Company. "Among School Children" from *Collected Poems* by William Butler Yeats. Copyright 1928 by Macmillan Publishing Company, renewed 1956 by Georgie Yeats; and by permission of Michael B. Yeats and Macmillan, London Ltd.

Subject Index

Acting, compared with interpretation, 266–267
Action
  defined, 211–212
  of a play, 268
Aesthetic distance, 304
Aesthetic entirety, 7, 129
Alliteration, 369
Allusions, 20, 171, 360
Ambiguity, 15
Analogy, 361
Analysis, literary, 6, 15
  of poetry, 38–43
  of story, 32–38
Angle of placement, 319–320
Anthologies, 8
Apostrophe, 362–363
Articulation, 88
Assonance, 369, 406
Audience
  adapting program to, 506–507
  communicating with, 4–5,
    319–320
  sense, 80–81
Auditory imagery, 123
Autistic gestures, 121
"Awareness exercises," 129

Ballads, 353
Blank verse, 365, 392, 393,
  399–400, 407
Body, use in oral interpretation,
  117–131
Breath control, 75–80
  exercises for, 77–78

Cadences, 173, 401–405
Caesura, 403
Chamber Theatre, 441–448
Characters
  creation of, 215–217
  in drama, 263, 268–274,
    278–281, 309–320
  embodiment of, 309–313
  interplay of, 315–317
  muscle memory and, 310–311
  in narration, 212–213
  physical focus of, 317–320
Chautauqua movement, 513
Climax, 21–29, 39, 268
Comedy, 263
Communication, interpretation
  as, 3–7
Compiled scripts, 449–452
Concrete poetry, 452–453
Conflict, 211–212
Connotation, 19–20
Consonance, 369
Content, 349–352
Copyright permission, 494, 495
Costuming, 312–313
Crisis, 22, 211, 268
Cues, 316–317
Cutting, 218–220, 321–322

Denotation, 19
Denouement, 268
Description, 174–175
Dialect, 88, 353
Dialogue, narration and, 213–217
Diaries, 178–179

Direct discourse, 213
Direction of group performance,
    493–497
Drama, 8, 263–345
    characters in, 263, 268–274,
        278–281, 309–320
    conflict in, 268
    mechanical details and, 285–286
    memorization in, 305–306
    narrator in, 269
    oral interpretation of, 263–345
    physical focus in, 317–320
    rhythm in, 281–282
    scenes in, 274–281
    scenography in, 283–285
    solo performance of, 263–286
    special problems of, 322–323
    structural elements of, 268
    style in, 282–283
    technique in, 303–324
Dramatic lyric, 358
Dramatic monologue, 358–359
Dramatic narrative, 357–358
Dramatic poetry, 357–359

Elegy, 355–356
Ellipsis, 367–368
Elocution, 510–514
Emotional climax, 21–22, 39
Emotive content, 6–7, 85, 349–351
Empathy, 84, 126–129
Enjambment, 401
Epic, 354
Epic Theatre, 447
Essay, personal, 177–178
Excerpting, 218–220, 321–322
Exhalation, 75–78
"Expression" courses, 513–514

Factual prose, 176–177
Feet, in poetry, 394–397
Feminine/masculine lines, 407
Figurative language, 359–365
Figures of speech, 171, 360–363
Filmscripts, 453
First-person narration, 205–207
Foot (metrical) prosody, 394–397

Free verse, 365, 392–393, 400,
    401, 405, 407
Fulcrum, 29, 39, 40
    balance and, 29, 170–171

Gesture, 120–121
Greek theatre, 437–438
Group performance, 435–490
    challenges of, 452–454
    Chamber Theatre, 441–448
    of compiled scripts, 449–452
    direction of, 493–497
    Readers Theatre, 436–441
Gustatory imagery, 123

Iambic pentameter, 396
Imagery, 44, 45
    literary, 360–365
    and the senses, 123–126
    types of, 123–126
Indirect discourse, 214
Individuality, 9–10, 15, 19, 38
Inflection, 83
Inhalation, 75–78
Intelligibility, of speech, 109–111
Interpretation. *See* Oral interpreta-
    tion
Intrinsic factors, in works of art,
    26–31, 41, 43, 45, 124

Japanese Noh drama, 447
Journals, 178–179

Kinesics, 121–122, 123
Kinesthetic imagery, 123
Kinetic imagery, 123

Lectern, 320–321
Lecture recital, 498–499
Letters (correspondence), 179–180
Line
    lengths, 399–401
    masculine/feminine, 407
    in poetry, 394–401
Literary criticism, 15
Literary imagery, 334–340

Literature
    communicating effect of, 5–7
    evaluation of, 8–15
    see also Drama; Poetry; Prose
Locus, 24–27
Logical climax, 21–22, 39
Logical content, 349–351
Lyric poetry, 354–357

Masculine/feminine lines, 407
Material, choice of, 7–15, 499–500
Mechanical details, drama and,
        285–286
Melody, 83–84
Memorization, 4, 305–306
Metaphor, 171, 361
Meter, 395
Metonymy, 361
Metrical foot, 394–396
Metrical prosody, 394–396
Metrical tale, 353
Mime, study of, 129
Monologue, dramatic, 358–359
Monotone, 83
Motif, 40, 41
Muscle memory, 121, 122, 123, 310
Muscle tone, 122, 123, 175

Narration, 203–233
    characters in, 212–213
    conflict in, 211
    defined, 203
    dialogue and, 213–217
    first-person, 205–207
    second-person, 207
    setting and, 217–218
    third-person, 208–211
Narrative, dramatic, 357–358
Narrative poetry, 352–354
Narrator
    language of, 37
    nature of, 35–36, 38
    in plays, 269

Ode, 356
Olfactory imagery, 123, 125
Onomatopoeia, 369

Oral interpretation
    analysis of selection for, 19–44
    as art of communication, 3–7
    basic principles of, 3–159
    body use in, 117–131
    choice of selection for, 7–15
    compared with acting, 266–267
    definition of, 3–7
    of drama, 263–345
    by a group, 435–490
    history of theories of, 509–517
    performance of, 45–46
    of poetry, 349–431
    program building for, 498–506
    of prose, 163–260
    synthesis and, 44–45
    technique in, 303–345
    voice development for, 75–89

Paragraphs, 164–165
"Paraliterature," 180–181
Pause
    in poetry, 401, 403
    in speech, 85–87
Performance
    analysis of, 45–47, 129–131,
        220–223, 322–324, 408–409
    group, analysis of, 454–456
    technique and, 117
Performance area, 440
Persona (speaker), 23–24, 27
Personal essay, 177–178
Personification, 362
Petrarchan sonnet, 356
Phrasal pause, 85
Phrases, in speech, 168–169
Physical contact, 314–315
Physical focus, in drama, 317–320
Pitch, 83–85
Playing space, 440
Plays. See Drama
Plot, 211–212, 268
Poetic content, 349–351
Poetic syntax, 366–368
Poetry, 349–431
    cadences in, 401–405
    concrete, 452–453

Poetry (*cont.*)
  content of, 349–372
  conventional, 391
  dramatic, 357–359
  figurative language and, 359–365
  language of, 349–372
  lines of, 394–401
  lyric, 354–357
  narrative, 352–354
  oral interpretation of, 349–431
  pause in, 401, 403
  rhyme in, 403–405
  stanzas in, 365–366, 393–394
  structure of, 391–408
  syntax of, 366–368
  titles of, 371–372
  tone color and, 368–371
Point of balance, 29. *See also*
    Fulcrum
Point of view, 204–211
Posture, 119
Programs, 498–508
  audience for, 506–507
  building of, 498–506
  compared with recitals, 498–499
  experimentation in, 502–506
  selection of material for, 499–500
  timing of, 507–508
  unification of, 500–502
Projection of voice, 80–83
Pronunciation, 87–88
Properties, 308–309
Prose
  aspects of, 163–181
  factual, 176–177
  narrative, 203–223
  personal essays, 177–178
  rhythm in, 173–174
  style, 164–176
  types of, 176–181
Prosody, 391, 394–399
  foot (metrical), 394–396
  stress, 397
  syllabic, 397–399
Punctuation, 168–169

Quality of voice, 83–85

Readers Theatre, 436–441
Reading stand, 320–321
Reflective lyric, 355
Reflexive activity, 314
Rehearsal devices, 303
Remembered action theory, 310
Rhyme, 405–408
Rhyme scheme, 391
Rhythm
  of content, 30–31, 43, 45
  of a play, 281–282
  in prose, 173–174
Rising action, 268

Scansion, 395
Scene setting, 306–308
Scenes, 274–281
Scenography, 283–285
Scripts, compiled, 449–452
Second-person narration, 207
Selection, analysis, 19–44
  choice, 7–15, 499–500
  synthesis, 44–45
Semantics, 20
Semiotics, 20
Sense imagery, 123–126
"Sensitivity sessions," 129
Sensory appeals, 363–365
Sentences, 165–171
Setting, 217–218
Shakespearean sonnet, 356, 357
Simile, 171, 361
Soliloquy, 359
Solo performance
  of drama, 263–286
  purpose of, 265–266
  technical problems of, 303–345
Sonnet, 356–357
Speaker (persona), 23–24, 27
Speech
  intelligibility of, 87–89
  rate of, 85–87
  Standard American, 88
  see also Voice development
Speech phrases, 168–169
Standard American Speech, 88
Stanzas, 365–366, 393–394

Storytelling (narration), 203–223
"Stream of consciousness," 125
Stress, 173
Stress prosody, 397
Structure
  content and, 6–7
  defined, 391
  meaning and, 8
  of poetry, 391–408
Style, 164–176
  defined, 164
  description in, 174–175
  in drama, 282–283
  paragraphs, 164–165
  prose rhythm, 173–174
  sentences, 165–168, 170–171
  speech phrases, 168–169
  tone color, 172–173
  word choice, 171–172
Suggestion, 10, 15, 19, 38
Syllabic prosody, 397–399
Synecdoche, 361
Syntax, poetic, 366–368
Synthesis, by interpreter, 44

Tactual imagery, 123
Technique
  control and, 304–305
  defined, 117, 303

  of drama, 303–324
  memorization and, 305–306
  in oral interpretation, 303–308
  scene setting and, 306–308
  as style of performance, 117
Theories of interpretation, 509–517
Theory of remembered action, 310
Thermal imagery, 123
Third-person narration, 208–211
Timbre, 84
Titles, of poems, 371–372
Tone color, 172–173, 368–371
Tragedy, 263

Universality, 9, 10, 12, 15, 19, 38

Visual imagery, 123
Vocal quality, 84
Voice development
  breath control and, 75–80
  exercises for, 81–82
  intelligibility of speech, 87–89
  pitch and quality, 83–85
  rate and pause, 85–87
  volume and projection, 80–83
Volume of voice, 80–83

Word choice, 171–172

Selections Index

Note: **Italicized page numbers in an entry show where the selection is reprinted in the "Selections for Analysis and Oral Interpretation" or at length elsewhere in the text; roman page numbers indicate where the selection is discussed or mentioned in the text.**

"A & P" (Updike), *98–104*, 205, 206

Adams, John Quincy, 509

"Adonais" (Shelley), 406

Aeneid, The, 354

Albee, Edward, *Who's Afraid of Virginia Woolf?* 274–281, *275–277*, 282, 438

All for Love (Dryden), *294–297*, 312

Angelou, Maya, "I Almost Remember," 355, 407, *423; I Know Why the Caged Bird Sings, 155–158;* "Phenominal Woman," *154–155*

Antony and Cleopatra (Shakespeare), 285, *297–299*

"Apfel" (Döhl), 453, 472

Apocalypse Now (Coppola), 451

Arnold, Matthew, "Dover Beach," *104–105*

"Ars Poetica" (MacLeish), 351

"Art of Love, The" (Wallace), 124, *145–146*

"As I Would Wish You Birds" (Ciardi), 366, 394, *411–412*

As You Like It (Shakespeare), *153*

Auden, W. H. "In Memory of W. B. Yeats," 356

"B Negative" (Kennedy), *463–464*

Babcock, Maud May, 515

Bald Soprano, The (Ionesco), 283, 290

Baraka, Imamu Amiri, "Preface to a Twenty Volume Suicide Note," *389*

Barzun, Jacques, 177

"Because I Could Not Stop for Death" (Dickinson), *54–55*, 128

Beckett, Samuel, *Endgame*, 263; *The Lost Ones*, 211; *Waiting for Godot*, 263

Bell, Madison Smartt, "The Naked Lady," 207, *238–242*

Belle of Amherst, 435

"Bells for John Whiteside's Daughter" (Ransom), *384*

Bennett, Arnold, 164

Beowulf, 354

Betrayal (Pinter), 283, *335–340*

Betts, Doris, "The Ugliest Pilgrim," 23, 206, *229–238*

Bierhorst, John, "The Night Chant," *111*

"Blessing, A" (Wright), *413–414*

Bloods (Terry), 451

Blue Highways (Moon), *111–114*

Bowen, Elizabeth, *The Little Girls,* 93–97

Brecht, Bertolt, *The Caucasian Chalk Circle,* 269, 285, 438, 447, *467–469*

Breen, Robert, 441

Browning, Robert, "My Last Duchess," 359, *421–422;* "The Pied Piper of Hamelin," 79; "Soliloquy of the Spanish Cloister," 23, 359, 366, 371, *385–387*

Bryan, C. D. B., *Friendly Fire,* 451

Burgh, James, 511

Burney, Fanny, 450

Byron, George Gordon, "The Prisoner of Chillon," 357

Caesar and Cleopatra (Shaw), 285, *291–294,* 307

Cameron, Peter, "Homework," 24, *59–65*

Candida (Shaw), 284–285

Canterbury Tales (Chaucer), 353

Capote, Truman, *A Christmas Memory,* 23, *49–50*

Caputo, Paul, *A Rumor of War,* 451

Carroll, Lewis, "Jabberwocky," *92–93*

Caucasian Chalk Circle, The (Brecht), 269, 285, 438, *467–469*

Chamberlain, William B., 515

Chaucer, Geoffrey, *Canterbury Tales,* 353

Chekhov, Anton, *The Three Sisters,* 268–274, 269–270, 282

Chief Seattle, "My People," *108–110*

"Child on Top of a Greenhouse" (Roethke), 24, 29, *409*

Chopin, Kate, "The Story of an Hour," 29, *32–35,* 36–38

Christmas Memory, A (Capote), 23, *49–50*

Ciardi, John, 351; "As I Would Wish You Birds," 366, 394, *411–412*

"Cinderella" (Sexton), *460–462*

Clark, Solomon H., 515

Common Reader, The (Woolf), 171

Congressional Record, 180

"Conversion of the Jews, The" (Roth), 215, 216, *252–257*

Coppola, Francis Ford, *Apocalypse Now,* 451

"Crown of Feathers, A" (Singer), 124, *135–141,* 218

Cruz, Victor Hernandez, "Today Is a Day of Great Joy," 394, *425–426*

Cummings, E. E., "Spring is like a perhaps hand," 350, 368, *416*

Cunningham, Cornelius Carman, 515

Curry, Samuel Silas, 513, 514, 515

Cyrano de Bergerac (Rostand), 86–87

Da (Leonard), 24, 305, 308, *329–335,* 448

Dann, John C., *The Revolution Remembered, 185–186*

"Dauber" (Masefield), 353

"Death of the Hired Man, The" (Frost), 353, 354

Delsarte, François, 512

"Detective, The" (Marshall), 212, 213, *249–251*

Dial, 505

Dickens, Charles, 514; *A Tale of Two Cities,* 124–125

Dickey, James, "The Hospital Window," *387–389*

Dickinson, Emily, 10, 13–15, 19, 22, 24, 47; "Because I Could Not Stop for Death," *54–55,* 128; "I Felt a Funeral," *11–12,* 29, 30, 38–43, 46, 350

Didion, Joan, "Holy Water," 178; "Slouching Towards Bethlehem," 451; *The White*

Album ("Georgia O'Keeffe"), 105–107
Dispatches (Herr), 451
Division Street (Terkel), 180
Döhl, Reinhard, "Apfel," 453, *472*
Donne, John, "Go and Catch a Falling Star," 371, *415*; "A Hymn to God the Father," 97–98
"Dover Beach" (Arnold), 104–105
Drayton, Michael, "Since There's No Help," *424*
Dry September (Faulkner), 124, *187–189*
Dryden, John, *All for Love*, 294–297
"Dulce" (Sherman), 24, 25, *56–58*, 122

Eating Together (Hellman and Feibleman), *191–194*
Eliot, T. S., 392, 393, 407; "Journey of the Magi," 400, 403, *412–413*
Emerson, Charles Wesley, 513
Endgame (Beckett), 263
"Eve of St. Agnes, The" (Keats), 353, 354
Everything We Had (Santoli), 451, *465–466*

Faulkner, William, *Dry September*, 124, *187–189*
Feibleman, Peter, and Lillian Hellman, *Eating Together*, *191–194*
Fifth of July (Wilson), *287–289*
"Finishing the Hat" (Sondheim), 124, *325–326*
First Corinthians, Chapter 13 (St. Paul), *189–190*
For Colored Girls Who Have Considered Suicide/When the Rainbow Is Enuf (Shange), *473–477*
Forster, E. M., 213
"Forsythia" (Solt), 452, *471*

"40 – Love" (McGough), *470*
Freneau, Philip, "The Wild Honeysuckle," *84*
Friendly Fire (Bryan), 451
Frost, Robert, 392, 393; "The Death of the Hired Man," 353, 354; "Wild Grapes," 24, *52–54*

"Garret Watts" (Dann), *186*
Genesis I: 1–16 (The Torah), 30, *248–249*
"Georgia O'Keeffe" (Didion), 105–107
Gilbert, W. S., and A. S. Sullivan, *Iolanthe*, 87
Giovanni, Nikki, "Nikki-Rosa," *375–376*
"Go and Catch a Falling Star" (Donne), 371, *415*
"Goblin Market" (Rossetti), *477–490*
"Golden World, The" (Wolfe), 125, 126
Good War, The (Terkel), 180
Gone with the Wind, 317
"Graduations" (Martin), *183–184*
"Greenleaf" (O'Connor), 214

Hales, Corrine, "Power," *381–382*
Hamilton, Virginia, "The People Could Fly," *456–459*
Hard Times (Terkel), 180
Hardy, Thomas, "In Church," *158*
"Heart's Place, The" (Masters), 360, *377–378*
Hedda Gabler (Ibsen), 310
Hellman, Lillian, *Pentimento*, 170, 173; and Peter Feibleman, *Eating Together*, *191–194*
Henry IV (Shakespeare), 167
"Her Story" (Madgett), *107*
Herr, Michael, *Dispatches*, 451
"Holy Water" (Didion), 178
Homer, 206; *The Odyssey*, 20
"Homework" (Cameron), 24, *59–65*

Hopkins, Gerard Manley, 24;
      "The Starlight Night," 22, 48,
      123; "The Windhover," 367,
      369, 371, 372–373
Horses Make a Landscape Look More
      Beautiful (Walker), 29, 394,
      426–428
"Hospital Window, The"
      (Dickey), 387–389
"Hound of Heaven, The"
      (Thompson), 361
Hoyt, Helen, "The Sense of
      Death," 10–11, 12, 14, 24
Hughes, Langston, "The Negro
      Speaks of Rivers," 150
"Hymn to God the Father, A"
      (Donne), 97–98

"I Almost Remember" (Angelou),
      355, 407, 423
"I Felt a Funeral" (Dickinson),
      11–12, 29, 30, 38–39, 40–43,
      46, 350
"I Hear America Singing"
      (Whitman), 84
I Know Why the Caged Bird Sings
      (Angelou), 155–158
Ibsen, Henrik, Hedda Gabler,
      310–311
"Idea of Order at Key West, The"
      (Stevens), 380–381
"In Church" (Hardy), 158
"In Memory of W. B. Yeats"
      (Auden), 356
"In My Craft or Sullen Art"
      (Thomas), 369, 376–377, 397,
      398
Iolanthe (Gilbert and Sullivan), 87
Ionesco, Eugene, The Bald
      Soprano, 283, 290

"Jabberwocky" (Carroll), 92–93
"Jack and Jill" (Loomis), 418–419
James, Henry, 204; "Letter to
      Grace Norton," 190–191
"Jane Gould Tortillot" (Schlissel),
      194–197

Joans, Ted, "The .38," 146–148
Johnson, Gertrude, 515
Johnson, Samuel, 264
Jones, Rodney, "The Mosquito,"
      124, 141–142
"Journey of the Magi" (Eliot),
      400, 403, 412–413
Julius Caesar (Shakespeare), 82
June Recital (Welty), 124, 181–183

Karnow, Stanley, Vietnam, 451
Keats, John, 24; "The Eve of St.
      Agnes," 353, 354; "Sonnet,"
      48; "To Autumn," 361, 362,
      363–364, 366, 369–370; "To a
      Nightingale," 360
Keillor, Garrison, Lake Wobegon
      Days, 89–92
Kennedy, X. J., "B Negative,"
      463–464
Kunitz, Stanley, "Open the
      Gates," 366, 383–384, 393,
      398, 399, 403

Lake Wobegon Days (Keillor), 89–92
Lawrence, D. H., program on,
      501–502
Leonard, Hugh, Da, 24, 305,
      329–335, 448
"Letter to Grace Norton" (James),
      190–191
Little Girls, The (Bowen), 93–97
Loomis, Charles Battel, "Jack and
      Jill," 418–419
Losing Battles (Welty), 208–210
Lost Ones, The (Beckett), 211

MacLeish, Archibald, "Ars
      Poetica," 351
McGough, Roger, "40 – Love,"
      470
Madgett, Naomi Long, "Her
      Story," 107
Malamud, Bernard, "The Prison,"
      213, 220, 223–229, 494
Marshall, Archibald, "The Detec-
      tive," 212, 213, 249–251

Martin, Judith, *Miss Manners'®* *Guide to Excruciatingly Correct Behavior* ("Graduations"), *183–184*

Marvell, Andrew, "To His Coy Mistress," 371, *373–375*

Masefield, John, "Dauber," 353

Mason, John, 511

Masters, Marcia Lee, "The Heart's Place," 360, *377–378*

Merchant of Venice, The (Shakespeare), 82

Metamorphoses, The (Ovid), 212, *242–245*

Millay, Edna St. Vincent, "Sonnet XXX," 403, *424–425*

Milton, John, "On His Blindness," *420–421*; *Paradise Lost*, 354, 435

"Miss Lizzie," (Morrill), 24, *66–72*, 218

Miss Lonelyhearts (West), *442–448*

Miss Manners'® Guide to Excruciatingly Correct Behavior (Martin), *183–184*

Moby Dick (Melville), 219

Moon, William Least Heat, *Blue Highways*, *111–114*

Morrill, Claire, "Miss Lizzie," 24, *66–72*, 218

Morrison, Toni, *Sula*, 220, *246–247*

"Moses Hall" (Dann), *185*

"Mosquito, The" (Jones), 124, *141–142*

"My Last Duchess" (Browning), 359, *421–422*

"My People" (Chief Seattle), *108–110*

"Naked Lady, The" (Bell), 207, *238–242*

Navajo ceremonial chant, "The Night Chant," *111*

"Negro Speaks of Rivers, The" (Hughes), *150*

Nelson, Severina E., 515

New Testament, The (St. Paul), *189–190*

New York Review of Books, 505

New York Times, 503–505

New Yorker, 505

Nicholas Nickelby, 435

"Night Chant, The" (Navajo ceremonial chant, translated by Bierhorst), *111*

"Nikki-Rosa" (Giovanni), *375–376*

O'Connor, Flannery, "Greenleaf," 214

O'Connor, William Van, 393

Odyssey, The (Homer), 20, 205

Oedipus the King (Sophocles), 22, 313, *341–345*

"Old Lady's Winter Words" (Roethke), 24, 25, 124, *151–152*, 366, 371

Olds, Sharon, "The Race," *148–150*

"On His Blindness" (Milton), *420–421*

One Writer's Beginnings (Welty), *142–145*

"Open the Gates" (Kunitz), 366, *383–384*, 393, 398, 399, 403

Our Town (Wilder), 441

Ovid, *The Metamorphoses* ("The Story of Baucis and Philemon"), 212, *242–245*

Paradise Lost (Milton), 354, 435

Parrish, Wayland Maxwell, 515

Pentimento (Hellman), 170, 173

"People Could Fly, The" (Hamilton), *456–459*

"Phenominal Woman" (Angelou), *154–155*

Phillips, Arthur Edward, 515

Phillips, Wendell, 514

"Pied Piper of Hamelin, The" (Browning), 79

Pinter, Harold, 282; *Betrayal*, 283, *335–340*

Pope, Alexander, "The Rape of the Lock," 354

Pound, Ezra, 401

"Power" (Hales), *381–382*

"Preface to a Twenty Volume Suicide Note" (Baraka), *389*

"Prison, The" (Malamud), 213, 220, *223–229*, 494

"Prisoner of Chillon, The" (Byron), 357

Quite Early One Morning (Thomas), 217–218

"Race, The" (Olds), *148–150*

Ransom, John Crowe, "Bells for John Whiteside's Daughter," *384*

"Rape of the Lock, The" (Pope), 354

Revolution Remembered, The (Dann), *185–186*

Rich, Adrienne, "A Woman Mourned by Daughters," *379*

"Ringing the Bells" (Sexton), *51*

Robb, Mary Margaret, 515

Roethke, Theodore, 123; "Child on Top of a Greenhouse," 24, 29, *409*; "Old Lady's Winter Words," 24, 25, *151–152*, 366, 371; "The Waking," 410

Romeo and Juliet (Shakespeare), 25, 308, *326–328*

Rossetti, Christina Georgina, "Goblin Market," *477–490*

Rostand, Edmond, *Cyrano de Bergerac*, 86–87

Roth, Philip, "The Conversion of the Jews," 215, *252–257*

Royal Shakespeare Company, 435

Rumor of War, A (Caputo), 451

Runyon, Daniel, 207

Rush, James, 511–512

St. Paul, 179; *The New Testament* (First Corinthians, Chapter 13), *189–190*

Santoli, Al, *Everything We Had*, 451, *465–466*

Schlissel, Lillian, *Women's Diaries of the Westward Journey* ("Jane Gould Tortillot"), *194–197*

"Second Coming, The" (Yeats), *132–133*, 451

"Sense of Death, The" (Hoyt), *10–11*, 12, 14, 24

Sexton, Anne, "Cinderella," *460–462*; "Ringing the Bells," *51*

Shakespeare, William, 24, 31, 392, 438; *Antony and Cleopatra*, 285, *297–299*; *As You Like It*, 153; *Henry IV*, 167; *Julius Caesar*, 82; *The Merchant of Venice*, 82; *Romeo and Juliet*, 25, *326–328*, "Sonnet 18," *55–56*, "Sonnet 29," 420, "Sonnet 130," 56

Shange, Ntozake, *For Colored Girls Who Have Considered Suicide/When the Rainbow Is Enuf*, *473–477*

Shaw, George Bernard, 164; *Caesar and Cleopatra*, 285, *291–294*, 307; *Candida*, 284–285

Shelley, Percy Bysshe, "Adonais," 406

Sheridan, Richard Brinsley, 510

Sheridan, Thomas, 510–511

Sherman, Deborah, "Dulce," 24, *56–58*

"Since There's No Help" (Drayton), *424*

Singer, Isaac Bashevis, "A Crown of Feathers," 124, *135–141*, 218

"Slouching Towards Bethlehem" (Didion), 451

"Soliloquy of the Spanish Cloister" (Browning), 23, 359, 366, 371, *385–387*

Solt, Mary Ellen, "Forsythia," 452, *471*

Sondheim, Stephen, *Sunday in the Park with George* ("Finishing the Hat"), 124, *325–326*

"Song of Myself" (Whitman), 416–418

"Sonnet" (Keats), 48

"Sonnet 18" (Shakespeare), 55–56

"Sonnet 29" (Shakespeare), 420

"Sonnet XXX" (Millay), 403, 424–425

"Sonnet 130" (Shakespeare), 56

Sophocles, Oedipus the King, 22, 313, 341–345

"Spring is like a perhaps hand" (Cummings), 350, 368, 416

"Starlight Night, The" (Hopkins), 22, 48, 123

Stein, Gertrude, 203

Stevens, Wallace, "The Idea of Order at Key West," 380–381

"Story of Baucis and Philemon, The" (Ovid), 242–245

"Story of an Hour, The" (Chopin), 29, 32–35, 36–38

Sula (Morrison), 220, 246–247

Sullivan, A. S., and W. S. Gilbert, Iolanthe, 87

Sunday in the Park with George (Sondheim), 124, 325–326

Tale of Two Cities, A (Dickens), 124–125

Tennyson, Alfred, Lord, "Ulysses," 20, 25, 133–135, 358, 403

Terkel, Studs, Division Street, 180; The Good War, 180; Hard Times, 180; Working ("Terry Pickens"), 180, 197–200

Terry, Wallace, Bloods, 451

"Terry Pickens" (Terkel), 180, 197–200

".38, The" (Joans), 146–148

Thomas, Dylan, "In My Craft or Sullen Art," 369, 376–377, 397, 398; Quite Early One Morning, 217–218

Thompson, Francis, "The Hound of Heaven," 361

Three Sisters, The (Chekhov), 268–274, 269–270, 282

Thurber, James, 118, 177

"To Autumn" (Keats), 361, 362, 363, 364, 366, 369–370

"To His Coy Mistress" (Marvell), 371, 373–375

"To a Nightingale" (Keats), 360

"Today Is a Day of Great Joy" (Cruz), 394, 425–426

Torah, The, Genesis I: 1–16, 248–249

"Ugliest Pilgrim, The" (Betts), 23, 206, 229–238

"Ulysses" (Tennyson), 20, 25, 133–135, 358, 403

Updike, John, 206; "A & P," 98–104, 205, 206

Vietnam (Karnow), 451

Waiting for Godot (Beckett), 263

"Waking, The" (Roethke), 410

Walker, Alice, Horses Make a Landscape Look More Beautiful, 29, 394, 426–428

Walker, John, 510–511

Wallace, Ronald, "The Art of Love," 124, 145–146

Welty, Eudora, June Recital, 124, 181–183; Losing Battles, 208–211; One Writer's Beginnings, 142–145

West, Nathanael, Miss Lonelyhearts, 442–448

"When I Heard the Learn'd Astronomer" (Whitman), 47

White Album, The (Didion), 105–107

Whitman, Walt, 24, 403; "I Hear America Singing," 84; "Song of Myself," 416–418, "When I Heard the Learn'd Astronomer," 47

Who's Afraid of Virginia Woolf?
    (Albee), 274–281, *275–277,*
    282, 438–440
"Wild Grapes" (Frost), 24, *52–54*
"Wild Honeysuckle, The"
    (Freneau), *84*
Wilder, Thornton, 438; *Our Town,*
    441
Wilson, Lanford, *Fifth of July,*
    287–289
"Windhover, The" (Hopkins),
    367, 369, 371, *372–373*
Wolfe, Thomas, "The Golden
    World," 125, 126

"Woman Mourned by Daughters,
    A" (Rich), *379*
Women's Diaries of the Westward
    Journey (Schlissel), *194–197*
Woolbent, Charles H., 515
Woolf, Virginia, 171
Working (Terkel), 180, *197–200*
Wright, James, "A Blessing,"
    413–414

Yeats, William Butler, "The
    Second Coming," *132–133,*
    451

Student Questionnaire

We hope that you will take a few minutes to fill out this questionnaire. Your response will help us to plan future editions of *Oral Interpretation*. Please answer the questions, detach the sheet, and mail it to the Communications Editor, College Division, Houghton Mifflin Co., One Beacon Street, Boston, MA 02108. Thank you.

Name of college or university _____

Name of course/department _____

Name of instructor _____

Other books assigned in course _____

Reason you are taking the course _____

1. The following selections were used for the first time in this book. Please rate them.

	EXCEL-LENT	GOOD	FAIR	POOR	DIDN'T READ
Chapter 2 Analyzing the Selection					
CAPOTE From *A Christmas Memory*	___	___	___	___	___
SHERMAN *Dulce*	___	___	___	___	___
CAMERON *Homework*	___	___	___	___	___
Chapter 3 Voice Development for Oral Interpretation					
KEILLOR From *Lake Wobegon Days*	___	___	___	___	___
CHIEF SEATTLE *My People*	___	___	___	___	___
NAVAJO CHANT From *The Night Chant*	___	___	___	___	___
MOON From *Blue Highways*	___	___	___	___	___
Chapter 4 The Use of the Body in Oral Interpretation					
JONES *The Mosquito*	___	___	___	___	___
WELTY From *One Writer's Beginnings*	___	___	___	___	___
WALLACE *The Art of Love*	___	___	___	___	___
OLDS *The Race*	___	___	___	___	___
ANGELOU From *I Know Why the Caged Bird Sings*	___	___	___	___	___
HARDY *In Church*	___	___	___	___	___
Chapter 5 The Interpretation of Prose					
MARTIN From *Miss Manners'® Guide to Excruciatingly Correct Behavior*	___	___	___	___	___
DANN (ED.) From *The Revolution Remembered*	___	___	___	___	___
HELLMAN AND FEIBLEMAN From *Eating Together*	___	___	___	___	___
SCHLISSEL (ED.) From *Women's Diaries of the Westward Journey*	___	___	___	___	___
TERKEL From *Working*	___	___	___	___	___
Chapter 6 Narration					
BELL *The Naked Lady*	___	___	___	___	___
OVID From *The Metamorphoses*	___	___	___	___	___
MARSHALL *The Detective*	___	___	___	___	___
Chapter 7 The Solo Performance of Drama					
WILSON From *Fifth of July*	___	___	___	___	___
SHAW From *Caesar and Cleopatra*	___	___	___	___	___
SHAKESPEARE From *Antony and Cleopatra*	___	___	___	___	___

	EXCEL-LENT	GOOD	FAIR	POOR	DIDN'T READ
Chapter 8 Technique in Drama					
SONDHEIM From *Sunday in the Park with George*	___	___	___	___	___
PINTER From *Betrayal*	___	___	___	___	___
Chapter 9 The Language of Poetry					
STEVENS *The Idea of Order at Key West*	___	___	___	___	___
HALES *Power*	___	___	___	___	___
Chapter 10 The Structure of Poetry					
CRUZ *Today Is a Day of Great Joy*	___	___	___	___	___
WALKER From *Horses Make a Landscape Look More Beautiful*	___	___	___	___	___
Chapter 11 The Group Performance of Literature					
HAMILTON *The People Could Fly*	___	___	___	___	___
SEXTON *Cinderella*	___	___	___	___	___
SANTOLI From *Everything We Had*	___	___	___	___	___
BRECHT From *The Caucasian Chalk Circle*	___	___	___	___	___
McGOUGH *40 – Love*	___	___	___	___	___
DÖHL *Apfel*	___	___	___	___	___
ROSSETTI *Goblin Market*	___	___	___	___	___

2. Were the questions at the end of the selections for analysis and oral interpretation useful? How did they help you? Was there any way in which they could have helped you more?

3. Are there any selections that you would like to suggest for the next edition of this book? Why would they be valuable to include?

4. Which chapter of this book did you like best? Why? Which one did you like least? Why?

5. Did you ever use any of the bibliographies that appear at the end of most chapters? How often did you use them and for what purpose?

6. Which selections did you perform during this course? Where did you perform them? If you chose the selections yourself, please explain why you chose what you did.

7. Please make any additional comments you wish about any feature of this book.

Thank you for your help.